Calfrey C. Calhoun

University of Georgia

MANAGING THE LEARNING PROCESS IN BUSINESS EDUCATION

WADSWORTH PUBLISHING COMPANY

Belmont, California
A division of Wadsworth, Inc.

Dedicated to
MARJORIE, MARIA, AND ALAN

Production Editor: Cobb/Dunlop Publisher Services, Inc.
Designer: Marsha Cohen
Technical Illustrator: Sirius Productions Ltd.

Printed in the United States of America

1 2 3 4 5 6 7 8 9 10—84 83 82 81 80

Library of Congress Cataloging in Publication Data

Calhoun, Calfrey C
  Managing the learning process in business education.

  Includes bibliographical references and index.
  1. Business education. I. Title.
HF1106.C25   658'.007   80-11113
ISBN 0-534-00834-8

preface

All business educators share a common concern: how to make teacher-learner efforts more productive. *Managing the Learning Process in Business Education* is a methods text for teachers and students of business education.

Need for the Text

All prospective business teachers and teachers in service need to see the entire scope of business education, regardless of the level on which they may be teaching or planning to teach. This text is committed to the premise that teachers and students should take a balanced approach to the study of business education instruction. Such a goal endorses a practical point of view toward business education; it recognizes that each business education course offers its own challenges and ensures that each student is motivated toward specific objectives.

A major goal of instruction is to promote personal development. This book directs itself to that goal. It offers help for those confronted with guiding student instruction and learning, based on a careful analysis of research and the experience of the author.

Purpose of Text

Designed for both pre-service and in-service teachers, the text provides a comprehensive treatment of basic methods, techniques, and knowledge that relate to the teaching of business education. Particular attention is given to strategies for individualizing instruction in a variety of business subjects. The module-within-chapter format lends itself readily to a group-centered or an individualized form of instruction.

Organization of Text

Managing the Learning Process in Business Education is organized into six parts. The chapters generally employ a flexible, modular format including criterion-referenced objectives, text, learning activities, and a self-test. Each chapter also contains references and suggestions for further study.

Part one covers the Foundations for Teaching Business Education—a rationale for learning processes, principles, and systems underlying instruction in the field. Part two treats Teaching Communication-Related Business Skills—the methodology of typewriting, shorthand and transcription, office practice, and business communication. Part three involves Teaching Computation-Related Business Skills—the methodology of bookkeeping/accounting, business mathematics, and business machines. Part four covers Teaching Information-Processing Business Skills—the teaching of data processing. Part five presents Teaching Basic Business Skills—the basic business courses and career education. Part six covers Related Business Instruction, including work-study programs in business education and working with student organizations.

Acknowledgments

The author expresses special appreciation to Roger Peterson and associates at Wadsworth Publishing Company, for their professional expertise, positive suggestions, and encouragement during each stage of the manuscript development; to the authors and companies who have given permission to quote from their writing and whose names are given in the references; to the reviewers— Carl H. Pollock, Jr., Portland State University; Caroll Dierks, University of Northern Colorado; Lloyd L. Garrison, Oklahoma State University; Robert M. Peters, University of Maryland; Adaline J. Eastman, Ball State University; Otto Santos, Ohio State University; and Robert E. Hoskinson, Washington State University—who provided constructive criticism; and to my wife, Marjorie, who assisted me in researching and writing.

Calfrey C. Calhoun

contents

FOUNDATIONS FOR TEACHING BUSINESS EDUCATION

chapter 1

BUSINESS EDUCATION IN PERSPECTIVE

Business education is interpreted in many ways. To some, it pertains only to those occupations that are carried out in the office by office workers. Others interpret its scope to include not only the jobs performed by office workers but also the functions of management and/or advancement in occupations related to the office. In addition, business education provides the student with the understanding and knowledge needed for handling personal affairs and using the services of the business world.

In America, business education first began with the preparation of book-keepers as apprentices. The colonial schools of the mid-1600s added bookkeeping and business arithmetic to their curricula. After the Civil War, the demand for bookkeepers increased to the extent that neither the apprenticeship system nor private tutors could supply enough workers. As a result, private business schools developed as commercial ventures to train clerks in the shortest time possible. These schools, which grew rapidly, offered bookkeeping, commercial arithmetic, shorthand, and business law.

Public high schools began teaching bookkeeping in 1824, three years after the English High School in Boston was opened. In 1827, Massachusetts passed a law requiring every township with more than 500 families to establish a high school, and bookkeeping became the first vocational course included in the curriculum. Shortly thereafter secondary schools throughout the country began teaching bookkeeping—the underlying objective was to develop specific skills for employment.

The business education curriculum in both private and public schools expanded steadily with the development and acceptance of the typewriter in the late 1800s. The growth of business education, especially in the public schools, has paralleled the public demand for typists, stenographers, secretaries, book-keepers, and clerical workers. Even during the depression years of the 1930s and the economic recession of the 1970s, which resulted in a widespread decrease in the demand for employees, business education has remained a strong and viable component of both secondary and postsecondary curricula. Many

3

students have vocational aims in pursuing business education; an even larger number, especially at the high school level, enroll in courses such as typewriting or consumer economics for their personal-use values.

module 1.1
BUSINESS EDUCATION IN THE CURRICULUM

After completing this module, you should be able to (1) identify the major objectives and goals of business education, (2) differentiate the objectives of business education at each educational level, (3) explain the role of business education in career education, and (4) summarize enrollment trends in the field.

GOALS OF BUSINESS EDUCATION

Although some elements of business education may be found in the elementary grades, the major emphases are at the middle school, secondary, and postsecondary levels. A review of the overall and specific objectives will set the stage for an understanding of the role of business education in the curriculum.

Business educators generally agree that business education has two major objectives: vocational or career preparation, and general or personal-use education. Within these two major objectives, business education recognizes several goals for the various educational levels. For the individual who is planning a career in business or who is already employed in a business career, the goals focus on:

1. developing occupational competencies for obtaining a job and/or advancing in a career
2. helping adjust to occupational change
3. promoting career awareness and exploration preceding occupational preparation
4. establishing a foundation for further study of the field of business
5. providing knowledge and understanding of the free enterprise system, thereby developing more competent producers of goods and services.

For *all* individuals, business education goals relate to:

1. promoting career awareness and exploration of business careers
2. preparing students to be competent consumers of goods and services

3. providing a basic knowledge of economics and the free enterprise system
4. developing skills and knowledge needed in managing personal business affairs
5. furthering competencies of a business nature that have special supportive value in other professions
6. inspiring respect for the value and dignity of honest work
7. providing general business knowledge, skills, and understanding.

The trend among educators is to translate these general objectives into specific competencies whose attainment can be more readily measured. In the following sections, the role of business education at various educational levels is examined.

Middle schools

The past decade has brought about a trend in American education toward regrouping or reorganizing the twelve elementary and high school grades into a 5–3–4 or 6–3–3 or 4–4–4 arrangement that includes a three- or four-grade middle school. Such an organizational plan is based on the belief that students in the middle school years (grades 5 to 8, 6 to 8, or 7 to 9) are different from students in either the elementary or high school and, consequently, require a curriculum adapted to their characteristics.

Business education in the middle grades is concerned primarily with *exploration*. These courses, sometimes organized into minicourses, permit students to explore various occupations and to become familiar with job preparation requirements, tools, and educational opportunities available. In addition, students develop simple business skills such as typing, acquire economic understanding through courses such as consumer economics or general business, and initiate a foundation for more advanced study in the business field.

High schools

The objectives of business education at the high school level may be grouped into two major categories—general education and vocational preparation (or job training). The general or nonvocational objective includes basic business education for all students, whereas vocational business education is provided for those desiring business or office employment upon graduation or advanced preparation. Vocational preparation includes the development of job skills and knowledge to a level of employability in an entry-level business environment. Business education programs are offered in comprehensive high schools that combine both traditional and vocational offerings, in traditional high schools that focus primarily on academic or college-preparatory programs, and in vocational high schools or centers that offer job-oriented courses.

The Policies Commission for Business and Economic Education[1] described the role of business education at the secondary level in its statement entitled "This We Believe About Business Education in the Secondary School."

Major statements of the purposes of education in America have identified a need for business education. Business education achieves its goals through

1. Specialized instruction to prepare students for careers in business.
2. Fundamental instruction to help students to assume their economic roles as consumers, workers, and citizens.
3. Background instruction to assist students in preparing for professional careers requiring advanced study.

In an effort to satisfy the needs of all students, secondary schools should provide sound programs of business education that provide instruction for and about business.

WE BELIEVE THAT

1. Business education is an effective program of occupational instruction for secondary students desiring careers in business.
2. Business education has an important contribution to make to the economic literacy of all secondary school students.
3. Business education is desirable for students who plan programs requiring postsecondary and higher education in the field of business.

Postsecondary vocational–technical centers

Postsecondary vocational–technical schools experienced their most rapid growth in the years following the passage of the Vocational Education Act of 1963, which provided funds for their construction and operation. These schools, which normally serve a multicounty geographic area, are designed to provide vocational training or retraining for adults and youth beyond secondary school age who may or may not have completed high school.

Business education programs in area vocational–technical centers seek to prepare students for gainful employment as secretarial, accounting, clerical, data processing, or management workers. Courses provide both theory and practical application of job fundamentals; thus students learn to relate their education to the specific goals of getting a job or advancing in a given job. The curriculum also develops basic competencies in business English and communication, psychology, human relations, and business mathematics. Many area vocational–technical centers make extensive use of simulation and open labs for developing job skills in specific business occupations, in contrast to training at the high school level which may be more oriented toward broad clusters of jobs and/or content. Such training is relevant to the needs of trainees and, at the same time, meets the requirements and standards of the business community.

Community colleges

Another rapidly growing institution is the community, or junior, college with over 1,000 institutions now serving more than 2,000,000 students.

Business education objectives in the community college parallel those of the institution itself and include (1) preparation of students for employment (the terminal objective), (2) preparation of students for advanced study (the college transfer objective), (3) contribution to the general education of students, (4) skill development for semiprofessional, technical, or avocational use, and (5) upgrading of existing skills (the adult education or community service objective).

Business education in the community college includes both vocational courses such as accounting, business law, business machines, typewriting, and shorthand, as well as general education offerings such as economics, consumer education, and personal typewriting. A specialty of growing importance at this level is the organization and operation of small business enterprises.

Independent business schools

Independent business schools have been a vital part of the educational system since the mid-1800s. Historically, their primary objective has been the intensive preparation of individuals for business employment. Much of the methodology of business education originated in the private business school which today offers specialized and intensive training of office workers of all kinds.

The curriculum of the independent business school varies in response to the employment needs of the community. Courses of study are basically organized into five major areas: accounting, clerical, data processing, management, and stenographic-secretarial programs. In addition to these skill-oriented courses, instruction in related areas such as business mathematics, communication skills, psychology, and human relations is offered.

One of the problems that has received special attention in the private business school field is quality control. The founding of an Accrediting Commission for Business Schools in 1952 marked the beginning of organized efforts to improve the management and educational programs of individual schools. Through the commission, schools have collectively developed criteria, and each institution is reviewed periodically for accreditation. Many states have brought the private school under the regular jurisdiction of the state department of education or other regulatory agency. Students in many private business schools may qualify for various forms of federal and state financial aid.

Colleges and universities

At the college and university undergraduate level, business education programs are concerned broadly with the preparation of individuals for professional careers in the general area of business management or in the specializations that serve management, such as accounting, economics, insurance, finance, marketing, office administration, data processing, statistics, and real estate. They are also concerned with the preparation of business education teachers for middle school, secondary, and postsecondary levels.

Increasingly, as the fifth year of college work is required by more and more states for full certification, business teachers may be expected to view the master's degree as a minimum level of preparation. Many institutions offer the specialist, or sixth-year, certificate or degree for business teachers who want a high level of instructional competence in the field. For those planning to teach at the four-year college or university level, the doctorate in business education is considered the minimum degree necessary.

RELATION TO CAREER EDUCATION

One of the significant educational emphases of the 1970s has been the career education movement. Although the concept was not new, in early 1971, Dr. Sidney P. Marland, then U.S. Commissioner of Education, provided the initial federal thrust toward implementing career education. Marland stressed the fallacy of dividing public education into *academic* and *vocational* components. He proposed an emphasis on *career education* in a blend of academic and vocational programs. Career education would be an integral part of the total curriculum from kindergarten through the adult level. Students completing high school programs would be ready to enter either higher education or the labor market with adequate entry-level skills.

At the elementary level, career education means helping pupils become aware of the world of work, the values of a work-oriented society, and the role of the individual. Business educators serve as resource persons for classroom teachers, providing information about careers in the broad realm of business. Career concepts are interwoven into the daily activities of pupils so that they may become conscious of how skills learned in traditional settings, such as arithmetic, are applied in business and office careers.

In the middle grades, exploration of business careers begins. Pupils select clusters, or families, of occupations and become familiar with the preparation requirements and the educational opportunities available for obtaining the necessary training. Occupations are viewed both individually and in relation to each other within the business clusters. Guidance and counseling are important because they help pupils realistically to correlate information about themselves with the various occupational choices open to them. In many schools, career education is implemented through the framework of traditional courses; in others, it may be presented through minicourses focusing on various occupational clusters such as those recommended by the U.S. Office of Education. Business teachers offer minicourses in data processing, clerical, secretarial, finance, and management areas in order to provide a broad exposure to these lines of work. Frequently, business education teachers serve as members of a schoolwide multidisciplinary team, planning ways to integrate career education into all courses as a prevocational emphasis.

At the high school level, as students begin the preparation phase, occupational choices are narrowed to one cluster or family of occupations, and their training provides specialized competency within that cluster. At this level, preparation centers around careers in bookkeeping and accounting, marketing and distribution, secretarial occupations, management or business ownership, clerical occupations, or data processing. Because the business teacher is in direct contact with students, he or she has the opportunity to incorporate career education objectives into each course in the business curriculum.

ENROLLMENT

It is difficult to obtain an accurate picture of total business education enrollment, especially at the secondary level, because all business education classes are not federally funded. (It was not until the Vocational Education Act of 1963 that business and office education received federal monies for training purposes.) Reports of federally funded enrollment, therefore, reflect only a portion of the total enrollment because of the distinction still being made between "vocational" and "nonvocational" objectives of students. For example, state or federal reports may not include beginning typewriting or beginning shorthand enrollments, the rationale being that these courses often serve only for personal use and do not result in entry-level job skills.

The *Digest of Educational Statistics,* 1977–78 edition,[2] reported 6,376,633 student enrollments in secondary business education programs throughout the country in 1973 (see Table 1.1). Of this total, 1,599,665 enrollments were reported in secondary vocational (federally funded) business and office education classes. Therefore, nearly 4,800,000 enrollments were either nonfederally funded vocational or nonvocational enrollments. In 1976, enrollments of 3,114,692 were reported in federally funded business and office education programs. They were classified as follows:[3]

Secondary	1,824,465
Postsecondary	620,102
Adult	670,125

The enrollment for federally funded business education programs in 1978 exceeded 3,200,000. These figures do not include middle school or nonfederally funded vocational and nonvocational secondary enrollments. Beginning typewriting, which has the largest single enrollment of any high school business course, is generally classified as a nonvocational subject and is not included in the projected enrollment.

An examination of secondary enrollment figures, as shown in Table 1.1, reveals that business education enjoyed the largest enrollment of any *elective* program at the high school level. As a percentage of total enrollment, however, business education has shown a decline at the secondary level in 1961 and 1973. This may be attributed, in part, to the increasing diversification of occupational offerings in comprehensive high schools.

table 1.1

NUMBER OF STUDENTS ENROLLED IN VARIOUS SUBJECT AREAS COMPARED WITH TOTAL ENROLLMENT IN GRADES 7–12 OF PUBLIC SECONDARY SCHOOLS: UNITED STATES, 1948–49, 1960–61, AND 1972–73

SUBJECT AREA	1948–49		1960–61		1972–73	
	NUMBER	PERCENT OF TOTAL	NUMBER	PERCENT OF TOTAL	NUMBER	PERCENT OF TOTAL
1	2	3	4	5	6	7
Total enrollment, grades 7–12..........	6,907,833	100.0	11,732,742	100.0	18,577,234	100.0
English language arts[1] ..	7,098,770	102.8	12,972,236	110.6	24,079,059	129.6
Health and physical education[1]...........	7,794,671	112.8	12,081,639	103.0	21,517,330	115.8
Social sciences	6,981,980	101.1	11,802,499	100.0	18,898,794	101.7
Mathematics...........	4,457,987	64.5	8,596,396	73.3	13,240,326	71.3
Natural sciences	4,031,044	58.4	7,739,877	66.0	12,475,429	67.2
Music	2,484,201	36.0	4,954,347	42.2	6,111,223	32.9
Business education.....	3,186,207	46.1	4,667,570	39.8	6,376,633	34.3
Industrial arts.........	1,762,242	25.5	3,361,699	28.7	5,726,138	30.8
Home economics	1,693,825	24.5	2,915,997	24.9	4,651,535	25.0
Foreign languages	1,234,544	17.9	2,576,354	22.0	4,510,947	24.3
Art..................	1,219,693	17.7	2,383,703	20.3	5,115,981	27.5
Agriculture...........	373,395	5.4	507,992	4.3	374,622	2.0
Vocational trade and industrial education ...	369,794	5.4	344,704	2.9	484,484	2.6
Distributive education ..	[1]	[3]	38,363	.3	129,549	.7
Other...............	111,053	1.5	106,467	.9	9,126	[4]

[1] Includes driver education and ROTC.
[2] Data not reported separately.
[3] Includes bilingual education only.
[4] Less than 0.05 percent.

Note: Percentages may exceed 100.0 because a pupil may be enrolled in more than one course within a subject area during the school year.

Source: *Digest of Educational Statistics*, 1977–78 ed. (Washington, D.C.: U.S. Department of Health, Education and Welfare, National Center for Educational Statistics, 1978), p. 48.

module 1.1
LEARNING ACTIVITIES

1. You are a high school business teacher in the Harrison County School System. The Board of Education has directed the curriculum supervisor to expand the business education program into the middle school as part of career education implementation. You are serving as a consultant in establishing this career exploration program. In one week you are to make a presentation to parents in which you explain the objectives of business education and career education in the middle school. You are to indicate how the program will differ both in objectives and content from the business education program at the secondary level. Write out what you will tell the parents.

2. Select three consecutive levels of business education and prepare a chart or table showing the major objectives of each. Explain differences and similarities among objectives at different levels.

3. Secure the latest copy of the *Digest of Educational Statistics* from your school library. Compare the business education enrollment figures with those shown in Table 1.1. Write a paragraph describing business education enrollment trends. If data are available to you, compare the business education enrollment figures in your state with national figures. Write a paragraph comparing business education enrollment trends at state and national levels.

4. You are a member of a panel making a presentation to elementary teachers on career education. Outline four to six points covering the role of business education as a component of career education in the elementary curriculum. As an alternative activity, outline two plans for implementing business career exploration at the elementary level.

module 1.1
SELF-TEST

_____ 1. The major objectives of business education are (a) career awareness and economic understanding, (b) consumer education and career preparation, (c) career preparation and general education, (d) career preparation and economic understanding.

_____ 2. Preparation for employment, preparation for advanced study, contribution to general education, upgrading of existing skills are all objectives of business education programs in (a) community colleges, (b) independent business schools, (c) postsecondary vocational–technical schools, (d) colleges and universities.

_____ 3. Career exploration is the primary career education objective at the (a) elementary level, (b) middle school level, (c) high school level, (d) postsecondary level.

_____ 4. Between 1960 and 1972, the percentage of total secondary business education enrollment compared to total secondary enrollment (a) increased significantly, (b) remained the same, (c) decreased, (d) increased slightly.

_____ 5. For each business education goal listed below, check the educational level(s) for which each goal is most appropriate.

	Middle	Secondary	2-Year Post-secondary	College
a. Developing occupational competencies for getting a job or advancing in a business career				
b. Helping people adjust to occupational change				
c. Promoting career awareness and exploration preceding occupational preparation				
d. Establishing a foundation for further study of the field of business				

e. Providing knowledge and understanding of the private enterprise system   _____

f. Promoting career awareness and exploration of business careers   _____

g. Preparing students to be competent consumers of goods and services   _____

h. Developing skills and knowledges needed in managing personal business affairs   _____

i. Furthering competencies of a business nature that have special supportive value in other professions   _____

j. Inspiring respect for the value and dignity of work   _____

k. Providing general business knowledges, skills, and understandings   _____

6. Explain the role of business education in career education at the (a) elementary level; (b) middle school level; (c) secondary level.

module 1.2
FACTORS INFLUENCING BUSINESS EDUCATION

After completing this module, you should be able to (1) explain the impact of technology on the field of business education, (2) cite four characteristics of emerging occupations, (3) differentiate among the various forms of employee mobility, (4) project basic employment trends for the labor force through the 1980s, and (5) explain the relationship of employment trends to business education.

TECHNOLOGY

The very nature of business education suggests that the business teacher should keep abreast of changing societal needs. Vital changes are being reflected in the effects of an accelerating technology on business and industry. The increasing pace of technological change can almost totally alter the nature of an occupation within the span of a few years. Thus an individual is likely to hold more than one job during his or her working years, and retraining is expected to become a continuing aspect of employment. Technological change not only causes some jobs to disappear; it also results in the upgrading of other jobs and the emergence of previously unknown occupations.

Emerging occupations generally differ from those being phased out in that (1) they usually involve fewer manual skills and more cognitive understandings; (2) they often call for the use of more technical knowledge; (3) their performance usually requires a more complete, functional general education than the jobs they replaced; and (4) in many cases the worker needs more maturity in order to fill the job successfully. Consequently, training programs should be viewed as open-ended and ongoing rather than terminal. Business teachers should be concerned with preparing office workers who are versatile and who possess the readiness and capacity for a lifetime of learning and relearning of job skills.

The effects of technology on business education is illustrated in the emergence of word processing systems in which secretarial jobs are organized according to functions related to correspondence and administrative support. Administrative and corresponding secretaries are the primary specialists in the word processing center. Often remotely located, linked by recorders and dictation devices, and supported by automated typing and copying equipment, these information-production specialists now require a new set of tools and facilities (frequently linked to a computer) to provide administrative services. Word processing systems are likely to increase in business use because of their potential for cost saving and increased efficiency. They represent a new configuration for providing facilitative office services and present important implications for the trainers of office workers.

MOBILITY

A unique characteristic of American society is its mobility. Approximately 20 percent of all Americans change their residence each year, with about 7 percent migrating across county or state lines. But geographic mobility is only one of several kinds of mobility. From the standpoint of labor market analysis, mobility is also classified as moving from one function to another, (that is, from teaching to business management), from one type of employer to another, or from one specialty to another. Moving from one specialty to another on the same job level (welding to electronics) refers to horizontal mobility; moving from one specialty to another (secretary to office manager) is also vertical (upward) mobility. Employees in the labor force change jobs on the average every three to five years; much of this change reflects movement to take advantage of new job opportunities.

There is a direct relationship among the level of training or education completed by an individual, the type of job for which he or she is qualified, and the amount of vertical mobility for continued growth and advancement. In reality, undereducated and well-trained individuals tend to be the most mobile —the former by necessity, the latter by choice. The undereducated often must move in an attempt to locate employment; the well-trained move voluntarily as an outgrowth of the expanding market for their services.

Occupational mobility is high among clerical workers. Approximately two-thirds of the projected workers needed through mid-1980 will be for replacement needs. A more detailed view of employment trends is provided in the following section.

EMPLOYMENT TRENDS

Employment trends have shifted considerably over the past several years, reflecting the changing nature of our society. In the opinion of a number of prominent social scientists, two major trends—postindustrialism and the "no growth" society—are expected to have a dramatic effect on the United States and other technologically advanced societies. The "postindustrial" society is already a reality. The "no growth" or "steady state" society, characterized by zero population growth and slow economic expansion, exists in theory. Its inevitability is predicated on the depletion of natural resources and the enormous costs of ecological imbalance. A major dimension of postindustrialism is a change from a goods-producing to a service-oriented economy, dominated by skilled professional and business services, requiring longer years of education and/or training of workers.

Some educators acknowledge that the current emphasis in most business education programs is on salability and transferability of specific applied skills, but that in years to come the emphasis is likely to change as the more salable skills become the more theoretical ones. New training approaches consistent with the changing requirements of many industries in the years ahead are needed in fields such as business education. Today's learning force is made up of persons in formative and continuing education. As career lines have changed from single to serial occupations, workers find that their initial occupation is unlikely to last a working lifetime. These observations point up the need to train for entry-level business occupations and, at the same time, to provide a basis for continuing business education. With broader-based training, including the cluster approach, career ladders, and coping skills, individuals may be better prepared to adapt to cyclical unemployment and changing skill requirements.

Clerical workers, numbering over 14.2 million, comprise the largest group of employees in the labor force; and employment in clerical occupations is expected to increase through the mid-1980s as jobs are created by growth and replacement. The overwhelming majority of clerical employees (seven out of ten) are female. More than half of all women who go to work after completing high school find jobs in clerical and related occupations. More than one out of five clerical workers are secretaries or stenographers, with bookkeepers and accounting clerks representing a little more than one-tenth of the total. At this point it is not clear whether recent federal legislation such as the Vocational Education Amendments of 1976 will have a significant effect in altering the predominantly female stereotype associated with business education.

Opportunities in the field of business exist for people with widely different educational backgrounds. Some jobs require only a high school education; others require specialized postsecondary training or a college degree. During the mid-1970s to mid-1980s, eight out of every ten jobs will not require a college degree; and the demand for white-collar workers, including clerical and sales employees, is expected to increase at double the rate for blue-collar workers. The broad business occupational clusters include clerical, bookkeeping and accounting, data processing, management, and business teaching; usually only the last two clusters require a college degree.

module 1.2
LEARNING ACTIVITIES

1. Outline a plan that you or another business education teacher could follow to keep up to date on major technological changes affecting business occupations. Be as specific as possible.
2. You have been asked to speak to (a) a middle school class or (b) a high school class or (c) a college class about employment trends in the office occupations. Summarize what you might tell them.
3. Prepare a chart, table, or diagram showing four kinds of employee mobility in business office occupations.
4. (Optional) Select one change (for example, word processing) that has resulted from technology. Compile a report on the implications of the change for business and for preparation of business employees.

module 1.2
SELF-TEST

_____ 1. The most mobile worker is (a) unskilled, (b) skilled, (c) clerical, (d) service.

_____ 2. One of the following is *not* a characteristic of emerging occupations: (a) more technical knowledge, (b) fewer manual skills, (c) more complete education, (d) fewer cognitive understandings.

3. List two qualifications that office workers should possess if they are to cope successfully with accelerating technological changes.
4. Describe briefly four types of employee mobility.
5. Opportunities in the field of business exist for people with widely different educational backgrounds. For each of the following levels of training, name at least three jobs that a graduate might hold:
   a. high school
   b. postsecondary vocational–technical school
   c. college or university
6. Identify the type of mobility involved in each of the following examples.
   a. Mary Adams, business teacher at West Taylor High School for the past seven years, has accepted a position as vocational director for the Taylor County School System.

b.   Jim Hinds, business manager of the Addison Office Equipment Company in Dayton, Ohio, has transferred to the Birmingham, Alabama, plant.

c.   Beverly Rhodes, secretary at the Doraville plant of General Motors, has accepted a position as secretary to U.S. Senator Hiram Livingston.

d.   Cynthia Simmons, former member of the stenographic pool, has completed training and is now employed as a programmer.

SUMMARY

Chapter 1 serves to place the field of business education in perspective by presenting an overview of its historical development, current and emerging objectives, relationship to career education, enrollments, effects of technology and mobility, employment trends in the office occupations, and contemporary issues related to business education instruction.

Historically, business education has emphasized two objectives: (1) education *for* business (the employment objective) and (2) education *about* business (the general education objective). At the middle school level, business courses are largely prevocational, exploratory, or personal-use in nature. High school programs develop specialized job skills for entry-level office employment. The postsecondary vocational–technical center, community college, and independent business school programs focus on preparation for employment and the upgrading or retraining of office workers. The college and university prepare business teachers, managers, and specialists who serve managers.

Business education is a vital vocational education and general education component in the broader concept of career education. Career education is implemented through the framework of existing business courses or as separate job-exploratory type minicourses.

Business education enjoys the largest enrollment of any of the elective programs at the high school level. As a percentage of total enrollment, however, the field showed a decline at the secondary level in 1961 and 1973.

The accelerating pace of technology indicates a need for higher-order technical skills and more cognitive understandings on the part of office workers of the future. The importance of ongoing training, especially in basic educational skills, is suggested. Occupational mobility is high among office workers, a fact that may be attributed largely to the predominance of part-time temporary workers. Because career lines are changing from single to serial occupations, broader-based business education is needed to prepare people for cyclical unemployment and changing skill requirements. Despite the effects of technology and changing labor requirements, the demand for office workers generally will continue to be strong throughout the 1980s as the trend toward white-collar service occupations continues.

References

[1]Policies Commission for Business and Economic Education, "This We Believe About Business Education in the Secondary School," *Business Education Forum* 25, no. 1 (October 1970): 8.

[2]*Digest of Educational Statistics,* 1977–78 ed. (Washington, D.C.: U.S. Department of Health, Education, and Welfare, National Center for Educational Statistics, 1978), p. 48.

[3]*Ibid.,* p. 144.

SUGGESTIONS FOR FURTHER STUDY

Barlow, Melvin L., ed. *The Philosophy for Quality Vocational Education Programs.* Yearbook 4. Washington, D.C.: American Vocational Association, 1974. Chapter 2.

Calhoun, Calfrey C., and Finch, Alton V. *Vocational and Career Education: Concepts and Operations.* Belmont, Calif.: Wadsworth Publishing Company, 1976. Part 1.

Kosak, Katherine B. "The Identification, Classification, and Evaluation of Issues in Postsecondary Vocational–Technical Business Education." Doctoral dissertation, University of Georgia, 1979.

Law, Gordon F., *Contemporary Concepts in Vocational Education.* Yearbook 1. Washington, D.C.: American Vocational Association, 1971. Chapters 1, 3, 5.

Nanassy, Louis C.; Malsbary, Dean R.; and Tonne, Herbert A. *Principles and Trends in Business Education.* Indianapolis, Ind.: The Bobbs-Merrill Company, 1977. Parts 1 and 2.

Popham, Estelle L.; Schrag, Adele F.; and Blockus, Wanda. *A Teaching-Learning System for Business Education.* New York: Gregg Division, McGraw-Hill Book Company, 1975. Chapter 1.

Rowell, Richard D. "Business Education Practices as Perceived by Business Education Leaders of the United States and Secondary School Teachers of New Hampshire." Doctoral dissertation, University of Georgia, 1975.

Strong, Merle E., ed. *Developing the Nation's Work Force.* Yearbook 5. Washington, D.C.: American Vocational Association, 1975. Sections 1–4

Woolschlager, Ruth B., and Harris, E. Edward, eds. *Business Education Yesterday, Today, and Tomorrow.* Reston, Va.: National Business Education Association, 1976. Parts II and III.

Worthington, J. Karl. "Identification and Analysis of Issues and Evolution of Trends in Selected Areas of Business Education in the Public Secondary Schools." Doctoral dissertation, University of Iowa, 1975.

chapter 2

LEARNING PROCESSES IN BUSINESS EDUCATION

In many respects, our knowledge of how we learn far surpasses our capability to make use of that knowledge. For example, we have only recently begun to apply knowledge that everyone learns in a *unique* manner "through perceptual strengths that either fortify or discourage acquisition of knowledge and skills, and with a learning style that tends to dominate ... every effort to achieve."[1]

As far as methods are concerned, there is no one best way to teach business subjects. Students learn under all kinds of conditions, depending on their unique learning styles. Some business education programs operate through traditional teacher-directed, subject-centered curricula. Other programs integrate content across subject matter lines through vocational block-time arrangements, where students participate as "employees" for two or more hours at a time within a simulated or model office setting. Still other programs teach office skills such as shorthand, typewriting, or business machines within a flexibly scheduled "open laboratory," with students entering and exiting as work is completed. Just how close each student comes to his or her maximum development is unknown. The teacher's role, in any event, is that of a guide or a change agent, providing a climate in which learning is most likely to occur. The business curriculum must be structured in such a way as to be meaningful in terms of how people learn.

Since each area of business education must be *learned,* the focus in this chapter is on theories and principles to guide learning. These concepts furnish a basis for deciding how to plan and manage the learning environment. We will see how representative theories of learning influence educational practice. Six types of learning outcomes are discussed, including associational, pure-practice, discovery-cognitive, appreciational-humanistic, perceptual-motor, and language-arts learning.

A variety of interrelated factors set the stage for student learning. These include *capacity, motivation, understanding, practice, transfer of training,* and *skill development.* From these, psychologists have proposed principles that help teachers to mesh effectively the needs of the learner with the content to be learned. These principles state relationships between two or more concepts, and they usually enable us to predict, explain, and control what goes on in the business classroom.

In Module 2.1, we examine several basic theories that explain how learning takes place. In Module 2.2, we focus on some of the guidelines for implementing these basic approaches to learning in business education.

module 2.1
LEARNING OUTCOMES IN BUSINESS EDUCATION

Theories of learning deal with the conditions that encourage or discourage learning. They are general concepts that apply to all learners, to all learning tasks, and to all situations where learning takes place. The major purposes of our analysis of learning in this module are to provide insights into some of the currently accepted theories of learning that have relevance for business education, and to extract useful implications for teaching. Educators have long been interested in developing and testing theories about how people learn. The newer theories tend to compete with the older ones rather than replace them; therefore, the educational beliefs and practices of most teachers reflect a variety of learning theories, some of which may be contradictory.

After completing this module, you should be able to (1) describe in educational terms what happens when a business student learns, (2) explain the major characteristics of six outcomes of learning and their application to business education, and (3) cite other variables affecting learning.

LEARNING DEFINED

Although psychologists differ in their definitions of learning, most agree that learning is a *change in behavior* that is not due to maturation, the effect of drugs, or psychological states. They also agree that learning is a continuous lifelong process that occurs under many and varied conditions. Gagne[2] describes learning as "a process which enables certain kinds of living organisms to modify their behavior fairly rapidly in a more or less permanent way, so that the same modification does not have to occur again and again in each new situation."

Experience is probably necessary for learning to take place, since an interaction of the individual and the environment is implied in all definitions. According to Hamachek,[3] learning is "a complex mix of intelligence, motivation, socio-psychological factors, and biochemistry. Learning is a continual, ongoing process of assimilating, integrating, reintegrating, and differentiating new experiences and information so that it makes a difference in behavior or attitude or both."

"Learning" itself cannot be observed. It can only be inferred by observing whether or not changes occur in the behavior or performance of an individual. The role of the business teacher in the learning process is one of shaping or modifying behavior so as to bridge the gap between what the student *knows* and what he or she *needs to know* to bring about learning or new behavior. How the teacher accomplishes this objective depends largely upon the learning theories to which he or she subscribes.

BASIC LEARNINGS*

Six types of learning outcomes that have grown out of educational theories are especially relevant for business education. These are: (1) *associational learning,* as in relationships of ideas or in remembering facts; (2) *pure-practice learning,* as in mere repetition for attaining automaticity; (3) *discovery-cognitive learning,* thinking and understanding, in formulating concepts and generalizations; (4) *appreciational-humanistic learning,* in developing attitudes and tastes; (5) *perceptual-motor learning,* where both the perceptual and the motor responses must be considered; and (6) *language-arts learning,* where it is important to make use of the learned medium so automatic that it is like speaking one's native tongue.

Associational learning

Associational learning occurs in every business course since each subject area has its unique vocabulary and its essential factual content that students need to know and remember. Associational learning involves recalling and verbalizing ideas. Students have certain ideas to learn; they connect them with other ideas and keep them in mind until they need to recall and recognize them. Generally, experiences that occur first in a series of events tend to be remembered first. Recent experiences are associated more easily than remote ones, and recent acquisitions tend to cause students to forget earlier ones.

*Portions of the material in this section are based on "Business Education in the Secondary School," Illinois Curriculum Program, Subject Field Series, Bulletin D-Three, 1963, pp. 169–84. Used with permission.

One of the teacher's tasks is to make the student conscious of techniques for learning and recalling quickly and effectively. Students should be encouraged to develop their own individual techniques and provide opportunities for demonstration. An *acrostic* is a convenient and common way of holding ideas together in a desired order while they are being memorized. For example, the word IDEA sugests the four points to be developed in a good sales letter:

> *I* stands for the interest aroused in the reader in order to keep reading the letter,
> *D* stands for the desire that must be created in the reader to want to own the product being sold,
> *E* stands for the increased emotion engendered in the reader for the product, and
> *A* stands for action aroused in the reader to purchase the product or send for it on trial.

An important part of associational learning is reinforcement. Correct responses (desired behavior) are reinforced to increase their chances of being repeated. In the early stages of learning shorthand symbols, it may be necessary to reinforce every correct response; in the next stage, responses can be reinforced intermittently, such as two or three times during a class period. Later, correct responses may have to be reinforced every other day, or once or twice a week. Periodic reinforcements are necessary to maintain desired behavior. The amount, kind, and frequency of reinforcement depend upon the individual. For some students, rewards of verbal praise are not enough. Several studies show that reinforcement such as free time leads to greater learning than verbal reinforcement. It should be noted that reinforcement comes *after* the correct response is given; it is not promised beforehand as a means of eliciting correct responses. However, the student should understand the conditions for earning or receiving rewards. Programmed instructional material is based on the reinforcement method. Learners know immediately whether or not their responses are correct and can progress at their own pace through the material. The principles of reinforcement are found in behavior modification. By rewarding desired behavior and ignoring, insofar as possible, undesirable behavior, the business teacher encourages positive performance in the classroom.

Pure-practice learning

Like associational learning, pure-practice learning is common to every business course. Unlike associational learning, it has less intellectual content. Pure-practice learning means that the student already knows how to perform a task and is merely doing additional practice to make the process automatic and to increase the ease and efficiency of performance. Expert stenographers and typists spend hours doing pure practice on certain words, phrases, and sentences for fast, easy execution.

Sometimes pure-practice learning results in overlearning that makes for erroneous responses. For the ending of a word, for example, the typist may respond with "ting" instead of "tion." Usually, however, pure practice, with proper motivation, brings beneficial results. Whenever people are called on to perform some task rapidly, they need the same pure-practice drill regardless of age or experience. An example occurs in the office machines class when fifteen division problems are to be done on the electronic calculator within fifteen minutes. The student who has practiced can do the fifteen problems in ten minutes or less, while the student who "knows how" but has not practiced becomes confused and perhaps cannot do even one problem under pressure of being timed. A certain amount of automaticity is required in all skills, and the sooner the student recognizes this fact and gains the self-discipline for pure practice, the more successful he or she will be.

Discovery-cognitive learning

Thinking and understanding learning, to some extent, pervades all learning as the student is expected to act with some degree of intelligence about the content of any course. To understand a concept in depth, the student must know the generic name for the group of objects; he or she must be acquainted with many of the objects included in this group and must be familiar with general statements indicating the relationship of these objects to other objects and ideas. The student, however, may have many experiences with concrete objects and still fail to arrive at abstractions and generalizations. For-mulating abstractions and generalizations involves ability of expression and participation in pertinent discussions, guided by a skillful teacher. The develop-ment of the concept of money serves as an illustration. As children, students first receive money as an allowance, feel it, count it, own it, and spend it for candy or ice cream. In grade school, they "play store" and do arithmetic problems involving money. Perhaps they collect pennies or other coins. They plan how to spend their allowance. In high school, they learn of the barter system and study the services of banks. They go on to further study of the function of money and its importance in the national economy and world trade. In developing their early concept of money, students have experiences with concrete forms of money until certain abstractions and general statements become part of their understanding of money. The concept of money, first represented by objects handled, became a generalized abstraction, with myriads of relationships not only to other concrete objects but also to other abstract ideas. A concept may be stated in terms of a generic class name, a generalization, a theory, or a principle.

When formulating objectives and competencies that involve concepts, one should have in mind definite meanings that can be stated in measurable form. For example, instead of "to gain an understanding of democracy," the objective might be "to discriminate between the economic systems of free enterprise and communism."

Concepts may deal with a more limited generalization that is derived from a given unit or topic. Illustrations are:

The purchase of a given product is a consumer-dollar vote for the continued manufacture of that product.

A budget for personal finances is good only if it controls the person's actions in earning and spending money.

Because he operates in a low-tax zone of the city and has low overhead costs, a merchant may not sell goods cheaper than a merchant in a high-tax zone who has a larger turnover.

How to get the student to think is an ever-present challenge to the teacher. The process of thinking may take the form of making generalizations from particulars (inductive reasoning) or the reverse (deductive reasoning); to perform these kinds of reasoning correctly requires disciplined effort. Thinkers alternate between inductive and deductive reasoning, and they use language facilities that present semantic problems. Thinking deals with cause-and-effect relations that are difficult to establish.

The use of inductive or deductive thinking in formulating or applying a principle or rule in shorthand or typewriting is a relatively simple process. The student must be willing to put forth the effort to memorize and to attend to details. On the other hand, thinking inductively or deductively on such topics as energy or inflation is a complex process because of the many variables. Students should realize that technical terminology and economic theories are definitely for the purpose of aiding their thinking about problems. For example, the use of macroeconomic and microeconomic analyses to differentiate the concepts that refer to the total economy from those that refer to the individual family or business firm is helpful. Many economic problems, such as the farm problem, must be viewed from the standpoints of society and the individual farmer.

Psychologists such as Jerome Bruner and Jean Piaget, who advocate learning by discovery, believe that students learn best when they have the opportunity to discover for themselves what they do not know. In terms of learning style, concrete learning precedes abstract learning. Thus, teaching mathematics principles in a business course is a way to provide abstraction in a highly concrete context, thus increasing the likelihood that mastery will occur. The discovery method is an outgrowth of the *cognitive field theory*, which stresses that learning is a mental process rather than a simple response to stimulation. Its proponents believe that the active process of discovering is what produces answers and develops self-reliance and self-confidence in the learner.

Though time-consuming and difficult to direct, thinking-and-understanding learnings are of extreme importance. All business employees need the ability to think, and the higher-level jobs gain their importance from their decision-making responsibilities. All citizens in a democracy need the ability and disposition to think. The talented student has unusual ability to think if given the opportunity, whereas the less talented has need for thinking to the best of his or her ability. Business courses offer tremendous possibilities for teaching thinking skills, and business teachers should meet these challenges in realizing their own greatest potential as teachers.

According to its advocates, learning by discovery allows individuals to develop their own schemes for learning; students are then in a much better position to continue the pursuit of knowledge on their own. One characteristic of the discovery method is that students are allowed to make errors in developing hypotheses and drawing conclusions. By analyzing their own errors, students discover faults in their logic and avoid repeating errors. Acceptance of this theory requires a classroom environment and a teacher tolerant of wrong hypotheses and conclusions.

Immediate feedback is not viewed as crucial in the discovery method. Instead, the emphasis is on discovery of error by the learner. According to Bruner,[4] "Knowledge of results ... should come at a point in the problem-solving episode when the person is comparing the results of his tryout with some criterion of what he seeks to achieve. Knowledge of results given before this point either cannot be understood or must be carried as extra freight in immediate memory."

Application of the discovery method can be made to advantage in courses such as business law, business math, economics, or general business where the learning outcomes stress concepts and relationships. There are, however, several shortcomings to discovery methods that should be noted: (1) students sometimes mistake their own wrong answers (or those of others) for "right" ones; (2) discovery learning, according to its critics, may seriously negate teaching; it is inappropriate for some students; it is very time-consuming and may encourage a jump to hasty conclusions.[5]

Appreciational-humanistic learning

Appreciational learning, which seeks to develop positive attitudes, appears in every business course because the student consciously or unconsciously makes value judgments and adopts certain attitudes and behavior patterns. In connection with business English, the student learns about the importance of the business letter, how to write an effective letter, and how to formulate strategic ideas, using correct grammar, spelling, and punctuation. In addition, the student should develop an appreciation for the business letter—an emotional feeling that causes him or her to try to create excellent letters. If students receive "A" grades in the units that deal with letters and yet fail to put forth the energy later when the need arises to write a business letter, then the appreciational learning is incomplete, and the "A" grade is misleading.

All teachers desire to inculcate certain appreciations in their students. They know that learning activities should be designed to present good examples to students so that they will develop good taste. In some cases, mere exposure to good examples is adequate; in other cases, the learning activities need to be more explicit. Appreciational learning appears in all courses because the student consciously or unconsciously makes value judgments. Appreciations are usually developed through a *humanistic approach* or one that is said to be personalistic, student-centered, self-actualizing, affective, intrinsic, internal, individualistic, nondirective, and relevant.

In the context of a structured business education classroom, elements of the humanistic approach can be applied. For instance, the planning of course objectives can set the stage for the achievement of goals considered important by teacher and students.

To promote appreciational-humanistic learning, teachers must see that a pleasant atmosphere is maintained, with congenial relations between themselves and their students. Teachers must avoid overdoses of monotonous drills and discouragement from strict grading. Their attitudes should be optimistic and buoyant, as they continue to show that they have faith in their students.

The teaching of appreciational-humanistic learning is a long-range objective, taking time and energy for careful planning, and requiring patience in waiting for results. These results cannot be clearly recognizable; in terms of what teachers hope for, results are usually fragmentary, and teachers must discipline themselves to accept the fragmentary.

The following suggestions can be considered when directing activities to develop attitudes and behavior patterns of appreciational-humanistic learning:

1. Businesslike attitudes and habits should prevail in the classroom. Students should be provided with desks conducive to developing efficient work habits. Students should be regular in attendance, get to class on time, and hand in their finished work in an orderly fashion. Teachers should make clear assignments and should begin and terminate the class on time.
2. Self-integrity and personality should be considered. Self-integrity in classroom situations and work experience programs prevents the students from striving merely for a personality that will enable them to "sell themselves" to a prospective employer. It enables them to develop into self-reliant individuals with a standard of ethics which they will not sacrifice as they work efficiently and honestly on the job.
3. Cooperation with coworkers and superiors should be stressed. Students learn to cooperate to the extent that they are given opportunities to work with a leader, to lead in activities, to organize and conduct groups, and to work in shared activities, planning, executing, and evaluating. They should be given an opportunity for positive behavior in showing interest, protecting, praising, understanding, and forgiving.
4. Lack of desirable attitudes and behavior patterns causes many workers to lose their jobs. How effective direct instruction for character education and personality development can be is an unsettled question—in the literature, there are varied opinions. Business teachers may find their experiments interesting, revealing, and challenging.

Perceptual-motor learning

Perceptual-motor learning is helpful as a category under which to organize what is known about teaching-learning activities in courses such as typewriting. "Perception" relates to a single unified meaning obtained from sensory processes while a stimulus is present. Visual stimuli reach the student from printed matter, auditory stimuli from voice sounds, and kinesthetic from internal bodily sources in the muscles. "Motor" relates to finger-hand reactions. This type of learning, then, on the perceptual side, consists of analyses and organization of sensory experiences for the eye, ear, and muscles; on the motor side, it consists of the coordination of muscular responses.

In some perceptual-motor learning, such as typewriting, the perceptual element is relatively simple while the motor response is complicated and difficult. Perceptual-motor learning in typewriting is the application of learning principles of sensory experience and muscular response. These motor-response movements are already fairly well under control, since the typist is capable of moving the fingers individually. Difficulties, however, arise because the typing movements must take place with such rapidity and precision in the perfected motor responses. In other words, using the keyboard in slow-motion typing is not hard to do; typing with rapid, smooth coordination does present real difficulties to the beginner and intermediate student.

The process of perceptual-motor learning follows a general pattern. The student engages in trial-and-error performances, making random approximate movements. He or she learns to identify and to reinstate those sensations that accompanied successful movements. He or she gives attentive practice in selecting right responses and inhibiting undesirable movements until correct response can be produced at will without the accompaniment of errors. The teacher furnishes the analysis that the student is unable to provide. At the proper times, the teacher supplies the necessary directions, using verbal comments and imitative demonstrations.

During the early stages of learning, the teacher directs the student's attention to superior methods of performance—first, to the moving parts of the body and, later, to the results of the movements rather than to the movement itself. In other words, the teacher directs the emphases on techniques in typewriting —on speed per se and on accuracy per se.

In general, it is better to start with complete patterns in the elementary movements than to give isolated training in single movements. The "complete pattern" requires learning units large enough for the student to experience the patterns of movements used in writing sensible copy. The results of first efforts are usually crude and imperfect. In succeeding activities, refinement of details and precision of performance gradually emerge.

Rapidity of movement is an essential aspect of this performance. According to motion-picture studies, a rapid performance is not just a slow performance speeded up. The movement paths of a rapid performance are different from those of a slow one. Speed must be included as a quality of the complete performance; it is practical to establish the speed-motion pattern before emphasizing strict accuracy. The concept of habit formation involves the belief that accidental successes emerge from random trials in contrast with the older view that perfect performance be demanded from the start.

The presence of "internal stimuli" in the muscles points to the need for practicing larger units of copy. For example, the letter in each word furnishes internal stimuli within the muscles and these direct the fingers to type the next word. When a single word is repeated in a repetitive drill, the last letter directs the fingers to repeat that word, which is an undesirable cue and not the objective in typing copy. The repetition of single words is useful for other purposes, such as overcoming awkward letter combinations, but it is a detriment if overdone.

A normal aspect of perceptual-motor learning is the presence of excessive and unorganized movements, called "initial diffused movements." For example, the student may bob his head, move his feet, pump his wrists up and down, move his elbows in and out, or utter sounds. These extra movements are likely to disappear in time. The early lessons should be based on the assumption that they will be present and the teacher should never put the student in a straitjacket, frustrating his efforts by negative directions. The teacher should rely on positive directions to tell the student what to do rather than negative ones to tell him what not to do.

A study of muscular responses reveals a distinction between tense and ballistic key stroking. In the ballistic responses, as studied in piano playing, there is alternate relaxation of opposite muscles in the fingers, resulting in quicker, stronger finger blows as well as periods of rest. In the tense responses, there is a pulling of opposite muscles all the time. The assumption is made that ballistic responses are preferred in typewriting, and in order to acquire ballistic stroking, which is economical of muscular energy, the student must learn to move his fingers rapidly in sequential stroking.

When measured, perceptual-motor learning in typewriting provides data revealing individual differences in the typing abilities of students. Some students have initial speed ability five times that of other students, and this wide disparity continues throughout the learning process. Since improvement rates in student skills also vary, students may start with the same speed rates and after a few weeks of practice show considerable differences in their speeds. The teacher can never safely predict what any given student may accomplish, no matter what his initial speed may be. The teacher should make provision in class assignments for sometimes unbelievable amounts of individual differences and should always be on the alert for a display of unusual progress by some students.

Perceptual-motor learning on the typewriter has been a favorite topic for research, since data can be measured with exactness and is readily handled by statistical formulas. Research studies show that fingers vary in abilities, with the index and middle fingers of the right hand strongest while the little finger of either hand is weakest. In addition, certain student errors are likely due to the difficulties presented by the arrangement of the keys.

For directing perceptual-motor learning, the teacher should possess a high level of the skill and should have studied the psychology of skills. The teacher's function is to analyze the students' learning and to shorten the learning process, thereby creating better learning outcomes than if the students had learned by themselves.

The intense interest of teachers and researchers in the early weeks of a typewriting class tends to make the later weeks appear less interesting. This situation should not exist; the teacher should find the class equally challenging later on. In this later period, the student needs a greater emphasis on pure-practice learning, with new kinds of motivation. There should also be a new emphasis on appreciation-humanistic learnings, which result in attitudes and behavior habits for doing excellent work and for mastering much factual information.

Psychologists agree that both teaching and learning of skill subjects, such as typewriting and shorthand, are most effective when both the whole and part methods are used. In shorthand, no attempt should be made to write the characters *perfectly* in the first lesson before going on to the next lesson. The learner runs through the whole system quickly, then polishes and perfects the shorthand skill as a whole without focusing attention on component parts.

Since individual keys make up the keyboard, and individual letters make up words, "the student must develop a kinesthetic response to the visual image of each letter which will create the correct movement through the fingers. These responses are first made on the stroke level and later on the word-recognition and combination levels."[6]

Easy material in the early lessons should be the rule. Some authors of typewriting manuals limit keyboard learning materials to words of one syllable only. After the skill has become automatic, the student may be guided through purposeful, distributed practice to develop new responses and to type more difficult material. The teacher must lead the student in identifying, developing, and using correct habits and techniques.

Russon and Wanous[7] believe that the contrast between motor learning and intellectual learning is more apparent than real.

> Basic typewriting such as skill involved in straight copy typing is a sensory-motor skill. When this basic skill is applied to problems beyond the simple typing of sentences, it becomes a perceptual-motor skill and requires some understanding and thinking. Then it is much more than an automatic skill and gradually becomes the office-type skill that is ultimately needed by the good typist.

One of the greatest contributions that a business teacher can make to the student's learning of perceptual-motor skills is through the ability to demonstrate good form and to furnish an immediate analysis of the learner's performance. An understanding of the psychology of skill development will help the business teacher to practice methods that are consistent with the way in which students learn most effectively.

For example, much objective evidence is available on the teaching and learning of shorthand. As in the learning of typewriting, educators generally agree on the psychology of skill development. Most of the following principles, reviewed by Leslie,[8] are applicable to both shorthand and typewriting instruction:

1. Skill in shorthand is best developed in short, intensive efforts of from 30 to 90 seconds.
2. Recreation, rather than mere repetition, is the cause of learning.
3. Language-arts like English, shorthand, and transcription are best developed by extensive rather than intensive practice.
4. Easy practice material develops speed more effectively than difficult practice material.
5. Consciousness or conscious direction of the mechanical details of the skill impair or inhibit the skill; perfect relaxation is necessary for the most effective skill development.
6. The period of initial diffuse movements in shorthand and typing is likely to last a few hours at the beginning of each new level of skill learning; teacher insistence at this point on perfect performance can be harmful.
7. The skill learner is training his mind rather than his hand.
8. Skill is best learned in the largest feasible wholes or subwhole.
9. The scope of the skill increases with the intensity of the skill—in shorthand, as the learner writes faster, he is able to write more different words, more difficult words, and more difficult thought concepts.
10. The learning process proceeds best when the learner has knowledge of his status and progress.

Many learners and teachers function effectively and efficiently with the preciseness and exactness of the reinforcement method. There are some major criticisms of the reinforcement method that should be noted: (1) extrinsic learning is overemphasized, (2) the teacher exerts too much control, and (3) reinforcement methods produce different effects on different students.[9]

Language-arts learning

Language-arts learning implies that dealing with thought content is a major ingredient of learning, such as fluency in expressing ideas in one's mother tongue or in a foreign language. The teacher who believes that shorthand is a language art tries to automatize responses without intellectualizing them. Language-arts learning is helpful as a category under which to organize what is known about the teaching-learning activities in shorthand. In language-arts learning, the student develops the ability to read in terms of ideas and to record the ideas in the new medium. The learner keeps his mind off mistakes in the early stages of the learning process. The intent here is to discuss language arts as a type of learning predominant in shorthand, not to develop any given method of teaching shorthand, although acceptance of the discussion may influence a teacher's method.

In connection with shorthand, the teacher's aims are to have the student (1) become adapted to reading shorthand so that he or she has the ability to read in terms of ideas, in contrast to deciphering words, one by one, and (2) become adapted to writing shorthand so that he or she has the ability to write and record ideas directly in the new medium, as contrasted with thinking in longhand or print and transferring the thought into shorthand outlines.

According to language-arts teaching principles, the teacher begins to teach the shorthand writing process and sets up the learning activities so that the student is not conscious of penmanship and does not laboriously struggle to write perfectly according to theory. While outlines at this time only approximate the desired patterns, the student is getting the movements in the proper timing. Whether writing or reading, the process is rapid in order to make it practically impossible for the student to devote attention to isolated elements of the shorthand.

After students have adapted to writing and reading certain materials, the teacher shifts to teaching refinement in these materials by using the analytical science method of teaching. In this method, students reflect, analyze, and synthesize, focusing attention on the details of the shorthand outlines. Instead of just *doing,* they divide their interest and effort between *doing* and *knowing what and how to do.* They isolate the elements—symbols, words, and phrases. They drill on the rules or theory of the shorthand system. They practice until they can write these beginning materials with a high degree of exactness, precision, and skill. They practice until they can read meaningfully and with facility; in this process, they are using pure-practice learning.

While students are working on the last of this adaptation-refinement cycle in the first unit of materials, the class period is partially devoted to adaptation to another unit of new materials; and as they progress toward refinement of them, new units are introduced for adaptation, and so on. Students extend their mastery of studied materials and enlarge their shorthand vocabulary until the day comes when they can handle a wide range of new materials without effort.

In teaching for the language-arts type of learning, the design of the learning exercises for the student, including size of learning unit, kind of materials used, rate of doing the exercise, and degree of perfection expected, is extremely important. One design may be diametrically opposed to another design. If the teacher, when teaching for language-arts adaptation, overemphasizes the science and pure-practice types of teaching, the design contains elements that are working at cross-purposes. For the teacher to prescribe designs of opposite intent may be as disastrous for the learner as if a physician prescribed a drug to raise body temperature at the same time that the patient was taking a drug to lower temperature.

Learning theories are not mutually exclusive but contain many similarities.

Fortunately, the business teacher does not have to choose one or another learning theory. Instead, one is able to select complementary elements from each theory that produce efficient learning outcomes in a given setting.

INCIDENTAL LEARNINGS

Along with basic learning outcomes, incidental learnings, sometimes called concomitant learnings, may also be achieved. The student's focal point of attention is surrounded by a peripheral area. When there are gaps or lags in time or interest, and students are not challenged to full attention, they use their background of past experiences and their imaginations to fill the gaps with ideas of their own. For example, they finish a phrase or complete the sentence ahead of a slow speaker. As panelists in a contest, they may start giving the correct answers before the questions are half stated. Students are capable of grasping and learning more than one thing at a time; thus, in certain situations, they add incidental learnings to the basic ones. By means of careful planning on the part of the teacher, students may add to their basic learnings.

Incidental learning means that the learning is not consciously sought by students or assigned by the teacher. If the teacher regularly expects students to restate the contents of a letter taken in shorthand, this learning is basic, not incidental. The teacher does not check definitely upon incidental learning, but frequently picks up evidence that it is occurring—for example, when students cheerfully report that they were able to answer test questions in economics because they learned the location of the mints or the law of diminishing marginal utility in their shorthand class. The teacher provides the opportunity, hoping the student will profit frequently.

Incidental learning may anticipate definite needs of the student for future objectives in a given course. The learning of new shorthand words incidentally in context illustrates the point. In typewriting, difficult words to spell may purposely be made a part of letters to be typed in early exercises of business letter forms in the hope that the student will pick up the correct spelling of these words for use later in transcription. In general business, the teacher may introduce the use of the 6 percent shortcut for figuring interest in order to cooperate with the accounting teacher who wants to stress that method the following year in accounting. A form of learning closely resembling incidental learning occurs when a teacher of business who does not teach formal English exercises insists upon checking the student's written papers for spelling, grammar, and punctuation. A teacher of economics may check an essay on price fixing for spelling. In these examples, the student is engaged in activities not specifically concerned with formal English exercises; their main concern is to express their ideas on economics exactly, not in a general manner. Of course, when planning for incidental learning, the teacher should exert care to avoid loading the learning situation with incidentals to the extent that the basic learning objectives are lost.

OTHER VARIABLES AFFECTING LEARNING

While theories of how we learn are very useful in themselves, in a practical sense, several other factors are involved in the learning situation. Among these are the student's age, intelligence, sex, capacity for mental imagery, maturity of speech, breadth of experience (through reading or other exposure), attention span, interest level, motivation, freedom of inquiry, memory, and expectancy and level of aspiration. Also to be considered are the level of difficulty of material to be learned, level of difficulty of presentation of material, communication ability of the teacher, as well as physical conditions in the classroom.

module 2.1
LEARNING ACTIVITIES

1. Using the information in this module and other sources as needed, write your definition of learning.
2. In teaching one business subject, list and explain the types of learning you would use.
3. There are many variables that influence learning. Observe a class and report on as many of the following factors as possible. Explain how you think each affected learning in the class you observed. For example, temperature can be a distracting factor if it is too high or too low.

student age	communication ability of teacher
student maturity of speech	student attention
student sex	freedom of inquiry
student interest	physical conditions in the room
student motivation	

4. Read and prepare a written or oral report on "The Process of Learning," Chapter 2, in *Essentials of Learning for Instruction* by Robert M. Gagne, 1975.
5. Select one business subject and describe the steps you would take to encourage discovery learning.
6. Try an experiment in a class or with some friends for several days. With one group, praise practically everything they do; with another group, use intermittent reinforcement or feedback; with a third group, give no feedback. After a few days, ask the students how they felt about the amount of praise or lack of it.

module 2.1
SELF-TEST

1. Explain how you as a teacher could infer that learning has occurred.
2. Briefly describe each of the following and cite one application of each to business education:
   a. associational learning
   b. pure-practice learning
   c. discovery-cognitive learning
   d. appreciational-humanistic learning

    e.   perceptual-motor learning
    f.   language-arts learning
3. List eight to ten variables that influence learning.

module 2.2
LEARNING PRINCIPLES

From the brief treatment of learning theories presented earlier, the reader is able to conclude that there are disagreements about the process of learning. Each learning theory has its unique characteristics and vocabulary. In spite of the disagreements, there are underlying principles on which authorities seem to agree. This module focuses on principles that provide foundations for developing and implementing various approaches to learning.

After completing this module, you should be able to (1) state one principle of learning related to each of the following conditions: differences, motivation, understanding, practice, transfer of training; (2) give an example of classroom application for each principle cited in (1) above; and (3) summarize the steps in the development of a psychomotor skill.

DIFFERENCES

Most business education classes are composed of students with varying general abilities, special aptitudes, and interests. For example, within a class of fifteen-year-olds, there may be a mental age range of ten years or more and a reading achievement range of five to twelve years. These potential differences make it necessary for the teacher to understand basic concepts regarding the capacity of student learners:

1. *Objectives should be established for each student that reflect his or her abilities, aptitudes, and interests.* To expect all students in a given class to achieve the same objectives is unrealistic. Objectives that are appropriate for low achievers are not necessarily adequate for high achievers, and vice versa. The most effective learning objectives fall within the range of challenge for all students; they are not too easy and not too difficult, and success is possible for all—but not certain.

2. *Most students experience similar results with regard to learning ability, rate of learning, and motivation for further learning—when provided with favorable learning conditions.* [10] In the past, a prevailing construct was that there were good learners and poor learners, and these attributes were rela-

tively permanent. Bloom and other researchers, however, now support the view that most students can learn what the schools have to teach—*if* the task is approached sensitively and systematically, that is, if individuals are provided with the time and help when and where they need it.[11]

If students are normally distributed with respect to aptitude for some subject and all students are given *exactly* the same instruction, then achievement measured at the completion of the subject will be normally distributed. Conversely, if students are initially normally distributed with respect to aptitude, but the kind and quality of instruction and learning time allowed are made appropriate to the characteristics and needs of each learner, the majority of students will achieve mastery of the subject.[12]

Bloom is convinced that many of the differences among students are due to environmental conditions in both the home and the school. Many of the individual differences in school learning may be regarded as man-made and accidental rather than innate.[13]

MOTIVATION

If learning is to take place, there must be a desire or a motivation to learn. These motives may stem from a number of sources both extrinsic and intrinsic. Some students are motivated by the desire to excel or succeed (mastery), others by the desire for approval or attention (social approval), and still others by the desire to conform to group or peer expectations.

To the extent that the value of education becomes its own reward, it can be said to have *intrinsic* motivation. Motivation of this type is most effective for learning. It can be contrasted with *extrinsic* motivation, in which external incentives are employed to get the student to learn. Sometimes the value of the external incentive transfers to the learning itself, thereby enhancing the learner's intrinsic satisfaction in learning.

There are several principles relating to motivation that should prove helpful to the business education teacher:

1. *Students generally persist in a learning task in direct proportion to their acceptance of objectives as meaningful.* A student's motivation affects the value he or she places on the learning of specific skills. For example, the student who wants to be a secretary may have a high incentive for learning to type a business letter, while the journalism student who wants to type newspaper copy may have a very low incentive. Immediate applicability of objectives generally is a stronger motivator than long-range goals.

2. *The attainability of goals serves as an incentive for the student.* Realistic goals that can be successfully attained by the student are essential. The business law student who plans to enter law school is likely to see more value in the intricacies of dissecting a legal case than does the student who is taking the course for personal-use reasons. Teachers and students should plan together to

select realistic goals so that the student can experience success or growth. The student should expect to succeed. The school that permits a student to fail repeatedly conditions him or her for failure. On the other hand, students should recognize and accept limitations and learn to set realistic goals for themselves. Students can, however, develop a tolerance for occasional failure by building up a firm foundation of successes.

It is possible that, by using relatively small steps in skill learning at first and gradually adjusting them to the developing capacity of the student (that is, focusing on many subcompetencies rather than on terminal performance), the student's successes can be multiplied. In this way, one's opportunities to develop a generalized desire to achieve through a background of successes are increased.

3. *Motivation should be appropriate to the task.* Motivation from within the student or from external sources should focus on the immediate attainable goal. The task should be adjusted to the level of the learner by focusing the student's attention on appropriate objectives. For example, by varying standards of grading and performance expectations for beginning and advanced typing students, the teacher uses motivation appropriately. Thus, in the initial stages of acquiring competencies, when the chances of errors are high or when tasks involve difficult discrimination, pressure to perform well should be kept at a low level. Anxiety resulting from intense motivation can cause students to make any response that comes to mind to questions and problem situations.

4. *Variety of materials, media, and instructional techniques stimulates the learning process.* "Variety is the spice of life" is a cliché, but it is applicable to the learning environment. Sameness in the classroom dulls attention and stifles student motivation. The degree of perseverance that the student brings to a task is an important factor in its mastery. The teacher should incorporate variety through the use of media, visual display, activities, assignments, and instructional procedures. The effective business teacher is sensitive to student reactions and adjusts material and techniques to provide motivation. For example, the office practice student might be asked to read the rules governing the filing of business names, be given a verbal explanation of the rules by the teacher or an instructional package, and be asked to apply the rules to a number of examples.

5. *Appropriate competition serves as an effective motivator.* Research findings indicate that relatively high motivation can be induced by rivalry. But instilling rivalry must be done with care. Rivalry can be produced by competition of groups, individuals, or with one's own previous performance. The general findings, according to Stolurow,[14] seem to be that group and individual rivalry among students are both questionable. With individual rivalry, it has been found that a person told that he has performed less well than his competitor tends to drop in performance, not only on the task used in making the comparison, but also on a subsequent task. Stolurow suggests that since (under this condition) one member of a pair is bound to fail, this factor will have an adverse effect on the performance of half of any group. Therefore, unless

extremely close matching is possible, instilling rivalry is to be avoided as a general classroom procedure. On the other hand, competition with one's previous record, coupled with guidance in the anticipation of the next level to be achieved, is not fraught with this difficulty. The teacher's choices are to offer specific rewards, to encourage competition of the learner with his previous performance, or both.

UNDERSTANDING

There is a positive relationship between meaningfulness and understanding. The more meaningful materials and tasks are to the learner, the more readily he or she will understand them. The business teacher can increase the relevance of new learning experiences by relating them to previous experiences of students, thus using an accepted principle of learning, that is, *proceed from the known to the unknown.* For example, students in bookkeeping may be introduced to the concept of *assets* by identifying things they own; likewise, the concept of *liabilities* may be associated with debts the student may incur. Further, the student is taken through the first bookkeeping cycle as early as possible in the course. In the initial cycle, the general ledger may be the only book of secondary account, and only a few accounts are learned. Each time the cycle is repeated, however, some new learnings are added. During the second time through the cycle, one or more subsidiary ledgers and more accounts and simple adjustments are added. In this way, the student is introduced to a constantly expanding bookkeeping cycle through a spiral of learning.

A second useful principle is that *learning progresses from the concrete to the abstract.* Ample practice should be provided at the concrete level before moving on to the abstract.

Learning experiences may be classified into three general categories: (1) doing, (2) observing, and (3) interpreting abstract verbal and visual symbols. Learning experiences or activities involving "doing" are the most concrete. Typing, taking dictation, using an office machine are examples of concrete "doing" activities. The student may observe an expert typist, noting her techniques, but he or she will not learn to type until firsthand experience is provided at a typewriter. The importance of concrete experiences can be observed in career exploration where students are provided opportunities for "hands on" experiences in business. Students need experiences at concrete levels before they can successfully handle abstract questions and problems.

PRACTICE

The role of practice in the learning process leads to questions by teacher and students. They want to know how much practice, the type of practice that is necessary, how long the practice sessions should be, when the practice should occur, and what conditions are necessary for effective practice. Practice itself does not result in learning but it does provide the opportunity for learning (or for whatever motivates it) to take place.

Through practice, we learn not only to make correct responses in the presence of particular cues, but also we learn to eliminate making incorrect responses. . . . Practice provides an opportunity for either the direct use of an existing habit previously learned or the realignment of the cue, mediation, or response processes. An example of the situation requiring realignment is that in which inappropriate or awkward movements appear in the initial states of learning a new skill.[15]

In planning for practice sessions, you may find the following guidelines helpful.

1. *Distributed practice is more effective than massed practice.* Klausmeier and Goodwin[16] suggest that "shorter practice sessions with an interval of time between sessions produce excellent results provided two conditions are met—the practice sessions must be sufficiently long to bring about improvements and the space between sessions must not be so long that forgetting occurs." The amount of time needed for practice depends on factors such as the kind of material being learned, the amount of thinking involved, interest and effect of the activity, and ability and aptitude of the learner.

2. *Amount and kind of practice vary according to individual needs.* Students do not need the same kinds and amounts of practice. Generally, the greater the student's rate of learning, the less practice he or she needs to learn a skill or concept. Slower students need longer, uninterrupted practice sessions to develop skills and become aware of the principles and concepts being presented.

Smith and Dechant[17] point out that, *in general, equalizing practice has been found to increase differences in performance.* "The complexity of the response to be learned must be considered. When the behavior that is to be acquired is so simple that both the good and the poor performance can achieve mastery, the differences decrease with practice and the variability within a group of learners becomes less. If the task is complex, the slow tend to stand still while the gifted advance and the variability in the group increases."

3. *Immediate knowledge of results is an essential condition for effective practice.* Learners are aided by information about their performance. Incorrect responses should be corrected immediately. When a student is observed using improper fingering at the typewriter or writing a shorthand symbol incorrectly, the error should be corrected *then* at the time and point of error. "A primary determiner of the efficiency with which students acquire any skill is the quality of the help given at the time incorrect movements or responses are made."[18]

TRANSFER OF TRAINING

The real test of learning is the application of previous learning to current problems. If an individual is able to apply what has been learned to new situations, then we can conclude that there has been transfer of training. The teacher should understand the following three major principles in order to assure automatic transfer of training.

1. *Transfer of training is more likely to occur when training conditions and application conditions are similar.* The more common the elements between the situations, the greater the chance for transfer. Most students should experience little difficulty in typing on two or three different makes of typewriters because of the similarities of the keyboard. More practice would be needed, however, in changing from a manual typewriter to an electric one, especially an executive or electronic typewriter, since several elements differ—for example, the touch and variable spacing.

The teacher should provide students with settings that as nearly as possible resemble the conditions under which the tasks will be performed. "This does not mean that it always will be most efficient to start the learner in the actual situation in which he will be required to perform the skill to be learned. It may be necessary to build skill components into larger and larger assemblies that eventually permit the learner to perform correctly in the criterion situation. The complexity of a task in relation to the student's ability is the determining factor."[19] In the initial stages of training stenographers, for instance, emphasis is placed on the development of typing and shorthand skills. However, as the student becomes proficient, the teacher adds variables that are more nearly like those in the business office, such as simulation or work experience, thus providing opportunities for application of skills in businesslike settings.

2. *The learner must perceive the similarities between the practice and application situations before transfer of training takes place.* We cannot assume that transfer of training will occur automatically, regardless of the similarity of conditions. The learner must recognize the common elements between the practice condition and the new application. The teacher can assist the learner by providing a variety of tasks to which the principle or skill being learned can be applied during the learning phase. The shorthand student who practices taking live dictation from several individuals and taking dictation via telephone is better prepared to take dictation under the varying conditions of the business office than one who has taken dictation only from the teacher.

3. *Transfer of training may be vertical or lateral.* In lateral transfer, the individual performs tasks of about the same difficulty as in the practice situation; an example would be transcribing letters from dictation in the practice situation and in the business office. In vertical transfer, the individual uses what is learned as a foundation for more difficult tasks. The student may build on basic typewriting skills by operating an automatic typewriter in a word processing center. "Transfer to the learning of more complex skills is dependent primarily on the prior learning of the simpler skills. The more basic skills must be mastered (overlearned) in the sense that they can be readily retrieved in order for transfer to take place to the learning of the more complex intellectual skills."[20]

DEVELOPING PERCEPTUAL-MOTOR SKILLS

Skill development is an important phase of business education. Consequently, the teaching and learning of skills are discussed separately from general learning principles even though these principles apply to skill development.

Skill learning has three basic phases: cognition, fixation, and automatization. During the cognition stage, the learner thinks about what he or she is doing. Movements are slow, unsure, and often inaccurate, and each one is planned. The individual eliminates unnecessary responses that interfere with accuracy. In the second stage, the learner is accurate according to objective standards, but responses are unnecessarily complicated and more labored than they need be. The third stage gradually emerges from the second. In it, actions become more rapid and precise with decreasing attention to the motor component—for example, the physical process of typing—and increasing attention to the perceptual component—that is, the material being typed. With one visual fixation, the skilled typist can perceive a series of words. In the third stage, the learner is crowding together the necessary and sufficient responses, thereby increasing speed. "The extent to which this compression develops is determined by (1) conditions of practice—pacing; (2) criteria used to evaluate performance—standards of correctness; and (3) the learner's capability."[21]

To learn a skill, according to Stolurow[22] "(a) the learner must have the required response in his repertoire—it must be something he can do, and (b) the learner must be sensitive to the cues with which the response is to be associated. In learning to type, for example, the learner must be able to make the required ballistic movements and he must make them in response to either seen or heard language materials."

The factors abstracted from these examples can be stated as principles and arranged into a convenient sequence such as that recommended by Stolurow:[23]

> (1) The teacher should motivate the learner, get him to want to learn the skill. (2) The teacher should identify clearly the stimuli that are to become the cues for the response and make sure that the learner can discriminate them. (3) The teacher should determine an efficient way to get the learner to make responses that will achieve the goal. (4) The teacher should set up the learning situation so that the desired responses can occur as close as possible to their cues. (5) The teacher should reinforce each response as soon as it occurs. (6) The teacher should provide the learner not only with opportunities to practice under the conditions just described, but also with cue and response conditions that vary from time to time. These variations should be deliberately introduced if the objective is to develop a high level of skill.

An alternate approach to the development of skills is offered by DeCecco and Crawford[24] whose five-step procedure is summarized below:

1. Analyze the skill in terms of constancies and sequences of movements.
2. Assess the entering behavior of the student in terms of component skills and psychomotor abilities.
3. Provide training in component units, skills, and abilities to allow the student to acquire missing links and to learn these links so well that he can concentrate on their coordination.
4. Describe and demonstrate the skill.
5. Provide for contiguity, practice, and feedback.

The first three steps in the above sequence relate to identification and assessment of prerequisite readiness skills and provision for development of missing skills or reinforcement of weak ones. This phase of skill instruction should not be neglected. If a student lacks the prerequisite skills, he or she cannot be expected to master new, higher-level ones. Stolurow's six steps in skill instruction expand and explain steps 4 and 5 of DeCecco and Crawford's instructional plan.

During the process of skill development, the teacher and student interact before, during, and after practice. Before practice begins, the teacher and student identify obtainable, well-defined objectives. Through the use of verbal instructions and live or filmed demonstrations, the student observes the skill or task to be practiced. During practice sessions, the teacher observes the student, giving cues or stimuli when needed ("Keep your eyes on the copy").

Any stimulus that impels action is an elicitor of that action. In most business education classes, we depend upon language and demonstrations to serve as elicitors. In psychomotor skills, the more nearly it is possible to identify stimuli that are efficient as cues and elicitors, the more efficient will be the learning situation. In the early stages of a beginning typing class, a training procedure that appears to fit these requirements is one that uses sharp vocalization combined with looking at the key as elicitors. Speaking combined with looking produces the desired key stroking most dependably, most quickly, and most accurately. As the student becomes more skilled, fewer teacher or external cues are needed.

The student who first writes the word *space* in Gregg shorthand in four virtually distinct segments later is able to write the latter parts of the outlines on the basis of sensations of movement or kinesthetic cues arising from having written the earlier strokes. "At this stage cues are produced by earlier responses rather than by letters or sounds in the external world. In skills, external cues gradually become less and less important as they are replaced by response-produced or movement-produced cues. This is described as the process of automatization, internalization of cues, or response chaining."[25]

As soon as possible the teacher provides feedback to the student, since the effectiveness of feedback is positively correlated with its nearness to the response. Improper responses that are not corrected immediately tend to be repeated.

Reinforcement is a necessary consequence of response if changes in performance are to take place. Performance or behavior can be said to be shaped by its consequence. A variety of reinforcing events are known, with much more known about some types than others. One or more of the following functional properties of stimuli characterize a reinforcer according to Stolurow: "(a) provides reward; (b) removes an intense stimuli or reduces it; (c) informs, provides knowledge of results, or (d) punctuates—produces an abrupt change or shift of attention to a new cue or to the same cue on another occasion."[26]

Effective practice is necessary if the skill is to become autonomous. This means that the teacher provides opportunities for immediate and continuous use of the skill, preferably in a variety of situations.

module 2.2
LEARNING ACTIVITIES

1. Using this module and other resources from your library, prepare a listing of learning principles that you plan to use in teaching.
2. Select one learning principle and explain specifically how you plan to implement it in the classroom.
3. Read and write a report on a current article involving one component of learning that interests you, such as motivation, reinforcement, or transfer of training.

module 2.2
SELF-TEST

1. For each of the following positive or negative behaviors or conditions, state an appropriate learning principle:
   a. At the end of the semester, the teacher expects each student to have achieved a typing speed of 40 words per minute.
   b. The teacher returns the general business test papers ten days after the test was given.
   c. At the end of two years of shorthand instruction, students take dictation at speeds ranging from 80 to 140 words per minute.
   d. Members of the economics class "buy" and "sell" stocks.
   e. The student who took dictation at 100 words per minute in class from the teacher was able to take dictation at only 70 words per minute on the job.
   f. A student is promised a part-time job next summer if he or she can type.
   g. A simulated office is the setting for an office practice class.
   h. The teacher divides the class into two groups. The group that takes dictation at the highest speed with the fewest errors gets 10 points added to its grades.
   i. Each typing student is expected to practice 40 minutes per day.
2. Outline a sequence of steps for effective instruction of skill courses.

SUMMARY

As a business teacher, you should be knowledgeable about the theory of learning so that you can provide a climate in which student learning is most likely to occur. Six outcomes of learning that have grown out of representative theories are especially relevant for business education. These include (1) associational learning, as in relating ideas or remembering facts; (2) pure-practice learning, as in repetition for attaining automaticity; (3) discovery-cognitive learning, as in formulating concepts and generalizations; (4) appreciational-humanistic learning, as in developing attitudes and tastes; (5) perceptual-motor learning, as in learning to use the typewriter; and (6) language-arts learning, as in learning to take shorthand.

The conditioners of success in learning are student differences, motivation, understanding, practice, transfer of training, and skill development. Objectives should be established for each student that reflect abilities, aptitudes, and interests. Most students experience similar results with regard to learning ability, rate of learning, and motivation for further learning—when provided with favorable learning conditions.

Students generally persist in a learning task in direct proportion to their acceptance of the goals or objectives as meaningful. Objectives should be attainable and motivation should be appropriate to the task. Variety in the use of materials, media, and instructional techniques serves as an aid to motivation.

The more meaningful materials and tasks are to the learner, the more readily are they understood. The teacher relates learning to the experiences of the students and progresses from the concrete to the abstract.

Through practice, the student learns not only to make correct responses in the presence of particular cues, but also to eliminate incorrect responses. The business teacher learns that distributed practice is more effective than massed practice, that amount and kind of practice vary according to individual needs, and that immediate knowledge of results is an essential condition for effective practice.

If an individual is able to use prior experiences under different conditions, we can conclude that transfer of training has taken place. Transfer of training is more likely to occur when training conditions and application conditions are similar. The learner must understand the similarities between the practice and application situations before transfer of training takes place.

Psychomotor skill learning involves three basic stages: (1) cognition—in which the learner thinks about what he or she is doing; (2) fixation—in which the learner is accurate according to objective standards, but the responses require more effort than necessary; and (3) automatization—in which the learner crowds together the necessary responses, thereby increasing speed. Reinforcement of responses and effective practice are essential if a skill is to become automatic.

References

[1]Rita Dunn and Kenneth Dunn, *Educator's Self-Teaching Guide to Individualizing Instructional Programs* (West Nyack, N. Y.: Parker Publishing Company, 1975), p. 19.
[2]Robert M. Gagne, *Essentials of Learning for Instruction,* exp. ed. (Hinsdale, Ill.: The Dryden Press, 1975), p. 5.

[3]Don E. Hamachek, *Behavior Dynamics in Teaching, Learning, and Growth* (Boston: Allyn and Bacon, 1975), p. 433.

[4]Jerome S. Bruner, "Some Theorems on Instruction Illustrated with References to Mathematics," in *Theories of Learning and Instruction,* ed. E. R. Hilgard, 63rd Yearbook, National Society for the Study of Education, Part 1 (Chicago: University of Chicago Press, 1964), p. 315.

[5]Hamachek, *Behavior Dynamics,* pp. 448–50.

[6]Allien R. Russon and S. J. Wanous, *Philosophy and Psychology of Teaching Typewriting* (Cincinnati: South-Western Publishing Company, 1960), p. 145.

[7]———, *Philosophy and Psychology of Teaching Typewriting,* ed. (Cincinnati: South-Western Publishing Company, 1973), pp. 120–21.

[8]Louis A. Leslie, *Methods of Teaching Gregg Shorthand* (New York: Gregg Division, McGraw-Hill Book Company, 1953), pp. 418–23.

[9]Hamachek, *Behavior Dynamics,* pp. 456–57.

[10]Benjamin S. Bloom, *Human Characteristics and School Learning* (New York: McGraw-Hill Book Company, 1976), p. x.

[11]Ibid., pp. ix, 1, 4.

[12]Ibid., p. 4.

[13]Ibid., p. 9.

[14]Lawrence M. Stolurow, "The Psychology of Skills, Part II: Analysis and Implications" in *The Delta Pi Epsilon Journal,* 2, no. 3 (June 1959):18.

[15]Ibid., pp. 27–28.

[16]Herbert J. Klausmeier and William Goodwin, *Learning and Human Abilities,* 2d ed. (New York: Harper & Row, 1966), p. 333.

[17]Henry P. Smith and Emerald V. Dechant, *Psychology of Teaching Reading* (Englewood Cliffs, N.J.: Prentice-Hall, 1961), p. 61.

[18]Klausmeier and Goodwin, *Learning and Human Abilities,* p. 336.

[19]Stolurow, "The Psychology of Skills, Part II," p. 28.

[20]Gagne, *Essentials of Learning,* p. 84.

[21]Stolurow, "The Psychology of Skills, Part II," p. 29.

[22]Lawrence M. Stolurow, "The Psychology of Skills, Part I: Basic Concepts and Principles," in *The Delta Pi Epsilon Journal,* 2, no. 2 (April 1959):27–28.

[23]Ibid., p. 29.

[24]John O. DeCecco and William R. Crawford, *The Psychology of Learning and Instruction,* 2d ed. (Englewood Cliffs, N.J.: Prentice-Hall, 1974), p. 285.

[25]Stolurow, "The Psychology of Skills, Part I," p. 21.

[26]Ibid., pp. 23–24.

SUGGESTIONS FOR FURTHER STUDY

Bigge, Morris L. *Learning Theories for Teachers.* New York: Harper & Row, 1964.

Gagne, Robert M. *The Conditions of Learning.* 2d ed. New York: Holt, Rinehart and Winston, 1970.

West, Leonard J. *Acquisition of Typewriting Skills.* Belmont, Calif.: Pitman Publishing Company, 1969. Chapter 2.

chapter 3

INSTRUCTIONAL SYSTEMS FOR BUSINESS EDUCATION

In recent years there has been renewed interest in instruction aimed at the individual, with the emphasis shifting from group norms to the individual's needs, interests, and capabilities. Still, the most significant factor in any instructional system is the teacher. In an individualized form of instruction, the teacher has the opportunity to do what he or she does best: (1) diagnose learner difficulties, (2) provide individual or small-group instruction as needed, (3) motivate and encourage learners, (4) prescribe appropriate objectives, learning activities, and materials, and (5) identify and encourage individual talents, strengths, and interests.

Individualized instruction, not to be confused with individual instruction, may incorporate instructional groups, teams, or one-to-one instruction. It is an approach that permits each student to learn at the peak of his or her potential, as described in Module 3.1.

One of the major problems of developing and implementing individualized instruction is the complexity of classroom management with a variety of activities being carried on by students with different interests at various levels of achievement. Module 3.2 is devoted to procedures involved in monitoring and managing an individualized instructional program.

module 3.1
DEVELOPING A CONCEPT OF INDIVIDUALIZED INSTRUCTION

Social, ideological, and technological circumstances of the past decade have produced the impetus and technical ability to allow schools to be oriented toward an instructional system sensitive to the needs and demands of individual students. It is likely that curricular reform in the decade ahead will require the development of instructional materials, processes, and arrangements to permit and encourage students to perform as independent learners.

When you complete this module, you should be able to: (1) explain the need for individualized instructional systems, (2) define systems approach, competency-based instruction, and individualized instruction by citing characteristic elements of each, (3) give examples of three levels of individualized instruction, (4) prepare a list of assumptions underlying individualized instruction, (5) illustrate ways of providing for three variables present in individualized instruction, (6) outline or flow chart a systems approach to curriculum employing individualized instruction, (7) cite several suggestions as to how teachers may move toward individualized instruction, (8) identify three advantages that individualized instruction has over traditional instruction, and (9) give three limitations of individualized instruction.

COMPETENCY-BASED LEARNING SYSTEMS

The *systems approach* to planning, organizing, leading, and controlling curriculum can help us to discover the whats and hows, wheres and whens of teaching. An instructional design model can be a tool for the teacher-manager.

What is the systems approach? The systems approach itself is a problem-solving process or set of processes applicable at various levels in education. In the systems approach we find that a certain objective is recognized; to discover ways and means for its realization requires the systems specialist (or team of specialists) to consider alternative solutions and to choose those promising optimization at maximum efficiency and minimal cost in a complex network of interactions. Working from the theoretical framework described as general systems theory, the systems specialist solves problems in a series of stages:

1. states or is given objectives and determines what ends are to be achieved
2. analyzes the complex network of interactions in the relevant system, that is, conducts a system analysis
3. outlines alternative solutions to the problem
4. determines which alternatives provide the best solution at maximum efficiency and minimum cost, that is, performs a system synthesis.

For the past twenty years educators have increasingly turned to systemic approaches (long used by business and the military services) to solve complex problems within the educational system. For example, instructional methods and organizational patterns within schools have reflected a strong desire to develop more effective techniques for coping with individual differences and needs of both students and professional staff. These efforts have generated a broad range of approaches and/or programs that may be characterized under the umbrella of *competency-based instruction.*

Within the context of systems models and competency-based education, one of the most pervasive themes dominating American education during the last decade has been a renewed interest in the concept of individualization of instruction. No other concept has had greater influence or impact upon the development of modern educational programs and the implementation of instructional changes.

We are living in an era of school accountability. With inflation and evidence of widespread general economic apprehension, school patrons are looking critically at public schools and centers of higher education. These institutions, with decreasing enrollments, continuing financial problems, and resistance of students to programs that appear to lack relevancy, are searching for solutions. Competency-based instruction appears to be one answer to these problems.

Contemporary competency-based curriculum designs are characterized by a trend toward learning that is student-centered rather than teacher-centered. Objectives, based on task analysis, communicate expected outcomes to the learner. The emphasis in instructional programs has shifted away from concern for the group norm toward concern for the individual. Individualized instruction thus requires that all educators make decisions that are relevant to each student.

Basically a curriculum model for competency-based, individualized instruction includes the following elements:[1]

1. selection and sequencing of instructional tasks and objectives
2. development and/or selection of instructional materials and activities for teaching each objective or for achieving each objective
3. evaluation for placing each student at the appropriate point in the curriculum
4. plan for developing individualized programs of study
5. procedure for evaluating and monitoring individual programs.

The major feature of competency-based instruction is the sequencing and modularization of curriculum into small, manageable units of instruction. Students, progressing through these units, demonstrate their competency (ability to meet specific stated performance objectives) on each module. This style of methodology can function at any level and within any discipline; however, business education is uniquely suited for it. Indeed, segments of competency-based instruction have been employed for many years by business educators.

Students receiving instruction in competency-based programs are made aware of broad program goals and specific performance objectives of each module within the program. The modular design permits students to progress through the many small segments of the program on an individual basis. This is the so-called "open-entry" and "open-exit" feature; they can "drop back in" if they "drop out."

Teachers, by means of their record system (which is quite time-consuming), have a constant progress profile of every student. They can identify which students are at the various levels within the training program. This system lends itself uniquely to idividualization of instruction and it provides for excellent program evaluation and monitoring.

The ultimate goal of most competency-based business education programs is to provide students with high-quality job skills. The schools must know, and the students must know, that these skills have been developed. Because there is real accountability established through students meeting performance objectives for all instructional units, there is a sense of assurance that the programs are fulfilling their purpose.

DEFINING INDIVIDUALIZED INSTRUCTION

Individualizing instruction may be defined as applying logic to the learning act, and then, by careful planning and organization, providing an efficient method whereby learners have the opportunity to acquire behaviors in their own way at their own rate. Thus, individualizing is a way to think about managing the classroom rather than a method of instruction. It is the way a teacher arranges students, equipment, and material so that each student can learn at the peak of potential, without undue stress and strain.

There are three research-based assumptions that undergird the national movement toward individualization:[2]

1. Every student has the potential for learning the next thing beyond that which he already knows.
2. Students use different modes and strategies in learning.
3. Students need different kinds of assistance from and stimulation by the teacher.

Bloom's learning for mastery strategy is based on the assumption that most students can master what is taught them, and it is the task of instruction to find the means that will enable them to master the subject matter under consideration.[3]

From these assumptions, educators have derived three dimensions of an individualized program that take into account each student's needs in terms of (a) a task at the correct level of learning difficulty, (b) the learning behavior and environment that will best enable the student to accomplish the task, and (c) the teaching decisions and actions that will best increase his or her learning.

An operational approach to a definition of individualized instruction requires the involvement of the student in

1. the diagnosis of the student's prior knowledge, skills, proficiency, interests, maturity, motivation, perceptual strengths, and learning styles
2. a prescription by the teacher through a cooperative effort of the student and teacher or by student self-direction of a plan of progress toward objectives

3. an assessment of the student's progress based on individualized evaluation of progress by the teacher or a cooperative teacher and student effort.[4]

Another way to look at individualized instruction is to compare it to a more traditional approach to teaching:

Traditional Instruction	*Individualized Instruction*
1. Everyone completes the lesson at the same time.	1. Student progresses at his/her own best rate.
2. Everyone starts at the same time.	2. Student can start anytime.
3. If student redoes a part he/she holds up the rest of the class.	3. Student can redo any part.
4. Teacher learns what is happening as a result of group tests.	4. Teacher knows how each individual student is doing.
5. Teacher is a lecturer and busy giving content.	5. Teacher is free to manage the learning process.
6. Everyone goes through the material whether he/she knows it or not.	6. Each student is taught only what he/she needs to know to do something.
7. Everyone goes through the lesson together or not at all.	7. Student works alone, with others, or with teacher.
8. Everyone does the same thing regardless of student differences.	8. Student meets personal needs.
9. Everyone takes the whole course.	9. Student can take part or all of a course.
10. Everyone does the same thing.	10. Each can work on different course material.

There are, however, some definite limitations associated with the practice of individualized learning. These are summarized by Hoover as follows:[5]

Individualized learning programs demand a vast quantity of materials to fill the various learning needs of students.

The program tends to limit teacher flexibility, for example, once a learning option has been selected, the activities are prescribed and outlined for the learner without much teacher involvement.

Current individualized learning programs are primarily applicable to the skills areas.

Some slow students have experienced difficulty in adjusting to existing individualized learning programs.

Individualized learning programs provide a minimum of pupil-pupil interaction.

Frequent testing is essential. Adequate placement tests especially are nonexistent in some subject areas.

Individualized learning programs demand a restructuring of existing facilities and instructional personnel relationships.

CURRICULUM DESIGN

A flowchart illustrating a systematic approach to organizing a curriculum employing individualized, modular instruction is shown in Illustration 3.1.[6]

Flowchart Explanation[7]

Step 1. Gather input data on students.   In this step, the curriculum or course developer collects and analyzes both individual and group data, such as official school records (standardized achievement tests, vocational interest and aptitude tests, criterion-referenced tests, extracurricular activities, and transcripts of grades), work experience records, and teacher and counselor observations. Results of these data make it possible to establish more accurately the level of skill development, knowledge, and attitudes that each student will bring into the classroom.

Step 2. Formulate student performance objectives.   All course, unit, and lesson objectives are stated in terms of student performance. Students know exactly what is expected of them and how they will be evaluated.

illustration 3.1
**A SYSTEMS APPROACH TO CURRICULUM DESIGN:
STRATEGIC AREAS**

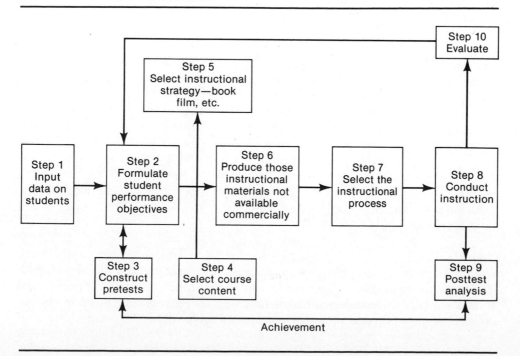

Step 3. Construct pretests. Each student is pretested to determine to what degree he or she has already mastered the unit objectives. The results of each pretest enable the teacher to diagnose learning requirements and to prescribe the proper learning package.

Step 4. Select course content. Course content is selected (only after the objectives have been determined) on the basis of the contribution it will make toward helping the student achieve the stated objectives.

Step 5. Select the instructional strategy. Once the content has been chosen, the media considered most suitable for its presentation is selected, including printed materials, films, audiotape, filmstrips, and other audiovisual media.

Step 6. Produce those instructional materials not available commercially. Although a great variety of instructional materials are available commercially, many cannot match specific teaching objectives. Therefore, a media production and duplication center should be established locally to help teachers develop the kinds of materials necessary to ensure achievement of the objectives.

Step 7. Select the instructional process. After the objectives, content, and media have been chosen, the instructional process thought to be most effective is determined. This learning environment includes large-group instruction, small-group interaction, independent research, or individualized instruction.

Step 8. Conduct instruction. Since the function of the teacher in this curriculum differs from the more conventional role as dispenser of information, there is little "talk and chalk." The teacher-manager in a systems-oriented curriculum diagnoses learning problems, prescribes the best learning sequences, conducts individual and small-group discussions, assists students who are experiencing difficulties, monitors student learning, and provides feedback on individual performance as needed.

Step 9. Analyze posttests. Upon completion of the instructional units and after consultation with the teacher, the student is tested. If there is a significant gain between the pre- and posttest scores, the student will then go on to the next learning sequence.

Step 10. Evaluate. Every phase of the instructional process is constantly being evaluated so that more effective procedures and strategies can be developed. This ongoing evaluation is the key element in the entire process. It is performed in conjunction with students, instructors, and employers interested in the instructional program and provides necessary data to revise the course, unit, and lesson objectives.

LEVELS OF INDIVIDUALIZATION

Many teachers feel that, as a method, individualized instruction has much to offer in improving classroom learning. However, with present facilities, materials, curricular organizations, and administrative restrictions, it is difficult to achieve total individualization. Individualized instruction is characterized by at least three levels of sophistication, thus allowing considerable flexibility in designing programs:[8]

Level 1. Self-paced—The simplest form of individualization to implement is one in which students are expected to acquire the same skills and knowledge with the same material, but the rate or pace at which each student progresses through the material varies.

Level 2. Alternate modes—The next level of individualization consists of providing more than one instructional mode for acquiring each competency. For example, this level involves the use of a variety of instructional modes for presenting the same concepts—tapes (auditory), sound-slides or filmstrips (auditory-visual), print (visual), and so on. In the initial stage, the teacher usually recommends the mode that each student should follow, based on observation and knowledge of the student's ability and learning style. In the next stage, two or three alternate modes are identified, and the student is allowed to choose the one he or she wishes to use. The final stage in level 2 (same competencies for all students, but different routes and rates) permits students to determine on their own the instructional mode best suited to their individual styles of learning.

Level 3. Independent learning—The ultimate goal in education is to help each student acquire the competencies necessary to become a truly independent learner, one who can assume personal responsibility for developing new attitudes, relationships, and skills. If the teaching-learning process is teacher-centered, if students are limited to what the teacher as an intermediary explains, if students never learn "how to learn" or how to become independent learners, then students are severely handicapped when they leave school. Although many teachers prefer the role of directly dispensing knowledge, they must be careful not to limit student learning to what they know and present in the classroom. The changing nature of our society makes it imperative that students know how and where to acquire new knowledge and new skills.

The individualized instructional system presented in this module was not described to sell it in toto. Do not make the mistake of thinking that individualized instruction is an all-or-nothing concept. As was said earlier, there are degrees of individualized instruction, and anything done in teaching that is in the direction of individualizing should be helpful to students. Here are some suggestions, provided by Burns, of things that can be done quite easily, either alone or in combination.[9]

1. Provide alternate reading materials at a variety of levels of difficulty.
2. Provide for a variety of topics to be studied.
3. Let learners select some topics they want to study.
4. Let learners help set the goals of instruction.
5. Let learners study using their own preferred study habits.
6. Encourage learners to locate their own sources of information.
7. Let learners proceed at their own pace (fast or slow).
8. Provide tutorial help.
9. Provide for a variety of modes for learning (auditory, visual, tactile).
10. Devise and administer diagnostic pretests to determine what learners already know.
11. If you know that learners have already acquired the desired instructional behaviors, excuse them from the instruction, but provide alternative things to learn.
12. Encourage learners to select and pursue related topics of learning on their own.
13. Provide for supplementary and concurrent projects for students to pursue.
14. Encourage students who have difficulty in learning to try new, alternative methods of study, until they find study techniques that work for them.
15. Provide a variety of visual, auditory, and tactile materials to aid learners.
16. Provide remedial instruction for learners who need it *before* they attempt to learn new sets of materials and *during* the learning of the new material.

In addition to individualizing instruction in terms of the three main variables—objectives, work habits, and time—it is helpful to consider other factors that will enhance learning, such as response confirmation-feedback and reinforcement, application or practice, and readiness.

Methods and teaching strategies such as team teaching and small-group techniques can contribute to an individualized instructional system. More closely related are micro techniques, flexible scheduling, continuous progress systems, contract methods, and independent study.

In summary, individualized instruction appears to be a natural way of learning, and in the long run it may be the answer to some of the problems currently facing school systems. Individualized instruction is not a single procedure in practice, which is done or not done, but a concept of instruction that takes into account learners' needs, habits of study, and time. With a little effort, each business teacher can find the means to provide one or more methods, strategies, or applications pointing in the direction of individualized instruction

module 3.1
LEARNING ACTIVITIES

(Select item 1 or item 2)
1. The Marion County Board of Education is considering the consolidation of two existing high schools into one comprehensive high school. The vocational teachers

recognize this as an opportunity to implement an individualized instruction system. You have been asked by the vocational coordinator to make a presentation to the board in which you explain, define, and justify individualized instruction in "layman's language." Write or tape-record your presentation, including any visual aids that you will use.

2. In an effort to better meet the needs of students, the postsecondary vocational-technical centers in your state are considering operation on a 7 A.M. to 11 P.M. schedule, with additional training programs to be offered on weekends (Friday evening, Saturday, and Saturday evening). A student may attend "class" from 7 to 8 A.M. one day and 4:30 to 5:30 P.M. the next. In order to accomplish this flexible schedule, an individualized instructional program must be implemented. Your task is to meet with the directors of the schools, explaining individualized instruction and justifying its implementation. (You may assume that the directors have a general understanding of the term, but know little about the mechanics of implementing such a program.) Write or tape-record your presentation, including any visual aids that you will use.

3. Mrs. Burns wants to improve her performance in her business math class. She knows that you have been individualizing instruction in your classes and comes to you for help. She has no prepared instructional modules, and the class has been meeting for one week. Outline specific suggestions that you will make to Mrs. Burns.

4. Read the material in this module, plus other references. (See References for Further Study.) Compile a list of assumptions that underlie the theory and practice of individualized instruction.

5. Interview two or more business education teachers at two different instructional levels as to the ways in which they provide for individual differences in the classes they teach. Share your findings with the group.

6. There are limitations to implementation of individualized instruction. List three limitations (disadvantages) and cite ways that a business education teacher could eliminate or lessen them.

module 3.1
SELF-TEST

1. The terms "systems approach," "competency-based instruction," and "individualized instruction" are closely related. List the major characteristics of each.
2. Illustrate a systems approach to curriculum by means of individualized instruction. (Prepare an outline or flowchart as part of your answer.)
3. *Learner needs, habits of study,* and *time* are three significant variables in individualized instruction. Explain each variable in terms of implementing an individualized instruction program in business education.
4. Identify and describe three levels of individualized instruction.
5. For each of the following characteristics of a *traditional class,* cite an advantage of individualized instruction:
   a. Everyone starts and completes the lesson at the same time.
   b. Everyone does the same thing.
   c. The teacher is a lecturer and busy giving content.

module 3.2
MANAGING INDIVIDUALIZED INSTRUCTION

Individualized instruction can offer a more efficient way to learn, as well as a more acceptable system to contemporary learning styles; it is also less expensive, more interesting and motivating, and more acceptable to students than traditional group-centered instruction. On the other hand, if the individualized system is not well-managed, it can be infinitely more costly and less effective than a traditional system in most of the areas mentioned. After completing this module, you should be able to (1) identify the four basic ingredients of an individualized learning system, (2) contrast the advantages of buying instructional materials versus developing them locally, (3) define the positions that may be involved in a system of differentiated staffing, (4) explain how the individualized instructional laboratory operates, (5) describe the role of the instructor in an individualized skills lab, (6) describe the form of keeping records and checking papers employed in the individualized instructional lab, and (7) explain how students are tested and graded in the individualized instructional system.

INGREDIENTS OF A SUCCESSFUL SYSTEM

A successful individualized learning system, whether it is a program in an institution or an entire institution, must have four basic ingredients:[10]

1. Staff—teachers, supervisors, administrators, consultants—who are trained or are willing to be trained in development and operation of an individualized system of instruction.
2. Instructional materials that are relevant to the task and developed according to acceptable standards.
3. Facilities, equipment, and organization that make possible the implementation of the system or program.
4. Students who are willing and able to profit from an individualized learning structure.

Failure to take into account any of the four factors could lead to setting of unrealistic objectives and to frustration when these objectives are not met.

Impact on student learning and instructional productivity and efficiency are probably the key issues in any decision to proceed with individualized instruction. The cost in personnel, time, materials, and equipment during development stages will be considerable, and the development program should not be started without considering the demands of an individualized program. Early benefits will bring increased program efficiency for the student, the school, and the public. Later the more sophisticated learning materials will greatly enhance student learning opportunities.

TO BUY OR BUILD A SYSTEM OF INDIVIDUALIZED INSTRUCTION

Availability of local funds, basic writing and development talent among the faculty, enthusiasm for writing, and time for materials development are some of the determining factors in deciding whether to purchase or to develop locally the individualized instructional material. There are some advantages to locally developed individualized materials and some advantages to the purchase of programs or segments. Locally developed individualized materials have the following advantages:[11]

1. *They are most likely to be "on target" with performance objectives of the program.* If the materials are developed with a reasonable level of skill, it is very likely that they will more nearly meet learning objectives than materials that were developed at a different location without the specific objectives in mind.

2. *There is better acceptance of the materials from students.* In comparing an instructor-developed system of materials with a purchased system of materials of equal "quality," the instructor-developed individualized instruction is more likely to "succeed" with students than the purchased program.

3. *There is an increased likelihood that the materials will be used by the instructor in the program.* While hard evidence does not exist on the subject, most instructors and vocational directors agree that instructors are more apt to utilize materials they helped to develop.

4. *They have better guarantee of continuity.* When we consider the dynamic and constantly changing nature of occupations and how vocational-technical education must change with it, it is easy to understand how a teacher who designed and built an instructional program will be better equipped to modify it than a teacher who purchased an individualized program without benefit of knowing how and where the various concepts and rationales were assembled.

5. *There are in-service education values.* It is not possible for an instructor to develop effective individualized instructional materials without a review or additional study of the ways people learn. This is of great value to the instructor in the interpersonal work with students so necessary in an individualized system.

6. *There is compatibility of the individualized instructional system.* If a business education department engages in the development of an individualized instructional system, it is possible to develop a reasonably standardized format.

Some of the identifiable advantages of purchasing totally or partially individualized instructional materials are:

1. *Quality is usually a known quantity.* The materials can be examined as a whole as a validity check, and sometimes formal validation data is available. This is in contrast to many of the materials developed in institutions where an inexperienced instructor may invest the institution's time and money and fail to produce a usable product.

2. *Price is a known quantity.* It is possible to look at the materials and make a judgment about whether or not the price is realistic.

3. *Purchasing is less of a strain on instructors.* Instructors who have been teaching in a conventional way for many years with little effort applied to curriculum development will probably be, at best, apprentice developers of individualized materials initially. The ability to develop and write individualized curriculum is a talent that is often, but not always, associated with ability to work well with students.

4. *The purchase price often may be less than the development price.*

STORAGE AND CONTROL OF MATERIALS

An individualized system involves the development and/or acquisition of a great deal of instructional materials, with considerable emphasis on audiovisual as well as print materials. If this material is not carefully cataloged and controlled, it will disappear; it will not be available to students when needed, and the individualized system will break down. Availability is the key word for storage and control of such instructional materials. The following suggestions are offered:[12]

1. For a single individualized program in a high school or an isolated program in a community college, an in-house instructional materials center may be located within the lab or classroom area under the supervision and control of the teachers or teacher aides.

2. For an individualized high school business department, for a department with compatible programs in the community college or vocational-technical school, a departmental instructional materials center, staffed with one or more trained aides or clerks is recommended. Materials should be checked in and cataloged under the supervision of a person trained in library science. There also should be provision for necessary audiovisual equipment, tables, and rooms for those individualized activities not requiring performance in the lab. Checkout cards should be used and should be replicated in some central location so that there is general information about individualized resources available to all in the institution.

DIFFERENTIATED STAFFING

Individualized instructional programs are well-suited to differentiated staffing, particularly if they are institutionwide. The range of positions usually includes student aide, learning resources secretary, instructor aide, instructor, senior instructor, lead instructor, and instructional manager. Instructor aides work with students during the instructional process under the supervision of instructors. Senior instructors have no duties except excellent instruction and preparation of materials. Lead instructors teach, but they also perform a coordinating function where there is more than one instructor teaching similar or identical programs.

If differentiated staffing is to function well, all participants, including students, must be aware of their role in the system and must also understand the function of the other participants in the system. In the individualized instructional mode, the lead and senior instructors will spend a proportionately larger share of their time working on the preparation and organization of instructional materials and less time conveying information to students. Paraprofessionals, such as instructional aides and library clerks, will spend time in putting students in contact with instructional materials, finding materials for students, assisting with the setup of audiovisual equipment and other lab apparatus, and answering student questions.

OFFICE-TYPE ATMOSPHERE

In a traditional course, the responsibility for learning is placed on the teacher who must set the pace for the class so that all the material will be covered by the end of the term. The teacher is concerned about "missed" class sessions and late work and students who have difficulty in keeping up with the pace of the class.

If the responsibility for completing assigned work is placed upon students, and if they accept this responsibility, there is an amazing change in their attitudes. They will now demand attention and want help; they will ask that papers be checked immediately so that they may progress without delay. They no longer have to "put in time" by sitting in class, but may finish courses in as many hours as it takes to complete the work in the manner required.

An additional benefit of the individualized approach is that there are many features that are similar to working conditions in the office. For instance, students must work with the teacher as they would an employer to turn out acceptable work. Work does not leave the office until it is "mailable," and in the lab, work should not be recorded until it is acceptable. Students develop a sense of respect for quality work.

Students learn to cooperate with others in the individualized lab concerning the use of equipment and materials. They must put things back in their proper places, clean up work areas, and perhaps wait to use equipment or materials. At times students may have to wait to see the teacher, just as in an office the employee may have to wait to see the employer. Students must develop patience and learn to make good use of their time until they can consult with the teacher or supervisor.

The office-type arrangement of desks and equipment adds to a businesslike atmosphere as does the freedom of students to talk with anyone in the lab (as in an office), and to do so without interrupting the work of others. Students also learn to work in an atmosphere where there are many activities going on at the same time. They find that they must concentrate on their own work in order to get it done.

OPERATION OF INDIVIDUALIZED LABS

In an open-entry, open-exit arrangement, students may come and go at any time within the lab hours scheduled. One way to check in/check out is to use a time clock and have students punch in and out using time cards. These can be put through a computer and a printout made of the time per week spent by each student. Or students may sign in and out on a time sheet that is checked occasionally to see when a student was last in the lab. All completed work is filed in a designated folder. The folder is used by the student for incomplete work to be left in the lab. The folder also serves as a repository where notes may be left for students if there is need to communicate with them after they have left the lab. (An optional method to this unassigned time approach is to assign a specific time for students to come to class; they may still progress at their own rates of speed, within the assigned times.)

The Business Education skills laboratory at the University of Georgia serves students enrolled in three levels of shorthand, two levels of typewriting, and business machines. All of the six areas of instruction are offered concurrently at each of five periods per day. Sixty stations are provided in the laboratory; therefore, accommodations for 300 student enrollments are possible. The lab staff consists of two teams, each comprised of a department faculty member, a graduate lab assistant, and one or more undergraduate teacher aides (senior methods students). Each team is responsible for two periods per day, and each member of the team is assigned to work with all courses and with all levels of students enrolled.

A combination of media are used, including film loops, tape/transparencies, slide/tape, self-instructional printed matter, practice sets, text materials, small- and occasionally large-group instruction. When the student has demonstrated the competencies required for the course at the level specified, he or she may continue work into the next course or terminate class activity for that quarter. Thus, the open-exit concept is practiced in the lab.

Standards have been established for each level of instruction, and each student is provided with a set of standards for the content area or level for which he or she is enrolled. Students may take a pretest to determine their level of competency or the level at which they should begin work.

In order to determine progress, students have an opportunity to perform self-checks at various points. When a student feels ready to take a section, unit, or final test, permission is granted. Prior to taking the test, the student will sign a roster indicating the test to be taken. All tests to be administered that day are pulled from the file and are monitored by one of the team members. Test papers are graded and returned to the student on the following day. Each student is encouraged to keep an evaluation record so that he or she knows the competency level attained at any point during the quarter and when the quarter is terminated.

Instructor assignments

An instructor should be in the lab at all times when it is open. Instructors who work in the lab should be able to answer questions dealing with all of the courses taught there. The lab is never canceled because of illness of an instructor; another teacher can easily substitute.

It is important for instructors to act as counselors because students feel much freer to discuss their career problems, as well as their personal problems, when they work on one-to-one basis with instructors. They talk with instructors each time they come into the lab because they must personally present work to be checked, and it is frequently checked on the spot. This means that the instructor must be able to diagnose problems in skill development or understanding, reteach areas that the student has temporarily forgotten, and generally prescribe for the student's problems. The teacher should provide supplementary drills, lessons, or units from previous courses or information to fill gaps in the student's knowledge—especially information pertaining to grammar, punctuation, mathematics, or business machine problems.

Keeping records and checking papers

In order to know the progress of each student, some kind of record must be kept. Illustration 3.2 provides an example of an achievement record. It includes a designation for each assignment given for the course, along with tests and a grading system. Additional information is collected for the student which can be used to identify his or her record of achievement.

There are several procedures the teacher may use in implementing and maintaining individualized programs. The following are some examples:

1. Prepare a 2 X 2 chart with the skills, concepts, or modules listed briefly on one axis and the students' names listed on the other axis. Record the date of completion in the appropriate block when the student satisfactorily completes each module, skill, or concept. Such an inventory allows the teacher to see at a glance where each student is working.

2. As in the previous illustration from the business machines course, prepare a list of skills or concepts on 8½ X 11 paper. Maintain this profile sheet on each student, recording the skills to be included in the program of study, the date students begin the work, and the date it is satisfactorily completed. This in-depth profile sheet can be filed in the student's folder to become the basis for individual conferences.

3. The next example illustrates a contract or learning agreement used at the secondary level for a student wishing to contract for an "A." The learning

illustration 3.2

BUSINESS EDUCATION SKILLS LABORATORY—STUDENT ACHIEVEMENT RECORD

Name_____ Course _EBE 311--Business Machines_ Period_____
Student ID No._____ Date Enrolled_____ Phone_____
Street Address_____ City_____ State_____ Zip_____
Date to be Completed_____ Date Completed_____ Grade Assigned_____

THIS IS YOUR RECORD. KEEP IT UP-TO-DATE. ALL WORK MUST BE COMPLETED BEFORE CREDIT CAN BE RECORDED.

PART I   Basic Skill Development on Two Calculators:
          Display and Printing

	Date Completed	Posttest
DISPLAY CALCULATOR		
Text Material, pp. 80-147		
TEST I Addition/Subtraction (Display Calculator)	_____	_____
TEST II Test on all Parts of Machine	_____	_____
PRINTING CALCULATOR		
Text Material, pp. 9-76		
TEST III Addition/Subtraction (Printing Calculator)	_____	_____
TEST IV Test on all Parts of Machine	_____	_____

PART I SHOULD BE COMPLETED BY END OF 5TH WEEK

PART II   Machine Application to Business Math

	Pretest	Posttest
Mathematics of Invoices	_____	_____
Mathematics of Selling at Retail	_____	_____
Mathematics of Borrowing and Lending	_____	_____
Mathematics of Stocks and Bonds	_____	_____
Mathematics of Percentage	_____	_____

PART II SHOULD BE COMPLETED BY END OF 8TH WEEK

PART III Machine Application to Accounting and
          Record keeping in Business and Industry

PRACTICE SET COMPLETED_____   PRACTICE SET TEST_____

PART III ALLOW MINIMUM OF TWO WEEKS FOR COMPLETION

GRADING SYSTEM:

PART I	Addition and Subtraction Test I	5%
	Addition and Subtraction Test II	5%
	Printing Calculator Test	10%
	Display Calculator Test	10%
PART II	Business Math-Machines Activities Achievement Tests (Average of 5 Tests)	35%
PART III	Practice Set and Test	35%

agreement is completed and signed jointly by the teacher and the student. Teacher and student cooperatively identify the skills and modules to be completed, providing for the student who needs to complete the entire program, who is able to exempt part of the program through pretesting, or who needs to review specific skills. After the topics are selected, each student is ready to begin working on a module. Notice the instructions to the student in the module that follows, "Handling Incoming Mail." After filling out the KNOW/TO BE STUDIED columns, he or she is ready to begin HIM–1, "Sorting Mail for Delivery," or to get the Pre/Post Check from the instructor and take the test to determine whether to begin HIM–1 or to take the Pre/Post Check for HIM–2. The first page of each instructional module is similar to the example. Each student can begin work or take a precheck on a module of his or her choice.

The amount of time the teacher spends introducing the individualized instructional program depends on the students' prior experience with individualization and the types of instruction the teacher plans to implement. The information students need to know should be listed before they are ready to start an individualized program. For example, if the teacher of business is planning to have students use instructional modules, they need to know where to get the modules, where to file their activities, where and how to check out equipment, how to monitor their progress, the standards of classroom behavior, housekeeping responsibilities, the grading system, and so on. This type of information should be gone over with the class and procedures posted in appropriate places in the classroom. At the audiovisual storage point, procedures should be posted for checking equipment in and out.

OFFICE OCCUPATIONS
LEARNING AGREEMENT FOR QUARTER 1   2   3

I, _____ , agree to complete the PLACE packages
                STUDENT
relating to these specific objectives checked below during this quarter. If I complete all of the objectives to the instructor's satisfaction, I shall have earned an A. At any time during the quarter, I may renegotiate with the instructor for additional objectives, but I cannot negotiate for fewer objectives. If all of the objectives are not completed, I, _____ , will grade
the student accordingly.   INSTRUCTOR

_____ Handling Incoming Mail	_____ Job Hunting
_____ Outgoing Mail Services	_____ Executive Typewriter
_____ Stencil Duplication	_____ Checking Account
_____ Spirit Duplication	_____ Machine Transcription
_____ Ten-Key Adding Machine	_____ Reference Sources
_____ Using the Telephone	_____ Payroll Accounting
_____ Invoices	_____ Human Relations
_____ Purchase Orders	_____ Word Processing
_____ Envelopes	_____ Alphabetic Card Filing
_____ Index Cards	_____ Numeric Filing
_____ Interoffice Memorandum	_____ Subject Filing
_____ Proofreading	_____ Printing Calculators

HIM PSG 1-7   NAME_____

PLACE SERIES GUIDE 13
HANDLING INCOMING MAIL
HIM 1-7

Mail is an important link of communication between a company and the "outside world." The proper flow of mail into a company is important for the efficient operation of the firm. Proper management of this responsibility is necessary for the continuous flow of information needed to run the business smoothly.

When you complete this PLACE Series, you will be able to

HANDLE INCOMING MAIL BY SORTING IT FOR DELIVERY, INDICATING .
AN EFFICIENT DELIVERY ROUTE, FOLLOWING PROCEDURES FOR OPENING
AND CHECKING THE MAIL, AND USING A MAIL REGISTER.

The PLACE packages listed below will help you to reach your objective.

INSTRUCTIONS: If you think you know something about one or more of the PLACE packages, make a check in the KNOW column. The teacher will give you a Pre/Post Check to find out how much you do know. If you do not know anything about the packages listed, check Complete Series space in the TO BE STUDIED column and begin with the first PLACE package in the series.

KNOW   TO BE STUDIED

____ HIM-1 SORTING MAIL FOR DELIVERY
____ HIM-2 DELIVERING THE MAIL   _____
____ HIM-3 SORTING THE MAIL BEFORE OPENING   _____
____ HIM-4 PROCEDURES FOR OPENING THE MAIL   _____
____ HIM-5 DATE/TIME STAMPING, SCANNING, AND ROUTING   _____
____ HIM-6 USING A MAIL REGISTER   _____
____ HIM-7 EVALUATION OF INCOMING MAIL PROCEDURES   _____

         Complete Series   _____

As practice lessons and evaluations are completed and the standards for completion are met for each assignment, they may be so marked on the record. It is advisable that the assignments be checked off only when they have been completed acceptably. Acceptable completion standards should be explained to students on the activities/assignment sheet or during the orientation session, and they should be cautioned to complete the assignments as instructed. Certain practice problems are checked by the student but may be spot-checked by the instructor. Keys to practice problems may be put in plastic sheets, in binders, at a convenient place for student use.

Testing and grading

Students should be allowed to take tests when they are ready. The assignment sheets should indicate exactly what is to be covered, so that they will know what they must be prepared to do. Because one of the advantages of the individualized approach is that students may progress at their own rate and may master each lesson before proceeding, evaluations should be passed with 90 to 95 percent accuracy or "A" grade level. If they are not passed at this level on the first attempt, students should be counseled as to the areas to review before trying the evaluation again.

Evaluations and quizzes should be checked immediately, or as soon as possible after being given, and they should be discussed. The immediate feedback is important to the student. Shorthand tests should be dictated by the teacher so that writing techniques may be observed and bad habits corrected immediately. (It is also a variation from the recorded lessons and good practice in taking dictation from "live" sources.) Papers may be returned to students as soon as they are checked and recorded. It is advisable to keep the evaluation and test papers, including dictation speed takes. Student files may be set up so that test papers can be kept until completion of the course. These files are for teacher reference, not for students.

Quizzes should be stressed as learning activities as well as checkpoints for the instructor. They should be constructed to include what the teacher wants the student to know or be able to do at a given point. (This will justify insistence on the student passing the test before going on.) The fact must be stressed that tests can be retaken and that no harm is done by not passing. The reason for lack of progress should be diagnosed carefully; it may be failure to follow directions in completing lessons, skipping assignments or shortcutting them, or requiring more time and practice to master the section under study.

Because students must complete all parts of assigned lessons and must pass the evaluations at an "A" level, they can justifiably be awarded an "A" for the course. Some students take much more time than others to complete lessons and reach the "A" level, but we know that individuals do not learn at the same rate. The assumption is that 95 percent of all students can master the material if given enough time.

Some variations in grading may occur in short courses when dictation and transcription rates are considered. However, even though a scale is used for dictation speeds and transcription rates, grades for these rates should be assigned at the end of the course and students should be allowed time for more practice on transcription or dictation, and permitted to retake the tests involved, in order to reach the "A" grade level. This could serve as additional motivation to reach the higher dictation and transcription rates. Students appreciate the fact that they are given the chance to obtain an "A." Those who have difficulty reaching the required standards after repeated attempts have been given every opportunity under this system. They can now determine for themselves whether they are, in fact, suited to this particular skill.

Monitoring the learning process

In traditional situations, the class is carried through learning experiences largely as a total group. The instructor relates to the class as a group, although he or she gives individual attention. When evaluating progress, two aspects are determined: (a) the progress of the group or (b) individual progress in relation to the group. A written test may be given to the class as a means of determining how many passed or failed, thereby discovering what percentage of the class is progressing at a satisfactory rate.

In individualized instruction, each person progresses at his or her own rate. The instructor is, therefore, more interested in individual progress. The monitoring and tracking role is different under these conditions. With many class activities progressing at the same time, each student must be pinpointed in his or her learning schedule, as well as being productively occupied. Because the teacher's role is different under individualized instruction, different methods of evaluating progress are necessary.

One of the best ways for the teacher to monitor and track progress is to walk through the area while students are working, watching for obstacles and situations where the learning process has broken down or is about to do so. A survey of the whole situation will reveal that most students are working. But are they learning? Are they learning *correctly*? First, learning obstacles must be identified. Watch the student repeat the project so that what he or she does or does not do that causes poor performance can be identified. The instructor must not step in and perform the task; presumably, students have already been given a demonstration. The student should be asked to perform the task again so that more detailed feedback can be collected. This is structuring a learning situation (in typewriting, shorthand, or business math, for example) so that monitoring may be performed more closely. A student may be wasting time, using incorrect motions or processes, or he or she may be finished and not know what to do next. Few people will admit that they do not know what to do—even in a classroom situation. They would rather pretend that they know perfectly well what to do next, but simply prefer not to do so! Maybe the work is too easy and the student is bored—so he or she "goofs off." Or perhaps the work is too difficult and he or she feels no progress is being made. Perhaps the work was not organized properly. In any event, the proper action for the teacher is to find out precisely what caused the learning process to stop and to help it start up again.

Housekeeping

Before the course begins, satisfactory housekeeping standards should be defined and the procedures stated by which students will maintain them. When a class ends, suppose one observes a dirty floor, clutter on learning surfaces and floor, and equipment, furniture, and materials scattered. The effect on students is that they learn poor work habits and transfer them to the job situation. They accept substandard surroundings and inefficient procedures as being the standard. The instructor has an obligation to influence by example. The following steps will help to establish correct learning of housekeeping standards:

1. Decide which housekeeping standards are necessary, being sure to include those needed to meet fire and safety codes or other legal restrictions.
2. Identify those services provided by the school's custodial staff.
3. Decide which housekeeping standards industry requires in performing the particular occupational skills being taught.
4. Set up appropriate responsibilities for students to carry out satisfactorily.

In defining housekeeping standards and assigning specific tasks to students, a work-assignment sheet such as the following may be kept:

CLEANUP RESPONSIBILITIES		
TASK	WEEK	NAME
Room arrangement	March 5–9	Cindy Jones
Chalkboard	March 12–16	Fred Miller
Equipment	March 19–23	Alan Greene

It is important that each student be responsible for cleaning up his or her own work station each day. Overall assignments, such as those indicated above, can be rotated.

module 3.2
LEARNING ACTIVITIES

1. The administration and faculty at
   (select an educational level of your choice: secondary, postsecondary, vocational-technical, community college, or university)
   is committed to the implementation of individualized instructional programs. The first phase will focus on skill courses. You have been asked to prepare a presentation to the board of education or board of trustees concerning individualized instruction in the field of business education. Your report should include (but not necessarily be limited to) these topics:
   a. Subject matter courses to be included
   b. Materials of instruction—justification for purchase or local development
   c. Staffing needs, staff orientation, and staff assignments
   d. Recordkeeping system including identification of objectives/skills/modules, individual progress, and so on
   e. Student orientation
   f. Grading, testing, and evaluation.
2. Arrange to visit a business education skills laboratory that trains students in typewriting, shorthand, or business machines. During your visit, note the size of the lab,

major items of equipment, the learning activities taking place, and the way students are going about their work. (You may wish to make an observation checklist.) In terms of managing the lab, talk with the teacher to get information about general management procedures, equipment maintenance, storage and distribution of supplies, policies covering lab use by others, orienting students to the management system in use, and managing lab activities in line with procedures and systems devised.

module 3.2
SELF-TEST

1. What are the *four basic ingredients* of a successful learning system?
2. Identify three advantages of local development of individualized instructional materials. List three advantages of purchasing such materials commercially.
3. Define the responsibilities of each of the following positions in a differentiated staffing setup: (a) paraprofessional (instructor aide), (b) instructor, (c) senior instructor, (d) lead instructor.
4. Explain briefly (a) how an individualized instructional lab is organized and managed, (b) how testing and grading are conducted in the individualized lab, and (c) how records of student achievement are kept in the individualized lab.

SUMMARY

During the past decade, there has been renewed interest in the concept of individualized instruction. Contemporary curriculum designs are increasingly characterized by a trend toward learning that is student-centered rather than teacher-centered. The major feature of competency-based, individualized instruction is the sequencing and modularization of curriculum into small, manageable units of instruction. The student's demonstrated ability to perform on each segment of the curriculum is the heart of the concept.

Individualizing is a *way to think* about managing the classroom rather than a method of instruction. It is the *approach* a teacher uses in arranging students, equipment, and materials so that each student can learn at the peak of his or her potential, without undue stress and strain. Individualized instruction permits the learning objectives, the means for achieving the objectives, and the rate for achieving the objectives to be adapted for each student. Student achievement of the objectives is based on predetermined levels of knowledge and skill.

Individualized instruction is not a *single* thing in practice; there are degrees of individualized instruction, ranging from varying the rate or pace students progress through the same material to independent learning in which students select appropriate objectives, instructional modes, and rates to acquire the competencies necessary to become truly independent learners.

Business teachers can find the means and time to provide one or more methods, strategies, or applications pointing in the direction of individualized instruction.

A well-managed individualized instructional system is essential for success in business education. A successful system has receptive staff and students, relevant instructional materials, and appropriate facilities and equipment. Several crucial decisions must be made prior to implementation of an individualized program; these include operational factors such as the storage and checkout of materials and equipment, assignment of responsibilities to instructional and support staff, provision for record keeping for each student, procedures for immediate evaluation and feedback of student performance, student and staff orientation to individualized instruction, and identification of housekeeping responsibilities.

References

[1]Calfrey C. Calhoun and Alton V. Finch, *Vocational and Career Education: Concepts and Operations* (Belmont, Calif.: Wadsworth Publishing Company, 1976), p. 277.

[2]Madeline Hunter, "A Tri-Dimensional Approach to Individualization," *The Education Digest* 43, no. 1 (September 1977):17–18.

[3]Benjamin S. Bloom, J. Thomas Hastings, and George F. Madaus, *Handbook on Formative and Summative Evaluation of Student Learning* (New York: McGraw-Hill Book Company, 1971), p. 43.

[4]Rita S. Dunn, "A Position Paper to Further the Individualization of Instruction in the School," *Audiovisual Instruction* 17, no. 9 (1972):49–54.

[5]Kenneth H. Hoover, *The Professional Teacher's Handbook,* abr. 2d ed. (Boston: Allyn and Bacon, 1976), p. 136.

[6]Calhoun and Finch, *Vocational and Career Education,* p. 270.

[7]Ibid., pp. 270–272.

[8]Ibid., pp. 277–278.

[9]Richard Burns, "Methods for Individualizing Instruction," *Educational Technology,* 11, no. 6 (June 1971):56.

[10]David J. Pucel and William C. Knaak, *Individualizing Vocational and Technical Instruction* (Columbus: Charles E. Merrill Publishing Company, 1975), p. 193.

[11]Ibid., pp. 199–201.

[12]Ibid., p. 208.

[13]Calfrey C. Calhoun, Project Director, *Office Occupations Program: The Development of an Individualized Instructional System for Selected Multioccupational Programs in the Area/Comprehensive High Schools of Georgia* (Athens: Department of Business Education, University of Georgia, 1975), p. 8.

SUGGESTIONS FOR FURTHER STUDY

Bishop, Lloyd K. "Individualizing Educational Programs." *Business Education Forum,* 25 (May 1971):13–14.

Bradshaw, James R. "Where Do We Stand in the Area of Accountability?" *The Balance Sheet* 58 (December 1976):166–67.

Bullock, R. V. "Individualizing Instruction on a Shoestring." *Audiovisual Instruction* 17, no. 2 (1972):37–39.

Calhoun, Calfrey C. "Individualizing Instruction in Business Education." *The Journal of Business Education* 49 (March 1974):252–54.

Davies, Ivor K. *Competency Based Learning: Technology, Management, and Design.* New York: McGraw-Hill Book Company, 1973.

Davis, Robert H.; Alexander, Lawrence T.; and Yelon, Stephen L. *Learning System Design.* New York: McGraw-Hill Book Company, 1974.

Dunn, Rita, and Dunn, Kenneth. *Educator's Self-Teaching Guide to Individualizing Instructional Programs.* West Nyack, N.Y.: Parker Publishing Company, 1975.

————. *Practical Approaches to Individualizing Instruction.* West Nyack, N.Y.: Parker Publishing Company, 1972.

Flanagan, J. C. "Individualizing Instruction." *Education* 90 (1970):191–206.

Furtado, Lorraine T. "Designing Instructional Systems." *The Balance Sheet* (November 1974):115–17.

Hayman, John L., Jr. "The Systems Approach and Education." *The Education Forum* 43 (May 1974):493–501.

Howes, Virgil M. ed. *Individualization of Instruction.* New York: The Macmillan Company, 1970.

Huffman, Harry; Brady, Mary M.; Peterson, Marla; and Lacy, Annell. *A Taxonomy of Office Activities for Business and Office Education.* Research 12. Columbus: The Center for Vocational and Technical Education, The Ohio State University, 1968.

Johnson, Stuart R., and Johnson, Rita B. *Developing Individualized Instructional Material.* Palo Alto, Calif.: Westinghouse Learning Press, 1970.

Lambreath, Judith. "Choices for Teachers Too—When They Individualize." *The Journal of Business Education* 50 (January 1975):148–50.

Mager, Robert F. *Goal Analysis.* Belmont, Calif.: Fearon Publishers, 1972.

Mohan, Robert, and Hull, Ronald E. *Individualized Instruction and Learning.* Chicago: Nelson-Hall Company, 1974.

Popham, James. *The Uses of Instructional Objectives.* Belmont, Calif.: Fearon Publishers, 1973.

Popham, James, and Baker, Eva L. *Establishing Instructional Goals.* Englewood Cliffs, N.J.: Prentice-Hall, 1970.

————. *Planning an Educational Sequence.* Englewood Cliffs, N.J.: Prentice-Hall, 1970.

————. *Systematic Instruction.* Englewood Cliffs, N.J.: Prentice-Hall, 1970.

Resources in Vocational Education 10, no. 5. Columbus: The Center for Vocational Education, The Ohio State University, 1977.

Wagoner, George A. "Individualizing Instruction: When and How." *Business Education Forum* 27 (May 1973):27–28.

Weisgerber, Robert A., ed. *Developmental Efforts in Individualized Learning.* Itasca, Ill.: F. E. Peacock Publishers, 1971.

————. *Perspectives in Individualized Learning.* Itasca, Ill.: F. E. Peacock Publishers, 1971.

West, Leonard J. "Individualization of Instruction." *Business Education Forum* 25 (May 1971):19–21.

Wood, Merle W. "Competency-based Instruction in Secondary Business Education." *The Journal of Business Education* 51 (October 1975):27–29.

chapter 4

MONITORING STUDENT PROGRESS

The role of student evaluation in the business education instructional program is to provide feedback to the student and the instructor regarding student performance. Evaluation is defined by Bloom and others as "the systematic collection of evidence to determine whether in fact certain changes are taking place in the learners as well as to determine the amount or degree of change in individual students."[1]

Business teachers are frequently less than enthusiastic about their role in evaluation. It is more interesting to stimulate thinking in a classroom or to encourage students to test their skills and knowledge. But the task of constructively criticizing student achievement in a manner that is acceptable to the learner requires careful judgment and sensitivity to students' reactions. Students sometimes view the assignment of a grade as a judgment of themselves as persons rather than as a measure of their achievement.

After completing this chapter, you should be able to (1) identify and explain at least four purposes of evaluation in business education, (2) cite examples of formal and informal evaluation in the field, (3) outline and demonstrate the steps in planning a test, (4) construct objective, subjective, and attitude test items, as well as performance items, (5) identify four sources of error in measuring student performance, and (6) explain three approaches to grading in business education.

PURPOSES OF EVALUATION

Evaluation of student learning is conducted for several reasons, most of which relate specifically to the student. Traditionally, one of the most frequent uses of evaluation is to *show the extent of student growth or change* (achievement) which serves as a *basis for grades* that represent, at best, value judgments of student progress.

Evaluation helps to *determine the student's readiness* to pursue subsequent steps in learning. An achievement test samples concepts that are basic to the next step in the learning sequence. An achievement test score on an instructional unit in a skills course (in which skills are sequenced on the theory that the mastery of one skill is essential to learning succeeding skills) serves as an indicator of the student's readiness (or lack of it) for the next unit. For example, in accounting, the first cycle presented is usually a service-type business and does not include adjustments. As the course progresses, the cycle is expanded to include various types of adjusting, closing, and reversing entries. The spiral of learning takes business students through a complete accounting cycle several times, each time building on what they learned previously but adding new processes, subject matter, and skills.

Another purpose of evaluation is to *diagnose.* Diagnosis is the process of identifying the point at which students need to increase their proficiency to master a task. Diagnostic tests are used both to place students at the onset of instruction and to discover the underlying causes of deficiencies in student learning as instruction unfolds. Students enrolled in typewriting at the postsecondary level, for example, may be given a typing proficiency test as a basis for placement in the proper course or instructional module. Diagnostic tests used to identify deficiencies should measure intensively in limited areas of subject matter, thus making it possible to locate specific weaknesses. Diagnostic tests are frequently given at the beginning of a business communication course to identify specific areas of weakness, such as grammar, punctuation, or spelling, as a basis for a prescription for learning. If a student demonstrates mastery of the task, he or she is certified as competent and is allowed to move on immediately to another task. If a student does not demonstrate mastery, he or she may undertake instruction in the task. At a point where the student wishes to demonstrate mastery, the test may be taken.

Tests are also used for *prediction.* The business student's present achievement level in English, for example, is one of the best indicators of future achievement in shorthand transcription.

Finally, student assessment is used as a basis for *individual guidance.* The teacher and/or guidance counselor uses a battery of aptitude, interest, and achievement tests as one means of assisting in career guidance. In any event, self-evaluation should be included as a vital part of the total evaluation process. One of the teacher's responsibilities is to provide opportunities and guidance for students in assessing their performance in all areas under study. Self-evaluation is an integral part of the instructional program in business education. Learning to evaluate oneself realistically is a valuable benefit of the learning process.

Current emphasis in student evaluation focuses on comparisons that are intraindividual rather than interindividual. This represents a change from normative comparisons (that is, comparisons with other persons, such as through the use of standardized tests) to absolute comparisons (that is, comparisons with absolute standards, as in a teacher-made, criterion-referenced test). Intrastudent evaluation is concerned with measuring *what* rather than *how much* the student has learned.

Assessments of student learning are conducted for reasons other than those relating specifically to students. A vital measure of the effectiveness of the business education curriculum is the performance of students. Evaluation of student achievement tells a teacher how effective he or she has been in designing and implementing instructional units. By completing an item analysis of tests, the teacher can pinpoint areas that students did not master. Thus tests may be analyzed for teaching inadequacies as well as for student difficulties.

METHODS OF EVALUATION

Evaluation devices are classified in a number of ways according to type, form, and function. They are grouped in this chapter into two main categories: formal techniques and informal techniques.

Formal techniques

The best known formal evaluation techniques are teacher-made tests. These tests may be oral or written, in-class or take-home, closed book or open book, group or individual, or speed or power in typewriting. In addition to these, the teacher may choose to use published tests that may or may not be standardized. Published tests that accompany many of the business education texts are available from the publisher. There are, however, a limited number of published achievement and aptitude tests in business education that the teacher may wish to use.

Tests may be classified into three categories: performance, essay, and objective. Performance tests are used widely in business education. Ordinarily, students respond to the test question or situation by an overt action. These tests generally require students to integrate a body of knowledge or a number of skills. Examples of performance tests include production tests in typewriting, transcription tests in shorthand, and problem tests in accounting. Essay tests contain questions or instructions that require the student to compose a more-or-less extensive, original written response. The questions frequently begin with words such as *discuss, explain, describe,* or *compare.* Objective tests generally sample specific items of knowledge. A simple, predetermined list of answers is usually prepared, thus eliminating much judgment or opinion in correcting the papers. Examples of objective tests include true-false, multiple-choice, matching, classification, completion, and short-answer types.

Other examples of formal evaluation techniques include case studies (used in business law and business principles and management), reports and term papers (used in social-business courses, such as comparative economic systems, consumer economics, and economics), projects and simulations (used in office practice), and practice sets and application exercises (used in accounting).

TESTS IN PRINT.   Published tests may be achievement- or norm-referenced, in which students are compared to other students, or they may be criterion-referenced tests, in which students are compared to a given standard. The results of norm-referenced tests are usually reported in percentiles. A student scoring at the 75th percentile has performed equal to or better than 75 percent of similar students who were used to establish the norms of the test. (By checking the test manual for a description of the population used to establish the norms, the teacher can decide whether or not his or her students have characteristics similar to those of students used to determine the norms.) Criterion-referenced results are reported in terms of the number of objectives achieved.

Examples of published business education tests are listed below along with the grade levels or groups for which each test is designed, the publisher, and a brief description of the test.

National Business Entrance Tests. Grades 11–16 and adults. National Business Education Association. Subtests available as separates; three series.

    a. General Testing Series (Series 2500), 1972. Six tests.
        1. Business Fundamentals and General Information Test
        2. Bookkeeping Test
        3. General Office Clerical Test
        4. Machine Calculation Test
        5. Stenographic Test
        6. Typewriting Test

    b. Short Form Series 1955
        1. Stenographic Test
        2. Typewriting Test

    c. Official Testing Series (Series 2000 and 2100), 1974. Administered only at NBET Centers which may be established in any community.
        1. Business Fundamentals and General Information Test
        2. Bookkeeping Test
        3. General Office Clerical Test
        4. Machine Calculation Test
        5. Stenographic Test
        6. Typewriting Test

Short Occupational Knowledge Test for Bookkeepers, Job Applicants. Science Research Associates, 1970. Score is pass, fail, or unclassifiable.

Clerical Speed and Accuracy: Differential Aptitude Test. Grades 8–12 and adults. Psychological Corporation, 1972, 1974. Measures speed and accuracy of perception and marking.

D.A.T. Spelling Test and D.A.T. Language Usage Test. Grades 8–12. Psychological Corporation, 1972, 1974. Two tests measuring command of correct English. Designed to predict effectiveness in secretarial and other jobs in which correctness of expression is essential.

Hay Clerical Test Battery. Applicants for clerical positions. Aptitude Test Service, 1972. Four tests: a) Test I: The Warm-up, b) Number Perception Test, c) Name-finding Test, d) Number Series Completion Test.

Minnesota Clerical Test. Grades 8–12 and adults. Psychological Corporation, 1959. Two scores: number comparison and name comparison.

Personnel Institute Clerical Tests. Clerical personnel and typists-stenographers-secretaries. Personnel Institute, 1967. Twelve tests.

    a. Preliminary Screening Interview
    b. Confidential Personal History Inventory
    c. Diagnostic Interviewer's Guide
    d. Work Reference Investigation
    e. Mental Alertness Test (formerly Otis Employment Test)
    f. Vocabulary Test
    g. Comparing Names Test
    h. Copying Numbers Test
    i. Arithmetic Test
    j. Grammar Test
    k. Spelling Test
    l. Typing Test

The Short Employment Tests. Clerical applicants. Psychological Corporation, 1972. Three tests: verbal, numerical, clerical.

Short Tests of Clerical Ability. Applicants for office positions. Science Research Associates, 1960. Seven tests: coding, checking, filing, directions, arithmetic, business vocabulary, language.

Survey of Clerical Skills: Individual Placement Series. Adults. Personnel Research Associates, 1966. Five scores: spelling, office math, office terms, filing, grammar.

Office Information and Skills Tests: Content Evaluation Series. High school. Houghton Mifflin Company, 1972. Four scores: office information, error location and correction, typewriting, transcription.

Appraisal of Occupational Aptitudes. High school and adults. Houghton Mifflin Company, 1971. Eight scores: checking letters, checking numbers, filing names, filing numbers, posting names, posting numbers, arithmetical computation and reasoning, desk calculator. Norms for women only.

Clerical Worker Examination. Clerical workers. McCann Associates, 1963. Five scores: clerical speed and accuracy, verbal ability, quantitative ability, total ability, total.

General Clerical Test. Grades 9–16 and clerical job applicants. Psychological Corporation, 1972. Four scores: clerical speed and accuracy, numerical ability, verbal facility, total.

Office Skills Achievement Test. Employees. Psychometric Affiliates, 1963. Seven scores: business letter, grammar, checking, filing, arithmetic, written directions, total.

Office Worker Test. Office workers. International Personnel Management Association, 1972. Eleven scores: reading, vocabulary, reasoning, arithmetic, checking, filing, spelling, punctuation, usage, information, total. Distribution restricted to member public personnel agencies and nonmember agencies approved by the publisher.

Secretarial Performance Analysis. Employees. Psychologists and Educators, 1969. Ratings by supervisors. Four scores: basic skills, executive skills, personal attributes, total.

Short Occupational Knowledge Test for Secretaries. Job applicants. Science Research Associates, 1970. Score is pass, fail, unclassifiable.

Typing Test for Business. Job applicants. Psychological Corporation, 1968. Restricted to personnel departments.

Agribusiness Achievement Test. Grades 9–12. Houghton Mifflin Company, 1972. Four subtests: animal science, plant and soil science, mechanics, and management.

Modern Economics Test. Grades 10–12. Houghton Mifflin Company, 1970. Covers four areas: the national income, monetary and fiscal policy, price systems, international economics and economic development.

Business English Test: Dailey Vocational Test, 1970. Grades 8–12 and adults. Houghton Mifflin Company. Tests spelling, punctuation, capitalization, and grammar. Covers the fundamentals of English involved in clerical, secretarial, and business careers.

Work Values Inventory. Grades 7–12 and adults. Houghton Mifflin Company, 1972. Measures fifteen values: intellectual stimulation, job achievement, way of life, economic returns, altruism, creativity, relationships with associates, job security, prestige, management of others, variety, aesthetics, independence, supervisory relations, and physical surroundings.

Vocational Planning Inventory. Grades 8–10, 11–12; 13 entrants. Science Research Associates, 1970. The battery consists of the SRA Arithmetic Index, SRA Pictorial Reasoning Test, SRA Verbal Form, Survey of Interpersonal Values, Mechanics subtest of the Flanagan Aptitude Classification Test, and the following subtests of the Flanagan Industrial Tests: Arithmetic, Assembly, Expression, Memory, Scales, and Tables. Tests cannot be scored locally; the student's copy of his or her test report presents predicted grades in nine or ten areas including agriculture, business, construction trades, drafting and design, electronics and electrical trades, home economics and health, mechanics and mechanical maintenance, metal trades, general academic, general vocational. The counselor's copy of an individual test report also presents national percentile rank norms for the component tests, single scores for the seven or eight nonpersonality tests, and twelve value scores on the two personality tests. Two levels. High school prediction program for vocational students in grades 8–10 for predicting success in grades 9–12 in areas listed above; post high school prediction program for vocational students in grades 11–12 and grade 13 entrants.

Wide Range Employment Sample Test. Ages 16–35 (normal and handicapped). Guidance Associates of Delaware, 1973. Manual refers to the test as The Jasak-King Work Samples, originally developed for use with mentally and physically handicapped persons enrolled in a rehabilitation workshop. Twelve scores: folding, stapling, bottle packaging, rice measuring, screw assembly, tag stringing, swatch pasting, collating, color and shade matching, pattern matching, total performance, total errors.

Informal techniques

Business teachers also make frequent use of informal means of appraising student performance. The technique that is used most often is observation. Checklist and rating scales are examples of observational tools that may be used to assess student process and product. In typewriting, for instance, teachers use checklists to rate student technique that is best evaluated through observation as opposed to an examination of the typescript. Observation techniques may also be employed when the teacher evaluates the finished product; for instance, the teacher or student may use a rating scale or a model when evaluating a letter that has been transcribed or a report that has been typed.

Observational procedures are one of the most valuable tools for process evaluation. The teacher moves around an office machines class, for example, providing assistance as needed—explanations, encouragement, instruction, and on-the-spot remediation.

Other informal techniques include student opinionaires, case studies, anecdotal records, interviews, self-rating scales, personal data forms, discussions, autobiographies, and role-playing incidents.

PLANNING A TEST

When business teachers prepare any test—pre- or posttest for an instructional module, short quiz, unit test, or end-of-course examination—they have to make a number of decisions. Planning a test may not be an elaborate, laborious process, but it should include adequate advance planning. Some of the decisions that teachers make in planning for testing are as follows:

1. *When or how often to test.* Within the framework of the grading period of the school or college (9 weeks, a quarter, a semester, and so on), the business teacher decides on the approximate number of tests and the tentative time for each when he or she plans the course or unit of instruction. Frequent testing, as opposed to once or twice a quarter, provides a more reliable basis for evaluation, whereas too frequent testing does not improve the instructional program and can result in test passing as the major goal for study. The frequency of testing is determined in part by the nature of the course itself. In courses such as typewriting, shorthand, and business machines, there are frequent, even daily, papers that provide a continuing measure of student performance. In such cases, unit tests may be spaced farther apart.

2. *What kinds of questions or items to use.* The most commonly used types of test questions in business education are performance, objective, and essay, in that order. The teacher selects the type of item most appropriate for the subject matter of the course, such as performance items in typewriting and shorthand, case problems in business law, and objective or essay items in consumer economics and general business. Essay and performance tests are easier to prepare than objective tests, but they take longer to score. The quality of the test depends upon writing satisfactory items, regardless of type, and including a representative sample of the various aspects of the content.

3. *How many questions or the length of the test.* To make this decision, the teacher needs to know the length of the testing period and the type of questions he or she plans to use. For instance, one essay question or two production

problems may take longer to complete than thirty multiple-choice items. Unless one of the criteria for the test is speed, as in typewriting and shorthand, the general trend is to include few items so that most students have time to attempt all of them. As a rule of thumb, students can usually complete true-false items at the rate of two per minute and multiple-choice items at the rate of one per minute. Naturally, one would need to extend this time estimate if items were long or complex.

4. *What emphases to give various aspects of content and taxonomic levels.* The emphasis on the various areas of content in a test (as reflected in the objectives) should be in the same proportion to the emphasis in the instructional program. For example, if the teacher plans to devote one class period of a unit on banking to installment loans, and only part of a period to types of banks, then he or she would plan for more test items on loans than on types of banks. To accomplish this, the teacher outlines the test specifications (see Table 4.1). On one axis of a 2 X 2 grid, the teacher lists the topics or content to be included and the relative importance or weight of each. On the other axis, he or she lists the taxonomic levels. The teacher then records the number of questions desired in each category. A majority of the test items generally fall within the cognitive domain (see Module 5.2). The taxonomic levels used in Table 4.1 are modifications of Bloom's original cognitive taxonomy. His modified system contains four levels: knowledge, understanding, application of knowledge, and application of understanding. *Evaluation of knowledge* requires assessment of the student's recall of specific information or responses previously practiced in learning experiences. At the *understanding* level, behaviors such as interpretation, translation, summarization, analysis, detection of similarities and differences, all of which demonstrate understanding as well as recall of knowledge, are evaluated. *Application of knowledge* calls for evaluating the student's ability to apply previously learned knowledge to the solution of known problems. The most

table 4.1
DEVELOPING TEST SPECIFICATIONS

CONTENT/SKILLS	RELATIVE WEIGHT	KNOW-LEDGE	UNDER-STANDING	APPLICATION OF KNOWLEDGE	APPLICATION OF UNDERSTANDING	
Axis 1						
Types of Banks	10	3	1			(4)
Deposits	20	3	2	2	1	(8)
Loans	20	2	2	2	2	(8)
Transferring Funds	10	2		2		(4)
Trust Services	10	2		2		(4)
Renting Safe Deposit Boxes	10	1		3		(4)
Keeping Deposits Safe	10	1	2	1		(4)
Federal Reserve System	10	1	1	1	1	(4)
Total		15	8	13	4	(40)

Axis 2 spans KNOW-LEDGE, UNDER-STANDING, APPLICATION OF KNOWLEDGE, APPLICATION OF UNDERSTANDING.

complex of the four levels is *application of understanding.* At least one element of the problem, either in the condition or in the solution required, must be new to the student; that is, it is expected that the student has not experienced this problem before.[2]

   5. *What level and distribution of difficulties are appropriate for the questions included in the test.* There are two approaches the teacher may consider in writing the test items. One is to identify criteria and write items to measure mastery of the criteria. The goal of this approach is mastery, so the teacher wants most of the students to answer most of the questions correctly. The second approach is to write questions that show relative levels of achievement among students; thus, a test would deliberately include easy, somewhat difficult, and difficult items.

   6. *How to draft the test items and write the directions.* Using the information from the preceding steps, the teacher selects the test items and directions.

The taxonomy of educational objectives

   Bloom and others[3] describe six different levels of educational objectives that have implications for the way in which test items are constructed. The first three levels (recall, comprehension, and application) illustrate, in the samples that follow, why some tests measure a person's understanding related to performance and others do not.

   The usefulness of a test is related to how and why it was written. A test developed to measure one's knowledge measures only whether a person can *recall* the facts. The following is an example written to measure a business student's *knowledge.*

What is the formula for calculating interest on a loan for one year?

(Answer: $I = P \times R$)

If students can answer this question, we know they can repeat the formula for figuring interest on loans. We do not know whether they understand the formula or whether they can apply it.

   Items written on the *comprehension* level are designed to determine if a student can use the knowledge in specified or taught situations. Such items allow the instructor to determine that a student understands the material in the situation given; the instructor cannot judge whether the student can use the material in a situation different from that taught. For example, if we assume that the student has been taught to calculate interest on a business loan for a three-year period, the following would be an example of a comprehension-level item.

Calculate the interest on $1,000 at 6% for 3 years.

(Answer: $1,000 \times .06 \times 3 = 180)

If a student can arrive at the correct answer to this question, we know that he can do what he has been taught. We still do not know whether he can apply the formula in a setting where a unique problem is encountered.

The third level at which meaningful business education test items can be written is the *application* level. At this level, the objective of the test item is to determine if students can apply their knowledge in new, untaught situations. This type of test usually requires the presentation of a real-life problem to which the student is asked to react. Assuming that the formula for obtaining interest was taught as shown above, the following would be an application-level item.

Jim Adams paid $10 interest on a loan of $800 for 90 days. What was the *rate* of interest?

(Answer: The interest charge of $10 for 90 days (¼ of a year) is equal to a charge of $40 for one year (4 × $10 = $40) or ($10 ÷ ¼ = $40). Hence, the rate of interest he paid was 5% ($40/$800 = .05 = 5%).)

As you can see, instructors can obtain more information about the ability of students to use the information they have learned if tests are designed at the comprehension and application levels instead of at the knowledge level only. Far too many tests are written to measure only the knowledge level. These kinds of items do not determine whether the student can use the information in a real-life or on-the-job situation. An instructor can only evaluate the effectiveness of a test if he or she is sure of the level the items are to assess. During the initial introduction of material, it is appropriate to test students' knowledge of basic facts (definitions, formulas, principles, and so on). Most instructors move from this stage to a series of highly prescribed examples to show basic applications of the information. Students are then tested with comprehension-level items to determine if they can apply the knowledge in those situations they were taught. Later, they are asked to apply and integrate many types of knowledge learned earlier to new situations. When they can apply the knowledge to situations they have never experienced before, they are ready to enter application level items and/or occupational placement.

Instructions or directions should be clearly written for each section of the test so that students know specifically what to do, how to do it, and where to place the response. If students are not familiar with the type of test items, a sample item should be included. The sample item should not be numbered, but rather indicated with an "x." After the teacher drafts the items, he or she should compare them to the test specifications, checking number and type of questions.

Each business teacher or department may want to develop a resource file of test items by subject or, more specifically, by objective. To begin the file, each test item should be written on a 3 × 5 card, coded to an objective, and filed behind the appropriate objective. Test items reflecting different levels of difficulty and taxonomic levels should be written for each objective and the items periodically revised, discarding inappropriate items and adding new ones so that a current selection of items is available to the teacher in constructing a test.

7. *What should be the order of the items.* The teacher considers several factors in arranging the test items; these include type of questions, difficulty of the items, and content. Items of the same type—true-false, multiple-choice, and so on—are generally grouped together. Within each section, test items are usually arranged in order of difficulty, beginning with the easiest items. Placing items relating to the same topic together aids the students in sequential thought processes.

8. *What to include in the scoring key.* A key for the test should be prepared, preferably at the time the test is put together. If some items have more than one correct answer, all possible responses should be included. For essay items, the main ideas should be listed and the number of points decided upon for the various aspects of the answer.

Readability of test items

When preparing test items, the teacher should remember that the function of a test is to determine whether a student understands what has been taught. The vocabulary level and sentence structure of the items should be clear and written at a level appropriate for students.

CONSTRUCTING WRITTEN TESTS

There are two major construction procedures used in developing instruments to measure competence in a given task. The first procedure is used for developing written tests of understanding. The second procedure is used in the development of instruments for the assessment of performance and attitude. The development of tests measuring understanding will be discussed first.

Essay tests

Essay tests can be used in business courses such as business law, general business, or consumer education. When constructing items, the teacher will find it helpful to keep several points in mind:

1. Ask questions or set up situations that require students to demonstrate their command of knowledge; that is, they are to select specific facts from the mass of information they possess, to organize their thinking, and to express ideas in their own words. Here are some examples of essay questions that can be asked:

Present arguments for and against . . .
Tell in your own words . . .
What would be the result of . . .
Suggest ways of correcting . . .
What are the differences . . .
Outline a method for . . .
Discuss the change in attitude . . .

2. Write the question so that students know specifically what they are to do. Avoid such questions as "Describe what you know about. . . ." In some items, it may be appropriate to specify a minimum length or minimum number of points to be discussed.

3. In general, construct several specific questions that can be answered somewhat briefly as opposed to one or two all-encompassing questions.

Short-answer tests

Another type of test used in business education courses is the short-answer test. One form is the completion item in which part of the information is given and part is omitted. Students select their answers from the many that come to mind; therefore, there may be a wide variety of responses.

In addition to one- or two-word completion items, other short-answer tests call for one or two complete sentences, definitions, lists, and so on. The information called for is generally factual; that is, list, name, define. If the student is to list objects or items in order, this should be indicated in the directions. For example, "List, in order, six steps in reconciling your bank statement."

Hardaway differentiates between essay and longer supply type items (short answer). "Essay questions may require no longer answers than the longer supply types. The differentiation is not in the length but in the mental processes being tested. The essay test should be reserved for situations where it is desirable to have the student 'describe,' 'compare or contrast,' and the like . . . testing the higher mental processes such as interpretation, analysis, synthesis, application, or evaluation should be the goal."[4]

Multiple-item tests

Multiple-item tests include multiple-choice, matching, and classification. Multiple-choice is the favorite of test experts and is widely used by teachers. Matching and classification items are appropriate for measuring factual information and vocabulary.

When planning multiple-choice items, the teacher should begin by reviewing the course/unit/module objectives and listing key ideas relating to the content. (This helps to ensure that test items will focus on important concepts and understandings rather than insignificant points.) The key ideas, principles, and generalizations from the course are used as the basis for developing sound items. Then, as nearly as possible, the items should be worded so that the student is required to apply knowledge rather than repeat facts.

The multiple-choice item usually begins with a stem question or an incomplete statement that can be answered concisely and for which it is possible to write *plausible* but incorrect answers. Four answers for each item are written to reduce the chances of guessing the correct response. The pattern of the *correct response* (that is, the length and grammatical structure) should be followed in writing the incorrect responses. Sometimes there is a tendency for the teacher to write the correct response more precisely and with greater detail, thus providing an irrelevant clue. All responses should be plural if the stem calls for a plural response and, if possible, the stem should be worded so that *a/an* is not the last word. *A/an* is included as part of the response if it is needed. If the choices are a series of numbers, as in a business math exam, the numbers are arranged in ascending or descending order.

After administering the multiple-choice items, the teacher may want to tally the number of student responses to each of the different answers. Choices that were not selected should be discarded or revised. (The teacher should revise items periodically if they are being retained as part of a pool of test items.)

It is generally a good idea to avoid questions that call for an incorrect response ("which of the following is *not* . . .") and those where the response is "none of these" or "all of these." The latter type might be used in business math when all or none of the responses are correct. The following is an example of a multiple-choice test item with directions.

Directions: In the numbered blank space on your answer sheet, write the letter that corresponds to the word or phrase that *best* answers or completes the question. The first item (X) is answered as a sample.

1. Harvey Johnson needs to purchase a new tractor for use on his farm, but he does not have enough cash. He goes to the bank to secure a loan. For which type loan would Mr. Johnson probably apply?
   A. Mortgage loan
   B. Personal loan
   C. Federal Reserve loan
   D. Commercial loan

Matching tests

Matching tests can be successfully used in business education subjects to evaluate knowledge of vocabulary, to classify entries by account in accounting, or to match shorthand words with corresponding longhand words. The most common type of matching test consists of related words, phrases, or sentences in each column to be selected or matched.

It is preferable to limit each section of a matching test to approximately eight to ten items, with two or three additional items, thus allowing ten to twelve items in the answer column. Care should be taken to see that two or three responses are not given for a single item. Matching tests have certain limitations, that is, only factual material is used and the statements must be true. The following example illustrates a matching item.

Directions: Match each description in Column I with one of the items listed alphabetically in Column II. Write your answer in the numbered blank space on your answer sheet.

	Column I		Column II
1.	Enforces Truth in Lending Act	A.	Better Business Bureau
2.	Approves drugs for use in the United States	B.	Department of Agriculture
3.	Inspects and grades meat	C.	Federal Consumer Commission
4.	Nonprofit agency that protects and informs consumers	D.	Federal Trade Commission
		E.	Food and Drug Administration
5.	Investigates fraud through the mails	F.	Interstate Commerce Commission
		G.	U.S. Department of Commerce
		H.	U.S. Postal Service

True-false tests

On the surface, true-false items may seem easy to construct. However, it is not easy to avoid ambiguous words or phrases and to construct items that are totally true or totally false. True-false tests are easy to administer and may be given orally by the teacher or placed on tape. The tests do, however, tend to measure knowledge of facts rather than the ability to reason. Some points for consideration when writing true-false items are as follows:

1. Prepare items that are entirely true or entirely false. (See true-false-neither alternative, pages 82–83.)
2. Use simple sentence structure and fairly short sentences. (Long sentences tend to be true.)
3. Avoid taking a sentence from a module or a book and making it false by changing a few words or inserting "not."
4. Guard against irrelevant clues such as specific determiners. Terms such as *always, all, never, none* are usually indicators of false statements, whereas words such as *some, often, usually,* and *sometimes* are indicators of true statements.
5. Limit each test item to one idea. Complex sentences that combine two or more ideas tend to be partly true and partly false.
6. Maintain a balance of true-false items over a period of time so that students do not pick up a teacher preference for one type item or the other.

True-false-neither tests

One alternative to the traditional true-false test is the true-false-neither test which eliminates the limitation that all items must be *entirely* true or false. True-false-neither items could include compound sentences in which one clause is true and one is false, or statements that are partially true or partially false, or statements that are true under some circumstances and false under others. True-false-neither format provides a plausible alternative for scoring disagreements, in which some teachers count an item true only if it is entirely true while others feel that items that are partially true should be marked true. It is important for the teacher to explain to students his or her own interpretation of true and/or false statements.

The following example illustrates a true-false-neither test.

Directions: Respond to each statement below by writing "T," "F," or "N" in the numbered blank on your answer sheet. Write "T" if the statement is true; write "F" if the statement is false; write "N" if the statement is neither entirely true nor entirely false or if the statement may be true under some conditions and false under others. "X" is a sample item.

1. It is economical to compose form letters to take care of common, recurring situations.
2. A medical examination is required before life insurance is issued to a person.

CONSTRUCTING PERFORMANCE TESTS

Performance instruments

The evaluation of performance requires a different methodology from that used when writing a test. While written tests usually measure knowledge or attitudes previously learned, performance measurement allows the teacher to judge performance as it is taking place. Performance appraisal in business education takes the form of performance tests or product evaluations. Performance tests are used when the teacher wishes to determine if the student can perform a process correctly as well as produce a usable product. Product evaluations are used when the teacher is primarily interested in determining whether the student can produce a usable product. In performance testing, the teacher observes the student as he or she completes the process to determine if the product is completed correctly. For example, in taking dictation in third-semester shorthand, the student is expected to write the outlines fluently, as opposed to drawing them, and to use correct motions in forming the characters. Thus, the teacher observes *how* students write outlines in addition to evaluating their transcripts. Performance tests are widely used in business education skill courses and may be administered on an individual or a group basis. In individualized classes, performance tests are administered on a one-to-one basis. If the test is long, it may cause problems since the teacher is not in a position to provide assistance to other students who may need help.

After correct techniques are developed by business students, and as they acquire more proficiency in their skills, product evaluations replace performance checks. The product test allows the teacher to evaluate the finished product rather than the process itself. It also allows more flexibility since it can be scheduled at a fixed class period or during times when other students do not require teacher assistance.

The procedure for developing performance tests involves three major steps: (1) specifying the objectives, (2) specifying the items to be observed, and (3) specifying the criteria that determine successful completion of a task. The three-part objective should likewise include (1) a statement of the conditions given within which the student must perform, (2) the performance expected of the student, and (3) the standard against which student performance will be evaluated. The level of the expected performance is of critical concern to the teacher in developing performance tests. Typically, almost any performance in business education skill courses is a combination of more elementary performances. In constructing a performance test, the teacher must be sure that the student brings to the task an appropriate background of prerequisite *knowing* and *doing* skills. For this reason, much care should be taken in writing the objective and in selecting the correct verb. Once the verb is selected and the student is told the nature of the expected performance, the context or "givens" should be described. The givens describe the tools, previous knowledge, machines, software, or prerequisites that the student will be required to use in demonstrating the behavior. The third part of the three-part objective—the performance standard—is used to judge whether a student has mastered a task. It communicates the quality of performance expected and provides a basis for the teacher to judge the quality of the product, as in the following example:

> Given 150 words of dictation at 90 words per minute, the student is able to *transcribe* a business letter into mailable copy.

In a performance test, the items are typically steps of procedure that the student must complete correctly in order to complete the performance. In a product evaluation, the items are related to a finished product that can be observed. To continue the previous example, in order to turn out a mailable letter, the student

> types with reasonable accuracy and speed
> takes dictation in shorthand notes at 90 words per minute
> checks shorthand notes for grammar, punctuation, special notations
> estimates the length and placement of the business letter
> transcribes shorthand notes at the typewriter
> makes punctuation, spelling, and other editing corrections, and
> proofreads the finished product.

The procedures used to determine the items for both performance tests and product evaluations are quite similar. They both start with a definition of the learning objective. The next step is to determine which items should be observed during the performance on the finished product. When identifying and stating steps, the following rules should be observed:

1. Begin each step with a verb (major verb categories include, for example, *call, check, compile, compose, deliver, determine, type, duplicate, file,* and so on).
2. Make each step independent of other steps. (Avoid evaluating the same performance in more than one step.)
3. Include only one task performance in each step.

After the performance steps have been identified following the above procedure, they are used together with the performance objective as the foundation for developing a product performance test. The most common form of a performance test is a performance checklist which summarizes (a) the objective the student was to achieve, (b) the procedural learning steps he or she should have taken, and (c) criteria for making a judgment about whether the student completed the task satisfactorily. After the basic instrument is constructed, the teacher must determine how it is to be scored. If 100 percent mastery is required, the student must complete each step satisfactorily in terms of what can be seen after the performance is completed. Illustration 4.1 incorporates these ideas into a product performance checklist.

The following points summarize the detailed procedures that should be used in developing performance evaluation instruments:

1. Specify the objectives.
2. Determine whether to evaluate using a performance checklist or a final product evaluation.
3. List the procedural steps if a performance checklist is to be used.
4. List the factors to be rated after the performance if a product evaluation is to be used.
5. Identify critical items. (Determine if student and/or instructor checkpoints are needed when using a product evaluation.)
6. Determine the criteria for judging satisfactory completion of each step.
7. Establish the acceptable mastery level score for the instrument.

Less formal measures that the teacher may use for performance evaluation (both process and product) include technique checklists, production problems, and practice sets. (Examples of these are given in the chapters dealing with typewriting, shorthand, and accounting.) In essence, the teacher is evaluating performance daily in skills classes as he or she observes students (and provides appropriate assistance as needed) and as finished products are corrected.

CONSTRUCTING ATTITUDE-EVALUATION INSTRUMENTS

Evaluation of student attitudes and feelings (affective domain) is a complex but important phase of the total instructional program in business education. Since the teacher cannot view characteristics such as dependability, cooperation, friendliness, and so on, he or she then must rely on observable student actions as evidence of their presence. Attitudinal assessments may include teacher observation instruments, student self-evaluations, and student questionnaires or opinionnaires. The instruments may be used to assess both school-related and job-related attitudes and cover feelings about course organization, instructional materials, attitudes toward selected careers, to teacher assessment of student attitudes displayed on the job through cooperative job stations.

The process of constructing attitude-evaluation instruments parallels that used in constructing performance-evaluation instruments; that is, determine the attitude to be evaluated, specify the items to be observed, and identify the

illustration 4.1
PRODUCT PERFORMANCE CHECKLIST

Transcribe business letter

Course: Shorthand, Third Semester
TERMINAL PERFORMANCE OBJECTIVE:
Given: 150 words dictation at 90 words per minute
Performance: Transcribe at the typewriter
Standard: Mailable copy within 15 minutes

INSTRUCTOR CHECK POINTS	ITEMS TO BE OBSERVED	SATIS-FACTORY	UNSATIS-FACTORY	CRITERIA
	1. Received dictation in person.	1	0	All dictation was recorded.
	2. Checked shorthand notes.	2	0	Corrections and punctuation were added.
	3. Transcribed dictation using acceptable form and placement.	2	0	Acceptable transcription
	4. Proofread typing.	2	0	Checked special copy notations.
	5. Corrected copy.	2	0	Spelling, typing errors neatly corrected.
	6. Obtained signature.	1	0	No visible errors.
Total Score Possible		10		
Minimum Mastery Level Score		10		Total Score _____

criteria for acceptable performance of each item. The items on the attitude-evaluation instrument should be constructed so as to assess student mastery of objectives which specify (1) the environment in which the behavior is to be exhibited, (2) the attitude to be exhibited, and (3) the observable behavior expected. An example of an objective is as follows:

> In the outer office of a company, the receptionist greets visitors promptly with a smile and speaks in a pleasant voice.

Using this objective, the teacher may follow the previously described process to construct an evaluation instrument:

1. Attitude to be evaluated: Greets visitors promptly and courteously.

2. Items to be observed: Greets visitors promptly; greets visitors with a smile, pleasant voice.

3. Criteria for acceptable behavior:

Stops work immediately to greet visitors;
greets visitors with a smile;
if using phone, smiles or shows other
nonverbal recognition of visitors;
terminates telephone conversation as
quickly as possible;
speaks in a pleasant voice.

A checklist, such as the product performance checklist in Illustration 4.1, can be constructed by the teacher using this data. Although attitude-related behaviors and criteria are not as precise as in a performance checklist, the teacher can identify job-related and school-related attitudes and assess student demonstration of these attitudes.

IMPLEMENTING TESTS

Where learning is individualized, if a student performs satisfactorily on the preassessment instruments, he or she is allowed to move on to other learning objectives. If he does not demonstrate satisfactory achievement on the test instruments, then his performance is reviewed to diagnose the particular intermediate learning steps he has not mastered, and a prescription is given for further work in these areas. When the student again feels ready to demonstrate mastery of the task, he is allowed to repeat the posttest, and if he satisfactorily completes each of the instruments, he is allowed to move on. If he does not perform satisfactorily, he repeats work on those objectives that have not been mastered. This process, shown visually in Illustration 4.2, continues until he masters the learning task.

illustration 4.2
MASTERY FORMULA FOR TASK LEARNING

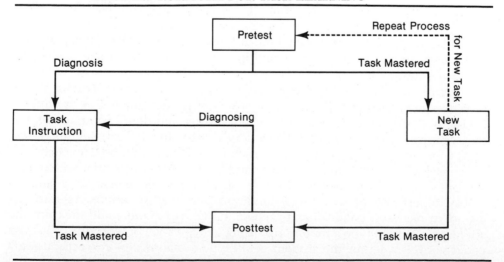

The assessment of student progress toward task objectives is complex, requiring measures of three aspects: knowing or technical information (cognitive), doing or performance (psychomotor), and attitude (affective). Each of these aspects is then evaluated by using more than one measure or instrument which results in separate scores. Another way to view multiple measures is to develop one instrument with more than one item measuring each specific objective in a learning package. The use of multiple assessments helps to improve the accuracy of measuring student performance.

Measuring student performance is subject to four sources of error. *Student error* can be minimized by motivating students to be careful and to do their best, but student mistakes can be corrected only by the students. *Instrument error* is the result of items being written in such a way that even careful students might misinterpret an item and write the wrong answer. Instrument error is usually due to inability on the part of the instructor to communicate with students through the evaluation instrument. One primary source of this error is the difference between the vocabulary of students and that of the instructor. This type of error can be controlled largely by the instructor as the test is developed or refined. *Scorer error,* made during the correction process, occurs when the instructor does not adequately indicate how to judge if the student responded with the correct answer. The instructor may think that he or she is being objective, and that judgments are free of personal bias, but many outside influences affect how one person judges another's performance. For example, if the person being judged is very similar to the instructor doing the scoring, the instructor tends to judge higher; if the overall general impression of the answer (form, grammar, neatness) is good, the instructor doing the scoring will tend to judge higher. These factors do not relate to how well a student has mastered the content but to other factors that the scorer cannot separate from his or her judgments. *Guessing error* occurs when students, not knowing the answer to a question, attempt to guess the answer. Guessing causes a student's score on an instrument to vary from one time to the next although his or her knowledge does not vary. Total scores may vary depending on how well the student is able to guess. Although there are many sources of error that can affect a test score, if the instructor uses multiple assessments, he or she can reduce error to a minimum.

Besides needing multiple measures to reduce error, the instructor should measure more than one dimension or aspect of performance. For example, it is usually desirable to measure both the knowing and doing components of a task. Many instructors feel that if a student's ability to "do" is being measured, then what he or she knows is already measured. This would be true perhaps if every possible "doing" activity that an individual encounters relative to a particular task could be measured. However, it is not possible to measure a person's ability to perform a task under all conditions and in all situations. Assume that a student has been taught how to type a manuscript. One could measure the student's ability to type a manuscript using a given style of footnoting, but one could not tell whether the student could type a manuscript correctly using a different form for footnotes. If students can perform the task in one situation and know the rules, principles, or generalizations for performing the task in other situations, one can be more assured that transfer of learning will take place. Assessments of knowing and doing that complement each other provide more information concerning whether a student has mastered a task than either a knowing or doing assessment alone. It is highly important for the learner to know *why*, in order to be able to apply what was learned to similar, but new, situations.

GRADING STANDARDS

A universal problem for teachers at all levels is how to grade. The problem centers primarily around the use of variable or fixed standards of performance as the basis for determining grades.

According to Ebel, there are at least two shortcomings of any grading system: "(1) the lack of clearly defined, generally accepted, scrupulously observed definitions of what the various marks should mean, and (2) the lack of sufficient relevant, objective evidence to use as a basis for assigning marks."[5]

Grading and individualized instruction

The traditional concept of grading has been based on the idea of a minimum standard, with the grade reflecting how far above or below the standard a particular student scores. In an individualized instructional program, there is no minimum standard for the class, but rather a standard for each student. The ultimate plan for grading/evaluating in individualized instruction is a checklist that includes the concepts and skills for each course. Ideally the teacher and student together identify objectives for a given period of time and then, at the end of that time, evaluate how well the student has done in reaching these objectives.

While some institutions use a checklist to report student performance, larger numbers of institutions use grades. One approach to grading individualized instruction is to base students' grades on the growth they have made at their own functioning levels since the previous grading period.

Relative scale

One method of grading is relative marking, that is, grades are based on students' relative standings within a class or classes, or in relation to performances of past classes. Hardaway recommends that grades which represent knowledge of subject matter should be based on relative standings.[6]

Absolute scale

In courses that develop technical skills for vocational purposes, fixed standards are usually the basis for grading. In this approach, expected (fixed) levels of performance for each grading period and for each grade are specified, and students' grades reflect the degree of achievement of the goals. (See chapters on typewriting and shorthand for examples of standards and grades.) Even with the use of fixed standards, there are considerable variations among teachers and schools. Standards tend to vary from one school to the next since school aims, school populations, and employment conditions and/or requirements vary from place to place.

In deciding on the grading system to use, the teacher needs to consider factors such as the policy of the school, the course itself, the makeup of the classes (relative heterogeneity or homogeneity), the advantages and disadvantages of each grading approach, the responsibility to the employment community, and the individual needs of students.

LEARNING ACTIVITIES

1. Review the manual and test covering one published business education test. Prepare a report to include (a) content area for which the test is designed, (b) date of publication, (c) author(s), (d) population used to establish norms, (e) how the results are reported (percentile, standard score, and so on).
2. Write four test items of any type and for any content area to illustrate Baldwin's four taxonomic levels (one item for each level).
3. Interview a business education teacher and report on the formal and informal techniques he or she uses to evaluate student performance.
4. Construct one of each of the following types of test items, using any business education subject area or task of your choice. Specify the taxonomic level of each item you write: (a) essay, (b) short-answer, (c) multiple-choice, (d) true-false or true-false-neither, (e) matching.
5. Write directions to accompany each test item you wrote for Number 4.
6. Select one of the following attitudinal traits, or specify one of your choice, and construct an attitude-evaluation checklist: friendliness, cooperation, enthusiasm, initiative, loyalty.
7. Construct a checklist covering the evaluation of *process of performance* for one of the following tasks. Refer to other appropriate chapters in this text if necessary.

     operating the ten-key adding or calculating machine in the related cooperative work experience class
     taking dictation at 90 words per minute in third-semester shorthand
     operating the keyboard in beginning typewriting
8. Construct a *product performance* checklist covering performance of a task from one of the following courses in which you will evaluate the production of a finished product.
     Advanced Typewriting
     Advanced Shorthand
     Office Practice
     Advanced Accounting
9. Select a business education subject of your choice and make the decisions regarding the first five steps in "Planning a Test." A decision regarding the criterion in Step 1 should be made in view of the course as a whole; decisions regarding criteria identified in Steps 2 to 5 should be made as related to one test.

SELF-TEST

1. Evaluation of learning may be best described as _____

   _____

   _____

2. For each of the following situations, state the *purpose* of evaluation:
   a. Alice Manders enrolls in the business education program at Forest Postsecond-ary Vocational Technical School. On the first day, the teacher gives Alice a typewriting test.
      Purpose: _____

      _____

   b. John Stanford uses an individualized instructional approach in Business Commu-nication. On Thursday, all of the students will take a test on punctuation.
      Purpose: _____

      _____

   c. During winter quarter exam week at Broxton Senior High School, Linda Mitch-ell gives a test in Business Law.
      Purpose: _____

      _____

   d. Sandra Roberts has completed the second instructional module in Business Math and signs up to take the posttest on Tuesday.
      Purpose: _____

      _____

   e. Wayne Lanier reviews the English grades of students enrolled in Shorthand II.
      Purpose: _____

      _____

3. List three examples of formal and informal evaluation techniques and cite at least one instance when you might use each.
4. Briefly explain the following:
   a. student error
   b. instrument error
   c. guessing error
   d. scorer error
5. In business education skills courses, the teacher should use absolute standards rather than flexible grading since he or she has an obligation to the prospective employer. (Defend or refute this statement.)
6. Outline the procedure for developing performance- or attitude-evaluation instru-ments.

SUMMARY

Evaluation of student progress in business education is necessary to (1) measure achievement, (2) determine student readiness for subsequent steps in learning, (3) diagnose deficiencies, (4) predict achievement, (5) serve as a basis for individual prescription and guidance, and (6) provide a measure of teacher instructional effectiveness. Current emphases in student evaluation focus on comparisons that are intraindividual rather than interindividual. Intrastudent evaluation is concerned with measuring *what* rather than *how much* the student has learned. This represents a change from normative comparisons to absolute comparisons.

Evaluation devices may be classified as formal or informal. Formal evaluation devices are teacher-made tests of the performance, essay, or objective type. A limited number of business education tests are available in print. Observation is a widely used informal means of appraising student performance; other means include opinionnaires, case studies, discussions, and simulated incidents.

Planning a test involves making decisions about (1) how often to test, (2) what kinds of items to use, (3) how long the test should be, (4) what weight to give to various items of content, (5) what level and distribution of difficulties are appropriate for test items, (6) how to write test items and directions, (7) how to order items, and (8) how to construct scoring keys.

The taxonomy of educational objectives may be used to ensure an appropriate range of learning objectives and, ultimately, test items. The first three levels are especially relevant to business education tests. Items written on the *knowledge level* serve to determine whether students can recall facts. Items written on the *comprehension level* discriminate whether students can use the knowledge in taught situations. Items written on the *application level* distinguish whether students can apply their knowledge in new, untaught situations.

While written tests usually measure knowledge or attitudes previously learned, performance measurement allows the teacher to judge performance as it takes place. In performance testing, the teacher observes students as they complete a process to determine if the process is completed correctly. Such tests are widely used in shorthand and typing on an individual or group basis. After correct techniques are developed by students, product evaluations (production tests) allow the teacher to evaluate the finished product.

Attitudinal evaluation instruments require the teacher to rely on observable student reactions. These instruments may be used to assess both school-related and job-related attitudes. The process of constructing attitude-evaluation instruments involves determining the attitude to be evaluated, specifying the items to be observed, and identifying the criteria for acceptable performance of each item.

While some schools use a checklist to report student performance, a larger number use grades. One method of grading is *relative marking* in which grades are based on the relative standing of students within a given class. However, in courses that develop technical skills for vocational purposes, *fixed standards* are usually the basis for grading. In this approach, levels of performance for each grade and grading period are specified, and student grades reflect the degree of achievement of the goals, which may be set on either an individual or group basis. Standards tend to vary from one school to the next since aims, school population, employment conditions, and requirements vary from location to location.

References

[1]Benjamin S. Bloom, J. Thomas Hastings, George Madaus, *Handbook on Formative and Summative Evaluation of Student Learning* (New York: McGraw-Hill, 1971), p. 8.

[2]Ibid., p. 864.

[3]Benjamin Bloom, ed., *Taxonomy of Educational Objectives: The Classification of Educational Goals, Handbook 1, Cognitive Domain* (New York: McKay, 1956), p. 18.

[4]Mathilde Hardaway, *Testing and Evaluation in Business Education,* 3rd ed. (Cincinnati: South-Western, 1966), pp. 96–97.

[5]Robert L. Ebel, *Measuring Educational Achievement* (Englewood Cliffs, N.J.: Prentice-Hall, 1965), p. 401.

[6]Hardaway, *Testing and Evaluation,* p. 418.

chapter 5

PLANNING FOR INSTRUCTION IN BUSINESS EDUCATION

In the past, many decisions were made by teachers on a short-term basis, often as a matter of expediency. Today this is no longer possible. Both short- and long-range decisions are becoming more necessary: these decisions may be called for at any time before the lesson, during it, or after it has ended. This demands an increasing degree of professionalism from teachers as well as a framework within which decisions can be made.

In its simplest terms, decision making involves determining precise, concrete objectives and then selecting a course of action that is most likely to lead to a successful outcome. This decision-making process is central to the teacher-manager's job, and the three terms *authority, responsibility,* and *accountability* are only meaningful within this management decision-making context. The business teacher has to choose what is to be done and who is to do it: when, where, and how. Virtually every decision that a business teacher makes must be geared within the framework of planning, organizing, leading, and controlling, although the character of decision-making processes varies according to the function involved.

Most schools today are better equipped physically than ever before to provide superior educational programs. But the inevitable key to educational success is still the teacher. Competency-based teacher education programs are graduating teachers with a better grasp of the teaching-learning process, especially in regard to the skills commonly associated with planning, monitoring, and evaluating the outcomes of learning. Module 5.1 describes some of the competencies associated with successful teaching in a learner-centered environment.

The business teacher's analysis and prescription of educational objectives are facilitated by the recognition and use of the cognitive, affective, and psychomotor taxonomies. The use of these classifications of educational objectives ensures appropriate coverage of subject matter for all levels of student interest and achievement. Module 5.2 is designed to help the business teacher to discriminate these domains, to properly fit business education objectives into the schema, and to learn how to write performance objectives.

The ability to plan for instruction is essential to successful teaching in business education. Instructional plans need to encompass the design of the whole course of study, the structure of each unit plan, and the construction of the individual daily lesson plan or instructional module. Each of these plans has a unique and essential purpose in the work of the class and each is dependent on the other to form a unified and rational curricular structure. Planning helps the teacher to view the instructional program as a whole system of learning and to make sure that every learning activity contributes to the ultimate goal. Prior planning of units and lessons permits the teacher to establish clearly defined objectives, secure the necessary instructional materials, and select varied activities to enhance learning. Teachers who do not preplan thoroughly tend to use a limited range of activities and to provide uneven coverage of the subject matter. Module 5.3 covers the mechanics of planning courses, units, lesson plans, and modules.

The concept of mainstreaming, now incorporated into law, challenges business educators to develop new understandings and skills for working with students with special needs. Teachers are learning to recognize various forms of learning disabilities and to modify their courses to provide appropriate educational opportunities for handicapped students within the regular class. Module 5.4 deals with the problem of providing for differences among students in business classes.

module 5.1
THE ROLE OF THE BUSINESS TEACHER

This introductory module emphasizes the key role of the teacher as a manager of learning. When you finish this module, you should be able to (1) explain the functions of the business teacher as a manager of learning, (2) characterize the behavior of a business teacher in a student-centered learning environment, and (3) describe the nature of competencies identified as crucial for beginning teachers.

TEACHER FUNCTIONS

The key to what is accomplished in a business education program is the teacher. Decisions about course objectives, use of multimedia materials, classroom organization and management, and instructional techniques, for example, are the crucial variables that make the difference in a learning situation. At one time, the teacher was considered the center of the classroom and the transmitter of knowledge. A more contemporary view focuses on the students as the center of learning, with the teacher serving as a guide, diagnostician, and director.

The functions of the business teacher in instruction may be classified into four major areas: (1) planning, (2) organizing, (3) leading, and (4) controlling. The *planning* function includes tasks such as defining objectives, sequencing instructional topics, allocating the time available, and budgeting resources. While all the functions are necessary and related, planning is the key without which none of the other functions could be performed. During the planning process, decisions are made on the means to bridge the gap between where the learners *are* and where they *should be.* Planning is a decision-making function upon which the other functions are built.

The *organizing* function involves arranging the learning environment and delegating responsibilities so as to realize the objectives in the most efficient, effective, and economical manner.

Through the *leading* function, the teacher is responsible for inspiring, motivating, and encouraging students to achieve a given set of learning objectives. The more knowledge the teacher possesses about students, the more effective he or she will be in leading them. Students differ widely in their interests, abilities, goals, and achievements; therefore, differing motivational techniques must be used.

The *controlling* function involves determining the success of the organizing and leading functions for reaching objectives. If objectives are not being realized, the teacher may need to adjust (1) the instructional objectives to more realistically fit student needs or (2) the learning resources and motivational techniques. Attempts should be made to modify the learning situation before changing the objectives. The controlling function is an ongoing one. Problems should be observed and adjustments made as needed during the learning process rather than waiting until the end of a unit to identify problems that students are encountering.[1]

Does the teacher still "teach" in a student-centered learning environment? The answer is a definite *yes,* whenever he or she is the best resource available. Thus, when assembling resources for realizing each objective, the teacher should be considered as a primary source. At times he or she is the best resource for clarifying, explaining, demonstrating for the entire class, for a small group, or for an individual.

The following list summarizes some vital business teacher behaviors in a student-centered learning environment: (1) prescribes objectives, resources, and activities in cooperation with students; (2) involves students in group and independent decision making; (3) guides students toward independence and self-direction; (4) diagnoses and prescribes learning experiences for each student; (5) uses a wide variety of instructional techniques; (6) provides multilevel and multimedia instructional materials; (7) provides for different learning styles and for different learning rates; (8) continues an ongoing assessment of student performance; (9) uses a flexible room arrangement, including a variety of instructional areas; and (10) works with students individually, in small groups, or as a total group as needed.

Drawing upon a consensus of teachers, administrators, and supervisors as to the competencies essential and desirable for beginning teacher effectiveness, University of Georgia researchers identified eighteen generic competencies.[2]

GENERIC TEACHER COMPETENCIES

Teaching Functions	*Competency Statements*
Planning Instruction	Plans instruction to achieve selected objectives.
	Organizes instruction to take into account individual differences among learners.
Instructing	Uses instructional techniques, methods, and media related to the objectives.
	Communicates with learners both orally and in writing.
	Reinforces and encourages the efforts of learners.
	Demonstrates a repertoire of teaching methods.
	Uses procedures that involve the learner in instruction.
	Demonstrates an understanding of the school subject being taught.
Managing Instruction	Organizes time, space, materials, and equipment for instruction.
	Adjusts instruction to changes in conditions.
Providing the Learning Environment	Demonstrates enthusiasm for teaching and learning and the subject being taught.
	Helps learners to develop positive concepts of themselves.
	Manages classroom interactions.

Evaluating

Obtains and uses information about the needs and progress of individual learners.
Refers learners with special problems to specialists.
Obtains and uses information about the effectiveness of instruction to revise it when necessary.

Being a Professional

Meets professional responsibilities.
Engages in professional self-improvement.

module 5.1
LEARNING ACTIVITIES

1. Compare the functions of a business manager and a business teacher. How are they alike? How are they different?
2. Write a one-page paper describing the current role of the business teacher in a student-centered learning environment.
3. Prepare a list of the ten most important competencies that a beginning business teacher should possess.
4. Rate each of the Georgia generic competencies for beginning teachers as follows:
   a. essential
   b. highly desirable
   c. desirable
   d. of little or no importance

module 5.1
SELF-TEST

1. Which of the four teaching functions identified in this module is most essential? Why?
2. List some of the activities that characterize the business teacher in a learner-centered environment.
3. In the Georgia survey of teacher competencies, which five items ranked highest?

module 5.2
CLASSIFYING AND WRITING INSTRUCTIONAL OBJECTIVES

Before we can effectively specify and measure instructional objectives, we must first determine the kinds of behavior reflected in the objectives. A classification of behavioral domains—cognitive, affective, and psychomotor—has been generally accepted by educators. After completing this module, you should be able to (1) discriminate among the cognitive, affective, and psychomotor domains, (2) classify behavioral objectives according to the three domains, and (3) construct appropriate performance objectives.

THE BUSINESS TEACHER AND INSTRUCTIONAL OBJECTIVES

One of the initial tasks confronting a business teacher is the selection of the objectives to be included in each course. This activity is highly important since the objectives chosen will condition other decisions about sequence, method of instruction, and evaluation. It is important to use sound criteria in the selection and development of learning objectives.

At least two teacher tasks may be identified in relation to learning objectives:

1. *The teacher analyzes student needs and goals.* Student data such as maturity level, interests, goals, achievement, abilities, and special learning needs are available through a variety of sources including cumulative school records, questionnaires and checklists prepared by students, group and individual discussions and conferences, parent interviews, schoolwide needs assessments, and other professional staff.

2. *The teacher frames learner objectives for lessons, units, and courses.* Several criteria should be considered in formulating learner objectives:

a. Objectives are written in terms of behavioral change, specifying both conditions and standards.
b. Objectives are clearly and concisely worded so as to be understood by teacher and student.
c. The student is involved in the selection of his or her learning objectives.
d. The objectives are attainable; that is, the student possesses the prerequisite skills, abilities, and achievement needed to realize the objectives within a reasonable time.
e. Necessary materials, equipment, and facilities are available.
f. Objectives are based on task analysis data, research and/or currently reliable literature designed to reflect the skills, knowledges, and attitudes needed by students.
g. Objectives selected are most appropriately learned in the school setting, as opposed to skills best learned on the job or through additional specialized training.

For a given group of students in the same course, perhaps some objectives will be the same for all students; others will be identical for some of the students, while additional objectives may be appropriate for only a small group of students. Whether the teacher chooses fixed objectives or variable objectives depends much upon the instructional plan preferred.

Instructional objectives are helpful both to the teacher and the student since they provide concrete help and direction. One can justify writing objectives because they limit the task and remove all ambiguity and difficulty of interpretation; they ensure that measurement is possible, so that the quality and effectiveness of learning can be determined; and they provide a complete but terse summary of the course that could serve as a "conceptual scaffold" or advance organizer for learning. Moreover, by classifying objectives, the teacher will be able to avoid concentrating on one category to the exclusion of another, to make sure that prerequisite objectives have been met before teaching more complex ones, and to assure that goals are *appropriately* evaluated.

Objectives may be classified in two ways: according to the principal type of behavior exhibited, and according to the complexity of the task. An examination of objectives shows that they may be classified further into one or more of three general categories: *thinking, feeling,* and *doing.* More specifically, these are commonly referred to as the *cognitive, affective,* and *psychomotor domains. Cognitive* objectives, which are the foundation of most educational programs, are concerned with information and knowledge. *Affective objectives* focus on attitudes, values, and emotions. *Psychomotor objectives* involve the manipulation of objects and the development of motor skills. Learning to type and to operate business machines are examples of psychomotor usage in business education. Very few objectives may be classified as being exclusively in one domain. The classification is usually based on the domain in which the principal type of behavior occurs. Even though it is difficult to isolate the three behavioral domains in practice, there is still some justification for placing an objective in one of the three categories from a practical standpoint. In addition, there is considerable overlap in the use of behavioral terms, even though some terms are more directly relevant to one category than to another.

Objectives in the cognitive and affective domains have been classified by Krathwohl and others into *taxonomies,* from simple to complex order, as listed in Table 5.1. These classifications provide a framework for analyzing learner objectives according to their complexity, thus assuring that a variety of objectives of differing degrees and levels are included. Each level of objectives is built on preceding levels. Therefore when a student has demonstrated knowledge of basic facts in business English, for example, higher order objectives and learning experiences should be planned. A student who demonstrates knowledge of parts of speech, basic rules of punctuation, paragraph writing, note taking, and research procedures is ready to progress to objectives requiring the use of these skills in problem situations.

In selecting objectives, the teacher should try to choose those that are written precisely; that is, those that contain action verbs, such as *write, list,* or *construct,* which are open to fewer interpretations than terms of a more general nature, such as *know, understand,* or *appreciate.* The learning activities in this module contain examples of action verbs that may be used at various levels of the cognitive and affective domains.

Research in the psychomotor domain has lagged behind that in the affective and cognitive domains. Ragsdale, Simpson, and Harrow each have developed models for classifying behaviors in the psychomotor domain. Table 5.2

table 5.1
**THE RELATIONSHIP BETWEEN THE COGNITIVE AND
AFFECTIVE DOMAINS**

COGNITIVE OBJECTIVES	AFFECTIVE OBJECTIVES
1. The cognitive continuum begins with the student's recall and recognition of KNOWLEDGE (1.0).	1. The affective continuum begins with the student's merely RECEIVING (1.0) stimuli and passively attending to it. It extends through his more actively attending to it,
2. It extends his COMPREHENSION (2.0) of the knowledge.	2. his RESPONDING (2.0) to stimuli on request, willingly responding to these stimuli, and taking satisfaction in this responding.
3. his skill in APPLICATION (3.0) of the knowledge that he comprehends,	3. his VALUING (3.0) the phenomenon or activity so that he voluntarily responds and seeks out ways to respond.
4. his skill in ANALYSIS (4.0) of situations involving this knowledge, his skill in SYNTHESIS (5.0) of this knowlege into new organizations,	4. his CONCEPTUALIZATION (4.1) of each value responded to,
5. his skill in EVALUATION (6.0) in that area of knowledge to judge the value of material and methods for given purposes.	5. his ORGANIZATION (4.2) of these values into systems and, finally, organizing the value complex into a single whole, a CHARACTERIZATION (5.0) of the individual.

Source: From *Taxonomy of Educational Objectives: The Classification of Educational Goals: Handbook
2: Affective Domain,* edited by David R. Krathwohl et al. Copyright © 1964 by Longman Inc., pp. 49-50.
Reprinted by permission of Longman.

summarizes these three models. Simpson's model is useful when analyzing a
particular skill movement, such as typewriting a table with several columns.
The learner goes through the phase of interpreting the stimulus (perception);
he or she then prepares for active response (set). Because the skill movement
is new, the learner must initiate what he or she perceives the task or movement
to be. After some imitation (guided response), the learner practices the movement through trial-and-error learning. When the learner has acquired confidence in his or her performance of the movement, he or she is at the
mechanism level; in other words, the movement pattern becomes habitual and
progresses into a smooth, complex overt response. When the learner has mastered the skill movement, he or she is able to modify it (adaptation) and then
to create movement patterns based on the acquired skill movement (origination).

An awareness of the hierarchy of psychomotor development presented in
the Simpson model should assist the teacher in developing sequential patterns
of skill development in business courses such as typewriting, business machines,

table 5.2
THREE MODELS FOR CLASSIFYING PSYCHOMOTOR BEHAVIORS

RAGSDALE MODEL	SIMPSON MODEL	HARROW MODEL
1 Object-Motor (Manipulating or acting with direct reference to an object)	1 Perception (Interpreting)	1 Reflex movements (Segmental reflexes, intersegmental reflexes, suprasegmental reflexes.)
	2 Set (Preparing)	
		2 Basic-Fundamental Movements (Locomotor movements, non-locomotor movements, and manipulative movements)
2 Language-Motor (Movements of speech, sight, handwriting)	3 Guided Response (Learning)	
	4 Mechanism (Automatizing)	3 Perceptual Abilities (Kinesthetic discrimination, visual discrimination, auditory discrimination, tactile discrimination, coordinated abilities)
3 Feeling-Motor (Movements communicating feelings and attitudes)	5 Complex Overt Response (Performing)	
	6 Adaptation (Modifying)	4 Physical Abilities (Endurance, strength, flexibility, agility)
	7 Origination (Creating)	
		5 Skilled Movements (Simple adaptive skill, compound adaptive skill, complex adaptive skill)
		6 Nondiscursive Communication (Expressive movement, interpretive movement)

Source: C.C. Calhoun and A.V. Finch, *Vocational and Career Education: Concepts and Operations.* (Belmont, Calif.: Wadsworth Publishing Company, 1976), p. 438.

and keypunch. The four levels that follow must be regarded as much more tentative than the taxonomies in the cognitive and affective domains.

1. *Observing.* The learner observes a more experienced person performing the activity, noting sequences and relationships as well as the finished product.
2. *Imitating.* At this level, the learner has begun to acquire the basic rudiments of the desired behavior, following directions and sequences under close supervision. The emphasis is on the student's deliberate effort to imitate a model.
3. *Practicing.* The entire sequence is performed repeatedly in sequence. Conscious effort is no longer necessary as the performance becomes habitual in nature. We might say that the person has acquired the skill.

4. *Adapting.* This level is often referred to as "perfection of the skill." The process involves adapting "minor" details which, in turn, influence the total performance. The teacher or the learner may imitate these modifications.[3]

It is obvious that the psychomotor domain also involves a graded sequence from simple to complex. By deciding upon the degree of skill development needed, the teacher is able to plan instructional activities more efficiently. Likewise, evaluational techniques will vary considerably with the different levels.

Sometimes psychomotor skills are primarily of a mental nature, as in spelling and writing shorthand; at other times, they are neuromuscular, as in typewriting. Objectives in this domain traditionally have been designated as "skills." Certain aspects of a skills taxonomy can be inferred from established methology in the field, sometimes called "drill techniques."

LEARNING ACTIVITIES

Cognitive domain

In the cognitive domain, behaviors are identified in terms of thinking (mental processes), beginning with the concrete behavior of knowledge and continuing through the more abstract processes of analysis and synthesis. Study carefully pages 104–106 of this module which illustrate the six levels of cognitive behavior under which educational objectives may be classified. Upon completion of this study, proceed to Exercise 1.

Affective domain

One must be concerned not only with the knowledge a student gains but also with his or her willingness to identify with a given subject. The more strongly a student is attracted to a subject, the more obstacles he or she is likely to overcome in order to stay in contact with that interest.

Writing objectives for the affective domain is quite different from writing objectives for the cognitive domain, primarily because of the difficulty of observing and measuring students' interests, attitudes, and values. However, we are not so much concerned with measuring and grading students on affective outcomes as we are in recognizing the relationship between cognitive and affective processes; that is, in developing a conscious awareness of how affective influences serve to shape our thoughts.

Study carefully pages 107–109 about the affective domain, keeping in mind that the explanations given are subject to discussion or revision. This material is designed to guide you in understanding the affective domain rather than to provide you with "right" answers. Upon completion of this study, proceed to Exercise 2.

(Continued on page 106.)

MAJOR CATEGORIES	GENERAL INSTRUCTIONAL OBJECTIVES	TERMS FOR STATING BEHAVIORAL OBJECTIVES
A. KNOWLEDGE: the recall of previously learned material from specific facts to complete theories. Although some alteration of the material may be required, this is a minor part of the task. All that is required is the bringing to mind of the appropriate information.	KNOWS common terms KNOWS specific facts KNOWS methods and procedures KNOWS basic concepts KNOWS principles	defines, describes, identifies, labels, lists, matches, names, outlines, reproduces, selects, states

EXAMPLE of a BEHAVIORAL OBJECTIVE:

Given the names of the major parts of the typewriter and a list of their respective functions, the student will be able to match each correctly.

MAJOR CATEGORIES	GENERAL INSTRUCTIONAL OBJECTIVES	TERMS FOR STATING BEHAVIORAL OBJECTIVES
B. COMPREHENSION: refers to a type of understanding in which the individual knows what is being communicated and can make use of the material or idea without necessarily relating it to other material. This may be shown by *translating* material from one form to another (shorthand symbols to words) by *interpreting* material (explaining or summarizing), and by *estimating* future trends (predicting consequences or effects).	UNDERSTANDS facts and principles INTERPRETS verbal material INTERPRETS charts and graphs TRANSLATES verbal material to mathematical formulas ESTIMATES future consequences implied in data JUSTIFIES methods and procedures	converts, defends, distinguishes, estimates, explains, extends, generalizes, gives examples, infers, paraphrases, predicts, rewrites, summarizes

EXAMPLE of a BEHAVIORAL OBJECTIVE:

Given a list of Brief Forms, the student will be able to transcribe each, giving the correct work meaning.

MAJOR CATEGORIES	GENERAL INSTRUCTIONAL OBJECTIVES	TERMS FOR STATING BEHAVIORAL OBJECTIVES
C. APPLICATION: refers to the ability to use learned material in new and concrete situations. This may include the applicaton of such things as rules, methods, concepts, principles, laws, and theories.	APPLIES concepts and principles to new situations APPLIES laws and theories to practical situations SOLVES mathematical problems CONSTRUCTS charts and graphs DEMONSTRATES correct usage of a method or procedure	changes, computes, demonstrates, discovers, manipulates, modifies, operates, predicts, prepares, produces, relates, shows, solves, uses

EXAMPLE of a BEHAVIORAL OBJECTIVE:

Given the account titles and their respective amounts, the student will be able to prepare a Balance Sheet.

MAJOR CATEGORIES	GENERAL INSTRUCTIONAL OBJECTIVES	TERMS FOR STATING BEHAVIORAL OBJECTIVES
D. ANALYSIS: refers to the ability to break down material into its component parts so that its organizational structure may be understood. This may include the *identification* of the parts, *analysis* of the relationships between parts, and *recognition* of the principles involved.	ANALYZES the organizational structure of a work RECOGNIZES unstated assumptions RECOGNIZES logical fallacies in reasoning DISTINGUISHES between *facts and inferences* EVALUATES the relevancy of the data	breaks down, diagrams, differentiates, discriminates, distinguishes, identifies, illusrates, infers, outlines, points out, relates, selects, separates, subdivides

EXAMPLE of a BEHAVIORAL OBJECTIVE:
Given several types of business transactions, the student will be able to analyze each in terms of its effect on the Balance Sheet accounts.

MAJOR CATEGORIES	GENERAL INSTRUCTIONAL OBJECTIVES	TERMS FOR STATING BEHAVIORAL OBJECTIVES
E. SYNTHESIS: is the putting together of elements and parts so as to form a whole—the process of working with pieces, parts, elements, and so on, and arranging and combining them in such a way as to constitute a pattern or structure not clearly there before. This may involve the production of a communication (letter), a plan of operations (research proposal) or a set of abstract relations (scheme for classifying information).	WRITES a well-organized theme GIVES a well-organized speech WRITES a creative letter PROPOSES a plan for an experiment INTEGRATES learning from different areas into a plan for solving a problem FORMULATES a new scheme for classifying objects, events, or ideas	categorizes, combines, compiles, composes, creates, designs, devises, explains, generates, modifies, organizes, plans, rearranges, reconstructs, relates, reorganizes, revises, rewrites, summarizes, tells, writes

EXAMPLE of a BEHAVIORAL OBJECTIVE:
Given dictation on a new and unfamiliar business letter, the student will be able to transcribe the letter correctly.

MAJOR CATEGORIES	GENERAL INSTRUCTIONAL OBJECTIVES	TERMS FOR STATING BEHAVIORAL OBJECTIVES
F. EVALUATION: is concerned with the ability to judge the value of material (statement, letter, report) for a given purpose. The judgements are based on definite criteria. The criteria may be those determined by the student or those which are given to him.	JUDGES the logical consistency of written material JUDGES the adequacy with which conclusions are supported by data JUDGES the value of a work (writing) by use of internal criteria JUDGES the value of a work by use of external standards of excellence	appraises, compares, concludes, contrasts, criticizes, describes, discriminates, explains, justifies, interprets, relates, summarizes, supports

EXAMPLE of a BEHAVIORAL OBJECTIVE:
Given several business letters typed by students in the class, the student will be able to evaluate each in terms of mailability.

COGNITIVE DOMAIN *(continued)*

EXERCISE 1, COGNITIVE DOMAIN

In the following exercise, try to recall the six categories of the cognitive domain. In the blank to the left of each sentence, write the correct category for the cognitive behavior. Refer back to the learning material, if necessary, in order to justify your response.

_____1. Given the five steps for *posting*, the student will be able to illustrate in diagram form the sequence of each step.

_____2. Given a list of *brief forms* and their respective word meanings, the student will be able to match each correctly.

_____3. Given several *balance sheets* prepared by students in the class, the student will be able to identify and appraise the correctness of the form.

_____4. The student will be able to explain in one or two short sentences the definitions of the terms *assets*, *liabilities*, and *capital*.

_____5. Given relevant information from checkbook stubs and a bank statement, the student will be able to prepare a *reconciliation statement*.

_____6. Given the job requirements for a specific secretarial position, the student will be able to compose a *letter of application*.

Check your responses with those given below. Then proceed to Learning Activity 2, Affective Domain.

Exercise 1 Responses

1. Analysis 2. Knowledge 3. Evaluation 4. Comprehension 5. Application 6. Synthesis

---

Psychomotor domain

The psychomotor domain focuses attention on the performance of a motor act and deals primarily with the observation and measurement of *external behavior.* (Measurements in the cognitive and affective domains of behavior assess what might be called *internal behavior.*) Instructional objectives in the psychomotor domain usually include cognitive and affective elements, but the demonstration of a motor skill is the dominant characteristic of the student's response. This overlapping of behavior from the different domains is, of course, not limited to performance skills. Learning outcomes in the cognitive area have some affective elements, while outcomes in the affective area have some cognitive elements.

Study carefully pages 110–113 which explain the psychomotor domain and provide examples of behavioral objectives. Then proceed to Exercise 3.

WRITING PERFORMANCE OBJECTIVES

The terms *performance objectives* and *behavioral objectives* are used synonymously to describe what the student is expected to be able to do after instruction that he could not do before instruction. There are several ways of writing behavioral objectives. In this module, we shall focus on two types. (The activities for this section are included in Module 5.3.)

(Continued on page 109.)

MAJOR CATEGORIES	GENERAL INSTRUCTIONAL OBJECTIVES	TERMS FOR STATING BEHAVIORAL OBJECTIVES
A. RECEIVING: refers to the student's willingness to attend to particular phenomena or stimuli (classroom activities, textbook, and so on); it is concerned with getting, holding, and directing the student's attention—from simple awareness that a thing exists to selective attention on the part of the learner.	LISTENS attentively SHOWS awareness of the importance of learning SHOWS sensitivity to human needs and social problems ACCEPTS differences of race and culture ATTENDS closely to the classroom activities	asks, chooses, describes, follows, gives, holds, identifies, locates, names, points to, replies, selects, sits erect, uses

EXAMPLE of a BEHAVIORAL OBJECTIVE:
Given the correct sounds for shorthand symbols (by the instructor), the student will be able to repeat the sounds correctly.

B. RESPONDING: refers to active participation on the part of the student. He not only attends to a particular phenomenon but also reacts to it in some way. This area emphasizes acquiescence in responding (reads assigned material), willingness to respond (voluntarily reads beyond assignment), or satisfaction in responding (reads for pleasure or enjoyment). Responding includes those instructional objectives that are classified under "interests"; that is, those that stress the seeking out and enjoyment of particular activities.	COMPLETE assigned homework OBEYS school rules PARTICIPATES in class discussion COMPLETES laboratory work VOLUNTEERS for special tasks SHOWS interest in subject ENJOYS helping others	answers, assists, compiles, conforms, discusses, greets, helps, labels, performs, practices, presents, reads, recites, reports, selects, tells, writes

EXAMPLE of a BEHAVIORAL OBJECTIVE:
Student volunteers to help a fellow student learn the Brief Forms in shorthand class.

C. VALUING: concerned with the worth or value a student attaches to a particular object, phenomenon, or behavior. This ranges from the more simple acceptance of a value (desires to improve group skills) to the more complex level of commitment	DEMONSTRATES belief in the democratic process APPRECIATES good literature (art or music) APPRECIATES the role of science (or other subjects) in everyday life SHOWS concern for the welfare of others	completes, describes, differentiates, explains, follows, forms, initiates, invites, joins, justifies, proposes, reads, reports selects, shares, studies, works

MAJOR CATEGORIES	GENERAL INSTRUCTIONAL OBJECTIVES	TERMS FOR STATING BEHAVIORAL OBJECTIVES
C. VALUING (continued) (assumes responsibility for the effective functioning of the group). Valuing is based on a set of specified values, expressed in the student's behavior and is consistent enough to make the value clearly identifiable. Objectives are classified under "attitudes" and "appreciation."	DEMONSTRATES problem-solving attitude DEMONSTRATES commitment to social improvement	

EXAMPLE of a BEHAVIORAL OBJECTIVE:
Student voluntarily shares with the class a magazine article discussing the qualifications of a good secretary.

MAJOR CATEGORIES	GENERAL INSTRUCTIONAL OBJECTIVES	TERMS FOR STATING BEHAVIORAL OBJECTIVES
D. ORGANIZATION: concerned with bringing together different values, resolving conflicts between them, and beginning the building of a value system—emphasis is on comparison, relating, and synthesizing values—concerned with the conceptualization of a value (recognizes the responsibility of individual improvement) or with the organization of a value system (develops a vocational plan). Objectives relate to the development of a philosophy of life.	RECOGNIZES the need for balance between freedom and responsibility RECOGNIZES the role of systematic planning in solving problems ACCEPTS responsibility for his or her own behavior UNDERSTANDS and accepts his or her own strengths and limitations FORMULATES a life plan in harmony with his or her abilities, interests, and beliefs	adheres, alters, arranges, arranges, combines, compares, completes, defends, explains, generalizes, identifies, integrates, modifies, orders, organizes, prepares, relates, synthesizes.

EXAMPLE of a BEHAVIORAL OBJECTIVE:
Student discusses with instructor and formulates an educational plan in prepara- for a secretarial career.

MAJOR CATEGORIES	GENERAL INSTRUCTIONAL OBJECTIVES	TERMS FOR STATING BEHAVIORAL OBJECTIVES
E. CHARACTERIZATION: At this level, the individual has a value system and has developed a characteristic "life style." Thus behavior is pervasive, consistent, and predictable. The major emphasis is on the fact that the behavior is typical or characteristic of the student. Objectives are concerned with the student's personal, social, emotional adjustment.	DISPLAYS safety consciousness DEMONSTRATES self-reliance in working independently PRACTICES cooperation in group activities USES objective approach in problem solving DEMONSTRATES industry, punctuality, and self-discipline MAINTAINS good health habits	acts, discriminates, displays, influences, listens modifies, performs, practices, proposes, qualifies, questions, revises, serves, solves, uses, verifies

AFFECTIVE DOMAIN *(continued)*

E. CHARACTERIZATION (continued):

EXAMPLE of a BEHAVIORAL OBJECTIVE:
Student takes initiative in recruiting new
members into the FBLA (Future Business
Leaders of America) student organization.

EXERCISE 2, AFFECTIVE DOMAIN

In the following exercise, try to recall the five categories of the affective domain. In the blank to the left of each sentence, write the correct category for the affective behavior. Again, if your answers differ from those shown at the bottom of the page, refer back to the learning material in order to clarify your response.

_____ 1. The student prepares a presentation on the requirements for becoming a CPA (Certified Public Accountant) for the advanced bookkeeping class.

_____ 2. The student offers to contact an accountant in the business community and invite him to speak to the bookkeeping class.

_____ 3. The student consistently demonstrates interest and commitment to his or her V.O.T. job.

_____ 4. Following a presentation of the important uses for financial papers and reports, the student participates in the class discussion.

_____ 5. The student is attentive to class presentation of the "beginning bookkeeping steps" and is not reluctant to ask question.

Check your responses with those given below. Then proceed to Learning Activity 3, Psychomotor Domain.

1. Organization   2. Valuing   3. Characterization   4. Responding   5. Receiving

Exercises 2 Responses

Mager-type objectives

Mager[4] considers that a clear objective should be written so as to exhibit three characteristics:

1. It identifies the terminal behavior.	Computes nine problems involving addition and the use of the subtotal and nonadd keys
2. It describes the conditions under which the behavior will occur.	Using a ten-key adding-listing machine
3. It specifies the criteria or standard of acceptable performance.	Correctly within a fifty-minute period

Thus, a Mager-type objective would be stated in the following manner: *Using a ten-key adding-listing machine, the student computes correctly within a fifty-minute period nine problems involving addition and the use of the non-add and subtotal keys.*

The Mager-type objective consists of five basic components:

1. WHO is to perform the desired behavior.

Example: the student   the learner

(Continued on page 114.)

MAJOR CATEGORIES	GENERAL INSTRUCTIONAL OBJECTIVES
A. PERCEPTION: is the first step in perforing a motor act. It is the process of becoming aware of objects, qualities, or relations by way of the sense organs—auditory, visual, tactile (touch), taste, smell, kinesthetic (muscle sense). Perception involves receiving and selecting *cues*—then determing their meaning in order to perform a particular motor act.	SENSITIVITY to auditory or visual cues AWARENESS of differences in cues RECOGNITION of operating difficulties with machinery through the sound of the machine in operation

EXAMPLE of a BEHAVIORAL OBJECTIVE:
As the instructor points to the shorthand outlines on the chalkboard, the student will be able to correctly read aloud each outline.

B. SET: Is a prepatory adjustment or readiness for a particular kind of action or experience (mentally, physically, and emotionally). Mental set is readiness in terms of using judgment in making distinctions. Physical set focuses on the needed sensory organs. Emotional set is readiness in terms of a favorable attitude toward the motor activity.	KNOWLEDGE of steps KNOWLEDGE of appropriate tools ACHIEVEMENT of bodily stance POSITIONING of hands preparatory to typing DISPOSITION to perform DESIRE to perform

EXAMPLE of a BEHAVIORAL OBJECTIVE:
As the instructor recites a few "easy" words, the student will be able to write the simple shorthand outlines.

C. GUIDED RESPONSE: is an early step in the development of skill. Emphasis is upon the abilities needed for the more complex skills—by imitation or by trial and error. Imitation is the response to the perception of another person performing the act. Trial and error is the act of trying various responses in order to meet the requirements of the task to be performed.	IMITATION of the process PERFORMING as demonstrated DISCOVERING the most efficient method DETERMINING the sequence of a performance through trial and error

EXAMPLE of a BEHAVIORAL OBJECTIVE:
Following a teacher demonstration of the correct typing response to a dictaphone belt, the student will be able to type a short letter from a dictaphone belt, using the correct procedure.

D. MECHANISM: At this level, the learned response has become habitual. The learner has achieved a certain confidence and degree of proficiency in the performance of the act. Also involved is some patterning in the carrying out of the task.	ABILITY to PERFORM a particular motor skill

EXAMPLE of a BEHAVIORAL OBJECTIVE:
Given shorthand dictation of a familiar letter, the student will be able to transcribe the letter into longhand.

MAJOR CATEGORIES	GENERAL INSTRUCTIONAL OBJECTIVES
E. COMPLEX OVERT RESPONSE: At this level, the individual can perform a motor act that is considered complex because of the movement pattern required. At this level, *skill has been attained.* The act can be carried out smoothly and efficiently, with minimum expenditure of time and energy.	SKILL in operating SKILL in setting up SKILL in performing

EXAMPLE of a BEHAVIORAL OBJECTIVE:

Given three business letters, the student will be able to type each within a specified time period, using correct letter form, as well as producing mailable letters.

F. ADAPTATION: Altering motor activities to meet the demands of new problematic situations requiring a physical response.	DEVELOPING a motor activity through adapting known abilities and skills

EXAMPLE of a BEHAVIORAL OBJECTIVE:

Given the data for inventories, purchases, and income statement accounts, and using the calculator, the student will be able to compute the cost of inventories and net income.

G. ORIGINATION: Creating new motor acts or ways of manipulating materials out of understandings, abilites and skills developed in the psychomotor area	CREATION of a new skill requiring psychomotor response

EXAMPLE of a BEHAVIORAL OBJECTIVE:

Given the present library holdings, the student will develop a new computer program and keypunch the data onto cards for keeping a current inventory of books and materials.

EXERCISE 3, PSYCHOMOTOR DOMAIN

In the following exercise, try to recall the categories of the psychomotor domain. In the blank to the left of each objective sentence, write the correct category. Keep in mind that the psychomotor domain includes cognitive and affective elements; however, the demonstration of a motor skill will be the chief concern of the objective.

_____1. Given a few simple number sets (1, 2, 3), the student will be able to add them on a ten-key adding machine, using the touch method.

_____2. Given the figures and the columnar headings, the student will be able to correctly set up a tabulation.

_____3. As the instructor calls out the "home keys" of the typewriter, the student will be able to type them without looking at his fingers.

_____4. Given a rough draft of a letter, the student will be able to type it correctly, without error, and specify the kind of letter.

EXERCISE 3 (continued)

_____5. Given dictation of an unfamiliar letter, the student will be able to type a mailable copy within a specific time period.

_____6. Following a teacher demonstration, the student wil be able to set up a tabulation, using correct procedures.

_____7. The student sets up a bookkeeping system for the high school bookstore.

Check your responses with those given below, and proceed to the Self-Test.

6. Guided Response   7. Origination

1. Set   2. Mechanism   3. Perception   4. Adaptation   5. Complex Overt Response

Exercise 3 Responses

SELF-TEST

A series of learning activities commonly found in business education classes are listed in Column 1 on the following form. Three blank spaces are given to the immediate right of each activity and represent either the cognitive, affective, or the psychomotor domains.

Directions

a. Decide whether the activity described *best fits* under the cognitive, affective, or psychomotor domain. (If you think it is a "50-50 deal" between two domains, you may check both.)

b. After determining the domain, decide the level (category) within that domain that this activity best represents.

COGNITIVE DOMAIN	AFFECTIVE DOMAIN	PSYCHOMOTOR DOMAIN
1. Knowledge	1. Receiving	1. Perception
2. Comprehension	2. Responding	2. Set
3. Application	3. Valuing	3. Guided Response
4. Analysis	4. Organization	4. Mechanism
5. Synthesis	5. Characterization	5. Complex Overt Response
6. Evaluation		6 Adaptation
		7. Origination

COLUMN 1 Learning Activity	COLUMN 2 Domain/Level		
	COGNITIVE	AFFECTIVE	PSYCHOMOTOR
1. A 5-minute typewriting speed test			
2. A bulletin board displaying three letters typed in different styles			
3. A 5-minute oral report by the student on the number of job openings in data processing			
4. A 5-minute warm-up drill on alphabetic sentences at the beginning of the hour in first-year typewriting			
5. Two students are asked to play the roles of the receptionist and the telephone caller to provide the introduction to the telephoning unit			

6. Transparencies showing the transcript of a letter dictated at 100 *wam* were used so that students could evaluate the mailability of their own transcripts		
7. A class field trip to Auto Owners Insurance Company to see their data processing center and become aware of the important role of the computer in business		
8. Prepare a job analysis for your career objective by interviewing an office worker who has that type of position, basically to perceive the importance of business education courses in relation to the job		
9. A matching test consisting of 50 bookkeeping terms and definitions		

COLUMN 1 Learning Activity	COLUMN 2 Domain/Level		
	COGNITIVE	AFFECTIVE	PSYCHOMOTOR
10. A production test in first-year typing involving the typing of a number of form letters			
11. Given a list of five different secretarial tasks, you should be able to arrange them in descending order of importance and provide a logical reason for each decision			
12. Given various pieces of business correspondence and a dictionary, you should be able to locate all typographical errors within 10 minutes			
13. Given three letters (of average length and difficulty) at 80 *wam*, you should be able to transcribe them into mailable form (with one carbon) within 20 minutes			
14. Given three weeks of instruction in telephone techniques, you will demonstrate correct procedures in a role-playing situation in which you work for a junior executive in a large firm			
15. Given the task of matching 50 words from the bookkeeping textbook, you should be able to match 48 of 50 with the proper definition on the first trial and in 30 minutes			
16. A student attends the FBLA meeting on Thursday evening (attendance is not required)			
17. Given a typewriter that is not working, you should be able to determine the reason for the malfunction within 5 minutes (for the common malfunctions)			
18. An in-basket in which students are asked to sort the jobs and arrange them in the order in which they should be done			

This is relatively easy to determine. Obviously the teacher wants the student, or in some cases, the class to demonstrate the behavior. In many objectives, however, the "Who" is omitted, and the objective begins with the action verb in Component 2.

2. The ACTUAL BEHAVIOR to be employed in demonstrating mastery of the objective.

Example: write   file   speak

This component of an instructional objective is the specific, observable act or behavior the learner is to perform. The aim should be toward the use of specific action verbs, such as telephone, transcribe, sort, list, duplicate, rather than general verbs, such as appreciate, understand, and so on.

3. The RESULT of the behavior, which will be evaluated to determine whether the objective is mastered.

Example: the speech   the letter

The third component is the PRODUCT or PERFORMANCE; that is, what the student is to do. To put it in the form of a question: What are the *consequences* of the learning experience? Including this component in the objectives ensures that the *result* of the instruction, rather than the instruction itself, will be the end product to be measured and evaluated. Here are some examples of statements that include the first three components. The portion of the statement that appears in all capital letters is the RESULT of the behavior (the object of the verb):

The student writes a SENTENCE.
The student types a LETTER.
The student files the CORRESPONDENCE.

To determine the result expected from students, the teacher must first decide what he or she wants them to do as a result of instruction, then identify what behavior is to be performed.

4. The RELEVANT CONDITIONS under which the behavior is to be performed.

Example: in a one-hour quiz   in front of the class

What are the "givens," the "limitations," the "restrictions" that are imposed on students when they are demonstrating the behavior? The following are some examples of stimulus conditions that might be included in an objective:

Using a ten-key adding-listing machine
Without the use of class notes or other references
After reading Chapter 5

The following are some suggestions to help determine the conditions:

    a. Specify the available materials or equipment that will help the student to perform the behavior required in the objective.

    b. Specify the materials or equipment that the student cannot use to perform the behavior.

    c. List as many of the actual conditions as possible under which the student might be expected to demonstrate the behavior in a real-life setting, and try to include as many of them in the objective as possible.

    5. The STANDARD (criterion) that will be used to evaluate the success of the product or performance.

    Example: 95 percent correct   four out of five   in 30 seconds

This component refers to the basis for evaluating the prescribed behavior, the criterion of acceptable performance. One way to indicate an acceptable level of performance is to specify a time limit when it is appropriate. Another way is to indicate the minimum number or percentage of acceptable correct responses. Still another way of describing the behavior is to define the important characteristics of performance accuracy, such as "a mailable letter," "accurate to the nearest whole number," or "a scaled drawing 1/10 its actual size." If, for example, the objective were stated as "The student will be able to type the writing at 60 words per minute with three or fewer errors," then "60 words per minute with three or fewer errors" is the *standard* specified for determining whether or not the student performed the task.

    Try numbering the five component parts of this objective:

        Given a 100-word business letter in unarranged copy, the student will type the letter in block style within three minutes with 100 percent accuracy.

Your answer should look like this:

                                       4   1
    Given a 100-word business letter in unarranged copy,   the student
    2   3
    will type   the letter in block style
                     5
    within three minutes with 100 percent accuracy.

    Another way to determine the content of a performance objective is by supplying the answers to five questions:

1. What is to be done?   (Type letter)
2. How is it to be done?   (Block style from unarranged copy)
3. How well is it to be done?   (100 percent accuracy)
4. How fast is it to be done?   (Three minutes)
5. How will I know it has been done?   (Visual inspection for correctness)

The answer to the fifth question may be written into the objective by using an expression such as "pass a module posttest." Or it may be specified in other directions to the student, such as "Turn in the completed work to the instructor for evaluation" or "Take the test at the end of the module." This step is designed to help the business teacher make decisions about evaluation that can be accomplished through a test, demonstration to the teacher, teacher inspection, tape-recorded presentation, or product such as a paper, report, and so on.

Gronlund-type objectives

Gronlund[5] notes that there are two ways of stating objectives as learning outcomes. One is to list the specific behavior students are to exhibit at the end of the instructional period. (This is similar to the Mager-type objective.) Specific learning outcomes would be:

List the steps
Define the terms
Write a sentence using each

"A second method is to state first the general instructional objectives and then to clarify each objective by listing a *sample* of the specific behavior we are willing to accept as evidence of the attainment of that objective."[6] This procedure would result in statements such as the following:

Understands economic concepts and principles
  Identifies examples of economic concepts/principles
  Describes economic concepts/principles in own words
  Points out the relationship of economic principles

Applies standard of mailability to letters
  Identifies criteria for mailable letters
  Selects mailable letter from two or more examples
  Types a mailable letter

This second procedure makes clear that the instructional objective is *understanding* or *applying,* not identifying, describing, or typing. Rather these latter types of behavior are *samples* of the types of performance that represent understanding and application. A different sample of specific types of behavior could serve equally well.

Teaching efforts should be directed toward general objectives of instruction and not specific samples of behavior selected to represent each objective.[7] For example, in teaching an understanding of technical terms used in business law, the teacher might have students study the textbook definitions, compare and contrast the terms during class discussions, and give examples illustrating the meaning of each term. On a test the students might be given a list of the technical terms and then asked to define each term in their own words, giving an original sentence using each term. This test, then, is designed to measure *understanding* of terms, rather than recall of previous learning.

At the training level of a task or skill, such as filing alphabetically, it is possible to list all the types of behavior involved in the task, teach these types of behavior directly, and include them all in an evaluation of student performance at the end of instruction. For higher levels of instruction, however, it is possible to list only a sample of the specific types of behavior that represent each instructional objective. For example, after the students have learned the rules and procedures for alphabetic filing, a general objective may be to demonstrate an understanding of principles of alphabetic filing. Sample behaviors include listing rules for alphabetic filing, arranging individual and company names in alphabetic order, or filing a set of cards alphabetically. A test of this objective might call for students to examine two lists containing individual and company names, determine items that are not in correct alphabetic order, and arrange them in the proper sequence.

Gronlund[8] suggests that there is an advantage to limiting statements to behavioral outcomes without a reference to subject matter. Then, a set of outcomes may be useful with various units of study. Read the following objectives for a unit in economics.

Objectives for a Unit in Economics[9]

1. Knows basic terms.
    1.1 Relates terms that have the same meaning.
    1.2 Selects the term that best fits a particular definition.
    1.3 Identifies terms used in reference to particular economic problems.
    1.4 Uses terms correctly in describing economic problems.
2. Understands economic concepts and principles.
    2.1 Identifies examples of economic concepts and principles.
    2.2 Describes economic concepts and principles in his or her own words.
    2.3 Points out the interrelationship of economic principles.
    2.4 Explains changes in economic conditions in terms of the economic concepts and principles involved.
3. Applies economic principles to new situations.
    3.1 Identifies the economic principles needed to solve a practical problem.
    3.2 Predicts the probable outcome of an action involving economic principles.
    3.3 Describes how to solve a practical economic problem in terms of the economic principles involved.
    3.4 Distinguishes between probable and improbable economic forecasts.
4. Interprets economic data.
    4.1 Differentiates between relevant and irrelevant information.
    4.2 Differentiates between facts and inferences.
    4.3 Identifies cause-effect relations in data.
    4.4 Describes the trends in data.
    4.5 Distinguishes between warranted and unwarranted conclusions drawn from data.
    4.6 Makes proper qualifications when describing data.

Notice that the objectives specify *how* the student is supposed to react toward the subject matter, but they do not identify the specific content. By adding the specific subject matter, the business teacher can relate the general and specific objectives to various units and to various courses. A word of caution is in order. The teacher should not write one set of general objectives and specific objectives and limit the instructional units and modules to the objectives. It is highly important to vary the objectives according to subject matter and student needs.

The levels of educational objectives in the cognitive, affective, and psychomotor domains should be a reference point for the business teacher in selecting and writing general objectives.

In summary, Gronlund's procedure for defining instructional objectives in behavioral terms includes the following steps:[10]

1. State the general instructional objectives as *expected learning outcomes*.
2. Place under each general instructional objective a list of specific learning outcomes that describes the *terminal behavior* students are to demonstrate when they have achieved the objective.
   a. Begin each specific learning outcome with a *verb* that specifies definite, *observable behavior*.
   b. List a sufficient number of specific learning outcomes under each objective to describe adequately the behavior of students who have achieved the objective.
   c. Be certain that the behavior in each specific learning outcome is relevant to the objective it describes.
3. When defining the general instructional objectives in terms of specific learning outcomes, revise and refine the original list of objectives as needed.
4. Be careful not to omit complex objectives (for example, critical thinking, appreciation) simply because they are difficult to define in specific behavioral terms.
5. consult reference materials for help in identifying the specific types of behavior that are most appropriate for defining the complex objectives.

The performance objectives written by business teachers include both Mager-type and Gronlund-type objectives. Mager-type objectives may be more appropriate for skill development, such as learning the typewriter keyboard, learning shorthand symbols, and performing calculations. Gronlund refers to these as minimum essentials, those skills everyone is expected to know. "The objectives are frequently stated as tasks to be performed rather than goals to work toward."[11]

At the developmental level, instructional objectives include some learning outcomes that encourage maximum development of the student. The teaching emphasis is on encouraging each student to progress as far as possible toward predetermined goals, and general and specific objectives, described earlier, are generally used. Evaluation is based on a sample of specific behavior. Table 5.3 summarizes a comparison of the relation of objectives to teaching and testing at "minimum essentials" and "developmental" levels of instruction.

table 5.3

SUMMARY COMPARISON OF THE RELATION OF OBJECTIVES TO TEACHING AND TESTING AT TWO DIFFERENT LEVELS OF INSTRUCTION

	MINIMUM ESSENTIALS LEVEL	DEVELOPMENTAL LEVEL
Teaching Emphasis	Shape and modify student behavior to fit a predetermined *minimum level of performance*.	Encourage and direct each student toward the *maximum level of development* he is capable of achieving.
Nature of the Objectives	Limited, specific, and completely defined tasks to be performed.	General goals that provide direction and are defined by a *representative sample* of specific behaviors.
Relation of Teaching to the Objectives	Teaching is directed toward the specific behavior stated in the objective. Each *specific behavior* is taught on a one-to-one basis.	Teaching is directed toward the *general class of behavior* that the objective represents, rather than toward the behavior listed in this particular sample.
Relation of Testing to the Objectives	Each specific behavior is tested directly on a one-to-one basis. Test items require students to demonstrate responses identical to those learned in class.	Only a *sample* of specific behavior is tested for each objective. Test items require students to demonstrate previously learned responses in situations containing some novelty.
Specifying Performance Standards	Standards of minimum performance are easily specified, but they are usually set in an arbitrary manner.	Performance standards are difficult to specify. Achievement is typically reported in terms of *relative* position in some known group.

Source: Normal E. Gronlund, *Stating Behavioral Objectives for Classroom Instruction* (New York: The Macmillan Company, 1970), p. 36.

module 5.3
PLANNING COURSES, UNITS, AND DAILY LESSONS

Careful teacher planning is essential for imparting purpose and direction to teacher and student effort in the business education classroom. After completing this module, you should be able to (1) plan a course outline, (2) construct a unit plan, (3) develop a daily lesson plan, and (4) write an instructional module.

PLANNING THE COURSE OF STUDY

When the business teacher or department staff begins planning a course of study, there are four basic questions to be considered:

1. What are the students to learn from this course? More specifically, what are the topics and course objectives? These should be selected on the basis of their value to students.
2. What course content or material will be used to achieve these objectives? This involves sequencing topics, including relevant content, and discarding material not consistent with the objectives.
3. How much time should be devoted to each topic or objective? These decisions keep the teacher from spending too much time on beginning topics and too little on topics scheduled near the end of the course.
4. How will student achievement of objectives be evaluated? This involves both formative and summative types of measurement.

Selecting and/or writing course objectives is the most important part of course planning, for it is from the objectives that the teacher determines the subject matter to be covered, the instructional techniques to be used, and the evaluation methods to be applied. After the objectives have been chosen or written, the next step is to arrange them in an appropriate learning order based on the nature of the course and the makeup of the class.

Identifying instructional units

With the course goals and objectives in mind, block out the major units. The following are suggestions of sources for unit topics:

1. *Curriculum guides.* These guides and courses of study developed by state education departments, regional curriculum laboratories, colleges, and universities will suggest ideas. Local conditions, of course, should be taken into consideration in selecting and modifying topics.

2. *Textbook for the course.* Student and higher level texts can be used to develop topics. Chapter divisions or combinations of chapters may become units of work. The texts may also suggest student learning activities appropriate to the topic. Textbooks are very convenient sources for units and are usually carefully developed, but they do have some disadvantages. They may be very general in nature, they may not be up-to-date, and they may not be entirely suitable for the local situation.

3. *Curriculum experts in business education.* Many research and development projects have produced materials that may be very useful. Check with the Business Education Service in the state education department, universities, and local business education or vocational education coordinators for sources of materials that have already been developed. In particular, look for material in the ERIC System and in the serial, Abstracts of Instructional and Research Materials in Vocational and Technical Education (AIM/ARM).

4. *Other business teachers, supervisors, and college professors.* Colleagues may be able to suggest significant or especially effective topics for units. They may be particularly helpful in suggesting topics related to current trends or local conditions in business education.

5. *Current events.* These should not be ignored in the search for stimulating unit topics. They often excite a great deal of student interest which can be directly related to an aspect of the course of study.

When planning courses and instructional modules specifically related to job entry, consider three kinds of information on which unit topics may be based: (1) technical information that workers must know in order to make decisions in doing their work; (2) general information that the workers should know to make their jobs more interesting and the workers more enlightened employees (in this category are topics relating to the social significance of the occupation, scientific basis, or economic importance); and (3) vocational guidance information that helps the worker to find and keep a job. Such topics as employment opportunities, employer-employee relations, job advancement, and labor laws are examples of the guidance information that can serve as the focus of units of work.

JOB DESCRIPTION. One source for identifying job-entry topics is a job description which details each of the kinds of activities performed by the worker as well as the conditions under which the work is done. *The Dictionary of Occupational Titles, Occupational Outlook Handbook,* and research studies are helpful sources for job descriptions and listings of tasks performed by workers. If no job description is available, or if the teacher wants a description tailored to a job in a particular location, then he or she will have to write one. This means identifying the kinds of tasks performed by office workers and any special conditions under which they are performed. Talking with persons on the job and/or observing them perform their tasks can be beneficial, especially if one has limited work experience. A job description for a file clerk might read as follows:

> The file clerk keeps records accurate, up-to-date, and properly placed. Clerks read the material to be filed and arrange it by number, alphabet, subject matter, or some other filing system. Aside from inserting new data into files, file clerks perform duties related to existing files, such as entering additional information on materials in the files, investigating file records, and tracing missing file data. Much of the time is spent retrieving information stored in the files. The clerk maintains records of materials removed from the files and sees that materials given out are returned. Other tasks include periodically destroying or transferring filed materials to inactive files, checking to ensure that materials are correctly placed, and preparing folders, labels, and index cards for use in the file. In small offices, file clerks may also type, sort mail, or operate office machines.

As seen in the example, each job is made up of a number of tasks, many of which form the basis for the instructional program. From the information in the job description, one can list all the tasks that might be included in the performance of a particular job. The tasks performed by a file clerk, for example, include (but may not be limited to) the following:

1. files by alphabet
2. files by subject
3. files by number

4. gets material from file
5. makes new files
6. inserts material in file in proper order

7. keeps record of material checked out of files
8. refiles material in existing files
9. locates misfiled material

10. determines material to be destroyed
11. transfers active files to inactive status
12. requests or orders filing supplies

Tentative topics should meet most or all of the following criteria: the topic must (1) be significant, (2) be relevant to students, (3) have focus or continuity, (4) be feasible and practical, and (5) have a goal.

Complete Learning Activity 1 at the end of this module.

TASK ANALYSIS. The first step in the task analysis is to list all the operations or details that are included in the performance of a task. (A task is a unit of work, or complete job element, required for the completion of a job objective.) Included in this list are those operations that seem very elementary. Some of the skills students will have already learned, possibly as prerequisites to this particular learning activity. One of the tasks of a secretary or stenographer is to transcribe business letters. The following example lists the details necessary to complete that task.

Task Example: Transcribes a business letter
List of task details involved:
1. Types with reasonable accuracy and speed
2. Takes dictation in shorthand notes with reasonable accuracy and speed
3. Proofreads typing
4. Checks shorthand notes
5. Makes punctuation and spelling corrections
6. Transcribes shorthand notes
7. Obtains signature
8. Makes necessary revisions and corrections
9. Types envelopes
10. Files copies of communication
11. Distributes communication
12. Mails communication
13. Duplicates communication
14. Locates addresses for communication

(In determining the relative importance of a task, one considers its frequency of performance and its learning difficulty.)

Before the teacher decides on the proper order in which these task details are to be performed, it would be helpful to list them on a form that acts as a guide in sequencing them (see Step 1, Table 5.4, Task Detail List). Then number the task details in the proper order, that is, the order in which they are actually performed (see Step 2, Table 5.4). Next, under the column headed "Level of Importance," indicate the relative importance of each task detail in terms of its value to the final product (Step 3, Table 5.4). Label each task detail as *1* (high), *2* (average), or *3* (low) to indicate its importance. These ratings of importance will help to determine which task details should be included in the learning activities and which can be omitted.

The second major procedure in the task analysis is to select from the list just completed those task details that must be performed in achieving the task (Step 1, Table 5.5, Task Detail Sequence). Place each task detail in proper sequence (Step 2, Table 5.5, Task Detail Sequence). (Did you notice that the task details are expressed in terms of what the student *does* when performing the task detail rather than in terms of what must be known?) After you have listed these detailed steps in the proper sequence, decide on the materials needed for each task step and indicate these in the column headed "Hardware/Software Required" (Step 3, Table 5.5, Task Detail Sequence). (Hardware covers equipment, while software refers to paper, books, and so on.)

In the column headed "Prerequisite Knowledge and Skill Required," indicate such items as accuracy and speed requirements, proficiency levels in related courses, or prerequisite courses or skills; in other words, anything the

table 5.4
TASK DETAIL LIST

Task Example: *Transcribe a business letter*

STEP 1	STEP 2	STEP 3
NO.	TASKS	LEVEL OF IMPORTANCE
1	Types with reasonable accuracy and speed	1
2	Takes dictation in shorthand notes with reasonable accuracy and speed	1
3	Proofreads typing	1
4	Checks shorthand notes	2
5	Makes punctuation and spelling corrections	1
6	Transcribes shorthand notes	1
7	Obtains signature	3
8	Makes necessary revisions and corrections	1
9	Types envelopes	2
10	Files copies of communication	3
11	Distributes communication	3
12	Mails communication	3
13	Duplicates communication	2
14	Locates addresses for communication	2

student must have acquired prior to beginning this particular job activity (Step 4, Table 5.5, Task Detail Sequence). Some of these items may have to be reviewed or taught.

In the last column (Step 5, Table 5.5, Task Detail Sequence) list the work habits and attitudes to be developed, such as personal care and appearance, maintenance of work station and materials, orderly work procedures, courtesy and the ability to work with others, punctuality and attendance, personal achievement and objectives, work simplification, cost consciousness, personal safety and safety of others, and pride in work.

After the beginning training stages, include tasks that require the student to exercise judgment or have the judgmental factor built in. Notice that Steps 2 and 4 in Table 5.5—"Checks shorthand notes for punctuation/spelling" and "Proofreads letter"—call for the student to do his or her own thinking and decision making.

table 5.5
TASK DETAIL SEQUENCE

Task Example: *Transcribe a business letter*

NO.	TASK STEPS	HARDWARE/ SOFTWARE REQUIRED	PREREQUISITE KNOWLEDGE AND SKILL REQUIRED	ATTITUDES OR WORK HABITS
1	Take dictation in shorthand	Note pad/ pencil/pen	Shorthand speed minimum 80 *wam* with 100% accuracy	
2	Check shorthand notes for punctuation/spelling		Good English background	Orderly work procedures
3	Transcribe dictation	Typewriter, business stationery, correction supplies	Typing speed: minimum 50 *wam* with 95% accuracy. acy. Letter format; mailability	
4	Proofread letter		Good English background; good spelling and punctuation skills	Pride in quality of work
5	Obtain signature; make necessary corrections or revisions			Courtesy
6	Type addresses on envelopes	Envelopes, typewriter	Address placement	
7	Duplicate letter	Copy machine	Duplicating	Cost consciousness
8	Mail original letter			
9	File letter-copy	Filing cabinet	Filing system	

Complete Learning Activity 2 at the end of this module.

FLOWCHARTS. The task steps just completed on the Task Detail Sequence could be further simplified by transferring them to a flowchart. A flowchart is a graphic representation of a sequence of steps required to carry out a performance objective. A flowchart is like a road map—through the use of symbols, which represent operations or equipment, the steps to be followed in the performance of the activity can be easily traced. (See an office management text for the details about preparing flowcharts.)

Sequencing instructional unit topics

Unit topics should be presented in a sequence that is most helpful to students, not necessarily what is most meaningful from the teacher's point of view. The sequence of units related to skill development in business courses should be based on the logical order of task mastery. In order to acquire certain skills, it is often necessary to demonstrate mastery of certain prerequisite skills; for example, learning the typewriter keyboard precedes typing a letter, and straight copy typing precedes typing a rough draft. The identification and analysis of tasks related to a job provide the teacher with data to be used in the sequencing of units and objectives and the selection of meaningful content. A basic question that the teacher must answer when sequencing units is "What does the student have to master before taking the next step?"

At least two other organizational patterns for sequencing skill units should be considered, especially where student motivation is a concern and students' dropping out of school before completing training is a possibility. Whenever possible, topics that are of *most interest* to students should be presented near the beginning of the course. Another approach to sequencing units is to teach first those *skills* that a student uses most frequently on the job; therefore, if a student leaves school before completing the course, he or she would possess some marketable skills.

What about the topics that are not specifically related to skill development? In courses such as general business or business law, establish the sequence on an arbitrary basis or by focusing on student interest and input in making these decisions.

After the topics have been identified and sequenced, the time needed for each unit should be established. This will depend on factors such as whether the goal is acquaintance, mastery, or review for content; the importance of the topic to the particular group of students; and the amount of material available.

After sequencing the unit topics and estimating the amount of time for each, select, adapt, and/or develop the instructional content for each unit. At this stage of planning, material identification consists basically of listing books and chapters, filmstrips, tapes, and guest speakers. At least three general criteria should be considered in the selection of such material: the content (1) is based on previously identified learner objectives, (2) includes a variety of difficulty levels and media to provide for student differences in achievement and learning style, and (3) is planned in relation to time and resources available.

General types of evaluation can be identified by topics. For a unit on "Using the Telephone," the evaluation would probably include student demonstration using the teletrainer, whereas a unit in business mathematics would likely be evaluated through problems, perhaps using a calculator.

Complete Learning Activity 3 at the end of this module.

DEVELOPING THE UNIT

After selecting the topics and general course objectives, the next task is to develop the teaching units. The following steps may be used in developing a unit:

1. *Select a topic.* The first step in organizing a unit of work is to decide on the topic. If the course of study plan has been completed, and the topics identified, this step has already been accomplished.

2. *Prepare for the unit.* The teacher who is preparing to develop a unit should know as much as possible about the topic. This may entail reading and reviewing the section in the text dealing with the topic as well as reading advanced texts for additional information. Curriculum guides may have more information or suggest other sources. Articles in periodicals can also offer information on new developments and the latest trends. Sometimes it is helpful to make visits and confer with people. If units related to word processing are planned, it would beneficial to visit a company with a word processing center. Depending on the nature of the unit topic, the teacher may also wish to prepare a reading list for students. Group or individual study can be encouraged by giving students leads on materials that they can find and use.

If a student project is a part of the plans for the unit, it should be thoroughly developed and tested during the planning stage. A worthwhile unit can be ruined by the inclusion of a project that fails because it is too difficult, it takes too much time, or the needed supplies or equipment are not available. If the teacher has not used the project before, he or she should go through the entire process to be sure it is practical. In some situations, examples of finished products to show students, such as manuscripts or business reports, should be available.

3. *Involve students in planning.* Student involvement in planning the instructional unit can be valuable to the business teacher. It can increase student interest and motivation, make the unit more relevant to students, and provide creative ideas and suggestions. There are, of course, definite limits to what students can select and change. Essential knowledge and necessary job-entry skills must be retained in the unit. There may be some tedious practice to be accomplished or some difficult theory that must be learned whether students particularly like it or not. Students are not aware of everything they

need to know. If there is a conflict between the suggestions of students and the teacher's best professional judgment, then the teacher must assume final responsibility and make the decision.

One can involve students by having them react to a tentative unit plan, discuss what they would like to learn in a unit, assist with presentation of parts of the unit (such as demonstrations), brainstorm ideas to be included in the unit plan, or suggest problems encountered in work situations that could be incorporated into the unit learning plan.

4. *Develop the content.* A unit follows a well-designed structure, and good ideas are the materials of its construction. Materials should be selected carefully to meet the objectives and needs of students. The first step in developing a unit is to select or write the objectives. (See Module 5.2 for details.) When writing objectives for skill courses, the teacher must not concentrate on skills objectives to the exclusion of all else. A unit is likely to be a richer learning experience for students if the objectives include some concern for each of the following: (a) concepts or "big ideas" related to the topic, (b) attitudes and values to be developed, (c) mental habits and ways of thinking to be introduced or reinforced, and (d) skills and work habits to be mastered. Not all types of objectives can be given equal emphasis in any one unit. Some units will be more appropriate for emphasizing the development of attitudes, others for skills, and so on. However, it is still possible in many units to plan for objectives in each of the three domains—cognitive, affective, and psychomotor.

5. *Select learning activities.* Learning activities are the experiences through which students achieve the objectives of the unit. In any unit there can be some learning activities that are required of all students, some that are highly recommended, and others that are completely optional. Students can be allowed some flexibility and choice in the learning activities they want to pursue. It is probably not possible to provide all of these factors in every unit, but one should try to select activities that provide for the following:

a. *Background knowledge and skills.* Students must possess the background knowledge and skills required so that they have a reasonable chance of completing the learning activities successfully. If the learning activity requires students to interview business leaders, be sure they know how to do so.

b. *Practice.* Students must have an opportunity to practice the kinds of behavior specified by the objectives. If the objectives call for them to be able to file material alphabetically, numerically, or geographically, be sure the learning activities include practice in filing material in order to apply the rules they have learned.

c. *Statement of purpose.* Students must have a perception of the purposes and value of the learning activity.

d. *Element of choice.* Students should be furnished some choice of learning activities depending on their individual abilities, interests, and previous knowledge.

e. *Feedback.* The learning activities should provide for prompt feedback, knowledge of results, and reinforcement.

It is easy for teachers to fall into a pattern of using the same two or three kinds of learning activities in their instructional plans. The following suggestions for unit learning activities are presented to stimulate creative thinking:[12]

a. *Reading parts of a textbook*—Students can be asked to read short, relevant sections dealing specifically with the knowledge required to reach the objective. This may be a single reference or it may be a number of alternative references from different books.

b. *Examining reference books*—You may have your students examine or gather data from standard reference books such as reference manuals for office personnel, secretarial handbooks, and so on.

c. *Working in programmed materials*—Students may complete one or more sections of a programmed text or other programmed material such as programmed English, business mathematics, or consumer economics.

d. *Reading special materials*—Students can be referred to materials available in the school library such as books, encyclopedias, periodical articles from bound volumes, and so on.

e. *Solving practice problems*—You could have students attempt to solve practice problems in the skills component, such as computational problems, exercises, and so on.

f. *Viewing or listening to audio or audiovisual materials*—On a large-group, small-group, or individual basis, students can gain information from media materials such as slidetapes, audiotapes, films, filmstrips, videotapes, and so on.

g. *Observing or operating models or mock-ups*—Working with such objects can help students to gain understandings of mechanisms or operating controls (for example, teletrainer, PBX board, and so on).

h. *Role playing of performance in a simulated situation*—Students may take the principal role of the employee or the participating role of the customer, the receptionist, the secretary, accountant, and so on. Role-playing activities should be one of the later activities in the student's learning experiences.

i. *Participating in real-life performances*—In these performances, the students function for short periods of time under controlled conditions in an actual work situation or a situation very close to real, such as a cooperative business student in a work-training station, acting as receptionist in school office, and so on. These also should be final learning activities.

j. *Observing the skilled worker in a real work situation*—This should be done with specific goals in mind, usually with some form of guide, observation instrument, or report form to give structure and purpose to the observation period (for example, student teacher or teacher aide observes the regular teacher).

k. *Videotaping student performance*—These tapes can be viewed and used by the student to evaluate and improve his performance.

l. *Participating in simulation experiences*—In simulations, a student goes through a "dry run" of the performance with the conditions controlled and consequences minimized as in simulated office situations or practice sets. Case studies, in which students write their reactions to the given situation, are also simulation experiences.

m. *Participating in small-group experiences*—These experiences give students a chance to discuss, plan, or evaluate their work (for example, discuss results of observations, plan for role-playing sessions, or evaluate the instructional value of their activities).

n. *Observing the instructor demonstrate an operation*—There are numerous situations in the business "skill" courses where the best approach is for the instructor to perform an operation and describe it as students observe. This may be done on an individual, small-group, or total class basis.

o. *Listening to guest speakers or outside experts*—These classroom experiences should be scheduled by the teacher at a time when many students are ready for the experience. Usually the nature of the topic is such that the whole group can benefit, even though they may not all be at the same point in their learning.

p. *Producing or constructing projects or services*—These must directly contribute to the objective and therefore must be carefully designed, be of limited scope, and require a limited amount of time (serve in school store).

q. *Completing problem-solving activities*—Some objectives may require solving problems involved in given situations. These may be relatively short experiences (for example, plan a travel itinerary involving a trip to three cities). It is very important in problem-solving activities that the student have the required skills, that he have access to the information needed to solve the problem, and that the problem not go beyond the performance objective.

r. *Completing skills practice exercises*—Some skilled operations may require that the student not only be able to perform them correctly once, but that the student be able to do them smoothly and flawlessly every time. Learning activities may therefore specify practice periods in terms of times, number of repeated experiences, or quantity of production (for example, three successful takes of dictation at 100 words per minute for three minutes).

s. *Memorizing information*—The performance objective may require that the student can best function if he has committed some information to memory (for example, the Gregg shorthand brief forms).

t. *Collecting objects*—Some performance objectives may be reached by asking students to collect real objects so as to become familiar with their characteristics, the variety available, the settings in which they may be found (for example, newspaper advertisements, business letters).

u. *Reading information sheets*—These are concise statements of very relevant information specifically prepared for the unit, geared to the student's level, and available from no other convenient source (for example, job sheets in office practice).

v. *Writing technical reports, reacting to case studies, preparing reports for class discussion*—This activity is particularly valuable in the business communication, office management, and office practice courses.

w. *Preparing audio and audiovisual materials*—Students can be asked to gather information and produce diagrams, drawings, slides, charts, graphs, tapes, layouts, design sketches, transparencies, and so on. Activities of this type are usually interesting to students, add variety to the learning experience, and tend to reinforce learning.

x. *Completing planning experiences*—Performance objectives may require that the student learn how to plan the job or operation. Planning may include selecting or designing the job, developing a sequence of procedures, figuring materials and costs, noting check-points and evaluation standards (for example, producing the school annual, newspaper, or commencement program).

y. *Completing critique or evaluation experiences*—The student is asked to rate or evaluate an example of a finished product or service, or to make a critical analysis of a performance of a specified skill, as in typewriting or shorthand class. The object of the evaluation is a work sample product, the work of a fellow student, the student's own work, as, for example, a transcript, word list, or examination paper. The final result may be a completed rating sheet, a grade, a written report, or an oral report.

z. *Participating in cooperative student experiences*—Though instruction may be individualized, there are situations when two or more students may work together in a learning experience. Many occupational tasks involve teamwork, and it is proper for the learning activities to incorporate this. Occupational activities that involve cooperative production techniques, worker interaction, and team problem solving are places where cooperative student experiences are applicable.

As a final check on the adequacy of the learning activities, the business teacher can apply these criteria: (a) each activity should relate to at least one objective; (b) the activity should seem worthwhile to the student; (c) the activity should be stimulating and thought-provoking; and (d) the activity should relate to the students' aims and interests and pertain to their lives both in school and out.

6. *Select evaluation procedures.* An important part of every unit is that of planning for student evaluation. Without an evaluation component, the teacher would not know the extent to which students have learned. The purpose of the evaluation procedure is to determine whether students can now meet the objectives of the unit. If one of the unit objectives calls for students to be able to write a letter of application for a job, the unit test should require them to write such a letter, and the teacher should evaluate the results to see how closely their performance meets that called for in the objectives.

Evaluation procedures should take into consideration the following guidelines:

a. *Number of items.* Prepare only as many items as necessary to find out how well the student is able to meet the objectives.

b. *Type of skill.* Require the same kind of student performance in the evaluation as called for in the objective. A cognitive objective would likely be measured by a pencil/paper test while a psychomotor objective would be measured by a performance test.

c. *Objectivity.* Try to make the evaluation process as objective and free from judgment or bias as possible.

7. *Write unit plans.* The ideas and plans assembled thus far cannot be left as vague notions and mental notes; they must be written down in some form that will give them substance and organization. The written document or format in which ideas for the unit are described is called a unit plan. It needs to be complete, structured, and clearly written. This plan will be used to prepare

for the lessons in the unit, to help collect the resource materials, to organize the learning activities, and to construct the evaluation situation.

There is no one best format for developing a unit plan. You will eventually settle on a format that works best for you and includes the kind of information you need. There are, however, certain basic components or elements that should appear in every plan, though they may have slightly different names and be given somewhat varying degrees of emphasis. A brief description of each unit plan element follows:

a. *Title of the unit.* The title should be stated clearly and briefly.
b. *Overview/introduction.* This describes the general scope of the unit, the significance of the topic, and/or statement of purpose or rationale.
c. *Student performance objectives.* Each objective should be stated in terms of what students are expected to be able to do at the completion of the unit.
d. *Outline of the contents of the unit.* This outline should be very condensed. As the lessons are developed, the content outline will be expanded.
e. *Student learning activities.* This is a list of the activities that will enable the student to reach the objectives, including the lessons to be presented by the teacher.
f. *Concluding activities and evaluation procedures.* This section describes in broad terms the kinds of measurement techniques that will be used to find out how closely each student's performance matches the objective.
g. *Instructional resource materials and/or bibliography.* This section includes lists of books, films, reference sheets, speakers, and so on, that may be used by the teacher and/or students. Items that are unusual or peculiar to the unit are noted in this section; for example, supplies required, special equipment, or other reminders are listed here.

Sample unit plan formats and checklist

Two suggested unit plan formats are included (see Illustrations 5.1 and 5.2). They should be expanded to meet particular needs. It is important to remember that instructional plans are made to fit the needs of students and teachers rather than to fit a form. A unit planning checklist is also included (Illustration 5.3) to assist in evaluating construction of a unit. An example of a model unit plan is included in Illustration 5.4.

Complete Learning Activity 4 at the end of this module.

DEVELOPING THE DAILY LESSON PLAN

The third type of planning carried out by the business teacher is a daily lesson plan. The length of the plan and its format depend on the person who is going to use it. While no two educators agree completely on the content and form of a lesson plan, the one point they all agree on is that *all* teachers must do some form of lesson planning. Beginning teachers need to prepare enough plans to guide their instructional efforts. In order to write a plan, you have to think through where you are going, how best to get there, and how to

illustration 5.1
FORMAT FOR A UNIT PLAN

UNIT PLAN

Unit Title _____

Subject _____ **Teacher** _____

School _____

I. Overview:

II. Topics to be Covered:

1.
2.
3.
etc.

III. Student Performance Objectives:

1.
2.
3.
etc.

IV. Student Learning Activities   Required Resources

1.
2.
3.
etc.

V. Student Evaluation:

VI. Resource Materials:

illustration 5.2
FORMAT FOR A UNIT PLAN

UNIT PLAN

Subject _____ **School** _____ **Teacher** _____

Unit Topic _____

Overview _____

_____

_____

Student Performance Objectives	Content	Learning Activities	Resources	Evaluation

illustration 5.3
UNIT PLANNING CHECKLIST

Directions: Place an X in the NO, PARTIAL, or FULL box to indicate that each of the following performance components was not accomplished, partially accomplished, or fully accomplished. If, because of special circumstances, a performance component was not applicable, or impossible to execute, place an X in the N/A box.

NAME _____

DATE _____

RESOURCE PERSON _____

LEVEL OF PERFORMANCE

	N/A	No	Partial	Full

In developing the plan, you
1. consulted curriculum guides and courses of study in the vocational service area for appropriate topics and content .... ☐ ☐ ☐ ☐

2. selected a topic which .... ☐ ☐ ☐ ☐

   a. is relevant to students .... ☐ ☐ ☐ ☐

   b. is significant .... ☐ ☐ ☐ ☐

   c. has a focus or continuity .... ☐ ☐ ☐ ☐

The objective(s) as stated in the unit plan:
3. are stated in terms of student behaviors or performances ...... ☐ ☐ ☐ ☐

4. provide for individual differences in student abilities .... ☐ ☐ ☐ ☐

The instructional content outlined in the plan:
5. is correlated with the student performance objectives of the unit . ☐ ☐ ☐ ☐

6. provides a variety of difficulty levels .... ☐ ☐ ☐ ☐

The student learning activities in the plan:
7. are based upon the student performance objective(s) of the unit ☐ ☐ ☐ ☐

8. are varied, to provide for a wide range of student interest, ability, and learning styles .... ☐ ☐ ☐ ☐

9. provide for student practice and application of the requisite performances .... ☐ ☐ ☐ ☐

The evaluation procedures specified in the unit plan:
10. are directly based on the objective(s) .... ☐ ☐ ☐ ☐

11. require the same kinds of student performance as called for in the objective(s) .... ☐ ☐ ☐ ☐

12. use techniques to gather data that depend as little as possible on the judgment, opinion, or attitude of the teacher .... ☐ ☐ ☐ ☐

LEVEL OF PERFORMANCE: All items must receive FULL, or N/A responses. If any item receives a NO, or PARTIAL response, revise your plan accordingly, or check with your resource person if necessary.

know when you have arrived. By means of a plan, you are visualizing just what you will accomplish in the classroom. In addition, through good planning, you can anticipate problems and work, in advance, to eliminate or overcome them. Planning also allows you to anticipate your needs for supplies, tools, equipment, and other support materials. All of these organizing efforts help to save time, to weed out the extraneous, and to cover the essential elements. In the classroom, the lesson plan serves as a handy guide during the presentation. Finally, since daily lesson plans grow out of unit plans, the daily plan helps to keep the teacher on track in his or her goals, thus providing for continuity in the course and in student learning.

Preparing the lesson plan

PRELIMINARY INFORMATION.   Somewhere at the top of the lesson plan certain information is identified. Various lesson plan forms list the subject, the date the plan will be used, the unit title, the title of the lesson, the grade level of the students, the hour or period the class meets, and the teacher's name. How much of this information is included will depend on individual needs. If you teach several different subjects, you may wish to specify *subject*, whereas if you teach five sections of typewriting, you will, no doubt, specify *class*.

LESSON APPROACH OR INTRODUCTION.   The critical components in this section are the aims or objectives and the lesson introduction. The aims or objectives are the "where you are going" portion of the plan; they name the specific changes to be expected in student behavior. The objectives should be written so as to allow for individual differences since content and activities that are too easy for one student may be too difficult for another. (With implementation of Public Law 94–142, which guarantees appropriate educational opportunities for *all* students in the least restrictive environment, business teachers can expect to have students in their classes with wide ranges of ability, achievement, and interest.) These objectives are drawn from the broader unit plan. (Writing student objectives is discussed in Module 5.2.)

In this section you determine how to acquaint students with the specified objective(s) for the lesson. Several major purposes are to orient students to (1) what the objectives of the lesson are, (2) how the lesson relates to them, (3) how it relates to their past classroom work, and (4) what will be expected of them. Two additional functions are to get the attention of the students and to motivate them sufficiently to hold their attention. There are various methods used to achieve these purposes: telling an interesting related story, giving a brief demonstration, asking provocative questions, or presenting background information. Preferably, students should be involved in some way, by suggesting answers to questions, assisting in the demonstration, sharing their related experiences, and so on.

LESSON DEVELOPMENT.   Once you have determined where you are going, and have decided how to introduce the lesson, you need to plan how to get there. This involves selecting the most appropriate learning experiences

illustration 5.4
MODEL UNIT PLAN

SUBJECT Vocational Education   **SCHOOL** Main-Chance Vocational   **TEACHER** Ernest Early

UNIT TOPIC Deal with Customers, Handle Routine Requests and Complaints.

OVERVIEW According to occupational analyses, beginning workers in this field will be in contact with the public and will frequently be dealing directly with customers. This unit is designed to provide students with a knowledge of the principles on which customer relations are based. A student successfully completing this unit will be competent in the skills needed to work with customers in routine situations.

Student Performance Objectives	Content	Learning Activities	Resources	Evaluation
The student will be able to:	Introduction to consumer relations	Listen to introductory lesson by the teacher.		Pretest and post-test; Occupational Attitude test, No. 17
demonstrate a positive attitude toward customers and toward the work of dealing with them.	Importance of good customer relations.	Read Chapter 4 in the test	Course textbook	
	The need to develop personal competence in this area.	Listen to presentation by personnel manager	Personnel manager of Stiles and Workman, Inc.	
	Job requirements in customer skills.	Participate in class presentations		
pass (80%) a 25 item objective test on the basic psychological principles of customer relations.	Value of knowledge of psychology when dealing with customers. Nature of typical customers.	Listen to teacher presentations on psychological bases and practical applications. Participate in class discussions.		Teacher-made test: 25 item objective exam developed from presentations and videotape on basic principles
	View videotape "People Awareness"... respond to taped questions. The psychological needs of the customer. Problem customers Examples of Applications	Videotape "People Awareness" Videotape playback unit		

by means of which students can achieve the objectives. When planning the activities, make sure that each one is related to an objective.

The instructional techniques and learning activities you select will be determined by such factors as individual needs, interests, and abilities; whether students are to learn a skill, an idea or concept, an attitude, or a value; the amount of time and the resources available. The following is a list of sample techniques and learning activities to get you started in thinking about appropriate methods and activities you can plan:[13]

audiotape	brainstorming	bulletin board
buzz groups	chalkboard	committees
community study	computer	debates
demonstration	discovery	discussion
displays	dramatizations	drill and practice
exhibits	field trips	research

illustration 5.4 (continued)

Student Performance Objectives	Content	Learning Activities	Resources	Evaluation
demonstrate competence (in a simulated situation) in techniques of dealing with customers in routine business situations. The level of performance should be that expected of beginning workers.	Appearance and dress requirements of the occupation. Manners expected of workers. Techniques and behaviors in dealing with customers.	Listen to teacher presentation on techniques for dealing with customers. Participate in class discussion.		Student performance of customer relations competencies, evaluated by checklist.
	Undesirable behaviors Handling routine customer situations: Requests and complaints	Critique the given case studies of customer relations situations. Participate in role-playing of customer and worker (participate in both roles).	Case study sheets with model answers Handouts describing role-play situations.	

LEVEL OF PERFORMANCE: Your completed unit plan should have included all the components and elements indicated in the Model Unit Plan. If you missed some points or have questions about the form of your unit plan, review the material in the information sheet, Writing Unit Plans, pp. 36–42, or check with your resource person if necessary.

film loops	films	filmstrips
flannel boards	flipcharts	games
graphics	homework assignments	illustrated talks
independent study	information sheets	investigation/reporting
laboratory work	large-group/small-group instruction	library research
listening		models
oral recitation	listing/diagramming	problem solving
programmed matter	panels/symposiums	question-and-answer
	projects	resource persons
reading aloud	real objects	simulation
review	role playing	step-by-step procedure panels
slides	speaking	
supervised study	team teaching	television
transparencies	verbal illustrations	videotape
visual illustrations	work-study	writing

The procedures should reflect not only student activities but also teacher activities. This means that you must include enough detail so that you know what to do and say, all of which necessitates including content as well as procedures in the plan. The format of this content section may vary. Some teachers organize the content in outline form, while others write in paragraph form. Many times the technique(s) determine how to plan the content. For example, if you chose "demonstration," you would need to list, in detail, the steps of the demonstration in the exact sequence they are to be performed. If you chose to give a brief explanation, you would need to outline the information, whereas if you chose discussion, you would need to prepare a list of key questions to guide the discussion and keep it moving. Remember, the content must relate to the achievement of objectives and to each individual in the class.

In this section, list also the resources and materials needed. This means that you must select appropriate aids to support the objectives and content of your lesson, and you must have these aids available.

LESSON SUMMARY. There are two major activities that occur in this section of the lesson: (1) summarizing the lesson and (2) evaluating students' attainment of the objectives. The summary component is the place in the plan where you determine ways of pulling together the loose ends, drawing conclusions, evolving generalizations, and/or reiterating major concepts. This may be done through teacher summary, student summary, short quiz, review, demonstration, or some other method. Of primary importance is to relate again to the lesson objectives what has occurred during class. In other words, the summary should reinforce for students where they were headed, where they have been, where they should be now, and where they will go next.

The evaluation component is the tool for determining if, in fact, the students are where they should be now. The method of evaluation selected should be based on the type of objective the student is trying to achieve. Directing questions to several members of the class, applying the new learning to a realistic product as in typing or shorthand, assisting students in deriving generalizations, and preparing summaries and drawing conclusions are indicators of student achievement.

OTHER INFORMATION. There are at least four other items that need to be considered in planning a lesson.

Assignments. Allow time in the lesson plan for making assignments, if appropriate. Calling to students as they rush out the door is an ineffective way to make an assignment. Assignments accomplish three purposes: (a) they set up the objectives of the new work; (b) they provide students with a plan for doing the work; and (c) they motivate students sufficiently to begin and complete the work. Some teachers prefer to make assignments at the beginning of the class while others make them near the end of the period.

Announcements. To make sure that items, such as a meeting of FBLA, the due date for independent study projects, and so on, are mentioned, any announcements should be noted in the lesson plan and scheduled for a particular time during the class period (that is, at the very beginning or the very end).

Time. It is especially valuable for beginning teachers to indicate beside each activity in the lesson plan how much time the activity may take. Comparing the estimated time to the actual time will allow a teacher to make more accurate estimates as time goes on. The following rules of thumb may be helpful in budgeting your time:[14]

1. Initially make your procedures too long. Inexperienced teachers tend to talk fast and move swiftly, not having enough material, whereas the experienced teacher is more likely to run out of time.
2. Provide a few minutes at the beginning of the period for announcements, taking attendance, and time at the end of the period for summarizing or clinching the lesson, straightening up work stations, and making assignments as appropriate. After allowing time for these administrative and teaching chores, you may find that a forty-minute film may be too long for a fifty-minute period.
3. Mark in your procedures, by an asterisk or underlining, the activities that must be covered during the period in case time starts to run out.
4. Give students time to learn. Points have to be made and remade. Introduce your points and follow them up with explanation, examples, and demonstrations as appropriate.
5. Don't panic if you do run out of material. Use the time for a review or to let students begin homework under supervision. For a while, the new teacher would be wise to have some extra activities planned for such an emergency.

Using the plan

Generally, beginning teachers should follow lesson plans fairly closely, but they should not feel bound to them. There are situations, such as the following, that justify deviation from the plan: (1) the lesson is more difficult than anticipated, calling for more detailed teaching than planned; (2) during the lesson, the teacher discovers that students need a review of certain prerequisite information or skills before they can proceed with the new material; (3) students raise questions during class that are *sufficiently important* to warrant immediate follow-up (usually a *brief* time devoted to the question is sufficient); (4) events may occur in or out of class to necessitate changes, such as an event of national, state, or local importance, or an exciting school event. (On some occasions, you may want to devote the entire period to the event; at other times, allowing students to talk about the event for a few minutes at the beginning of the period is sufficient.)

In using the lesson plan, the teacher should exercise a reasonable degree of flexibility, being sensitive to student reactions and making necessary and desirable adjustments to ensure the orderly flow of instruction and learning. Suggestions for planning, organizing, and teaching specific business subjects are found in the chapters devoted to the content areas.

Lesson plan formats

The form of the lesson plan is best that yields the most service to you, the teacher. You will probably experiment with different formats until you find one that permits you to teach with maximum effectiveness and efficiency. Different types of business education courses call for different lesson plan formats. Sample lesson plan forms for use with informational, manipulative skills, and problem-solving or managerial objectives follow (see Illustrations 5.5, 5.6, and 5.7). A Checklist for a Preliminary Lesson Plan (Illustration 5.8) will help you evaluate the plans you have prepared.

Complete Learning Activities 5 and 6 at the end of this module.

---

illustration 5.5
MODEL LESSON PLAN: INFORMATIONAL

UNIT:	Job Opportunities
LESSON TOPIC:	Ways of Getting a Job: The Résumé
OBJECTIVE:	Given four sample résumés, the student will develop his own résumé containing complete information in each of the necessary categories as indicated by the samples.

INTRODUCTION:

5 minutes

This past week we have been talking about various ways of getting a job. Today, I want you to assume that you will be completing vocational training soon and have been watching the "help wanted" column in the local newspaper. This morning you noticed a job opening that appeals to you, but the ad suggests that you send a résumé to Box 47 in care of the local paper.

The only way that you can secure further information regarding this position is by sending your résumé to a box number. What are you going to do, give up? What is a résumé? What will the prospective employer do with it? Where can you get one? These are a few of the questions that we will try to answer using some sample résumés. At the completion of this lesson you will have a personal résumé that you have developed. When that job opening comes along, you will be prepared.

METHOD: Discovery
Supervised Individual Activity

LEARNING ACTIVITY: Students will study the four samples individually to discover for themselves the
10 minutes   types of information contained in a résumé and the format required.

20 minutes   Based on what they have discovered, each student will prepare his own résumé, rough draft.

RESOURCES: Copies of four teacher-prepared sample résumés for each student.

EVALUATION: Students will pair off, trade papers, and discuss each résumé, evaluating the completeness of each on the basis of the four samples. Each student will then
15 minutes   make a final draft of his résumé incorporating any necessary revisions. Final evaluation will be made by the teacher using the four samples as guidelines.

SUMMARY: Question and Answer

15 minutes   Point #1: The objective of this lesson was to develop a résumé containing information appropriate for job application.

Point #2: What is a résumé?

Point #3: What information should a résumé contain?

Point #4: Why should careful attention be given to the preparation of the résumé?

WRITING THE INSTRUCTIONAL MODULE

The instructional module provides the means for working effectively with low-, average-, and high-ability students within a single-class setting. An instructional module has two essential and unique characteristics. First, the teaching function becomes an integral part of the learning module. The teacher's role is modified to become that of a teacher-manager, human relations specialist, guidance counselor, evaluator, and coordinator of learning experiences. Second, opportunities for the student to make choices are built into the module. Within the framework of assignments or activities provided, the student may choose specific activities to meet specific objectives and may work at greater depth if he or she wishes.

The structure of the module depends on clearly stated behavioral objectives that students understand they must accomplish in order to progress. The module contains a highly structured assortment of media, modes, and learning levels so that an individual student can choose an appropriate route in meeting these objectives.

Rationale

The first step in developing the instructional module is to write the rationale. The purpose of the rationale is to explain to the learner why it is important to achieve the objectives of the module. It is a conditioner, and it is usually short and easy for the student to comprehend. Here is an example of a rationale:

> Since the principles of debit and credit are basic to all manual and machine accounting, when to debit and when to credit are basic concepts to be understood and mastered. Learning *how* to debit and credit will involve knowing *why*. Learning why will come to you as you progress from one stage to the next in learning how. Thus, debiting and crediting are reasoned actions—not procedures merely to be memorized.

Complete Learning Activity 7 at the end of this module.

Performance objectives

The second step in constructing a module is to write the performance objectives. (See Module 5.2 for details of writing performance objectives.)

Complete Learning Activity 8 at the end of this module.

---

illustration 5.6
MODEL LESSON PLAN: MANIPULATIVE SKILLS

Unit _____
Lesson _____

JOB (or operation):

AIM (or purpose):

TOOLS AND EQUIPMENT:

MATERIALS:

TEACHING AIDS:

REFERENCES:

I.   PREPARATION (of the student)

II. PRESENTATION (of the skills):

Operations or Steps	Key Points (things to remember to do or say)

(Additional blank sheets can be ruled into two columns for notes for presentation step.)

illustration 5.6 (continued)

Operations or Steps	Key Points (things to remember to do or say)

III. APPLICATION (practice by student under close supervision)

IV. TEST (performance of skill to acceptable standards)

Suggested Reading for Student:

illustration 5.7
MODEL LESSON PLAN: PROBLEM-SOLVING OR MANAGERIAL

UNIT:

LESSON TOPIC:

OBJECTIVE:

INTRODUCTION: [Identification of Problem (informal)
Statement of the Objective (formal)]

time

METHOD: [Problem-Solving or Managerial]

KEY QUESTIONS TO ASK TO IDENTIFY FACTORS	FACTORS TO BE IDENTIFIED

time

RESOURCES: [list of resources for students to use in locating information needed to solve problem]

time

SUMMARY: [draw conclusions to the problem]

time

EVALUATION:

illustration 5.8
CHECKLIST FOR PRELIMINARY LESSON PLAN

Directions: Place an X in the NO, PARTIAL, or FULL box to indicate that each of the following performance components was not accomplished, partially accomplished, or fully accomplished. If, because of special circumstances, a performance component was not applicable, or impossible to execute, place an X in the N/A box.

Name _____

Date _____

Resource Person _____

LEVEL OF PERFORMANCE

	N/A	No	Partial	Full
1. There is a stated **objective** in the plan	☐	☐	☐	☐
2. The objective is stated in terms of a single student behavior	☐	☐	☐	☐
3. The objective contains the conditions under which the objective will be achieved, and the criteria via which achievement will be measured	☐	☐	☐	☐
4. There is an **introduction**	☐	☐	☐	☐
5. The introduction contains information or techniques meant to motivate students and orient them to the lesson objective	☐	☐	☐	☐
6. There is a statement in the plan indicating what **methods, techniques,** or **learning experiences** will be used to help students achieve the lesson objective	☐	☐	☐	☐
7. Students are given an opportunity to apply what they learned	☐	☐	☐	☐
8. The necessary **content** for the methods selected (i.e., key questions, information outline, step-by-step procedures) is included in the plan	☐	☐	☐	☐
9. There is a **summary**	☐	☐	☐	☐
10. The summary contains information or techniques meant to pull loose ends together, restate major points, and relate the lesson to the objective	☐	☐	☐	☐
11. A method of **evaluation** is provided	☐	☐	☐	☐
12. **Resources** are included in the plan	☐	☐	☐	☐

LEVEL OF PERFORMANCE: All items must receive FULL, or N/A responses. If any item receives a NO, or PARTIAL response, the teacher and resource person should meet to determine what additional activities the teacher needs to complete in order to reach competency in the weak areas.

Pre/post test

The objective of the pretest is to determine whether the student needs to work through the module. In many cases, the student already exhibits the behavior called for in the module. (It is conceivable that the entire module is a test; if the student completes it, he or she has learned it. The module that you are constructing is such an example.) Short of having the student complete the entire module, there are means for the teacher to determine whether or not the student needs to continue through the module:

1. *Teacher knowledge of the student.* A student enrolled in beginning typewriting at the secondary level with no prior knowledge of the keyboard would begin with module 1, based on your knowledge of the student. However, a student enrolled in beginning typewriting at the postsecondary level, with some prior instruction, would be given a placement test. The decision as to whether or not to require a performance pretest can be made on the basis of teacher information about the student and the content of the module.

2. *Have student answer questions.* Depending on the specifications of the performance objectives, the teacher may construct pencil-and-paper test questions to measure student knowledge.

3. *Have student perform part of the operation.* If the performance objective specifies that the student will take new-matter dictation at 80 words per minute, then the test would involve dictation at this rate and verification of an acceptable result.

Mager and Beach[15] offer the following guidelines for the preparation of the pre/post test:

1. *Use the objectives as your guide.* Prepare as many items as necessary to find out how well the student meets each objective. In some cases, only one item is appropriate; in other cases, you may feel that several items are needed to make an accurate assessment.

2. *Create items that call for the same behavior specified in the objective.* If the objective calls for a student to use a certain piece of equipment, then create test items that make him or her use the equipment. In such cases it would be inappropriate to ask him or her to write an essay about the use of equipment. On the other hand, if an objective requires a student to explain something rather than do it, then an oral item or an essay item is appropriate.

If the objective calls for the student to demonstrate a specific skill, the pretest may be as simple as this:

Do you know how to reconcile a bank statement? If your answer is yes, ask your teacher for the Posttest. If your answer is no, turn to the next page and begin work on this module.

The posttest for this objective might be the following:

> The checkbook on January 31 has a balance of $1,009.50 and the bank statement balance is $1,007.83. After examining the statement, you discover that a deposit of $100.00 is not listed on the statement, and neither are the following checks: #69 ($9.33) and #74 ($92.00); a service charge of $1.00 and a charge for collection of a note, $2.00, are not listed. Reconcile the account.

The sole purpose of the posttest is to determine whether the student exhibits the behavior called for in the objective. If the objective states a specific learning outcome, then test items should be constructed to measure that behavior. If the objective states a general learning outcome with samples of behavior, then the test items are samples of behavior that are evidence of student mastery of the objective. (The samples of behavior in the test are not necessarily the same as those in the objective. See the writing of performance objectives in Module 5.2.)

The pre/post test may be the same or the teacher may prepare two equivalent forms. The student may score the pretest, but the teacher usually scores the posttest to determine whether the student has exhibited the behavior specified in the objective.

You may want to reread Chapter 4 and refer to specific content-area chapters for additional information on test construction and evaluation of student performance.

Complete Learning Activity 9 at the end of this module.

Learning activities and assignments

The "heart" of a module is the learning activities section. Writing objectives is probably the most difficult part of writing the module, but locating and developing learning activities takes the most time. It is in this section that you *teach,* and you have several alternatives:

1. Briefly organize explanations in written form or select appropriate written material from textbooks and other sources.
2. Use illustrations, such as flowcharts or diagrams.
3. Prepare cassette tapes of the lesson to be taught or select appropriate cassette tapes.
4. Make or select sound slides, filmstrips, film loops, films, and transparencies illustrating some segments of the lesson.
5. Plan group discussions, teacher/student demonstrations, and individual or group presentations in addition to the material presented in the module.

KINDS OF ACTIVITIES.   Learning activities fall into three general groups: *required, recommended,* and *optional.* (In many modules, the activities are divided into two groups: required and optional.) *Required* activities are those that every student must complete if assigned the objective. Activities should not be classified as "required" without considerable thought. The "required" label cuts down on the flexibility of the program and denies the learner choices, but it can be justified. *Recommended* activities are those that the teacher considers valuable in helping the student attain the objective. *Optional* activities are in the nature of what is sometimes called "enrichment." Optional activities should be especially interesting or contain special features; thus, they can be enrichment activities for gifted students or remedial activities for students needing additional drill or practice. The learning activities selected and/or written will be based upon the teacher's imagination, the availability of materials, time, facilities, and equipment, as well as student interests, abilities, needs, and career goals. (See pages 128–130 for examples of learning activities.)

ARRANGING ACTIVITIES.   The business teacher may find it helpful to make a flowchart to illustrate how the student can proceed through the objectives. Using a sequenced list of steps as a basis for planning, prepare activities for each objective; try to include two or three activities utilizing different media. Note the following sample objective and activities.

Sample Objective: Prepare a master in four colors that requires typing, drawing, and lettering and run ten correct copies on 5 × 8 cards within an hour-and-a-half time limit.

Sample Activity:
A. 1. Review your choice of filmstrips and cassettes:
        #C1–2a Introduction to Spirit Duplication
        #C1–2b How to Prepare a Master
        #C1–2c How to Operate the Spirit Duplicator
        Rewind the cassette.
    2. Review the teacher-prepared instructions for operating an electric spirit duplicator.
    3. Review Resource #3, CLERICAL OFFICE PRACTICE, pp. 364–70.
    4. Review Resource #4, DUPLICATING MACHINE PROCESSES, pp. 64–71, 83–87, and 93–94.
    5. Review Resource #5, LIQUID DUPLICATING SYSTEMS, pp. xxvii, xxviii, and 14–22.
    6. Review Resource #6, CLERICAL OFFICE PROCEDURES, pp. 373–79.
B. From Resource #4, DUPLICATING MACHINE PROCESSES, read p. 81, "Prepare the Duplicator." Adjust the directions for a 5 × 8 card instead of a postal card.
C. Complete Assignment #4 in Resource #1, *Spirit Duplication,* according to the directions on p. 22.
D. Alternate Problem: Complete the assignment on p. 41 in Resource #5, LIQUID DUPLICATING SYSTEMS, according to the directions given for Assignment #4 in Resource #1, *Spirit Duplication.*

Business teachers at postsecondary vocational-technical schools have used the format shown in Illustration 5.9 to arrange the learning activities for individualized instruction. This Unit Guide Sheet illustrates, in compact form, both the work flow and interrelationship of different materials and evaluation.

Complete Learning Activity 10 at the end of this module.

Materials and resources

The final step in writing an instructional module is to list the materials and resources the student may use to complete the activities. The following is a list of some of the types of instructional materials you should consider:

Written materials: Textbooks, supplementary texts, handbooks, periodicals, pamphlets, programmed materials, reference books, documents, and clippings.

Hardware: Equipment, tools, machinery, computers.

Audiovisual aids: Films, filmstrips, single-concept film loops, radio, television, records, tapes, pictures, drawings, paintings, slides, slidetapes, videotapes, audiotapes, transparencies, microfilms, maps, globes, graphs, charts, diagrams, models, mock-ups, posters, collections, specimens, actual objects, flannel boards, chalkboards, magnetic boards, flip charts.

Any materials that you consider using should be previewed. When previewing materials, ask yourself these questions.[16]

1. Does the content match my lesson objective(s)?
2. Will the material fit with the instructional method(s) I plan to use?
3. Is the content up-to-date? totally? in part?
4. Is the content logically sequenced?
5. Is the material appropriate for the grade level of my students?
6. Can each of my students handle the vocabulary used?
7. Will this material motivate each of my students?
8. Is this material geared to the abilities, needs, and interests of all my students? some of my students?
9. Will this material fit into my time constraints?
10. Do I have access to the equipment (projector, tape deck, and so on) necessary to use this material? Is it in good operating condition?
11. Do I have the facilities necessary to use this material effectively?
12. Do I have access to the funds necessary to purchase or rent this material?
13. Is this material produced well technically? (Is the film sound clear and audible? Is the print in the text easy to read?)
14. Does the material have validity? (Does the author or producer indicate that it has been proven that it will do what it is intended to do?)

illustration 5.9
UNIT GUIDE SHEET

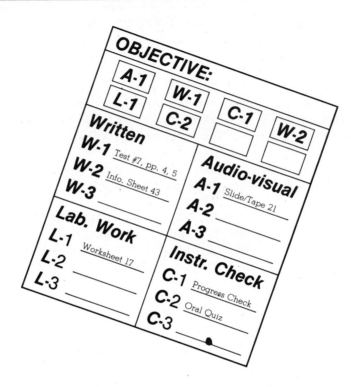

1st: Read the "OBJECTIVE"

The student learns what he must do as a result of having performed this unit.

2nd: Follow the "FLOW CHART"

Here the first block is "A-1." At "A-1" below, the student is told to view slide/tape number 21. Here the second block is "W-1." At "W-1" below, the student is told to read text #7, pages 4 and 5. Here the third block is "C-1." At "C-1" below, the student is told to check with the instructor, and so on.

illustration 5.9 (continued)

MAJOR DIVISION   *Computational Skills*   UNIT   *MCH 103*

OBJECTIVE   *Using a ten-key adding-listing machine, complete and record correct answers to a minimum of 24 problems involving multiplication during a ten-minute period.*

START → Math Unit → L-1 → A-1 → L-2 → W-1 → L-3 →

→ C-2 → W-2 → L-4 → C-2 → L-5 → C-2 → L-6 →

→ C-1 → A-2 → W-3 → L-7 → C-2 → C-3 → C-1

WRITTEN

W-1   Text: Read and study, page 18

W-2   Text: Read and study, page 26

W-3   Text: Read and study, page 20

W-4   _____

W-5   _____

W-6   _____

W-7   _____

W-8   _____

W-9   _____

AUDIO-VISUALS

A-1   Slide/Tape MCH 103-1

A-2   Slide/Tape MCH 103-2

A-3   _____

A-4   _____

A-5   _____

A-6   _____

A-7   _____

A-8   _____

A-9   _____

LABORATORY

L-1   Pretest MCH 103 (optional)

L-2   Job Sheet 103-1

L-3   Assignment MCH 103-1

L-4   Assignment MCH 103-2

L-5   Assignment MCH 103-3

L-6   Job Sheet 103-2

L-7   Assignment MCH 103-4

L-8   _____

L-9   _____

CHECK POINT

C-1   Instructor Check

C-2   Student Check

C-3   Unit Examination 103

C-4   _____

C-5   _____

C-6   _____

C-7   _____

C-8   _____

C-9   _____

If you are looking for materials for demonstration purposes or student use such as hardware (tools and machinery) or software (consumables such as typing paper, pencils, erasers, correction materials), you must check a few additional items. These materials should be the same as those the students would be expected to use on the job. They should be in good operating condition. With consumables, there should be a sufficient supply to allow for a number of restarts or waste. The degree of student participation will also indicate how much material or how many machines of pieces or equipment you will have to make available. For example, it takes only one piece of equipment if students watch the teacher demonstrate a skill, but more is required if each student is to perform the skill independently.

Readability level

Readability level of materials and reading levels of students are a major consideration in selecting materials. Methods for determining the reading level of written material have been constructed by Flesch,[17] Spache,[18] Dale and Chall,[19] Gunning,[20] Bormuth,[21] Fry,[22] and others. Fry's formula and graph for estimating readability follow (adapted from "A Readability Formula That Saves Time" by Edward Fry).

Directions for using the Readability Graph:
1. Select three 100-word passages from near the beginning, middle, and end of the book. Skip all proper nouns.
2. Count the total number of sentences in each of the three 100-word passages (estimating to nearest tenth of a sentence). Average these three numbers.
3. Count the total number of syllables in each 100-word sample. There is a syllable for each vowel sound: for example, cat (1), blackbird (2), continental (4). Don't be fooled by word size: for example, polio (3), through (1). Endings such as -y, -ed, -el, or -le usually make a syllable: for example, ready (2), bottle (2). It is convenient to count every syllable over one in each word and add 100. Average the total number of syllables for the three samples.
4. Plot on the graph (Illustration 5.10) the average number of sentences per 100 words and the average number of syllables per 100 words. Most plot points fall near the heavy curved line. Diagonal lines mark off approximate grade level areas.

Example	Sentences per 100 words	Syllables per 100 words
100-word sample, page 5	9.1	122
100-word sample, page 89	8.5	140
100-word sample, page 160	7.0	129
	$3\sqrt{24.6}$	$3\sqrt{391}$
	8.2	130

Plotting these averages on the graph, we find that they fall in the 5th grade area; hence the book is about 5th grade difficulty level. If great variability is encountered either in sentence length or in the syllable count for the three selections, then randomly select several more passages and average them in before plotting.

Complete Learning Activity 11 at the end of this module.

---

module 5.3
LEARNING ACTIVITIES

Course content of business education skill courses is directly influenced by the tasks that office employees perform on the job. In this activity, you will be identifying and analyzing tasks as a basis for determining course content and objectives.

1. Select one office occupation position and prepare a job description for it.
2. In order to complete this activity, you will need (a) one blank copy of the Work Sheet, (Illustration 5.11), (b) one blank copy of the Task Detail List (Table 5.4), and (c) one or two blank copies of the Task Detail Sequence (Table 5.5).
    a. List the tasks the worker performs in order to do the job described in Learning Activity 1 above. Star those tasks you would include in your instructional program. Include decision-making as well as performance-type tasks.

illustration 5.10
FRY'S READABILITY GRAPH

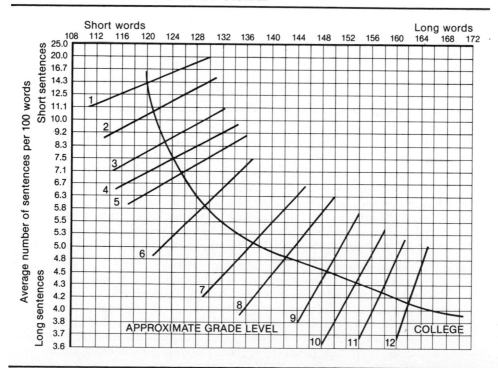

illustration 5.11
WORK SHEET

COLUMN 1	COLUMN 2	COLUMN 3 SKILLS AND KNOWLEDGE REQUIRED	COLUMN 4 Hardware/Software REQUIRED	COLUMN 5 ATTITUDES OR WORK HABITS TO BE EMPHASIZED
TASK:	STEP 1. ____ STEP 2. ____ STEP 3. ____ STEP 4. ____ STEP 5. ____ STEP 6. ____	1. ___ 2. ___ 3. ___ 4. ___ 5. ___	1. ___ 2. ___ 3. ___ 4. ___ 5. ___ 6. ___	1. ___ 2. ___ 3. ___ 4. ___ 5. ___ 6. ___
TASK:	STEP 1. ____ STEP 2. ____ STEP 3. ____ STEP 4. ____ STEP 5. ____ STEP 6. ____	1. ___ 2. ___ 3. ___ 4. ___ 5. ___	1. ___ 2. ___ 3. ___ 4. ___ 5. ___ 6. ___	1. ___ 2. ___ 3. ___ 4. ___ 5. ___ 6. ___
JOB TITLE: ____ TASK:	STEP 1. ____ STEP 2. ____ STEP 3. ____ STEP 4. ____ STEP 5. ____ STEP 6. ____	1. ___ 2. ___ 3. ___ 4. ___ 5. ___	1. ___ 2. ___ 3. ___ 4. ___ 5. ___ 6. ___	1. ___ 2. ___ 3. ___ 4. ___ 5. ___ 6. ___
TASK:	STEP 1. ____ STEP 2. ____ STEP 3. ____ STEP 4. ____ STEP 5. ____ STEP 6. ____	1. ___ 2. ___ 3. ___ 4. ___ 5. ___	1. ___ 2. ___ 3. ___ 4. ___ 5. ___ 6. ___	1. ___ 2. ___ 3. ___ 4. ___ 5. ___ 6. ___
TASK:	STEP 1. ____ STEP 2. ____ STEP 3. ____ STEP 4. ____ STEP 5. ____ STEP 6. ____	1. ___ 2. ___ 3. ___ 4. ___ 5. ___	1. ___ 2. ___ 3. ___ 4. ___ 5. ___ 6. ___	1. ___ 2. ___ 3. ___ 4. ___ 5. ___ 6. ___

b. List the job title and tasks you have selected in Activity "a" on the Work Sheet, column 1.

c. Select one task from the Work Sheet, column 1, and complete a Task Detail List (Table 5.4), and a Task Detail Sequence (Table 5.5). See Table 5.6, Major Verb Categories, for a sample of action verbs.

d. Record the information from the Task Detail Sequence on your Work Sheet. (The data you assemble on a work sheet allows you to review the proposed content "as a whole." The tasks then become the basis for instructional modules.)

Self-Check: Before submitting Learning Activities 1 and 2 to your instructor, check to determine whether you have (a) written a job description, (b) listed tasks, (c) decided importance of tasks, (d) picked tasks to be included in course content, (e) selected one task from Step "C", (f) listed task details, (g) sequenced task details, (h) selected task details to be included in content, (i) identified hardware/software/supplies; skills/knowledges; attitudes/habits for each task detail, (j) recorded appropriate information on Work Sheets.

table 5.6
MAJOR VERB CATEGORIES

CALL	Wire (page, phone, telephone)
CHECK	Adjust, Correct, Inquire, Oversee, Proofread, Scan, Test, Verify (confirm, examine, inspect, update)
COMPILE	Arrange, Attach, Batch, Bind, Collate, Collect, Cut, List, Obtain, Select (choose, gather, get, make)
COMPOSE	Convert, Draw, Sign, Write (make up)
DELIVER	Deposit, Destroy, Disburse, Distribute, Issue, Place, Refer, Request, Route, Send, Transfer (give to, hand to, present, put, submit, transmit)
DETERMINE . . .	Assign, Devise, Evaluate (decide, design, formulate)
DUPLICATE . . .	Photograph (copy, mimeograph, photocopy, Xerox)
FILE	Destroy, Hold, Locate, Maintain, Pull, Refer, Remove, Search, Sort (extract, find, go through, look up, take from, trace)
MAIL	Address, Insert, Label, Open, Route, Seal, Send, Stamp, Wrap (forward, stuff, transmit)
RECEIVE	Answer (phone), Greet, Hold, Obtain, Request, Take Dictation
TYPE	Teletype, Transcribe

3. This is an ongoing activity to be completed over a period of time such as a quarter or a semester. Select a business education course of your choice.
   a. Using a variety of resources, prepare a course-of-study plan.
   b. Select one topic or unit from the course plan and develop a unit plan.
   c. Develop a one-day lesson plan from the unit.
4. Examine the sample unit plan in this module (Illustration 5.4). Rate it using the Unit Planning Checklist (Illustration 5.3).
5. You have been invited to speak to an undergraduate methods class about planning a daily lesson. Outline in detail, write, or tape-record your presentation. Prepare a transparency to illustrate the lesson plan format you recommend.
6. Secure a lesson plan from your instructor or select one you have prepared and evaluate it using the Checklist for Preliminary Lesson Plan (Illustration 5.8).
7. The learning activities in items 7–12 are designed to lead you through a step-by-step process of developing an instructional module. You will use the task for which you completed the Task Detail List and Task Detail Sequence as the basis for each activity. At this point, the extent to which you are able to complete the activities of the module is dependent upon your knowledge of the subject matter involved. You may want to refer to specific content chapters in this book for additional information. The objective of activities 7–12 is to acquaint you with the process of writing an instructional module. *Now, read the section in this module entitled "Rationale." Then write a rationale for your module, focusing on the task selected. Ask your instructor to evaluate your rationale and to give you suggestions for revision. Then rewrite it and submit for instructor approval.*

8. Study the section in module 5.2 (pp. 106–119) entitled Writing Performance Objectives.
   a. In Module 5.2 questions were presented as a guide for writing Mager-type objectives. Answer one set of questions after writing one performance objective for the task you are using as a basis for these activities. If you have difficulty, reread the module or read references 4 and 5, listed at the end of Chapter 5.
   b. You may want to state some learning outcomes as "Gronlund-type objectives." Using the task from your Work Sheet, or a task/concept/skill of your choice, write an appropriate objective. Include general and specific objectives and specify subject matter. If you have difficulty, reread the module or read references 4 and 5, listed at the end of Chapter 5.
   c. Reread the task and task details/steps from the Work Sheet. How many objectives do you need to specify what the student is supposed to do? Write the performance objectives for the module you are constructing. Check your objectives against the characteristics described in this module; revise as necessary, then go over the objectives with your teacher.
9. Study the section in this module entitled "Pre/Post Test." Then construct a pre/post test to measure student achievement of objectives identified in Learning Activity 8.
   a. List each objective and specify how you will measure student behavior.

Sample Objective	*Pre/Post Test*
Using a ten-key adding-listing machine, complete and record correct answer to a minimum of twenty-four problems involving multiplication within a ten-minute period (specific objective).	Performance Test. Twenty-four multiplication problems.
Understand technical terms relating to contracts.	Pencil/paper test. Define and give example of each term.

   b. Select one objective from Learning Activity 9a and construct one or more test items to measure student behavior. (See Chapter 4 and related content-area chapter.)
   (Note: When constructing a test covering all the objectives of a module, compare each test item with your objectives and code the question to the objective to which it relates. If you have written a question not covered by an objective, reevaluate your objective. Compare your test items with the objectives. Do you have items for each objective? Ask your instructor to review your pre/post test.)
10. Study the section in this module entitled "Learning Activities and Assignments." Select one of the objectives you identified in Learning Activity 8 and write activities for it. (The task details, skills/knowledges, hardware/software, and attitudes/habits recorded on your Work Sheet provide the basis for selecting the learning activities to include.) Try to include (a) required, recommended, and optional activities and (b) one or more activities in which students can select the method of presentation (print/tape/film, sound slides, and so on). Now, reread your activities. After completing them, should the student be able to exhibit the behavior specified in the objective? Make an appointment with your instructor to review your learning activities.

11. Study the section in this module entitled "Materials and Resources."
    a. List the materials, equipment, and supplies the student will need to complete the activities specified in Learning Activity 10. Cite complete references.
    b. Select one of the textbooks or printed resources identified in Learning Activity 11a, or pick a book of your choice to determine its readability using Fry's Readability Formula.

    Reread your activities. Have you listed *all* the materials, supplies, and equipment the student will need?

module 5.3
SELF-TEST

In this module, the self-test is built in, and your achievement is reflected in your completion of previous learning activities.

module 5.4
PROVIDING FOR STUDENT DIFFERENCES

As the business teacher plans the instructional program, he or she is confronted with the task of accommodating students with a wide range of achievements, abilities, aptitudes, learning styles, preferences, and special needs. Current trends toward mainstreaming—a practice in which students with special needs are instructed in the regular classroom by special education instructors working with classroom teachers on a resource basis—require that teachers and school systems provide instructional programs flexible enough for *all* students. These challenges point up the need for a variety of multilevel, multimedia materials if the teacher is to provide appropriate learning experiences for each student.

When you have completed this module, you should be able to: (1) Cite examples of how a business teacher can provide for individual differences; (2) Identify the characteristics of various categories of students with special needs; (3) Describe the adaptations that a business teacher could make to accommodate students with the following types of special needs: (a) shorthand student in a wheelchair, (b) typewriting student with one hand, (c) consumer economics student with hearing loss, (d) business machines student who is a slow learner, (e) learning disability student in bookkeeping, (f) legally blind student in typewriting, (g) educable/mentally retarded student in general business; (4) Explain the use of simulation, open lab, model office, demonstration, lecture-discussion, and individualization as instructional strategies in business education; (5) Explain the use of grouping as an instructional strategy.

THE BUSINESS TEACHER PROVIDES FOR INDIVIDUAL DIFFERENCES

In the past, when the business teacher prepared for a class in typewriting, accounting, general business, or business English, he or she had one textbook for the class which was supplemented primarily with lectures, demonstrations, or class discussions. The chalkboard was the primary visual tool. Today the business teacher has access to a variety of instructional materials including audiotapes, filmstrips, sound slides, and printed materials, including the textbook, to provide for varying learning styles and special needs such as those of the poor reader, the auditory-minded student, and the visually-impaired student.

Each learner has his or her own preferred path for acquiring information. Factors such as noise, lighting, heating, time of day, motivation, persistence, classroom organizational arrangement (group versus independent learning), and perceptual strengths contribute to an individual's learning style. Of these, perceptual strengths (auditory, visual, tactile) is probably the most widely recognized single factor used to identify preference in learning. Most students can be classified as average; that is, they possess sufficient adequacy in visual, auditory, and tactile modalities to perform satisfactorily in a number of situations. Others—perhaps as many as 25 percent—have one modality that is strongly dominant, with the others relatively weak. For example, auditory-minded students learn better when material is explained to them; visually-oriented students fare better when they see the information before them. Even in a classroom in which the business teacher individualizes instruction, the auditory-minded student is handicapped if the information is presented visually in a textbook or all-print package. The basic task for the teacher, then, is to determine for a unit or lesson both group and individual learning experiences based on the individual differences of students. Let us turn our attention now to some of the ways in which this can be done. Most schools use several approaches to try to solve problems that result from individual differences among students.

Perhaps the most widespread approach is the practice of grouping students according to their interests, in courses such as accounting, business management, secretarial, or retailing. Or students may be grouped on the basis of prior achievement or ability, as reflected in grades or test scores, into basic or honors courses. Some high schools and postsecondary institutions have established individualized instructional programs.

Differentiated assignments is one of the ways in which teachers can cope with individual differences in the classroom. This can be done by varying the length of the assignment, the difficulty, and the type. By varying the length and difficulty of assignments, the business teacher provides for differences in achievement. Of course, this means that a variety of materials on different reading levels must be available. By providing options in the type of work required, the teacher capitalizes on students' special talents and interests; for example, accelerated students may be encouraged to undertake research projects, while others may elect to make a graph or prepare a bulletin board to illustrate a concept.

Grouping within the classroom is often an effective means for organizing students for instruction. Differentiated assignments may then be made to each group (see pages 167–168, "Grouping Students for Instruction").

Through differentiated assignments, the teacher can provide for the academically talented student. Assigning *more* problems or *longer* problems or providing *more* drill does not adequately provide for the accelerated student. Instead, these students can be allowed to move at a faster pace than their classmates and may be given assignments entirely different from those of the rest of the class. Through this arrangement, these students will complete their regular class work before the end of the year, and the teacher will need to provide meaningful work for them. In some schools, students are allowed to start the next course if it involves a sequence of skills, as in typewriting. In many classes, however, the teacher will have to plan with the student for additional activities. (Procedures for setting up an individualized instructional program are discussed in Chapter 3.)

In the next section we shall consider the characteristics of students with *special* needs and some of the modifications that can be accomplished effectively in business education classes.

PLANNING FOR STUDENTS WITH SPECIAL NEEDS

When planning instruction to meet the needs of each student, the business teacher should expect to encounter learners with special needs—that is, students who are (1) physically handicapped, (2) emotionally and socially maladjusted, or (3) educationally handicapped. As a prerequisite for certification, many states require teachers to enroll in special education courses to ensure that they will be able to recognize and deal with such handicaps. To meet the needs of these students, adaptations are often necessary in methods, materials, media, and sometimes in arrangement of facilities. In this section, we shall review briefly the characteristics of students with special needs and summarize some suggestions for instruction.

Physically handicapped

Students who fall into this category include the orthopedically handicapped, blind and partially sighted, and deaf and hard-of-hearing. Orthopedically handicapped students are those with poliomyelitis, muscular dystrophy, multiple sclerosis, and congenital amputations. A special desk may be needed for the student who is in a wheelchair. In many instances, these students are not educationally handicapped, so no modification is required in instruction. If the student has one arm or hand paralyzed, is missing fingers, or has a deformed hand or arm, he or she should still be able to function in the business education classroom. By focusing on the student's abilities, the teacher and student can devise ways to compensate for the disability.

If a student is able to write, he or she should be able to succeed in shorthand since it is more dependent on mental than physical skills. No major difficulties will be encountered in other business subjects with the possible exception of typewriting. Typewriting requires more adaptations, but skill can be developed by focusing on the student's strengths. An electric typewriter should be provided because of the ease of carriage return, evenness of touch, and uniformity of stroking. A one-handed typist should sit to the side of the typewriter opposite from his or her usable hand; that is, the right-handed typist should sit to the left of the machine and the left-handed typist to the right of the machine. Operations requiring two hands, such as using the shift key, present a problem. An arm stub may be used to depress the shift key, or a string may be attached to it so that it may be operated with the toe or foot. Illustration 5.12 shows possible keyboard positions for students with one hand or with missing fingers. The student, however, may make his or her own adjustments, depending on strengths.

Visually handicapped

The visually handicapped student (the blind or partially sighted) can function satisfactorily in the majority of business education classes if the teacher offers adequate verbal descriptions and explanations. The typewriter provides the visually handicapped student with an excellent communication tool. Since a good typist learns to type by touch, the visually handicapped typist should not be at a marked disadvantage in speed or accuracy in straight-copy work.

The tape recorder is a valuable instructional tool for the visually handicapped student. By recording class discussions, explanations, and directions, the visually handicapped student can review independently. Through agencies such as Recording for the Blind, the student may obtain "talking" copies of textbooks, thus allowing him or her to complete assignments independently. Students who read well can record instructional materials for the visually handicapped student. Learning activity packages on tape and recorded tests offer the student an opportunity to make use of his or her learning style and progress toward becoming an independent learner. Here, again, the student can respond to tests by typing or by recording responses.

Large-print copies of textbooks for students with limited vision are often available from state departments of education. Requests are usually made in the spring for the following school year. The local director of instruction or special education director will have information on materials available and procedures for obtaining it. In addition, some books are available in braille. Some school systems have resource personnel who work with classroom teachers in adapting instruction for the blind and who assist in preparing materials in braille.

illustration 5.12

FINGER POSITION FOR ONE-HANDED TYPIST

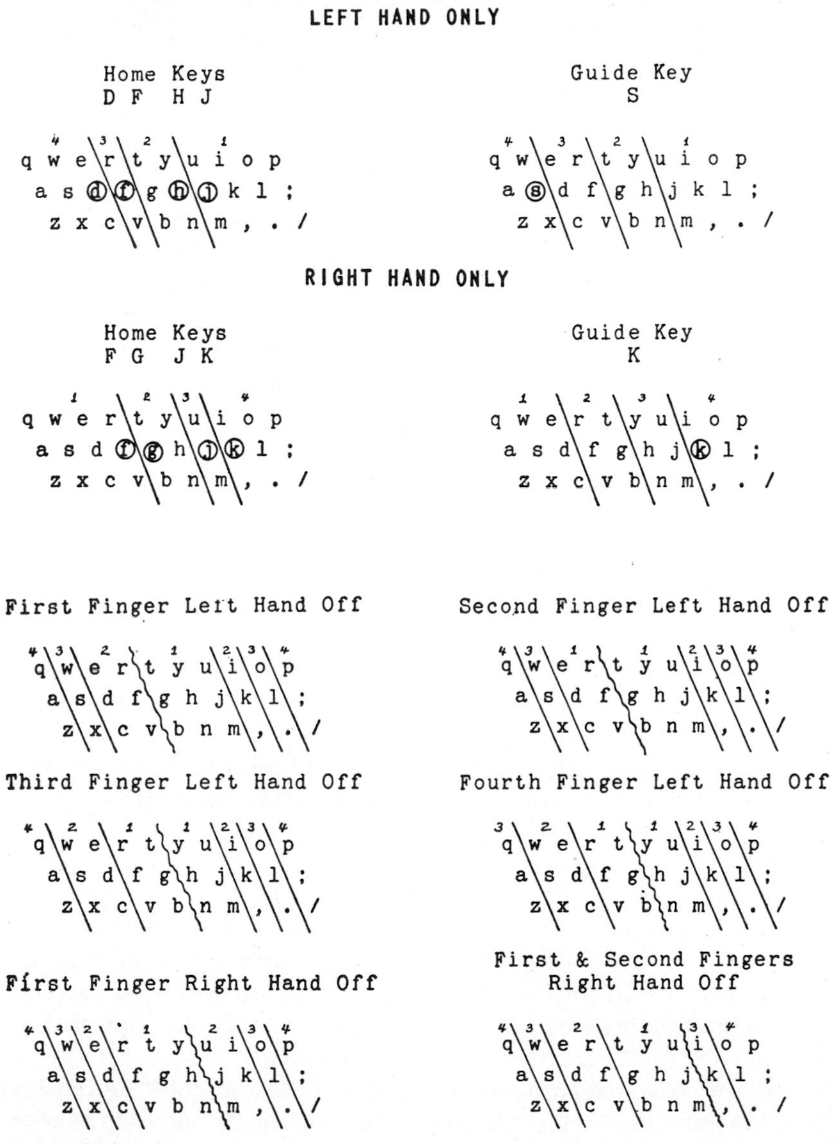

LEFT HAND ONLY

Home Keys
D F H J

Guide Key
S

RIGHT HAND ONLY

Home Keys
F G J K

Guide Key
K

First Finger Left Hand Off

Second Finger Left Hand Off

Third Finger Left Hand Off

Fourth Finger Left Hand Off

First Finger Right Hand Off

First & Second Fingers
Right Hand Off

Source: Jane E. Clem, *Techniques of Teaching Typewriting,* New York: Gregg Publishing Division, McGraw-Hill Book Company, 1955), p. 154.

What modifications should the teacher make if a visually handicapped student enrolls in typewriting? On the first day, the student should become familiar with the physical arrangement of the room. The teacher, or a student, can explain the arrangement as the visually handicapped student touches the object being described. Directions and explanations should be specific—"four steps to your left is the teacher's desk" instead of "the teacher's desk is over there." Don't forget to warn the student in the event you rearrange the room.

In introducing the parts of the typewriter, the teacher explains the name, location, and function of each part of the machine while the student examines each part as it is being described. The appropriate hand used to operate each part should be identified. Given a tape recording of the description, location, and function of the machine parts as they are introduced for a lesson, the student can practice as often as necessary. Verbal descriptions and instructions should be followed immediately by student practice. Frequent checks can be made by the teacher to assure that (1) directions and explanations are clear and (2) the student is correctly following the instructions.

Dictation or recording is the most effective and efficient method of providing copy for the student. When the student has to compose a rough draft, he or she could record it or write it out in braille.

Although the emphasis is on correct technique, the visually handicapped student can learn to correct errors of which he or she is aware. The use of correction tape is the simplest procedure to use in teaching the student. One typewriting task that the visually handicapped student cannot perform is proofreading.

In addition to the blind and visually impaired, there are other visual handicaps that occur frequently in the school population, such as the nearsighted, farsighted, amblyopic (lazy eye), and cross-eyed. If the student only wears glasses, additional classroom adjustments such as seating arrangements may be necessary, and vision checks may have to be made frequently.

Deaf and hearing-impaired

Deaf students more than likely will receive their instruction in special schools for the deaf. However, there are numbers of students with hearing impairments in your classes. Students with identified, correctable hearing losses who wear hearing aids should exhibit no special difficulties in the classroom.

Students with hearing impairments are often not detected, but instead may be classified as retarded or inconsiderate. The teacher should note students who do not respond when spoken to if he or she is not looking at the speaker, who do not correctly follow oral directions, or who do not recall information presented orally to the class. These students may have hearing loss and should be examined by a specialist.

Students with hearing loss should be seated near the speaker so that they may observe the speaker's lips. The teacher needs to enunciate words clearly.

The tape recorder is also a valuable instructional aid for the hearing-impaired student because he or she can adjust the volume. Earphones are available with a volume control for each ear.

Some students have hearing losses that are not medically correctable. Usually the first sounds they lose are word endings such as "s" or "ed." These students should also be seated in the classroom so that they can observe the speaker's lips.

In typing, students are encouraged to keep their eyes on the copy, but for hearing-impaired or deaf students, this is a problem since they cannot hear the bell. The Technology Department at Golden West College, Huntington, California, designed a special bright light on the corner of a regular electric typewriter. When the bell rings, the light flashes on, making the student aware that he or she is approaching the end of the line. Other adaptations for the deaf or hearing-impaired student include the inset of an interpreter along with demonstrations and comments by the teacher on videotapes.[23]

Emotional and social maladjustment

The emotionally disturbed student is one with emotional problems so severe that he or she cannot function effectively. These students are unable to do what is expected of their peers. Behavior may range from withdrawal to aggressive destruction. Emotionally disturbed individuals should receive professional treatment by mental health specialists who can provide assistance to the teacher if the student is in school.

The socially maladjusted student is encountered more frequently in school. This is an individual who continuously violates the rules and customs of society. Such a student is often classified as a delinquent. In the majority of cases, the individual who is socially maladjusted is lacking in academic skills, even though he or she may possess average or above average ability. This student needs a structured classroom in which the teacher is firm, but kind. The parameters of acceptable behavior and performance are identified and consistently maintained. Instructional activities and assignments should be brief since the student usually has a short attention span. This may necessitate breaking down a long assignment into two or three parts, each of which must be completed before the student is given another part. As nearly as possible, the course content should be related to the student's interests and immediate needs.

Acceptable and appropriate behavior should be reinforced as soon as possible. For example, a student could "earn" free time to look at a magazine, listen to a record or radio (with earphones), or "do nothing" as a reward for successful completion of an assignment. Resource persons such as behavior disorder specialists, school psychologists, and mental health counselors can be called on for suggestions and assistance in working with socially maladjusted students. Carrels or individual work stations are used in some schools to provide quiet work areas with a minimum of distraction.

Educationally handicapped

Students with three types of educational handicaps are of special concern to the business teacher: the educable mentally retarded (EMR), the slow learner, and the student with a learning disability.

EDUCABLE MENTALLY RETARDED. The educable mentally retarded student is one who falls within an IQ range of 50 to 70. He or she is characterized by a limited capacity to learn, an academic achievement ranging from third to sixth grade at age 16, difficulty in engaging in abstract thinking and handling symbols, difficulty in generalizing and transferring information (knowledge), and a short attention span. EMR students may be enrolled in typewriting, general business, consumer economics, record keeping, clerical office practice, and other business courses. The teacher should keep in mind the general characteristics described above and the following suggestions when planning an instructional program.

The following guidelines have been found effective in working with EMR students in business education classes:

1. Divide activities into small sequential parts.
2. Progress slowly from the simple to the complex so as to ensure successful experiences.
3. Provide activities that are useful and based on life situations.
4. Explain or show how experiences are related.
5. Since the EMR student cannot learn all that other students do, select those needs identified as critical.
6. Select attainable goals for students.
7. Use multisensory simulation since it is more effective than a one-dimensional approach.
8. Provide concrete experiences.
9. Provide more practice for mastery than for the average student.
10. Deliver instruction in small steps as in programmed instruction.

EMR students can be trained to satisfactorily perform a number of low-level (entry-level) jobs in business. They can learn to do repetitive tasks that require little decision making on their part. In courses such as typewriting and clerical office practice, emphasis should be placed on the mastery of basic skills. However, these students should not be expected to accomplish tasks such as typing a final copy from a rough draft in which they have to make decisions about format, spelling, grammar, and so on. Students enrolled in general business cannot be expected to realize the same objectives as students with more ability. Instructional material may have to be rewritten to lower the readability level and to focus on the specific facts, principles, or concepts being taught. Printed material should be supplemented liberally with pictures or illustrations and verbal explanations.

One of the problems of teaching EMR students is that they need to know concepts associated with their chronological age, such as borrowing money, using guarantees, buying insurance, and so on, but they lack the achievement and maturity to understand the concepts. The EMR student, whether in elementary, middle, or secondary school, is unable to perform tasks at the time that society expects him or her to do so.

Evaluation of EMR students should, of course, reflect in a realistic way the objectives they are striving to reach. Performance items and recall or simple comprehension questions are more appropriate than higher-level items of evaluation or synthesis.

SLOW LEARNER.   Between the EMR students and the "normal" students is a group who are of major concern to most teachers—the slow learners. These students, whose IQs range between 70 and 90, learn at a rate slower than "normal" students but not as slow as the educable mentally retarded.

The following characteristics may be found in varying degrees among slow learners. Some are similar to those identified as EMR characteristics, while others are observed in students who are in the low normal range. Slow learners

1. are below grade level in achievement (at age 16, when working at a level equal to mental age, can achieve at seventh to eighth grade level)
2. have poorer reasoning ability than normal students
3. are slow to see cause/effect relationships, to make inferences, to draw logical and valid conclusions, to transfer learning, and to generalize
4. need more repetition to reinforce learning
5. respond to immediate goals
6. have poor work habits
7. are below average in immediate and long-term memory
8. have little self-motivation to learn
9. have a difficult time following directions
10. need more praise and encouragement than average learners
11. may have difficulty controlling emotions
12. have poorly developed language and communication skills.

Slow learners are probably enrolled in all business courses and should be able to achieve success if attention is given to their special learning needs. When planning learning experiences for them, the teacher should incorporate guidelines such as the following:

1. Allow more time for mastering skills, learning, concepts, and principles. Slow learners develop their abilities in much the same manner as normal learners, but at a slower pace.
2. Offer opportunities for additional practice and review.
3. Provide more activities in which the student uses and reuses the skill and/or knowledge in meaningful context.
4. Provide more details and simplified explanations and directions. Demonstrations, both live and on film, and concrete examples may be needed. In most instances, directions in textbooks are too difficult. These should be rewritten or recorded in simpler, step-by-step terms.

5. Use concrete illustrations, related to the learner's experiences.
6. Define short-term goals.
7. Use multisensory aids to reinforce verbal instruction and material.
8. Provide learning experiences and activities in small segments.
9. Reward the student with frequent praise and encouragement when there is tangible evidence of progress. Progress charts in typewriting, for example, provide the student with a concrete record of progress toward speed and accuracy goals.
10. Vary the number of directions and instructions according to student ability. Experiment to determine how much direction each student can follow both orally and in written form. Some students can complete tasks if one-, two-, or three-step directions are given. If certain procedures are to be used daily, prepare a chart in which the steps are listed in 1-2-3 order, and display it prominently so that students can refer to it as needed. For example, the rules for vertical and horizontal centering on a half sheet or full sheet of paper could be displayed. Assignments should be concise, short, and specific.

LEARNING DISABILITY. A group of students receiving an increasing amount of attention in recent years is that classified as having a learning disability; the term calls attention to the fact that there are individuals attending school who have difficulty in learning despite the fact that they have no apparent physical, sensory, intellectual, or emotional defects.[24] A learning disability may be general so that the student has difficulty in many subjects, or it may be specific with the student experiencing difficulty in only one subject area. The student whose learning disability is in reading, for example, frequently sees letters and words reversed or in a distorted manner. Other general characteristics of the learning disabled student include poor eye-hand coordination, a high level of distractibility, and an inability to reproduce words or designs even if identified by the student. The student may also be unable to distinguish letters correctly.

The typewriter is being widely used as a communication tool for the learning disabled student since it removes the added factor of having to form the letters when writing.

Learning disabled students are not unable to learn. They do, however, need individualized help. To determine how the student can best be taught, the teacher should try teaching a skill using various techniques. Some students have learned to compensate for their reading disabilities by depending primarily on an auditory approach. In this connection, many of the suggestions for working with visually handicapped students are equally appropriate for the learning disabled student. Instruction for these students should be planned with the following suggestions in mind.

Create a learning environment with as few distractions as possible. A carrel or learning station painted in a neutral shade could be provided for the student, thus removing him or her from the distractions of other students, colorful classroom walls, various displays and learning centers, and a variety of learning activities occurring simultaneously. Give specific instructions: instead of "Pay attention," tell students what they are to hear, observe, and so on; for example, "Look at the illustration on the screen while I explain. . . ."

Since learning disabled students are more likely to confuse letters or words that are similar, these should be taught in contrasting pairs, calling attention to their similarities and, particularly, their differences. Having the student verbalize how the words/letters/symbols are alike or different may prove helpful. There are no readily packaged answers for teaching the learning disabled student. If the student fails to learn, look for a different method of teaching, constantly checking on the effectiveness of each approach.

Another group of students who also tend to reverse letters and numbers are those with mixed dominance; that is, whose right eye is dominant and whose left hand is dominant. A quick informal check of eye dominance can be made as follows: (1) Tear or cut a small square from the center of an 8½ X 11 inch sheet of unlined paper; (2) Give the paper to the student, telling him or her to hold it with both hands down in front or in his or her lap if seated; (3) Stand approximately 3 to 4 feet from the student, holding a pen or pencil at his or her eye level; (4) Ask the student to quickly bring the paper up and to look through the opening in the paper at the pencil you are holding. (Most people bring the paper to their dominant eye.) The student should not be alerted to the purpose of your check since this causes him or her to respond in other than a normal manner. Characteristics of mixed dominance include reversals of letters when writing or typing a word, reversals of digits when writing numbers, and so on. Students with this problem must learn to proofread carefully and to refer to mental images of the sequence of letters in a word or the digits in a number when in doubt about their order.

THE BUSINESS TEACHER SELECTS INSTRUCTIONAL STRATEGIES

The business teacher may choose from a variety of instructional techniques, ranging from reading a textbook to on-the-job work experience. All techniques are not equally effective for each student or for teaching each objective. Techniques are not viewed as "good" or "bad," but are evaluated in relation to their appropriateness for the student, the objective, and the learning situation. Instructional strategies are presented in two categories: grouping students for instruction and instructional procedures.

Grouping students for instruction

Students may be grouped or arranged in several ways for instruction, ranging from an individual basis in a machines laboratory to a total group in a business math class. When choosing a grouping plan, you should consider its appropriateness for learner style, for meeting instructional objectives, and for use with materials and space available.

The *total group arrangement* is based on the assumption that students are alike, that they need the same learning experiences, that the material is appropriate for all, and that learning styles and rates are the same. The major advantage is economical use of teacher time; only one preparation and one presentation are necessary for the entire group. Total class grouping is appropriate when the entire group requires the same information. Introducing a unit, summarizing key points learned, and giving directions are examples of situations that lend themselves to the use of total group arrangement.

Achievement level grouping is an attempt to minimize the spread of achievement within each group. Materials, rates of instruction, and instructional objectives may vary from one group to another, but they are primarily the same within a given group. This grouping arrangement may result in placing students in classes according to ability or achievement, sometimes known as *tracking*, a practice not in vogue.

Specific purpose grouping involves the use of flexible or short-term grouping of students for a special reason. Under this arrangement, students with similar problems or deficiencies may be grouped for instruction in that particular skill. The group is dissolved after the skill has been taught. For example, a small group might be organized for fifteen to twenty minutes of instruction and practice in using the tabulator key in typing or for a few days of review of grammar or punctuation in a business communication class.

Interest groups represent another method of grouping students to capitalize on their special interests. Groups ranging in size from two to five or six students may be homogeneously arranged to accomplish a common interest or project. Usually such groups are organized on a short-term basis. In skill classes such as typewriting or shorthand, students can progress at their own rate and, therefore, are instructed on an *individual basis,* with other grouping arrangements used as needed.

Choosing instructional procedures

Variety in teaching procedures makes the learning process more interesting to students. Business teachers can choose from a wide range of techniques that are appropriate for the specific objectives, students, and learning situations (that is, facilities, equipment, and materials available) under consideration. This section contains a brief explanation of selected techniques.

In an attempt to provide realism in instruction, business teachers often use *simulation.* It is an effort to bridge the gap between business and the classroom by providing an officelike atmosphere, where students assume the role of office employees, and by providing businesslike assignments that must be completed according to business standards of acceptability. Simulation activities require the student to incorporate a variety of skills, including decision making as well as application. A number of simulated practice materials are available commercially.

A form of simulation is the *model office* which provides students with the opportunity to experience the function of an office in the school environment. The model office incorporates the physical arrangement, various office positions (office manager, receptionist, clerk-typist, secretary, bookkeeper), work input and tasks, and interaction of workers in a setting that is representative of the service or manufacturing firm that is being simulated.

The *open lab* is used especially for skills courses. In this arrangement, students come to the lab at any period or time during the day (when there is space available) for machine, shorthand, or typewriting instruction. An individualized, multimedia approach is, of necessity, used, with the teacher available to assist students as needed. Through the use of instructional packages, videotapes, sound slides, film loops, filmstrips, and other media, the student progresses at his or her own pace. The availability of material, the development of a management and record-keeping system, and the establishment of a systematic procedure for assessment and prescription are essential to the success of individualized instruction in an open lab. Because of the variation in motivation and responsibility among students, the teacher may find it necessary to establish minumum short-term and intermediate goals. Without interim guidelines, some students cannot discipline themselves to follow through on long-term assignments.

Individualized instruction is a philosophy, not a method of instruction. Using this concept, the teacher arranges students, facilities, and materials so that each student can learn at his or her peak. It takes many shapes in the classroom—individual activities; group activities; use of multimedia material; diversified objectives, content, materials, and pacing. Individualized instruction is organized around varying fixed and flexible requirements of objectives, content, materials, proficiency, and time. For example, the objectives and content may be fixed for all students, but the materials, proficiency, and time for completion of the objectives are flexible.

Individualized instruction can be implemented within a one-room arrangement or in an open lab if the teacher provides appropriate instructional opportunities for all students. A successful individualized learning system requires careful planning, relevant material, adequate facilities and equipment, and an efficient management and evaluation system.

The *lecture method* is teaching by telling in which the student is, for the most part, a passive participant. Therefore, the amount of time devoted to lecturing should be limited. The lecture method can be used effectively, however, in those instances when time is limited, a lesson is being summarized, new material is being introduced, the subject matter is simple and appropriate for the students, and an experience is being described. In a lecture presentation, the teacher is competing with untold numbers of stimuli for the listeners' attention. Consequently, the teacher has to use a variety of techniques to capture and hold that attention. Examples include change in voice volume and pitch; varying of pace in delivery of message; staccato sentence; humor; clear enunciation; timely, interesting, and associative information; some physical activity; appropriate eye contact and facial expression; gestures; and some movement around the room.

The business teacher should more often combine the lecture with visual presentations and/or opportunities for discussion. The *illustrated lecture* incorporates slides, filmstrips, transparencies, or charts, and adds the visual or "showing" dimension. Another variation of the pure lecture method is the *lecture-discussion* in which students are encouraged to participate by asking questions, interjecting ideas, or indicating impressions. Both illustrated lectures and lecture-discussions are more desirable than lectures alone. The *question-and-answer* technique is widely used in conjunction with the lecture method. Typically the teacher uses questions in initiating a unit to find out what the students already know about the subject or as a means of stimulating interest in the topic. Throughout the lecture, questions are used to hold attention of the group or to review important concepts that have been presented. The art of questioning is one that should be cultivated by the business teacher; questions can be a valuable tool for teaching if they are interesting, relevant, and timely.

Demonstration is highly important to the business teacher in such courses as data processing, shorthand, and typewriting. In demonstrating, the teacher performs a given task, showing how it is done, explaining the procedure as he or she goes along. In addition to live demonstration by the teacher or another student, filmstrips, loops, slides, and videotapes provide excellent means for showing the student how to perform a given procedure. If filmed demonstrations are available, one student or a group of students can review a procedure as often as necessary. In live or taped demonstrations, the student should be able to see what is happening and to hear the explanations. Weaknesses of live demonstrations are apparent in that (1) it is sometimes difficult for all to see and hear; (2) individuals who need to see the demonstration more than once are often reluctant to ask; and (3) since students progress at differing rates, an excessive amount of teacher time may be taken up with the same demonstration to different groups.

Other valuable instructional techniques include role playing, case studies, case incidents, field trips, independent projects, panel-discussions, debates, and resource speakers.

module 5.4
LEARNING ACTIVITIES

1. Read at least two articles in one area of special needs. Briefly summarize the articles and explain how you would provide for students with that particular special need in a specific business education course.

2. Defend or refute the following assumption:

   The business teacher should be expected to provide instructional programs for all students with special needs who wish to enroll.

3. Interview the special education coordinator in your school system to determine (a) the nature and extent of special education needs in your school, (b) assistance now

available to schools through Public Law 94–142, Education for All Handicapped Children Act, (c) how individual education plans for special education students are developed, (d) what business teachers can do to assure all students equal educational opportunities under the law, and (e) ways in which business teachers can accommodate the special needs of students in business classes.

4. Suggest at least one situation in which you would use the following instructional techniques: (a) demonstration, (b) simulation, (c) open lab, (d) lecture, and (e) model office.

module 5.4
SELF-TEST

1. Explain, using an example, how a business teacher can provide appropriate instruction for an "auditory-minded" student.
2. List at least four characteristics of each of the following learners: (a) slow learners, (b) students with learning disabilities, and (c) educable mentally retarded students.
3. What is the rationale for grouping students for instructional purposes?
4. Describe the use of each of the following as instructional strategies for use with all students: (a) simulation, (b) demonstration, and (c) individualization.

SUMMARY

The teacher is the key to what happens in the business education classroom. His or her functions may be classified into four major areas: (1) planning, (2) organizing, (3) leading, and (4) controlling. One of the first tasks confronting the teacher is selecting writing instructional objectives. Objectives, which are stated in terms of learner outcomes, may be classified according to the types of behavior exhibited and the complexity of the task. Thus, objectives are generally divided into three categories: (1) cognitive, (2) affective, and (3) psychomotor. Cognitive objectives emphasize intellectual outcomes, such as knowledge, understanding, and thinking. Affective objectives emphasize feeling and emotions, such as interests, attitudes, and appreciations. Psychomotor objectives emphasize motor skills, such as writing, typing, and operating machines. Learning objectives should be written so as to tell students in what way their behavior will be changed after instruction.

After learning objectives are identified, the next task is to sequence them and to select appropriate content. Objectives related to skill development may be sequenced according to the order of task mastery, frequency of use, or, in some instances, student interest. In selecting, adapting, or constructing teaching units to implement objectives, the business teacher plans activities and appropriate materials and evaluation procedures. When developing the daily lesson plan, or when writing instructional units, the business teacher is careful to provide for all students regardless of achievement, ability, aptitude, interest, learning style, and special needs. This means that objectives, resource materials, instructional procedures, and evaluation measures are appropriate for the auditory-oriented as well as the visually-oriented; for physically, socially, emotionally, or educationally handicapped students as well as so-called average or gifted students. The teacher can draw upon a variety of grouping arrangements and instructional procedures when planning for instruction. Such strategies should be selected according to their appropriateness for the learner and his or her objectives. No one grouping pattern or instructional procedure is best for all students. Rather, an appropriate mix should be provided in line with the purposes of instruction, the prior achievement and learning goals of the students, and the learning resources available to the teacher.

References

[1]Ivor K. Davies, *Competency Based Learning: Technology, Management, and Design* (New York: McGraw-Hill, 1973), pp. 24–25.

[2]Georgia Department of Education, "Beginning Teacher Evaluation Project" (Athens: University of Georgia, College of Education, 1976).

[3]Kenneth H. Hoover, *Learning and Teaching in the Secondary School*, 2d ed. (Boston: Allyn and Bacon, 1968), p. 54.

[4]Robert F. Mager, *Preparing Instructional Objectives* (Palo Alto, Calif.: Fearon Publishers, 1962).

[5]Norman E. Gronlund, *Stating Behavioral Objectives for Classroom Instruction* (New York: The Macmillan Company, 1970), p. 4.

[6]Ibid., p. 4.

[7]Ibid., p. 5.

[8]Ibid., p. 9.

[9]Ibid., p. 40.

[10]Ibid., p. 17.

[11]Ibid., p. 33.

[12]The Center for Vocational Education, The Ohio State University, *Develop a Unit of Instruction*, Module B–3, Professional Teacher Education Module Series (Athens, Ga.: American Association for Vocational Instructional Materials, 1977), pp. 26–29.

[13]The Center for Vocational Education, The Ohio State University, *Develop a Lesson Plan*, Module B–4, Professional Teacher Education Module series (Athens, Ga.: American Association for Vocational Instructional Materials, 1977), p. 9.

[14]Leonard H. Clark and Irving S. Starr, *Secondary School Teaching Methods*, (New York: The Macmillan Company, 1976), pp. 131–32.

[15]Robert F. Mager and Kenneth M. Beach, Jr., *Developing Vocational Instruction* (Belmont, Calif.: Fearon-Pitman Publishers, 1967), pp. 40–41.

[16]The Center for Vocational Education, The Ohio State University, *Select Student Instructional Materials*, Module B–5, Professional Teacher Education Module Series (Athens, Ga.: American Association for Vocational Instructional Materials, 1977), p. 8.

[17]Rudolph Flesch, *How to Test Readability* (New York: Harper and Bros., 1951).

[18]George D. Spache, *Good Reading for Poor Readers*, 6th ed. (Champaign, Ill.: Garrard Press, 1966).

[19]Edgar Dale and Jeanne S. Chall, "A Formula for Predicting Readability," *Educational Research Bulletin* 27 (January 21, 1948): 11–20; and 28 (February 18, 1948): 37–54.

[20]Robert Gunning, *The Technique of Clear Writing* (New York: McGraw-Hill Publishing Company, 1968).

[21]J. R. Bormuth, "Cloze Tests as Measures of Readability," (Ph. D. diss., Indiana University, 1962).

[22]Edward Fry, "A Readability Formula That Saves Time," *The Journal of Reading*, 11 (April 1968): 514.

[23]Joyce Kupsh, "Working with Hearing-Impaired Students," *Journal of Business Education*, 53, no. 3, (December 1976): 115.

[24]Allen O. Ross, *Psychological Aspects of Learning Disabilities and Reading Disorders* (New York: McGraw-Hill Book Company, 1976), p. 1.

SUGGESTIONS FOR FURTHER STUDY

Alcorn, Marvin D.; Kinder, James S.; and Schunert, Jim R. *Better Teaching in Secondary Schools.* New York: Holt, Rinehart and Winston, 1970.

Aldrich, Julian C. *How to Construct and Use a Resource Unit.* New York: Joint Council on Economic Education, n.d.

Allen, Paul, et al. *Teacher Self-Appraisal.* Worthington, Ohio: Charles A. Jones Publishing Company, 1970.

Andrew, Michael D. *Teachers Should Be Human Too.* Washington, D.C.: Association of Teacher Educators, 1972.

Armstrong, Robert J., et al. *The Development and Evaluation of Behavioral Objectives.* Worthington, Ohio: Charles A. Jones Publishing Company, 1970.

Bloom, Benjamin S., et al. *Taxonomy of Educational Objectives: The Classification of Educational Goals, Handbook I, Cognitive Domain.* New York: David McKay Company, 1956.

Calhoun, Calfrey C., and Hillestad, Mildred, eds. *Contributions of Research to Business Education.* Washington, D.C.: National Business Education Association, 1971.

Chesler, Mark, and Fox, Robert. *Role-Playing Methods in the Classroom.* Chicago: Science Research Associates, 1966.

Clark, Cecil D. *Using Instructional Objectives in Teaching.* Glenville, Ill.: Scott Foresman and Company, 1972.

Gayles, Anne R. *Instructional Planning in the Secondary School.* New York: David McKay Company, 1973.

Gorman, Alfred H. *Teachers and Learners.* 2d ed. Boston: Allyn and Bacon, 1974.

Gramb, Jean D., et al. *Modern Methods in Secondary Education.* New York: Holt, Rinehart and Winston, 1970.

Gronlund, Norman E. *Stating Behavioral Objectives for Classroom Instruction.* New York: The Macmillan Company, 1970.

Heitzmann, William R. *Educational Games and Simulations.* What Research Says to the Teacher Series. Washington, D.C.: The National Education Association, 1974.

Hunkins, Francis. *Questioning: Strategies and Techniques.* Boston: Allyn and Bacon, 1972.

Hyman, Ronald T. *Ways of Teaching.* 2d ed. Philadelphia: J. B. Lippincott Company, 1974.

Kibler, Robert J., et al. *Behavioral Objectives and Instruction.* Boston: Allyn and Bacon, 1970.

———. *Objectives for Instruction and Evaluation.* Boston: Allyn and Bacon, 1974.

Kirk, Samuel. *Educating Exceptional Children.* 2d ed. Boston: Houghton Mifflin Company, 1972.

Krathwohl, David R., et al. *Taxonomy of Educational Objectives, Handbook 2: Affective Domain.* New York: David McKay Company, 1964.

Kruper, Karen R. *Communication Games.* New York: The Free Press, 1973.

Livingston, Samuel, and Stoll, Clarice. *Simulation Games.* New York: The Free Press, 1972.

Mager, Robert F. *Developing Attitude Toward Learning.* Belmont, Calif.: Fearon Publishers, 1968.

Meacham, Merle H., and Tombaugh, Tom N. *Changing Classroom Behavior.* New York: Intent Educational Publishers, 1974.

Public Law 94–142, Education for All Handicapped Children Act.

Tanner, Daniel. *Using Behavioral Objectives in the Classroom.* New York: The Macmillan Company, 1972.

Wiener, Daniel N. *Classroom Management and Discipline.* Itasca, Ill.: F. E. Peacock Publishers, 1972.

part two

TEACHING COMMUNICATION-RELATED BUSINESS SKILLS

chapter 6

TEACHING TYPEWRITING

In recent years, the typewriter has become the medium that is used almost universally as a method of written expression. In fact, the typewriter can be thought of as a tool of literacy. It is difficult to imagine anyone who expects to pursue a high school or postsecondary school course who would fail to benefit from the mastery of typewriting. The ability to type is second only to handwriting in the communication skills.

There are approximately 5,000,000 persons employed as typists, stenographers, and secretaries whose combined annual job openings exceed 500,000; many other employees use the typewriter at least part of the time. The continuing increase in the number of clerical workers in the labor force means that the ability to type will continue to be an effective aid in securing employment.

An analysis of office tasks performed by employees in eight functional business areas (see page 237) as identified in the New Office and Business Education Learning Systems Study (Development of Performance Goals for a New Office and Business Education Learning System[1]) revealed that typewriting was a common requirement in all areas.[2] Erickson found that typewriting was a basic component or a supportive activity in over half (167) of the 300 jobs he studied;[3] and Cook and Lanham's study revealed that 85 percent of all jobs open to high school graduates that required any skill, required typewriting skill.[4]

In addition to the wide use of typewriting in business, large numbers of people use the typewriter as a personal communication tool. At the high school level, one-half or more of the students enrolled in typewriting selected the course as a general education elective though many of these students may eventually use typewriting as a vocational tool.

module 6.1
TYPEWRITING GOALS AND THE PSYCHOLOGY OF SKILL

After completing this module, you should be able to (1) compare the major objectives of typewriting at the elementary, middle school/junior high, secondary, and postsecondary levels; and (2) explain at least eight principles of learning that are related to typewriting skill development.

ELEMENTARY SCHOOL TYPEWRITING

Typewriting at the elementary school level is used largely as a vehicle for learning other subjects, especially the language arts. Research studies have focused on improvements in spelling, composition, reading, word meaning, and language usage through typewriting. Use of the typewriter at this level motivates interest and improves pupils' attitudes toward their work. The course content of elementary typewriting reflects the interests and achievement levels of pupils who compose poems, seasonal greetings, letters to friends, items for school newspapers, descriptions of pets, riddles, answers to questions, and one-word, one-sentence, and multiple-sentence responses to complete a sentence or story.

Elementary grade pupils can learn touch typewriting and can use the typewriter as a communication tool. However, typewriting is offered at the elementary level on a very limited basis partly because of the unavailablity of machines and the lack of teachers trained to teach typewriting. Materials are modified to fit the interest and reading levels of elementary pupils. Pupils with special needs, such as those with visual impairments or learning disabilities, benefit substantially from typewriting as a communication tool.

MIDDLE SCHOOL/JUNIOR HIGH TYPEWRITING

In the middle school or junior high school, typewriting is offered both as a part of career exploration and as a separate subject. As a part of career exploration, the student is introduced to the typewriter and investigates careers in which typewriting skills are needed. Although the student becomes familiar with the keyboard and types simple exercises, the objectives of career education at this level emphasize exploration rather than competence in typewriting. Its value as a career education tool outweighs the possibility of developing incorrect techniques as a result of the limited instructional time given to developing the skill.

Typewriting offered as a separate course at the middle school or junior high level has as its major focus personal use—typing letters, reports, manuscripts, and outlines. As at the secondary level, keyboard competence is a major objective. Other objectives include learning proper use and care of the machine, developing some fluency in straight-copy material, typing assignments for other courses, developing skill in composing at the typewriter, setting up simple tabulations and centering, acquiring proofreading skills, and using carbons.

HIGH SCHOOL TYPEWRITING

Typewriting is the most popular elective course offered in high school. Approximately one-fourth of all high school students select at least one quarter of typewriting. The number of quarters, semesters, or years of typewriting available at the high school level varies from one school to another. Factors affecting the amount of typewriting offered include the number of students with prior training at the junior high school level, the organization of skill courses in the eleventh and twelfth grades (whether separate courses in typewriting and shorthand are offered, or whether these skills are advanced through an integrated office practice or office simulation), the size of the school, typewriting enrollment, and demand for the course.

During the first semester, the goal of the student makes little difference in the objectives and content of the typewriting course since everyone is acquiring facility at the keyboard. Consequently, students with personal-use or vocational objectives may be enrolled in the same beginning typewriting class. Content of the beginning course usually includes learning the keyboard, developing speed and control, applying typewriting skill to simple situations such as letters or envelopes, centering, writing reports or papers for other courses, proofreading, composing, and learning to take care of the typewriter.

In advanced typewriting, the emphasis shifts toward development of employable skills through sustained production typewriting. A second-year student, for example, might be expected to type an invoice from arranged or unarranged copy in correct form with no errors; to type two purchase orders from unarranged copy in acceptable form and verify the totals in twenty minutes; or to arrange and type the four terms in the heading of an interoffice memorandum in three different ways on a plain sheet of paper with 100 percent accuracy. Examples of other topics included in production typewriting are business letters, business forms, tabulations, rough drafts, statistical charts and tables, stencils, spirit masters and other masters for copying processes, legal forms and documents, manuscripts and reports, envelopes, carbon copies, financial statements, telegrams, programs, minutes of meetings, dictation at the typewriter, composing at the typewriter, proofreading, and correction techniques.

POSTSECONDARY LEVEL TYPEWRITING

The major emphasis of typewriting in community colleges, independent business schools, and vocational-technical centers is the development of vocational competence. At least two major differences may be noted in typing expectations at the postsecondary level compared with the high school level: (1) the postsecondary student is expected to cover the material at a faster pace than the secondary student and (2) a higher level of competence is expected and required of postsecondary than of secondary students. Since students enter postsecondary institutions with varying levels of typewriting skill, as well as differing levels of ability, an individualized approach is effective. After being tested to determine their prior achievement, these students can begin at an appropriate level of instruction and progress at their own rate.

Typewriting at the four-year college or university level focuses on developing personal-use skills, job-related skills, or complete vocational competency. Students from various departments and colleges enroll in one quarter or semester of typewriting for personal use. Other students from areas such as journalism, pharmacy, law, or the arts and sciences use typewriting as a job-related skill. Prospective business teachers develop vocational competencies which serve as the content-basis for teaching typewriting. Secretarial or office administration students develop vocational competence needed for employment where typewriting is a significant part of the job. As with other subject areas in community colleges or vocational-technical centers, higher levels of competence are expected than at the secondary level.

THE PSYCHOLOGY OF TEACHING TYPEWRITING

The teaching of typewriting is based upon psychological principles of skill building, with classroom procedures built around these principles. The following are some of the basic principles, previously introduced in Chapter 2, upon which skill building in typewriting rests.

1. *The greatest learning takes place when students understand the goals toward which they are working and when these goals are set in terms of each student's capabilities.* Each activity in the classroom has a definite goal that is known not only to the teacher, but also to the student. In reaching this goal, the student competes against his or her own record of performance rather than against that of the rest of the class. Knowledge of long-term goals (such as gaining employment as a secretary or acquiring skill to type term papers for personal use) is not sufficient motivation for a student to persist in the day-by-day tasks in typewriting. Short-term goals that may be reasonably attained should be established and known by the student.

2. *Students learn best when an appeal is made to as many senses as possible.* The teacher not only tells the student how to type, but also demonstrates each aspect of typewriting. Thus, students hear and see performance at the expert level. When being introduced to letters of the keyboard, the students look at the keyboard, get the "feel" of the keys and the distance between rows, look away, and try to imitate the teacher's stroke sound.

3. *The amount and kind of practice vary according to individual needs.*

Since students enrolled in typewriting differ in aptitude, achievement, and rate and style of learning, the amounts and kinds of practice appropriate for each student also differ. In addition to assigning practice that meets an individual's unique needs, the teacher should be aware of the student's ability to stay on task and should stop the practice when the student's concentration begins to wane and the practice becomes ineffective. This may mean assigning the student a different typewriting task and, at a later time, returning to the original one.

4. *Distributed practice is more effective than massed practice.* An ultimate goal in typewriting is for the student to be able to type for sustained periods of time. However, during the learning stages, practice sessions should be short. This means that the teacher breaks up the daily typewriting class into short practice periods with a variety of activities—warm-up exercises, speed drills, technique drills, new content, and so on, with a definite goal for each. A skill that is developed during a short practice period can be maintained through continued, systematic practice that is gradually increased in length. Short-term practice will not in itself bring about improvement in a given skill.

5. *Immediate knowledge of results is an essential condition for practice.* Immediate knowledge of results serves several desirable purposes. First, it motivates the student. Since "nothing succeeds like success," the student who knows that he or she has completed a task satisfactorily is motivated to attempt the next task. Immediate is the key word, for the student is interested in knowing the results as quickly as possible. Immediate knowledge helps the teacher to decide on the subsequent step in instruction—whether to use remediation for a skill not mastered or to advance to the next objective. Typewriting is built on this step-by-step process of skill development: the mastery of one skill is necessary for mastery of the next. Consequently, the student and the teacher need to know the degree of student mastery of a given skill before making decisions regarding future instruction. When the student does not know, for example, that he is incorrectly typing a footnote and is allowed to continue, the practice reinforces the incorrect procedure, and it becomes more difficult to correct.

6. *Each element of skill development is best learned in isolation before being put into a composite situation.* In presenting the various components of the expert pattern of typewriting, the teacher drills for mastery of each component. Then he or she teaches the application. For example, the use of the backspace key is mastered before horizontal centering is introduced. Problem typewriting is not taught until students have a mastery of the keyboard.

7. *Skill results from the development of expert techniques.* The teacher constantly stresses the development of correct techniques. His or her role in the classroom is that of a coach. The teacher analyzes the difficulties encountered by each student and shows how to overcome them.

8. *Skill develops more rapidly when time is devoted to sheer drill on each element of the skill.* The teacher develops speed and accuracy in typewriting

classes through a series of short takes (one-half-minute, one-minute, and two-minute drills) and repetitive practice on material that presents no problem and is well within the student's capability. Five-minute timed writings are used only to measure the ability to maintain a sustained speed. They are not used as learning devices because lengthy timed writings do not contribute to the building of basic skill.

9. *Transfer of learning is more likely to occur when training conditions and application conditions are similar.* As nearly as possible, the business teacher should provide practice materials and settings that approximate those on a real job. Model offices and simulations provide examples of instructional arrangements in which students may practice office-type production problems in a businesslike setting. For example, a clerk-typist in a model office setting might complete the following tasks in sequence:

a. Receive purchase order requisition from office manager.
b. Type purchase order in triplicate on appropriate form.
c. Proofread the copy.
d. Clip purchase order requisition to top of purchase order and return to office manager.

It is not only important for the training conditions and application conditions to be similar but also *the learner must perceive the similarities between the practice and application situations* before transfer of learning takes place. For the teacher to know the relationship between an exercise in centering and typing the title or cover page for a report is not enough; the student must also be aware of the similarities. In the early stages of typewriting, and particularly when working with slow learners, it is often necessary for the teacher to lead students toward recognizing similarities through direct, guided questions.

10. *In learning a skill, a student makes many random movements initially. Excessive movements decrease as the learner progresses from the cognition to the automation stage of skill development.* From the beginning of typewriting instruction, the teacher should demonstrate the correct pattern for the student. During the early stages of learning a specific motor skill, the student is also using cognitive skills; that is, when he sees the letter f, he says f to himself, mentally fixes where the key is on the typewriter, and decides which finger to use when striking the key. The movement used in striking the key is exaggerated and excessive. As the student becomes more proficient, he eliminates these excessive movements. For example, in the initial stages, the student returns to the home-row keys after striking each letter. The teacher does not stress accuracy until opportunity has been given for the elimination of random movements by the development of correct keyboarding techniques. He or she concentrates on facility of manipulation with all practice directed toward an even, steady flow of motion.

module 6.1
LEARNING ACTIVITIES

1. The business education staff in your school believes that typewriting is a functional skill for all students. Write a justification for a minimum of one semester of typewriting for all high school students that you would present to the faculty.
2. The business education staff in your school district is preparing a course guide for typewriting. Using the information in this module and other sources such as those found in the reference section,* list the objectives for typewriting at these levels: (a) middle school, (b) secondary school, and (c) postsecondary school.
3. Select four principles of learning identified in this module and explain how you would implement each in a typewriting class.
4. Using the *Reader's Guide*, the *Education Index*, and/or the *Business Education Index*, locate, read, and report on an article on typewriting at the elementary school, middle school, or high school levels.

module 6.1
SELF-TEST

A. Discussion Questions
1. What are the major objectives of typewriting at the following levels? (a) elementary, (b) middle school/junior high, (c) high school, (d) postsecondary.
2. List six principles of learning and explain the importance of each in teaching typewriting.

B. Multiple Choice

_____ 3. At the elementary school level, typewriting is offered largely for its value as a (a) communication tool, (b) guidance tool, (c) career education device, (d) prevocational course.

_____ 4. The purpose of junior high school typewriting is (a) career exploration and personal use, (b) personal use and low-level job skill, (c) guidance and personal use, (d) career exploration and guidance.

_____ 5. The content of second-year typewriting at the high school level (a) appeals to students bound for college, (b) is largely employment-oriented, (c) is integrated into office practice, (d) emphasizes a high level of straight-copy skill.

_____ 6. Typewriting at the four-year college level focuses largely on (a) personal-use skills, (b) job-related skills, (c) vocational skills, (d) all of these skills.

C. True or False

_____ 7. A multimedia approach is superior to a demonstration approach in teaching the keyboard.

*See also the *Business Education Index, Reader's Guide to Periodical Literature*, and *Education Index*.

_____ 8. Some problem typing should be done by students before they have mastered the keyboard.

_____ 9. Short practice periods in beginning typewriting are preferred to sustained practice.

_____ 10. The amount and kind of practice prescribed for a typewriting student is based on the common needs of the class.

_____ 11. Immediate knowledge of results is an essential condition for practice.

_____ 12. Accuracy in typewriting is more important in the early stages of learning the keyboard than even, rapid motions.

_____ 13. The major criterion for success in typewriting is technique.

_____ 14. Transfer of learning is fostered by the use of office simulations.

_____ 15. Longer timed writings (five to ten minutes) contribute greatly to the building of basic skill.

_____ 16. The teacher should establish uniform, short-term goals for each typewriting class.

module 6.2
TEACHING AND LEARNING THE KEYBOARD

The keyboard learning stage is a crucial period in typewriting instruction and learning because it is during this stage that the foundation is laid for the development of correct typewriting technique.

After completing this module, you should be able to (1) explain the use of the _skip-around method_ for teaching the typewriter keyboard, (2) identify the horizontal and vertical methods for teaching the keyboard, (3) discuss the effects of rate of presentation and pacing on keyboard learning, and (4) describe a method for teaching figures and symbols.

THE SKIP-AROUND METHOD

Although research does not reveal one method to be clearly superior to another, the _skip-around method_ of presenting the typewriting keyboard is the most widely used. Actually, the skip-around method is a sequential plan for initiating control of the keys that combines the approaches used in the home-row and vertical plans; that is, the home-row keys are taught first, and then other keys are presented vertically from each of the home-row keys. For example, the *i* key is taught by locating it in relation to the *k* key which the student has already learned.

Russon and Wanous[5] describe the skip-around method as a plan consisting of the following procedures:

> The home row is taught first. This is an important principle because a feeling of security is built up in the typist by giving him a base of operation in the home keys. The new keys following the home row are then presented in logical fashion. Each day two to four new letter keys are presented. The choice of letters to be presented together follows certain principles: (a) some left- and some right-hand strokes are presented together; (b) some easy reaches and some not-so-easy reaches are presented together; (c) some first- and second-finger keys are combined with some third- and fourth-finger keys; and (d) some upward reaches are combined with some downward reaches.

The skip-around method results in the early typing of words and sentences, makes use of the strong fingers and easy reaches first, and avoids introducing alternate keys that are the subjects of substitution errors (such as *i* and *e*) in the same lesson. The typing of nonsense letter combinations should be kept to a minimum. Copy consisting of short, balanced-hand words in phrases, clauses, or sentences should be the predominant type of copy used during the initial stage of instruction. However, the teacher may successfully use such drill copy as *ftf ftf ftf tf tf tf* when teaching new keys and reaches to promote the development of good stroking and correct fingering habits.

THE HOME-ROW OR HORIZONTAL METHOD

In the *home-row* or *horizontal method,* the student is taught the home keys (*asdf jkl;*) first, using all fingers from the start. After the home row has been taught, the third row of keys is presented, followed by the bottom row. Since there is only one vowel in the home row, however, some of the drill material is made up of nonsense typing. One way to minimize nonsense drill is to use the home-row approach in conjunction with other approaches; that is, present the home-row keys and quickly move to another approach, such as the skip-around or vertical method.

THE FIRST-FINGER-FIRST OR VERTICAL METHOD

In the *first-finger-first* or *vertical method,* the student is first taught all the keys struck by the strong index fingers (*f* and *j*). When these keys have been presented, all keys struck by the second fingers (*d* and *k*) are taught, and so on. This approach crowds most of the difficult reaches into a limited number of lessons, and there is a tendency to make mistakes on letters typed by the same fingers on opposite hands. It also forces the learner to use many one-hand word patterns that are difficult to type before unskilled fingers are able to execute even, easy reaches with ease.

Learning the keyboard means learning to make a number of different motions toward *each* key rather than learning the forty-four key locations. Compare the different motions used in making *t* in these words: a*rt, ta*ll, t*r*ip, ma*te.*

Students should initially learn the location of each new key by a sight-approach method, that is, by actually looking at the keyboard to see the new key's location and the distance and direction the finger must reach to strike it. Students may then make a few trial reaches to the new key while watching their fingers. They should then attempt to type, by the touch method, using the newly learned key and all other previously learned keys. For example, the letter *e* is typed with the *d* or left middle finger. To make a reach, extend your *d* finger upward. Your little *a* finger can serve as an anchor for home position. *Watch* as you reach several times to the *e* key and back to the *d* key. Type *ede ede ede* as you look at the keyboard. Can you type *e* by moving *only* your finger and no other part of your hand or arm? When you think you have mastered the reach, type the following line twice *without looking* at the keyboard: *ded ded ede ede deed.*

While learning keyboard reaches, students should be allowed to glance at the keys occasionally to help them learn to control newly learned keys by touch, but the habit of looking at the keyboard frequently or generally should not be allowed to develop. Such an improper technique habit will be hard to break later on. Students who persist in watching their fingers should retype keyboard drills that appear in earlier lessons. Requiring such practice is not a punishment but a remedial device to eliminate some of the causes of keyboard watching, such as lack of mastery of preceding lessons, insecurity, or lack of confidence in one's ability to type by touch.

RATE OF PRESENTATION

The rate of presentation of the alphabetic keyboard varies in typewriting texts from one week at the college level to three weeks at the junior high school level. Approximately six to ten class periods may be the optimum time to spend in making the initial keyboard presentation. All keys previously introduced should be reviewed each class period before any new keys are presented. The teacher may find it helpful for some students to have one or two review lessons during the keyboard learning stage when no new keys are presented.

When an individualized approach is used, the student progresses through the keyboard lessons at his or her own pace. Some teachers, however, prefer to keep the class together during keyboard presentation before implementing an individualized approach.

As soon as the student learns the alphabetic keyboard and the location of the shift key, comma, and period, he or she is ready for several days of practice before learning to type figures and symbols.

Control of the stroking rate allows the teacher to control the interval between motions during which the beginner gets set for and organizes his or her motions. The earliest stages of practice benefit from stroke-by-stroke pacing by the teacher. Dictation of each letter in the copy in a sharp, clipped voice will foster striking (or light tapping strokes on an electric machine) instead of pressing motions. However, stroke-by-stroke pacing should be confined to no more than a fraction of a minute on any given occasion and to the earliest practice of each new key during keyboard learning because "(1) Such pacing is metronomic, and the best typing rhythms are anything but metronomic; and (2) any given rate will necessarily be too fast or too slow for some members of any class."[6]

The main emphasis in the keyboard learning stage should be on the development of proper typewriting techniques: sharp, fluent stroking on the manual; light tapping on the electric; action centered in the fingers, not in the hands or arms; eyes on the copy; comfortable posture. Very little emphasis should be placed on accuracy of the typescript during the keyboard presentation stage. Overemphasis on correctness of typescript at the start tends to lead to hesitant motions, frequent glancing at keys, and pressing rather than striking (or lightly tapping) the keys. Immediate error recognition and correction, on the part of the student, can be an important aid to learning. "During keyboard learning practice, the learner who notices a mistake *as soon* as he makes it should immediately follow it with the correct stroke or should space once and retype the word."[7] This does not mean that the student should constantly watch the typescript for errors, but if an error is noticed, it should be retyped correctly (that is, *tge* for *the*).

Students should spend the major portion of each class period typing. Several short "rest" breaks, however, can be distributed throughout the class period during which the teacher explains problems and procedures, demonstrates techniques, and motivates the students.

What should be done if, despite the teacher's guidance, students develop poor technique habits? Students who have previously used a hunt-and-peck method can overcome such an inefficient technique and learn proper fingering and touch operation of the keyboard. Unlearning an incorrect technique and substituting a correct one for it may be more difficult than merely learning a new skill, but the teacher and the learner should put forth sufficient effort to accomplish the task since technique greatly conditions the development of skill.

FIGURES AND SYMBOLS

Control of the number and special character keys by touch should be taught in the same manner as the alphabet keys, distributing their initial presentation over at least three or four class periods and beginning their introduction a week or two after the alphabet keys have been presented and learned fairly well.

The teacher may select one of two basic methods in presenting the keyboard: the conventional (home-row) method or the pipe-organ method. In the conventional method, the student's hands remain on the home row and he or she moves the finger from the home-row position to the appropriate number key, such as *f* to *4*. When using the pipe-organ method, the left hand moves to the number row while the right hand remains on the traditional home row to strike the comma, period, space bar, shift key, and *1* key (on some machines). On most typewriters, this plan calls for the fourth finger on *2*, third finger on *3*, second finger on *4*, and first finger on *5*.

The following procedures may be used to assist students in mastering numbers and symbols:

1. Present a limited number of figures or symbols in one lesson. Two or three are probably enough since sufficient drill must be allowed for mastery of each key.
2. Have students look at the location of the new key and practice moving the finger from the home-row and striking the new key several times (home-row method).
3. Have students move the fingers from home row to the number row without typing the intervening key (home-row method).
4. Gradually provide drills that contain a mixture of words and figures when students demonstrate a level of proficiency of approximately 100 digits per minute.
5. Frequent reviews, drills, and timed writings on the number and special character keys should be given to develop and maintain number-row mastery. Touch control of the number keys is essential for most typists.
6. Teach digits as a group rather than as individual numbers—43, not 4–3. This is accomplished by dictating number drills and by having students visualize groups of digits from their copy as a whole rather than individual numbers.
7. The typewritten copy should be compared with the original copy to check for number errors. Students should be reminded of the seriousness of number errors.

At least two different plans are used successfully in teaching symbol keys. One plan is to delay teaching symbol keys until the number keys have been taught, thus teaching the symbols in relation to the corresponding numbers. A second plan is to teach a number key in one lesson and the corresponding symbol key in the following lesson.

PARTS OF THE MACHINE

Machine parts should be taught as they are used. At that time, the student should become familiar with the location, operation, and purpose of the particular part. Only six or seven nonkeyboard parts of the typewriter are used frequently during the actual typing process; these are the space bar, shift keys, backspace key, carriage return key or carriage return lever, margin release, and the tabulator keys. The speed of operating these parts should be appropriate to the stroking speed. To develop skill, the teacher should provide drills that incorporate the use of the nonkeyboard parts.

module 6.2
LEARNING ACTIVITIES

1. Prepare a demonstration minilesson designed to teach two to four letters of the keyboard. Your plan should include what you will say, a listing of the visual aids you will use, and a description of the demonstrations you will conduct. You may use a typewriting textbook or other references as needed.
2. Using typewriting textbooks, resource guides, or other references, prepare a lesson plan for teaching one nonkeyboard part of the typewriter. You may wish to use the format described in Chapter 5.
3. Prepare a chart explaining and/or illustrating the finger motions used in making an *n* in the following words: name, autumn, nut, setting.
4. Review typewriting texts from the junior high, high school, and college levels. How many lessons are devoted to keyboard presentation of the alphabet? How many lessons are devoted to numbers and symbols? What approach is used in presenting the keyboard in each book?

module 6.2
SELF-TEST

A. Discussion Questions
1. What procedures characterize the skip-around method of teaching the keyboard?
2. What difficulties does the business teacher encounter in using the horizontal and vertical methods of teaching the keyboard?
3. Why should the business teacher be concerned about pacing in the early stages of teaching beginners to type?
4. Describe how you would present the numbers, figures, and symbols in a beginning typewriting class.

B. Multiple Choice

———— 5. Primary emphasis in the keyboard learning stage should be on the development of (a) correct posture, (b) fast stroking, (c) proper technique, (d) correct typescript.

———— 6. The number of class periods most frequently used in initial presentation of the alphabet section of the keyboard is (a) three to seven, (b) six to ten, (c) seven to eleven, (d) twelve to sixteen.

———— 7. The correct method of operating the nonkeyboard parts of the typewriter (a) should not be taught, (b) should be taught at the outset, (c) should be taught as needed, (d) should be taught if questions arise.

———— 8. Research about teaching and learning the keyboard suggests that (a) some typing methods are definitely superior to others, (b) students prefer the vertical (first-finger-first) method, (c) teachers prefer the horizontal (home-row) method, (d) no one individual procedure is clearly superior to another.

module 6.3
DEVELOPING TECHNIQUE

After completing this module, you should be able to (1) recognize correct position at the typewriter and proper operating techniques; (2) demonstrate proper techniques in using the operating controls of manual and electric typewriters; (3) diagnose student behaviors that inhibit the development of typewriting skill, and prescribe corrective procedures to improve students' basic operating techniques; and (4) explain and/or show good demonstration techniques.

From the first day, the teacher should emphasize development of correct techniques in typewriting—the form used by the expert typist. In a general sense, *technique* denotes the whole manner of operating the machine; it is everything that affects *how* students type. In a specific sense, technique denotes the habits and motions used in a particular operation; we speak of "backspacing technique" and "paper insertion technique." The business teacher recognizes that to develop speed, accuracy, and efficiency at the typewriter, the student must develop good techniques.

PLANNING FOR TECHNIQUE

Good techniques are not learned incidentally. Rather, the teacher plans for and incorporates technique development in daily lessons, demonstrates correct techniques to students, observes them to see that they are exhibiting proper techniques, provides remediation when needed, and evaluates students' papers for evidence of good and poor techniques. In the early stages of typewriting instruction, the teacher should place major emphasis on developing good technique and avoid stressing accuracy too soon. In the initial phases, the instructional approach is technique, then speed, then accuracy. A major portion of the grade for the first marking period is based on technique.

A three-technique plan to be included in daily lessons that was recommended by Lloyd[8] is appropriate for ensuring that proper techniques are developed. He recommended that each lesson provide for

1. *new techniques*, involved in the new learnings of the lesson, to be presented and taught—such as backspacing to center a whole table, tabulating across the page, or backspace centering a title
2. *familiar techniques*, involved in the new learnings of the lesson, to be reviewed thoroughly—such as clearing and setting tab stops, using the tabulator, or backspace centering a title
3. *follow-up techniques*, given attention as a follow-up to a recent presentation or as a necessary step in general improvements—such as returning the carriage without looking up, capitalizing, or number-key stroking.

The purpose of technique drill is to develop habits that should become automatic. Therefore, such drills may be used to introduce a new technique, such as using margin stops; to refine a technique, such as using the shift-lock key; or to correct a faulty technique, such as looking back and forth from the copy to the typescript. To be effective, each technique drill should focus on one goal that is known to the student. During the early stages of typewriting instruction, the techniques that are emphasized may be classified into two general categories: position at the typewriter and operating technique. Later, special operating techniques such as centering, spreading and squeezing, and editorial decisions such as spacing after punctuation, and expression of numbers are included.

POSITION AT THE TYPEWRITER

"Every learner should be allowed to select, within generally appropriate limits, a posture comfortable to him. Occasionally small shifts in position are desirable and maximum stroking efficiency is the result of relaxation rather than of deliberate effort to confine movements to the fingers."[9] West is not suggesting that any posture—such as sitting on one foot or slumping in the chair—is acceptable in typewriting. Placing the feet flat on the floor instead of resting the heels of shoes on the rung of the chair results in less fatigue. Whether or not the student places one foot slightly ahead of the other is a matter of preference. In fact, as the student tires, it is natural to make small shifts of the feet for relaxation and rest.

How far a student sits from the typewriter depends on his or her size. A good rule of thumb is to properly curve the fingers on the second-row keys and to sit at a distance so that the elbows are slightly ahead of the body. A common fault of beginning typists is sitting too close to the machine. The typewriter frame should be even with the front of the desk so that the student does not have to reach across the front edge of the desk to gain access to the keyboard.

EYE MOVEMENTS

After the initial instructional period, students must keep their eyes on the copy while typing. Looking back and forth is detrimental to their progress. Keeping the eyes on the word in the copy while it is being typed is an aid to concentration. Reading ahead causes errors, such as transposition of letters or words and insertion and omission of characters. Students should be reminded that continuous typing boosts their skill faster than sporadic typing. The copy should be placed to the right of the machine to prevent blocking the student's view of the copy if the typewriter has a movable carriage.

TECHNIQUE CHECKLIST

Authorities do not agree on whether to use a technique checklist in typewriting classes. However, many feel that it is a fundamental tool of instruction, and they recommend its use to evaluate each student on the basic techniques. Such a checklist may be of value to beginning business teachers in analyzing typewriting techniques of students. The following checklist suggests the corrective action needed to improve basic operating techniques. Based on the results of this rating, remedial work should be planned to help students overcome these faults. Improvement results from correct practice, not quantity of practice. However, a student usually needs several days of remedial drill to correct a bad habit. Remedial drills may be practiced for as long as two weeks on a spaced-interval-practice basis.

When correcting poor technique habits, the teacher and student should follow these steps:

1. Teacher identifies specific technique to be corrected.
2. Student observes the correct technique demonstrated by the teacher (or via audiovisual such as film loop, slidetape, videotape, and so on).
3. Student verbalizes to the teacher the correct procedure for executing the technique.
4. Student demonstrates correct technique to teacher.
5. Teacher prescribes appropriate drill.
6. Student practices drill for short period daily for one to two weeks depending on severity of poor habit and degree of progress.
7. Teacher observes student periodically to determine whether problem is corrected.

CONDUCTING DEMONSTRATIONS

The art of demonstrating is a valuable form of guidance in the typewriting classroom, and the teacher should use it frequently. Developing good technique and learning complex skills are aided by observing an effective model.

Most aspects of technique involving machine operation can be effectively demonstrated by the teacher. Some demonstrations, such as paper insertion, need to be seen, and others, such as the sound of stroking at a particular speed, need to be heard. If you want students to hear the sound of stroking, raise or pull forward the paper rail (bails) so that the type bars or type font makes loud noises as you type.

There are several points you will want to keep in mind in demonstrating:

1. Do not attempt to demonstrate while some students are typing or talking. Have students put a clean sheet of paper in their machines before you begin demonstrating, to prevent their typing as you talk.
2. Stand where students can observe the demonstration. Visual demonstrations are useless unless students can see exactly what you want them to see. If you are using a demonstration machine on a movable stand at the front of the room, you may have to repeat the demonstration at two or three locations, moving the stand as necessary.

illustration 6.1
TECHNIQUE CHECK SHEET

BASIC TECHNIQUES AND CONDITIONERS

RATINGS:		Rating Periods									
Excellent . . . . 4 points Good . . . . 3 points Average . . . . 2 points Acceptable . . . . 1 point		1	2	3	4	5	6	7	8	9	10

POSITION AT TYPEWRITER
1. Sits in a comfortable, relaxed position directly in front of typewriter.
2. Keeps feet on floor for proper body balance.
3. Keeps elbows in relaxed, natural position at sides of body to provide correct hand position.
4. Keeps wrists low and relaxed, but off frame of typewriter.
5. Keeps fingers well curved, upright, and in typing position.

Point Average

KEYSTROKING
1. Keeps fingers curved and upright over home keys.
2. Makes quick, snappy strokes with immediate key release.
3. Maintains uniform keystroking action (force).
4. Keeps hands and arms quiet, wrists low.
5. Strikes each key with proper controlling finger.

Point Average

SPACE BAR
1. Keeps the right thumb curved—on or close to space bar.
2. Strikes space bar with a quick, down-and-in (toward the palm) motion of right thumb.
3. Releases space bar instantly.
4. Does not pause before or after spacing stroke.

Point Average

CARRIAGE (OR CARRIER) RETURN
1. Returns carriage (or carrier) quickly at ends of lines.
    MANUAL: Quick, flick-of-hand motion.
    ELECTRIC: Quick, little finger reach.
2. Keeps eyes on copy during and following return.
3. Starts new line without break or pause.

Point Average

SHIFT KEYS
1. Reaches quickly with little fingers; keeps other fingers in typing (home-key) position.
2. Holds shift key all the way down as the letter key is struck—capitals are uniformly on the line of writing.
3. Releases shift key quickly after letter is struck.
4. Does not pause before or after shift key stroke.

Point Average

TABULATOR
1. Reaches quickly with controlling finger; keeps other fingers in typing (home-key) position.
2. Uses minimum hand and arm motion.
3. Continues typing immediately after tabulating—without pause or interruption.

Point Average

3. Keep the demonstration machine uncovered with paper inserted throughout each class period so that you can step over to it quickly and perform those two-or-three-second demonstrations to emphasize a point.
4. Have the necessary materials at hand when you begin demonstrating.
5. Follow a demonstration routine, such as
   a. Students watch as teacher demonstrates.
   b. Students and teacher perform together step-by-step.
   c. Students perform independently as teacher observes.

If instruction is being provided in an individualized, multimedia context, the media and the explanation that accompanies it should be carefully synchronized. Such demonstrations in typewriting are more effective when shown on film loops or videotape rather than slides or still pictures since the former media incorporate motion. Even in the individualized classroom, there will be situations in which you will have to use live demonstrations for helping a student.

DRILLS FOR DEVELOPING TECHNIQUE

The typewriting teacher will want to build up an inventory of technique drills to use for introduction, reinforcement, and/or remediation purposes. One approach is to prepare a technique drill resource kit using index cards or quarter sheets of paper filed behind the appropriate technique heading. (Laminated cards last longer and are easy to clean.) You will want to make multiple copies of some of the drills for use with groups. Single copies of several different drills are useful for remediation and for an individualized approach.

The technique drills by Lloyd,[10] shown on pages 195–197, are examples of the type of drill you can collect for your file.

TEACHER OBSERVATION

A good typewriting teacher emphasizes technique and, as a result, is constantly observing and helping students. He or she does not sit behind a desk at the front of the room, but rather moves about the room, up the aisles, and around individual work stations. The following are examples of student behaviors to watch for, their possible causes and their corrections.[11]

1. Watch for Moving Heads. Is the student lost? (Were your directions clear? Was (s)he paying attention?) Is the student done? (Directions should include continuing activities when student finishes immediate activity.) Is (s)he untangling keys? (The student must look up for this.) Is (s)he a real peeker? (The student needs to develop confidence, so stop grading the work for a while; assign retyping of earlier lessons.) Did (s)he think you said to stop? (Be consistent with your signals.)

TYPING TECHNIQUE DRILLS

Sample Drills for Improving Keyboard Proficiency

A.   TO IMPROVE RHYTHM:

1.	3-Letter Run	The man and the boy did not get the pay for the one day off.
2.	4-Letter Run	They said that they will lend them some more cash very soon.
3.	5-Letter Run	Those eight steel firms found their hotel bills would mount.

B.   TO MAKE STROKING BRISKER, SHARPER:

4.	Rows 2 and 3	They would help you quite a lot if you would ask their aid.
5.	Row 3 only	We owe it to you to try to write or to type up your poetry.
6.	Repetitives	She told us that she had told us that he had told us that.

C.   TO KEEP HANDS LOW, HUGGING THE HOME KEYS:

7.	Stroke Drill	ffaf jj;j ffsf jj1j ffdf jjkj aasa ;;1; aada ;;k; aafa ;;j;
8.	Home Stress	Karl was afraid the girl had had salad dressing in the jar.
9.	Anchor Stress	Get a top; a small car; a ball; a mitt; and, perhaps, a bat.
10.	End-on-Homes	Harold asked if Fred would like a cold glass of fresh milk.

D.   TO IMPROVE SHIFTING FOR CAPITALS:

11.	Easy 2-Counts	Lou Art Jim Dan Ina Sam Joe Wes Lyn Sal Una Cal Lil Ada Kim
12.	Fast 1-Counts	May Roy Ken Ann Mac Vic Lew Sol Pam Rue Hal Don Max Flo May
13.	In Context	We saw Dr. and Mrs. J. N. White at the Hamon-Whitney Hotel.

E.   TO IMPROVE THE SPACE-BAR STROKE: Words

14.	Short Words	None of us like the man who will not do all that he can do.	12
15.	End-Start Words	Jack knew why you used data about the early years so often.	12
16.	Comma-Space	Well, the art, or skill, of typing is, or will be, helpful.	12
17.	Period-Space	Mr. Ray paused . . . smiled wanly . . . and fell. I raced.	12
18.	Downhill Run	Polishing usually results from what men try to do to do it.	12

F.   TO SPEED UP NUMBER STROKING:

19.	We-23 twos	we 23 up 70 or 94 it 85 ow 92 pi 08 re 43 yo 69 to 59 we 23	12
20.	We-23 threes	wet 235 you 697 ore 943 pie 083 tie 583 ire 843 two 529 529	12
21.	Number Race	The 1 the 2 the 3 the 4 the 5 the 6 the 7 the 8 the 9 Etc.	--
22.	Number Race	To 1 or 2 or 3 or 4 or 5 or 6 or 7 or 8 or 9 or 10 or Etc.	--

G.   TO ELIMINATE PAUSING BEFORE LONG WORDS:

23.	Uphill Run	To be the one who wins will always reward victors suitably.	12
24.	Springboards	To tolerate or organize an analysis of offerings is simple.	12
25.	Hit 'Ems	An elementary way to emphasize a new concept is functional.	12
26.	Derivatives	Prac practice practical practicing practically practitioner	12

H.   TO IMPROVE EYES-ON-COPY HABIT: START HERE

27.	Back Words	them. of one even for pay not did and keys the all lost She	12
28.	Back Strokes	.uoy rof prit eht ekam ot ekil dluow yeht taht dias nem ehT	12
29.	Alphajumble	h e b ; y v s p m ? j g d a x u , r o l i f c z w . t q n k	12

Sample Drills for Improving Basic Manipulation of Machine Part

I.   TO SPEED UP THE CARRIAGE RETURN:
(Type each word on a separate line, using single spacing)

		Electric Machines	Manual Machines	
30.	Very, Very Easy	join kink limp pony link	dear base tree crew fast	--
31.	Very Easy	lend hand jams lake melt	dogs rule slow wilt ride	--
32.	Easy	John Jump Hill Pump Holy	Fred Drew Bart Bess Dear	--
33.	Fairly Easy	Jane Kent Lane Park Lady	Riva Alan Tina They When	--
34.	Fairly Hard	Dora Ruth Fred Dave Stew	Jinx Hulk Long Lily Pink	--

J. TO SPEED UP CARRIAGE RETURN WITH INDENTION:

35.	Special	(Repeat 32, 33, 34; indent carriage 5 spaces on each line.)	--
36.	Double-Spaced	I am sure you will wish to visit with us as soon as it	12
37.	Single-Spaced	is possible for you to do so.	18

K. TO SHARPEN ATTENTIVENESS TO WARNING BELL:
(Type each line 6 times. The first time, begin the line
at the margin; each subsequent time, indent the lines 10 more
spaces. If typed correctly, lines will end evenly at right.)

38.	No Hyphens	To arrange work that will look well, the bell must be heard.	12
39.	With Hyphens	Word division should be considered negatively distractional.	12

L. TO IMPROVE BACKSPACING: Words

40.	1-Backs	lab lad law lax (and) rat raw ram ran (and) tar tab tam tan	12
41.	2-Backs	rot ret rut rat (and) sit sat set sot (and) mit mat mut met	12

M. TO QUICKEN THE USE OF THE MARGIN RELEASE:

(Copy line for line, with margin stops set at 15 and 71.)

42.	1-Mores	I wanted to raise it, but I did not have enough strength.	12
43.	2-Mores	We had some doubts about him, but he finally came through.	12
44.	3-Mores	When we heard what he was up to, we all felt quite alarmed.	12

N. TO IMPROVE USE OF SHIFT LOCK AND RELEASE:

45.	Separates	CHAIRMAN: Wasn't that in JANUARY, rather than in FEBRUARY?	12
46.	Consecutives	MR. PARK: The WORLD ALMANAC says so, but I AM NOT CERTAIN.	12
47.	On-Offs-On-Offs	CHAIRMAN: Well, DOW-JONES says so; and SPEAR-MOODY agrees.	12

Sample Drills for Improving Special Operating Techniques

O. TO IMPROVE BACKSPACE-CENTERING:

(Center each part of each line; the letter I will align.)

48.	Evens	It WILL Give Rich Confidence in INITIATIVE	--
49.	Odds	DESIGNS for Buildings Involving the Major Principles	--
50.	Spreads	S P I R I T D U P L I C A T O R G U I D E S	--

P. TO DEVELOP EXPERTNESS IN HALF-SPACING:

	Sentence:	She said that she wished that she could do exactly as I do.	12
51.	Spreading	(Type above sentence twice; second time, change she to he.)	11
52.	Crowding	(Type above sentence twice; second time, change she to they.)	13

Q. TO DEVELOP ALERTNESS IN TABULATING:

(Set tab stop every 12th space from the left margin.)

		M	T	T	T	T	
53.	Standard	Martin	3-75-441	69.42%	$ 99,000	6 ft. 11 in.	--
54.	Inspaced	Davis	384-080	7.18%	103,000	3 ft. 2 in.	--
55.	Backspaced	Jarvis	11-38-161	100.00%	2,116,000	10 ft. 10 in.	--
56.	Mixed	Harmon	8-66-044	8.21%	$1,372,000	9 ft. 9 in.	--

TYPING TECHNIQUE DRILLS *(continued)*

Sample Drills for Improving Editorial Performance

R.   TO SHARPEN EDITORIAL ATTENTIVENESS:

57. Insert missing vowels	Mr. W-1s-n: W- -r- pl--s-d t- -ckn-wl-dg- --r r-c--pt -f y--r l-tt-r -f F-br--ry 22, -b--t y--r -v-rd-- p-ym-nts.	11 23
58. Insert missing words	My ---- Mrs. Coe: If --- --- arrange -- visit with us some---- next ----, we should -- ---- to discuss ---- bill.	11 23
59. Untangle word inversions	Our office not may be able to within stay its budgeted expenses. We need shall to trim every away extra activity.	11 23
60. Fix punctuation	Dear Mr. Solon: We fear-- rightly or wrongly --that you ask the impossible; however, I'll do what I can to conform.	

2. Watch for Bobbing Shoulders. Has he or she crossed legs? Is (s)he wearing out? (Plan on more short rest periods.) Is the machine faulty? (The typewriter may be too high or too low; if the ribbon is worn, the student must slug the keys to get readable print; if the key is sticking, the student must strike it very hard.) Is bad posture causing fatigue? Hunching, leaning back, or slumping? Do his or her elbows stick out? (S)he may be too close to the machine. (Exceptions must be made for individual body structures, however. Not everyone can assume correct hand position with his or her elbows held to his or her sides.)

3. Watch for Massaging. Are students rubbing forearms? (This is due to too much continuous typing, too heavy a hand on the keys. Check touch control and ribbon.) Does (s)he rub shoulders or back? (The machine is probably too low or too high.) Does (s)he rub neck? (Student may be holding chin too high; may be sitting too far to the left—center the student opposite the *j* key. Copy may be too close to or parallel to machine—turn copy so that it points to two o'clock, and be sure the copy is elevated. Is (s)he rubbing a leg? (This is probably due to crossing the legs or not placing both feet flat on the floor, thus causing undue pressure from the front edge of the chair against the back of the thigh resulting in impeded circulation.)

4. Watch for Keystroking. Is his or her typing jerky? (Assign rhythm drills.) Does (s)he hold some keys down instead of releasing them quickly? ((S)he may be holding home position too rigidly or may be heavy-fingered —give drill in which finger is used for two or more successive strokes.) Does (s)he hit two keys at once? ((S)he may be resting wrists on frame of machine—assign upper row word drills. (S)he may be holding hands too high or bouncing them, and probably isn't curving fingers enough.) Is student "off center" so that hands are not in proper position? (Center body opposite *j* key.) May be "swaying" in a swivel chair because both feet are not on the floor to anchor his or her body. As (s)he sways slightly, the hands move a bit to the right or left of the normal home-row position. (Adjust height of chair so that feet are on the floor.) Is (s)he too close to the machine? (A sharp, crisp stroke requires hands to be close enough together so that thumbs could lock—this is not possible if (s)he is too close.)

module 6.3
LEARNING ACTIVITIES

1. Assemble a resource file for technique drills. Try to have at least two different drills for each technique you choose to include. (This should be an ongoing activity that you will want to continue on the job.)
2. Observe one typewriting student in a high school, college, or vocational-technical center. Check the techniques needing improvement, using the checklist in this module or another of your choice.
3. Prepare a chart or slide that you can use with a beginning typewriting class, demonstrating correct posture at the typewriter.
4. Prepare a live or taped demonstration showing the proper technique for operating an electric and a manual typewriter. Cover touch; position of elbows, forearms, wrists, and hands; keyboard and carriage return controls; and symbols and punctuation.
5. Prepare a list of all the desirable techniques used by a proficient typist. (This could be an individual or a group project.)
6. One of your students inserts paper into the typewriter incorrectly. Outline your plan for remediation, describing your demonstration. (You may substitute a typing skill of your choice.)
7. For each of the following problems, list the probable cause(s) and the corrective measure:
   a. jerky typing
   b. rubbing shoulders
   c. hitting two keys at once
   d. holding down keys
   e. student off-center
   f. elbows sticking out
   g. peeking at hands and typescript
   h. rubbing a leg

module 6.3
SELF-TEST

A. Multiple Choice

_____ 1. The instructional approach recommended in this module for developing good typewriting technique is (a) speed, then accuracy, then technique, (b) technique, then speed, then accuracy, (c) accuracy, then technique, then speed, (d) technique, then accuracy, then speed.

_____ 2. Remedial drills to correct poor typewriting habits are best practiced (a) for sustained lengths of time for a few days, (b) on a spaced-interval practice basis for up to two weeks, (c) sparingly, since they focus on errors the student has already made, (d) on a regular basis with the entire class participating.

_____ 3. A common fault of beginning typists is (a) crossing the legs, (b) slumping in the chair, (c) sitting too close to the machine, (d) failing to keep feet on the floor.

——————— 4. The teacher should observe the position of the student's copy to ensure that it points to (a) 12 o'clock, (b) 3 o'clock, (c) 11 o'clock, (d) 2 o'clock.

——————— 5. Students who strike two keys at once are probably (a) holding their heads too high, (b) sitting in an off-center position, (c) leaning back or slumping forward, (d) resting wrists on the frame of the machine.

——————— 6. To improve rhythm, the business teacher should prescribe (a) back words or back strokes, (b) long words, (c) 3-, 4-, or 5-letter runs, (d) fast l-counts.

B. True or False:

——————— 7. Students should try to read ahead in the copy as they type.

——————— 8. In an individualized classroom, demonstrations are most effective when they are developed using slide tapes.

——————— 9. To aid a student's transfer from an electric to a manual machine, or vice versa, use familiar, fluent material.

——————— 10. If students elbows stick out, they may be too close to the machine.

——————— 11. At the typewriter, the student should sit so that he or she is centered opposite the *f* key.

C. Discussion Questions

12. Describe correct position at the typewriter.
13. List and explain four characteristics for effective demonstrations by the teacher.
14. Describe the characteristics of correct stroking on a manual and an electric type-writer.

module 6.4
DEVELOPING SPEED AND ACCURACY

After completing this module, you should be able to (1) identify and explain six guidelines for developing speed and accuracy; (2) compute syllabic intensity and stroke intensity of copy; (3) classify typewriting errors into three major categories; (4) identify two approaches for building speed and accuracy; and (5) compute gross words a minute, correct words a minute, net words a minute, and gross words a minute with an error limit.

Both speed and accuracy are necessary when typing straight copy and when planning and typing practical business and personal papers such as letters, tabulations, manuscripts, invoices, and envelopes. The development of rapid and accurate typewriting skill depends primarily on correct fingering and stroking techniques and on a strong desire to attain a high level of speed with control.

Developmental goals for students include greater speed, improved technique, and increased control or accuracy as evidenced by decreasing errors. Teachers must become aware of and skilled in conducting drills designed to develop sharp stroking and skillful movements.

SPEED AND ACCURACY GUIDES

The development of accuracy must coincide with the development of speed for effective application in production typewriting. However, specific instructional procedures used for the development of speed often differ from those used for accuracy because there is usually a need to emphasize one of these factors more than the other.

Through the years, business teachers have not been able to agree on how to develop typewriting speed and accuracy. At one time, teachers believed that accuracy should precede speed and they required perfect copy on all drills. Those following the accuracy approach believed that if one mastered accuracy, speed would develop automatically. Later, teachers turned their attention to developing speed before accuracy. In this approach, the emphasis was on speed followed by attention to quality of work. A student would work toward a speed goal, such as 40 words per minute, and when it was achieved, he or she would drop back to 35 words per minute and concentrate on accuracy.

A more appropriate approach for developing speed and accuracy may be one that incorporates both, but with the principal emphasis on correct *techniques*.

> In the technique with appropriate speed approach, *relative* speed of stroking receives initial emphasis as a part of the correct technique, and errors in typescript are of secondary importance in the early lessons.... The goal of the technique approach is not a page of usable typed material during the first weeks of the course but the starting of the techniques that will bring typing power later on.[12]

It is important to build typing skills to a production level. As soon as this is accomplished, the emphasis in teaching can be shifted to production typing techniques. The following instructional procedures are generally used by business teachers in realizing this goal.

1. *Separate drills should be conducted for speed and accuracy.* The techniques involved in building speed and accuracy are different. When students are pushing themselves for higher stroking rates, they may want to forget temporarily about accuracy. When working on accuracy in the typescript, speed becomes a secondary consideration. Gradually, as keyboarding skills increase, speed and accuracy merge.

2. *To build speed, force the rate.* When students increase their speed, two things happen: (a) they decrease the time between perceiving the copy and making the stroking response and (b) they decrease the time between one

stroking response and the next. Speed does not develop unless the student makes a determined effort to gain it. That is, if the student makes no additional errors during speed practice than when typing at a normal rate, he or she is not pushing enough to realize any substantial gains in speed. On the other hand, the student should not push so hard that he or she loses control of the machine.

3. *Focus continuously on speed or accuracy goals until substantial gains are made.* The student does not make gains in speed or accuracy if he or she switches back and forth between the two types of drill every day or two. The student should focus on speed, for example, until gains of approximately 4 to 8 *wam* are achieved.* Then the student should drop back for control.

4. *Short timings should be used for building speed and accuracy.* The goal, of course, is to transfer the speed and accuracy achieved in short timings (1–2 minutes) to longer periods of time, such as 5 minutes, which more nearly approximates uninterrupted typing time in business or personal use. Initially, the timed writings may be one-half minute in length on easy copy. As students develop their speed, more difficult copy is used and the length of the writings is gradually increased.

5. *Set goals on an individual basis.* All students in a given class do not need the same amount and kind of practice at any one time. Thus, individual goals should be used in the development of speed and accuracy. By establishing individual goals, each student can concentrate on improving weaknesses. One student may be working to reduce errors while another may have an immediate goal of increasing his or her stroking rate by two words per minute. As soon as one goal is reached, another should be set.

6. *Use a variety of materials for skill-building purposes.* For overall skill development in both speed and accuracy, the teacher should select a variety of materials. Some special practice materials are helpful for initial learning or remedial purposes. For instance, material consisting of 3- and 4-word sentences provides practice in using the shift key for capitals and for spacing between sentences. In the beginning phase of instruction, students who typewrite speed sentences, return-the-carriage drills, and guided writings for speed seem to increase their speed more than do students who simply type "all-purpose" exercises and practical typewriting problems without specific speed-building drills. Special-purpose drills to improve basic techniques, to review the keyboard, and to eliminate particular types of errors are effective in developing both speed and accuracy. Some research seems to indicate that in the later phases of instruction, "all-purpose" exercises and problems are effective.

It is helpful to the student if the teacher has available a package of material for speed and accuracy development including drills taken from ordinary prose as well as special practice materials. An example of a collection of such practice material is *Guided/Timed Writings* by Rhodes and Calhoun[13] which contains 38 units, each composed of two 100-word alphabetic paragraphs which are graduated in 2 *wam* increments from 10 to 46 *wam*.

---

*Note that the abbreviations *wam* (words a minute) and *wpm* (words per minute) are used interchangeably.

A sample guided writing from the Rhodes and Calhoun material follows.

THE GUIDED WRITING

2½ Min.	Min. 5							
		0		1		2		
		0	1		2		3	
0	0	A guided writing has only one purpose. That
2	4	one purpose is to motivate you to type at a speed
4	8	that is just a bit faster than the speed at which
6	12	you now type. This is how it works. A signal is
8	16	given at the end of every fifteen seconds, and as
10	20	the signal is given, the typist should have typed
12	24	to the point in the copy above which a guide mark
14	28	is printed. The typist can now see if his typing
16	32	speed is fast enough to make his typing goal. If
18	36	not, he now knows that he must type a bit faster.
20	0	Each time you type a guided writing you play
22	4	a game. The rules of this game place you against
24	8	a stop watch. If you type fast enough to keep up
26	12	with the guide calls and thus can reach your goal
28	16	before the signal to stop, you are the one who is
30	20	the winner. But, if the signal to stop typing is
32	24	given before you have typed to your goal, old man
34	28	time wins. No typist ought to expect to beat the
36	32	clock in all of the games. Should you be able to
38	36	do this, the game would be much less fun to play.

	0		1		2		3	
	0			1			2	

Speed and accuracy drills

While many workable instructional plans have been implemented, the following procedures, suggested for use with *Guided/Timed Writings,* are based on a student Speed-Control Cycle:

Initially the student is to type a 2½-minute timed writing to determine his entry speed goal. As an example, assume the student types 11 *wam.*

1. The student enters the writing at the unit having guided writing checkpoints for the next speed level, 12 *wam.* This *wam* goal is to be attained on one paragraph of each unit.
2. Upon accomplishing the speed goal of step 1, the student then engages in control typing. (S)he does a guided writing at a reduced rate of 2 *wam* (10 *wam*). The student is to type at the rate of 10 *wam* with no more than 2 errors a minute (5 total errors). As with the speed goal, the control goal is to be attained on one paragraph of each of the 10 *wam* units.
3. On completing the accuracy objective, a new speed-control cycle is begun. The initial speed goal of the new cycle is 2 *wam* above that attained in step 1 of the previous cycle, or 14 *wam.*
4. Periodic evaluations, perhaps weekly, are made of the student's keystroking skill by administering nonpaced 2½- or 5-minute timed writings. These writings are evaluated in terms of both speed and errors. The rate is acceptable without penalty only if the error rate is no more than 2 errors a minute. The student grade is read from the *wam* Progress Chart and is based on *wam* rate and week of typing instruction.[14]

In the early stages of learning to type, speed and accuracy are best developed through the use of easy copy. Then, as the student develops more skills, advanced copy is used. The timed writings shown on page 204 have been used successfully by the author in developing speed and accuracy in typewriting classes.

Copy difficulty

A number of indices of copy difficulty have been developed, such as incidence of high-frequency words, sentence length, word length, and number of syllables per word. Two of these—average word length or stroke intensity, and average number of syllables per word or syllabic intensity—are used frequently because of the ease of computation. The majority of typewriting textbooks specify the stroke intensity and syllabic intensity of the copy. The computation of these indices may be illustrated through this sentence: *Please have the manager return my call.* The sentence contains 7 dictionary words,

TIMED WRITINGS

Directions. Type your name at the top of the paper. Set the machine for a
70-space line. Use a 5-space paragraph indention and double-spacing. If you
complete a paragraph before time is called, start again at the beginning.

Timed Writing A   Time: 5 minutes

	Strokes
Some people think that good typists are born and not made. Many	65
others think that good typists are the product of correct practice.	134
You will agree, I am certain, that a person must have at least a normal	206
sense of coordination if he is to type well. You will also agree that	277
a person needs to practice good typing habits if he is to reach the top	349
in typing. Does it not follow, then, that good typists must have been	420
first born with the right faculties for good typing, but must have trained	495
those faculties by working with good form? I think you will agree with	567
both of these thoughts. You may wonder how many of us are born with	636
the faculties we need for good typing. You need wonder no longer, for	707
the answer is that almost all of us have the muscle control and nerve	777
response we need to type well. If most of us have the aptitude for typing,	853
then aptitudes are not the answer to why some can type better than others.	927

Score (cwam) _____

Timed Writing B   Time: 5 minutes

	Strokes
Yesterday I saw a new film on typing and from it learned the answer	68
to success in typing. The performer in the film was an expert who could	141
make a typewriter hum like a motor. He said that the secret of good	210
typing is correct typing. It is as simple as that. After we learn and	282
practice as we should, we shall be able to type with speed and control.	355
Always strike the keys sharply, but with a motion of the fingers, not of	428
the hands. Use correct posture; keep the eyes on the copy; and type	497
with confidence. His motto was: If you desire to type with speed and	568
accuracy, you can, but only if you practice properly. Since some people	641
do as they should, while others do as they want to, some learn to type	712
better than others. If you want to learn to type well, learn good typing	786
habits; then use those habits in your typing at all times.	844

Score (cwam) _____

Directions for Scoring. Determine the gross strokes typed; divide by 5 to
get the gross words; deduct one for each error; divide by the time of the
test to get the correct words per minute (cwam).

Formula: Gross strokes ÷ 5 = gross words - errors = correct words ÷ time = cwam

10 speech syllables, and 39 characters and spaces. *Syllabic intensity* equals the number of syllables divided by the number of words: $(10 \div 7 = 1.43)$. *Stroke intensity* equals the number of strokes divided by the number of words: $(39 \div 7 = 5.57)$. In both measures, the lower the number, the easier the copy.

Rowe, Lloyd, and Winger[15] offer the following Syllabic Intensity index as a guide to the difficulty of the copy.

DIFFICULTY INDEX	
SYLLABIC INTENSITY	DIFFICULTY
1.00+	Very Easy
1.15+	Easy
1.25+	Fairly Easy
1.35+	Normal
1.45+	Fairly Hard
1.55+	Hard
1.65+	Very Hard

7. *Purposeful repetition is essential to the development of typewriting skill.* Repetition occurs when straight-copy timed writings are repeated or when letter combinations or words reoccur in the typewriting copy. Words such as *the, and, if, of,* and so on, can be typed quickly because they appear frequently in ordinary straight-copy material. Repeating a timed writing enables students to build their speed rapidly. Clem[16] points out that skills are best learned through re-creation rather than repetition. Repetition means typing the same word or sentence over and over; re-creation is typing a word or words but in a different context each time. The student *performs* each time rather than *repeating* one performance.

8. *The development of correct technique underlies the development of stroking speed.* As the student learns to complete each typing operation more skillfully, he or she will be able to increase speed. (For technique drills and instructional procedures, see Module 6.3.) Continuity of writing is essential in maintaining an effective rate of production. One of the characteristics that distinguishes beginning typists from expert typists is the ability of the advanced learner to type for long periods of time without hesitation. "The majority of typists could increase their present speed an average of 25 percent if they would eliminate one habit only—hesitation."[17] Hesitations not only reduce typing speed but also increase errors. To reduce hesitations, students must learn to concentrate on the copy, maintain correct reading speed, reduce the number of times they look from the copy to the machine, and eliminate pauses between strokes.

9. *Accuracy development includes concentrating on development of proper techniques, relaxation, and continuity.* A terminal typewriting objective of each student should be to produce accurately typed copy at an acceptable rate. To guide students in developing accuracy, the teacher must first be able to identify major kinds of errors. Errors can be classified into three catego-

ries: those that need to be ignored, those that need to be studied, and those that need to be erased and/or corrected.[18]

Errors to be ignored

Errors made on typewriting drills.   The general purpose of typewriting drills is to modify behavior; therefore, each drill has a specific purpose inherent in its design. When these drills are used in typewriting practice, the student's entire attention should be on the purpose of the drill; and other errors should be ignored.

Errors made on first practice of problem material.   When the student takes up some new typewriting application for the first time, the purpose is to acquaint him or her with a new arrangement of typed material and an appropriate procedure for typing the problem; the arrangement is the important result. Therefore, the errors should be encircled but not corrected.

Errors made on timed practice of problem material.   The purpose of this exercise is to help the student develop fluency. During this practice, the emphasis is entirely on building skill in the activity; therefore, errors should be encircled but not counted.

Errors made on beginning lessons in elementary typewriting.   In beginning typewriting, many errors are due to chance and do not have a specific cause or remedy. Most of these will disappear naturally and it is not necessary to be concerned about them.

Errors to be studied and used as guides

When typewriting students reach the control stage, errors should be studied and their cause determined. Typewriting teachers must understand *why* errors are made—just knowing that they are made is not enough. Such errors are generally classified into two broad areas: (1) those that can be discovered by examining the typescript and (2) those that can be detected only by observing the student at work. Errors that can be detected from the typescript include those related to spacing; faulty use of the shift key; failure to return the carriage at the right time; faulty stroking—strikeovers, piling, crowding, ghost letters; arranging; centering; reading copy—omissions, additions, substitutions. Students can and should learn to evaluate their typescript for these errors. The teacher should provide a correct copy for students to use in checking their papers. For diagnostic purposes, the teacher can use student errors as a guide for prescribing future assignments, including special remedial drills and practice, and as an indicator of when to shift the emphasis from building a faster stroking rate to dropping back in speed to improve accuracy.

Errors to be erased and corrected

The best time to present erasing/correcting is when students first apply their skill to production typewriting, which is usually near the end of the first semester. (See Module 6.5, Developing Production Competencies.) Clem suggests a classification of errors that she believes to be simpler and, therefore, more practical for students as well as for teacher use:[19]

1. *Reach error: m* for *n*—misdirected; *3* for *e*—overreach; *k* for *i*—underreach; *g* for *b*—too high; *h* for *y*—too low.
2. *Substitution error:* use of the wrong finger or hand for the correct one, as *a* for *s* and *e* for *i;* wrong word for the correct one.
3. *Manipulation error:* faulty shift giving raised capitals or misplaced small letters after the shift; double-spacing between words due to prolonged space stroke; piling of letters; ghost letters; keys sticking and piling up at printing point.
4. *Machine error:* indented or extended margin; irregular spacing between lines; double-spacing between words; or any error due to failure of the machine to function properly.
5. *Speed error:* failure to space between short words; crowding and piling due to forcing the machine too fast; raised capital letters due to hasty shifting, clipping off the first or last letter of a word.
6. *Accidental error:* finger glancing off a key; returning the carriage too soon; leaving out words when changing paper; turning two pages of the copy; starting errors, such as forgetting to indent or releasing the shift; stopping errors, when time is called.
7. *Ignorance:* any error made because the writer did not know it was an error, like long or short lines caused by not knowing the rule, wrong spacing after punctuation marks, or short pages.
8. *Omission of letters or spaces:* when weak fingers strike so lightly that the letter fails to register, like *tht* for *that;* forgetting to space between words.
9. *Addition of letters or spaces:* holding space bar too long; striking space bar too high so *n* is written in space between words; doubling up the last letter or any letter of a word, like *plann* for *plan* and *ommission* for *omission.*
10. *Transposition of letters or words:* mind working one step ahead of the fingers; slow typist transposes letters, like *hte,* and the fast typist transposes words, like *the of.*
11. *Anticipation error:* letting the mind run ahead of the writing, so that some letter in a word ahead is written instead of the letter that should have been written, like *womorrow* for *tomorrow,* or as with the faster writer, some word ahead may be anticipated and written. This error belongs to the fast reader.
12. *Motorization error:* made through the influence of a motorized vocabulary. The sequence of letters in a word suggests a sequence that has been motorized, like *withing* for *within* or *enought* for *enough.*

13. *Inattention error:* mind wandering causing changes in word or letter sequence; omission or repetition of words, phrases, or a line; misspelling a word, like *judgement* for *judgment;* spacing in the body of a word. When the eyes move to the beginning of a new line of the copy, they may drop down two lines or pick up the same line if the writer is thinking of something else.

14. *Distraction error:* results when the eyes are taken away from the copy because of some other influence, like someone entering the room; omission, insertion, or repetition of words, phrases, or lines.

15. *Mechanics of writing:* errors due to incorrect capitalization, paragraphing, punctuation, syllabication, and so on.

After the teacher and/or student identify the errors that need correcting, the teacher demonstrates and/or explains the proper procedure to be used and assigns appropriate drills and exercises. (See Module 6.3, Developing Technique.) One aid in individualizing instruction is for the teacher to prepare sound slides, film loops, or other audiovisual materials illustrating and explaining proper technique. He or she may wish to assemble a resource file of drills and exercises for practice and review, or to use one of the published drill books with a good index so one can easily locate an appropriate drill to correct a specific problem.

From the earliest stages of typewriting instruction, the teacher should emphasize proper use of operating controls. Special drills and exercises, such as return-the-carriage drills, columnar typing, and sentences with many capital letters, are important in developing correct technique and speed in using controls.

Some typewriting errors would be eliminated if the reading ahead tendency could be reduced. Students should be taught to read copy carefully and at a speed that matches their typewriting rates. Close attention must be paid to the exact sequence of letters in each word. Poor reading habits result in spelling, punctuation, and paragraphing errors as well as the addition, omission, and transposition of words. Correct habits of reading for typewriting require the typist to move his or her eyes smoothly and continuously along the lines of copy, reading slowly, carefully, and attentively. Typists read about one second ahead of their fingers. For a beginning typist, this is about one letter ahead of his or her fingers; for more advanced typists, one word. The student should be reminded that the eye is to supply the copy to the hands as needed. Receiving a stimulus for striking keys, not comprehension, is the major purpose of reading for typewriting. But paying attention to the thought of the material being typed is also necessary if the typist is to typewrite sense regularly and consistently.

Immediate error recognition and correction is important. Students should be reminded that much practice is of no value unless the stroking error is immediately recognized and corrected.

SPEED AND ACCURACY DEVELOPMENT PLAN

Speed and accuracy are not developed incidentally but are the result of systematic instruction and practice. The following procedure illustrates how a teacher might go about organizing an instructional plan for a student. It is important to remember that (1) speed and accuracy are set up on an individual basis and (2) in the early stages of typing, *relative* speed of stroking precedes accuracy emphasis, but the principal emphasis is on technique.

Speed development

1. Assign each student a practice exercise at a rate of speed slightly above (2–3 *wam*) previous speed goal.
2. When speed in Step 1 is reached, the student progresses to material of the next longer length (for example 27–28 *wam*) and practices until he or she completes it in the time allowed. Only gross speed is figured; errors are disregarded. If students are not earnestly trying to follow the copy, you may decide to set some error limit as a criterion for progressing to the next level.
3. Continue the procedure in Step 2 (in increasing increments of 2–3 *wam*) until the student reaches the immediate speed goal: for example, 30 *wam* for students beginning at 25 *wam* in Step 1.

Have available a resource file of materials containing writings of increasing increments—such as 2–3 *wam*. Some teachers have the student complete two different writings at the immediate speed goal before he or she changes speed objectives. Record scores on individual progress charts. Also indicate the goal for the next practice session so the student will know whether he or she is to continue with speed or change to an accuracy drill. Teachers should check progress charts regularly to determine whether or not students are, indeed, alternating goals.

Zimmer suggests a six-step method for developing speed in typewriting classes:[20]

1. Each student establishes his or her previous speed per minute and then determines the quarter of a minute speed. (For example, the student typed 20 *wam* or 5 words per quarter minute.)
2. The student sets a speed goal that is between 4–8 *wam* higher (20 words plus 4 words = new goal of 24 words).
3. Student determines the quarter-minute speed required to achieve this goal (4 words divided by 4 = 1 word in one quarter of a minute).
4. The student adds this figure to the quarter of a minute speed (5 words + 1 word = 6 words per quarter minute).
5. In the practice copy, the student circles every sixth word (30 strokes) for a one-, two-, or three-minute writing.
6. While being timed, the student pushes to reach each circled word as the instructor calls "quarter minute."

The student's speed goal is determined by his or her present speed and the length of the timed writing. Higher speed goals should be set for one-minute and two-minute timed writings than for five-minute writings. A lower goal is set for a student who types at a lower rate of speed than for one with a higher rate of stroking. A study by Hudson as reported by West suggests the following increases for practice sessions of five minutes:[21]

20–29 *gwam*	less than 5 *wam*
30–39 *gwam*	less than 9 *wam*
40–49 *gwam*	less than 12 *wam*
50–59 *gwam*	less than 15 *wam*

Accuracy

1. Upon reaching the speed objective (such as 30 *wam*), the student drops back to a paragraph or sentence writing 3–4 *wam* below that speed (26–27 *wam*). The goal then is to complete the writing in the time allowed within the error limit established by the teacher—usually 2–3 *wam*.

2. When the student has achieved the objective in Step 1, he or she moves to sentences at an increased rate, working toward the previous speed goal (30 *wam*) while staying within the error limit. When this goal is achieved, the student is ready to return to a new speed goal.

Timed writings for both speed and accuracy usually begin with one-minute writings and gradually move to five-minute writings. Rest time between timed writings is in proportion to the length of the writing, ranging from fifteen to twenty seconds between one-minute writings to one minute between five-minute writings.

MEASURING SPEED

Typewriting authorities do not agree on how to measure speed on straight copy. Some feel that the teacher and student should not be concerned with errors during speed practice on straight-copy matter and that the student's speed is his or her *gross words a minute* (total words divided by total number of minutes typed. Five strokes, including characters and spaces, equals one word. If a student types 200 words in 5 minutes, *gwam* score would be 40). Others feel that a one-word or five-word penalty causes the student to exhibit greater care. To figure the *correct words a minute* using a one-word penalty for errors, subtract the number of errors from the total number of words and divide the result by the number of minutes typed. Thus, the same student who made 5 errors in 200 words in 5 minutes would compute *cwam* as follows: 200 words – 5 errors = 195/5 = 39 *cwam*. A popular method now used to figure speed is *gross words a minute with an error limit*. This means that the total number of words are divided by the number of minutes with no deduction for errors. Errors are listed separately and are usually limited to one or two per minute. The above student's *gwan* with error limit score would be 40/5.

Another method of measuring speed is net words a minute. The *nwam* procedure is to subtract 10 words for each error from the total words and divide by the number of minutes. Therefore, using the previous example, 200 words − 50 (10 X 5 errors) = 150 words ÷ 5 minutes = 30 *nwam.* This method has several disadvantages, especially when used in the first and second semesters: (1) the heavy error penalty is discouraging to the beginning typist, (2) figuring the score is time-consuming, and (3) the composite score does not reflect the actual speed/accuracy skills of students.

module 6.4
LEARNING ACTIVITIES

1. Begin a collection of drills for developing speed and accuracy in the typewriting class.
2. Prepare a minilesson (live or soundtape) in which you introduce timed writings to students. Indicate the educational level—middle school/junior high, high school, or postsecondary.
3. Analyze the errors on one student's typewriting paper and classify them according to Clem's classification. Select three of the errors, give the possible causes, and indicate the corrective measures the student should follow.
4. Select a paragraph from a book, periodical, or other source. Calculate the syllabic intensity and the stroke intensity of the copy. Classify the copy as easy, average, or difficult. In which semester of typing would it probably be most appropriate to use?
5. Take a speed test or secure one from a student. Compute the speed using *gwam, cwam, gwam* with error limit, and *nwam.*
6. Read and report on at least two articles by different authors dealing with the use of timed writings as a teaching-learning device.
7. Review at least two different typewriting books (junior high, high school, or college level). At what point are speed-oriented timed writings introduced? At what point are timed writings introduced for writings developing accuracy? What is the length of the initial writings? What is the length of timed writings contained in each book? What is the syllabic intensity and stroke intensity of speed timings at several points throughout the text?
8. Select one type of error that may be hindering a student's speed and/or accuracy development. Prepare a self-instructional package to correct the error. (Your package might contain a cassette tape, script, slides; film loops; or small charts or illustrations.)

module 6.4
SELF-TEST

A. Discussion Questions
1. Explain two different approaches for developing speed and accuracy. Indicate which you prefer and why.
2. Identify five guidelines for developing speed and accuracy in typewriting.
3. Explain the plan you prefer for measuring speed in a given quarter or semester of typewriting. Tell why you prefer this plan.

B. True or False

_____   4.   Normally it takes less time for a student to progress from 40–50 words per minute than from 20–30 words a minute.

_____   5.   Errors made on timed practice of problem material should be ignored.

_____   6.   In the earlier stages of instruction, "all-purpose" drills are as effective for speed-building purposes as are specially devised drills.

_____   7.   In a procedural sense, repetition in typewriting is more important than Clem's concept of re-creation.

_____   8.   Students should be taught to read copy somewhat slower than their normal typing rate.

C. Multiple Choice

_____   9.   The total number of words typed divided by the number of minutes equals (a) *twam,* (b) *nwam,* (c) *cwam,* (d) *gwam.*

_____   10.   In the early stages of typewriting instruction, copy with a syllabic intensity of (a) 1.03, (b) 1.18, (c) 1.27, (d) 1.50, would be most appropriate for speed development.

_____   11.   Initially, the technique approach gives (a) equal emphasis to speed and accuracy, (b) little emphasis to speed and accuracy, (c) equal emphasis to technique, speed, and accuracy, (d) emphasis to technique and relative speed.

_____   12.   The length of initial timed writings in class should be (a) one-quarter minute, (b) one minute, (c) three minutes, (d) five minutes.

_____   13.   A characteristic that distinguishes the beginning typist from the expert typist is (a) rhythm, (b) continuity, (c) error, (d) intensity.

_____   14.   Students should be taught to read typewritten copy (a) several words at a time, (b) on a letter-by-letter basis, (c) at a rate matching their typing speed, (d) at a rate faster than their typing speed.

module 6.5
DEVELOPING PRODUCTION COMPETENCIES

After completing this module, you should be able to (1) define production typewriting and describe the content of production tasks, (2) explain a plan for developing competence in production typewriting, (3) describe two methods of proofreading, (4) demonstrate two correction techniques, and (5) explain three methods of scoring production typewriting.

The long-range goal of all typewriting instruction is production; that is, students produce a sufficient quantity of typewritten work for personal or professional use in a given period of time. When your students achieve a speed of twenty-five to thirty gross words per minute on five-minute writings, they are ready to begin applying their basic skills to production-type tasks. This means that the concept of production typing is introduced in the first-semester course, with the difficulty and length of the production period gradually increased as students improve in speed and accuracy, and as they develop the confidence and ability to handle the varied tasks.

Production typewriting differs from straight-copy typewriting in that generally it includes *all* the activities that go into the preparation of typewritten papers, from reading the directions and planning the total job to correctly disposing of the completed papers. Thus, students have to handle the materials, adjust and operate the typewriter, produce copy in acceptable form, proofread the copy, and make necessary corrections. To complete a production assignment, they use several skills other than those specifically related to basic typewriting. These skills include problem solving, decision making using reference sources, handling materials efficiently, and evaluating the final product against a predetermined standard. Production jobs differ in their complexity and in the number and kinds of skills needed to complete them.

Muhich[22] found that the time spent by the student in planning, paper handling, adjusting the typewriter, making decisions, and other similar nontyping activities often exceeds the time spent in keystroking. As production tasks become more complex, the contributions made by raw or basic typewriting skill to the production of those tasks become fewer. If nontyping tasks contribute at least as much as typing tasks in production rate, then teachers should provide instruction and practice in these tasks.

PRODUCTION TYPEWRITING APPROACHES

There are several different approaches to developing competency in production typewriting; all of these incorporate three general areas of emphasis. First, students are introduced to new or difficult features of the production task and they are drilled on the appropriate technique—such as sequence and placement of parts of a business letter. Second, students learn and practice standards and optional procedures in typing various production tasks—such as those involved in letter placement and differing letter formats. Third, students draw on the knowledge acquired in previous steps and assignments to complete all of the activities related to a production job including planning, implementing, and evaluating steps.

Russon and Wanous[23] propose a six-step plan for developing production typewriting competence.

> Step 1. *The approach in production typewriting.* In this step, the student is introduced to the general nature of the form and to new or unique features of the task.

Step 2. *Problem skill building.* During this phase, students are drilled in the techniques of production typewriting. Examples of these drills include time-comparison drill, drill on parts of the problem, guided writing on problem copy, timed writing on production-type copy, work-habit drill, and judgment-placement drill.

Step 3. *Presenting optional procedures.* In this step, students review standard and optional procedures involving width of margins, punctuation, and letter styles.

Step 4. *Problem solving and decision making.* This step requires the student to make his or her own decisions in production tasks. The tasks used in developing these problem-solving, decision-making skills should be graduated in difficulty. For example, in the first task, the student should have to make only one decision.

Step 5. *Developing good work habits.* Production typing requires the student to read directions carefully before starting to type, to assemble needed materials, and to arrange the materials to make them accessible. In planning the design of the typewriting work area, students should keep the following principles of layout in mind:

a. There should be a standard place for each tool and type of material needed.
b. There should be adequate space for each activity.
c. Needed materials should be separated and properly labeled.
d. All materials needed should be within easy reach of the typist.
e. Double and triple handling of materials should be avoided.[24]

Step 6. *Measurement and evaluation.* To be realistic, measurement should include all the activities that are essential to the job. These activities include such items as reading directions, assembling and inserting papers into the typewriter, making machine adjustments, typing, proofreading, correcting errors, and disposing of the finished product. An acceptable standard of production work is mailability or usability, accomplished in a reasonable period of time. Although the standards may vary from teacher to teacher, there is agreement on the following quality standards:

a. In content, the copy should be a faithful reproduction of the original document.
b. All typographical errors should be neatly erased and corrected.
c. The type should be uniformly clean and even.
d. Spelling, punctuation, capitalization, and word division must be correct.
e. Standard practices in preparing the paper must be observed.
f. Decisions made on variable practices must be in good taste and lend to the readability of the document.[25]

Several different methods are used in introducing a new problem to students. In one approach, the new elements may be part of the total problem. The *orientation problem* focuses on the new elements and frequently is a portion of the problem. After typing the orientation problem, the student types the complete problem, including the new skill introduced in the orientation, as shown in the following example on page 215.[26]

40B ■ **HORIZONTAL CENTERING:**   LINES [15] twice (Half sheets; DS; begin on Line 9)

<table>
<tr><td colspan="2">Get Ready to Center</td><td colspan="2">How to Center</td></tr>
</table>

Get Ready to Center

1. Insert paper with left edge at zero.
2. Move left margin stop to 0, right margin stop to end of scale.
3. Clear all tab stops.
4. Set a tab stop at horizontal center of paper.

How to Center

1. Tabulate to center of paper; from center, backspace *once* for each *two* letters, figures, spaces, or punctuation marks in the line: as ST (backspace) EP (backspace) S space (backspace).
2. Do not backspace for an odd or leftover stroke.
3. Begin to type where the backspacing ends.

Line 9
10
11
12
13
14
15
16
17
18
19
20
21
22
23
24

                    STEPS IN HORIZONTAL CENTERING
                                                TS

          Move margin stops to ends of scale
                                            DS
                Clear all tabulator stops

      Move carriage (carrier) to exact center of paper

          Set tabulator stop at center of paper

                Backspace "once for two"

      In backspacing, disregard odd or leftover stroke

            Begin to type where backspacing ends

To triple-space when the machine is set for double spacing, (1) operate the carriage return once and (2) space forward one line space by hand, using the cylinder knob.

40C ■ **PROBLEM TYPING:**   CENTERED ANNOUNCEMENTS [17] (Half sheets)

1. Place typed copy of 40B, page 67, beside your typewriter for easy reference.
2. Follow those steps in typing Problems 1 and 2.

Problem 1: On a half sheet, center each line of the announcement at the right. Begin on Line 13. Use single spacing (SS).

Problem 2: Repeat Problem 1, double-spaced (DS). Begin on Line 11. TS after heading.

	Words
WALNUT CREEK PLAYERS *TS*	4
announce casting tryouts for	10
"Sound of Music"	13
3:30-5:30 p.m. in the	18
Little Theater of the Music Building	25
Monday-Friday, October 2-6	30

In another approach, the students are provided a model of the problem with directions for typing it.[27] Directions are repeated and new terms are identified on the model itself, as shown in the example on page 216.

In a third approach, the teacher "talks" the students through the task, as shown in the following example:

Set your margins 1½ inches from the left and the right edges of your paper; single space; set a tab stop at 50; twirl your cylinder knob to about two inches from the top of the paper (approximately twelve to fifteen spaces down from the top); tab to 50 and type today's date. Twirl your cylinder knob so that the paper is moved up about an inch (approximately six line spaces from the date); type the inside address at the left margin.

The teacher should dictate and type with the class—Mr. John J. Johnson (return); 234 First Avenue (return); New York, New York (depress space bar three times 1, 2, 3); type Zip Code number, 10036; (return and space again).

Dear Mr. Johnson (return and space again); begin the first paragraph of the letter.[28]

U G A
Business Education, Inc.

April 4, 19--

(DS)

SPECIAL DELIVERY (Mailing Notation)

(DS)

Mr. Ralph E. Wilson, Office Manager (Inside Address)
Commerce Office Equipment, Inc.
P.O. Box 3749
Commerce, GA   30529

(DS)

Dear Mr. Wilson   (Salutation)

(DS)

The information that you requested about letter styles and features is being forwarded to you under separate cover. The booklet describes those features that are most universally used in the business world today.

As you read the booklet, you should note that paragraphs   (Body) are indented five spaces in the Modified Block Letter with indented paragraphs. Other features shown in the sample indicate that the date, the complimentary close, the company name, and the writer's name are begun at the center of the paper. When punctuation marks are omitted after the salutation and complimentary close, we describe this as Open Punctuation.

Special mailing notations (AIR MAIL, SPECIAL DELIVERY) are typed in all capital letters at the left margin, a double space below the date line.

The company name in the closing lines is used when a letter is typed on plain paper instead of letterhead. However, we have placed it in our illustrations so you can see its correct placement. The writer's name and title are used in the closing lines along with the typist's reference initials.

Thank you for requesting our booklet on letter styles. After you have had opportunity to review it, we would appreciate your comments about it.

(Complimentary Close)   Sincerely yours

(DS)

(Company Name)   UGA BUSINESS EDUCATION, INC.

(3 blank lines -- type on 4th line)

(Writer's Name & Title)   J. Stephen Jones, Director

bbj (Reference Initials of Typist)

Keep the letter short; your main emphasis here is on placement of the letter. You may want to dictate one or two sentences or have the students use the first sentence or two from a letter in the typewriting book. Continue dictating the script for and the placement of the complimentary close and the position for the typed name.

West recommends carrying students quickly through several exercises followed by typing the same letter from the typewriting book or a copy provided by the teacher. Connelly recommends that after the demonstration students be given an opportunity to practice each part of the letter separately—for example, to type the inside address three times. A good related drill is to have students practice estimating distance. For instance, have them twirl the cylinder knob to about two inches from the top of the paper and type a *1;* then reinsert the paper and space down two inches or twelve line spaces and type a *2;* compare the closeness of the *1* and *2.*

Following a principle of problem-solving skill development, the teacher assigns problems of graduated difficulty and frequently evaluates student performance in unguided writings to identify those students needing additional guided practice. Since problem solving and decision making constitute a major portion of vocational typewriting, students should have as much practice as possible using a variety of materials. Leonard[29] used articles from newspapers, television ads, football programs, and so on, to give students practical experience in typing tables, manuscripts, tabulation, and centering. She selected articles of varying difficulty—some required only one or two decisions, such as deciding on a heading and column headings before typing a table with horizontal and vertical placements. Others were more difficult, such as having to decide how much information to include, selecting a title, subtitle, and column headings, as well as placement on the page. The teacher wrote directions in longhand for each activity. Since the activities were different, each student had to work independently although the teacher helped students, as needed, with specific problems. When the student was satisfied with his or her work, he or she took it to another student to be evaluated. The evaluation was then signed by the student examiner. The teacher also checked the paper, circling in red those errors that were not discovered by the student examiner.

As part of the instructional process, the teacher makes sure that students can perform (providing instruction when necessary) certain related skills that are needed to complete various production tasks. To produce mailable copy on letters, reports, forms, and manuscripts, students need to know how to center vertically and horizontally; to set up tables; to divide words at ends of lines; to spell, punctuate, and capitalize copy correctly; to proofread; and to make acceptable corrections. It is important to provide instruction and practice so that students can apply these skills in a number of different situations. For instance, instead of telling students where to set the margins and tabulator to address business-size envelopes, teach them to type the address halfway down and five spaces to the left of center of the envelope. The student can then apply these directions to envelopes of all sizes. Judgment-placement drills focusing on determining the half-way down point on the envelope are an example of relevant related instructional content.

Multimedia learning packages covering related skills provide a means for individualizing instruction. Packages can be used for initial instruction, review, or remediation, depending on student needs. Having these types of materials available allows the teacher more time for individual and small-group instruction, diagnosis of student progress, and prescription of instruction.

PROOFREADING

Proofreading is one of the related typewriting skills that students need to master, and it is a skill that must be taught. For effective proofreading, the student is taught to read the copy slowly, word for word two times, once for meaning and again for correctness of details. A commonly used method of proofreading is the paper-bail method; the proofreading is done before the work is removed from the typewriter. The student follows the typewritten line along the paper bail, making corrections as needed. As each line is proofread, the student turns the cylinder. When the proofreader-copyholder method is used, students work in pairs. The typist reads aloud from the original and the partner checks for errors in the copy. For important documents, the procedure should be repeated in reverse.

The business teacher provides a list of errors for students to locate in the copy and conducts drills to help students become efficient proofreaders. Proofreading errors may be classified into four categories: arrangement; technical information; thought conveyance; and figures, dates, and amounts. One procedure in checking production work is to "check the problem until an error is found. Then the teacher marks the problem unacceptable and returns it to the student so that he or she is still responsible for locating the error(s) which have been overlooked."[30]

The overhead projector and individualized packages provide effective mediums for instruction in proofreading. In one sense, it is psychologically more effective to reward students for finding and correcting their errors than to penalize them for not finding and correcting them. On the other hand, penalizing students for errors can be justified in view of what happens on the job. In any event, proofreading is an important business skill that must be learned.

CORRECTION TECHNIQUES

Many typewriting specialists recommend that erasing and other correction techniques, such as (1) the use of correction paper and liquid correction fluid, (2) strikeovers that are acceptable, and (3) squeezing and spreading letters, be taught in the application phase of typewriting.

To make a neat erasure, the typist should (1) roll the paper forward (or backward if the error is at the lower third of the page); (2) lift the paper bail; (3) move the carriage, using the margin release, to the side nearest the error, making sure that erasures will not fall into the type basket, (on electric machines, move the element to the right or left); (4) gently erase the error using an up-down stroke, blowing the crumbs away as they accumulate. (See typewriting text for method of erasing carbon copies.) Illustration 6.2 shows the advantages and disadvantages of various types of correction methods.

There are some strikeovers that are acceptable—that is, the error is not detectable. Examples include the following:

ERROR	ACCEPTABLE STRIKEOVER
c	e,d,o
o	p
i	f,t
n	h
b	B
.	,

Procedures for squeezing and spreading letters vary according to the kind of typewriter. Typewriting textbooks provide these directions.

The teacher should stress that applied exercises and drills must be handed in with all errors neatly corrected. Students should be given timed drills periodically in which they are to make various corrections. The teacher will find ample drills and exercises in typewriting books or he or she may want to construct some.

PRODUCTION STANDARDS

There are several measurements for the business teacher to consider in evaluating the student's work. A commonly used measure is net production rate a minute (*n-pram*). Errors are erased and corrected, and a penalty (usually 10 words for each error) is deducted for each uncorrected error. The number of gross words minus the penalty is divided by the length of the writing (number of minutes) to determine *n-pram*. For example, if a student typed 750 words in 15 minutes with 5 uncorrected errors, the *n-pram* would be 47 (750 −50 = 700 ÷ 15 = 47).

Another measurement is mailable words a minute (*mwam*) which penalizes students 26 seconds for each error in the timed writing. (According to Balsley, 26 seconds represents the average amount of time for making a correction without a carbon copy.[31]) To figure *mwam*, add 26 seconds for each error to the time of the writing and divide this amount of time into the total words typed. Thus the student who typed 750 words in 15 minutes with 5 errors would have a *mwam* score of 44 (5 errors × 26 seconds = 130 seconds = 2 minutes 10 seconds; 15 mintues + 2 minutes 10 seconds = 17 minutes 10 seconds; 750 words divided by 17 1/6 = 44).

The following plan is recommended by Hoskinson:[32]

illustration 6.2
CORRECTION METHODS—ADVANTAGES AND DISADVANTAGES

	ERASER	CORRECTION FLUIDS		CORRECTION PAPER	CORRECTION RIBBON	CORRECTING TYPEWRITER
		CHEMICAL	WATER-BASE			
TIME REQUIRED	Done correctly, the most time consuming method.	Fast-dry formula dries in 10–12 seconds.	Takes about 45 seconds to dry.	Extra backspace time is needed.	Extra backspace time is needed.	Fast.
PERMANENCY	Permanent.	Permanent.	Permanent.	Temporary; chalky substance may flake off in mail or file.	Temporary; chalky substance may flake off in mail or file.	Permanent.
EFFECT ON PAPER	Makes indention on paper surface; can make paper fuzzy.	Bonds itself to paper making like-new surface for typing.	Bonds itself to paper making like-new surface for typing.	Chalklike substance adheres to paper.	Chalklike substance adheres to paper.	Lifts carbon ink off or covers carbon ink with chalklike substance.
TECHNIQUE INVOLVED	Practice needed to acquire technique.	Practice needed to acquire technique.	Practice needed to acquire technique.	Little technique needed.	No technique needed.	Knowledge of correcting typewriter required.
MATERIALS REQUIRED	Eraser, index cards, type cleaner, metal letter protector.	Bottle of correction fluid, thinner.	Bottle of correction fluid.	Appropriate type of correction paper for paper being corrected.	Correction ribbon.	Self-correcting typewriter, special ribbons.
CORRECTIONS ON COLORED PAPER	Many times erases pigment; spots.	Comes in white and colors.	Comes in white and colors.	Comes in white and limited colors.	Comes in white only.	Corrects on all colors.
OTHER POSSIBLE CORRECTIONS	Corrects typewritten or pen errors; corrects before or after removed from typewriter.	Corrects typewritten or pen errors; corrects before or after removed from typewriter.	Corrects typewritten or pen errors; corrects before or after removed from typewriter.	Corrects only typewritten errors; once removed from typewriter, very difficult to reinsert.	Corrects only typewritten errors; once removed from typewriter, very difficult to reinsert.	Corrects only typewritten errors; once removed from typewriter, very difficult to reinsert.
CARBON COPIES/ PHOTOCOPIES	Corrects carbon copies; smears chemical surface on some photocopies.	Corrects carbon copies; can smear some photocopies.	Corrects carbon copies; will not smear photocopies.	Corrects carbon copies; will not correct photocopies.	Will not correct carbon copies or photocopies.	Will not correct carbon copies or photocopies.

1. Select enough problems to challenge better students in 30 minutes. (Try to parallel job requirements in the later stages.)
2. Assign 12 points for each problem. (You may use variable points for problems of varying difficulty, but be sure the total points for each problem are divisible by 4.)
3. Deduct 2 points for each error.
4. For a problem not finished when time is called:
   award 9 points if it is approximately ¾ done
   award 6 points if it is approximately ½ done
   award 3 points if it is approximately ¼ done.
5. Determine total points and assign a letter grade, using a "curve" tempered with judgment.

Timed writings for production typing are ordinarily twenty-five to thirty minutes in length and generally consist of a mixture of three or four different tasks such as preparing a rough draft, a letter, or an invoice. The number of tasks depends on the length and difficulty of each part and the test time interval.

An alternate type of evaluation consists of restricting the test to problems or units of the same type, such as addressing envelopes or typing business letters, with all units being of the same difficulty. Enough letters can be duplicated on one legal size sheet to take care of a test twenty-five to thirty minutes in length. An example of two business letters is given to illustrate this type of problem typewriting.

module 6.5
LEARNING ACTIVITIES

1. Using typewriting books and professional journals for references, begin a collection of timed writings for production typewriting, indicating your standards.
2. Prepare visual(s) demonstrating two different correction techniques.
3. Take a production test or obtain one from a typewriting class and compute the rate using *n-pram, mwam,* and total number of points according to Hoskinson's plan.
4. Prepare a chart that you can display in your classroom, specifying mailability standards for production typewriting tasks.
5. Review literature as needed and prepare a business letter incorporating the most frequently made errors. Put the letter on a transparency so that you may challenge your class to find all the errors.
6. Observe and time an advanced student in a production typewriting assignment. What percentage of the time was spent on nontyping tasks? How could the student improve his or her production typing efficiency?
7. Select one skill related to production typewriting, such as tabulating, proofreading, or centering, and prepare a self-instructional unit or module to teach the skill.

module 6.5
SELF—TEST

A. Discussion Questions
1. Outline a plan for developing production typewriting competencies.
2. Why is problem solving an important skill in production typewriting?

PRODUCTION TEST ON BUSINESS LETTERS

LETTER STYLE: ___ Full Block   PUNCTUATION: ___ Mixed
                 ___ Modified Block   ___ Open
                 ___ Modified Block with   ___ Closed
                       Indented Paragraphs
                 ___ AMS Simplified

1. (148 words)   Current Date

    Mr. Richard Rowell, 812 Dillon Building, Atlanta, Georgia 30303
    Dear Mr. Rowell: I am answering your letter to our manager, Mr. Johnson,
    in which you asked him whether he could talk to the meeting of your
    national council, which will be held in Philadelphia on April 16. I am
    afraid that Mr. Johnson will have to disappoint you. For the past several
    weeks, he has been busy with the reorganization of a number of our plants
    in Mexico; consequently, he may have to leave for that country on a moment's
    notice. (P) I think, though, that you might like to invite Mr. Frank Brown,
    who is director of public relations for our organization. If you will invite
    him, I think he will be happy to accept. (P) If at any time I can help
    you in any other way, I hope you will be sure to write me. Very truly yours,
    Wyatt-Bigelow Company, Clifton A. Baxter, President (S)

2. (146 words)   Current Date

    Mr. Walter L. Bishop, 1484 Whiteford Avenue, Belmont, California 94002
    Dear Mr. Bishop: We are sorry to hear of your decision not to let us
    publish your book. While we regret your decision, we must accept it as
    final. (P) As I told you, we think very highly of your manuscript; and
    we think it would have had a good sale if it had been published under the
    plan that I have outlined to you. I am sure you realize, though, that no
    publisher can tell in advance the actual success that any book will enjoy;
    consequently, we find it necessary to protect ourselves by arranging a
    contract such as the one we offer you. (P) If at any time in the future you
    wish to take up the matter again, we shall be very glad to hear from you.
    In the meantime, we are returning the manuscript to you. Very truly yours,
    Standard Press, Inc., Richard R. Bennington, President (S)

3. List the tasks (activities) a student might perform in order to complete a production
    typewriting assignment.

B. Multiple Choice

_____   4. Timed production typewriting includes (a) all activities that go into the
preparation of typewritten papers, (b) more typing than nontyping tasks, (c) all tasks
from listening to directions to proofreading the copy, (d) both five-minute and
thirty-minute writings.

_____   5. For copy to be *mailable*, the student should (a) make no errors, (b)
correct all errors, (c) correct most of the errors, (d) correct some of the errors.

_____   6. One of the following is *not* a method of introducing a new problem to
students during production typing: (a) using an orientation problem, (b) providing
students with a model problem, (c) giving students extra time to study the problem,
(d) providing drill on related skills.

module 6.6
PLANNING FOR INSTRUCTION

After completing this module, you should be able to prepare a lesson plan, indicating ways of meeting student differences. Appropriate planning is the key to an effective instructional program. How much and what kinds of plans depend on the teacher's experience and the nature of the class.

PLANNING THE COURSE

When the teacher plans the typing course, he or she writes the general objectives, selects the units to be included, and determines the emphasis for each, taking into consideration the amount of time available (quarter, semester, year), the purpose of the course (vocational, personal use), and the students. These factors are essential to planning a traditional course and/or developing or selecting instructional modules for an individualized course.

The authors of most typewriting textbooks organize the course content into units or cycles, indicating the amount of emphasis for each topic by the number of lessons assigned, as shown by the following example:[33]

Cycle 1   Basic Typing

PHASE 1: BASIC TYPING SKILLS		
Unit	*Lesson*	
1	1–15	The Letter Key
2	16–20	Improving Stroking Precision
3	21–30	Figures and Basic Symbols
4	31–33	Reading/Typing Response Patterns
5	34–37	Special Symbols
6	38–39	Evaluating Basic Typing Skills
PHASE 2: BASIC TYPING APPLICATION		
Unit	*Lesson*	
7	40–51	Centering/Tabulating/Composing
8	52–63	Personal/Business Communications
9	·64–71	Themes/Outlines/Report Manuscripts
10	72–75	Inventory/Measurement

It is important that the teacher not be restricted by the content, organization, and time periods recommended in the textbooks, but plan lessons and select materials to meet the needs of students. For the beginning teacher, a good textbook provides a framework for teaching skills normally included in a typing course.

LESSON PLANNING

Planning effective lessons is a necessary skill for business teachers. The lesson plan must be so organized that when you meet your class you are fully prepared to start the lesson promptly and carry it through to a successful conclusion.

In an individualized setting, the teacher selects the appropriate module and drills for each student. Normally, if the student has satisfactorily completed a module, he or she begins the next one in the series. The teacher monitors student progress through the modules, giving help as needed. If the student cannot satisfactorily complete the module, the teacher prescribes the appropriate alternate modules or instruction. In a conventional class, the teacher prepares daily lesson plans. The following is a sample lesson plan that a teacher might prepare for a beginning typing class. Notice that content and procedures are indicated in the plan.

Typewriting I

Before class:
1. Assemble transparencies:
   keyboard
   words aligned at center
   names centered horizontally and off-center
2. Overhead projector
3. Student folders with drills for Activity 4 listed

Objectives:
1. To be able to use backspace key to align words at center of page.
2. To be able to center horizontally three lists of names in fifteen minutes or less.

Materials: Textbook, Lesson 13, pp. 30–33
   Transparencies (see "Before class")
   Drills

Activities:
1. Conditioning Practice
   Warm-up
   Speed check—two half-minute timed writings
   Accuracy—repeated double letters
2. Introduce Backspace Key
   Show backspace key on transparency
   Demonstrate using key, verbalizing steps
   Students locate key, observing moving finger from home-row position to backspace key; practice reach two to three times without watching finger
   Show example of words aligned at center on transparency
   Demonstrate aligning words, verbalizing steps
   "Talk" students through example—write words to be used on chalkboard
   Students type exercise from book

Observe students as they type
3. Center Names Horizontally
    Show sample of names centered and off-center on transparency
    Briefly discuss ways of centering
    Demonstrate backspacing, verbalizing steps
    "Talk" students through problem, write name on chalkboard
    Students type problem from book
    Observe students at work, providing help as needed
    Students turn in papers in proper basket
4. Individualized Practice
    Students work on drills prescribed by teacher, in student folder
    Observe students, noting technique, and so on
5. Clean Up Work Station

Evaluation:
1. Examine problem-horizontal centering, identify students needing additional help
2. Observe student typing individual drills, noting areas of strength and weakness.

Once the basic keyboard skills have been learned, the most effective approach to teaching typing is a well-implemented individualized one in which students progress at their own pace and the teacher prescribes the specific objectives, drills, and activities for each student. (See Chapters 3 and 5 on developing and implementing individualized instruction.) If the teacher is unable to implement an individualized program because of lack of materials and facilities or insufficient knowledge and skills, he or she can modify instruction in a traditional classroom. The following are some examples of modifications that a teacher might make to better provide for the learning needs of students.

1. Assign drills based on needs. Remedial technique drills, additional practice on skill presented in textbook. (Remember, some students need more *time* than others to master a skill or technique.)
    Teacher has multiple copies of a variety of drills so that differentiated assignments can be made.
2. Vary difficulty and length of problems covering same skill. (Some students always finish the textbook problem early! They should not be penalized by typing "more of the same.")
    Teacher needs multiple copies of a variety of materials of differing lengths and difficulty levels to be used for problems. (Don't forget sources such as newspapers, football programs, magazines.)
3. Use a variety of visual and auditory techniques to present new materials, skills. The majority of the class may be able to learn a new skill from the procedures described in the textbook and demonstration/explanation. Some students will need more help—taped step-by-step explanations that the student can play as often as needed; slides, film loops, filmstrips, transparencies illustrating the procedure that may be accompanied by a script or recorded explanation.

As the teacher develops and/or acquires more materials, then the student can work toward mastering each skill before beginning a new one. This is not always the case when the entire class moves together through the same material at the same pace.

module 6.6
LEARNING ACTIVITY

1. Using an outline similar to the sample in this module, the sample in Module 5.3, or one approved by your instructor, prepare a daily lesson plan for Typing 1 or 2. Indicate how you would provide for individual differences.

module 6.6
SELF-TEST

1. Using Illustration 5.8 in module 5.3, evaluate the lesson plan developed in the learning activity for this module.
2. Describe two ways for meeting individual differences in a conventional setting.

module 6.7
EVALUATING TYPEWRITING PERFORMANCE

After completing this module, you should be able to (1) explain and give an example of two different methods of evaluating student performance in typewriting, (2) illustrate at least two methods of scoring straight copy and production typewriting, (3) identify standards for straight copy and production typewriting, and (4) select factors and relative weight of each that comprise grades in typewriting.

The purposes of evaluation in typewriting are generally the same as those for any business subject. Primarily, the teacher uses evaluation to diagnose weaknesses, to measure achievement in terms of course objectives and vocational standards, to motivate students, and to serve as a basis for determining grades.

METHODS OF EVALUATION

The business teacher uses two general methods to assess changes in student behavior in typewriting. One—subjective evaluation—is the primary method for assessing techniques and work habits. The only way to evaluate body position at the typewriter, for instance, is to observe the student at work. A sample Technique Check Sheet is included in Module 6.3. Each student should be given a copy of the rating scale or one should be on display in the typewriting room so that students know the techniques and work habits or traits on which they are being evaluated. In teaching the keyboard, teachers stress and evaluate techniques, especially during the first and second semesters. During the first semester, techniques may make up as much as 40 percent of the grade. Techniques continue to be stressed to a lesser degree in other semesters of typewriting instruction.

Work habits and traits are also evaluated by observation. It is important that the teacher spell out performance indicators of good work habits and traits that students need to exhibit and identify the degree of evidence that corresponds to given grade levels such as A, B, or C. Examples of expected behaviors include being on time, bringing necessary materials to class, listening when someone else is talking, and so on.

The second method the teacher uses is objective evaluation which includes knowledge tests and performance tests. The real measure of whether or not a student knows basic information such as spacing rules, syllabication, or punctuation is the extent to which he or she uses them in production or application settings. Occasionally the teacher may want to use objective tests to assess student knowledge of information such as components of the typewriter, parts of letters, and rules related to typewriting performance. These tests should, however, supplement other methods of evaluation. As Anderson and Pullis[34] point out, "Students will continue to regard typing usages and knowledges as unimportant unless the typing teacher includes these items among the factors considered in measuring and evaluating progress in the typing course."

Another type of objective test is the performance test which is used to measure students' keystroking ability and the application of basic skills to problem-solving situations. Straight copy or timed writings and production tests are examples of performance tests.

Regardless of the methods of measurement and evaluation the teacher uses, it is important that he or she specify precisely the expected student performance and behavior in the form of objectives. It is essential that students know of these expectations from the beginning of the course.

Some of the methods used by business teachers to measure and evaluate performance are discussed in other modules in this chapter. The use of Gross Words a Minute (*gwam*), Correct Words a Minute (*cwam*), Net Words a Minute (*nwam*), Words a Minute with Error Cutoff, and Gross Words a Minute with Percentage of Accuracy are examples of methods of scoring straight-copy timed writings. In the first semester of instruction, Gross Words a Minute is a widely used method of measuring performance, often giving way to a combination *gwam* with error limits after the first ten to twelve weeks. To determine *gwam*, divide the number of words by the length of the writing. To determine accuracy, the teacher may choose to set an absolute error limit; that is, to decide on the number of allowable errors for each grade, such as one error for an A, two or three errors for a B, and so on. Another way to figure accuracy is to set an error limit and not record a grade for any paper that contains more than this error limit, such as four errors per minute in the first semester.

In production typewriting, Net Production Rate a Minute (*n-pram*) is an often used method of scoring. (The teacher may want to use Gross Production Rate a Minute in the early stages of production development and not penalize the students for errors.) In this method, the errors are corrected, and a penalty, usually ten words per error, is deducted for each uncorrected error. *N-pram* equals the number of words typed, minus the penalty, divided by the length of time. A variation of the formula is expressed as

$$\frac{\text{Total Acceptable Words} + 1/2 \text{ Unacceptable Words}}{\text{Time}} = n\text{-}pram$$

Other plans of evaluation include Mailable Papers an Hour. In this method, you count the number of mailable papers typed in a certain time interval, such as thirty minutes. One disadvantage of this method is that materials are not of the same difficulty which makes it harder to measure true progress. Since the content of the copy increases in difficulty during the grading period, the quantity completed may remain the same, showing no progress in output. Mailable Words a Minute (*mwam*) is discussed in Module 6.5.

Russon and Wanous [35] describe a scoring plan that incorporates quantity and quality, Gross Words a Minute Plus Bonus.

> In this method, the total words typed is divided by the time of the test as *gwam*. Bonus points for accurate work are added as follows: 10 bonus points for verbatim papers, 5 bonus points for mailable papers, 0 bonus points for nonmailable papers. Student A types 6 papers totaling 900 words in 30 minutes. The time of the test is divided into the words; therefore, student A's production speed is 30 *gwam*. Assuming that three of these six papers were verbatim, two were mailable, and one was non-mailable, the total bonus is figured as follows:

$$10 \times 3 = 30$$
$$5 \times 2 = \underline{10}$$
$$\text{Total Bonus} = \overline{40}$$

$$\text{The Bonus is added to } gwam = 30$$
$$\text{Student A's Score} = \overline{70}$$

STANDARDS AND GRADING

Before the teacher begins the typewriting course, he or she should determine the objectives, standards, and grading plan that will be used. Several questions must be answered in order to make these decisions.

1. *Will the objectives be the same for all students in the course?* If so, am I providing for individual differences—the slow learner, the mentally retarded, the gifted student? If not, how do I justify differentiated objectives? Do I have an obligation to business standards to expect certain performances from all students? What plan for individualizing instruction will I follow: (a) objectives and material constant, time flexible? (b) objectives and material flexible, time constant? (c) objectives, material, and time flexible?

2. *On what will I base the standards for the course?* Will they be flexible from class to class or from year to year, with the best performances receiving an A, and so on? Will I use external criteria such as performance objectives and assess students according to their degree of achievement of the objectives? Will I base the external criteria on standards of local business or will I select them from the literature in the field?

3. *How will I translate student performance into grades?* Can I use Pass–Fail to indicate achievement of objectives? If a student does not achieve the objectives by the end of the grading period, do I assign an incomplete or a grade based on performance to that date? What factors combine to form the basis for a grade? How important is each factor? Do I set a scale so that a certain number of points on these factors equals a certain letter grade?

How the business teacher answers questions such as these influences his or her decisions about standards and grading. Standards need to be established and students should be aware of them from the beginning of the course. Teachers are not in agreement as to what these standards should be, but they do agree that students should be given goals that are challenging and attainable.

The following standards for straight-copy timed writings are suggested by Russon and Wanous:[36]

	HIGH SCHOOL		COLLEGE	
First Semester, 5 Minutes	45+	GWAM—A	45+	GWAM—A
	39–44	GWAM—B	41–44	GWAM—B
	32–38	GWAM—C	37–40	GWAM—C
	22–31	GWAM—D	33–36	GWAM—D
Second Semester, 5 Minutes	55+	GWAM—A	60+	GWAM—A
	47–54	GWAM—B	53–59	GWAM—B
	37–46	GWAM—C	46–52	GWAM—C
	30–36	GWAM—D	30–45	GWAM—D
Third Semester, 5 Minutes	55+	NWAM—A	67+	NWAM—A
	50–54	NWAM—B	60–66	NWAM—B
	43–49	NWAM—C	54–59	NWAM—C
	38–42	NWAM—D	45–53	NWAM—D

Zimmer[37] suggests the following grading chart:

SUGGESTED GRADING CHART FOR TIMED WRITINGS

SPEED GRADING

Week	Maximum Errors	A (90–100)	B (80–89)	C (70–79)	D (60–69)
4	—	20 or more	15–19	10–14	8–9
5	—	22	17–21	12–16	10–11
6	—	24	19–23	14–18	12–13
7	3 per minute	26	21–25	16–20	14–15
8	3 per minute	28	23–27	18–22	16–17
9	3 per minute	30	25–29	20–24	18–19
10	2 per minute	32	27–31	22–26	20–21
11	2 per minute	34	29–33	24–28	21–23
12	2 per minute	36	31–35	26–30	22–25
13	1 per minute	38	33–37	28–32	24–25
14	1 per minute	40	35–39	30–34	25–29
15	1 per minute	40	35–39	30–34	25–29

ACCURACY SCORING

Formula: (1) From 100, subtract the lowest passing grade.
(2) Multiply the number of minutes by the number of allowable errors per minute.
(3) Divide the figure derived in (1) by the figure derived in (2).

Example: (1) If the lowest passing grade is 60, $\dfrac{100}{-60}{}\Big/ 40$

$$\frac{\begin{array}{r}100\\-60\end{array}}{40}$$

(2) Multiply 5 minutes by 1 error per minute = 5.
(3) $40 \div 5 = 8$ points per error.

Error Penalty Guide*
(Assumes 60 is lowest passing grade)

			Penalty Per Error			
2	3	5				
		1 error per minute	−40	−20	−13	−8
		2 errors per minute	−20	−10	−6	−4
		3 errors per minute	−13	−6	−4	−3

Penalty is rounded off for greater ease in using.

Kaisershot's method[38] of grading timed writings combines gross words a minute with an error tolerance as shown in the table on page 231.

It is perhaps even more difficult to establish standards for vocational or production typewriting. Even among actual businesses, there are wide variations in standards due in part to the fact that every business office has different needs.

Douglas, Blanford, and Anderson[39] suggest the following standards in relating production output to basic typing skills:

SUGGESTED STRAIGHT-COPY STANDARDS IN TYPEWRITING

SEMESTER ONE

THREE-MINUTE TIMED WRITINGS—WEIGHT APPLIED TOWARD SEMESTER GRADE=40 PERCENT

GWPM		*Total Errors*
45+	A	0–2 = One bonus grade
40–44	B	3–4 = Grade remains
32–39	C	5–6 = Minus one grade
31	D	

(Example: 34/4 = C; 34/2 = B; 34/5 = D)

SEMESTER TWO

FIVE-MINUTE TIMED WRITINGS—WEIGHT APPLIED TOWARD SEMESTER GRADE = 40–45 PERCENT

GWPM		*Total Errors*
55+	A	0–3 = One bonus grade
50–54	B	4–5 = Grade remains
40–49	C	6–7 = Minus one grade
39	D	

SEMESTER THREE

FIVE-MINUTE TIMED WRITINGS—WEIGHT APPLIED TOWARD SEMESTER GRADE = 30–35 PERCENT

GWPM		*Total Errors*
65+	A	0–2 = One bonus grade
58–64	B	3–4 = Grade remains
48–57	C	5–6 = Minus one grade
47	D	

SEMESTER FOUR

GWPM		*Total Errors*
70+	A	0–2 = One bonus grade
62–69	B	3 = Grade remains
54–61	C	4–5 = Minus one grade
53	D	

Naturally, these standards serve only as rough guides since there are many variables that enter into each typewriting production job.

Grades and standards are tied together, with grades usually reflecting the degree to which standards are met. In translating student performance into grades, the teacher has to make several decisions. First, he or she must decide what factors make up the grade—technique? timed writings? work habits? production? production improvement? Next, the teacher has to decide the *relative* weight or importance to assign to each factor. The importance of the factors themselves will vary from semester to semester. For instance, technique is not as important for grading purposes in the fourth semester as in the first semester of typing instruction.

Russon and Wanous[40] suggest that these scales might be appropriate for four semesters of grading in typewriting:

Typing letters, with carbons and envelopes	½ to ⅔ basic typing rate (8–10 average length letters an hour)
Addressing envelopes	50 percent of basic rate or minimum 2 envelopes per minute
Typing rough drafts	40 to 60 percent of basic typing rate
Manuscripts with footnotes	60 to 75 percent of basic typing rate
Tabulations	25 to 50 percent of basic typing rate
Stencils	4 single-spaced stencils an hour
Transcription from voice-recording machine	25 words per minute
Typing medium-length form letters with envelopes	10 to 12 an hour

Zimmer[41] proposes a grading scale for end-of-semester based on speed, accuracy, and production, with the teacher deciding on the relative weight of each factor.

FACTORS TO BE EVALUATED AND GRADED	WEIGHTED PERCENTAGES
1. First Semester	
Techniques	30%
Basic skill competencies (straight copy, statistical copy, rough draft copy, script copy, etc.)	40%
Problem and/or production work	20%
Work attitudes and habits	10%
2. Second Semester	
Techniques	10%
Basic skill competencies	40%
Problem and production work	40%
Work attitudes and habits	10%
3. Third Semester	
Techniques	10%
Basic skill achievement	30%
Production achievement	30%
Production improvement	20%
Work attitudes and habits	10%
4. Fourth Semester	
Basic skill competencies	20%
Production achievement	40%
Production improvement	30%
Work attitudes and habits	10%

The preceding suggestions are examples of standards the business teacher may set. Each teacher must, of course, select standards and a grading system appropriate for his or her students and school setting.

module 6.7
LEARNING ACTIVITIES

1. Prepare a chart showing the factors and weights you will use to determine typewriting grades for semesters 1, 2, 3, and 4.
2. Construct an objective test covering the knowledge aspects of typewriting such as spacing, parts of the letter, and so on.
3. Examine the teachers' editions of typewriting textbooks by two different authors. What standards and grading plans does each author recommend?
4. Defend or refute the following statement: The school's primary responsibility is to the student. Therefore, different objectives should be set for each student in typewriting and he or she should be graded on the extent to which these objectives are achieved.
5. Interview two or three typewriting teachers employed at the same educational level. What standards does each use for beginning and for advanced typewriting instruction? How do they translate these standards into grades?
6. Read at least two articles on individualizing typewriting instruction. Prepare a report for the class explaining how standards and grading are handled.
7. Discuss the following: Employers (can) (cannot) furnish reliable production standards for the classroom typewriting teacher. Why or why not?
8. Should classroom training standards be identical with employment standards for students who are taking a job where typewriting is a crucial skill? Why or why not?

module 6.7
SELF-TEST

A. Discussion Questions
1. Justify the use of the following to evaluate student performance in typewriting: (a) subjective evaluation, (b) objective evaluation.
2. Explain how to compute *n-pram, gwam,* and *cwam* with error limit.
3. How do standards for straight-copy timed writings at the high school level compare with those at the college level?

B. True or False

_____ 4. Evaluation and grading are equivalent terms.

_____ 5. In production typing, net production rate a minute is a widely used method of scoring.

_____ 6. The advanced typing student should be able to type letters at one-half to two-thirds of his or her basic typing rate.

SUGGESTED PLAN FOR END-OF-SEMESTER EVALUATION

(Assumes 60 is lowest passing grade; adjust according to your own needs.)
Factors that you may desire to consider in arriving at a final grade include:

Speed

Accuracy

Production Record

1. How to determine speed grade:

    a. During the last 3 weeks of classes and on the scheduled final examination day, give a number of 5-minute timed writings.

    b. Using this chart, determine the numerical grade for each:

    Below 25 wpm is not considered an acceptable passing speed for the course.

Gross Speed	Grade	Gross Speed	Grade
25	60	35	80
26	62	36	82
27	64	37	84
28	66	38	86
29	68	39	88
30	70	40	90
31	72	41	92
32	74	42	94
33	76	43	96
34	78	44	98
		45	100

    c. Average the 3 best scores to arrive at the final speed grade. (Using 3 scores ensures against an "accidental" high score.)

    Assume: 38 wpm   86 with 2 errors

               42 wpm   94 with 4 errors

               40 wpm   90 with 2 errors
               $270 \div 3 = 90$ as the final grade for speed

    d. Using the accuracy scoring guide on page 230, determine the accuracy grade for each and then average the three.
       2 errors x 8 = 100-16 = *84*

       4 errors x 8 = 100-32 = 68

       2 errors x 8 = 100-16 = 84
               $236 \div 3 = 78.6$ as the final grade for accuracy

234

e.   Production work grades may be averaged as the basic for the production grade *or* the instructor may develop his own production examinations.

Assume 85 as the production grade.

f.   The three grades may be given equal weight.

Speed	90
Accuracy	79
Production record	85

$254 = 3 = 85$ or B (B+ where used)

or

The items way be weighted. Assume that you consider speed and accuracy as being of equal value but that production work should be doubled in value:

	Grade		Weight		Weighted Value
Speed	90	x	1	=	90
Accuracy	79	x	1	=	79
Production	85	x	2	=	170
					$339 \div 4 = 85 = B$
			but		
Speed (25 wpm)	60	x	1	=	60
Accuracy	90	x	1	=	90
Production	80	x	2	=	160
					$310 \div 4 = 77.5 = C$ or C+

_____   7.   An advantage of Mailable Papers an Hour is the speed with which a teacher can compute individual progress in output.

_____   8.   If the teacher plans to grade the typing student on technique, it should be done late in the typing course.

SUMMARY

The importance of typewriting both as a communication tool and as a vocational skill is illustrated by the large numbers of students who enroll in the course. At the elementary level, typewriting is used as an aid in learning language arts skills; at the middle school level, its major focus is personal use and career exploration. At the high school and college levels, typewriting is offered both for personal use and job competency.

The teaching of typewriting is based on psychological principles that emphasize student recognition of goals, multisensory approaches, systematic but distributed practice, immediate knowledge of results, mastery learning, and the automatization of responses. The skip-around method of presenting the typewriter keyboard, which combines the approaches used in the home-row and vertical plans, makes possible the early typing of words and sentences. The main emphasis during the keyboard learning stage, which lasts from one to three weeks, is on development of proper typewriting techniques. The instructional approach is technique, then speed, then accuracy. Technique drills are effective in helping students to develop habits that become automatic. Learners are taught correct posture and proper reading habits. They learn to use a ballistic stroke, to keep fingers curved and close to the home keys, to release the key quickly, and to pass on to the next stroke without a pause. Attention is given to the differences between the manual and electric typewriter.

A technique checklist is a valuable tool for assisting teacher observation and evaluation of basic student techniques. Based on the results of the technique rating, remedial work can be prescribed to help students overcome their faults. The teacher also uses demonstration frequently as a means of guiding typewriting instruction.

In building typing skills to a production level, a variety of short, separate drills are conducted for speed and accuracy until substantial gains are made. Purposeful repetition and correct techniques underlie the development of typing skill. The teacher should know which errors to ignore and which to study as a basis for corrective work by the student. Speed and accuracy development plans are outlined along with the formulas for measuring speed.

Production typewriting incorporates three general approaches. First, students are introduced to new or difficult features of the task and are drilled on the appropriate technique. Second, students learn and practice standards and optional procedures in typing various production tasks. Third, students draw on knowledge acquired in previous steps to complete all of the activities related to a production job, including planning, implementing, and evaluating steps. Students are given an opportunity to practice each part of the production task separately, then to put it together. The teacher assigns problems of graduated difficulty. Simultaneously, proofreading and correction techniques are taught. At the production level, students are graded on a net word a minute basis, mailable words a minute, or on a point system in which timed writings for production are somewhat extended.

A sample lesson plan is presented in this chapter; it includes objectives, materials, activities, and evaluation components. Once the basic keyboard skills are fixed, the teacher may prescribe objectives, drills, and activities on an individualized basis. Through the use of drills, problems of varying length and difficulty, and a variety of visual and auditory techniques, the teacher is able to modify instruction so as to meet learning needs of all students.

The business teacher uses two general methods for purposes of evaluation in typewriting. Subjective evaluation is the primary method for assessing techniques and work habits. Objective evaluation is used to measure knowledge and performance. The performance test is widely used to measure students' key-stroking ability and the application of basic skills to problem-solving situations. Standards for the course should be determined objectively and should be known by the students from the outset of the course. Suggested standards are included in this chapter.

References

[1]Frank W. Lanham, principal investigator, *Development of Performance Goals for a New Office and Business Education Learning System* (Columbus: Center for Research and Leadership Development in Vocational and Technical Education, The Ohio State University, USOE Project No. 8-0414, April 1970).

[2]Calfrey C. Calhoun, project director, *Purpose-Centered Curriculum for Florida Office and Business Education* (Tampa: University of South Florida, 1970).

[3]Lawrence W. Erickson, *Basic Components of Office Work—An Analysis of 300 Office Jobs,* Monograph 132 (Cincinnati: South-Western Publishing Company, 1971).

[4]Fred S. Cook and Frank W. Lanham, *Opportunities and Requirements for Initial Employment of School-Leavers and Emphasis on Office and Retail Jobs,* USOE Project No. 2378 (Wayne State University, 1966).

[5]Allien R. Russon and S. J. Wanous, *Philosophy and Psychology of Teaching Typewriting,* 2d ed. (Cincinnati: South-Western Publishing Company, 1973), p. 171.

[6]Leonard J. West, *Implications of Research for Teaching Typewriting,* Delta Pi Epsilon Research Bulletin, no. 4 (St. Peter, Minn.: Delta Pi Epsilon, Gustavus Adolphus College, 1974), p. 5.

[7]Ibid, p. 9.

[8]Alan Lloyd, "The Typing Teacher as a Technician: The Care and Feeding of Good Typing Technique," *Business Education World* 38, no. 6 (February 1958): 14. Reprinted with permission of BUSINESS EDUCATION WORLD, Gregg Division, McGraw-Hill Book Company, copyright February 1958.

[9]Leonard J. West, *Acquisition of Typewriting Skills* (New York: Pitman Publishing Company, 1969), p. 100.

[10]Alan Lloyd, "The Typing Teacher as a Technician: The Selection and Remedial Use of Technique Drills," *Business Education World* 38, no. 7 (March 1958): 30-32.

[11]Alan Lloyd, "The Typing Teacher as a Technician: What to Watch for When Observing Typing Students," *Business Education World* 38, no. 8 (April 1958): 24-25.

[12]Russon and Wanous, *Philosophy and Psychology of Teaching Typewriting,* pp. 154–55.

[13]George S. Rhodes and Calfrey C. Calhoun, *Guided/Timed Writings,* 1976. (Marietta, Ga.: Philip Page Printing Co., 1976) p. 10.

[14]George S. Rhodes and Calfrey C. Calhoun, "Guided/Timed Writings," Instructor's Guide, 1976, unpublished, pp. 1–2.

[15]John L. Rowe, Alan C. Lloyd, and Fred E. Winger, *Gregg General Typing 1,* 2d ed. (New York: Gregg Division, McGraw-Hill Book Company, 1967), p. 34.

[16]Jane E. Clem, *Techniques of Teaching Typewriting,* 2d ed. (New York: Gregg Division, McGraw-Hill Book Company, 1955), p. 103.

[17]Ibid., p. 238.

[18]Parker Liles and Zenobia T. Liles, *A Guide for the Improvement of Typewriting Instruction* (Atlanta: Georgia State Department of Education, 1968), pp. 61–63.

[19]Clem, *Techniques of Teaching Typewriting,* pp. 196–97.

[20]Kenneth Zimmer, Teacher's Guide and Key for *Typewriting for the College Student* (New York: Glencoe Press, 1972), pp. 4.3.2–4.3.3.

[21]West, *Implications of Research,* p. 254.

[22]D. Muhick, "Key-Stroking vs. Decision-Making Factors in Proficiency at Office Typing Tasks," (Master's thesis, Southern Illinois University, Carbondale, 1967).

[23]Russon and Wanous, *Philosophy and Psychology of Teaching Typewriting,* pp. 318–31.

[24]Ibid., p. 329

[25]Ibid., pp. 330–31.

[26]D. D. Lessenberry, T. James Crawford, Lawrence W. Erickson, Lee R. Beaumont, and Jerry W. Robinson, *Century 21 Typewriting,* Complete Course (Cincinnati: South-Western Publishing Company, 1972), pp. 67–68.

[27]Business Education Department, University of Georgia, "Modified Block Style Letters," Learning Activity Package 3, EBE 305 Course, 1975.

[28]Mary E. Connelly, "Building Production Speed" in *Methods of Teaching Typewriting,* Eastern Business Teachers Association Yearbook, Vol. 38 (Somerville, N.J.: Somerset Press, 1965), p. 91.

[29]Jane A. Leonard, "Typing: Creating a Laboratory Atmosphere," *Journal of Business Education* 52, no. 2 (November 1976): 81–82.

[30]Lloyd V. Douglas, James T. Blanford, and Ruth I. Anderson, *Teaching Business Subjects,* 2d ed. (Englewood Cliffs, N.J.: Prentice-Hall, 1965), p. 158.

[31]Irol W. Balsley, "A Study to Determine the Validity of Methods of Measuring Straight Copy Typing Skill," (Ruston, La.: Polytechnic Institute, December 1956), p. 9.

[32]Robert Hoskinson, Unpublished notes on production standards.

[33]Lessenberry et al., *Century 21 Typewriting,* Table of Contents.

[34]Ruth I. Anderson and Joe Pullis, "Measurement and Evaluation in Typewriting," in *Methods of Teaching Typewriting,* Eastern Business Teachers Association Yearbook, Vol. 38 (Somerville, N.J.: Somerset Press, 1965), p. 193.

[35]Russon and Wanous, *Philosophy and Psychology of Teaching Typewriting,* pp. 346–48.

[36]Ibid., pp. 352–53.

[37]Kenneth Zimmer, Teacher's Guide and Key for *Basic Intermediate and Advanced Typewriting for the College Student* (New York: Glencoe Press, 1972), pp. 5.2.1–5.2.2.

[38]Alfred L. Kaisershot, "Consider These Typewriting Standards," *Journal of Business Education* 51, no. 6 (March 1976): 267.

[39]Douglas, Blanford, and Anderson, *Teaching Business Subjects,* pp. 175–76.

[40]Russon and Wanous, *Philosophy and Psychology of Teaching Typewriting,* pp. 355–56.

[41]Zimmer, *Basic . . . Typewriting for the College Student,* pp. 5.3.1–5.3.2.

SUGGESTIONS FOR FURTHER STUDY

Century 21 Reporter. Cincinnati: South-Western Publishing Company. Published twice yearly. See all issues.

Coleman, Marion G., and Hanson, Oleen M., eds. *Effective Secretarial Education,* NBEA Yearbook, No. 12. Reston, Va.: National Business Education Association, 1974. Part III.

Erickson, Lawrence W. "The Teaching of Typewriting." In *Contributions of Research to Business Education,* NBEA Yearbook, No. 9, edited by C. C. Calhoun and Mildred Hillestad, pp. 17–37. Washington, D.C.: National Business Education Association, 1971.

Typing News. Cincinnati: South-Western Publishing Company. Published twice yearly. See all issues.

Winger, Fred E. "Typewriting." In *Changing Methods of Teaching Business Subjects,* NBEA Yearbook, No. 10., edited by Leroy Brendel and Herbert Yengel, pp. 84–97. Washington, D.C.: National Business Education Association, 1972.

Woolschlager, Ruth, and Harris, E. Edward, eds. *Business Education Yesterday, Today and Tomorrow,* NBEA Yearbook, No. 14. Reston, Va.: National Business Education Association, 1976. Chapters 6, 18.

See *Business Education Index,* published annually by Delta Pi Epsilon, for extensive listing of typing articles.

chapter 7

TEACHING SHORTHAND AND TRANSCRIPTION

Much has been written and said about the teaching and learning of shorthand. Authors, researchers, and teachers differ considerably in their statements of objectives, methods, and placement of shorthand in the curriculum. In today's world, changes in technology and the applications of technology constantly create new demands and requirements for employment in business occupations. However, analysts of the job market are nearly unanimous in their forecast of an undiminished demand for stenographers and secretaries who are proficient in the use of shorthand systems.

Shorthand is a vital skill for the modern secretary. Many beginning jobs offer the secretary an increase in salary of 25 percent or more if he or she can write shorthand. This is a significant improvement in salary for a very small investment in time. Shorthand students generally take stenography in school for a period ranging from nine to fourteen months. Most students spend one hour in class daily, five days a week. This amounts to a maximum of 280 hours —a small investment of time to gain a skill that will reap big dividends and provide an open door to employment in the eighties.[1]

Three main elements are basic to a successful shorthand system: (1) a highly motivated student who has a keen desire to learn shorthand and an ability to master the content of shorthand instruction, (2) a teacher who is well-grounded in the theory and application of the shorthand system and is able to utilize teaching strategies in harmony with current research and psychological skill-building principles, and (3) a system of shorthand that will provide adequately for the transcription of shorthand notes to assist in meeting the career objectives of students.[2]

module 7.1
GOALS AND OBJECTIVES

Any discussion of the goals and objectives of shorthand systems must take into account the goals of the student, the time available for instruction, and the conditions under which the skill is to be acquired. The effectiveness of instruction and learning in shorthand also depends on the application of sound psychological principles of perceptual-motor-skill learning.

After completing this module, you should be able to (1) specify the objectives for varying levels of symbol shorthand, and (2) identify several guidelines for the application of learning principles to the teaching of shorthand.

OBJECTIVES

Shorthand, primarily a vocational skill, is offered at the secondary and postsecondary levels. Regardless of the instructional or educational level, the ultimate performance goal is for the student to develop the skills needed to take dictation in a business office with sufficient speed and accuracy to produce mailable copy. Dictation rates of 100 to 120 words per minute are frequently cited as the goal needed for a marketable skill. Mitchell[3] recommends a minimum rate of 120 *wam* because average conversational speeds range from 120–140 *wam*. "The often stated 'average' dictation speed of 80 *wpm* is deceiving. A dictator's pauses may contribute to an average of 80 *wpm*, but a secretary or stenographer with an 80 *wpm* skill will have great difficulty in keeping up when the dictator is speaking at the 120 *wpm* rate. A safe marketable skill is 120 *wpm*."

At the secondary level, two years or four semesters of shorthand/transcription instruction are recommended. The length of shorthand instructional programs at the postsecondary level varies, ranging from three quarters to six quarters or four semesters. In an individualized program, however, the emphasis is on mastery of skill, with the time flexible and dependent on student progress.

First year/beginning shorthand

The major emphasis in the first semester of shorthand is on shorthand theory, vocabulary building, and shorthand dictation. During the second semester, the emphasis is on further speed building and transcription. According to Anderson,[4] the objective by the end of the second semester should be the recording of new-matter business letter material at 80 words per minute. Students should be able to transcribe a minimum of two mailable letters in thirty minutes.

The following are minimal objectives for first-year shorthand as reported in the Iowa Business Education Handbook:[5]

1. During the first semester, the student will be able to pass periodic theory tests with a minimum of 70 percent accuracy by writing the correct outline next to the longhand word. This should not be a timed test.
2. At the end of 9 weeks of instruction, a student will be able to transcribe from the text into longhand or typewritten form at a minimum rate of 60 words in a period of 3 minutes with a maximum of 5 errors, not including errors in punctuation or spelling. The student knows

beforehand a group of 3 lessons from which the test material will be chosen.

3. At the end of the first semester, the student will be able to write all the brief form outlines, dictated one every 3 seconds, with a minimum of 95 percent accuracy for outline formation.

4. At the end of the first semester, the student will be able to write the brief forms dictated at a rate of one every 3 seconds and transcribe with a minimum of 95 percent accuracy on the longhand response.

5. At the end of the first semester, the student will be able to write the outlines for a comprehensive longhand theory test with a minimum of 95 percent accuracy on outlines. This should not be a timed test.

6. At the end of the first semester, the student will be able to read orally from shorthand homework notes at a minimum rate of 60 words in one-half minute.

7. At the end of the second semester, the student will be able to read orally from shorthand homework notes at a minimum rate of 90 words in one-half minute.

8. At the end of the second semester, the student will be able to take dictation over unpreviewed, new material for 3 minutes at a minimum rate of 60 *wam* and transcribe for 30 minutes at a minimum rate of 20 *wam* with 95 percent accuracy.

Second year/advanced shorthand

The second year of shorthand instruction includes either one semester of speed building and one semester of transcription, or the two skills will be emphasized simultaneously in a full-year course. Lamb[6] suggests the following goals for second year, or advanced shorthand:

1. Record practiced matter dictated at 100–120 *wam* for five minutes and new matter of average difficulty dictated at 80–100 *wam*.

2. Transcribe these "takes" on the typewriter in usable form at first trial at a minimum transcription rate of 12–25 *wam*.

3. Record matter dictated at uneven rates, including "spurt dictation."

4. Transcribe notes requiring correction or special attention in acceptable form at a reasonable rate of speed, the actual rate to be determined by the situation.

5. Intelligently solve problems connected with dictation and transcription: asking for repetition of a word or name not heard in dictation; making satisfactory substitutions for words omitted from notes; detecting discrepancies in thought within a letter; checking own errors and working toward their elimination, and so on.

6. Habitually apply job skills learned in class to daily shorthand work: keeping a neat notebook, with used pages separated from unused pages by a rubber band; dating each day's dictation; marking with a light vertical line the dictation that has been transcribed; indicating by means of a paper clip or special mark those letters to be transcribed first; marking dictated matter to indicate insertion of mate-

rial; and other miscellaneous job skills that make up the "know-how" of stenographic work.

7. Understand the personal traits and attitudes required for success in stenographic work.

If students are to develop marketable shorthand/transcription skills, there are specific abilities that they must demonstrate. The student should be able to take dictation with ease, type smoothly and easily from shorthand notes, make word selections and spell accurately from thinking of the word recognized in outline form, judge copy placement by scanning shorthand notes, grasp the meaning of material being transcribed so that a continual judging of its adequacy is possible, produce copy at an acceptable rate of speed, and proofread with impeccable accuracy.[7]

Transcription, which begins in the first semester of shorthand instruction, is a complex process. To transcribe accurately and produce mailable copy, the student must be able to demonstrate mastery of shorthand, composition, grammar, punctuation, basic rules of format, and typewriting. Some view transcription as a fusion of skills already developed and facts already known. To others, it means the development of new skills never before encountered. For the teacher, the final objective is the integration of all types of teaching into the ability to produce a usable product in a reasonable period of time.

APPLYING LEARNING PRINCIPLES TO THE TEACHING OF SHORTHAND

Learning theories and principles of learning that underlie the teacher's decisions regarding the instructional program are presented in Chapter 2. Principles of learning specifically related to skill development are discussed in Chapter 6, Module 1. In this module, we will consider shorthand skill development. The following principles can be of enormous benefit to the teacher who understands them and applies them to the teaching of shorthand.

1. *Learning experiences proceed from simple to complex.* The components that need to be organized in a simple-to-complex pattern for dictation/transcription skill development include: speed of dictation—slow to fast; familiarity of vocabulary—very common to less common words; subject matter of content—common, generally known to technical and specialized; spelling and word choice—easy, familiar words to difficult, unfamiliar ones; punctuation—simple, limited use to complex, more extensive use; length of sustained effort—short items requiring little time to record and transcribe to long items, or several items requiring a substantial block of time for completion.[8]

2. *Learning experiences are sequenced in logical steps.* "New theory must be presented in 'bite size,' since one day's presentation builds on the preceding one."[9] The important message is that the proper sequence of learning enables one to avoid the mistakes that arise from omitting essential steps in the acquisi-

tion of knowledge. In shorthand, each step is a prerequisite to the next. Skipping any lesson in shorthand, especially in the early part of the course, may prove harmful to the point of discouraging some students from proceeding with the next course.[10] Such a sequence in shorthand instruction is (a) reading, (b) writing from practiced material, (c) writing from new material, and (d) transcribing.

3. *Desired student behavior is the result of reinforcement of that behavior.* This principle, drawn from the behaviorist model, has implications for shorthand instruction. Students take turns reading short passages from the previous day's homework. Knowing that the material will be read in class is reinforcement for doing the work. Students take dictation from material covered five lessons back. This represents delayed reinforcement for work done earlier. It is incentive to work on the current lesson so that five lessons hence it may be taken down in shorthand with greater ease. Graphic progress charts maintained by students tend to induce them to better their own scores. It is reinforcement for a continually increasing effort on the part of the student.[11]

4. *Skills are best developed by actual use in a setting that most nearly approximates actual use.* Appropriate practice is essential to skill development. Educators have long endorsed the concept of learning by doing. This principle suggests that shorthand students should be given opportunities to begin taking dictation as soon as possible, working gradually toward office-style dictation.

5. *Systematic review is necessary for skills to become automatic.* Planned, systematic incorporation of theory application, brief/forms/speed/forms, and phrases in the daily lesson for three to five days after initial introduction is necessary for the student to internalize the skills and for them to become automatic. Planned review throughout the course is important.

6. *The instructional process incorporates several modes of presentation.* Bruner[12] believes that the developing human being has three means of acting upon the environment: through direct action, through imagery, and through language. To apply Bruner's theory, if a student has difficulty understanding a principle in shorthand, the teacher can direct him or her to the three modes of learning: watch a demonstration (the teacher at the chalkboard or with the overhead projector or film/loops); read the shorthand notes and figure out the principles from the patterns followed by the outlines; read the textbook or listen to the teacher, or to a tape.

7. *Repetition is necessary for skills to be learned.* "This principle may be a difficult one for a teacher to observe. There is a natural desire to keep moving to new areas of learning."[13] Shorthand students, in most cases, need several opportunities to practice the same activity or skill, preferably in modified settings. Repetition does not mean doing the same thing in an identical way. Business teachers, for example, may have students copy two different letters instead of copying one letter twice.

8. *Regular practice is essential for skill development.* "Regularity of practice is a key factor in the development of any skill. Intermittent, long sessions are not as effective as shorter, more frequent ones. Frequent practice reinforces and simplifies mastery."[14]

9. *Speed in a skill is best developed on familiar material.* When the objective of shorthand activity (or lessons) is speed development, the teacher uses material that is familiar to the students.

10. *Terminal goals should simulate actual job situations.* "This principle means that the student must progress to the level of office-style dictation. It also implies that, in the transcription segment of the shorthand program, the student must by the end of the program be able to prepare mailable copy just as he or she would in an office."[15]

module 7.1
LEARNING ACTIVITIES

1. Your department is preparing for a visit from a regional accreditation team. One of your assignments is to write the objectives for your courses in shorthand. Using the information presented in this module and in other sources as needed, list the objectives for four semesters of shorthand instruction.
2. Select at least five learning principles discussed in this module and give one or more examples illustrating the application of each in the shorthand classroom.
3. Using the *Business Education Index* and/or other references, identify, read, and report on at least one article about shorthand goals and objectives at the secondary or postsecondary level.

module 7.1
SELF-TEST

1. Identify the major instructional emphasis for (a) the first semester of shorthand, (b) the second semester of shorthand, and (c) the second year of shorthand.
2. "Transcription is a complex process." Explain this statement as related to goals and objectives.
3. List a minimum of five principles of learning that apply to shorthand.

module 7.2
PLANNING FOR INSTRUCTION

Planning, more than any other single factor, is a crucial component in the success of your shorthand course. Effective planning and prior preparation on the teacher's part ensure a balance of activities and content on a day-to-day basis. Planning also does much to ensure effective use of time, as well as providing for variety and interest in classroom activities.

After completing this module, you should be able to (1) summarize the learning activities in the shorthand classroom and their relative importance over four semesters, (2) illustrate how a 40–50 minute class period could be used (after writing has been introduced) in terms of learning activities and time allowance, and (3) identify the components of a lesson plan for a given lesson before writing begins.

FACTORS TO CONSIDER

As the business teacher plans the shorthand course, he or she identifies objectives, units of instruction, standards and testing plans, instructional strategies, materials and equipment needed (and available). The length of the course (one or two years), offering of related courses (such as office practice), student characteristics, availability of instructional hardware and software, and occupational opportunities and standards influence the teacher's decisions. Content in shorthand courses focuses on theory, brief forms and phrases, reading, practiced and new-matter dictation, typewritten transcription, and review of related English skills.

Shorthand instruction may be individualized, by use of commercial material or teacher-made materials, or may be teacher-directed. Even within the teacher-directed class, provision must be made for individual differences such as the rate at which students take dictation, amount of review, and remediation of English for individual students. In an individualized approach, the business teacher continuously monitors the performance of each student, giving help when needed, diagnosing and prescribing appropriate instructional modules, and evaluating student progress. In the teacher-directed class, the instructor plans each lesson thoroughly, secures the materials and equipment needed, practices the shorthand outlines at the chalkboard or with the overhead projector as appropriate, reviews dictating at various speeds, and uses a stopwatch. Each lesson is planned to include a variety of activities, and the teacher incorporates varied instructional techniques to introduce and reinforce a given skill. Note in the following lesson pattern the varied instructional activities designed to review, introduce, practice, and preview:[16]

> *Alternation of Classroom Activities.* For many reasons it is desirable to alternate classroom activities. Learners very quickly tire of any one activity, and the mere change from the one activity to the next renews their interest and attention briefly. In changing back and forth from one activity to another during the shorthand period, it is important to be sure that no time is lost. If only one minute were to be lost at each change of activity, it would easily be possible to lose ten minutes or more in a period.
>
> What are the possible profitable activities in the shorthand classroom? (1) Concerted spelling and reading from the teacher's chalkboard outlines. (2) Individual spelling and reading of outlines from the chalkboard. (3) Individual reading of connected matter from the manual and workbook. (4) Individual reading from brief-form charts or similar material from the manual. (5) Taking dictation from practiced material. (6) Individual reading back from dictation. (7) Individual and concerted reading from shorthand filmstrips. (8) Individual and concerted reading from shorthand transparencies.

Suggested Lesson Pattern During Reading Approach. Assume that the teacher is presenting Lesson 8. The 40-minute period might be divided approximately as follows:

7 minutes presentation of brief forms in paragraph 48.
4 minutes reading from connected matter in Lesson 7, the previous day's homework.
1/2 minute recall of brief forms, which have been left on the chalkboard.
3 minutes presentation of -ly in paragraph 49.
4 minutes reading from connected matter in Lesson 7.
1 minute recall of brief forms and -ly.
3 minutes presentation of amounts and quantities in paragraph 50.
4 minutes reading from connected matter in Lesson 7.
1/2 minute recall of everything on the chalkboard.
2 minutes discussion of Business Vocabulary Builder in paragraph 51.
3 minutes reading from connected matter in Lesson 7.
·3 minutes sight-reading from Reading Practice in Lesson 8, which is tomorrow's homework.
3 minutes recall of theory of Lesson 8 with Gregg Shorthand Filmstrips or Gregg Shorthand Transparencies.

Careful planning and preparation help the teacher avoid continuing one activity too long and losing time in going from one activity to another. The following sample teaching plan, the Fifth Day, is recommended by Christensen and Bell:[17]

SAMPLE TEACHING PLAN, FIFTH DAY

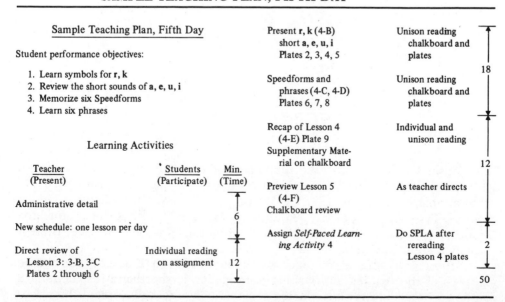

Sample Teaching Plan, Fifth Day

Student performance objectives:

1. Learn symbols for **r, k**
2. Review the short sounds of **a, e, u, i**
3. Memorize six Speedforms
4. Learn six phrases

Learning Activities

Teacher (Present)	Students (Participate)	Min. (Time)
Administrative detail		6
New schedule: one lesson per day		
Direct review of Lesson 3: 3-B, 3-C Plates 2 through 6	Individual reading on assignment	12

Present **r, k** (4-B) short **a, e, u, i** Plates 2, 3, 4, 5	Unison reading chalkboard and plates	
Speedforms and phrases (4-C, 4-D) Plates 6, 7, 8	Unison reading chalkboard and plates	18
Recap of Lesson 4 (4-E) Plate 9 Supplementary Material on chalkboard	Individual and unison reading	12
Preview Lesson 5 (4-F) Chalkboard review	As teacher directs	
Assign *Self-Paced Learning Activity* 4	Do SPLA after rereading Lesson 4 plates	2
		50

The format for the Typewriting Lesson Plan in Module 6.6 is equally appropriate for shorthand. The plan incorporates both content and procedures.

Developing skills in reading, writing, and transcribing shorthand requires drill and repetition. One of the tasks of the teacher, then, is to incorporate variety in approach and materials in order to maintain student interest. For instance, during the first weeks when students are developing skill in reading shorthand, the teacher employs techniques such as total class reading in unison, reading by rows or by individuals, half the class reading, reading by the teacher immediately followed by reading by an individual, or a group, or the class. These techniques focus on repetitive practice, but do not result in following a dull routine.

module 7.2
LEARNING ACTIVITIES

1. Outline a daily lesson plan in shorthand before or after writing has begun. Include performance objectives, as well as student and teacher learning activities.
2. Prepare a chart for a shorthand class period after writing is introduced. Identify the types of learning activities you would use and the time allowance for each.

module 7.2
SELF-TEST

1. Theory knowledge in shorthand is emphasized most in the _____ semester.
2. Dictation speed building assumes least importance in the _____ semester.
3. Typewritten transcription assumes major importance in the _____ semester.
4. Automatization of brief forms/speed forms should take place in the _____ semester.
5. Reading skill is emphasized primarily in the _____ semester.

module 7.3
INSTRUCTIONAL STATEGIES FOR TEACHING SHORTHAND

Methods of teaching symbol shorthand are commonly divided into two groups: (1) the Reading Approach, often referred to as Language-Arts teaching or the "Functional Method," and (2) the Writing Approach, often characterized as Science-Type teaching or the "Traditional Method." Most business educators identify with one or the other method although, in actual practice, there is usually a combination of the two approaches.

After completing this module, you should be able to (1) identify the characteristics of the reading and writing approaches to shorthand instruction, (2) outline a procedure for introducing shorthand symbols, (3) explain the role of reading in beginning shorthand instruction, (4) identify and explain sound practices to be incorporated in developing good writing skills, (5) name four possible theory errors and suggest at least one teaching strategy for preventing or remedying each.

TWO APPROACHES

In order to differentiate the components of the two primary approaches to teaching shorthand, the characteristics of each are compared below:[18]

Writing Approach	Reading Approach
part method	whole method
conscious control	subconscious control
physical skill	mental organization
accuracy and refinement of shorthand characters	fluency and correctness in taking dictation
correction of shorthand outlines	correction of transcripts only
end in itself—conformity with the textbook	means to an end—transcription
verbalized rules	no rules
problem solving	habit forming
intensive repetitive home practice	extensive nonrepetitive home practice
emphasis on word lists	emphasis on connected matter
vocabulary building	constructional ability

THE WRITING APPROACH

The older science-type method views shorthand as a science; that is, outlines are constructed after rules have been presented by the teacher and learned by the student. The method is logical and orderly and emphasizes understanding the *why* as well as the *how* of writing shorthand. "Those who are opposed to the writing approach say that teaching rules develops a hesitant style of writing and that the method focuses attention on the strokes making up each outline rather than the meaning of the entire sentence."[19]

Characteristics

Douglas, Blanford, and Anderson[20] describe the following characteristics of the writing approach:

1. *Use of rules.* Knowledge of the rules of constructing outlines is considered important. Usually the rule is presented, followed by words illustrating the application of the rule.
2. *Use of word lists.* Word lists are practiced extensively in the writing approach.

3. *Early introduction to writing.* Shorthand outlines are copied from the text on the second or third day of class instruction.
4. *Penmanship drills.* Penmanship is considered important in the writing approach. Special drills are practiced emphasizing the proportion of the strokes, relative size of the vowels, shorthand slant, and placement on the line of writing.
5. *Vocabulary tests.* The student's ability to write accurate outlines is tested frequently. These tests may be given on words previously practiced or on new applications of rules that have been learned.
6. *Use of formal reviews.* Teachers using this approach often give formal review on previous lessons at regular intervals.
7. *Extensive reading and writing.* In this method the students are instructed to read and write certain letters in the text several times. They are not required to read and write as extensively as are students following the reading approach.
8. *Varied activities from the beginning.* From the first days of the shorthand course, students perform many different activities. These activities include reading shorthand, copying shorthand plates from the text, recording practiced material from dictation, recording new-matter dictation, and transcribing plate material into longhand.

Presenting the first lesson

With the writing approach, the teacher presents the shorthand alphabet in the first lesson. After the alphabet is presented, the teacher explains the joining of alphabetic characters to form words. For example, the teacher writes *p–a–y* on the chalkboard or overhead projector and asks which letter is not pronounced. The class answers *y*. The teacher then writes the shorthand outline *p–a* on the chalkboard, and the students are asked to write the word in their notebooks, explaining that the two letters *p* and *a* are joined together to form the word *pay*.

Homework in the writing approach

The writing approach emphasizes the spelling and reading of outlines as they are presented. This spelling and reading is done aloud, both in class and for homework. One lesson is assigned each day. Students spell and read the new outlines and write each outline. The connected matter is read and copied. Many teachers using this approach assign part of a lesson rather than all of it and instruct the class to copy this portion two or three times.[21]

THE READING APPROACH

Introduced in 1934 by Louis A. Leslie, the reading approach is a concentrated effort on reading for the first four weeks of the shorthand course. Douglas, Blanford, and Anderson identify the following features of the reading approach:[22]

1. *Emphasis on reading.* The first four weeks of the semester are devoted to reading. Writing is deferred until the beginning of the fifth week.
2. *No rules taught.* Rules as such are not taught in the reading approach. Students are discouraged from asking questions regarding shorthand theory, since it is believed that extensive reading and copying of accurate shorthand outlines from plates will answer most questions more effectively than will class discussions.
3. *Use of the key.* A printed key to the plate material in the text is included at the back of the text. The key is provided to assist students in studying and to enable them to read more extensively and with greater fluency than would otherwise be possible.
4. *No word lists.* In theory the reading approach never makes use of word lists. In actual practice, however, word lists are found at the beginning of each lesson. No emphasis is placed on the lists other than to present the new family of words included in the lesson.
5. *No formal penmanship practice.* No penmanship practice is considered necessary since the students are reading and practicing so much correct shorthand plate material each day.
6. *No repetition practice.* Students are instructed to read and copy the shorthand plates in the text only once.
7. *No formal review.* The reading approach stresses that the acquisition of shorthand skill is a cumulative process with each new lesson built on the preceding lessons.
8. *Fewer papers to correct.* The reading approach deemphasizes the correcting of shorthand notes. It is believed that the transcript is the important element and that if the student transcribes correctly, his outline is satisfactory.
9. *No tests except for administrative purposes.* This approach also deemphasizes the giving of tests in the first semester. Only those necessary for reporting grades are given.
10. *Simplified early learning situation.* Advocates of the reading approach point out that the introduction of only one learning activity at a time greatly simplifies the beginner's problem of mastering shorthand.

Proponents of the reading approach believe that it eliminates the initial diffuse movements that are characteristic of beginners when writing is attempted too soon. The learner sees so many well-written examples of the various shorthand symbols that he or she begins to observe exact shapes and their differences. The extensive methodology employed by the reading approach enables the learner to cover additional ground more rapidly. Ease of learning is also cited as an advantage of the reading approach since the learner need not cope with the many problems that present themselves when reading and writing are presented from the very beginning.

Perhaps the greatest disadvantage of the reading approach is that students naturally want to write at the beginning of instruction. If the opportunity to write is postponed too long, they may lose interest.

Presenting the first lesson

The shorthand alphabet needed only for the first lesson is presented on the first day of instruction. Then the class is shown how the alphabetic characters are joined to form words. The emphasis is placed on reading, as follows:

> If we write *pay* by sound, what letter do we omit? (Teacher writes *pay* on the chalkboard, erasing or crossing out the *y* when the class responds that *y* should be omitted.) Yes, so we join *p* and *a* (writing the letters separately as they are pronounced) to form the word *pay* (writing it). Let's spell and read it together: *p–a, pay; p–a, pay; p–a, pay.*

Homework

"The homework assignment for the reading approach for the first four weeks is to read the new lesson once. Beginning with the fifth week, the assignment is to read the new lesson once and write it once."[23]

Introduction to writing

"Beginning with the fifth week, the class is introduced to writing by asking them to turn to an early lesson in the text (such as Lesson 3) and to copy from the shorthand plate as the teacher dictates."[24]

COMBINING THE APPROACHES

Most teachers actually use a combination of methods instead of adhering exclusively to one method. For instance, a teacher may modify the reading method by teaching some rules and by introducing writing before the fifth week (or whenever the textbook calls for it). On the other hand, a teacher using the writing approach may delay writing for a few days.

The following procedure, which combines reading and limited writing, may be used to introduce symbols for alphabetic sounds:

1. Direct student attention to the new shorthand alphabetic symbol in the textbook; point out the direction and character of the symbol; enunciate the sound the symbol represents; pronounce distinctly each letter, sound, or word represented by the symbol; and then write the symbol on the chalkboard or overhead transparency—perhaps two or three times to be certain all students have a visual image of the symbol/outline as it is being written.

2. Direct students to write each symbol three times in their notebooks to give them the feel for the motions involved.

3. Write on the chalkboard or transparency the first word used in the textbook to apply the symbol or principle. Sound/spell and pronounce the word as you write it.

4. Have students sound/spell and pronounce the word as many times as needed to achieve initial mastery (recognition) and write the outline three times.

5. Steps 3 and 4 are repeated for each of the words provided in the textbook for a particular sound.

6. After all illustrative words for a sound have been presented by means of the procedures described in Steps 1 to 5, they are reviewed in a reading activity—first in the sequence presented and then again in random order, the teacher pointing rapidly to each of the outlines and sound/spelling those outlines on which the students hesitate.

Limited writing of symbols and word outlines as theory is presented helps students to clinch recognition of symbols, and it improves sound/spelling. Remember to have students observe you writing an outline before they attempt to write it. Similar procedures may be used to introduce brief forms and phrases *except* that they are not sound/spelled but are memorized for instant recognition in reading and immediate recall in writing.[25]

Knowledge of shorthand theory is essential for it is the foundation upon which shorthand writing and transcription are based. Business dictation is about equally composed of outlines based on theory and nontheory outlines, which means the student must not only memorize nontheory outlines but also must develop a solid foundation for writing outlines from sound. Nontheory elements include arbitrary word signs, composed of speed forms (brief forms) and related words, common phrases, correspondence forms, contracted forms, and special outlines for longhand abbreviations.

READING PRACTICE

The development of strong reading skills is an important objective in beginning shorthand, for it is related to the development of good writing ability. From the first day it is desirable for students to sound/spell shorthand outlines by pronouncing each symbol within the outline before saying the word. Example: M A K make. The amount of time spent in sound/spelling decreases as students become more proficient in reading shorthand. After two to four weeks, students should sound/spell only when they encounter an outline that they cannot readily identify. When connected material is being read, theory words not immediately recognized should be sound/spelled. To foster fluent, rapid reading, however, the teacher will find it helpful to then have students reread the same material without sound/spelling.

Reading practices include both group and individual drill and incorporate word-by-word and word-group units. Gregg, Leslie, and Zoubek recommend that group procedure be used primarily in reading word lists from the chalkboard, while connected matter should be read by individuals. (Initially, teachers use group drill in reading simple phrases and sentences from the board and from the textbook plates.) "The learners must be trained to read both loudly and fast. They must be trained to spell and pronounce any word the instant the teacher's finger points at the shorthand outline, to cease reading instantly and become absolutely quiet the moment the teacher's finger is lifted, and to resume reading the moment the teacher's finger is placed on the blackboard again."[26]

There are five characteristics of reading and spelling (sound/spelling) from the chalkboard:

1. *Rapid.* Rapid reading sets the pace for rapid writing.
2. *Repetitive.* Frequent and immediate reading and spelling help students attain the high spelling and reading speed that is necessary and provide the drill needed to recognize alphabetic symbols and the manner in which they are joined.
3. *Random.* Unless spelling and reading of symbols is in a random order, students may memorize the order of the words instead of reading each outline.
4. *Unaided.* In most word lists, the teacher will have to read and spell the first word because it will contain one new alphabetic character or word beginning or word ending the students do not know. The remaining words should be read without teacher aid.
5. *Concerted.* Reading word lists in concert allows for the participation of all students, giving confidence to the slower or more timid students.

Students should be expected to achieve a minimum oral reading rate of 50 to 60 words a minute by the fourth week of instruction; some students may be nearer the 80-word-a-minute level by then. A minimum level of 120 to 130 *wam* should be achieved by the end of the first semester.

Langemo[27] recommends setting specific goals in minutes and seconds for completing the reading portion of homework assignments. As a rule of thumb, students should be expected to read shorthand twice as fast as they can write it. To determine the reading goal, add the number of words in all of the letters of a shorthand lesson and divide by the desired reading speed to obtain the time that should be allowed. Thus a lesson containing 315 words to be read at 90 *wam* would have a reading goal of 3.5 minutes ($315 \div 90 = 3.5$). Reading goals should be individualized, reflecting student performance.

Using a variety of reading drills, such as the following, helps to maintain student interest:

1. *Catch the Ball.* The teacher calls on a student to begin reading. Every few words a different student is called upon to read. The objective is not to repeat a word or to delay in reading when called upon.
2. *Help the Teacher.* The teacher begins reading, then pauses after every few words and calls on a student to read the next word or words.
3. *The Corrector.* One student begins reading. The first student to note an error or hesitation is challenged to pick up the reading just as soon as the error or hesitation occurs.
4. *The Assistant.* One student is called upon to read and another student is called on to supply any outline that causes hesitation or that is incorrect.[28]

WRITING PRACTICE

While the initial emphasis in beginning shorthand is generally on reading, it gradually changes to writing, so that by the end of the first semester, a majority of in-class and out-of-class activities are devoted to writing shorthand. "As actual shorthand writing begins to assume a larger role in the practice activity, an effective strategy is to have most of the writing done on the simpler, previously read plates of the preceding lessons. Students can, generally, read more difficult copy than they can write with fluency; therefore, a several-lesson lag between reading and writing is desirable."[29] Early writing activities should be brief and should focus on easy, thoroughly familiar materials. In the beginning stages, student writing should be preceded by teacher demonstration of the material on the chalkboard or overhead projector. (The teacher demonstration and/or explanation should include form, size, and proportion of the symbols, when necessary.)

During the early stages of writing, it is important that the teacher move around the room and carefully observe student writing of outlines, giving assistance and instruction as needed. Initially, the writing *process* is more revealing than the writing *product*.

The development of good writing skills requires that attention be given to several priorities:[30]

1. "A rapid elimination of the tendency to *draw* rather than to *write*." Writing under time pressure and using drills that force increasingly rapid outline construction can assist students in writing with fluency and speed.
2. "The development of consistency in constructing shorthand symbols." Special writing precision drills help to improve consistency. The teacher and student should periodically evaluate the student's shorthand notes, identifying writing practices that need correcting or remedying.
3. "A sensitivity to good proportion in the formation of shorthand characters." Writing drills in which similar but different symbols occur in the same outline are helpful in developing sensitivity to good proportion.
4. "An appreciation for the importance of correctly written outlines." Students need to be aware of the relationship between correctly written outlines and the increased likelihood that the outlines will be transcribed without error.
5. "Extra practice on those shorthand principles, symbol joinings, and other system components which some students find less easy to master than others." From the beginning, the teacher must be aware of individual differences in learning style and rate and provide appropriate drills and activities.

Out-of-class practice is recommended for students in order to develop skill in reading and writing shorthand. Writing the material from shorthand plates is one activity frequently used. Students must realize, however, that it is possible to copy the outlines without knowing the content of what they are writing. A self-dictation procedure encourages students to write rather than copy the textbook shorthand letters. The procedure is as follows: (1) the student reads a few words from a letter; (2) turning from the textbook, the student repeats the words he or she has read—"self-dictating" the words so that he or she must "re-create" the shorthand outlines rather than only copy them; and (3) the student continually and rapidly repeats the process to self-dictate the entire lesson.[31] Self-dictation goals may be set for students by dividing the number of words in the letters by the desired speed. Thus 300 words at a self-dictation rate of 40 *wam* is a self-dictation goal of 7.5 minutes.

Students should use a fine point pen that writes smoothly for shorthand. (An extra pen should be on the desk.) It is a good idea to have students use separate notebooks for homework and classroom dictation. The teacher should explain and demonstrate the proper use of the notebook, including turning pages, using rubber bands to hold pages, writing down half the column of the notebook, moving the page up so the writing is near the center of the notebook, and dating the bottom of the page.

Theoretically, correct shorthand outlines can be transcribed much more accurately than incorrectly written ones. Teachers should know the guidelines underlying the construction of outlines and the principles for writing vowels. Illustrations 7.1 and 7.2 summarize these guidelines as applied to Gregg shorthand.

With regard to shorthand theory, business teachers should remember that English is often an inconsistent language; therefore, any shorthand system

illustration 7.1
GUIDELINES FOR CONSTRUCTING GREGG OUTLINES

Panel 1: A Hierarchy of Guidelines for Constructing Outlines in Gregg Shorthand

The following five guidelines are listed in the order of priority in which they are applied; for example, if a choice is possible between applying Guideline 3 and Guideline 4, Guideline 3 should take precedence.

1. Preserve the primitive form whenever possible; that is, try to include as much of the root word as possible in its derivatives. For example, in the primitive word *refer*, the e in the second syllable is written because the vowel is accented; thus, in the derivative *reference*, the second e is still written even though the vowel is no longer accented:

refer   reference

2. Other things being equal, write monosyllables in full in order to ensure perfect legibility. The abbreviating devices that may be employed in longer words are not generally applied to monosyllables:

man   deaf

3. Use the symbols or principles that apply (blends, word beginnings and endings, etc.), even when doing so combines the syllables:

to mor row   de ter
ter mi nal

4. Preserve the syllable whenever possible, when s occurs between strokes with no intervening circle vowel, write the s with the syllable to which it belongs:

in stru ment   re sort

5. Whenever a choice exists as to which of the dual characters to use, write the character that would normally be joined to the preceding character. When s or th occurs between conflicting strokes (that is, the preceding stroke requires one form of s or th and the following stroke requires the other form), use the form that would join to the character that comes first:

first

Source: B. Scot Ober, "A Word to the Whys: A Discussion of the Construction of Gregg Shorthand Outlines," *Business Education World*, 55, no. 5 (May–June 1975): 14. Reprinted with permission of BUSINESS EDUCATION WORLD, Gregg Division, McGraw-Hill Book Company, copyright May–June 1975.

illustration 7.2
PRINCIPLES FOR WRITING VOWELS IN GREGG SHORTHAND

Panel 2: Principles for Writing Vowels in Gregg Shorthand

1. The circle vowel is omitted in these combinations:

k-r, g-r, k-l, g-l

courage   eager

legal

p-n, p-t, p-d, b-n, b-t, b-d

open   rapid   habit

p-k

respect   picture

2. The diphthong *u* is omitted before *r* and *l* in the body of an outline:

accurate   popular

3. The *oo* hook generally represents *u* after *t, d, n, m*:

tutor   duet   news

4. The *oo* hook is omitted between *r* and *l* and a straight downstroke:

crucial   solution

5. The vowel is always omitted in the following word endings:

-vity, -city

activity   capacity

-fect, -ject

perfect   project

-tract, -trict, -truct

contract   strict

-vent, -vention

event   convention

-sive

massive   expensive

6. The vowel is omitted when the following word endings are *not* stressed:

-en, -an, -on, -in

even   organ

origin

   but: begin

     complain

-el, -al, -ial, -eal

level   legal

material

   but: reveal

     conceal

-er, -ar, -or

folder   sugar

error   *but:* confer

     infer

The vowel is also written when *-er, -ar, -or* follow *ī*, left *s*, or a straight downstroke:

prior   closer

washer

7. The vowel is written only when the endings *-ant, -ance, -ent, -ence* follow *ī, n, r, l*:

covenant   finance

talent

   but: constant

     influence

8. The ending *-ion* is expressed by *oo-n* after *n,* by *n* alone in other cases:

union   champion

Source: B. Scot Ober, "A Word to the Whys: A Discussion of the Construction of Gregg Shorthand Outlines," *Business Education World* 55, no. 5 (May–June 1975): 15. Reprinted with permission of BUSINESS EDUCATION WORLD, Gregg Division, McGraw-Hill Book Company, copyright May–June 1975.

based on the English language can never be bound by hard and fast rules for which no exceptions are allowed. The system must provide flexibility because there is a constant trade-off between brevity in writing and clarity in transcribing. In the final analysis, the primary consideration must be the student's ability to accurately record and transcribe dictation. In reaching this point, the student must be able to overcome a variety of errors.

THEORY ERRORS

In this section, we shall examine five major types of theory errors and suggest teaching strategies for reducing these errors.[32]

1. *Failing to apply joining/direction patterns properly.* The word *make* can be used as a simple example of the proper application of joining/direction patterns. When the shorthand symbols required to represent *make* (mak) are written in the proper direction, the *m* stroke is made with forward motion, the *a* vowel with dominant to the left motion, and the *k* stroke with downward motion. The result is a theoretically correct Century 21 shorthand outline:

Writing any of the three symbols in the wrong direction or joining them incorrectly results in a theoretically incorrect outline. If both consonants are written in the proper direction, but the *a* is written with right motion, at least two incorrect responses can be made:

Teaching strategy. The key to preventing joining or direction errors is to insist upon properly constructed symbols and outlines when students write them for the first time. Before student writing begins, demonstrate symbol and outline construction on the chalkboard or transparency so they can see the outlines being written properly. Emphasize sound/spelling. Pronounce the word and then sound/spell it aloud as you write the outline. Have students sound/spell the outline with you as they first watch and then imitate your writing patterns.

Call symbol direction aloud as students write outlines: "up with *m*" "left motion *a*," "down with *k*," and so on. After initial board demonstration and student imitation, move around the room correcting improper joining/direction patterns.

2. *Failing to distinguish among differences in vowel sounds.* Writing errors caused by the subtle differences in English sounds are likely to be the most common ones made as well as the most difficult to eliminate. Not only does each vowel have several barely discernible differences in sound, but different vowels also represent very similar sounds.

Vowels in *er* endings, for example, are shown in the dictionary as having neutral, or *schwa,* sounds. Since neutral vowel sounds are not written when they occur in the body of a word, the sound of *er* in the outline is expressed without writing the vowel: waiver (waver)

| waiver | wavǝr | |
| visitors | vizǝtǝrs | |

A similar, yet not exactly the same, *er* sound is contained in several other words. The dictionary shows the vowel as being distinct in *expert, shirt, word, nurse,* and *encourage.* The outlines for these words should be written with the *e* vowel:

expert	eks pert	
shirt	shert	
word	werd	
nurse	ners	
encourage	en ker ij	

Teaching strategy. No method of teaching can completely eliminate the problems inherent in the English language. Two suggestions should be considered. In the initial stages of theory learning, sound/spelling is an effective technique to use. Later, as emphasis shifts to building notetaking speed, previewing those outlines that contain likely candidates for vowel sound problems is probably the best way to help students learn to express vowel sounds more precisely.

3. *Failing to utilize the derived alphabet.* While any English words can be written by using only primary alphabet symbols, the resulting outlines will be longer and often difficult to write fluently. The writing advantage gained by using shortened repetitive word elements will be lost. Using *b* to represent *ble,* for instance, reduces the writing burden in words that contain this word ending:

| assembling | ǝ sem bling | |

Teaching strategy. Teach derived alphabet elements as unit sounds rather than as separate symbol sounds. Sound/spell the derived alphabet as follows:

concern	*con* s e r n
payment	p a *ment*
making	m a k *ing*

Preview words containing derived alphabet symbols, especially the less frequently used word beginnings and endings, prior to dictation practice containing these words.

4. *Failing to write symbols in proper proportion.* Although the sense of the sentence will often solve problems resulting from improper proportion, outlines where *a*'s and *e*'s are written with circles of nearly the same size or where *m*'s and *n*'s are practically the same length can technically be considered theory errors. Inability to make a great enough distinction between symbols that are written alike except for size can be a contributing factor to reading and transcribing difficulties.

Teaching strategy. In the beginning stages of writing, constantly stress the importance of good proportion by illustrating well-written outlines on the chalkboard. Later, during lower speed takes, when the speed forcing is relaxed, encourage students to concentrate on making definite distinctions in symbol size. Intersperse writing drills that specifically call attention to problems of proportion. Dictate outlines that will require proper proportion to distinguish between them:

call _____   and fall _____

wrote _____   and road _____

about _____   and appreciate _____

5. *Failing to place outlines in correct relation to the line of writing.*

People (pepl) when it is written

and *above* (abuv) if written

are examples of errors in placement.

While not usually a problem in systems that do not use position to represent various sounds, shorthand outlines not placed according to the basic placement rule are theoretically incorrect.

Teaching strategy. A simple explanation and demonstration of the basic placement rule when writing begins will normally solve this problem. Students who understand the rule and who see only outlines properly placed on the line in their texts should experience no difficulty. If placement questions arise, you may want to draw a line on the board to indicate correct outline placement.

module 7.3
LEARNING ACTIVITIES

1. Outline a procedure that you will use in introducing shorthand symbols. Be prepared to demonstrate a mini-lesson to the class.
2. Practice writing shorthand outlines, brief forms, phrases on the chalkboard and on an overhead projector transparency. Ask a fellow student or your instructor to

observe you as you write. Are you exhibiting the characteristics (proper motions, direction of outlines, correct proportion of characters, and so on) that you expect your students to use in writing?

3. Prepare a mini-lesson on reading shorthand from the chalkboard or from textbook plates. Incorporate at least two different reading drills. Be prepared to demonstrate to the class.

4. Select one of the five theory errors discussed in this module and prepare a remediation lesson. You may wish to structure it in the form of an instructional module or a drill, using tape, transparency, and printed material.

module 7.3
SELF-TEST

1. Summarize the characteristics of the reading and writing approaches to teaching shorthand.
2. Why is reading shorthand an important part of the instruction for beginning shorthand?
3. Explain a self-dictation procedure that a student may use in writing shorthand out of class.
4. List four priorities underlying the development of good writing skills in shorthand.
5. Name and briefly describe five characteristics associated with reading and spelling from the chalkboard.

module 7.4
DICTATION AND SPEED DEVELOPMENT

Developing student speed in writing shorthand is of primary importance in reaching a marketable level of skill. The successful shorthand teacher follows a well-defined overall procedure for introducing dictation and building speed. Several effective speed-building plans are described in this module, including the (1) one-minute plan, (2) stair step plan, (3) spurt dictation, (4) progressive dictation, (5) three-by-four plan, (6) pyramid speed-building plan, and (7) reducing speed/extending time plan. Techniques for developing writing skills, the role of dictation by semester, office-style dictation, methods of handling student differences, and accuracy development are also covered in this module.

After completing this module, you should be able to (1) outline a procedure for introducing (a) dictation, and (b) new-matter dictation; (2) explain and/or demonstrate the steps involved in at least four speed-building plans; (3) summarize the essence of speed-building procedures involved in four semesters of shorthand instruction; (4) demonstrate the ability to dictate at varying rates of speed; (5) outline procedures for providing for individual differences in speed building; (6) describe a plan for reviewing the shorthand alphabet; (7) explain at least eight techniques the teacher may use in developing writing skills in shorthand; and (8) identify at least five characteristics of office-style dictation.

INTRODUCING DICTATION

Developing student skill and speed in writing shorthand is of primary importance. According to Leslie:[33] "You can write (shorthand) as fast as your mind can think the outlines. The shorthand learner must be given every possible opportunity to stock his mind with good shorthand characters, every opportunity to use these characters correctly, and as little opportunity as possible to use those characters incorrectly." Most shorthand writing in the classroom should be from dictation. Early dictation, of course, is from easy, familiar, practiced material. Many teachers prefer to use material the students have practiced reading several days earlier. The use of easy material encourages students and gives them confidence in their ability to write shorthand. Before beginning to dictate, it is well to preview outlines, phrases, or brief forms/speed forms that may give students difficulty. Additional review after the dictation will be necessary if students are still having difficulty with certain outlines.

When introducing dictation, dictate at 40 to 60 words per minute with frequent pauses. Initially the teacher may dictate for 15 seconds, pause for 5 to 10 seconds, then dictate for another 15 seconds. Then the length of dictation may be increased to 20 seconds followed by a 5- to 10-second pause, followed by dictation for 30 seconds with a 5-second pause. Gradually the teacher works up to a full minute of dictation with no pause. During the very early stages of writing, the teacher may not want to time the dictation. This delay could be for two or three days or as long as two weeks, depending on teacher preference and student abilities.

Permitting students to have their textbooks open while taking dictation should be limited to the early stages of writing. To help ensure that students are listening to the dictation and not copying from the textbook, occasionally change simple words. One approach that might be considered a bridge between practiced and new-matter dictation is to rearrange the content of the letters from the textbook plates and construct "new" letters on the same topic and composed of the same words, but arranged in different order. Thus, the students are writing familiar material that is arranged differently.

NEW-MATTER DICTATION

Shorthand teachers are not in agreement as to when to begin new-matter dictation. Russon[34] developed an early new-matter approach to the teaching of shorthand in which dictation is introduced during the second week of instruction. Leslie,[35] on the other hand, believes that students are not prepared to begin new-matter dictation until they can write practiced material at the rate of 80 to 100 *wam* on 60-second repetitive dictation. The combined problems of (1) the high dropout rate between first- and second-year shorthand and (2) the development of marketable skill, whether in one or more years of instruction, may cause the business teacher to consider seriously a relatively early introduction of new-matter dictation. For example, very simple material that has been liberally previewed on the chalkboard/overhead projector may be introduced during the latter part of the first semester. During the second semester, the teacher gradually increases the amount of new-matter dictation for speed building.

Regardless of when new-matter dictation is introduced, the teacher should use easy material—short, simple sentences composed of easy words—that has been thoroughly previewed. Initially, 30-second dictation at a speed the class can write is recommended.

Speed building is a key factor in developing a marketable shorthand skill. The longer a student is allowed to remain at a given speed, the more difficult it becomes to move to his or her eventual goal. The writing motions made at one speed are not simply the same ones speeded up at a higher level; the motions change as the student increases speed. Thus when a student remains at one level too long, his or her writing habits become more difficult to alter.[36] In order to force speed in writing shorthand, the teacher should keep these principles in mind:[37]

1. Dictation for speed building should be short, faster than the previous one, until the last dictation, which is given for quality of writing.
2. Announce the speed of each dictation so that learners may become accustomed to judging speed for themselves.
3. Practice for speed development must be done without regard for legibility; the learner must learn to write faster than he can write. As each new speed advance is consolidated, it will be possible to write that speed legibly; meanwhile, the learners will be learning to write illegibly the next higher speed. Give very short dictations, repeated at higher and higher speeds, with no responsibility for legibility. Finally, in order to avoid the permanent loss of legibility, give the learner an occasional opportunity to write at a speed that is slow for that learner with no responsibility except for accuracy and legibility of outlines—about every fourth or fifth dictation. This alternation between writing for speed, without regard for legibility and for legibility without regard for speed, has proved to be the surest and most rapid road to the desired combination of speed and legibility.

SPEED-BUILDING PLANS

The business teacher will want to use a variety of plans for building speed in writing shorthand. Since students acquire writing speeds in varying degrees, the teacher should present enough alternatives to meet the needs of each student. In this section we shall review some well-known plans that have been used successfully.

One-minute plan

One of the most widely used plans for developing speed is the one-minute plan. Several variations of the plan are given in the literature. The following procedure is excerpted from Leslie:[38]

Assume that a class is able to write 400 words in an exercise at about 60 words a minute.

1. Place on the chalkboard the preview (about 10 outlines) for the first 100 words of the dictation. These previews are read at random as the teacher points; they are not written by the learner.
2. Dictate the first 60 words in 1 minute. Have learners who got the dictation raise their hands after each dictation. Whenever more than one-half raise their hands, dictate 10–15 words a minute faster. *Allow 10 or 15 seconds for the slower writers to complete writing at the end of each dictation.*
3. Take 10–15 seconds to have the learners reread the preview quickly from the chalkboard.
4. Dictate in the minute 75 words—that is, 60 plus an additional 15. Ask how many got it. Have the material read back—although not more than one dictation in ten should be read back.
5. Have the learners read the preview again from the blackboard in 10–15 seconds.
6. Redictate, this time at 90 *wam.*
7. Reread the preview in 10–15 seconds and redictate at 100 *wam.* Not all the learners may get this fourth dictation, but urge them to get as much as they can consecutively. They are not to drop a few words and then resume writing.
8. Redictate the first 75 words in 1 minute with these instructions to the learners: "This will be only 75 *wam.* It will seem very slow. Write the very best shorthand you can; you will have lots of time to make good outlines."
9. Repeat Steps 1–8 (all the above) for the next 100 words of the dictation.
10. Dictate at 90 *wam* the two takes just completed.
11. Repeat the first eight steps for the next 100 words and again for the following 100 words.
12. Finally, redictate the entire 400 words at about 80 *wam.* Exact speed will vary with the class and with the difficulty of the matter.

Different material may be given, of course, at different rates. You might use 60, 70, 80, 90, 100—70. On very easy material, the dictation rates might run 60, 80, 100, 120—80, and so on.

Stair step plan

The stair step plan has been described by Grubbs as a method for building speed, endurance, and new-word skills. Illustration 7.3 shows the plan graphically, and the following discussion explains how to use it. The speeds and letters shown in the chart were chosen to illustrate the method. The plan could be used in any speed range and with any business letters.

First, choose four or five business letters as the dictation material for the plan. The exact number of words is unimportant, but letters of 80 to 100 words in length are recommended. Remove the letter endings to keep them short, and this is important at the beginning of the semester.

Having chosen your letters and with your stopwatch and chalk ready for instant use, Grubbs recommends these steps:[39]

1. Preview letter 140 at the chalkboard or overhead projector. Dictate letter 140 at 80 *wam* (or any other appropriate speed). Determine how many of your students got the take. Write additional outlines on the board or overhead if requested. If almost all of your students got letter 140, move to Step 2. If they did not, repeat the letter at 80 or at a lower rate if it appears that 80 is inappropriate.

2. Dictate letter 140 at 90 *wam* (or 10 words faster than your initial rate) and, without pausing between the complimentary close, dictate letter 141 at 80 wam. Determine how many of your students got the take, and place additional outlines on the board or overhead as needed. Read aloud and in concert all the words now on the board or overhead. This step may be repeated if necessary until all or almost all students get both letters. Then move to Step 3.

3. Dictate letter 140 at 100 *wam.* Follow immediately without pause with letter 141 at 90. Follow immediately with letter 142 at 80, placing the unfamiliar outlines in this letter on the board or overhead. Read all the words you have accumulated to this point, adding any that may be requested. Step 3 may be repeated if necessary.

4. Dictate letter 140 at 110 *wam,* letter 141 at 100, letter 142 at 90, and the new letter 143 at 80 *wam.* Place selected outlines from letter 143 on the board or overhead. Have all the words read in concert and either repeat Step 4 or proceed to Step 5.

5. Dictate letter 140 at 120 *wam,* letter 141 at 110, letter 142 at 100, letter 143 at 90, and letter 144 at 80 *wam.* Place selected outlines from letter 144 on the board or overhead. Have all the words read in concert and either repeat Step 5 or proceed to Step 6.

6. Dictate letters 140, 141, 142, and 143 without pause at 90 *wam.* This will be a take of about 3 1/2 minutes' duration. The rate, 90 *wam,* is enough below the maximum to which you have pushed your students, and there have been sufficient repetitions so that they should be able to get this take with ease and with confident control.

If you use five letters without repeating any steps, you can complete the procedure in 25 minutes. If you use only four letters, the plan consumes about 17 minutes. If you elect to use only three or four letters in the stair step procedure, operate the plan twice, using two separate sets of letters for maximum vocabulary experience.

Spurt dictation

The business teacher can relieve the monotony arising from continuous use of evenly spaced dictation by giving students an opportunity to take spurt dictation. This carefully planned *uneven* dictation is helpful in assisting students to break away from skill plateaus. The brief spurts to high rates will

illustration 7.3
STAIR STEP PLAN

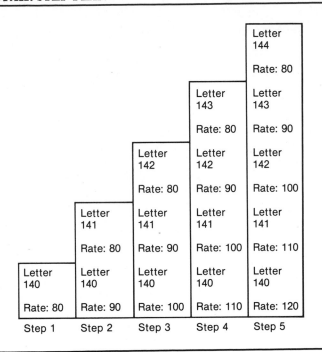

Source: Robert L. Grubbs, "Rx for Effective Shorthand Teaching: How to Build Skill in Second-Semester Shorthand," *Business Education World* 41, no. 6 (February 1961): 25. Reprinted with permission of BUSINESS EDUCATION WORLD, Gregg Division, McGraw-Hill Book Company, copyright February 1961.

help them exceed their present speed ceilings. The easiest way to use spurt dictation is to choose some material and type it in a spurt pattern of your choice. Then dictate it by the line rather than by the familiar 20 standard word groups. To make dictation very easy, plan to use a 6-second dictation interval per line. Since 6 seconds is one-tenth of a minute, the approximate rate for any line is determined by multiplying the number of 5-stroke words on the line by 10. For example, lines of 9 words (45 strokes) each dictated in 6 seconds will be dictated at the rate of 90 wam (9 x 10). The chart shows the rate per line for a number of lines when the dictation interval is one-tenth of a minute, or 6 seconds. The sample letter illustrates how a short letter might look when typed for spurt dictation.

Progressive dictation

Progressive dictation is continuous dictation that accelerates in a uniform fashion to higher and higher rates. To arrange your material for progressive dictation, simply follow the same procedure used in arranging material

ARRANGEMENT FOR SPURT DICTATION

If you dictate in 6 seconds a line of	Your dictation rate is
25 strokes - 5 words	50 *wam*
30 strokes - 6 words	60 *wam*
35 strokes - 7 words	70 *wam*
40 strokes - 8 words	80 *wam*
45 strokes - 9 words	90 *wam*
50 strokes - 10 words	100 *wam*
55 strokes - 11 words	110 *wam*
60 strokes - 12 words	120 *wam*
65 strokes - 13 words	130 *wam*
70 strokes - 14 words	140 *wam*

Source: Robert L. Grubbs, "Rx for Effective Shorthand Teaching: How to Build Skill in Second-Semester Shorthand," *Business Education World* 41, no. 6 (February 1961): 27. Reprinted with permission of BUSINESS EDUCATION WORLD, Gregg Division, McGraw-Hill Book Company, copyright February 1961.

LETTER FOR SPURT DICTATION

(Dictate each line in 6 seconds)	*wam* Rate per line
Dear Mr. Welsh: Are you planning to move	80
your factory to some other part of the	80
country? If so, one of your immediate	80
problems is to get complete information	80
about sites that are available. That is	80
where the Central Railroad can serve you. Our men have all	120
the facts necessary to help you pick the location that is	120
best suited to your needs. They can give you accu-	100
rate answers to any questions that you may want	90
to ask. They have complete information	80
on hundreds of sites in various parts of	80
the country. This service, which has proved of value to	110
the heads of large and small businesses alike, is described in our	130
booklet, "How to Find a Home for Your Busi-	80
ness." Send for a copy right now. Yours truly	90

Source: Robert L. Grubbs, "Rx for Effective Shorthand Teaching: How to Build Skill in Second-Semester Shorthand," *Business Education World* 41, no. 6 (February 1961): 27. Reprinted with permission of BUSINESS EDUCATION WORLD, Gregg Division, McGraw-Hill Book Company, copyright February 1961.

for spurt dictation, except that you will type it in steadily increasing line lengths. The following example shows a letter arranged for progressive dictation. Each line is to be dictated in 6 seconds and the rates are marked at the right. Use it only occasionally to help move students from a speed plateau.

LETTER FOR PROGRESSIVE DICTATION

(Dictate each line in 6 seconds)	Approximate *wam* Rate per line
Dear Mr. Collins: Thank you for your ap-	80
plication of October 7 in response to our	80
advertisement in the local newspapers. The	80
facts you have provided on the application	80
indicate that you are well qualified for the posi-	100
tion that is open, except that you do not seem to	100
have had very much selling experience. If you have	100
had such experience but have not indicated it on	100
your application, won't you please give us further information.	120
I am enclosing a booklet that describes our organization and	120
its functions. In the back of the booklet you will find a copy	120
of the agreement under which you would work as well as a sched-	120
ule of the commissions that we pay. As we stated in our advertisement,	140
we pay a big commission from which we expect our representatives to pay	140
their own expenses. The commission is 50 per cent of the first year's	140
business and 10 per cent for the next five years. I think you will agree	140
that this is a generous arrangement. Very truly yours,	110

Source: Robert L. Grubbs, "Rx for Effective Shorthand Teaching: How to Build Skill in Second-Semester Shorthand," *Business Education World* 41, no. 6 (February 1961): 28. Reprinted with permission of BUSINESS EDUCATION WORLD, Gregg Division, McGraw-Hill Book Company, copyright February 1961.

3 X 4 Plan

A skill-building plan recommended by Russon,[40] the 3 X 4 plan is well adapted for second-year shorthand classes. Assuming that the class is working for 100 words a minute, the procedure is as follows:

First, preview the first 3 minutes of a 5-minute 100 *wam* take (this will represent about 10 percent of the total, or 30 outlines).

1. Dictate for one-half minute at 140 *wam.*
2. Dictate the next one-half minute at 140 *wam.*
3. Now dictate the first minute at 120 *wam.*
4. Next, dictate the third half minute at 140 *wam.*
5. Now dictate the fourth half minute at 140 *wam.*
6. Next, dictate the last two half minutes at 120 *wam.*
7. Finally, dictate the entire take (3 minutes) at 100 *wam.*

Blanchard's pyramid speed-building plan

The objective of this plan is to increase the shorthand student's speed 20 *wam* on a 5-minute take. Assume that the class has reached a speed of 100 *wam* for 5 minutes on new matter, and that you want to increase their speed to 120 *wam* on a 5-minute take of new matter that has been liberally previewed. Assuming that a student can write for ½ minute at a speed 50 *wam* faster than he or she can write for 5 minutes, he or she can write for 1 minute at a speed 40 *wam* faster than he or she can write for 5 minutes. Therefore, your first goal is to raise the student's speed to 170 *wam* for ½ minute, then to 160 *wam* for 1 minute, then to 150 *wam* for 2 minutes, then to 140 *wam* for 3 minutes, then to 130 *wam* for 4 minutes, and finally to 120 *wam* for 5 minutes. (See Illustration 7.4.)

Step 1: Select from the student's text two or more easy business letters totaling approximately 600 words. Do not dictate any addresses during the timed dictation.

Step 2: Prior to the dictation period, assign for study a preview of 10 percent of the words in the take (60 in this case). Instruct the students to practice them from three to five minutes each and to know definitions.

Step 3: (At the class period following the study assignment, dictate for 2 minutes on easy matter for a warm-up.) Place the practiced preview on the chalkboard in large outlines. Have students read them rapidly and write them once from dictation at the rate of one outline a second. Leave outlines on the board for reference. (6 minutes)

Step 4: Dictate 300 words of the take at 100 *wam.* This gives the students the satisfaction of knowing they can write the new take at their present speed. (3 minutes)

Step 5: Have one or two students read back the first half of the dictation. (2 minutes)

Step 6: Dictate four half-minute takes at exactly 170 *wam*, stopping a few seconds between each dictation. Instruct students to finish each take. This will cover the first 340 words. Have one of the takes read back, preferably the second one. (3 minutes)

Step 7: Redictate the four half-minute takes as two one-minute takes at 160 *wam*. (2 minutes)

Step 8: Have the last half of this take read back. (1 minute)

Step 9: Repeat the procedure in Step 6, giving two more half-minute takes at 170. At the end of this step, you will have dictated the entire take. Have the last half-minute take read back. (2 minutes)

Step 10: Redictate these two half-minute takes at 160 *wam* without stopping and have the first half read back. (2 minutes)

Step 11: Let students rest a minute and then redictate the first 300 words of the take without stopping and have half of it read back. (2 minutes)

Step 12: Have students write the entire take at 120 *wam*—the goal. Have 200 words read back beginning in the middle of the take. (9 minutes)

Reducing speed/extending time plan

This plan[41] is recommended for building sustained writing speed. Using this approach, students read back frequently which allows them an opportunity to rest their writing hands. These steps are employed:

1. Select two or three letters from the text that total approximately 300 words.
2. Preview the unusual outlines that appear in the first 75 to 80 words. Have the class write each word several times.
3. Dictate the first 75 to 80 words at a speed of 140 words a minute.
4. Preview outlines in the next 75 to 80 words in the same way.
5. Dictate this word group at 140 words a minute.
6. Proceed in the same manner for the third and fourth groups of 75 to 80 words.
7. Challenge students to scribble-write the first half of the letter at 140 words a minute.
8. Allow 20 to 30 seconds for students to look over the outlines in the text.
9. Dictate the first half of the letter at 120 words a minute and ask students to try getting it all down. Then have someone read the material from notes as the rest of the class checks what they have written.
10. Repeat Steps 7, 8, and 9 for the second half of the letter.
11. Dictate the entire letter at 100 *wam*. Students can be called on to read while the rest of the class check their notes.

TECHNIQUES FOR DEVELOPING WRITING SKILLS

When dictation begins, the teacher should observe carefully the students' writing to ensure that outlines are written in the correct proportion and in the right direction. There are many ways to vary the procedure for giving dictation so that student interest and motivation are maintained at a high level. The following techniques are offered by Driska:[42]

illustration 7.4
PYRAMID SPEED-BUILDING PLAN

Timing aid for material counted in twenty standard-word groups:

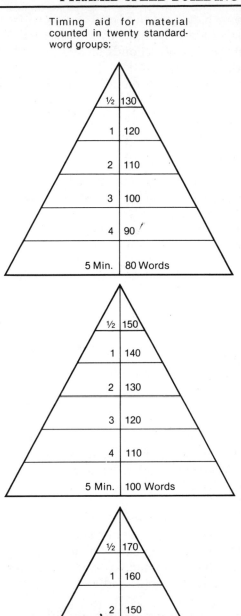

½	130
1	120
2	110
3	100
4	90
5 Min.	80 Words

½	150
1	140
2	130
3	120
4	110
5 Min.	100 Words

½	170
1	160
2	150
3	140
4	130
5 Min.	120 Words

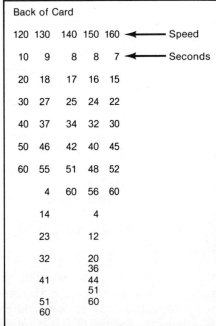

Front of Card

Speed →	60	70	80	90	100	110
Seconds →	20	17	15	13	12	11
	40	34	30	26	24	22
	60	51	45	40	36	33
		8	60	53	48	44
		25		6	60	55
		42		20		6
		60		33		17
				47		28
				60		39
						50
						60

(3 x 5 inch card)

Back of Card

Speed →	120	130	140	150	160
Seconds →	10	9	8	8	7
	20	18	17	16	15
	30	27	25	24	22
	40	37	34	32	30
	50	46	42	40	45
	60	55	51	48	52
		4	60	56	60
	14			4	
	23			12	
	32			20	
				36	
	41			44	
				51	
	51			60	
	60				

1. Have students memorize a shorthand sentence every week or two. In class for practice, they can write their sentence over and over in shorthand; you may want to time them on the sentence for 30 seconds or one minute. This process will help the students to write fluently.

2. To develop word-carrying capacity during dictation, have faster students occasionally wait until the end of the first sentence before beginning to write. When these students catch up with you, encourage them to wait until you are a sentence ahead. If a student practices this procedure occasionally, he or she will remember more of the dictation at a speed that will be a little faster for him or her.

3. Dictate newly previewed materials at a very rapid speed, 140 *wam* and up, announcing to students beforehand that whenever you stop dictating and call *stop*, each student must stop writing immediately. Make a game of this; the aim is to take all the dictation before *stop* is called. The number of stops depends upon the length of the material. Frequent, unexpected stops motivate the students to try harder each time. After the material has been dictated in this manner one or two times, repeat the material without interruptions at a specific rate such as 120 *wam.*

4. Dictate a personal letter addressed to the entire class or to an individual student. These short letters or postscripts added to a regular letter come as a surprise to the student.

5. For variety in homework in second-year shorthand, occasionally duplicate and distribute double-spaced typewritten material. Instruct students to write the shorthand outlines directly above the longhand words. Students will have to construct their own outlines and therefore will not be simply copying shorthand from the text.

6. In advanced shorthand, sprinkle letters with instructions. One day a week in your advanced classes, dictate some kind of special notation for several of the dictated letters. Students may make an extra carbon copy for you (cc); make a blind carbon copy (bcc); send a letter by registered mail, special delivery, certified mail, and so on.

7. When the dictation is too slow for the students, they should draw an additional line on each side of the printed vertical line in their notebooks, and then write each phrase of the dictation across the page as many times as they can. When the dictation is too fast, the students should write until they become confused. Then they should leave space in the notes and begin the next sentence.

Balsley suggests the following strategies for developing writing skills in shorthand:[43]

1. *Repetitive dictation.* This device is especially useful in situations where there is a wide speed range. The instructor states that thought phrases are going to be repeated as he or she dictates. The students are instructed to try to take the dictation every time it is repeated, but are to go on with the dictation as soon as they hear a new thought phrase. The rate at which the thought phrases

are dictated and how many repetitions are given are determined by the rate range of the entire class. When the letter has been completely dictated in this fashion, then the teacher redictates "straight" at middle-of-the-range speed for the class. If the letter began, "Dear Miss Owen: Our annual conference will be held again this year in Ocotober in Dallas . . . ," the repetitive dictation might sound something like this: "Dear Miss Owen . . . Dear Miss Owen . . . Our annual conference . . . Our annual conference . . . will be held again . . . will be held again . . . ," and so on. This device has proved to be one of the most effective for convincing students that they can write shorthand as fast as they can think it.

2. *Double take.* If the class has a wide range of note-taking speed, this device is useful. The teacher asks students to try to "double take" everything dictated. He or she then dictates at a rate at which the slowest students can get the dictation down once and which will probably challenge the speediest writers in their efforts to write everything twice. For example, an instructor might dictate at 40 words a minute. If a student were able to "double take" all of the dictation, he or she would, in effect, be taking the dictation at 80 words a minute. After the "double take" dictation, the letter/memo should be dictated "straight" at a rate 10 or 20 words above the original rate.

3. *Accelerated dictation.* This device is useful in two ways: it helps students become accustomed to the uneven dictation characteristic of the office, and it develops the ability to "hang on" when they fall behind the dictator. The teacher dictates each successive quarter minute at a 10-word higher rate for a minute and then drops back to the starting speed. For example, the first quarter minute might be at 40; the second, 50; the third, 60; and the fourth, 70. Each successive minute would follow the same pattern. This pattern could also be used with 20-word groups rather than on a quarter-minute basis.

4. *Zigzag dictation.* This device, like accelerated dictation, is helpful in getting students to "hang on" and to stretch themselves for short periods of time. It is best used with a letter or memo of several paragraphs of somewhat equal lengths or with a series of short letters. The pattern of dictation would be something like this:

P	1	60 wam
	2	70
Ps	1, 2	60
P	3	60
	4	70
Ps	3, 4	60
	1–4	60

There would be a pause of a few seconds between the dictation of each paragraph or group of paragraphs.

The dictation might also be of the opposite timing; that is, of raising the speed for the combined paragraphs, in which case the pattern would be:

P	1	60
	2	60
Ps	1, 2	70
P	3	60
	4	60
Ps	3, 4	70
	1–4	70

5. *Retention.* In this device, the teacher selects a group of sentences to be used over a period of time, each one longer by a word or two than the preceding one. They might be, for instance, 10 words, 12 words, 15 words, and so on. The student listens to the entire sentence and then writes it in a notebook. Over a period of several weeks, students can raise their ability to hold dictation in their minds by several words.

6. *Eyes-on-copy recording.* This device is helpful if there is a wide speed range in the class. The speed is announced, and the students are told that if they can take dictation at that speed they are to do so; those knowing the speed is too high for them are instructed to keep their eyes on the plate notes and write in their notebooks *without looking in the notebook.* They should be told that their outlines may be on top of each other because they are not looking in the notebook. The important fact is that the students will be seeing the outline for the word as it is dictated and they will be executing at the rate being dictated. When the dictation has been completed, it should be repeated at a lower rate. The students who attempt to take the material without looking in the book can check the plates quickly for any outlines on which they stumbled and then join the dictation.

7. *Potential rate-builder.* This device may also be identified as "The Sprint." Its purpose is to bring out the fact that one can write shorthand as fast as one thinks it. The teacher presents the sentence to be used—the first one should probably be no more than 10 words. Then he or she directs students to start writing the sentence when it is dictated and to write the sentence as many times as possible before "Stop" is called. Students then compute their rates. First the student counts the total number of times the sentence has been written. Next, the student multiplies the number of words in the sentence by the number of times it was written completely. Any words in a partially completed sentence are added on as well. This total number of words is multiplied by whatever figure is needed to get the rate per minute. For instance, if the timing period was 20 seconds, the students would need to multiply the total number of words by three to get the rate per minute.

8. *Phrase automatization.* A quick review of families of phrases can be accomplished by directing students to try to write each phrase dictated as many times as possible before they hear the next one. Such a group might be: *to be, to pay, to be able, to go,* and so on. The teacher can dictate at so many seconds a phrase or can simply watch the students to determine the proper pace.

Another device for building phrase capabilities is to dictate a paragraph or short letter "loaded" with phrases, asking students to note how many they wrote; then dictate the same material a second time.

9. *Geographical briefs.* In "everyday" dictation, only limited opportunity to write names of countries, states, and cities may be provided. Short sentences or paragraphs can be dictated that are "loaded" with geographical names.

10. *Briefform/speedform stress.* Short paragraphs "loaded" with briefforms/speedforms provide intensive review as a relief from word drills on the chalkboard.

11. *Intensive theory.* As with speedforms, short paragraphs "loaded" with outlines illustrative of certain theory can be dictated. Such "loaded" material should not, of course, be used for high speed development but rather for expanding shorthand vocabulary.

12. *Previewing and postviewing.* Some variety can be provided in dictation sessions by sometimes previewing a take and other times by postviewing.

13. *Precision practice.* Since in any symbol system many strokes differ only in proportion, brief practice in precise writing is desirable. Sentences containing several outlines in which poorly written outlines could be misread are dictated and the students asked to read back their notes.

14. *Sustained dictation.* Dictation without pause for 5 to 10 minutes occasionally helps students get the "feel" of actual dictation sessions. Such sustained dictation should probably not be attempted until the end of the beginning semester or during the second semester.

15. *Office-style dictation.* Even in beginning shorthand, students should be introduced to office-style dictation. This early introduction helps students realize the need for accurate outlines and gives them a clearer picture of their ultimate goal. Such dictation would, of course, be short.

16. *High-low.* In this device the teacher dictates at, say, 80 *wam* on the 60-word base. To do so, she dictates for 15 seconds at 80 *wam,* pauses for 5 seconds (bringing her watch to 20 seconds); dictates for 15 seconds at 80 *wam,* pauses for 5 seconds (bringing her watch to 40 seconds); and dictates for another 15 seconds at 80 *wam,* pauses for 5 seconds (bringing her watch to 60 seconds). Students should be encouraged to write fast enough to be waiting for the teacher to resume dictation before the 5-second pause has expired.

17. *Change-of-pace.* Several techniques can be used to inject variety in the skill-building process. Students can be asked to trade notebooks after a take and read each other's notes. The students should know that, in some emergency situations, a secretary may be asked to transcribe notes taken by somebody else. The students can be asked to stand while they take dictation, since such a situation sometimes occurs in the office. Students may be asked to take dictation with notebooks on their laps or with the notebook on the edge of the desk, simulating taking dictation while seated at the side of the dictator's desk.

OFFICE-STYLE DICTATION*

A commonly used teaching device is office-style dictation. Limited amounts of easy office-style dictation can be introduced in beginning shorthand, with more liberal amounts being used as students develop proficiency. The major emphasis in shorthand classes, however, is on developing speed and accuracy and making a mailable transcript. The best way to provide students with experiences in office-style dictation is through work experience—that is, on the job "live" dictation. Another technique is to have business persons come to class or prepare tapes and dictate answers to their correspondence. The business teacher can provide office-style dictation by dictating unrehearsed responses to his or her business letters.

For the teacher who wishes to cover them systematically, the usual types of office dictation include the following:

1. *Deleting and substituting word(s).* The dictator may change words as the sentence is being dictated:

> Extrusion produces a tougher and more reliable metal—no, a more *durable* metal . . .

Sometimes the dictator will decide to delete or change words several sentences later. In this case, he or she will have the stenographer read back the sentence and indicate the changes as the sentence is being read back:

> Delete *durable* and make it *rust-resistant.*

Deletions can be easily recognized by running a long diagonal mark through the words to be removed. The substituted word can be written above the one removed.

2. *Restoring words previously deleted.* Occasionally the dictator wishes to restore words as originally dictated:

> Extrusion produces a tougher and more rust-resistant metal—go back and make it a tougher and more *durable* metal.

In this case, the stenographer will cross out *rust-resistant* and rewrite the word *durable.*

3. *Transposing words, sentences, or paragraphs.* When the dictator makes a short transposition of a word, it can be indicated by using the sign:

> Extrusion produces a metal that is ⌐stronger⌐and⌐better⌐.

---

*At least three features distinguish office-style dictation from other dictation in the shorthand class: (1) the material is dictated only once, (2) the material may or may not be dictated at an even rate, and (3) corrections and instructions are incorporated into the dictation.

Occasionally, a whole sentence or paragraph is transposed by circling the material and making an arrow to the point where the material is to be placed. Material to be transposed to another page is treated as an insertion.

4. *Making insertions.* A very frequent change in office-style dictation is the insertion of a word or words using the caret. The dictator may give specific instructions (as in the following example) or he or she may not:

> Extruded aluminum is better than other—go back and put in *and lighter*—is better and lighter.

If the stenographer has already written *extruded aluminum is better than,* the

insertion may be made by the use of the longhand caret ($\wedge$).

Long insertions occur frequently and the stenographer must be prepared for them. The employer may interrupt the dictation or at the end of the dictation say:

> Go back and insert this paragraph right after the paragraph about the manufacturing process.

In this case, the stenographer should immediately mark a capital A with a large circle around it at the point where the new paragraph is to be inserted. Then in the next blank space in the notebook, write in shorthand "Insert A" with a circle around it. After the dictation of the insert is completed, write in shorthand "End of Insert A" with a circle around it. It is important to indicate the end as well as the beginning of any long insert. If the stenographer finds that the dictator constantly adds long inserts, as often happens in legal dictation, it is recommended that he or she write in only one column of the notebook, leaving the other column blank for inserts.

5. *Indenting material.* If the dictator indicates before beginning that he or she wishes to indent material for purposes of emphasis, the stenographer can actually indent the shorthand notes. The indented material should be enclosed on both sides by brackets ([   ]) to show that it is to be indented in the transcript and that the typewritten margins are to be changed.

6. *Noting special instructions.* Instructions about spelling and capitalization should be recorded in the briefest way possible. If the dictator indicates that a certain word is to be capitalized, simply put two dashes under the shorthand outline. Likewise, if punctuation is specified, it should be recorded within a circle. In other words, do the thing that is to be done rather than recording the instruction itself.

During the dictation, the employer will frequently think of special instructions: "By the way, send a carbon copy of this letter to Sanders." Instructions of this type should always be placed immediately at the beginning of the shorthand notes for that letter so that the transcript is completed *with* the extra letter. A few blank lines can be left before beginning a letter for purposes of making such notations.

Occasionally the nature of these instructions is such that they are most effectively kept at the point within the communication where they were actually dictated:

> These units can be offered to you with the following accessories—*list the options we have available*—with delivery in thirty days.

Such instructions can be effectively noted by writing them briefly in shorthand, separated from the preceding and following parts of the letter by a bold line above and below the instructions.

These and many other types of changes will be encountered in office-style dictation. Invariably, the dictator will be interrupted and will ask the stenographer to "read it back." Whenever such interruptions occur, the stenographer should immediately begin reading back the letter on which he or she is working. The business teacher should give shorthand students some practice in finding and reading back passages of letters being dictated.

ROLE OF DICTATION BY SEMESTER

Russon[44] summarizes the changing role of dictation speedbuilding in four semesters of shorthand. (When shorthand is offered for less than four semesters, the teacher would have to modify the procedures to help students acquire a usable shorthand skill.)

FIRST SEMESTER. The one-minute plan is used most of the time in the first semester, with the inverted pyramid plan used about one-quarter of the time. Speed intervals are usually increased by 10 *wam* (40, 50, 60 *wam*, and so on).

New-matter dictation (introduced early according to Russon's plan) is presented very slowly. The difference between 20 *wam* and 60 *wam* dictation is largely the time between the thought phrases, not the rate of dictating the words or phrases themselves. Punctuation is dictated in the first semester. After the first three weeks of dictation, however, periods are no longer dictated. Students are instructed to write periods whenever the dictator's voice indicates the end of a sentence. All other punctuation marks, however, are dictated. Students should read back punctuation marks when reading their notes.

SECOND SEMESTER. The one-minute plan is still used most of the time; the inverted pyramid plan, about one-quarter of the time; and the progressive plan, occasionally. The speed interval is increased from 10 *wam* (40, 60, 80, and so on). The teacher does not dictate punctuation in 3- and 5-minute takes. Have students read the punctuation mark where it should go in the transcript when reading back from their notes.

THIRD-FOURTH SEMESTERS.   During these semesters, the 3 X 4 plan is used about half the time, the one-minute plan about one-quarter of the time, and other plans are used occasionally. No punctuation or paragraphs are dictated in these semesters, but students should read punctuation marks when they read back their notes. Specific vocabulary drill should be incorporated into the instructional program. Dictation skill comes from the elimination of pauses; vocabulary practice will help cut down on the pauses that are bound to occur when the student hears an unfamiliar word. Difficulty of vocabulary in all dictation materials should increase with each semester.

Several speed-building plans are discussed in this module. The teacher should, of course, select the plans appropriate for the level of instruction and for individual learner needs.

One of the skills that the business teacher must develop is dictating at an appropriate pace. Dictation should be given in thought units, not word-by-word, and the teacher has to learn to dictate these thought groups at the various rates. A stopwatch is a necessary tool, and teachers should practice dictating, pacing themselves with the watch, before attempting to dictate to the class. Most of the prepared dictation material is marked off in groups of 20 "standard" words. "Standard" words are words that contain an average of 1.4 syllables. Every 28 syllables are equivalent to 20 standard words (28 divided by 1.4). The number of actual words that comprise 20 "standard" words varies. To properly pace dictation, the teacher must determine the length of time necessary to dictate 20 standard words. This is calculated as follows: Standard Word Count/Desired Rate X 60 Seconds = Seconds for Group. In pacing dictation at 60 *wam* , 20 standard words would be dictated every 20 seconds (20/60 X 60 = 20). Illustration 7.5 shows the number of seconds used to dictate 20-word groups at dictation rates ranging from 40 to 140 *wam*. You may want to make copies of this chart and fasten them to the front of each book or collection of dictation material.

Some of the dictation material is counted and marked to be dictated at specific rates, such as 60, 70, 80, 90 *wam*. You may, however, want to use these materials at other rates. Illustration 7.6 indicates how to change the pace of material counted for 15-second dictation intervals at designated speeds to other speeds. For example, the material marked in quarter-minute intervals for 60 *wam* would be dictated in 15 seconds (¼ minute). If you wished to use the same material at 90 *wam*, dictate each quarter-minute interval in 10 seconds.

INDIVIDUAL DIFFERENCES

Effective shorthand instruction must be organized so as to provide for individual differences. For years business teachers have done this to some extent, for example, by dictating at different rates. While varying the rate of dictation is one way to provide for individual needs, the business teacher must also vary the time that dictation is introduced, the amount and kind of out-of-class assignments, the amount and kind of practice drills, and the time that illustration 7.5

STOP WATCH SETTING FOR DICTATING AT VARIOUS RATES FROM MATERIAL COUNTED IN GROUPS OF 20 STANDARD WORDS

Rate Desired for Dictation (*wam*)

	40	45	50	55	60	65	70	75	80	85	90	95	100	105	110	115	120	125	130	135	140
Elapsed	30	27	24	22	20	19	17	16	15	14	13	13	12	11	11	10	10	9	9	8	8
Time in	60	53	48	44	40	37	34	32	30	28	26	25	24	23	22	21	20	19	18	17	17
Seconds		20	12	5	60	55	51	48	45	42	40	38	36	34	33	31	30	28	27	26	25
						14	8	4	60	56	53	51	48	46	44	42	40	38	37	35	34
										11	6	3	60	57	55	52	50	47	46	44	42
														9	6	3	60	57	55	53	51
																		6	4	2	60

To use this chart, look under the column headed by the rate at which you wish to dictate. The figures under each column heading indicate the number of seconds which should elapse as each 20-word group is dictated. For example, to dictate at 65 *wam,* the first 20-word group should be dictated in 19 seconds, the second 20-word group should be dictated by the time 37 seconds have elapsed, and so on.

These time indications have been rounded and carried through the first minute, but may be used when dictating for longer periods: If the last figure is 60, simply repeat the cycle; if the last figure is other than 60, return the sweep hand of the stop watch to zero when the last figure is reached, then repeat the cycle.

Source: Edward L. Christensen and R. DerMont Bell, *Teacher's Manual, Century 21 Shorthand,* Book 1 (Cincinatti: South-Western Publishing Company, 1974).

illustration 7.6

CONVERSION CHART FOR DICTATING AT VARIOUS RATES FROM MATERIAL MARKED IN QUARTER-MINUTE INTERVALS AT A GIVEN RATE

Rate Desired for Dictation (*wam*)

Rate at Which Copy Is Counted	40	50	60	70	80	90	100
40	15	12	10	9	7/8	7	6
50	19	15	12/13	11	9	8	7/8
60	22/23	18	15	13	11	10	9
70	26	21	17/18	15	13	12	10/11
80	30	24	20	17	15	13	12
90	34	27	22/23	19	17	15	13/14
100	37/38	30	25	21	19	17	15

Elapsed Time in Seconds

When double figures are given, alternate the two time intervals. For example, to dictate at 80 *wam* from copy counted at 40 *wam,* dictate the first quarter-minute segment in 7 seconds, the second segment in 8 seconds, the third in 7 seconds, and so on. An easy way to do this is to return the hand of the stop watch to zero after each segment of dictation.

Source: Edward L. Christensen and R. DerMont Bell, *Teacher's Manual, Century 21 Shorthand,* Book 1 (Cincinatti: South-Western Publishing Company, 1974).

new-matter dictation is introduced, as well as the amount of theory introduced each day.

Every student should have some dictation at his or her speed every day. If the teacher does not have access to equipment or materials for providing dictation at varying rates, then he or she provides all the dictation and, by necessity, some of the dictation will be too fast or too slow for some students. Therefore, students should be instructed as to what they are to do in these circumstances.

If the dictation speed is too slow, students should draw vertical lines on their notebook pages to make four columns rather than two and write each phrase of dictation as many times as possible across the page. The student may wait until the teacher has dictated part or all of a sentence before beginning to write. When the dictation speed is too fast, the student should write fluently until a state of confusion sets in. At this point the student leaves a space in his or her notes and begins the next sentence. If the dictation is much too fast, the student may trace over the outlines of a slower take. This is done with a pen, actually writing over the previous outlines. If the dictation is from the textbook, the student may trace over the outlines in the plate with the back of a pen. Another technique, sometimes called scribble writing, is for the student to look at previous takes or the textbook and write in his or her notebook one outline over the other without looking at the actual writing.

Because all students hesitate when an unfamiliar word is dictated, the teacher should give instruction in writing unfamiliar words. The teacher might suggest that students make one of the following responses quickly: (1) write the word in longhand, (2) write the first syllable of the word in shorthand or long-hand, or (3) skip the word. Actual drill on one or two sentences containing difficult words should be given once or twice a week until students have become adept at responding without hesitation.

Many schools have dictation equipment so the teacher can provide more readily for individual differences. The number of dictation speeds available for student use depends on the number of tape recorder/players or lab channels available. With one tape recorder and listening station, the teacher can provide for two dictation speeds simultaneously by giving live dictation to one group. The availability of inexpensive cassette tape players makes it possible for each student to have access to a tape player and thus take dictation at any speed at any time. In a shorthand laboratory, each student desk is wired and the student selects the dictation speed by turning to the appropriate channel. Shorthand labs may have dictating as well as playing facilities, and the number of channels available depends on the size of the lab. Through the use of commercial and/or teacher-made tapes, students can take dictation at their desired speed, without waiting for the teacher to dictate at speeds that are too slow or too fast. And they may come to the shorthand room any time there is an available space. By providing for dictation through tapes, the teacher is available to assist students on an individual basis as needed. Some schools provide dictation practice via telephone. The student calls and requests a specific tape and takes the dictation over the telephone. (Students are furnished a list of tape numbers and titles that specify the type and rate of dictation.)

In keeping with the increased emphasis on individualized instruction, some schools and commercial companies are preparing individualized instructional programs in shorthand. Through the use of film loops, tapes, sound slides, transparencies, and printed materials, the student progresses at his or her own pace. Some teachers prefer to individualize the entire shorthand course, while others instruct students as a group through the theory lessons and then begin an individualized program. By means of an individualized program, the teacher becomes available for diagnosing and prescribing for individuals as well as for small groups as needed.

Brookdale Community College's Business Management Institute developed an individualized shorthand instructional program with minimum standards as follows: Shorthand I—60 *wam*; Shorthand II—80 *wam*; Shorthand III—100 *wam*; and Shorthand IV—120 *wam*. The program was designed for vocational skill development, with each succeeding course preparing students to enter the business world at a higher level of job responsibility. Upon completion of Shorthand I, for example, the student was qualified for employment in an office position requiring minimal dictation and transcription skills for an "occasional" letter or memo. The student completing Shorthand II could fill a position in a small office where "light stenography" was required; he or she might also be considered for employment as a junior stenographer, defined by one company as "a position requiring spelling, reading comprehension, vocabulary, grammar, and stenographic training, but calling for little or no work experience." It was assumed that most students, however, would require a minimum of three semesters of shorthand to compete successfully in companies as junior stenographers with the ability to take and transcribe dictation at a moderate rate of speed, that is, not over 100 words a minute. Upon completion of Shorthand IV, the student could assume advanced stenographic or secretarial responsibilities involving decision making, follow-up and supervisory activities.[45]

DEVELOPING ACCURACY

After theory lessons have been taught and the majority of class time is being devoted to reading and writing shorthand, the teacher may discover that some of the students either did not learn or have forgotten parts of the shorthand alphabet. The omission of words, phrases, and/or sentences is a handicap for transcription. Gaffga [46] recommends systematic, frequent review of the alphabet, all small characters, or all large characters, dipthongs, and other groupings. This should not take more than two to three minutes at the beginning of class. She suggests the following techniques for assisting in the teaching and learning of accuracy in shorthand:

1. Intensive reteaching of the alphabet.
2. Increased use of theory tests.
3. Frequent review of brief forms and their derivatives.

4. Regular use of vocabulary drills and phrases.
5. Quick check with the Shorthand Dictionary for uncertain outlines.
6. Skill development of acceptable substitutions for illegible outlines.
7. Continued emphasis of written outlines based on sounds, not spelling.

module 7.4
LEARNING ACTIVITIES

1. Prepare or assemble material and be prepared to demonstrate four speed-building plans of your choice.
2. Begin a collection of motivational techniques relating to speed-building. Try to add at least five techniques not described in this module.
3. Prepare a mini-lesson in which you introduce dictation or new-matter dictation. Write a script containing what you will say and do; be prepared to demonstrate to the class or to videotape your presentation.
4. Review the speed-building plans in this module and from other sources. Then outline a four-semester speed-building procedure, specifying the plans you will use in each semester.
5. Using this module and other references, list at least three ways to handle individual differences during speed building.
6. Prepare three office-style dictation tapes. Incorporate at least two different correction/addition/deletion instructions in each.
7. Select some material and prepare a tape on which you dictate the material at 60, 80, 100 *wam*.
8. Outline the procedures you might use to review the shorthand alphabet in second- or third-semester shorthand class.

module 7.4
SELF-TEST

1. Briefly explain at least two points of view as to when to begin new-matter dictation. When do you recommend beginning new-matter dictation? Explain your answer.
2. List three different speed-building plans, giving the objectives for each.
3. Name and explain at least five different circumstances an employee might encounter when taking dictation from an employer.
4. List eight different techniques a teacher might use to stimulate interest and develop skill in writing shorthand.

module 7.5
TRANSCRIPTION

The most valid measure of achievement in shorthand is the student's ability to transcribe. In this module, attention is given to the introduction of transcription, pretranscription instruction, and phases in the development of transcription skill. Examples of drills for developing speed and accuracy in transcription are also included.

After completing this module, you should be able to (1) identify factors having a bearing on the point at which transcription training should begin, (2) specify skills associated with pretranscription or introduction to transcription, (3) describe five phases of transcription development, and (4) cite examples of drills appropriate for developing transcription speed and accuracy and be prepared to demonstrate drills.

The ultimate goal of shorthand instruction is the production of mailable transcripts. Shorthand competency is ultimately measured by one criterion only: the ability to transcribe. While business educators agree with this goal, they do not agree on the best way to achieve it. Transcription is a complex skill that incorporates shorthand, typewriting, and English, as well as new skills, facts, and problem solving. Tonne et al.[47] summarize three new basic skills involved in transcription:

1. The student must learn to read in thought groups when he or she transcribes;
2. The student must learn to type from the shorthand symbol, which includes decisions about spelling, homonyms, and punctuation; and
3. The student must make decisions about punctuation at the time of typing.

Business educators are not in agreement as to when to introduce transcription. Russon[48] recommends beginning simple transcription at the end of the fourth week of the first semester when the student has completed at least one and preferably two semesters of typewriting. Douglas, Blanford, and Anderson[49] suggest that if only one year of shorthand/transcription is offered, the teacher should concentrate for the last six weeks on transcription. Pullis[50] states that there is probably no one best time for introducing typewritten transcription. The introduction of transcription may vary according to the composition of the shorthand class; that is, the percentage of students who enroll in second-year shorthand; the percentage who have completed at least one year of typewriting instruction before enrolling in the shorthand course; the length of the daily class period; the rate of class progress in mastery of the shorthand system; the ability level of the students in handling mechanics of English usage; and the extent to which the shorthand classroom is equipped for transcription training.

If transcription is introduced during the first six months of instruction, care must be taken to avoid spending an inordinate amount of time in transcribing to the neglect of basic shorthand writing skill. One cannot transcribe what one is unable to record. Prerequisites must also be carefully controlled. If transcription is begun early, all students should have completed at least one year of typewriting and preferably be enrolled in second-year typewriting concurrently with first-year shorthand. When transcription is deferred, the teacher must never assume that transcription skill will "take care of itself."

Since the majority of high school students will complete only one year of shorthand instruction, the ability to record dictation in the first year course must not become an end in itself. The ultimate value of the shorthand program will depend upon the extent to which students are capable of producing acceptable typewritten copy from shorthand notes recorded at reasonable rates.

INTRODUCTION TO TRANSCRIPTION

The development of the skills needed in transcription begins in typewriting, shorthand, and business communication classes. In addition to developing keyboard competencies in typewriting classes, students learn letter placement and good correction techniques. In business communication and other English courses, students develop skills in grammar, punctuation, spelling, and vocabulary. In shorthand, students find marginal notes in their texts dealing with the conventions of written English, such as spelling, punctuation, and grammar.

Langemo[51] suggests the following procedures for practice punctuation usage in shorthand classes. Have students omit all punctuation marks except the period and paragraph when self-dictating a lesson. After completing the self-dictation, the students read through their lessons and insert all punctuation marks and missing words in each letter with red ink. Occasionally have students read parts of the letters in class, explaining where they placed missing punctuation and missing words and giving the reasons for their decisions.

Russon[52] believes that the teacher will have better success if he or she reviews needed skills in English mechanics as transcription is introduced. She recommends illustrating certain punctuation rules as follows:

Review Punctuation

At the beginning of each semester, a simple review of punctuation is in order. The writer suggests *pictures* to explain certain punctuation rules. One reason students have trouble learning the rules of grammar and punctuation may lie in the language with which these rules are commonly stated. The seven rules follow:

1. ○, ◯, and ◯

(Rule: In a series of three or more, use a comma before *and*.)

This rule is taught, even though there is a trend to drop the comma. I believe that it is easier to *ease up* on rules than it is to relearn in cases where they are necessary. Because, in technical writing, the comma before *and* is often necessary, it seems to be easier to teach it as a rule.

2. If_____,
    (Rule: When the dependent clause comes first, a comma follows the dependent clause.)

3. _____, and _____
    (Rule: With two independent clauses separated by *and* [or other conjunction], use comma before *and*.)

4. _____, _____, _____; and __
    _____
    (Rule: When an independent clause or an item in a series contains internal commas, use a semicolon to separate the independent clauses or items, even before *and*.)

5. _____; _____
    (Rule: If two independent clauses have no *and* [or other conjunction] between them], use a semicolon to separate them.)

6. _____ , ⟨ ⟩ _____

    (Rule: Any portion of the sentence that is not needed for the sense of the sentence is set off by commas before and after.)

7. TIME_____
    (Rule: Any expression of time [hour, day, week, month, year] at the beginning of a sentence is *not* followed by a comma.)

If the teacher draws these *pictures* on the chalkboard and explains them thoroughly, instructing the class to copy them in their notebooks and refer to them when in doubt, the problem of punctuation is somewhat simplified.

SKILL DEVELOPMENT

The business teacher directs the student through several phases in the process of developing skill in transcribing. During *the first phase,* which lasts only a day or two, students transcribe from familiar shorthand plates. Select a letter and preview it with the class, having several students read the letter. The preview should also include punctuation and spelling. The purpose of the preview is for students to become thoroughly familiar with all aspects of the letter so as to avoid hesitations when transcribing. Encourage students to read in thought groups and to keep the typewriter going steadily all the time. The first attempts at transcribing are not timed. After students have transcribed the letter a couple of times, have them transcribe the same letter one final time, and raise their hands when they have finished so that you can note how long it took them to complete. From the beginning, stress the importance of keeping the typewriter going at all times and not stopping to read.

Some business teachers recommend using double-spaced manuscript form for the first few weeks of transcription. Others, however, feel that students should begin transcribing in letter form from the beginning, with the teacher giving the exact margin stops. For the first two or three weeks, students should indicate errors with light pencil marks rather than erasing or correcting them.

The second phase of transcription instruction is transcribing familiar home-work notes. Some teachers omit the first phase and begin immediately with this one. In this phase, students are assigned a short, simple letter for homework. The letter is previewed in class, noting punctuation and spelling. Students then transcribe the letter from their notes, first without being timed, then timed, and are encouraged to make each transcript a little faster.

During *the third phase*, students transcribe practiced dictation material. The teacher dictates letters the students have practiced out of class (as home-work). They again transcribe, both untimed and timed.

In *the fourth phase*, students transcribe from new-matter dictation. Ini-tially, one or two simple letters that present no problems of English, punctua-tion, or typing style are dictated. Short previews of shorthand outlines of words or phrases are completed prior to dictation in order to review difficult items. Again, students transcribe on an untimed basis followed by timed transcription. After a couple of days, the teacher begins transcription under time, using simple letters. Students can now compute the speed of transcription (see Module 7.6). Gradually, the number and difficulty of letters will be increased. During this phase, the teacher incorporates drills, gradually moves toward student determination of margin stop settings, introduces corrections and, to-ward the end, tapers off and finally omits previews for new matter.

During *the final phase*, students integrate the skills developed in previous phases. The teacher dictates a series of letters that are transcribed under time. All the letters in a series are dictated at the same speed. This means that, in order to provide for individual differences, three to four letters would be dic-tated live or via tape, for example, at 60 *wam*, another group at 70 *wam*, and so on. The transcribed letters should be evaluated on the basis of mailability or usability; that is, a letter should be mailable if the student is to receive credit for it.

Shorthand speed development continues to be important during transcrip-tion. A portion of every period in the transcription class should be devoted to speed building. Unfamiliar, unpreviewed dictation should also be continued. The rate of dictation for transcription should be 10 to 20 words per minute below the students' shorthand dictation rate. Thus, for students whose dictation speed is 80 *wam*, the dictation rate for transcription should be 60 to 70 *wam*. Remember that students are expected to produce a mailable letter, and a 5 percent error allowance in dictation will probably not result in mailable copy.

When shorthand transcription is offered for one period a day, the teacher usually devotes one day to shorthand dictation and the following day to tran-scription. Since students need to develop the ability to transcribe for sustained lengths of time, this arrangement is an effective one. After the introductory phases of instruction, enough material should be dictated for 30 to 40 minutes of transcription. Some teachers vary the introduction to transcription by having students transcribe words, phrases, and simple sentences from the chalkboard or overhead projector before transcribing from shorthand notes.

TRANSCRIPTION DRILLS

Transcription drills are necessary when transcription is being introduced and, periodically, to increase speed and accuracy. Douglas Blanford and Anderson provide the following examples of good transcription drills.

1. Comparison of typing and transcription rate—the first day in transcription the students may be given a five-minute timed writing on some straight-copy material to determine their typing rates. They may next be given a five-minute timing on the same material written in shorthand. The transcription rate on straight copy is then compared with the typing rate.
2. A drill emphasizing the importance of accurate typing—the teacher may use a straight-copy drill to compare the typing and transcription rates of the students when they are required to correct all their errors.
3. Comparison of typing and transcription rates on letter copy.
4. Transcription of the same letter from shorthand notes two or three times in order to increase the student's transcription rate.
5. A preview of the difficult shorthand outlines in the letters to be dictated for transcription.
6. Comparison of typing and transcription rates on letter copy.
7. Transcription power drive (shorthand sentences with increasing line lengths).
8. Transcribing in thought units—the material to be transcribed is marked in thought units with dotted or colored lines, and the students are instructed to read and transcribe in thought units, keeping the carriage moving at all times.[53]

TRANSCRIPTION ACCURACY

During the transcription stage, students should be alert for possible errors that may creep in during the course of the dictation. Employers are only human, and they will occasionally make a mistake in dictation, such as an incorrect pronoun or verb. The stenographer is expected to catch such errors and not transcribe them mechanically. Some mistakes will be of a more serious nature and should be called to the attention of the dictator; others will not be obvious until transcription begins. Students should place a large X at the point where the error occurs—if it is obvious—so that the correction can be made later.

In order to provide training along these lines, the business teacher may initially include some rather obvious errors in the dictation, telling students that they should make the necessary corrections when they transcribe. Gradually, as students become aware of the need to be constantly alert to errors, the teacher can dictate letters containing more serious errors, warning the class about mistakes and stressing the importance of finding them.

Students should be told to watch for common mistakes such as incorrect dates and amounts, errors in names and titles, and omissions.

Letter placement

Your students will find transcription more interesting and realistic if you allow them to transcribe on real or simulated letterhead, preferably several different types. *Gregg Transcription* teaches letter placement by judgment in three stages:

1. Short letters—approximately 100 words
2. Average letters—100 to 200 words
3. Long letters—200 words or more.

The placement of short, average, and long letters is taught, as suggested by Leslie and Zoubek, as follows:[54]

> *Placing short letters.* The teacher might introduce the first stage in this way:
>
> Before you hand a letter to your employer to sign, you must, of course, be sure that you have transcribed the letter as it was dictated. You must, in addition, make sure that it is correctly punctuated and that there are no spelling errors. And you must also be sure that it is attractively placed on the letterhead. The placement of the letter is the first thing the reader will notice. If it is unattractively placed, it will lose some of its effectiveness and may even give the reader a poor impression of your firm.
>
> In this course we will learn to place letters attractively by judgment just as a stenographer in a business office places them. If you have ever watched an experienced stenographer transcribe, you have noticed that she simply glances at her notes, sets her right margin "about here" and her left margin "about there." She taps the carriage return a few times, and types the date; a few more times and types the inside address—and off she goes with the body of the letter.
>
> Today we will learn how to set up short letters—those containing about 100 words. First turn to Letter 23 of *Gregg Transcription*. (Have individual learners read back from Letter 23, spelling aloud any words that may cause difficulty. Then dictate Letter 23 from the *Student's Transcript*. Dictate slowly enough so that all learners can get the dictation easily.)
>
> Note carefully how much space this letter occupies in your notebook. Did this letter take half a column? A full column? The space you required to write this letter depends on your style of writing. If your shorthand notes are large, perhaps you required as much as a full column. If your

notes are small, you may have been able to write the letter in half a column.

Hereafter, when a letter requires about the same amount of space in your notebook as Letter 23 of *Gregg Transcription,* it is a short letter. This is the way that you are to place all short letters that you transcribe:

1. Insert the paper (preferably a letterhead) in you machine.
2. Set your margin stops for 2-inch margins.
3. Type the date two lines below the last line of the letterhead.
4. Start the first line of the inside address 4 inches from the top of the letterhead if your typewriter has elite type or 3 1/2 inches from the top if it has pica type. Use the inside address given on the model letter on page 31 of *Gregg Transcription.* Now transcribe the letter from your own notes. Use the closing given in the model letter on page 31 of *Gregg Transcription.*

(After the learners finish transcribing, compliment them on their attractively placed letters!)

To sum up, class, there are two things to remember about the placement of a short letter:

1. Your margins are 2 inches on each side.
2. You start the inside address 4 inches from the top if you are typing on an elite typewriter or 3 1/2 inches from the top if you are typing on a pica typewriter.

During the first few weeks of the transcription course, the learner's path will be smoother if his dictation is confined to letters of approximately 100 words.

Placing average letters. Sometime during the second month, the placement by judgment of letters of average length should be introduced, following the procedure suggested for the placement of short letters. With average letters, the learner should remember that

1. His margins are 1 1/2 inches on each side.
2. He should start the inside address 3 1/2 inches from the top of the letterhead on an elite typewriter or 3 inches from the top on a pica typewriter.

Placing long letters. Sometime during the third month, the placement of long letters should be introduced, once again following the procedure suggested for placing short letters. At this point the learner should remember

1. His margins are 1 inch on each side.
2. He should start the inside address 3 inches from the top of the letterhead on an elite machine or 2 1/2 inches from the top on a pica machine.

This simple method of teaching placement by judgment will always produce an attractively placed letter.

During the first month or two, have the learners tell you the following after the dictation of each letter to be transcribed: (a) the size of the letter—short, average, or long; (b) the number of inches from the top that they should allow before typing the inside address; and (c) the margins they will use.

module 7.5
LEARNING ACTIVITIES

1. Prepare or assemble an instructional module or several independent activities that would be appropriate for reviewing punctuation, capitalization, or other grammar skills related to pretranscription instruction.
2. Begin a file of transcription drills. Collect at least three that were not included in this module. Be prepared to demonstrate a drill of your choice with the class.
3. Develop a one-day lesson plan for Phase One or Phase Two of transcription development.
4. Prepare the script for a letter that you could use in developing transcription accuracy.
5. Read at least an article on one of the following: (a) when to begin transcription, (b) developing transcription speed and accuracy, (c) shorthand, typewriting, English skills needed in transcription.

module 7.5
SELF-TEST

1. When should transcription instruction be introduced? Justify your answer.
2. List prerequisite skills that students should possess before you begin transcription instruction.
3. Name and briefly summarize five phases of transcription instruction.

module 7.6
STANDARDS, TESTING, AND GRADING

Student achievement in shorthand is fostered by goals and skill development plans that are well understood by teacher and students. Immediate feedback is highly important to students, and it provides a basis for further progress. This module presents some basic principles underlying evaluation as well as a schedule of testing and grading. Evaluation measures or components of a good shorthand testing and grading system are also discussed along with a plan for grading daily and weekly transcripts.

After completing this module, you should be able to (1) identify some of the basic principles underlying an effective system of grading in shorthand, (2) develop a four-semester plan for testing and grading high school or postsecondary shorthand, (3) summarize the types of evaluation measures that should be used in evaluating student progress in shorthand, and (4) grade daily and weekly student transcripts.

MOTIVATION THROUGH MEASUREMENT

Knowledge of results is important, in a psychological sense, to student progress in shorthand. Learning theory underscores the importance of reinforcement, through positive feedback, of the results of learning. Immediately after a test or practice, the student needs to be told how well he or she did.

The student must always be aware of the goal toward which he or she is working so that progress can be checked against it. The student should be able to report his or her score at once in order to sustain a feeling of success. He or she can record an improvement in speed, fewer omissions in the dictation, increased accuracy on a transcript, or additional passes on a progress chart. These aspects of learning serve to motivate the student through positive knowledge of results.

PRINCIPLES OF GRADING

Since almost everything that happens in the shorthand class reflects the skills students have acquired, only limited amounts of formal testing and grading are needed. Business teachers observe their students reading and writing shorthand daily, allowing for informal evaluation of student progress and remediation for students needing special help.

It is important to remember that skills should be thoroughly fixed before they are tested or graded. Premature testing of a student's work may inhibit skill development. Since skill learning increases when the learner competes with him- or herself, a portion of the total grade should include an improvement factor. Of course, the weight given to any activity should reflect the total time devoted to that activity. Some teachers find that recording only passing test grades is highly motivational to students. These points are elaborated by Russon as follows:[55]

Grade One Paper a Week. The shorthand course is made up of many different activities. All of these activities must improve at the same time. Much of the time in a shorthand class is spent on dictation, for example. This dictation is *practice;* it is not graded. Each day there is some time spent on reading from shorthand—either from plates or the students' notes. This, again, is *practice*. Once a week, in all semesters except the first, twenty minutes may be spent improving the students' transcribing ability. This transcription activity is *practice*. No attempt should be made to grade or evaluate in any way the practice activities of shorthand students.

Each activity must be graded periodically, however. The interval between grades will depend on the time spent in class. If the shorthand class meets two hours a day, one for shorthand and one for transcription, each activity may be graded once a week. If the time available for both shorthand and transcription is only one hour a day or less, each activity need be graded only once every two weeks.

Teach Thoroughly Before Grading. Surprise tests are harmful in skill courses. The shorthand class should have a well-defined testing and grading plan set up at the beginning of the semester, and it should be followed. Any change in the pattern is announced before the change is made. Self-confidence comes first; skill building follows. The teacher who *springs* tests in shorthand undermines the self-confidence of the students.

The day chosen for testing and grading each activity is important. The end of the weekly practice period is best for dictation tests. Monday is a good day for *reading for speed*. Wednesday is good for transcription speed practice. The reasoning back of these choices is that sufficient time must be allowed for building speed increases before testing for the increase. There is always a loss of skill over a weekend; therefore, the skill must be built up through the week and is best tested on Friday. Monday is a good day for speed reading because repeated readings with rest periods between are facilitated on weekends. Wednesday is a good time for transcription speed practice because this skill is based on integration of many skills rather than the building up on one skill. The middle of the week is good for integrated activities.

Avoid Letter Grades if Possible. Skill learning increases best when the student is working for his own improvement. The minute letter grades are assigned to his work, he is competing with other class members. For this reason, the shorthand teacher should avoid giving letter grades except when necessary, as at the end of a grading period. All other scores should be in terms of points increased and words a minute. Certain standards are set for each activity, and the student knows how he is doing in terms of this standard.

Three- and Five-Minute Takes. Dictation takes, either for three or five minutes, are marked "Pass" or "Not Pass" (never "Fail"). The passing takes are recorded. On the takes not passing, the teacher might write some comment to encourage the student to keep trying. The official standard of 95 percent accuracy is satisfactory. Three- and five-minute takes are the *motor activity* of shorthand. As such, they have little value beyond their function as sign posts to tell the student and the teacher how he is doing. They are not the standards the office worker will use when he is on the job. As aids to skill building, however, they are highly motivational.

Production Tests. Beginning with the second half of the second semester, production tests are given. The production test is the activity that is closest to actual use of the student's transcription skill in business. In this test, six to eight letters are dictated; the students transcribe for 30 minutes. A method of grading these tests that is both valid and reliable is as follows: Score equals words per minute plus bonus points. Bonus points are awarded for verbatim and mailable letters. With production tests, about half the time of the transcriber is spent in nontyping activities; therefore, wpm transcription speeds will be low. Assuming that a student's *wpm* score is 22 and that he earned 30 points bonus, his score would be 52 points. It is better for the students if no grade is assigned on production tests except at the end of the grading period. Instead, each student will attempt to raise his own score each time he takes a production test. At the end of the grading period the final production test is given a letter grade.

Transcription Speed Tests. A third activity, which may be tested on Wednesdays in the second year, is transcription speed. The scores on transcription speed tests are, like dictation tests, expressed as "Passing" or "Not Passing." No letter grades are assigned.

Grade on Improvement. A part of the skill grade must be on achievement, but some of the final grade should be on improvement in skill. The ratio between achievement and improvement changes from the beginning to the end of the course. At the beginning of each skill learning, the percentage of the grade that is based on improvement is greatest. At the end of the course, most of the grade is based on achievement. The vocational nature of the course makes achievement of a marketable skill the final standard.

Assign Weights According to Importance. The weight assigned to any activity in the shorthand course is dependent upon the importance of that activity. For example, three- and five-minute dictation tests (like straight-copy tests in typing) are more important at the beginning of the course than they are at the end. On the other hand, production tests are not given at all in the first semester of shorthand. By the last semester, they are the most important activity.

The following grading schedules are suggestions only. Teachers who stress other activities may wish to add them to the schedule. One caution is necessary, however: Too many items should not be averaged in a final grade. Three to five items with varying weights totaling 100 percent seem to be the best.

First Semester. There are two main goals in the first semester according to the philosophy of the method described in these chapters. These goals are dictation speed and accuracy and brief forms. A less important goal is shorthand theory. The grading schedule is:

New Matter 3-Minute Takes............× 7 (70%)

Brief Form Test........................× 2 (20%)

Complete Theory Test..................× 1 (10%)

Standard for 3-minute dictation takes (average of three best takes) are:

80+.........................A

50–67.......................B

40–47.......................C

Standards for the brief form test (134 brief forms dictated at the rate of 12 brief forms a minute, only the shorthand graded) are:

Errors	Grade
0	A+
1	A
2	A−
3	B+
4	B
5	B−
6	C+
7	C
8	C−
9	D+
10	D
11	D−
More than 11	F

Standards for the complete theory test (100 words dictated at the rate of 12 words a minute, only the shorthand graded) are:

80% and up..................A

60–79%.....................B

40–59%.....................C

Second Semester. In the second semester production tests are added to the activities to be graded. The grading schedule follows:

New Matter 5-Minute Takes............× 4 (40%)

Speed Improvement....................× 2 (20%)

Production Tests......................× 2 (20%)

Brief Form Derivatives................× 1 (10%)

Complete Theory Test..................× 1 (10%)

Standards for 5-minute dictation takes (average of three best takes) are:

80+.........................A

70–77.......................B

60–67.......................C

Standards of improvement on 5-minute takes (based on the achievement of about the third week of the semester) are:

30 wpm +....................A

20–29 wpm...................B

10–19 wpm...................C

Standards for production tests at the end of the second semester are 4 mailable letters in 30 minutes.

Standards for the brief form test (based on 100 brief form derivatives) are the same as those for the brief form test in the first semester. The brief form derivatives are dictated at the rate of 12 words a minute. Only the shorthand is graded.

Standards for the complete theory test (100 words dictated at the rate of 12 words a minute, only the shorthand graded) are:

90% and up....................A
80–89%.......................B
70–79%.......................C

Third Semester. In the third semester transcription speed tests and mailable-letter projects are added to the grading schedule. Theory and brief form tests are dropped. The grading schedule for the third semester includes:

New Matter 5-Minute Takes.............× 3 (30%)
Speed Improvement.....................× 1 (10%)
Mailable Transcripts...................× 1 (10%)
Transcription Speed....................× 1 (10%)
Production Tests.......................× 4 (40%)

Standards for 5-minute dictation takes (average of three best takes) are:

100+........................A
90–97........................B
80–87........................C

Standards of improvement on 5-minute takes (based on the achievement of about the third week of the semester) are:

25+.........................A
15–24.......................B
10–14.......................C

Standards for mailable transcripts follow. In the third semester four letters are dictated at a medium rate; these projects may be given daily or weekly, depending upon the time available.

All Letters Mailable.............A
One Letter Nonmailable........B
Two Letters Nonmailable.......C
Three Letters Nonmailable......D

Standards for transcription speed tests follow. These standards are based on 5-minute transcription takes similar to 5-minute straight-copy typing tests.

40+.........................A
30–39.......................B
20–29.......................C

Standards for production tests at the end of the third semester are 5 mailable letters in 30 minutes.

Fourth Semester. In the fourth semester speed improvement is dropped from the grading schedule, which includes:

New Matter 5-Minute Takes.............× 3 (30%)
Mailable Transcripts...................× 1 (10%)
Transcription Speed....................× 1 (10%)
Production Tests.......................× 5 (50%)

Standards for 5-minute dictation takes (average of three best takes) are:

120+ . . . . .A
110–117 . . . . .B
100–107 .C

Standards for mailable transcripts are the same as for the third semester.

Standards for transcription speed tests are:

60+ . . . . .A
50–59 . . . . .B
40–49 C

Standards for production tests at the end of the fourth semester are six mailable letters in 30 minutes.

	TABLE VII							
	SCHEDULE OF WEIGHTS FOR GRADING VARIOUS ITEMS IN THE FOUR SEMESTERS OF SHORTHAND							
Semester	Dictation Speed	Brief Form Tests	Theory Tests	Speed Increase	Mailable Trans.	Trans. Speed	Production Tests
I	7	2	1				
II	4	1	1	2			2
III	3			1	1	1	4
IV	3				1	1	5

GRADING PLAN FOR PRODUCTION TESTS

The following method of assigning grades is based on the standard deviation. The method is statistically sound; if it is used, it must be followed exactly.

Scoring Production Tests

The suggested plan for scoring production tests is transcription words per minute plus bonus. The total words transcribed (including incomplete letters) are divided by the time of the test. To this figure are added bonus points for accurate work: 10 bonus points for verbatim letters and 5 bonus points for mailable letters. No bonus points are added for nonmailable letters.

For example, Student A transcribes six letters, totaling 900 words. The time of the test is 30 minutes; therefore, Student A's transcription speed is 30 wpm. Let us assume that three of these six letters are verbatim; two are mailable; one is nonmailable. The total bonus is figured as follows:

$$10 \times 3 = 30$$
$$5 \times 2 = \underline{10}$$
Total Bonus 40

Next, the bonus is added to the transcription wpm, as follows:

Transcription wpm = 30
Total Bonus   = $\underline{40}$
Student A's Score = 70

Assigning Grades

Letter grades are assigned to raw scores by taking a percentage of the highest score attained on the test. In the average transcription class there is a wide range of acceptable work. It is suggested, therefore, that 30 percent of the top score be set as the low passing score. Assuming that the top score is 110 points, grades are assigned as follows:

$$\begin{array}{r} 110 \quad \text{(Top Score)} \\ \times\, 30\% \\ \hline 33 \quad \text{(Low Passing Score)} \end{array}$$

$$\begin{array}{r} 110 \quad \text{(Top Score)} \\ -\ 33 \quad \text{(Low Passing Score)} \\ \hline 77 \quad \text{(Passing Range)} \end{array}$$

$$11\ )\ \overline{77} \qquad 7 \quad \text{(Passing Increment)}$$

The top score is multiplied by 30 percent to get the low passing score. This amount (33) is then subtracted from 110 to get the passing range. There are 11 grade intervals from A + to D −; therefore, the result (77) is divided by 11, giving 7 as the passing increment from one grade to the next. Now, starting near the bottom of the following scale, with 33 next to 11, the grades are assigned, adding the increment of 7 each time. Below the passing grade, the increment is subtracted.

Grade		
A +	0	110
A	1	103
A −	2	96
B +	3	89
B	4	82
B −	5	75
C +	6	68
C	7	61
C −	8	54
D +	9	47
D	10	40
D −	11	33
	31	26
F	14	19
	15	12

Recording Grades

The letter grade closest to the score is recorded on the student's paper. Student A, with 70 points, would be given the grade C +. The letter grade, however, is not recorded in the teacher's roll book. Instead, the corresponding number (in this case, 6) is recorded. It is now a simple matter to average these low numbers when assigning final grades. If the passing increment is an even number (such as 6), a score of 69 is given a B − and recorded as 5.5. When the increment is an uneven number, however, fractions are not used.

Assigning Final Grades

At the end of the grading period, the teacher assigns final grades as follows:

FOURTH SEMESTER

Student	Production Tests × 5	Speed Takes × 3	Mailable Letters × 1	Trans. Speed × 1
Brown, Donna	5.3	3.0	2.0	6.0

RUSSON'S TESTING AND GRADING PLAN *(continued)*

To determine final grades, the weight assigned each item is multiplied by the number representing the average for the item. For example, production tests in the fourth semester are weighted by 5; therefore, the production test grade is multiplied by 5. This procedure is followed with all of the items to be weighted, as follows:

Donna Brown

Production (5)	$5.3 \times 5 =$	26.5
Speed (3)	$3.0 \times 3 =$	9.0
Mailables (1)	$2.0 \times 1 =$	2.0
Trans. Sp. (1)	$6.0 \times 1 =$	6.0
	Total	$43.5 \div 10 = 4.35$ or B

MAKEUP TESTS

Makeup tests are an added burden on the shorthand teacher. An alternate suggestion is to assign a grade for the test that is missed. It is best to attach some penalty for missing a test, yet the penalty should not be extreme. The suggested grade, then, for a missing test is one grade below the lowest grade earned by the student during that grading period. If the student's tests were all A grade, and he missed one test, the grade assigned for the missing test would be B. If three tests are given during a certain grading period and a second student earns a B on the first and a C on the second, with the third test missed, he would earn a D for the missing test. The average test grade for the second student would thus be C.

If a student is absent for an extended period because of illness, it is usually better to assign a grade of "Incomplete" for that grading period. The incomplete grade is then changed to the grade the student earns in the following grading period.

EVALUATION MEASURES

Although business teachers do not agree as to the types of items and the relative weight that should be given to each in evaluating student progress in shorthand, the following discussion summarizes some of the measures used:

Reading rates

During the first semester, students read in class from shorthand plates and from their notes. The business teacher may wish to record two or three reading rates for each student within the grading period, noting the rate and/or errors.

Longhand transcription

One test used to measure students' reading ability is longhand transcription from shorthand plates. The students can be graded on the number of words they transcribe correctly during the three-to-five-minute test. Teachers may find it helpful to score separately the shorthand and nonshorthand errors. Thus a student's score may be C/A or A/C with the first grade indicating the ability to transcribe, and the second, the use of conventions of written English. This type of scoring provides diagnostic information to the teacher, who may then prescribe individualized instruction in spelling, punctuation, grammar, and so on. An average grade of B (C/A or A/C would equal B) would not give the teacher information as to the student's strengths and weaknesses in shorthand or English.

Theory and briefform tests

Some teachers recommend the use of theory and briefform tests during the first year of shorthand instruction. These tests usually include about 100 words or brief forms dictated at a rate of twelve per minute, or one every five seconds. Students write the words in columns.

Word list tests

Century 21 shorthand includes a learning performance word list test for each of the first sixteen five-lesson units. Each test includes theory words, speed forms, and high-frequency phrases that are emphasized in the unit. The authors suggest ways of using the tests, as follows:[56]

1. Dictate the items in sequence, collect the papers, and check the accuracy of the shorthand outlines.
2. Dictate the items, have the students transcribe their notes, collect the papers, and check both the shorthand outlines and the transcript.
3. Dictate the items and have students check their own work as the teacher writes the correct outlines on the chalkboard.
4. Duplicate the list of items, distribute copies to the students, ask the students to write the correct shorthand outlines adjacent to the printed words, and then collect and check the students' work.

The authors of Gregg shorthand[57] feel that word lists are no longer necessary or desirable types of shorthand tests. If a teacher wishes to use word list tests, however, the authors of Gregg shorthand recommend timing the dictation so that the student must construct the outlines at a specific speed or omit the words. They also urge that students transcribe the outlines and that only the transcript be graded.

Dictation tests

Dictation tests are considered the best type of shorthand test. Initially the tests are taken from practiced material and are preannounced. When to begin dictation tests varies among teachers. Douglas, Blanford, and Anderson,[58] for instance, suggest dictation tests when students are able to take practice dictation at 60 *wam*. There is also a wide variation in teacher attitudes toward error allowances in the transcripts of dictation tests, ranging from teachers requiring a perfect transcript to those allowing 5 percent or more error in the transcript. Some teachers indicate a 3 percent error allowance or allow errors equaling 10 percent of the speed of dictation, such as 10 errors in dictation at 100 *wam*.

Students should be able to pass two or three tests, with the error limit chosen by the teacher, at a given speed before progressing to the next level. The teacher should allow ample time, however, for students to practice between presentation of new material and testing it. During the first year, three-minute dictation tests are usually given; five-minute tests are given in the second year. Near the end of the first semester and during the second semester of shorthand, new-matter dictation tests replace tests of practiced matter. These tests are continued even after mailable letter transcription tests are initiated. The teacher may want to continue giving two grades on the shorthand transcript, one for transcription and one for nonshorthand errors.

Mailable letter transcription tests

The final test of shorthand competence is the mailable letter. Every teaching period of transcription is, in reality, a testing period.

> The use of mailable letters as a standard is realistic in light of vocational demands. A mailable letter is one a teacher would sign and send through the mail as his or her own. Variations that may occur in letters and that may be considered acceptable include: (1) letter placement slightly off center, (2) second choice paragraphing, (3) erasures of limited number and degree, (4) second choice punctuation, (5) altered dictation but unaltered meaning, and (6) minor missyllabication. A letter containing any of the following errors would be unmailable: (1) misspelled words or names, (2) material omitted or words that would change meaning, (3) noticeable strikeovers, (4) careless erasures, (5) serious misplacement, (6) omission of date, (7) transposed words, (8) errors in figures, (9) smudge marks, (10) raised capital figures, and (11) one-letter syllabication.[59]

GRADING DAILY AND WEEKLY TRANSCRIPTS

Grading mailable transcripts can be difficult. The following suggestions are based on Leslie and Zoubek's plans as described in the Instructor's Handbook for *Gregg Transcription.*[60]

Grading daily transcripts

If the teacher wants to grade students' transcription on a daily basis, the following plan is recommended. It is most easily described in the form of a hypothetical example:

Learners have been transcribing for a month or more. In 10 minutes, the teacher dictates at about 80 words a minute, five business letters containing approximately 800 words. In a 40-minute period at the typewriter, Learner M transcribes 4 1/2 letters, a total of 760 words. This gives him a gross transcribing speed of 19 words a minute. In the 4 1/2 letters transcribed, he had made a total of 6 errors, any one of which would have made a letter unmailable. (Ignore errors that would not cause a letter to become unmailable.) From the gross transcribing speed, the number of unmailable errors is deducted to get the learner's score for the day. His gross transcribing speed was 19 *wam*; he made 6 unmailable errors; his score for the day is 13.[61]

This plan counts the number of unmailable errors regardless of the letters in which those errors occurred, rather than the number of mailable letters.

Grading weekly transcripts

The authors of *Gregg Transcription* recommend a weekly grading plan based on a point system. This plan distinguishes between the perfect letter and the mailable letter, with the perfect letter getting twice as much credit as the mailable letter. An unmailable letter receives no credit (see Table 7.1). The minimum passing grade for each week would be the number of possible mailable points for all letters to be transcribed during the week. If the students transcribed 8 letters during the week, with each letter consisting of between 126–150 words, then the passing grade for the week would be 16 points (8 letters X 2 points each, mailable = 16). See Table 7.1 for point value.

As shown in Table 7.1, the point value of a letter is determined in blocks of 125 words. A perfect letter of 125 words or less would be given 2 points, whereas a mailable letter of 125 words or less would receive 1 point. The number of words in the letter includes the inside address and the firm signature, which may not be counted in the dictation book but would be included in figuring the gross transcription speed. In order to get a uniform and comparable basis for figuring transcription speeds through the year, it is suggested that the following additions be made to each letter to fit the circumstances: Add 15

table 7.1
POINT SYSTEM GRADING SCALE FOR LETTERS

NUMBER OF WORDS IN LETTER	POINTS		
	Perfect	*Mailable*	*Unmailable or Correctable*
Up to 125	2	1	0
126–250	4	2	0
251–375	6	3	0
376–500	8	4	0

Source: Louis A. Leslie and Charles E. Zoubek, *Instructor's Handbook for Gregg Transcription*, Diamond Jubilee Series, 2nd Ed. (New York: Gregg Division, McGraw-Hill Book Company, 1972),p.21.

words to compensate for writing the inside address and the firm signature. Add an additional 20 words to compensate for making one carbon copy. Add an additional 10 words for addressing an envelope. Thus, if a letter containing 211 standard words is transcribed with an inside address and firm signature, 15 words would be added, for a total of 226 words. If a carbon was made, an additional 20 words credit would be given, making a total of 246 words. If an envelope was also prepared, here would be an additional 10-word credit, making a total of 256 words. This letter, if typed perfectly, would earn 6 points.

In order to save time and work in the classroom, the teacher may use a Weekly Transcription Report, as shown in Table 7.2. As each day's transcripts are read back by the teacher and corrected by the students, the student records the results on this form, which is turned in at the end of the week with the transcripts attached. The large 27(A) in the upper left corner of the sample is the student's number. (Alphabetize student names and assign each student a number; numbers are easier to locate than names, thus making it easier to record points in your grade book.) The sample report represents a double period of shorthand and transcription each day. One day of the week (as should be done) was reserved for shorthand and typing speed tests and drill work. For the week shown on the sample report, that day was Wednesday (B) when the learner made 38 errors on the 120 *wam* test and 9 errors on the 100 *wam* test.

On the weekly sheet, the numbers of the letters dictated are listed in Column 1, as the teacher reads back the transcribed letters for correction. At the same time, the teacher reads the total number of words in each letter, including the credits for inside addresses and other additions. These are listed in Column 2 by the students. The students then add the number of words in the letters listed in Column 2, putting the total each day in Column 5. (The note at the foot of Table 7.2 gives the students directions about recording incomplete letters.) At the end of the week, Student 27 totaled Column 5 and found that he had transcribed 3,811 words and put that figure in Column 8. The week's average speed per minute is found by the student in the chart in the lower right-hand corner of the Weekly Transcription Report. This chart was figured for four transcription periods of 40 minutes net—a total of 160 minutes of actual transcription time. The student transcribed 3,811 words; the closest approximation to that is 3,840, giving a transcribing speed of 24 *wam*. The figure 24 is placed in Column 10. Columns 3 and 4 show the number of points for perfect and mailable letters. Note that letter 230 had 72 words and was unmailable (0 in Column 4). The next letter, 231, containing 107 words, was transcribed perfectly; in Column 3, the figure 2 indicates 2 points for a perfect letter of less than 125 words. At the end of the week, students total Columns 3 and 4 and transfer that figure to Column 9. The score of Student 27 is 48:24, or 48 points for the week with an average transcription speed of 24. Double the average speed for the week and add to the total number of points to arrive at the student score for the week. By doubling the average speed, the student is rewarded for additional transcription speed. When scores are arranged in order, the teacher can then compute school grades. (NOTE: If the shorthand transcription class

table 7.2
WEEKLY TRANSCRIPTION REPORT

Ⓐ → **27**
Number

Name *Rader, Charles*   Week Ending *Nov. 12*   Score **96**

WEEKLY TRANSCRIPTION REPORT--BLANKTOWN SCHOOL

1	2	3	4	5	6	7	8	9	10	11
Letter Number	Number of Words	Points P.	M.	Day's Total Words	Day's Total Points	Day's Trans. Speed	Week's Total Words	Week's Total Points	Week's Average Speed	Score for the Week
230	72		0				3,811	48	24	96
231	107	2								
232	127		1							
233	147		2							
234	145	4								
235	176	4								
236	185		0	959	13	24				
237	129	2								
238	105		0							
239	150		2							
240	151	4								
241	136	4								
242	168		2							
243	158		0	997	14	25				
120-38 100-9										
244	67	2								
245	97	2								
246	118		1							
247	150	4								
248	155		2							
249	354		—	941	11	23				
250	78		0							
251	35		—							
252	149	4								
253	187		2							
254	465		4	914	10	23				

Ⓑ → { (marks rows 120-38 / 100-9)

SCORE is obtained by adding twice the week's average speed to the week's total points.

160 Minutes
Total Transcribing Time
(Take nearest average speed)

Total Words	Week's Speed
2400	15.
2480	15.5
2560	16.
2640	16.5
2720	17.
2800	17.5
2880	18.
2960	18.5
3040	19.
3120	19.5
3200	20.
3280	20.5
3360	21.
3440	21.5
3520	22.
3600	22.5
3680	23.
3760	23.5
3840	24.
3920	24.5
4000	25.
4080	25.5
4160	26.
4240	26.5
4320	27.
4400	27.5

Note: If a letter is completed but unmailable, place a zero in Column 4. If the letter was not started, place a dash in Column 2 and a dash in Column 4; if not completed, a dash in Column 4 and the number of words completed in Column 2.

Source: Louis A. Leslie and Charles E. Zoubek, *Instructor's Handbook for Gregg Transcription,* Diamond Jubilee Series, 2nd ed. (New York: Gregg Division, McGraw-Hill Book Company, 1972), p. 23.

meets one period per day, with transcription two days per week, the score would be computed by adding the average speed for the two days to the total points for the two days *without* multiplying the speed.)

The scale given on the weekly report will save time in computing average transcription speed and will ensure accuracy. The teacher can make up a scale based on the actual time of transcription available each day in his or her class. For example, two 40-minute transcription periods per week would equal 80 minutes, and the total words would be half those shown in Table 7.2.

The weekly report serves as a diagnostic instrument for the teacher. The two speed tests show that Student 27 writes 100 *wam* very easily and can almost pass a test at 120 *wam* for 5 minutes with the maximum of 30 errors (95 percent accuracy). This student is a slow, steady worker. Notice the lack of fluctuation in the four daily transcription speeds shown in Column 7. The teacher evidently discovered that too few students completed the long letter, 249. Students were instructed to begin transcribing on Friday with letter 252 and to transcribe 250 and 251 at the end of the period. The student completed 252, made some error on 250 that rendered it unmailable, and failed to complete 251. Perfect scores on ten of the letters indicates a good knowledge of English and good all-around transcribing skill. Examples of other diagnostic information the teacher can gain from the weekly report are: zeros in Column 3 indicate inaccurate speed; dashes in Column 4 indicate the learner is a little slow and is failing to complete the last letter of the day. Dashes in Columns 2 and 4 indicate extreme slowness; the learner is not even beginning some of the letters. Columns 6 and 7 give an indication of the learner's steadiness. There should not be wide fluctuations from day to day in Columns 6 and 7.

module 7.6
LEARNING ACTIVITIES

1. Review carefully the standards and grading plans presented in this module and from other sources of your choice. Develop a standards, testing, and grading plan for shorthand (by semesters or quarters) at the educational level of your choice. Include the relative importance of each component, such as reading rates, speed takes, mailable letters, transcription speed, and production tests.
2. Prepare a chart or transparency that explains and/or illustrates your standards for mailable letters. Indicate what makes a letter unmailable.
3. Secure one student's shorthand transcripts for two days. (Ask your instructor if these can be obtained from a college class or secure them from a local high school or postsecondary school.) Complete as much of a Weekly Transcription Report as possible (see Table 7.2). Summarize your interpretation of the student's performance.

module 7.6
SELF-TEST

1. In one sentence each, identify three principles underlying effective teaching of shorthand.

2. According to Russon's testing and grading plan for shorthand:
    a. The grading schedule in first-semester shorthand emphasizes

    _____

    b. The grading schedule in second-semester shorthand emphasizes

    _____

    c. The grading schedule in third-semester shorthand emphasizes

    _____

    d. The grading schedule in fourth-semester shorthand emphasizes

    _____

    e. The suggested plan for scoring production tests is

    _____

    f. Letter grades are assigned to raw scores by

    _____

    g. At the end of the grading period, the teacher assigns final grades using these four components and weights:

Component	Weight
(1) _____	(1) _____
(2) _____	(2) _____
(3) _____	(3) _____
(4) _____	(4) _____

3. How are each of the following components used in testing and grading: (a) reading rates, (b) longhand transcription, (c) theory and brief form tests, (d) word list tests, (e) dictation tests, (f) mailable letter transcription tests?
4. Learner 1 has been transcribing for two months. In ten minutes, you dictate five business letters at 80 *wam* containing 800 words. In a 40-minute period at the typewriter, Learner 1 transcribes all five letters, a gross transcribing speed of _____*wam*. A total of eight unmailable errors were made. Point score for that day is _____.

SUMMARY

The goals of the student, the time available for instruction, and the conditions under which the skill is to be acquired are important conditioners of success in shorthand. Dictation rates of 100 to 120 *wam* are a goal for marketable skill. Major emphasis in the first semester is on shorthand theory, vocabulary building, and shorthand dictation. Emphasis in the second semester is on further speed building and transcription. The second year of shorthand instruction includes one semester of speed building and one semester of transcription, or the two skills are emphasized simultaneously in a full-year course. Learning experiences in shorthand proceed from simple to complex in a well-defined sequence. Emphasis is placed on reinforcing student behavior, work-like settings, systematic review for automatization of skills, repetition, and regular practice.

Planning for instruction is a major responsibility of the shorthand teacher. In the traditional setting, the teacher identifies objectives, units of instruction, standards and testing plans, instructional methods, materials, and equipment needed. In the individualized setting, the teacher continuously monitors the performance of each student, giving help when needed, diagnosing and prescribing appropriate instructional materials, and evaluating student progress. In both settings, provision must be made for individual differences with respect to such activities as the rate at which students take dictation, amount of review, and remedial work in related English skills. Each lesson is planned to comprise a variety of activities and instructional techniques, including spelling and reading outlines, individual and group reading of connected matter and brief forms, and dictation.

The two primary approaches to teaching symbol shorthand are the writing approach and the reading approach. The writing approach views shorthand as a science and emphasizes the use of rules, word lists, vocabulary tests, and early introduction to writing. The reading approach views shorthand as a language art and emphasizes extensive early reading, with writing deferred until the beginning of the fifth week. The reading approach does not stress rules, word list practice, repetition practice, or formal review. In practice, most shorthand teachers follow a combination of methods and approaches. The development of strong reading skills is an important objective in beginning shorthand since it is related to the development of good writing ability. By the end of the first semester in shorthand, the emphasis is on writing. The teacher must be alert to strategies that will reduce the major types of theory errors.

The successful shorthand teacher follows a well-defined procedure for introducing dictation and building speed. Among the commonly used speed-development plans are the following: one-minute, 3 × 4, pyramid, stair step, spurt and spread plans. Strategies for developing writing skills include repetitive dictation, accelerated dictation, zigzag dictation, dry-penning (eyes-on-copy recording), phrase automatization, previewing and postviewing, sustained dictation, and office-style dictation. Many schools use individualized instruction in the form of tapes, film loops, and packages of semiprogrammed material that allows the student to progress at his or her own pace. Some teachers individualize the entire course, while others instruct students as a group through the theory lessons and then begin an individualized approach. By means of such an approach, the teacher becomes available for diagnosing and prescribing for individuals as well as small groups as needed.

The most valid measure of achievement in shorthand is the student's ability to transcribe acceptable typewritten copy from shorthand notes recorded at reasonable rates. Important prerequisites to transcription include good typewriting skills, knowledge of letter placement, correction techniques, and English grammar, punctuation, spelling, and vocabulary. Transcription skill development follows a sequence of transcribing from (1) textbook shorthand plates, (2) familiar homework notes, (3) practiced dictation material, and (4) new-matter dictation. Many drills are available for increasing speed and accuracy in transcription.

Frequent positive feedback of the results of student learning is important to motivation and success in shorthand. Also, limited amounts of formal testing are needed to evaluate student progress, provide remediation, and assign grades for a given period. The shorthand teacher makes use of a schedule of weighting for grading various items in the four semesters of shorthand; these items include dictation speed, brief form tests, theory tests, speed increase, mailable transcription, transcribing speed, and production tests. Many teachers use a daily and/or weekly grading plan based on a point system which distinguishes among letters that are perfect, mailable, and unmailable.

References

[1]A. J. Lemaster, "The Present and Future Outlook for Shorthand," *Business Education World* 52, no. 3 (January–February 1972): 21.

[2]Dean Clayton, "Essential Elements of Shorthand Instruction," *Business Education Forum* 29, no. 3 (December 1974): 12.

[3]William Mitchell, "A Maxi Approach to Shorthand Teaching," *Business Education Forum* 25, no. 1 (October 1970): 12–13.

[4]Ruth I. Anderson, "Methods of Instruction in First-Year Shorthand," in *Effective Secretarial Education*, Marion G. Coleman and Oleen M. Henson eds. (Reston, Va.: National Business Education Association, 1974), p. 33.

[5]*A Handbook for Business Education in Iowa* (Des Moines: State Department of Public Instruction, Business and Office Education Service, 1972), pp. 168–69.

[6]Marion M. Lamb, *Your First Year of Teaching Shorthand and Transcription* (Cincinnati: South-Western Publishing Company, 1961), p. 23.

[7]Mary Ellen Oliverio, "Goals, Assumptions, and Activities in Teaching Shorthand Dictation/Transcription," *The Balance Sheet* 56, no. 3 (November 1974): 100–101.

[8]Ibid., p. 101.

[9]Irol W. Balsley, "Basic Conditions of Effective Shorthand Learning," *The Balance Sheet* 61, no. 6 (March 1975): 245.

[10]Charles T. Laurie, "Shorthand Instruction in Light of Recent Theories of Learning and Instruction." *Delta Pi Epsilon Journal* 18, no. 3 (May 1976): 4.

[11]Ibid., p. 2.

[12]J. S. Bruner, "The Course of Cognitive Growth," *American Psychologist* 19, (1964): 1–15.

[13]Balsley, "Basic Conditions," p. 246.

[14]Ibid.

[15]Ibid.

[16]Louis A. Leslie and Charles E. Zoubek, *Instructor's Handbook for Gregg Shorthand*, Functional Method, Diamond Jubilee Series, 2d ed. (New York: Gregg Division, McGraw-Hill Book Company, 1971), pp. 17–19.

[17]Edward L. Christensen and R. DerMont Bell, *Teacher's Manual, Century 21 Shorthand*, Book 1 (Cincinnati: South-Western Publishing Company, 1974), p. 54.

[18]Louis A. Leslie, *Methods of Teaching Gregg Shorthand* (New York: Gregg Division, McGraw-Hill Book Company, 1953), p. 4.

[19]Allien R. Russon, "Methods of Teaching Shorthand," Monograph 119 (South-Western Publishing Company, 1968), p. 11.

[20]Lloyd V. Douglas, James T. Blanford, and Ruth I. Anderson, *Teaching Business Subjects,* 2d ed. (Englewood Cliffs, N.J.: Prentice-Hall, Inc. 1965), pp. 194–95.

[21]Russon, "Methods of Teaching Shorthand," p. 11.

[22]Douglas, Blanford, and Anderson, *Teaching Business Subjects,* 2d ed., pp. 195–96.

[23]Russon, "Methods of Teaching Shorthand," p. 13.

[24]Ibid.

[25]Christensen and Bell, *Teacher's Manual, Century 21 Shorthand,* p. 16.

[26]Leslie and Zoubek, *Instructors Handbook for Gregg Shorthand,* p. 25.

[27]Mark Langemo, " 'Surefire' Shorthand," *The Journal of Business Education* 48, no. 6 (March 1973): 255.

[28]Steve Rosen and Beverly Korn, "I Like Shorthand But . . . ," *Business Education Forum* 26, no. 8 (May 1972): 44.

[29]Christensen and Bell, *Teacher's Manual, Century 21 Shorthand,* p. 19.

[30]Ibid., p. 20.

[31]Langemo, " 'Surefire' Shorthand," p. 255.

[32]Berle Haggblade, "Strategies to Assure Shorthand Theory Mastery," *Century 21 Reporter* (Fall 1974): 6, 9.

[33]Leslie, *Methods of Teaching Gregg Shorthand,* p. 168.

[34]Russon, "Methods of Teaching Shorthand," p. 13.

[35]Leslie, *Methods of Teaching Gregg Shorthand,* p. 169.

[36]William Mitchell, "Using Shorthand Speed-Building Plans to Develop Marketable Skills," *Business Education World* 53, no. 3 (January–February 1973): 25.

[37]Leslie, *Methods of Teaching Gregg Shorthand,* pp. 172–73, 176.

[38]Ibid., pp. 174–75.

[39]Robert L. Grubbs, "Rx for Effective Shorthand Teaching: How to Build Skill in Second-Semester Shorthand," *Business Education World* 41, no. 6 (February 1961): 24–25. Reprinted with permission of BUSINESS EDUCATION WORLD, Gregg Division, McGraw-Hill Book Company, copyright February 1961.

[40]Russon, "Methods of Teaching Shorthand," pp. 26–27.

[41]Mitchell, "Using Shorthand," p. 25. Reprinted with permission of BUSINESS EDUCATION WORLD, Gregg Division, McGraw-Hill Book Company, copyright January–February 1977.

[42]Robert S. Driska, "Motivate Students in Advanced Shorthand and Transcription," *The Balance Sheet* 59, no. 3 (November 1972): 104–5, 119.

[43]Irol W. Balsley, "Strategies for Developing Reading/Writing Skills in Shorthand," *Century 21 Reporter.* (Fall 1975): 5–6.

[44]Russon, "Methods of Teaching Shorthand," pp. 30–31.

[45]Jane M. Banks, "Individualized Shorthand Instruction: Installation of an Innovation," *Business Education World* 55, no. 2 (November–December 1974): 12–13.

[46]Ruth Gaffga, "Shorthand Accuracy," *The Journal of Business Education* 51, no. 8 (May 1976): 355.

[47]Herbert A. Tonne, Estelle L. Popham, and M. Herbert Freeman, *Methods of Teaching Business Subjects,* 3rd ed. (New York: Gregg Division, McGraw-Hill Book Company, 1965), p. 223.

[48]Russon, "Methods of Teaching Shorthand," p. 34.

[49]Douglas, Blanford, and Anderson, *Teaching Business Subjects,* p. 250.

[50]Joe M. Pullis, "The Shorthand Teacher's Dilemma: When to Begin Transcription?" *The Balance Sheet* 55, no. 2 (October 1973): 74, 94.

[51]Langemo, " 'Surefire' Shorthand," pp. 255–56.

[52]Russon, "Methods of Teaching Shorthand," pp. 34–35.

[53]Douglas, Blanford, and Anderson, *Teaching Business Subjects,* pp. 242–43.

[54]Louis A. Leslie and Charles E. Zoubek, *Instructor's Handbook for Gregg Transcription,* Diamond Jubilee Series, 2d ed. (New York: Gregg Division, McGraw-Hill Book Company, 1972), pp. 15–16.

[55]Russon, "Methods of Teaching Shorthand," pp. 51–57.

[56]Christensen and Bell, *Teacher's Manual, Century 21 Shorthand,* p. 27.

[57]Gregg, Leslie, and Zoubek, *Instructor's Handbook for Gregg Shorthand,* pp. 45–46.

[58]Douglas, Blanford, and Anderson, *Teaching Business Subjects,* p. 229.

[59]Mark Langemo, "Methods of Instruction in Second-Year Shorthand," in *Effective Secretarial Education,* Marion G. Coleman and Oleen H. Henson eds. (Reston, Va.: National Business Education Association, 1974), p. 45.

[60]Leslie and Zoubek, *Instructor's Handbook for Gregg Transcription,* pp. 20–25.

[61]Ibid., p. 20.

SUGGESTIONS FOR FURTHER STUDY

Hillestad, Mildred. "Cognitive Learning Processes and Research in Shorthand Teaching." *Delta Pi Epsilon Journal* 19 (January 1977): 14–25.

Hoskinson, Robert. "How Does Your Stenography Testing Program Measure Up?" *Century 21 Reporter,* (Spring 1977): 1–2, 8–11.

Nadler, Charles D. "Brief Form Learning and Retention." *Journal of Business Education* 52, no. 8 (May 1977): 381–83.

Nanassy, Louis C. "Current Research in Shorthand/Transcription." *Century 21 Reporter* (Fall 1977): p. 15.

Reese, Don, and Smith, E. Ray. "Shorthand: A Textbook Analysis." Monograph 129. Cincinnati: South-Western Publishing Co., 1976.

Streety, Beverly. "A Systematic Approach to Constructing Shorthand Theory Tests." *NABTE Review* 4 (1977): 86–88.

chapter 8

TEACHING OFFICE PRACTICE

Office practice is sometimes spoken of as a "capstone" course in business education because it ties together and integrates on a vocational level the knowledges and skills gained in other business courses, as well as introducing new, related subject matter that will result in a more competent office worker. The modern business office reflects a high level of change both in its technology and its social aspects. Likewise, the office practice course is dynamic; it provides a constantly changing content and structure in order to keep the student abreast of business practices. Both teacher and student realize a sense of accomplishment as they approach the task of applying previously learned and new skills to the solution of business problems in office practice.

The vocational objective of business education focuses on the preparation of students for employment. Office practice is designed to establish a link between the school and business. The course covers the information, procedures, and machines with which all workers need to have familiarity before accepting an office position.

module 8.1
CONTENT AND OBJECTIVES

Office practice courses should be flexible enough to meet the needs of all students in the business education program, whether their major area of interest is bookkeeping/accounting, clerical, stenographic/secretarial, or data processing. In larger schools, separate courses in secretarial/stenographic and clerical/bookkeeping office practice may be offered. Many schools, on the other hand, provide for all types of office practice in one course. In a single, intensified course, the teacher identifies instructional units or topics that are common to all groups of students as well as those that apply to each specialized area.

After completing this module, you should be able to (1) identify instructional areas/units of an office practice course and (2) explain and illustrate five types of objectives generally associated with an office practice course.

311

CONTENT

The content of office practice courses should reflect the skills and knowledges required in business. An analysis of the eight functional areas listed in the NOBELS study* (New Office and Business Education Learning System) resulted in the identification of forty-five instructional units. Twelve of these units were found to be common to all of the functional areas of business: computational skills, filing, grooming, human relations, keeping records, handling mail, operating office machines, problem solving, processing forms, proofreading, telephoning, and typewriting. These forty-five units of instruction were identified by teacher-participants in the Vocational Business Education Currculum Workshop for Senior High School Teachers at the University of South Florida in 1970.†

The New York State Department of Education Office Practice Syllabus recommends that subject matter in the course be divided into eight instructional areas: advanced typewriting, adding and calculating machines, machine transcription, duplicating machines, filing and records management, data processing, communications, and human relations.[1]

The following units are included in *Secretarial Office Procedures* by Oliverio and Pasewark: The Secretary, The Secretary and Word Processing, Preparing Mailable Letters, Letter Writing, Typewriting Reports, The Secretary and Data Processing, Using Mail and Shipping Services, Meeting the Public, Rapid Communication Services, The Secretary and Reprographics, Filing Records, The Secretary and Records Management, The Secretary and Travel Responsibilities, The Secretary and Financial Records, and You and Secretarial Work.[2]

OVERALL OBJECTIVES

Instructional objectives for office practice will vary from one school to another, from one type of course to another (stenographic or clerical, for example), and from one educational level to another. Certain basic features, however, are reflected in the overall objectives of the office practice course.

One type of objective centers around the integration of previously acquired knowledges and skills and their application to the requirements of a job. For example, typing letters from dictation requires the student to draw on previously developed skills in typewriting, shorthand, transcription, and business English to prepare letters according to a standard of mailability.

A second objective focuses on the development of new skills. Filing, office machines, rapid communication services, and mail and shipping services are examples of new skills that may be developed in the office practice course.

A third objective involves attitudes, work habits, and personality and char-

*Accounting, computing; electronic data processing; personnel; production; purchasing, shipping, and receiving; sales and client-related; stenographic; and other communication.
†George Vanover, Project Coordinator, and Calfrey C. Calhoun, Project Director.

acter trait development. Business courses such as accounting, shorthand, type-writing, and business machines provide limited opportunities for the treatment of topics such as human relations, interviews, job applications, and grooming.

A fourth type of objective concentrates on the further development of previously introduced skills and knowledges. For example, students enrolling in office practice with one year of shorthand instruction will have the opportunity to develop transcription skills.

A fifth type of objective focuses on assessment of personal goals in relation to the opportunities and requirements of a career in office work. This objective also involves helping the sutdent toward a better understanding of the role of the office within the total system of the business enterprise. The following specific course objectives illustrate the types of objectives cited above.

Specific objectives

1. To acquaint the student with the nature of secretarial work and its requirements
2. To guide the student in the proper development of personal qualities to ensure success on the job
3. To acquaint the student with the numerous opportunities and requirements common to secretarial positions
4. To familiarize the student with basic reference sources used in the office
5. To teach the importance of orderly work flow and a high level of accuracy in job performance
6. To give the student practice in making decisions involving the setting of priorities, planning, organizing, and evaluating work performance
7. To teach the procedures involved in handling incoming and outgoing mail
8. To develop proper dictation and transcription (including machine transcription) procedures
9. To develop proper telephone techniques and to acquaint the student with telecommunication services
10. To teach the secretarial handling of travel details
11. To acquaint the student with the financial and legal duties of the secretary
12. To provide information that will enable the student to intelligently select office supplies and equipment
13. To teach the student how to write a letter of application and how to prepare a personal résumé
14. To develop the student's ability to organize and record meetings and to prepare business reports
15. To acquaint the student with postal and shipping facilities.

module 8.1
LEARNING ACTIVITIES

1. Choose an educational level (secondary, postsecondary, vocational-technical, junior college, college or university), and prepare the following information for inclusion in an office practice curriculum guide:

    a. Rationale
    b. Objectives—at least one for each of the five types of objectives generally associated with an office practice course
    c. Instructional units (list)
    Use this module and other references of your choice in completing this activity.

2. Interview an office manager or employer to determine new skills needed by beginning office workers. Prepare a written or oral report.

3. Read one or more articles from business education or office management publications (such as *Administrative Management* or *The Office*) and prepare a report on emerging trends that will influence the training of office workers.

4. Compile a list of new instructional units and/or machines that you would recommend adding to an office practice curriculum to better prepare beginning office employees for the modern business office.

module 8.1
SELF-TEST

1. Examples of specific objectives for an office practice course are found in Module 8.1. On your paper, write the number of each objective, then indicate which of the five general types of objectives described in this module each illustrates.

module 8.2
ORGANIZATION AND INSTRUCTION

In an office practice course, the business teacher encounters students with various career objectives and different levels of achievement in related skills. On the basis of these factors, as well as objectives and content of the course, facilities, equipment, and materials available, the teacher selects the instructional techniques and organizational plans that are most appropriate. Several plans and techniques successfully used by business teachers are described in this module.

After completing this module, you should be able to (1) explain the use of the following organizational patterns/plans in teaching office practice: (a) total group, (b) rotation, (c) individualized instruction, (d) simulation, (e) model office; (2) explain and/or demonstrate the use of the following instructional techniques in office practice: (a) demonstrations, (b) lecture-discussions, (c) job sheets, (d) contracts, (e) committees, (f) instructional units, (g) in-baskets; (3) describe/illustrate at least two different ways of organizing an office practice classroom; and (4) prepare a list of equipment for an office practice classroom.

TOTAL GROUP INSTRUCTION

The teacher may wish to present some units to the entire class. For example, teacher time can be saved by introducing and explaining the organization of the course to the entire class at the same time. Total group instruction is appropriate for units such as developing interpersonal relationships or getting a job. Discussions throughout the course will be pointed toward employment. Students will have practiced desirable office personality traits, and they will have some understanding of job availability and job requirements in the employment community. The final portion of the course can be devoted to such activities as (1) studying the background and business outlook for potential employers, (2) evaluating positions in terms of their qualifications, (3) writing letters of application for criticism by the class, (4) filling in data sheets similar to those used in business, (5) preparing for personal interviews and practicing interviews with cooperating businesses, (6) making applications for positions at the end of the school year, and (7) discussing these interviews with the class.

ROTATION PLAN

The rotation plan is employed by the office practice teacher to allow students, in small groups or individually, to work at machines or other assignments different from those of the remainder of the class. At periodic intervals, depending upon the equipment and facilities available, the individual or group shifts to a different activity. In a typical one-year course, the rotation schedule might be used for sixteen weeks to introduce students to such activities as adding/listing machines, calculating machines, production typewriting, voice writing, clerical work, filing, and duplication. At the postsecondary level, more specialized equipment such as the automatic typewriter, accounting machine, and various types of reprographic and copying machines may be commonly included as part of a quarter or semester course. It is important that the teacher plan the entire course before beginning rotations to ensure that he or she has allowed adequate time for the various activities.

The business teacher may wish to follow these procedures in planning for the use of rotation:

1. Decide which learning activities you will include in the rotation plan. After identifying these activities, indicate the amount of time to allow for each activity.

2. Divide the class into two or more groups depending on the number of activities you wish to initiate. When students in one group complete a given set of activities, they rotate to the next group of activities. In assigning students to rotation groups, allow for a mixture of academically strong and weak students, as well as those who are quiet and those who are more outgoing.

3. Divide the activities into, for example, three equal groups and assign student groups to each as follows on page 316.

Activity Group I	Activity Group II	Activity Group III
Student Group 1	Student Group 2	Student Group 3
Student Group 3	Student Group 1	Student Group 2
Student Group 2	Student Group 3	Student Group 1

Rotation Schedule

Student Names	Time Period_____ Activities	Time Period_____ Activities	Time Period_____ Activities
Group 1 (list names)	Group 1 activities	Group 2 activities	Group 3 activities
Group 2 (list names)	Group 2 activities	Group 3 activities	Group 1 activities
Group 3 (list names)	Group 3 activities	Group 1 activities	Group 2 activities

INDIVIDUALIZED INSTRUCTION

By using individualized instructional materials, each student may work through modules or units appropriate to the instructional or career need. Such instructional packages, accompanied by appropriate media, can provide a vehicle for remedial work, additional practice on previously learned skills, or acquisition of new skills and knowledges. The teacher and student plan together the instructional units to be completed during a given quarter or semester. Each student progresses through the material at his or her own pace, with teacher assistance as needed. (See Chapters 3 and 5 for further discussion of the mechanics of individualized instruction.) The material in Illustration 8.1 shows individualized experiences appropriate for an office practice course at the high school level.

SIMULATION

As the course title implies, a major purpose of office practice is to provide students with opportunities to apply their skills in officelike settings. One approach that is widely used to accomplish this purpose is simulation. These activities are designed to provide students with realistic office situations under simulated conditions. Generally, students have acquired basic skills prior to beginning the simulation so that the simulated activities can focus on integration of these previously acquired skills. The actual uses of simulation vary widely. One approach is to employ a culminating simulation unit using teacher-prepared or commerical materials. Hanson and Parker illustrate three possible time schedules when stimulation is used simultaneously with the entire class, as shown in the chart on page 323.

Another approach using commercial simulation materials involves rotating one-third of the students through the simulation while the remainder rotate

illustration 8.1

TAKING MESSAGES USING THE TELEPHONE

OBJECTIVE

The skill of taking a message is developed in this PLACE. When you complete this PLACE, you will be able to:

TAKE A MESSAGE BY ACCURATELY COMPLETING THE NINE ITEMS REQUIRED TO RECORD THE MESSAGE.

RESOURCES

To help you learn to take a message, refer to the following resources which are on the resource list for this PLACE series.

MEDIA

Books:
1. TELETRAINING FOR BUSINESS STUDIES, (Published by Southern Bell)
2. Wood & McKenna, THE RECEPTIONIST, Gregg Publishing Company.
3. Meehan, Pasewark, Oliverio, CLERICAL OFFICE PROCEDURES, 5th Ed., South-Western Publishing Company.

illustration 8.1 (continued)

INSTRUCTIONS: *Choose one activity from Group A. Do Activities B and C. Activity D is optional.*

ACTIVITY

A. Choose one to read:

From Resource #1, TELETRAINING FOR BUSINESS STUDIES, pp. 20-23, 24-25. Omit the exercises.
From Resource #2, THE RECEPTIONIST, pp. 127-128.
From Resource #3, CLERICAL OFFICE PROCEDURES, pp. 306-308.

B. Complete the following exercise on taking messages.

You work for Mr. A. R. Keller. On March 9, at 1:10 in the afternoon, Mr. Charles Robertson, telephone number 555-1236, extension 421, calls to tell Mr. Keller that his company will accept the terms of the preliminary contract they discussed. Mr. Keller is not in, and will not be available until at least four o'clock. In the space below write out the information you think you should pass on to Mr. Keller:

_____

_____

_____

Now look at the form shown below. See how much easier it is to give all the necessary information, using a form like this than when you write it out yourself.

To_____
Date_____ Time_____

WHILE YOU WERE OUT

M_____

of_____

Phone_____

	Area Code	Number	Extension
TELEPHONED		PLEASE CALL	
CALLED TO SEE YOU		WILL CALL AGAIN	
WANTS TO SEE YOU		URGENT	
	RETURNED YOUR CALL		

Message_____

_____

_____

_____

_____

Operator

illustration 8.1 (continued)

Now see how well you can do on the problems given below. When you have finished the problems, check your answers with the answer sheet on page 4.

SECURE A PAD FOR TAKING MESSAGES FROM RESOURCES TO COMPLETE THESE PROBLEMS. (Forms for this purpose may vary slightly, but the information required is generally the same.)

Read the following "calls." Then write the necessary information on the Memo of Call pad.

Call #1.   At 10:15 the telephone in your office rings, and you answer it. Mr. Arthur Smith wants to speak to your employer, Mr. Tremont. Mr. Tremont is not in. Mr. Smith says that the call is personal and that he wants to hear from your employer before 4:30 p.m. today, at 247-6099, ext. 333.

Call #2.   You work for Mr. Miller, who has left the office for the day. At four o'clock the telephone rings. The following conversation takes place:

   You: Mr. Miller's office, Miss Jackson speaking.

   Caller: May I speak to Mr. Miller, please?

   You: May I ask who is calling, please?

   Caller: This is John Adams of the Modern Furniture Company.

   You: Oh, yes, Mr. Adams. I'm sorry, but Mr. Miller has left the office for the day. May I help you?

   Caller: No, thank you. I'll call back.

   You: Are you calling about an order, Mr. Adams?

   Caller: No. Mr. Miller is interested in some new fireproof files. I'll call him tomorrow.

   You: Thank you, Mr. Adams. I'll tell him to expect your call.

illustration 8.1 (continued)

CHECK

Check your filled-in forms with those shown below. The actual wording of the "Message" section may vary, but all the important information should be included. If you have any questions about the acceptability of your messages, have your teacher check it for you.

#1

To *Mr. Tremont*
Date *today's date* Time *10:15* (A.M.)

WHILE YOU WERE OUT

Mr. *Arthur Smith*

of _____

Phone *247-6099 333*
Area Code / Number / Extension

TELEPHONED	✓	PLEASE CALL HIM	✓
CALLED TO SEE YOU		WILL CALL AGAIN	
WANTS TO SEE YOU		RUSH	
	RETURNED YOUR CALL		

Message *personal call – return by 4:30 today*

Your name a initials
Operator

AD 5

#2

To *Mr. Miller*
Date *today's date* Time *4:00* (P.M.)

WHILE YOU WERE OUT

Mr. *John Adams*

of *Modern Furniture Co*

Phone _____
Area Code / Number / Extension

TELEPHONED	✓	PLEASE CALL HIM	
CALLED TO SEE YOU		WILL CALL AGAIN	✓
WANTS TO SEE YOU		RUSH	
	RETURNED YOUR CALL		

Message *called about fireproof files.*

Your name f initials
Operator

AD 5

illustration 8.1 (continued)

ACTIVITY

D. The following optional activities will give you a chance to practice your message-taking skill:

1. Work with another student and choose one of these calls to record: Teletrainer calls 5 and 6, Pages 83-86 of Resource #1 by Southern Bell, or Teletrainer situations 6 and 7 on Page 103.

   Plan your call and record it. You should play the part of the receiver of the call. Play back the tape and evaluate your conversation with a checklist like the one on Page 6.

   If you rate poorly on two or more items, choose another call, record it, and ask a classmate to evaluate your conversation using another checklist (from the resource center)

2. Work with another student and make up a script that will require at least two of the following:

   a. getting information
   b. taking a message
   c. giving information

   Record your script. Play it back and evaluate it on your checklist.

illustration 8.1 (continued)

CHECKLIST FOR RECORDED SCRIPTS

Listen to the recorded telephone conversation and answer these questions by checking the appropriate column.

	GOOD	FAIR	POOR	DOES NOT APPLY TO THIS CALL
<u>Beginning of the Call</u>				
1. Answered promptly and pleasantly.	___	___	___	___
2. Identified self/company.	___	___	___	___
<u>Development of the Call</u>				
1. Volunteered to help the caller.	___	___	___	___
2. Asked caller's name and telephone number.	___	___	___	___
3. Offered to take a message.	___	___	___	___
4. Asked if employer could return the call.	___	___	___	___
5. Supplied information that would help the caller without giving out company information which should be kept confidential.	___	___	___	___
6. Took message accurately.	___	___	___	___
7. Message easy to read.	___	___	___	___
<u>Closing of the Call</u>				
1. Left a pleasant impression.	___	___	___	___
2. Was certain conversation was ended before hanging up.	___	___	___	___
<u>Voice Personality</u>				
1. Pleasant tone of voice.	___	___	___	___
2. Sounded sincere, interested.	___	___	___	___
3. Spoke loudly enough.	___	___	___	___
4. Did not speak too loudly.	___	___	___	___
5. Used proper grammar.	___	___	___	___
6. Enunciated words clearly.	___	___	___	___
7. Courteous.	___	___	___	___

·POSSIBLE OFFICE SIMULATION SCHEDULES

I.	(27 weeks)				(9 weeks)		
	Learning Units				Simulation		

II.	(13 weeks)	(4 weeks)	(13 weeks)	(4 weeks)	(2 weeks)		
	Learning Units	Simulation	Learning Units	Simulation	Review and Evaluation		

III.	(9 weeks)	(2 weeks)	(7 weeks)	(2 weeks)	(7 weeks)	(7 weeks)	(2 weeks)
	Learning Units	Simulation	Learning Units	Simulation	Learning Units	Simulation	Review and Evaluation

Source: Garth A. Hanson and E. Charles Parker, "Simulation," in *Changing Methods of Teaching Business Subjects,* LeRoy Brendel and Herbert Yengle, eds. (Washington, D.C.: National Business Education Association, 1972), p. 235.

through other activities or units such as filing, office machines, proofreading, using references, and so on. In this approach, the conventional classroom is converted to form "offices" for part of the quarter, semester, or year, or a portion of the classroom is arranged in an office-type setting for the entire year. A temporary or permanent partition may be used to separate the "office" from the remainder of the classroom. Another plan, used more often at the post-secondary level, is the model office, in which the entire classroom is set up as an office for the total instructional time. (See section on the model office.) The classroom facilities and equipment are usually more sophisticated than in previously discussed plans. These characteristics are generally typical of total model-office simulations.[4]

1. The student spends sufficient time in the simulation to experience the routine, the excitement, the monotony, the promotions, and the over-all feeling of the real office world.
2. Since this type of simulation is usually large enough to warrant several positions within several departments, the student learns how to participate in such a large departmental atmosphere as in stenographic pools, clerical typewriting pools, duplicating departments, and payroll departments.
3. Since the instructor acts as president of the company and usually teaches more than one section of simulation, he has time to devote to implementing procedures and improving the package. Communications with the students are conducted through normal office procedures such as staff meetings, memos, and so on. Routine lesson plans and learning units are not used as they are in other simulation plans.
4. The simulation package is extensively structured with many employee manuals and organizational charts providing a standard operating procedure for most situations.
5. Students work for promotions much the same as they do in a real office situation. This experience provides the setting for competitive work among students. . . .

The business teacher will find a variety of commercial simulation materials available as well as materials from colleges and local and state departments of education. These vary in the number and kind of office positions and the amount and type of equipment and hardware needed. The teacher should review the available materials and select or construct a simulation package that most nearly prepares students for the types of initial employment available in the employment community. Hanson and Parker recommend asking these questions about a package:[5]

1. What documents will be coming across the desks of each person involved in the simulation?
2. What kind of action is taken with each of the documents?
3. Does this action coincide with the objectives established for your course?
4. What kinds of communications will be used in the simulation other than the written document, and how will they be used?
5. How will the work flow from position to position?
6. How difficult is it to introduce the material into the simulation?
7. What equipment will one need to perform the office duties?
8. What kind of interaction will occur between students, between student and teacher, and between teachers?
9. How will one be able to evaluate the students?

MODEL OFFICE PLAN

The model office plan is a form of simulation. This discussion, however, focuses on the model office as an organizational plan for a total office practice course. In the Michigan block-time plan, "the model office brings students as close as possible to actual work situations. Students are given time for adjustment and an opportunity to determine the areas of practice needing more work. The model office further develops human relations skills, knowledge of work flow, and ability to adjust to various situations. The student employee learns that others depend on his or her work and are held up if he or she does not finish or is too slow. The student learns that absenteeism puts additional strain on those present and makes the person who is absent a less efficient worker because he or she loses continuity. Students need to learn to work cooperatively with people of varying abilities."[6] Through a block, the teacher can provide instruction that builds advanced skills, integrates realistic practice in a simulated office environment, and offers time flexibility to meet the learning needs of individual students. Of course, an obvious disadvantage of the block-time plan is that it restricts the scheduling of other courses that may be needed to complete the student's program.

Material for a model office may be purchased or constructed by the teacher. Davis developed and implemented a model office simulation for postsecondary vocational-technical students. Her simulation centers on three skills clusters and includes the following job positions:

Accounting Cluster: (1) bookkeeper and cashier
(2) payroll and file clerk
(3) machines operator

Personnel Cluster:

(1) personnel assistant
(2) records clerk
(3) reservations, research, and file clerk

Communications Cluster:

(1) executive secretary
(2) stenographer
(3) clerk-typist
(4) duplicating, central supply, and postal clerk
(5) receptionist
(6) switchboard operator[7]

After identifying the skills clusters and/or department of the company and the job positions, she then completed a job assignment for each position. The job assignments were placed in individual packets in the desk for each job station. The work flow chart for each completed job assignment is shown in Illustration 8.2. A form for assigning point values to job assignments is illustrated in Illustration 8.3, and a weekly evaluation and point value employee rating sheet is shown in Illustration 8.4.

Point value system

If the employee's work was acceptable, the employee received a "point value sheet" from the office manager which was left with the payroll clerk for salary data.

If the employee's work was unacceptable, the employee returned to the station to rework the job assignment in whatever way was necessary to make it acceptable, and then returned it to the office manager for evaluation. (Note: This "unacceptable" cycle was repeated until the job was acceptable. All work redone resulted in a loss of time to earn points during working hours or caused the student to spend overtime hours without pay in order to meet minimum standards expected on the job.)

Upon acceptable completion of each job assignment, the Job Assignment Point Value Sheet (Illustration 8.3) was filled out and filed in the employee's record until the end of the week. At that time, the payroll clerk secured this form from the office manager and posted on it each individual job assignment point value earned by the employee during the week.

At the end of the week, the office manager rated the employee, using the Weekly Evaluation and Point Value Employee Rating Sheet (Illustration 8.4). The payroll clerk completed this form by posting the point values earned on the individual job assignments.

This procedure of completing job assignments continued until the employee had worked a full week (two hours per day for five days per week constituted a normal "work" week) equated with a "real world" forty-hour work week.

On the last day of the employee's work week, the time card was brought to the payroll clerk and left for payroll check computations. The payroll

illustration 8.2

EMPLOYEE WORK FLOW FOR EACH COMPLETED JOB ASSIGNMENT

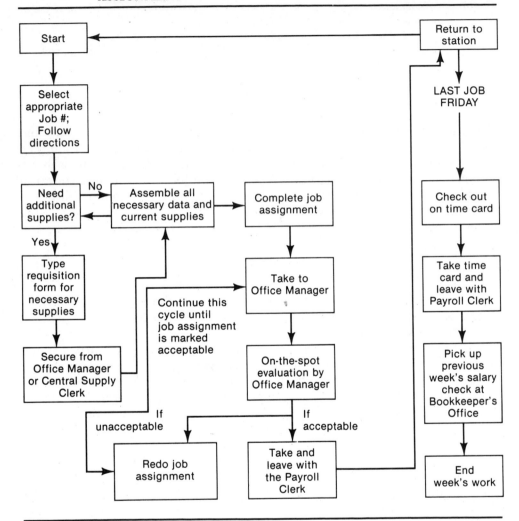

schedule was always one week behind. Therefore the employee picked up the previous week's paycheck when turning in the current week's time card.

The employee took as long as necessary to complete each job position before rotating to a new job station. There were two stations (duplicates) for each position within the lab utilized for the office simulation.

The office simulation lab was open from 8:00 A.M. to 10:00 P.M. daily, Monday through Friday, which allowed fourteen hours multiplied by twenty-three (duplicate setup for eleven job position stations plus one

illustration 8.3
JOB ASSIGNMENT POINT VALUE SHEET

Point Value Scale: 30 and above = A = _____
                               24-29   = B = _____
                               12-23   = C = _____
                               11 and below = F = _____

Major Strengths:

Major Weaknesses:

Suggestions for Improvement:

Weekly Point Value Accumulation:

1.   Weekly Office Manager Evaluation   <u>Points</u>

2.   Jobs: # _____   _____
                  # _____   _____
                  # _____   _____

NAME:_____

STATION:_____   DEPARTMENT:_____

DATE:_____

Job Packet Assignment # _____

       Point Value Given _____

                                     _____
                                     Office Manager
                                     "Secretaries, Incorporated"

switchboard operator). This allowed 1,610 hours of operational space for utilization by the students (fourteen hours of time usage per job station, divided by two, since each student could use the job station for two-hour intervals, equals seven students per station per day). With twelve separate job stations (in duplicate) in the office simulation, a total simulation enrollment of 168 students could be accommodated at one time. A sign-up chart for the quarter was kept at the office manager's station so that students could sign up for available times for the particular job station at which they were working.

illustration 8.4
WEEKLY EVALUATION AND POINT VALUE EMPLOYEE RATING SHEET

Student's Name_____

              (last)   (first)   (middle)

Job Station_____ Department_____

Date_____

General Evaluation	Excel-lent	Good	Satis-factory	Unsatis-factory
1. Dependability				
2. Promptness				
3. Appearance				
4. Following instructions				
5. Getting along with others				
6. Wise use of time				
7. Ability to work without constant supervision				
8. Skills:				
a. Shorthand				
b. Typing				
c. Office Machines				
d. Telephone				
Totals	_____	_____	_____	_____
	_____ ×3	_____ ×2	_____ ×1	_____ ×0
	_____ +	_____ +	_____ +	_____

GRAND TOTAL _____

Office manager

The office manager was, of course, the instructor in charge. The manager's overall duty was to keep the company simulation running smoothly. All students, or "employees," were kept functioning within the office by constantly producing work from the instructor-developed materials packets or through the production of "live" work substituted by the office manager.

The office manager rated the "live" work as to difficulty and the length of time needed to produce it. After determining these items, he or she assigned salary point values to be earned on the "live" work before "employees" accepted the work assignments. The office manager also had the perogative of accepting or rejecting actual "live" work that came into the simulation from inside or outside the school.

The weekly evaluation sheets were kept on each employee by the office manager who rated performances and assessed and assigned penalty points prescribed weekly. All final productions on both "live" and instructor-prepared materials were checked and evaluated by the office manager, who either instructed the employee to redo the work on his or her own time (not for salary hours) or assigned the points earned by the employee on the point value sheet.

In addition, the office manager conducted all initial interviews of applicants for each job station of the simulation.

In actual practice, many business teachers use a combination of organizational plans in implementing an office practice course. One example of a combination is the following:

2 Weeks	16 Weeks	6 Weeks	9 Weeks	3 Weeks
Total Group	Rotation	Model Office Simulation	Rotation	Total Group

Other plans include total group activities interspersed throughout the quarter, semester, or year; three six- to ten-week simulations for one-third of the class with the remainder of the class in an individualized or rotation plan. Small-group instruction is provided throughout the quarter as needed by means of teacher-directed instruction or individualized instructional packages.

INSTRUCTIONAL TECHNIQUES

Office practice lends itself to the use of a variety of instructional procedures, both singly or in combination. Each teacher will have to decide which procedures are most appropriate based upon the specific unit being taught, the facilities available, student abilities and needs, teacher preparation and skill, organizational patterns, and the length of time allotted to the course. (In addition to the following discussion, you may want to review Chapters 3 and 5 and related instruction Chapters 6, 7, 9, 10, and 11 for additional information on instructional techniques.)

Demonstrations, role playing, skits, and dramatizations

In any unit involving skill development, demonstrations are effective. Live or taped (filmed) demonstrations may be presented by the teacher or by students who possess a high degree of skill to illustrate procedures and techniques involving the use of office machines. Demonstrations involving more than one person, such as role playing, skits, or other forms of dramatization, are effective tools for teaching units such as grooming, getting a job, telephone techniques, and office behavior since they help students to become aware of acceptable behavior.

Lecture-discussion

While not a technique generally associated with teaching office practice, lectures (and discussions) can be used effectively on occasion. The lecture may be employed in combination with a demonstration or to supplement other procedures in conducting units related to total group learnings. In office practice, it may be effective to lecture under the following conditions:

1. When the teacher, or outside speaker, has information not readily accessible to students, such as specific job opportunities and requirements—or job experiences related by former students.
2. When the teacher wants to reinforce work presented by another method. Before or after students study a topic, the teacher may wish to reinforce learning by lecturing so that there is, in effect, a repetition of the main idea.
3. When the teacher wishes to change the pace or vary the learning situation. Any method used exclusively results in loss of attention on the part of students.
4. When economy is a factor. Through a well-planned and illustrated lecture, the teacher can synthesize many sources, giving all students coverage on a topic that would have been unrealistic to assign.

Job sheets

In use in business and industry for many years, the job instruction sheet offers the office practice teacher an efficient route to the development of many job skills. Job instruction sheets provide a minute breakdown of office tasks, including the method to be used, the sequence of operations, the machines, the materials, the standard time allowance, and the conditions requiring special attention. Job instruction sheets describe for the student the detailed steps to be followed in performing each operation.

PREPARATION OF JOB SHEETS.   For classroom purposes, job instruction sheets should include the following information: (1) the name of the equipment and materials necessary, (2) the steps needed to complete the task, (use an action verb to begin each step and list in sequence), and (3) key points and special techniques numbered to correspond with the related step so as to remind the student what he or she must know about each step in order to perform the job correctly. The teacher should perform the operation with the breakdown as a guide before giving it to the student.

USING THE JOB SHEET.   It is important that the teacher spend a few lessons demonstrating the use of job instruction sheets so that students can become familiar with the process and can follow instructions with a minimum of teacher direction. When introducing job sheets, the teacher should:

1. Explain to students the task to be learned or accomplished via the job sheet.
2. Distribute one packet of supplies, including the job sheet, to each student.
3. Demonstrate the operation at the expert level:
   a. Follow the steps in the breakdown exactly.
   b. Students should watch the demonstration, not the job sheet.
4. Demonstrate the breakdown a second time, pausing before each step of the operation to read the directions. (This slow-moving performance enables the student to see each step of the operation in detail and allows ample time for explanation of key points.)
5. Read the directions for the first step with the student.
6. Execute the first step with students according to the directions.
7. Continue with each step until all steps are completed.[8]

After this step-by-step introduction, the student should be able to progress at his or her own pace through the job sheets. It is a good idea to have all the students (1) read each job sheet carefully as many times as necessary to familiarize themselves with the content; (2) observe a live or taped demonstration of the skill at a vocational level of competency, if necessary, while following the job sheet; (3) perform the complete operation as many times as necessary until they are completely familiar with each step; (4) perform the operation for teacher observation and get assistance, if necessary; and (5) file the job instruction sheet in their personal folders for future use, if copies can be provided for each student.

When students are in the learning stage, you may find it helpful to have them work in pairs with one reading the directions and the other completing the tasks, and then reverse roles. For the student, concomitant learnings are significant, as he or she uses the operation breakdown or job instruction sheet.

> The student learns to follow written directions and to become independent in the operation of equipment and the performance of step-by-step procedures. She observes the technique of giving instructions in a logical manner. She may have the opportunity to assist in the development of a breakdown if her teacher permits or encourages it. She participates in the identification of operations for a task consisting of more than one operation. She must keep her materials in order in her own file and keep an orderly well-organized work area. Preparation of the work area, arrangement of materials and supplies, and cleaning up are frequent steps in operation breakdowns.[9]

A sample job instruction sheet illustrating the use of the telephone directory is shown in Illustration 8.5.[10]

illustration 8.5
ILLUSTRATIVE JOB INSTRUCTION SHEET: COMMUNICATION

USING THE TELEPHONE DIRECTORY
(The Introductory Pages)

Pupil's Name_____   Evaluation_____

Period_____ Date Started_____   Date Finished_____

Approved_____ : _____
              (Instructor)   (Person for whom work was done)

EQUIPMENT AND MATERIALS: A telephone directory for each one or two pupils.

INTRODUCTION: Telephone directories are reference books which serve many purposes. In addition to listing names, addresses, and telephone numbers of subscribers, the directory aids in locating businesses, churches, and professional personnel, provides useful information about the locality, provides a source for checking the spelling of names, and serves as a guide to the use of telephone services. New directories are published annually to include the names of additional customers and to make other changes. Directories are usually organized into three sections: (1) introductory pages, (2) alphabetical pages, (3) yellow pages. In very large cities and metropolitan areas, the yellow pages may be a separate volume.

Steps	Key Points
1. The introductory pages located at the front of the book provide basic information concerning the telephone. These include: a. Calling in emergency situations - fire, police, ambulance. b. Localities served by the directory.	1. a. Using the introductory pages of the directory, find the number you would call for: (1) fire department (2) information operator (3) assistance on a call. (4) having a telephone moved (5) requesting repair services (6) police (7) ambulance (8) making a mobile call (9) making an overseas call (10) discussing a change in a directory listing

illustration 8.5 (continued)

Steps	Key Points
c. Dialing instructions for local and out-of-town calls.	b. What information can you find about (1) direct distance dialing (2) sending telegrams
d. Area codes for some cities.	
e. Placing service calls.	
f. Obtaining weather and time reports.	
g. Information about reduced rates for out-of-town calls.	
h. Information about sending telegrams by telephone.	
i. Information about long distance and overseas calls.	
j. Information about available equipment and services.	
2. Read through these pages very carefully.	

RELATED QUESTIONS:

1. Name several kinds of information found in the introductory pages of a telephone directory.

2. What is the area code of Chicago? Denver? Phoenix?

3. Explain how you would send a telegram by telephone.

Contracts

A contract is a system of individualizing instruction that involves students directly in the selection of assignments. Contracts are written descriptions of specific work to be completed by individual students within a certain period of time. Students may contract for basic course requirements for a grade of *C*, additional work for a grade of *B*, and a greater amount of work for a grade of *A*. Brady recommends the following points for consideration when using contracts:[11]

1. The assignments for different grade levels, (A, B, C) should be varied and of increasing difficulty.

2. Standards of quality as well as quantity must be established. Work must be done correctly before a grade is given, and the number of repetitions should have an effect on the grade.
3. Time limits must be established for completing the contract.
4. The unit test must be based only on the C work if it is given to all students.
5. To earn an A grade, the student's work should show signs of original thinking, initiative, and planning.

A skill-building unit in duplicating could be taught effectively using the contract plan. The *C* contract might require the preparation of spirit and stencil master sheets, art work, correction of masters, and operation and care of machines. The *B* contract could include, in addition to the *C* requirements, the care of machines and supplies for wet-process and dry-process photocopiers, as well as knowledge of limitations and advantages of the spirit and stencil duplicators. A contract for an *A* could include an investigation into the criteria for selection of duplication methods—spirit, stencil, wet-and-dry process photocopiers, and high-volume reproduction (offset and multilith)—with recommendations for the use of each type of reproduction method.

Committees and small groups

Committees and small groups provide a valuable means for integrating skills and knowledges needed by students in advance of employment. Students are encouraged to work together on activities and are provided with opportunities to assume responsibility. Committees may be assigned by the teacher, or the students may select the topics they wish to investigate. Topics may be identified by the entire class as a group before individual selections are made. Topics for investigation might include job supply and demand in office occupations, office careers, job application procedures, office layout and design, copying methods and machines, and the uses of data processing in business. After the committee has organized and selected a chairperson, the members should outline what is to be done, secure the teacher's approval and suggestions, determine the research procedures to be used, and plan for writing up and presenting a report. While the subject matter covered is directly related to the content of office practice, much of the work can be accomplished outside the class period. Committees or small groups are useful for short- or long-term projects, ranging from a few days to a few weeks, depending upon the topics chosen and the interest and maturity of the group. The values of teamwork and cooperation are realized by students as they investigate, acquire, organize, and appraise business information and procedures.

Instructional units

One technique that is frequently used for organizing and carrying out learning experiences is the instructional unit. The units may be used with the entire class simultaneously, such as "getting a job," or for individual or group activities, such as "teaching" office machines. Suggestions for planning and developing units were discussed in detail in Chapter 5.

In-baskets

Problem-solving or "in-basket" activities describe typical situations or duties that an employee might encounter on the job. These situations usually require decision making and organization of work into logical sequences. In-baskets provide an especially effective technique for developing problem-solving skills. The activities and the time involved in an in-basket will vary depending on student expertise. The teacher will find activities appropriate for in-baskets in office practice textbooks and periodicals.

FACILITIES

The office practice room or laboratory should be designed and equipped as nearly as possible to represent the offices students will encounter as employees. The room should be large enough to arrange work stations or clusters to implement teaching plans, and it should have sufficient wiring, lavatory facilities, and storage.

How the business teacher organizes the office practice room is determined by the instructional plan he or she proposes to use. One arrangement is to set up the space as a model office. In this case, room arrangement will reflect the positions in an office and the flow of work. For example, there could be work stations for a receptionist, office manager, accountant, accounting clerk, secretary, sales manager, sales clerk, and shipping clerk.

Another plan is to make use of instructional clusters. The room could be arranged to include areas for typing, shorthand and transcription, business machines, duplicating, filing, and office management.

The least effective organizational pattern may be the traditional classroom in which student desks are arranged in rows facing the teacher. It is difficult for students to acquire the "feel" for an office in such an arrangement.

EQUIPMENT

The following equipment is recommended for adequate coverage of the office practice course:

Typewriter, one electric per student; at least one long carriage
Desks, one per student; may be L-shaped or double-pedestal
Chair, one per student, preferably posture
Spirit duplicator, one per class
Stencil duplicator, one per class
Photocopy machine, one per class

Electronic printing calculator
Electronic display calculator
Printing calculator
Ten-key adding machine
Rotary calculator

Dictation/transcription machine
Transcribing machine

Mimeoscope, one per class
Mimeoscope stylus, one per class
Mimeoscope lettering guide, one per class

Filing cabinet
Guides, folders
Copy holder
Interval timer
Paper cutter

Postage scale
Staple remover
Stapler
Scissors
Rulers

Collator
Stopwatch
Reference library
Telephone, one per office desk or at least two trainer telephones, such as Teletrainers from the telephone company

Other instructional equipment, such as teacher's desk and chair, bookcases, demonstration stands, film projectors, sound-slide machines, overhead projectors, cassette recorders, and so on, should be accessible from the school or department for use on a regular basis.

module 8.2
LEARNING ACTIVITIES

1. Select one level from (a) and (b) and complete the following activities in a, b, c, below:
   (a) high school, junior college/postsecondary vocational-technical college/university
   (b) clerical office practice, secretarial office practice, combined office practice
   a. List the instructional units to be included in the course. (You may need to refer to Module 8.1, office practice textbooks, articles from periodicals, and so on.)
   b. Identify the organizational plans you will use for each unit. Justify/explain your choices.
   c. List the equipment. Explain your choices.

2. Begin a collection of in-basket activities. (See sources such as *The Secretary* and/or write your own.) Assemble at least two different in-baskets.
3. Design a contract format you might use in an office practice course. Incorporate tasks, time, standards, any special directions, and so on. Ask your instructor to evaluate your contract.
4. Begin a collection of job sheets. Continue this activity in Chapter 12, Teaching Business Machines
5. Review one set of simulation material and describe it to the class. Include number of stations, length of simulation, equipment/facilities needed, types of tasks, and so forth.
6. Draw a floor plan for an office practice classroom.

module 8.2
SELF-TEST

1. Define the following organizational plans and instructional techniques as related to office practice:

simulation   job sheet
rotation   model office
in-basket   total group
individualized instruction

module 8.3
EVALUATION

The ultimate success or failure of an office practice course is determined by its product—a well-prepared student who is capable of securing, maintaining, and advancing in office positions. Just as the office practice course integrates isolated skills and knowledges in officelike applications, so evaluation in office practice focuses on an examination of the total student as a prospective office employee. Thus, evaluation plans should incorporate affective, cognitive, and psychomotor domains. Evaluation of student performance cannot be limited to factors such as net words per minute or mailable letters, but should include elements such as interpersonal relations, work habits, attitudes, and decision-making abilities, which often require more subjective assessment. Teacher evaluation, student evaluation, and outside evaluation of student performance are discussed in this module. After completing this module, you should be able to (1) explain at least two ways of measuring cognitive and psychomotor skills; (2) outline a plan for assessing affective skills such as attitudes, human relations; and (3) explain the importance of student self-evaluation in office practice.

EVALUATION OF SKILL

A part of most office practice courses is devoted to upgrading of existing skills (such as typewriting, shorthand, accounting) and to developing new skills (such as filing or business machines). Techniques, standards, and scales for measuring isolated skills are discussed in each respective chapter. The teacher may find it helpful to record individual student performance in skill areas on student profile sheets when specific skills are listed.

PERFORMANCE APPRAISAL

Evaluation of officelike activities is probably the most difficult type of evaluation with which the teacher is confronted. The teacher observes attitudes, organization, and appearance as well as work production in evaluating total student performance. "Although the evaluation of work production can be somewhat structured, a degree of subjectivity must be applied to both work production and the other qualities essential for an efficient office worker. However, teacher subjectivity has a foundation that forms the basis for evaluation. Familiarity with the requirements for office workers dictates this foundation."[12]

Some of the criteria in employee performance appraisal include acceptance of responsibility, accuracy, attitude, work habits, judgment, knowledge of job, reliability, quantity of work, quality of work, flexibility, and adaptability. Three of four descriptive statements or performance indicators, ranging from excellent to poor, are usually provided for each characteristic, as indicated below:

Attendance and Punctuality: Consider frequency of absences as well as lateness	Record is excellent	Occasionally absent or late	Frequenty absent or late without reason	Undependable: absent or late without reason

Illustrations 8.3 and 8.4 in Module 8.2 are examples of evaluation sheets used by Davis in her model office simulation. Illustration 8.6 is also an example of an appraisal form that might be used in a simulation or model office. Note that the forms incorporate cognitive, psychomotor, and affective skills. Occasionally it is helpful to have the student as well as the teacher complete a performance appraisal and discuss the results.

STUDENT EVALUATION

If the student is to become a competent employee, he or she needs to acquire the ability to evaluate his or her own work; to locate and correct errors; to assess decision-making abilities; and to evaluate work habits, attitudes,

illustration 8.6
WORK APPRAISAL FORM

Name_____ Office_____

Employer_____ Date_____

Company_____ From_____ To_____

EMPLOYER'S EVALUATION OF Office Practice STUDENT'S ON-THE-JOB WORK

Please check the following traits as (0) unsatisfactory, (1) average,
(2) above-average, (3) excellent.

Personal Traits   Skill Performance

    Grooming   0 1 2 3   Typing   0 1 2 3
    Suitability of dress 0 1 2 3   Shorthand   0 1 2 3
    Personal hygiene   0 1 2 3   Transcription   0 1 2 3
    Conduct   0 1 2 3   Filing   0 1 2 3
    Speech   0 1 2 3   Grammar   0 1 2 3
    Interest in work   0 1 2 3   Mathematics   0 1 2 3
    Cooperation   0 1 2 3   Spelling   0 1 2 3
    Initiative   0 1 2 3   Punctuation and   0 1 2 3
    Ambition   0 1 2 3   capitalization
    Adaptability   0 1 2 3   Proofreading   0 1 2 3
    Tact   0 1 2 3   Office machines   0 1 2 3

Ability   Business Techniques

    Follow directions   0 1 2 3   Use of telephone   0 1 2 3
    Take criticism   0 1 2 3   Use of sources of 0 1 2 3
    Understand   0 1 2 3   Information
      instructions   Office housekeeping 0 1 2 3
    Attend to details   0 1 2 3   Meeting people   0 1 2 3
    Keep on the job   0 1 2 3   Use of supplies   0 1 2 3

Times Absent_____

Times Tardy_____

General rating of student: (A) Excellent   (B) Above-average
                             (C) Average   (F) Unsatisfactory

Please list any points that should be improved.
    1.
    2.
    3.

                                  _____
                                     (Employer's signature)

                         DATE:_____

and interpersonal relations. The business teacher should plan specific opportunities, activities, and instruments for student self-assessment.[13]

The Student Work-Appraisal Sheet (see Illustration 8.7) shows a form that the student can use for self-appraisal of his or her work.

Role playing or case incidents based on office-related material such as that contained in *Human Relations for Office Workers: A Case Approach* (Calhoun and Finch) provides students with opportunities to assess their interpersonal relations. By tape-recording or videotaping role-playing exercises (or by means of student performance in a model office), the student and/or teacher can realistically evaluate strengths and weaknesses.

In-basket activities, described in Module 8.2, can be used to evaluate the student's decision-making abilities.

illustration 8.7
STUDENT WORK-APPRAISAL SHEET

Name_____ Date_____

Time Spent on Job_____ Estimated Time_____

I have proofread my work carefully: _____YES _____NO

My appraisal of each of the following items is:

	Good	Fair	Poor			Good	Fair	Poor
Original Copy	___	___	___	Erasures		___	___	___
Carbon Copies	___	___	___	Clean Type		___	___	___
Placement	___	___	___	Planning		___	___	___

I have studied and followed the directions to the best of my ability:
_____YES _____NO

My criticism of my work is:_____
_____
_____
_____

Improvements I suggest making in my work:_____
_____
_____
_____

Would I be proud to put this work on my employer's desk as a sample of my
production ability? _____YES _____NO

Would I be justified in asking for a raise if my work were consistently of
this caliber? _____YES _____NO

Grade I think I deserve on this assignment:_____

Instructor's comment:_____
_____
_____
_____

Instructor's Grade   _____

OUTSIDE EVALUATION

The teacher may occasionally call on the program's advisory committee to evaluate office simulation activities. Business persons can lend a realistic viewpoint to student evaluations and can help to augment the attempt toward realism in the classroom. Illustration 8.8[14] shows a form on which the business person can indicate an evaluation of a student's work. The teacher supplies the student's name and time taken to complete the work; the business person indicates whether he would promote the office worker, keep in the same job, keep on probation, or dismiss based on the quality of the work and the completion time.

module 8.3
LEARNING ACTIVITIES

1. In Module 8.2, you outlined instructional units for an office practice course. Describe the evaluation procedures you would use for each unit.
2. Choose one evaluation instrument in this module and revise it to more appropriately assess student performance and attitudes.
3. Visit a business in your community and obtain a copy of the personnel appraisal form. Report on the content and format of the instrument.

illustration 8.8
EVALUATION BY THE BUSINESS PERSON

TIME TO COMPLETE WORK_____

_____ WOULD PROMOTE

_____ WOULD CONTINUE WITH SAME STATUS

_____ WOULD KEEP ON PROBATION

_____ WOULD DISMISS

_____
Signature

Student_____

4. Collect two or three samples of an office practice student's work. Evaluate the product, using a standard of your choice. Compare your evaluation with that of a business person.

module 8.3
SELF-TEST

1. Why is student self-appraisal important in office practice?
2. Describe at least one way to evaluate affective, psychomotor, and cognitive skills in office practice.

SUMMARY

The office practice course, offered near the time when the student will enter the labor market, is designed to tie together and integrate, on a vocational level, previously learned skills and knowledges as well as new subject matter. While specific objectives vary from course to course, five basic types of objectives appear to underlie them all: (1) integration of previously acquired knowledges and skills; (2) development of new skills; (3) development of appropriate attitudes, work habits, and personality and character traits; (4) extension and further development of previously introduced skills and knowledges; and (5) assessment of personal goals in relation to career requirements and opportunities.

The nature of the course lends itself to the use of a variety of organizational patterns, including total group, rotation, individualization, simulation, model office, as well as other generally recognized teaching techniques.

Evaluation procedures should be planned to assess cognitive, psychomotor, and affective learnings. The teacher and student (and occasionally a business person) need to systematically evaluate student progress.

References

[1] *Office Practice Syllabus* (New York: The University of the State of New York, the State Education Department, Bureau of Secondary Curriculum Development, 1972), p. v.

[2] Mary Ellen Oliverio and William R. Pasewark, *Secretarial Office Procedures,* 9th ed. (Cincinnati: South-Western Publishing Company, 1977), pp. vi–viii.

[3] *Office Occupations Program: Using the Telephone*; The Development of an Individualized Instructional System for Selected Multioccupational Programs in the Area/ Comprehensive High Schools of Georgia, Revised, Norma N. Givens; Director, Calfrey C. Calhoun (Athens: University of Georgia, Department of Business Education, 1975), pp. UT: PP3.1–3.6

[4] Ibid., pp. 232–33.

[5] Ibid., p. 228.

[6] *Guide to Organizing and Operating the Block-Time Simulation Program,* vol. 1. 2d ed. (East Lansing: Michigan State University, Department of Secondary Education and Curriculum, 1975), p. 76.

[7]Mary Alice Davis, "The Development of a Systematic Structure, Method, and Sample Materials for Implementing a Secretarial Office Simulation for Post High School Vocational-Technical Programs" (Ph.D. diss., The University of Georgia, Athens, 1973), pp. 30, 50–56.

[8]*Office Practice Syllabus,* p. 30.

[9]Ibid., p. 31.

[10]Ibid., p. 32–33.

[11]Mary M. Brady, "Methods of Teaching Clerical Practice Classes" in *The Clerical Program in Business Education,* ed. Harry Hoffman. (Somerville, N.J.: Somerset Press, 1959), p. 280.

[12]*Guide to Organizing and Operating the Block-Time Simulation Program,* p. 79.

[13]Ibid., p. 82.

[14]Ibid., p. 83.

SUGGESTIONS FOR FURTHER STUDY

Booth, Phyllis D. "Student Involvement in Clerical Accounting Simulation." *Business Education Forum* 30, no. 1 (October 1975): 12–14.

Butler, Tommie, and Smith, Phyllis. "People's Trust of Little Rock," An Office Job Simulation. Cincinnati: South-Western Publishing Company, 1978.

Calhoun, Calfrey C., and Finch, Alton V. *Human Relations for Office Workers: A Case Approach.* Columbus: Charles E. Merrill Publishing Company, 1972.

Grieshop, Sister Mary Xavier, O.S.F. "Creative and Challenging Clerical Office Practice." *Business Education Forum* 29, no. 1 (October 1974): 21–22.

Jones, Adaline D. "Evaluating the Office Laboratory." *The Balance Sheet* 55, no. 2 (October 1973): 62–63, 90.

Lauer, William C. "Teaching Filing with Office Procedures." *The Balance Sheet* 52, no. 5 (February 1971): 200–201.

McClean, Gary N. "Effectiveness of Model Office, Cooperative Office Education, and Office Procedures Courses Based on Employee Satisfaction and Satisfactoriness Eighteen Months After Graduation." *Delta Pi Epsilon Journal* 19, no. 4 (October 1977): 21–28.

McCammon, Lillian. "Potpourri of Methods in Clerical Office Procedures." *Business Education Forum* 28, no. 7, (April 1974): 30–31.

Poland, Robert. "Various Types of Simulated Office Programs." *Business Education Forum* 27, no. 8 (May 1973): 22–24.

chapter 9

TEACHING COMMUNICATION SKILLS FOR BUSINESS

Communication in business involves numerous letters and written reports. But even more business time is taken up with oral communication—telephone calls, interviews, dictation, conferences, meetings, giving instructions, and so forth.

The communication process, oral and written, involves three levels of effectiveness. (1) Direct face-to-face communication is the most effective for two reasons: (a) it provides instant feedback, both verbal and nonverbal, and (b) it permits use of nonverbal techniques to reinforce the message; (2) Indirect, two-way communication, such as the telephone, offers the availability of instant verbal feedback; and (3) One-way communication, such as letters, reports, or radio, lacks both instant feedback and nonverbal communication cues.

People in business spend up to 80 percent of their time in some form of communication using the spoken or written word. But communication has two sides. Students receive instruction in delivering communications, but little help in the related skills of reading business letters and reports and listening while someone else speaks. All these aspects of effective communication are treated in this chapter, which contains modules related to effective speaking, listening, writing, and reading.

module 9.1
THE IMPORTANCE OF COMMUNICATION

The successful business employee knows how to communicate effectively. Research studies indicate the importance of communication skills in business, as measured by the amount of time spent in communicating and the high value assigned to communication ability by employers. Many companies now place a priority on employees' mastery of basic English skills such as grammar, spelling, punctuation, sentence structure, and vocabulary. However, courses in business English and communication have traditionally been among the most neglected of the business education curriculum, especially at the high school level.

After completing this module, you should be able to (1) differentiate the role of business communication at the secondary and postsecondary levels, (2) summarize the communication tasks commonly performed by business employees, (3) explain the importance of individualized instruction in the business communication course, and (4) illustrate the relationship of communication to other business education courses.

Business English at the secondary level is usually offered in the business education program. The course emphasizes basic English skills, especially as related to business letter writing. Little attention is typically given to the *total* communication process. At the postsecondary level, the courses offered frequently emphasize written communication, primarily business letters, business report writing, and a review of basic English skills. The term "business communication" is preferred to "business English" since the former implies written and oral communication. The emphasis of the course should be to help students to communicate more effectively.

Changes in instruction are emerging at the high school level as teaching materials reflect a more comprehensive coverage of business communication, including oral as well as written communication and basic English skills. Likewise, some postsecondary communication courses now include communication process and theory, the psychology of communication (including human relationships), oral communication, listening, and nonverbal communication, in addition to written communication.

The skills of reading, writing, listening, and speaking have no content of their own. They are developed through content areas. The course in business communication concentrates on the application of these skills and processes in meaningful, practical, and realistic situations related to business. The student *reads* an article about the economy, *writes* down an order taken over the telephone, *follows written directions* for changing a typewriter ribbon, *composes* an advertisement for the sale of merchandise, *writes* a letter making a hotel reservation. These business-related activities represent the content of business courses taken by the student. The same communication skills are used in each content area, and it is the teacher's responsibility to develop appropriate skills within the framework of each course at the time the skills are needed.

Therefore, we may conclude that business communication should be taught as a separate course, preferably by the business teacher who can make appropriate applications to business, in order to allow for in-depth treatment of skills and communication processes, but it should also be taught within each business course as the skills apply.

Before identifying appropriate instructional strategies, we should review briefly the topics to be included in a comprehensive business communication course. The general topics include (1) communication process and theory; (2) human relations and psychology; (3) speaking, listening, and nonverbal communication; (4) written communication, including writing and reading; and (5) basic English skills and vocabulary.

Students' prior achievements and their needs and interests help to guide the teacher in determining (1) the degree of emphasis in each topical area, (2) the specific objectives, and (3) the appropriate instructional methods and materials. For example, at the high school level, communication process and theory may be treated on an awareness level. In a college course, the same topic would be treated in depth.

Objectives and materials for high school programs should be geared primarily toward entry-level business situations. Postsecondary programs prepare students for both entry-level and more advanced positions; consequently, objectives and materials should reflect varying levels of job content. Research studies such as NOBELS[1] and V-TECS[2] are good sources for identifying specific communication competencies needed by office workers.

Communication tasks

The following tasks were extracted from the V-TECS study:

Supervise clerical workers
    give clear and complete directions
    explain and demonstrate procedures and equipment
Complete forms
    accident reports, expense statements, invoices, requisitions
Decide on least expensive and most desirable way to communicate
    specific messages to internal and external publics
    memorandums, newsletters, letters, telephone, meetings
Edit and revise original correspondence and reports
Inspect and verify data
Use reference materials
    maps and atlas, dictionary and thesaurus, company manual and secretarial
    handbook, telephone directory, zip code directory
Use telephone
    place calls, receive calls, take and deliver messages
Take sales orders in person
Greet callers and visitors
Take dictation at typewriter
Take minutes of meetings and prepare minutes

Regardless of the organizational pattern in a school—traditional classroom, individually prescribed instruction, or open education—communication skills are most effectively developed through a variety of instructional strategies. Both the traditional classroom (where everyone studies the same topic at the same time) and those using an individualized approach (where students progress at their own rates) offer appropriate situations for both lecture-discussion instruction and small-group or individual activities. The lecture-discussion technique is effective for introducing a topic, reviewing and summarizing key points, clarifying issues and concepts, and instructing groups on identified skills.

However, ample time must be provided for directed "hands on" experiences which are best implemented on an individual or small-group level. (A small group is often necessary in developing oral communication skills since both a speaker and a listener are required.) Through the use of instructional modules, programmed material, learning centers, listening stations, and so on, the teacher is able to provide the activities and experiences each student needs at the appropriate level of difficulty so that the student can progress at his or her own pace. (Some suggested individual and small-group strategies are described later in the chapter.)

Through the use of diagnostic, criterion-referenced tests, which are designed to measure mastery of a given set of instructional objectives, the teacher identifies those skills each student has mastered as well as those needing additional development. Then, by using individualized techniques, each student works through the needed material at his or her own pace. For example, a pretest in basic English skills may serve as a means of identifying the strengths and weaknesses of each student as a basis for assignment of specific learning experiences. A pretest could cover one skill, such as the use of commas, or a combination of skills, such as punctuation rules. For more advanced students, a pretest could incorporate all the basic skills. The test can be prepared in the form of sentences to be corrected, a letter to be proofread and corrected, or a writing assignment in which the student is required to use appropriate skills. A combination of items would be most appropriate since many students have "learned the rules" and can correct sentences but cannot or do not use the rules correctly in application situations.

module 9.1
LEARNING ACTIVITIES

1. Compare an old edition of a business communication textbook with a current one for the same level. Note similarities and differences in topical content and percentage of the book devoted to each topic.
2. List the topics that in your opinion are, or should be, included in a course in business communication at the high school or post high school level, and the amount of emphasis for each topic—acquaintanceship, review, or in-depth treatment:

Topic	Include HS	Post HS	Acquaint HS	Post HS	Review HS	Post HS	In-depth HS	Post HS

3. The Business Education Department at your school uses a traditional class organization. Prepare the copy for a brief talk that you might give explaining why business communication should be individualized.
4. Read an article on communication in business and deliver an oral report to the class or prepare a written report.
5. Interview a business person regarding the importance of communication skills in his or her business and the communication skills beginning employees most need.

module 9.1
SELF-TEST

1. Explain why communication is a part of every business education course.
2. What areas of content are currently being added to the business communication course at the secondary level? At the postsecondary level?
3. State two reasons why individualized instruction is essential in business communication.
4. Summarize the topics normally included in a business communication course at the secondary level. At the postsecondary level.
5. List at least two examples each of *reading, writing, listening,* and *speaking* communication tasks performed by business employees.

module 9.2
ORAL COMMUNICATION: SPEAKING

Persons engaged in business may spend up to 80 percent of their day in communication activities, and a large portion of this time is spent in oral communication. Examples of these activities include conversing (face to face and by telephone); giving and receiving directions or instructions; leading or participating in conferences, meetings, and informal discussions; delivering speeches and talks; interviewing; making introductions; and dictating. Oral communication is developed both *incidentally* as a part of other subjects, when the student is engaged in speaking or listening, and *deliberately,* when instruction and activities are provided to develop the skills.

After completing this module, you should be able to (1) cite examples of oral communication situations encountered in business and personal life, (2) describe and illustrate a format for developing oral communication skills, (3) outline five activities appropriate for developing oral communication skills, and (4) compare oral communication skill development in business communication courses and other courses such as office practice.

Speaking is a behavior that is learned by conscious or unconscious assimilation of speech models perceived on a daily basis. The business education teacher is concerned with the improvement of speech patterns and the development of skills in business speaking. Thus, planned instruction in oral communication is not only a part of the business communication course, but also is incorporated into courses such as office practice and related cooperative work experience. In these classes, instruction and practice are provided in skills such as greeting and introducing visitors, using the telephone to place and receive calls, and interviewing for a job. Students, then, have opportunities to apply the oral communication skills in real or simulated settings. (See Module 2.2, sections on Motivation and Transfer of Training.)

The learning of a skill is not a single-exposure process. No matter how good the first experience, little real learning will result unless there is provision for repeated practice of the new skill, preferably in a variety of settings. Thus, oral communication skills introduced in a business communication course should be reinforced in other courses and settings including clubs, meetings, and cooperative work experiences.

INSTRUCTIONAL CYCLE

The following eight-step instructional cycle suggests a format that you may wish to use in developing or reviewing oral communication skills: pretest; development of appropriate knowledge base; examination of models; evaluation of effective and ineffective models; preparation-evaluation-revision of speech; demonstration of skills; evaluation; and feedback. Let's examine the application of these steps to the teaching of public speaking.

Pretest

Depending on the prior experience of the students, you may wish to (1) eliminate the pretest and involve all students in the learning experiences or (2) have each student prepare and deliver a brief speech or (3) have each student evaluate a speech and recommend changes. The first option is desirable in a student's initial formal instruction in oral communication/public speaking, while the second or third options are appropriate if the skill is being reviewed or reinforced in another course.

Development of knowledge base

Before demonstrating competencies in speaking, the student must become acquainted with the "what" and "how to" of tone, rate, location and use of materials, and nonverbal messages. By varying the instructional procedures and learning activities, the teacher can incorporate both theoretical background and practical applications in developing effective speaking skills.

Instructional methods for developing the needed information base include lecture-discussion, small-group activities, reading assignments, taped presentations, and observations. Charts and posters, displays, and bulletin boards are visual aids that reinforce in the learning stage and serve as a review and/or reference at a later date.

Each person develops his or her own style of speechmaking. However, there are basic guidelines that are applicable to most speeches. These may be classified into three general areas of competency: voice, content, and nonverbal cues.

VOICE.   *The student demonstrates the appropriate use of pitch, volume, rate, and tone in each speaking situation. Pitch* refers to the tone on a musical scale that one uses most often when speaking. Women generally speak in higher pitched voices than men. Both use pitches above and below the normal pitch for variety and emphasis. Read a sentence in your normal voice, noting the inflections or variations in pitch that you have used. Then try reading the same sentence without any variation. In this way you can observe the effects of pitch in your own voice.

Circumstances such as size of the room, distance from the audience, purpose for speaking, and distractions help to determine the *volume,* or loudness, of speech. The breath stream, not raising the pitch, increases the volume. What volume is normal in the following situations?

1. an irate customer complaining to a salesperson
2. a speaker at a political rally
3. a receptionist greeting a visitor in an office

The average *rate* of speaking is around 150 to 180 words per minute. However, rate is influenced by the purpose for speaking. A slower rate is used sparingly for emphasis, for giving directions, or for dictation. Have you ever listened to an auctioneer? What did you notice about the rate of speech? Rate can be changed by varying the amount of time needed to say a word and by changing the length of pauses between words. Try using a different rate for giving direction, recalling an exciting event, or telling a joke. What is the effect on the listener?

Communicating to the listener involves both denotative (dictionary) and connotative (emotional implication) meaning of words. The *tone* of the voice is used to express connotative meaning. For example, say the word "Alan." Now repeat it to express feelings of surprise, anger, joy, or amusement. (Prepare a series of sentences or have students prepare sentences and identify the emotions to be expressed. Invite a student to select one and read it to the class while students guess the emotion or connotative meaning being illustrated.)

CONTENT.   *The student prepares and delivers a speech appropriate for the audience and the occasion.* The student should practice six steps in order to demonstrate mastery of this competency. The first step is the selection of a subject. In choosing a topic, three points should be considered: the speaker

—his or her knowledge of and interest in the topic; the audience—their interest or the speaker's potential ability to interest them in the topic; and the occasion —the topic should be in good taste.

The second step is the identification of purpose; it may be to inform, to persuade, or to entertain. Many speeches usually contain elements of all or parts of these.

The third step is the collection of material. Information may come from reading, personal knowledge, research, or from other informed persons.

Organizing and outlining the material constitutes the fourth step. The material may be arranged chronologically, logically, psychologically, or ranked by importance.

Writing the speech is the fifth step. The opening and closing sentences are most important. Opening sentences catch the listener's attention—or they fail. The closing sentences provide summary ideas for the listener to remember. Choice of words, sentence structure, and use of illustrations throughout depend on the speaker, the audience, and the occasion.

The sixth step is practicing or rehearsing the speech. Through the use of a tape recorder and a mirror, or videotape, the speaker and other students may analyze both what is said and how it is presented. Self-evaluation and peer evaluation provide important feedback for revision.

NONVERBAL CUES. *The student demonstrates the use of nonverbal cues to reinforce the verbal message.* Nonverbal communication is sometimes called body language. It falls into three categories: posture, movements, and gestures. Since the body constantly transmits meanings and attitudes to others, often subconsciously, the task is to develop body language that effectively reinforces positive verbal communication.

After developing a knowledge base—including topics such as differing types of body language, their role in speaking and listening, adapting body language to the occasion, and so on—the teacher may use the following activities for reinforcement purposes:

1. Teacher videotapes students or employees in different settings. From their actions (body language), students decide what the individuals may be saying.
2. Students and teacher assemble a collection of photographs, and teacher has students label the emotion that each expresses.
3. Students pantomime situations and ask others in the class to guess the action.
4. Students and teacher prepare two oral presentations, one using body language to reinforce the speech, the other using body language to contradict or distract from the message.
5. Students observe and report situations in which body language greatly helped or hindered oral communication.
6. Students role play examples of ways in which nonverbal communication by the listener can encourage or distract speakers.

Examination of models

Live or taped speeches are excellent for presenting basic information because the student can observe the principles or concepts in their functional settings. These models may be introduced at appropriate points during the development of a knowledge base (see activities for nonverbal cues).

Evaluation of models

A highly essential procedure is student examination and evaluation of a variety of speeches, both effective and ineffective. Students critique the speeches, noting particular strengths and weaknesses and suggest ways of improving ineffective presentations.

Preparation-evaluation-revision

At this point instruction becomes highly individualized, regardless of the classroom organization. Each student begins preparation of his or her own speech. Some students will select a topic independently, prepare an outline for teacher approval, collect the data, and prepare the speech with minimum help from the teacher. Others will need suggestions for topics, assistance in preparing an outline, guidance in using library facilities to collect data, and individual help in developing the content.

Demonstration of skills

In this phase of the instructional cycle, the students deliver their speeches. As each student presents his or her speech, other members of the class should be practicing the related skill of listening (see Module 9.3).

Evaluation

Ideally, speeches should be videotaped so that the student and the teacher can evaluate the presentation. Even a tape recording of the speech will allow the student to judge the speech in terms of use of voice and content. You may also wish to have class members critique speeches. Five students, for example, may be assigned to evaluate each speaker. Thus in a class of twenty-five, each student would evaluate and be evaluated by five speakers. These student evaluations would provide feedback to the speaker and would help to determine the extent to which students are able to apply their knowledge base in an evaluative setting. This is a high-level cognitive skill, and students should be familiar with the evaluative criteria to be used. The criteria used for judging speaking in Phi Beta Lambda or Future Business Leaders of America contests may be used as a guide.

Feedback

No instruction is complete without feedback to the student. In the case of public speaking, feedback would include teacher response, student response, and the student's own response based on a tape recording or video-tape of the speech.

This instructional cycle is recommended for developing skills in discussion, dictating, interviewing, making introductions, giving directions, using the telephone, or carrying on face-to-face conversations. The amount of time spent in the instructional cycle depends on the complexity of the skill and the students' prior knowledge and experience.

Applications

The following are examples of teaching strategies and activities that may be used with students in developing and reinforcing skills in speaking:

1. Pair students and place a divider on a table to separate them. Give each student identical sets of blocks, and give one of them a design to be made from the blocks. While reproducing the design, the student gives directions for making the design to the other student. No questions may be asked. Compare results with an illustration. Variations include giving directions for drawing an object or design.
2. Write scripts or have students prepare scripts for role-playing interviews. Allow other class members to evaluate the interviews and decide which candidate they would employ and why. Be sure to specify the evaluative criteria in advance.
3. Have students plan and give speeches. This activity could be used in conjunction with public speaking contests sponsored by various clubs in the school.
4. Ask a small group of students to plan and demonstrate a discussion on a topic of their choice. Record the discussion to allow for self-evaluation as well as class evaluation.
5. Have students preside at meetings. (Use in conjunction with FBLA, FSA, OEA, Phi Beta Lambda, Pi Omega Pi, and so on.)
6. Have students practice dictating letters and memorandums using dictating equipment or by dictating to a student enrolled in shorthand.
7. Ask students to demonstrate use of the tele-trainer with a teacher-prepared script or with student-prepared dialogue.
8. Give students directions for completing a task, for getting to a specific location, and so forth. Begin with two- or three-step directions and increase the difficulty and number of steps.
9. Have students role play the greeting and introducing of guests, including men and women, persons with titles such as mayor, senator, college dean or president, and judge.

module 9.2
LEARNING ACTIVITIES

1. Using this module and other references such as the *Occupational Outlook Handbook*, prepare a chart showing oral communication tasks that might be performed by a (a) receptionist, (b) office manager, or (c) secretary.

2. Select an oral communication skill other than public speaking and outline procedures for implementing the eight-step instructional cycle. (Include "what" and "how.")
3. Write a role-playing scene for each of the following: an interview, an introduction, a telephone call.
4. Develop an activity for giving directions.
5. Prepare a live or videotaped slide presentation for use in nonverbal communication.

module 9.2
SELF-TEST

1. List eight steps in an instructional cycle for developing oral communication skills.
2. Give five examples of oral communication skills used in a business office.
3. Explain the different emphases that you would place on oral communication skill development in (a) the business communication course and (b) the office practice course.

module 9.3
ORAL COMMUNICATION: LISTENING

The daily lives of individuals—on the job, at school, at play, at home—are dominated by spoken communication. And a large percentage of this time is spent in listening. Many teachers have taken for granted that listening develops naturally and does not require teaching. This is not true; listening and hearing are not synonymous, although one depends upon the other.

Studies have shown that there is little improvement in listening skills above the elementary grades *without instruction.* In fact, children in the primary grades are the best listeners (considering mental age), while adults are the poorest listeners. There is an inverse relationship between the level of listening effectiveness and the age of the individual. Above the elementary grades, listeners absorb an average of 25 to 30 percent of what they hear, implying that training is greatly needed to develop listening skills.

After completing this module, you should be able to (1) justify formal listening instruction in business courses, (2) identify four skills that are prerequisites to effective listening, (3) explain a minimum of two teaching techniques or activities for developing each of the prerequisite skills, and (4) demonstrate procedures for effective listening.

TEACHING LISTENING THROUGH BUSINESS SUBJECTS

Listening, like the other aspects of communication, is a skill to be developed, and it has no content of its own. Every business teacher is responsible for developing listening skills needed for his or her particular course. Shorthand transcription and machine transcription require careful listening skills so that each word can be transcribed verbatim. Students in a general business course are more concerned with listening for main ideas and concepts. Within the business communication course, students should be provided with opportunities to develop listening skills in the context of businesslike situations.

In the process of becoming an effective listener, the student demonstrates mastery of certain prerequisite skills. The following section identifies selected prerequisite skills and provides suggested teaching strategies and activities that may be adopted for use either in a traditional classroom or for individualized instruction.

The student identifies and gives examples of purposes for listening. The individual's purpose for listening determines to a large extent the way in which he or she listens. Examples of teaching strategies and activities to develop this competency include the following:

1. Individuals, small groups, or the total class compile lists of different purposes for listening in the various environments in which students function and in which business operates.
2. Individuals or teams of students interview business employees and prepare an inventory of listening situations in business.
3. Business employers speak to class members or prepare tapes on the role of oral communication in business.
4. Individuals keep logs of the amount of time spent in listening over a given period and record the purposes for listening.
5. Teacher prepares a tape or an article for student use on the purposes for listening. The following list represents one means of classifying these purposes:
   a. Courtesy—respecting the rights of others to speak or perform without interruption.
   b. Appreciation—listening to a record, speaker, play, radio, or television for entertainment.
   c. Conversation—listening to one or more persons so as to respond to their comments and/or questions.
   d. Purpose—acquiring information, using it or storing it for future use. Purposeful listening involves obtaining information, solving problems, sharing experiences, or following directions.
   e. Critical Thinking—requiring critical thought as we listen. We must understand important events or concepts, evaluate statements, separate fact from opinion, decide when to agree or disagree, and make judgments.

The student enumerates factors influencing listening. How a person listens is influenced by a variety of factors including maturity level, emotional and physical health, intelligence, experience, motivation and interest, vocabulary, physical environment, preparation for receiving the message, rate of speaking, fluency, visibility, use of gestures, and audibility of the speaker.

Using teaching techniques such as group discussions, brainstorming sessions, role playing, simulation, and so forth, the teacher should lead students in the identification of factors that influence their listening ability.

The student identifies and gives examples of barriers or hindrances to listening. The value of this objective lies in the student's ability to evaluate his or her own listening behavior and to identify those factors that hinder effective listening. Emotional interference, prejudice, boredom, anxiety, physical and environmental conditions are examples of barriers. Nichols and Stevens identify six habits that prevent effective listening:

1. Faking attention—the habit of trying to look like a listener in order to give the speaker assurance.
2. I-get-the-facts listening—trying to listen for each and every fact and, as a result, missing the major point.
3. Avoiding difficult listening—turning off the radio, television, or our minds if the subject seems too difficult.
4. Prematurely dismissing a subject as uninteresting—rationalizing our poor listening as being caused by an uninteresting subject.
5. Criticizing delivery and physical appearance—deciding in advance that a speaker has nothing interesting to say because his appearance and manner of delivery do not meet our preconceived standards of an interesting personal appearance and delivery.
6. Yielding easily to distractions—seeking a distraction to release us from the listening task.[3]

Ongoing activities for each student are (1) periodic personal evaluation of listening behavior to identify hindrances, and (2) development and implementation of plans for eliminating barriers to effective listening.

The student identifies and demonstrates procedures for effective listening. Effective listening is an active process, with the listener as well as the speaker sharing responsibilities. The following guidelines are typical of those that could evolve from activities for improving listening ability:

1. Get ready to listen—assume the right mind set to concentrate on what you will hear and see. Select environmental conditions as free from distractions as possible.
2. Determine the purpose for listening—entertainment, gain information, follow directions, respond to conversation or discussion, and so forth.
3. Give speaker full attention—look at the speaker. If listening to a tape, look at the recorder, accompanying visuals, or neutral surface. Some people find that closing their eyes while listening to a tape tends to cut out extraneous distractions.
4. Sit away from distractions—doors that will open or close, persons who talk, and so on.

5. Concentrate on the verbal message—weigh evidence, review portions of the talk completed thus far, listen "between the lines" for meanings not put into words, and observe the tone of voice being used.

6. Observe nonverbal messages—do posture, movements, and gestures contradict or reinforce the verbal message?

7. Take meaningful notes if appropriate—record name of speaker, date, place, time, main idea, or outline of phrases or key sentences.

Applications

Endless opportunities present themselves each day for the development of listening skills. The following are examples of teaching procedures and activities that may be used to help develop and reinforce effective listening behaviors.

1. Occasionally have the class stop and write the information that has just been presented. If they cannot remember, ask them to write down why they could not remember or to comment on trouble spots such as not understanding the meaning of terms used, daydreaming, or thinking that certain information is not important to them.

2. Avoid repetition of directions. This takes patience and consistency on your part. While conditioning students for "one-time" directions, it may be necessary to ask several students to repeat or to explain the directions after you have explained them.

3. Give students a purpose for listening. ("I am going to explain how I want you to . . ." or "Listen to this tape to find out . . ." or "Mary will explain and demonstrate the procedures you are to use. . . .")

4. Have students listen to a recorded speech both with and without taking notes. Give a test on the content of the speech. Wait several days and test again to determine the value of taking notes as opposed to listening and remembering.

5. Have three or four students listen to a taped speech, news report, or directions. Ask each student to report to the class about what he or she heard. (Other students who are participating in the activity are out of the room while each student reports.) Compare reports of students.

6. Tape background noises that might be heard in business. Give directions with background noises being played on tape. Students write down information, repeat instructions or information to someone else, and/or follow directions. Discuss the effects of noise on listening.

7. Have students close their eyes and listen for two or three minutes to sounds around them in class. Have them make a list of sounds heard; compare lists made by students.

8. Ask persons with different dialects or accents to dictate to students in shorthand class or to prepare tapes for transcription.

9. Prepare listening guides for students to use with taped speeches or presentations. Discuss with the class the effects of the guides on listening.

10. Set the stage for listening to a speaker or a taped lecture by establishing the purpose and providing necessary background information on the speaker and/or topic, including vocabulary that may be unknown to students.

11. Use a commercial listening improvement program such as EDL's (Educational Development Laboratories) *Listen and Think* (for middle grades); Xerox Corporation's *Effective Listening* (for high school and postsecondary); and Xerox Corporation's *Advanced Effective Listening* (for postsecondary and advanced high school students).
12. Design role-playing activities such as interviews or telephone conversations involving messages to be received and transmitted.
13. Give multiple-step oral directions for students to follow.

module 9.3
LEARNING ACTIVITIES

1. You recognize that the improvement of listening skills has not been a stated objective of the Business Education Department of your school. Summarize the rationale you might use in speaking to the departmental staff about incorporating listening skills into the curriculum. (Identify the educational level involved.)
2. Sketch a bulletin board that you would use as an aid in teaching students to overcome barriers or hindrances to listening. (Indicate the educational level.)
3. Write at least three role-playing situations for use with your students to illustrate three different purposes for listening. (Indicate the educational level.)
4. For two business courses (preferably a skill course and a basic business course), list and briefly explain three or more activities that you could use to improve listening skills. (Identify the educational level.)
5. Review a test for measuring listening ability, and report on its strengths and weaknesses to the class.
6. Review one of the commercial programs for developing listening skills, and report on its strengths and weaknesses to the class.
7. Prepare a chart or other visual aid to illustrate the procedures for effective listening.

module 9.3
SELF-TEST

1. Formal instruction in listening is needed in business education courses at the high school and adult levels because

   a. _____

   b. _____

2. Identify four skills that are prerequisites to effective listening.
3. Name five practices that should help one improve listening effectiveness.

module 9.4
WRITTEN COMMUNICATION: WRITING

Written communication plays a vital role in modern business and industry. The increasing volume and cost of correspondence, reports, and publications emphasize the need for improved efficiency and cost effectiveness in the written communications generated by a firm. Billions of dollars are spent each year on written communications at an estimated cost of over one cent per word. Some companies may handle up to one million pieces of mail per week.

After completing this module, you should be able to (1) cite examples of the use of written communications in business; (2) explain a procedure for beginning a class or unit on written communication; (3) explain the difference in instruction in business writing and instruction in composition or creative writing; (4) describe at least one technique for developing skill in each of the following areas: choice of words, sentence construction, paragraph construction, and planning for writing; (5) describe an instructional procedure for teaching business letter writing; and (6) explain an instructional procedure or activity for four writing tasks, excluding letter writing.

The tasks performed in business that require writing skills range from writing down messages taken over the telephone or in person to writing manuals and reports. More specifically, writing tasks include such items as these:

Composing letters, memorandums, telegrams, orders, and reports
Filling in pre-printed forms
Making notes of phone calls, messages, interviews
Taking and transcribing minutes of meetings and conferences
Composing copy for advertising or news releases
Writing manuals—service, office, sales
Preparing outlines and agendas
Writing speeches and talks
Preparing a résumé, application, and follow-up letters.

Written communication has been identified as the most difficult form of effective communication since the elements of immediate feedback and use of nonverbal communication are not possible. Therefore, it is important to provide guided direction in the development of skills in writing.

Business communication should be taught in a businesslike setting; that is, the teacher should select or construct exercises, examples, activities, and assignments that reflect business environments. Likewise, student performance should be evaluated in terms of business standards. "Business standards are high, and a misspelled word or an unclear sentence should be measured in terms of its effect on the person who reads the messages containing such errors —not merely because it is right or wrong."[4] High standards with respect to spelling and basic grammar are expected by business, and these should be firmly established in the classroom.

Instruction in business writing differs from instruction in writing/composition in traditional English classes in that the emphasis is on writing letters, memorandums, and reports as opposed to themes or creative writing. Human relations are also important in written business communication instruction since business is concerned both with what is said and how it is said. Effective human relations is a vital part of effective communication.

During the first few days of class, you may find it helpful to spend some time discussing with students your procedure for handing in assignments and making up work missed, the basis for grades, the general plans for evaluation, the objectives of the course, your standards for legibility, and whether letters and reports should be typed. At the first class meeting devoted to written communication, you may wish to assess the writing abilities of the class by having students write a brief report explaining their career objectives and the importance of communication skills in their future profession. This pretest helps to determine the amount and kinds of initial learning and the review and reinforcement activities students need in basic English skills as well as in principles of writing.

PRINCIPLES OF WRITING

Regardless of the form taken by the written message, there are certain basic principles that apply in teaching business writing. They fall into three general categories: choice of words, writing sentences and paragraphs, and planning for writing—including decision making. Incorporated into the treatment of these topics is the development of the seven "C-Qualities" of writing: correctness, conciseness, clarity, completeness, concreteness, consideration, and courtesy.

Choice of words

The accurate choice of words is positively related to clear and interesting writing. Guidelines for word choice include the use of (1) short and simple words, (2) as few words as needed to convey the message adequately, (3) concrete nouns and action verbs, and (4) words that are appropriately suited to the reader.

Practice in choosing words, which is directly related to vocabulary development, is more effective when treated throughout the course than when emphasized intensely by the teacher for a few days. A few minutes of a class period two or three times per week can be devoted to development of general and specialized vocabulary. (Don't overlook the newspaper and trade journals as sources for new business-related vocabulary.) Other exercises include substitution of synonyms for trite phrases, or practice in selecting concrete nouns and action verbs. When given lists of words such as *interrogate, utilize, mitigate, approximately,* and phrases such as *at the present time, as of this writing,* and so on, the student should be capable of choosing appropriate synonyms. You may also wish to list wordy expressions (or sentences containing them) and have students substitute more concise words.

One exercise for developing use of concrete nouns and action verbs is outlined below:

1. Student writes a sentence or is given a sentence by the teacher, such as "Our house is on a hill overlooking a lake."
2. Replace general nouns with specific nouns; for example, "Our cabin is on a wooded knoll overlooking Lake Blue Ridge."

3. Replace "be" verb with an action verb; for example, "Our cabin perches on a wooded knoll overlooking Lake Blue Ridge."

For exercises of this type, you will need to have dictionaries and a thesaurus or two available.

Sentences and paragraphs

The business teacher will have to consider two ways of dealing with sentences. First, they should be reviewed from a grammatical point of view, including the parts of a sentence and how they fit together. Rhetoric should be considered next, that is, making the sentences serve the writer's purpose.

By making an evaluation of student writing, the teacher can quickly identify those individuals who need to review or develop basic skills in sentence construction. Programmed material, instructional packages, and learning centers are examples of approaches the teacher may use to accommodate individual needs.

To help the student develop skills in sentence structure and variety, select examples of weak sentences from letters or books. Discuss with students the reasons for weaknesses and suggest ways of improvement. Ask them, individually or in pairs, to rewrite the sentences. One way to relate sentence construction to a businesslike setting is to have students write opening and closing sentences for letters.

Principles relating to sentence/paragraph construction may be presented using a deductive or an inductive approach. English grammar textbooks are usually written deductively; that is, a rule or principle is given, and illustrations and exercises follow. Many teachers prefer an inductive approach in which examples are given (such as sentences illustrating active and passive voice) and students are guided through discussion to a statement of the principle.

Paragraphs are peculiar to the written language. They exist only to help the reader follow the writer's thinking and, therefore, should be arranged in logical order. Characteristics such as *unity, coherence,* and *emphasis* on a central idea are essential to effective paragraphing. Here is one way to introduce or review these characteristics:

1. After defining a topic sentence, have each student write from three to five topic sentences. Emphasize the need for only one idea per paragraph.
2. Describe and illustrate patterns of developing paragraphs (through examples, details, explanation of cause, contrast, comparison, repetition, and definition).
   a. Read examples and identify development pattern.
   b. Underline topic sentence.
3. Have students select and develop one topic sentence, using one or more methods identified.
4. Describe and illustrate unity in a paragraph.

5. Have students check paragraph for unity. Does each sentence relate to the topic sentence?
6. Describe and illustrate coherence.
7. Have students check paragraph for coherence. Do the sentences follow in a logical order?
8. Explain and illustrate deductive and inductive organization of ideas.
9. Have students check paragraph for emphasis on the main idea, such as a strong closing sentence that restates the main idea.
10. Revise paragraph.
11. Have students practice writing other paragraphs using different patterns of developing and organizing paragraphs.

Planning for writing

Before beginning to write, the student should complete several planning and decision-making steps that are essential to effective and efficient writing. These steps include determining the purpose; visualizing the reader; selecting, organizing, and sequencing ideas to be used.

Guide students through activities such as the following:

Directions: Read each of the following items. For each, (1) specify the purpose for writing, (2) describe the reader, (3) outline topics to be included.
  a. A new popular record is being featured by a record club. Write a letter to members.
  b. Mrs. Jones has written to the president of a company reporting foreign matter in a can of soup. Write a letter to Mrs. Jones.
  c. The 1965 high school graduating class is having a reunion. Write a letter telling where, when, and what time the reunion will be held.

TEACHING STRATEGIES AND SUGGESTIONS

The following suggestions may be helpful in developing skills in business writing:

1. Walk around the classroom while a writing activity is in progress, and inspect the work; observe errors and correct them with the student. This procedure is more effective than having the student make the corrections at a later time.
2. Collect samples of a student's writing for evaluation. You may allow the student to evaluate his or her own material and then submit the best example for evaluation.
3. Require best writing at all times for material that is submitted (spelling, grammar, neatness, and so on).
4. Incorporate revision in the writing process from the beginning. It is essential to effective writing. The first writing is concerned with *what* to say, the second with *how* to say it.
5. Talk through what is to be written before actual writing may prove helpful for some students.

Two examples of writing are treated in this module: business letter writing and report writing. Instructional procedures described have applicability in the development of related writing skills as well.

Letter writing

The primary function of the business letter is to communicate with persons outside the firm. Specific functions or categories of letters in business are shown in Illustration 9.1.

At least three factors must be considered in writing: (1) content—What is the purpose of this letter? What is the message to be conveyed? (2) mechanics —choice of words that are appropriate and clear, effective sentence and paragraph structure, correct use of grammar, proper correspondence format; and (3) human relations—use of the "you" attitude, planned with the reader in mind. Thus, these competencies might be expressed as follows: (a) *The student writes a letter that conveys the intended meaning clearly, concisely, and effectively;* (b) *The student demonstrates correct use of mechanics in letter writing;*

illustration 9.1
LETTER FUNCTION IN BUSINESS

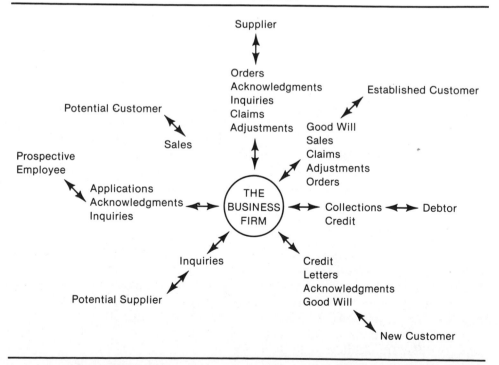

Source: From BUSINESS COMMUNICATIONS: PRINCIPLES AND METHODS, Fourth Edition, by William C. Himstreet and Wayne Murlin Baty. © 1973 by Wadsworth Publishing Company, Inc., Belmont, California 94002. Reprinted by permission of the publisher.

and (c) *The student demonstrates the "you attitude" in business letter writing.* The teacher should identify the necessary performance indicators by which mastery of these competencies can be determined; for example, words spelled correctly, positive attitude, choice of words appropriate for reader, and so forth.

At one time it was thought that the best way to teach business letter writing was to have the student write many different letters. We now know that better results may by obtained by writing fewer letters, but rewriting more often and devoting time to studying models of good style and to evaluating letters.

Basic principles of letter writing can be effectively taught by using examples of good letters to illustrate the concepts being presented. An overhead projector is an invaluable aid for demonstrating examples and may be used with individuals, small groups, or the entire class.

After reviewing basic principles covering the type of letter and content under consideration, the next step (or a concurrent step) is to present effective models. For example, if sales letters are being studied, show examples of effective letters, calling attention to the basic principles of selling as illustrated in the letters. Also, show examples of ineffective letters, leading the students in discussions of weaknesses and ways of correcting them. After studying models of effective and ineffective sales letters, the student is ready to evaluate examples. Assemble several sales letters and have students evaluate them and explain their decisions.

When students can recognize effective and ineffective letters, they are ready to begin writing. Before making the writing assignment, it is best to review briefly such basic questions as "What action do I want the reader to take?"

After students have written their letters in draft form, allow them to exchange drafts for proofreading and suggested changes. A few examples may be chosen for review by the entire class. Drafts of letters are now returned to the students for revision. A corrected copy is prepared following acceptable business standards, and submitted for teacher evaluation. For additional experience, students should practice writing the same message to audiences of different ages, educational levels, backgrounds, and interests.

Reports

Report writing, both formal and informal, should be preceded by a discussion of the types of business reports, their purposes and organizational styles. A logical transition from letter writing to report writing can be accomplished by comparing common and different elements. Both letters and reports begin with a purpose that determines the organization and presentation of the material. Both aim for messages that are clearly and concisely written. Business reports differ from letters in at least five ways:[5]

1. the formats are different
2. most reports stay within the company

3. letters use first person; reports can use first, second, or third person
4. reports are usually more complex
5. reports are usually more objective.

As with preparing to write letters, students should examine models of effective and ineffective reports, noting their strengths and weaknesses. In the initial stages, the teacher may want to provide notes or information to be organized and used as the basis of a report by the students. (Assignments would vary according to student achievement and capability.) In later stages, the student would be responsible for choosing the topic, organizing the outline, collecting the data, and writing the report.

Applications

Additional activities for developing competencies in written communication are listed below.

1. Have students write directions or instructions and try them out by asking others to follow them.
2. Have students listen to taped speeches or discussions, take notes, and write summaries or abstracts. Compare summaries written by several students who listened to the same tape.
3. Assemble copies of typical preprinted forms used in business. Teach any special vocabulary needed. Ask students to read the directions and complete the forms.
4. Have students read articles from journals, newspapers, and so on, and prepare a summary. (Be sure that the articles are on a reading level appropriate for the student.)
5. Have students take minutes of a meeting; then write them up and distribute them to those attending the meeting for approval.
6. Have students compose copy for a news release relating to an activity at school. (Proofreading by the student should be an integral part of all writing assignments.)

module 9.4
LEARNING ACTIVITIES

1. a. Identify four business writing tasks (excluding letter writing) and describe at least one activity you might use for developing each.
   b. Select one writing task (excluding letter writing) and prepare a learning center for use in developing the skill.
2. Outline in as much detail as possible your plans for the first day of instruction in written communication.
3. Using the module and a business communication text, outline the content and method and assemble or prepare necessary visual aids for teaching business letter writing.

module 9.4
SELF-TEST

1. List four to six different business writing tasks.
2. Justify the separating of instruction in business writing from writing instruction in traditional English classes.
3. Explain the importance of each of the following to written communication:
   a. choice of words
   b. sentence/paragraph construction
   c. planning for writing

module 9.5
WRITTEN COMMUNICATION: READING

One of the major problems confronting business teachers is the inability of large numbers of students to read textbooks or other printed materials. You may wish to refer to Chapter 5 for further suggestions for working with students with special reading problems.

After completing this module, you should be able to (1) summarize four general reading skill competencies needed by students and relate each to business, (2) cite one or more ways to develop each competency, (3) prepare or assemble instructional materials to assist in developing competency, and (4) explain the business teacher's responsibility in developing reading skills.

An understanding of an effectively written communication depends largely on the ability to read well. The enormous quantity of written information available and the constantly increasing amount of paper work in business make it necessary that prospective employees develop effective and efficient reading skills.

Specialized vocabulary, skills, and concepts are best taught in the specific context of the curriculum area in which they are used. As indicated in Chapter 2, it is easier to motivate and instruct students when they recognize the need for developing the skill. The student who must proofread a typescript sees immediately the need for deliberate step-by-step reading. Today more and more teachers above the elementary school level recognize the need for providing effective reading instruction—not necessarily the result of poor teaching in the elementary school. Rather, the business subjects at these levels require more refined levels of skill. Business education teachers should teach the vocabulary, reading skills, content, and understandings that are applicable to the field of business and industry.

READING SKILL COMPETENCIES

There are at least four competencies that the business student should exhibit in order to demonstrate proficiency in reading skills.

1. *The student identifies the purpose(s) for reading and uses appropriate rate and approach for each.* The purposes for reading are varied, and the first task of the reader is to decide his or her reason for reading a particular communication. The purpose may be to determine the main idea; locate information; make comparisons; draw conclusions; understand relationships; locate answers to specific questions; realize the author's purpose; draw inferences; select fact from opinion or fiction; acquire general information; interpret charts, maps, graphs, pictures; classify and/or arrange information; interpret and use formulas; or read for pleasure. The purpose may be suggested to the student by the teacher or another person ("Read these two proposals and tell me which one provides the most economical long-range solution to the problem."), or the reader may initiate the purpose ("I'll use this directory to find the zip code for . . .").

After identifying the purpose, the next step is the selection of approach and rate. When reading an article, report, or longer message, it is helpful to preview the material first. By reading headings, words in bold face or italics, first and last paragraphs, and illustrations, the reader receives an overview or outline of the content of the message. The teacher can assist students in learning to preview materials and to become aware of the amount of information that can be obtained from previewing. It is important to prepare questions that the students are to answer after previewing the material or article.

One of the most valuable skills for business employees to develop is learning to adjust their reading rate. The purpose for reading dictates the rate to be used for careful reading, cursory perusal, skimming, or scanning. Careful reading is deliberate, step-by-step reading for following directions, proofreading, reading formulas, and so on. Learning to read and understand directions is a skill that must be taught. Knowing the words does not ensure accurate performance. In developing this skill, the teacher begins with one-step directions ("Label the parts of this letter."), proceeds to two, three, or more simple steps, and finally introduces directions for which the steps are not stated specifically (such as classifying a number of items).

Cursory reading is done rapidly, with occasional pauses to read details of interest. The reader focuses on key words (nouns and verbs), skipping some of the less important words. One technique for quickly determining the main idea is to read the first paragraph, the first and last sentence of each succeeding paragraph, and the last paragraph. The main idea is most often stated in the first or last sentence of the paragraph.

Skimming is allowing the eyes to travel quickly over the page, stopping here and there to absorb ideas. To find the answer to a specific question, the reader should scan the material, that is, hastily glance over several lines at a time looking for the particular information. A reader would scan the page to find a telephone number, ZIP Code, or the cost of an item.

For practice in identifying the purpose and rate for reading a variety of materials, exercises such as the following are appropriate.

Directions: For each of the following situations, specify in Column A the purpose for reading and in Column B the rate of reading.

	A Locate Information	B Scan
Telephone Number		
1. Newspaper article reporting a seminar sponsored by your company.	_____	_____
2. Letter stating when and where you are to meet program chairman.	_____	_____
3. Article from a professional journal.	_____	_____
4. Letter before mailing.	_____	_____
5. Graph showing company profits/losses for past five years.	_____	_____

Another practice exercise is to pair students, giving one a stopwatch and a list of cities and their ZIP Codes. This student calls out the name of a city and records how long it takes the second student to locate the ZIP Code from a similar list.

Proofreading requires slow, careful reading. The following activity represents an effective way to provide student practice.

Directions: Read Paragraph A, then proofread Paragraph B, circling any errors.

A. How fast should you type? It is fairly certain that you can and should type much faster than you now typewrite. Much of the speed you gain during this course will depend upon your desire to improve and upon the form with which you type. Now is the time to make increasing your speed your new goal.

B. How fast should you type? It is fairly certian that you can and sould type much faster than yuo now typwrite. Much ofthe speed you gain during this course will depend upon your desire to improve and upon your desire to improve. Now is the right time to made increasing your speed your new goal.

An original copy or model is not always available with which to compare the completed product. The following is an example of such a proofreading activity.

Directions: Proofread the outline below, marking any errors.

HOW TO STUDY

I. ORGANIZATION FOR STUDY ·
   A. A Place to Study
   B. A Time to Study
   C. A Desire to Study

II. STRATEGY FOR EFFECTIVE STUDY
   A. Survey
   C. Question
   B. Read
      1. Read actively
      2. Read everything
      3. Note important terms as you read
   D. Recite
   E. Review
   G. Other Study Aids
      1. Take notes as you study.
      2. Make an outline of what you study.
      3. Evaluate and summarize what you have studied.

2. *The student demonstrates comprehension, interpretation, and critical reading skills.* The goal of reading is to obtain meaning from printed material and, more specifically in business communication, to obtain the writer's message. The first level of reading skill involves comprehending what is stated directly. An exercise in comprehension follows:

A. *Directions:* Read the following paragraph and answer the questions.

Additions or omissions. It is quite common for a typist to skip a word or two, or even to omit a line of material. This occurs frequently when two successive lines end with the same word. Occasionally, extra words are inserted. If you do not read the material to determine whether it makes sense, omission and insertion errors are difficult to locate. It is almost impossible to detect these errors if you are concerned only with the details of the copy.

1. Under what condition is a typist likely to omit a word or two?
2. What should be the purpose when proofreading for additions or omissions?

The next level, interpretation, is extracting deeper meaning from what is read, that is, inferring relationships and drawing conclusions from what is known. Through the effective use of questions, students can be guided by the teacher to use the information that is given and to read between the lines. A typical exercise in interpretation is illustrated in Sample B.

B. *Directions:* Read the statement to determine the author's purpose.

Moving lips and throat muscles, or silently pronouncing words, slows down the rate of reading. Through practice, these habits can be broken and the individual can learn to read with the eyes only, thus enhancing his or her ability as a communicator.

From this statement we can conclude that (1) there is a positive correlation between rate of reading and comprehension, (2) reading with the "eyes only" can increase speed of reading, and (3) "vocalizing" or "lip-reading" has little relationship to effective reading.

The third level encountered by the student is critical reading, in which the reader not only understands what he or she reads but must also react to it—separating facts from opinion, truth from partial truth, information from emotion. Determine whether each of the following statements in Sample C is fact or opinion.

C. 1. Face-to-face communication is the most effective level of communication.
C. 2. Women are more influenced by the speaker's appearance than by the message.
C. 3. Quality of work rather than quantity of work is more important to the employer.
C. 4. The most important characteristic of an effective letter is conciseness.

3. *The student correctly interprets charts, graphs, diagrams, and other illustrations.* Interpreting charts, graphs, diagrams, and so on, requires that the reader understand what is stated directly as well as what is implied. Initially, attention is drawn to mechanical aspects such as the title, the values being compared, and the meaning of symbols. Then the reader is expected to extrapolate meaning from the illustration. The questions following Table 9.1 are typical of those teachers ask to elicit factual and inferential information.

1. State in your words the purpose of Table 9.1 on p. 371.
2. How many participants were enrolled in adult education programs of four-year colleges and universities in 1972?
3. What was the change in percentage of enrollments of adult education participants in private schools between 1969–1972?
4. Compare the 1969–1972 enrollments in public elementary and secondary schools with the 1969–1972 enrollments in two-year colleges and technical schools.
5. If the trend for participant enrollments in adult education by source identified continues, what may we expect for 1982?

table 9.1

PARTICIPANTS IN ADULT EDUCATION, BY SOURCE OF INSTRUCTION: UNITED STATES, 1969 AND 1972

SOURCE OF INSTRUCTION	PARTICIPANTS (IN THOUSANDS)		PERCENT CHANGE 1969 to 1972
	1969*	1972	
1	2	3	4
Total......................	13,041	15,734	20.7
4-year colleges and universities......	2,831	3,367	18.9
Employers	2,274	2,613	14.9
2-year colleges and technical institutes	1,650	2,561	65.2
Public elementary and secondary schools	1,970	2,200	11.7
community organizations	1,564	1,996	28.4
Private trade, vocational, and business schools................	1,504	1,393	− 7.4
Other (labor unions, professional associations, hospitals)	2,562	3,380	31.7
Not reported.....................	54	98	81.4

*Data for 1969 are for public schools only.

NOTE: Details do not add to totals because some participants receive instruction from more than one source.

Sources: U.S. Department of Health, Education and Welfare, National Center for Education Statistics, Adult Education Participants and Participation, 1969, Full Report, and Adult Education Participants and Participation, 1972, Full Report.

4. *The student uses the proper source(s) for locating information.* There is a difference between knowing how to read and using reading skills as a tool for learning and/or locating information. With the expansion of mass media and technical devices for communication, an important task is knowing where to locate needed information. This, in turn, is followed by the development of skills in selecting, evaluating, and applying the information.

After discussing the use of major sources of information, such as dictionaries, ZIP Code directories, telephone directories, reference manuals, and so forth, and the kinds of information found in each, the teacher might employ an activity such as the following.

REFERENCE SOURCES

Directions: Answer each of the following questions. In the blank at the end of each line, write the letter of the best reference source: (A) National ZIP Code Directory, (B) Dictionary, (C) Telephone book, (D) Reference Manual for Office Personnel

1. What is the abbreviation for Minnesota? _____
2. Do you single-space or double-space footnotes? _____
3. In what time zone is Hawaii located? _____
4. What is the area code for Alaska? _____
5. What is the past tense of ring? _____

6. What is the ZIP Code for 376 Peach Orchard Road, Waterbury, CT? _____
7. Your boss dictates: "The (grey, gray) suit you
   returned was certainly defective. Thank you for
   bringing this to our attention." How would you
   spell the word in parenthesis?   _____
8. Can you draw a postal money order for $150?   _____

Since reading skills are learned, guided instruction is needed before the student can apply the skills to the reading situations encountered. The degree of mastery of skills varies to such an extent that pretests are necessary to determine each person's level of performance. The content of the tests should be typical of that encountered by the individual in business—letters, reports, books, reference manuals, and so forth.

Analysis of the pretests helps the teacher to determine which skills students need to develop. If the student is deficient in skills other than locating material, then teaching strategies should focus on guided oral activities followed by guided reading experiences. These discussions, demonstrations, observations, video-, and audiotapes are examples of techniques that may be used to provide the student with the necessary background information. To illustrate, if students cannot interpret a chart or graph, the teacher should:

1. Select a simple graph, prepare a copy for each person, or prepare a transparency of the graph for use with an overhead projector.
2. Explain where the title is located; ask students to locate the title on their graphs; call on students to read the title.
3. Check comprehension by asking the students to paraphrase the title. Using the same procedures (explanation followed by application), identify variables being compared and meaning of symbols.
4. Explain the procedure for reading information from the graph—the cost of a letter in a given year—and illustrate the procedure on the transparency.

When students demonstrate their ability to answer specific questions, such as letter cost, present a question that requires several steps. For example, what component accounts for the largest percentage of the cost of a business letter? Which method is most economical for reproducing 250 letters? Call on students to explain the procedures.

The explanation, demonstration, and guided application steps are followed by independent activities in which students interpret a graph.

Through the use of videotapes, films, film loops, filmstrips, or sound slides, instructional modules may be constructed for developing this skill, thus freeing the teacher to monitor application of skills and to provide additional individual help as needed.

Persons such as librarians (or media specialists) and reading specialists provide excellent sources for the teacher in developing these skills, both in supplying information and in teaching mini-units for groups of students needing special help.

Applications

In addition to activities suggested throughout the module, the following are recommended for use with students to reinforce their reading skill development:

1. Read a newspaper article; underline the facts and circle the opinions.
2. Read the subheadings in an article or report and restate them as questions.
3. Read three or four business letters and state each writer's purpose.
4. Read three paragraphs from your textbook, an article, or other source. Write the main idea of each paragraph in one sentence. Compare your answers with those of other students.
5. Interview two or more employees with different jobs within a given job cluster. How are the reading requirements of their jobs alike? How are they different?
6. Spend five or ten minutes each day on reading improvement by practicing these suggestions: (a) give your full attention to the message; (b) read silently (do not lip-read or vocalize); (c) avoid regressing (try moving an index card continuously down the page, one line behind where you are reading); (d) look at groups of words; and (e) mentally review what you have read.

module 9.5
LEARNING ACTIVITIES

1. Begin a file of learning activities for developing reading skills related to business education. Classify each activity according to purpose, such as proofreading, scanning, finding the main idea, following directions, graph/map reading, summarizing, drawing inferences, distinguishing fact from opinion, and so on. Assemble at least four different activities.
2. Using this module and other resources such as those listed in "References for Further Study," prepare a module or learning center for developing a reading skill.
3. Read and summarize South-Western Publishing Company Monograph 128, *The Development and Refinement of Reading Skills in Business Education.*
4. Compute the readability of a business communication textbook, advertisement, business letter, or selection of your choice. (See Module 5.3.) What is the target population for using the material? (For example, high school juniors or seniors.) Do you think the material is too easy, too difficult, or about right?
5. Prepare a visual aid that demonstrates reading skills used in business offices.

module 9.5
SELF-TEST

1. List and briefly explain four general reading skill competencies needed by students.
2. Explain the responsibility of business teachers in developing certain vocabulary and reading skills.
3. List three to five purposes for reading that you might encounter in a business situation.
4. Justify the development of flexible reading rates as a business-related goal for reading.

SUMMARY

Persons in business spend up to 80 percent of their time in some form of communication. The increased volume and cost of communication emphasize the need for improved efficiency and cost effectiveness. Communication skills must be taught both in a separate course and as part of existing business courses. It is the responsibility of the teacher to develop appropriate communication skills within the framework of each business course at the time the skills are needed.

Skills in oral and written communication as well as in basic English and vocabulary should be incorporated into the business communication course. More recently the content has been expanded to incorporate communication process and theory, psychology of communication, and nonverbal communication.

Skills in speaking, such as giving and receiving directions, directing conferences and meetings, presenting speeches, interviewing, and making introductions are also an important part of the planned activities and instruction in business communication. Such skills may be developed through an eight-step instructional cycle that includes pretesting, development of appropriate knowledge base, examination of models, evaluation of models, preparation-evaluation-revision, demonstration of skills, evaluation, and feedback.

Listening skills are directly related to speaking and must be developed through planned activities and instruction. In the process of becoming an effective listener, a student demonstrates mastery of certain skills. These include identifying and giving examples of the purposes for listening, enumerating factors influencing listening, identifying and giving examples of barriers or hindrances to listening, and identifying and demonstrating procedures for effective listening.

Instruction in business writing should include exercises and activities that reflect actual business environments. Regardless of the form of written communication, planned instruction should incorporate these elements: choice of words, writing sentences and paragraphs, and planning for writing—including decision making. Best results in business letter writing may be obtained by writing fewer letters, but rewriting more often and devoting time to models of good style and the evaluation of letters. At least three student competencies relating to letter writing may be identified: (1) the student writes a letter that conveys the intended meaning clearly, concisely, and effectively; (2) the student demonstrates correct use of mechanics in letter writing; and (3) the student demonstrates the "you attitude" in business letter writing.

An understanding of written communication depends largely on the ability to read well. Business teachers should teach the vocabulary and reading skills that are applicable to business and industry. There are at least four competencies that business education students should exhibit to demonstrate proficiency in reading skills: the student (1) identifies the purpose(s) for reading and uses appropriate rate and approach for each; (2) demonstrates comprehension, interpretation, and critical reading skills; (3) correctly interprets charts, graphs, diagrams, and other illustrations; and (4) uses the proper source(s) for locating information.

References

[1]Frank W. Lanham et al, *Development of Performance Goals for a New Office and Business Education Learning System,* U.S. Department of Health, Education and Welfare, Project No. 8–0414, Grant No. OEO–0–0–080414–3733(083) (Columbus: Center for Research and Leadership Development in Vocational and Technical Education, The Ohio State University, 1970).

[2]Vocational-Technical Education Consortium of States, *Performance Objectives and Criterion-Referenced Measures, Secretarial, Stenographic, Typing, and Related Occupations* (Blacksburg: Virginia Polytechnic Institute and State University, Division of Vocational-Technical Education; and Richmond: Division of Vocational Education and Division of Educational Research and Statistics, State Department of Education, 1975).

[3]Ralph G. Nichols and Leonard A. Stevens, *Are You Listening?* (New York: McGraw-Hill Book Company, 1957), pp. 104–13.

[4]Marie M. Stewart, Frank W. Lanham, and Kenneth Zimmer, Teacher's Manual and Key for *Business English and Communication,* 3d ed. (New York: Gregg Division, McGraw-Hill Book Company, 1967), p. 4.

[5]Herta A. Murphy and Charles E. Peck, *Effective Business Communication* (New York: McGraw-Hill Book Company, 1972), pp. 584–85.

SUGGESTIONS FOR FURTHER STUDY

Barker, Larry L. *Listening Behavior.* Englewood Cliffs, N.J.: Prentice-Hall, 1971.

Bonner, William H. "The Teaching of Business English and Communication." In *Contributions of Research to Business Education,* edited by Calfrey C. Calhoun and Mildred Hillestad, Chapter 12. Washington, D.C.: National Business Education Association, 1971.

Calhoun, Calfrey C., and Finch, Alton V. *Human Relations for Office Workers.* Columbus, Ohio: Charles E. Merrill Publishing Company, 1972.

Ellenson, Ann. *Human Relations.* Englewood Cliffs, N.J.: Prentice-Hall, 1973.

Kitzhaber, Albert R., ed. *Is Anybody Listening?* New York: Holt, Rinehart and Winston, 1974.

Maier, Norman R. *Problem-Solving Discussions and Conferences.* New York: McGraw-Hill Book Company, 1963.

Perfetto, Edda. "Communications." In *Changing Methods of Teaching Business Subjects,* edited by Leroy Brendel and Herbert Yengel, Chapter 14. Washington, D.C.: National Business Education Association, 1972.

part three

TEACHING COMPUTATION-RELATED BUSINESS SKILLS

chapter 10

TEACHING BOOKKEEPING AND ACCOUNTING

Instruction in bookkeeping and accounting can be traced to the early nineteenth century when the English High School was opened in Boston in 1824. Accounting instruction continues to be offered at the secondary, vocational-technical/community college, college and university, and graduate levels for individuals desiring careers in accounting such as full-charge bookkeeper or accountant; for persons whose jobs require specialized accounting knowledge such as payroll clerk, accounts receivable clerk, or audit clerk; for those who perform their jobs more efficiently with a basic understanding of the accounting cycle such as secretary, cashier, or manager; and for persons who use the information for private use and as a basis for making decisions as a citizen. The duration and content of accounting courses vary according to the occupational needs and interests of students.

module 10.1
OBJECTIVES AND CONTENT

Automated data processing is increasing in importance as a tool of bookkeeping. Consequently, course objectives, content, and methods should be reviewed and revised frequently to reflect the role of automation.

> Today's accounting teachers recognize that the modern business world has undergone a veritable revolution in practices and procedures—a revolution sparked by the impact of automation, data processing, and the techniques of system analysis. The manual procedures for processing financial data are being rapidly supplemented or displaced by the use of office machines, punched card and punched tape equipment, and computers. Thus in any accounting course offered today, the emphasis must be shifted from the mastery of manual techniques along to the mastery of concepts that apply to all techniques.[1]

After completing this module, you should be able to (1) explain the role of accounting instruction in the overall preparation of office workers, and (2) identify content that is appropriate for students with various personal-use and career objectives.

Illustration 10.1 summarizes the accounting skills and knowledge needed by individuals in selected occupations:[2]

illustration 10.1
MEETING CAREER OBJECTIVES IN ACCOUNTING

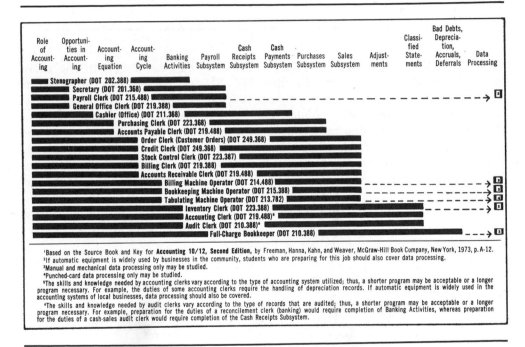

[1]Based on the Source Book and Key for **Accounting 10/12, Second Edition**, by Freeman, Hanna, Kahn, and Weaver, McGraw-Hill Book Company, New York, 1973, p. A-12.
[2]If automatic equipment is widely used by businesses in the community, students who are preparing for this job should also cover data processing.
[3]Manual and mechanical data processing only may be studied.
[4]Punched-card data processing only may be studied.
[5]The skills and knowledge needed by accounting clerks vary according to the type of accounting system utilized; thus, a shorter program may be acceptable or a longer program necessary. For example, the duties of some accounting clerks require the handling of depreciation records. If automatic equipment is widely used in the accounting systems of local businesses, data processing should also be covered.
[6]The skills and knowledge needed by audit clerks vary according to the type of records that are audited; thus, a shorter program may be acceptable or a longer program necessary. For example, preparation for the duties of a reconcilement clerk (banking) would require completion of Banking Activities, whereas preparation for the duties of a cash-sales audit clerk would require completion of the Cash Receipts Subsystem.

OBJECTIVES

The objectives of accounting instruction fall into two categories: overall general objectives and specific content objectives.

Overall objectives

A primary objective of accounting is vocational use; that is, preparation for employment within a wide range of careers in business such as those shown in Illustration 10.1. Some students enroll in bookkeeping for *semivocational* reasons; that is, they plan to operate a business of their own or to hold a temporary business position and they know that bookkeeping skills will be beneficial. In addition to career-related objectives, accounting offers *personal-use* values—for example, those involved in preparing financial records such as income tax returns. A further overall objective of the accounting course is to develop students' abilities to interpret *general business* records (such as financial statements of a business or personal nature) as they relate to the financial aspects of business practice. Thus students learn how business operates and the importance of business in our private enterprise economy. Finally, accounting has *general education* values that serve to develop good work habits such as orderliness, and the ability to work in groups and to follow directions. Most of these general goals are reached in the first accounting course.

Specific objectives

Specific course objectives vary depending on the length and purpose of the course as well as the level at which it is offered. At the high school level, the following objectives help to define the outcomes of instruction in accounting:

The student will be able to:

1. journalize transactions in combination, special, and general journals
2. post to general and subsidiary ledgers
3. prepare a trial balance
4. complete a worksheet with simple adjustments
5. prepare basic financial statements such as the income statement, the capital statement, and the balance sheet
6. record simple adjusting and closing entries in a journal, post to the ledger, rule the accounts that are closed, and balance and rule the accounts that remain open
7. prepare a post-closing trial balance.

The *Mississippi School Bulletin* illustrates the differences in specific objectives for the first and second courses in accounting at the high school level:[3]

Accounting I:
1. To provide the student with a basic understanding of the accounting equation.
2. To develop a comprehensive vocabulary of accounting technology.
3. To instill in the student the importance of following instructions accurately and thoroughly.
4. To help the student acquire an understanding of the accounting cycle.
5. To acquaint the student with business forms commonly used.
6. To develop the ability of the student to analyze transactions and to solve problems.
7. To develop the use of arithmetic, penmanship, and spelling needed for proficiency in accounting.
8. To acquaint the student with different types of business organizations.

9. To provide an integrated and realistic review of the accounting principles to be applied during a complete fiscal period by the use of simulation sets.
10. To show the relationship of automated equipment to accounting principles and procedures.

Accounting II:
1. To review the current practices in payroll procedures, taxes, and related reports.
2. To develop the ability of the student to apply accounting principles and procedures to departmental records and understand the relationship of all departments.
3. To enrich the student's understanding of the purposes and use of valuation accounts for accounts receivable.
4. To develop an understanding of various methods of determining depreciation, maintaining fixed asset records, and recording the related transactions.
5. To reinforce the student's understanding of the special problems of controlling accounts and of deferred and accrued items.
6. To develop the student's ability to understand the organization of partnerships and corporations and to prepare and analyze their financial statements.
7. To develop an understanding of the control of financial operations of a business through the use of the voucher system, inventory control systems, and budgetary control systems.
8. To develop proficiency in accounting for sales tax, property tax, and income tax.
9. To reinforce the student's knowledge of the purpose, use, form, and content of negotiable instruments and other business reports.
10. To relate the use of automated data processing procedures to accounting.
11. To acquire an understanding of the essentials of cost accounting and apply these principles to a service department and a manufacturing business.
12. To develop proficiency in recording installment, credit card, COD, and consignment sales.
13. To develop an understanding of management use of accounting data through decision making.

At the postsecondary level, the course becomes more oriented toward specialized objectives, such as those related to cost accounting or income taxation.

CONTENT

At the secondary level, one or two years of accounting are usually offered. The courses include basic accounting theory and principles with a heavy emphasis on the recording phase. In a modular or individualized approach, a student can enroll for the particular units of instruction needed to meet his or her career objectives.

Weaver suggests the sequence of accounting units as shown in Table 10.1.[4] By referring to Illustration 10.1 in this module, the teacher can select instructional units appropriate for students·with various career objectives.

The following are examples of instructional units that may be included in Accounting I: Starting an Accounting System, Stating the Fundamental Bookkeeping Equation, Journalizing Transactions, Posting the Ledgers, Preparing Trial Balance, Completing the Worksheet, Preparing Elementary Financial Statements, Recording, Adjusting and Closing Entries, and Preparing a Post-Closing Trial Balance. The following are examples of units included in Accounting II: Review of Basic Accounting Procedures, Departmental and Payroll Accounting, Updating Accounts by Adjustments, Partnership Accounting, Control Accounting, Accounting for Taxes, Notes, and Drafts, Corporation Accounting, Automated Accounting Systems, Cost Accounting, Special Problems of Sales Accounting, and Use of Accounting Data by Management.[5]

In a research study, Smiley identified forty concepts that should be included in the course content of first-year accounting.[6] Concepts were drawn from textbooks used by first-year accounting teachers in Ohio. These concepts provide a comprehensive and appropriate underpinning for the first-year course in accounting (see Table 10.2).

module 10.1
LEARNING ACTIVITIES

1. Select ten of the concepts identified by Smiley and review a beginning accounting textbook to determine whether or not the concepts are included.
2. Write a brief statement explaining the role of accounting instruction in the preparation of office workers.
3. The amount of accounting instruction needed for differing careers or for personal use varies. Your school administrator has asked you to outline a plan to meet the instructional needs in accounting for students whose career objectives include becoming (a) an accountant, (b) an accounting clerk, (c) a secretary, (d) a plumber. Include a brief summary of the content for each career objective.
4. Read an article about the impact of automated data processing on accounting systems. Write a report on the article and ask your instructor to evaluate it or give an oral report to the class.
5. Consult the latest edition of the *Occupational Outlook Handbook* and write a brief report on the occupational projections in accounting and bookkeeping.

module 10.1
SELF-TEST

1. How is instruction in accounting affected by automatic data processing?
2. Briefly explain the career and personal-use values or goals of accounting instruction.

table 10.1
FLOW OF UNITS IN A CAREER-ORIENTED ACCOUNTING PROGRAM

ROLE OF ACCOUNTING: Explains what accounting is and its function in business. Includes a discussion of the characteristics of the free enterprise system and various forms of business ownership.

OPPORTUNITIES IN ACCOUNTING: Introduces career opportunities in the accounting, computing, and data processing field and relates accounting to individual student career goals.

ACCOUNTING EQUATION: Presents the fundamental elements of accounting and the analysis of transactions in terms of their effect on the fundamental elements. Introduces financial statements (balance sheet and income statement) to provide an overview, and shows how this knowledge can be applied to processing data by hand, by machine, by punched-card equipment or by computer.

ACCOUNTING CYCLE: Takes students through the nine steps of the accounting cycle for a service business.

BANKING ACTIVITIES: Covers banking activities and petty cash procedures, expanding the first step of the accounting cycle (the origination of data) to familiarize students with the source documents and procedures used in handling cash.

PAYROLL SUBSYSTEM: Presents payroll accounting and procedures early in the program. Covers payroll records and procedures, as well as payroll tax returns.

CASH RECEIPTS SUBSYSTEM: Presents information on the source documents, accounting records, equipment, procedures, controls, and personnel involved in handling cash receipts. Emphasizes the procedures and controls for handling the asset, not just for recording it.

CASH PAYMENTS SUBSYSTEM: Completes the handling of cash. Includes the procedures and controls for handling cash payments and an intensive examination of cash proofs.

PURCHASES SUBSYSTEM: Acquaints students with procedures, controls, forms, and jobs for handling and recording purchases. Covers the accounts payable ledger, the schedule of accounts payable, transportation costs, purchase discounts, trade discounts, purchase allowances, and purchase returns. Presents all skills and knowledge relating to purchases without interruption for a discussion of such things as taxes on sales.

SALES SUBSYSTEM: Includes procedures, controls, forms, and jobs. Covers the accounts receivable ledger, aging accounts receivable, the schedule of accounts receivable, sales taxes, sales returns, sales allowances, delivery charges, and sales discounts.

ADJUSTMENTS: Presents adjustments for merchandise inventory and prepaid expenses. Ties together the entire sequence of skills and knowledge completing the accounting cycle. (Most students will eventually be working in the first four steps of the cycle—originating data, journalizing, posting, and proving the ledgers—covered in the subsystems.)

CLASSIFIED STATEMENTS: Presents the various types of assets and liabilities and covers the various financial statements.

BAD DEBTS, DEPRECIATION, ACCRUALS, DEFERRALS: Covers procedures for estimating and recording bad debts, depreciation, accruals, and deferrals.

DATA PROCESSING: Presents the four basic data processing methods—manual, mechanical, punched card and electronic. Covers procedures and equipment, as well as application to accounting activities.

*The order of the last two units may be reversed.

3. How does the content of Accounting I differ from that of Accounting II, as outlined in Module 10.1?

module 10.2
INSTRUCTIONAL STRATEGIES FOR TEACHING ACCOUNTING

One of the teacher's responsibilities in teaching accounting is to plan the instructional program to involve students in those activities that best help them learn necessary skills and knowledges. However, since all students do not learn in the same way, the teacher must plan to incorporate a variety of methods.

According to Boynton, "Accounting is comprised of both knowledge and skill. These are not learned in the same way. Knowledge of facts can be acquired by hearing, seeing, feeling, tasting, smelling, and associating or reasoning. Skill in bookkeeping requires actual practice, drill, and repetition."[7] Since students vary widely in their rate and style of learning, the business teacher needs to plan for meeting individual needs. (See Chapter 5.) Instructional techniques discussed in this module are appropriate for individual, small-group, or large-group instruction.

After completing this module, you should be able to (1) explain how to provide for individual differences in teaching bookkeeping and accounting; (2) identify at least six different kinds of materials that are appropriate for use in accounting instruction; (3) differentiate among journal approach, account approach, balance sheet approach, equation approach, and systems approach; (4) outline procedures for introducing the instructional program in accounting; (5) outline a procedure for teaching the journals, incorporating the influence of electronic data processing; (6) outline the procedure for teaching the worksheet, adjusting and closing entries, and for preparing the financial statements; (7) explain and/or prepare five techniques for developing accounting concepts and vocabulary; (8) explain and/or demonstrate one or more activities for review, remediation, or development of math skills related to accounting.

STUDENT DIFFERENCES

In courses such as accounting, typewriting, or shorthand, it is important that students master each level of skill before they begin the next one, since the subject matter "pyramids"; that is, each new skill or concept is built on the preceding one. Frequently, total group instruction does not provide this foundation for all students, since learning rates and styles vary.

table 10.2
TABLE OF CONCEPTS FOR THE FIRST-YEAR HIGH SCHOOL COURSE

1. The management of a business enterprise needs data about every facet of its operations, much of which is made available through accounting.
2. A balance sheet summarizes the financial condition of a business as of a particular date by identifying the assets, liabilities, and the owner's equity.
3. A business maintains accounting records on a periodic and/or annual basis in order to compare one period's or year's performance with another and to satisfy tax requirements.
4. The classification of accounting data into accounts makes it possible to summarize the data into financial reports.
5. A separate account is maintained for each asset, liability, and owner's equity item.
6. In double-entry accounting, a business transaction affects at least two separate accounts by increasing or decreasing the respective account balances.
7. Whereas an income statement summarizes the revenues and expenses for a period of time, the balance sheet summarizes an accounting equation on a given date.
8. The interrelationship between the income statement and the balance sheet is reflected in the owner's equity section of the balance sheet.
9. Accounts provide a means whereby business events as recorded in the journals may be classified and summarized.
10. The significance of petty cash and the bank reconciliation statement is that both represent means of exercising control over cash.
11. Each transaction has an effect on one or more of the fundamental elements.
12. A fundamental consideration in the design of an accounting system is to provide a measure of control over accuracy and to safeguard assets.
13. Each business enterprise requires a separate set of accounting records.
14. A record of each transaction is made so as to provide a log of events or conditions affecting the financial position of the enterprise.
15. Journals are one means of providing a listing of business events in chronological sequence.
16. A sequence of procedures, called the accounting cycle, is followed in maintaining the accounting records during each accounting period.
17. The equality of the total debits and the total credits in the ledger should be verified at regular intervals.
18. The statement of owner's equity summarizes the changes in owner's equity resulting over a fiscal period.
19. The recognition of estimated bad debt expenses through an adjusting entry provides a more accurate valuation of accounts receivable on the balance sheet and a more accurate net income amount on the income statement.
20. Closing entries are the media whereby the results of operations for an accounting period are transferred to an owner's equity account.
21. Income transactions result in an ultimate increase in owner's equity whereas expense transactions result in an ultimate decrease in owner's equity.
22. An income statement summarizes for a given period of time the revenue, costs, and/or expenses and reveals the net profit or net loss.
23. A relationship exists between the method used to compute the depreciation charge and (1) the amount of reported income and (2) the book value of the depreciable assets.
24. When a business sells merchandise or services on credit, provisions should be made to allocate the losses resulting from bad debts to the accounting period in which the merchandise was sold or the services rendered.

table 10.2 (continued)

25. A relationship exists between the form of business organization and procedures designed to account for such items as profit distribution and owner's equity.
26. A relationship exists between the statement of cost of goods manufactured and the income statement in that the total cost of manufacturing goods appears in the cost of goods sold section of the income statement.
27. The significance of a voucher system is that it is a control system composed of records, methods, and procedures employed in (1) verifying and recording liabilities and (2) paying and recording cash payments.
28. A merchandising business differs from a service business in that provisions must be made in the merchandising business to account for the purchase and subsequent selling of merchandise.
29. An accounting system provides for the flow of data from the point of origination to the final reports.
30. An accounting system must provide the means of determining the net amount of sales of goods or services.
31. An accounting system encompasses the entire network of communications employed by a business organization to provide for its informational requirements. The system may employ manual, mechanical, and electronic means of processing financial data.
32. Tax legislation necessitates the maintenance of certain types of financial data, i.e., the amount of sales tax payable, FICA taxes payable, and withholding tax payable.
33. The journalizing of transactions increases the accuracy of accounting data by providing, in one location, an analysis of each business event.
34. Since the management and ownership of a corporation are often separate, accounting data are needed to report the results of management's operations to the owners.
35. Assets are recorded at the lower value of cost or market, thus recognizing possible losses but not possible gains.
36. The significance of the "cost of goods sold" figure is that it facilitates the determination of gross profit on sales and thus provides a measure for evaluating performance.
37. A reference or audit trial should be provided for each transaction so that the data can be traced from its origination (beginning) to its use (end).
38. From an accounting point of view, the single proprietorship is the simplest form of business organization.
39. Adjusting entries are reversed to update certain accounts and separate expired costs and expenses from unexpired costs and expenses and earned income from unearned income, thereby facilitating the determination of the income or loss.
40. The postclosing trial balance provides a means of verifying that the total debits equal the total credits after the adjusting and closing entries have been made to the accounts.

The heavy vocabulary and concept load in accounting texts makes it essential for the business teacher to build certain features into an individualized plan. As with any individualized material, the first requisite is to specify performance goals so that the student knows what he or she is to learn. Second, printed materials (textbook, teacher-made, commercially-prepared) should be presented in small segments with ample definitions, illustrations, and examples to aid in comprehension. Comprehension checks for each segment of printed material help to assess student understanding of concepts. Third, explanations should be given prior to making reading assignments. Unlike some business subjects in which students can read the textbook or printed material and complete activities or prepare for group discussions with a minimum of teacher explanation, each segment of accounting instruction should begin with teacher explanation/demonstration prior to students' reading the printed material. Through the use of audiovisual aids, the teacher can provide live and/or taped explanations when each student needs them (dependent on his or her ability and achievement). Fourth, provision should be made for students to apply the knowledge gained in the printed/illustrated material in specific activities. This involves breaking down large problems such as those at the end of a textbook chapter into segments corresponding to those in the printed material, or preparing activities related to the information covered in the printed material. Fifth, teacher and/or student assessment should be built into the module or assignment so that the student becomes aware of his or her performance. Through this feedback, teacher and student can decide whether the student is ready to progress to the next module, whether it needs to be repeated, or whether remediation should be provided for a portion of the content.

Based on the range of student abilities and achievements within a class, the expertise of the teacher, and the amount of material available, the teacher may opt for all students to use individualized materials or just for some to use them. When the entire class is working at individual rates, the teacher has an introductory period with the total group after which students progress at their own pace through the appropriate modules for their career objectives. The teacher provides assistance and instruction as needed on a one-to-one or small-group basis.

In some situations, the teacher may wish to teach part of the class as a group, while others work on an individualized basis. This is often done to allow capable students to move at a faster pace. "Individualized learning guides and the accompanying transparencies and cassettes do not replace the teacher. The most they do is change the class organizational pattern and alter the way in which the teacher uses the time available. The teacher using individualized materials has a role that is in many ways more demanding that that of the teacher in a traditional instructional setting. Only if the teacher commits much time and energy to the individualized program can it succeed."[8]

When the class is organized for instruction into small or large groups, the teacher will need to use a combination of methods to assure that students acquire both knowledge and skills. Discussions, lectures, and demonstrations using various audiovisual devices such as transparencies, chalkboards, slides, charts, and so on, are of much value to the business teacher in helping students to acquire an understanding of the vocabulary, concepts, rules, and processes of accounting. Problems, practice sets, simulations, and worksheets are examples of learning activities used to develop skills.

MATERIALS

The bookkeeping/accounting teacher uses many materials and media to support the instructional program in accounting, selecting and/or developing materials that are appropriate for each student or group of students.

The textbook is one of the fundamental tools used. Because of the heavy vocabulary and concept load in textbooks, the teacher should acquaint students with vocabulary and concepts prior to making reading assignments. It is important to spend some time explaining how to "read" and interpret illustrations. Short reading assignments followed by problems and activities in which the concept is applied make effective use of the textbook. Most textbooks are accompanied by a workbook that reduces student time for routine repetitive tasks and allows the student to focus on the concepts being presented. The workbooks, available from the textbook publisher, correlate with the text and contain study guides and application-type problems with the necessary forms. You may wish to have your students complete these problems individually, in small groups, or as a total group either in class or at home. The study guide may be used as a pretest of students' knowledge of a topic or it may be used by the student as a self-evaluation device. If used for self-evaluation, students will check their solutions in class and confer with you for any additional work needed.

Since accounting involves both knowledge and skill, students need opportunities to apply accounting principles in activities that approximate those found in business. Most publishers of accounting textbooks offer business simulation sets designed to integrate principles learned in the accounting course. Simulations vary in the length of time needed to complete them, ranging from a few days for those covering very simple transactions to several weeks for complex sets. In beginning bookkeeping, some teachers prefer to use a simulation set immediately after students have covered the first simple cycle and then a more complex set in the latter part of the year.

If students are grouped for instruction, the teacher will probably want the group to work together for two or three days to be sure that everyone understands the work. Students should then be encouraged to progress at their own pace. The teacher, however, should specify minimum progress expectations prior to beginning the simulation.

Other instructional materials available include income tax kits from the Internal Revenue Service, social security kits from the Social Security Administration, wall charts, transparencies, sound-slides, films, and filmstrips.

INSTRUCTIONAL APPROACHES

On-the-job accounting/bookkeeping activities proceed through six basic steps, as follows: (1) journalizing business transactions, (2) posting to ledger accounts, (3) preparing a trial balance and completing a worksheet, (4) preparing financial statements, (5) closing the ledger, and (6) preparing a post-closing trial balance. Weaver et al. identify nine basic steps of the accounting cycle: (1) originate data; (2) record transactions in journal; (3) post to ledgers; (4) prove ledgers and prepare worksheet; (5) prepare financial statements; (6) record adjusting entries and closing entries in journal and post to ledger; (7)

balance and rule ledger accounts; (8) prepare post-closing trial balance; and (9) interpret financial information.[9]

Through the years, business teachers have used a variety of approaches to teach the steps in the accounting cycle. The various procedures used have, in general, grown out of these approaches which may be characterized as follows:

Journal approach

In this approach, the steps in the accounting cycle are presented in the order in which they occur on the job. From the beginning, a two-column journal is used and the students make a series of transactions. Heavy emphasis is placed on the learning of rules. Major weaknesses include a lack of reasons given students for what they are doing and little or no explanation of the relationship of each step to the total bookkeeping cycle.

Account or ledger approach

This approach begins with the account, the hows and whys of account balances, and their debits and credits. The usual order of presentation is to "move ahead to proving the equality of debits and credits by taking a trial balance, then journalizing, posting, and proceeding to the preparation of financial statements."[10] One weakness of this approach is the lack of reasons given students regarding the processes. Also, because instruction begins in the middle of the cycle, moving back to the journal and then forward, students may be unclear as to the process.

Balance sheet approach

The balance sheet approach may be described as a *why* approach since it begins by showing students to what use bookkeeping/accounting records will be put and why they are necessary. "One common order of presentation is to proceed to an understanding of the need for accounts, the meaning of debit and credit, and the use of the ledger. This is then followed by the use of the journal for recording transactions, posting transactions, taking a trial balance, preparing a worksheet, preparing financial statements, and finally the closing of the books and taking a post-closing trial balance at the end of the fiscal period."[11] Criticisms of this approach include the fact that it starts at the end of the bookkeeper's normal duties rather than at the beginning. Then, too, balance sheets are usually prepared by accountants rather than bookkeepers. Finally, a disproportionate amount of emphasis is placed on the balance sheet in this approach.

Equation approach

The equation approach emphasizes the *why* of accounting from the beginning. Students develop the ability to analyze business transactions by learning the relationship of the elements of the accounting equation, the effects that various transactions have upon these elements, and the reasons behind the rules of debit and credit. In this approach, students are introduced first to the balance sheet equation and then gradually to the balance sheet as a whole. This approach is commonly used in secondary level accounting texts.

Systems approach

One method of teaching the modern concept of the accounting process is the systems approach. Through this approach, students learn how any given business activity fits into an accounting system. "Flowcharts are used to show the sequence of procedures and flow of data through an accounting system and to help students trace the interconnection of the various parts of the system."[12] Illustration 10.2 is an example of a Systems Flowchart of the Accounting Process.

The systems approach is used in conjunction with other instructional approaches such as the equation approach. At the college level, the instructor may wish to use a flowchart such as the one shown in Figure 10.2 to introduce the accounting process, often in the first lesson. At the high school level, the business teacher may want to wait until the accounting cycle has been presented to introduce the flowchart.

Kaluza suggests four advantages for a systems approach:[13]

1. Previous learning is related to modern practices. The teacher can tie in the various steps in the accounting cycle to the overall accounting process.
2. The student observes that the functions of recording, classifying, and summarizing are only a part of the accounting process. At this point the teacher emphasizes the distinction between bookkeeping (recording, classifying, and summarizing) and accounting.
3. The student should understand that there are two important branches of the accounting process: managerial accounting and financial accounting. Financial accounting requires the study of generally accepted accounting principles, while managerial accounting does not necessarily include this study.
4. The student is presented with the main objective of the accounting process: to provide financial data for proper analysis and interpretation so that useful decisions can be made by parties both inside and outside the firm.

INITIAL INSTRUCTION

In the initial stages of bookkeeping/accounting instruction, the teacher tries to build student interest in the subject. One method of motivation

illustration 10.2
SYSTEMS FLOWCHART OF THE ACCOUNTING PROCESS

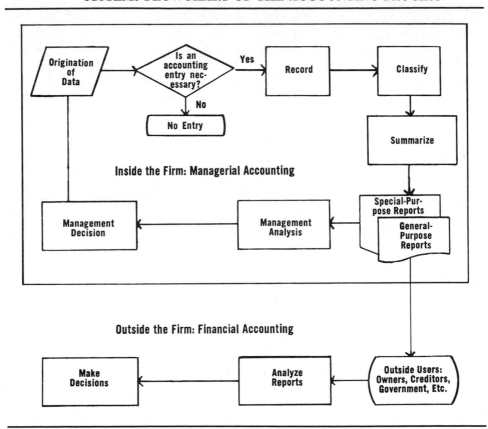

Source: Henry Kaluza, "Teaching the Modern Concept of the Accounting Process: The Systems Flowchart," *Business Education World* 53, no. 2 (November–December 1972): 18. Reprinted with permission of BUSINESS EDUCATION WORLD, Gregg Division, McGraw-Hill Book Company, copyright November–December 1972.

is to relate the objectives of the course to a simple service business, such as a motel or a laundry. This can be done by using a balance sheet as a starting point for the accounting system, to show the meaning of assests, liabilities, and capital. You may want to use the ledger account form to stress the principle of equality of debits and credits and to build an image of the accounting equation. Or you may wish to list on the chalkboard or a transparency what the business owns —money, property, and so forth. Label this "Financial Worth of ——— Company." Next, list what the business owes. Ask how you might find out the Net Financial Worth (Capital) of the business. One or more students will likely suggest subtracting what is owed from what is owned. Write this formula on the chalkboard: Owns – Owes = Net Financial Worth. Don't forget to discuss the meaning of "net." If necessary, write another example of what the business owns and owes on the chalkboard or a transparency and have students determine the net worth.

Debit and credit

Accounting teachers recognize the importance of developing a firm foundation in the basic principles of debit and credit as a basis for understanding the accounting cycle. When introducing debit and credit, the teacher should thoroughly illustrate each rule, principle, and step. Transparencies for use with an overhead projector are excellent visual tools. The teacher and/or student can write on the transparency (and erase items written with a grease pencil); transparencies can be projected on a screen so that all students can see the illustration; they can be indexed to topics or chapters, and can be used more than once so that the teacher can build up a variety of resource materials.

Illustration 10.3 is an example of a visual that can be made into a transparency to illustrate the basic accounting equation. "After the basic accounting equation has been carefully reviewed, another transparency is used to introduce 'T' accounts and the rules of debit and credit as shown in Illustration 10.4. Further emphasis is added by having students go to the chalkboard and indicate increases and decreases on the transparency overlay, which shows up quite well on a green or black chalkboard."[14] As in all phases of accounting instruction, it is necessary for students to have practice involving the basic principles of debit and credit if they are to develop skills as well as knowledge.

Students can more easily understand the whys underlying the basic principles of debit and credit if they plan business transactions in T accounts by answering these questions: (1) What is the name of each account affected by the transaction? (2) What is the classification of each account affected? (3) How is the balance of each account affected?

illustration 10.3
THE BASIC ACCOUNTING EQUATION

Assets	= Liabilities + Owner's Equity
Cash + Receivables + Inventory + Fixed Assets = Payables + Capital	
Transactions can then be written on the transparency and the students asked to state the effect of the transaction by using " + " or " − " signs, then "increase" or "decrease," and finally, the terms "debit" and "credit."	

Source: Andrew J. Potts, "Teaching the Modern Concept of the Accounting Process: The Systems Flowchart," *Business Education World* 54, no. 5 (May–June 1974): 27. Reprinted with permission of BUSINESS EDUCATION WORLD, Gregg Division, McGraw-Hill Book Company, copyright May–June 1974.

illustration 10.4
THE T ACCOUNT FOR DEBIT AND CREDIT

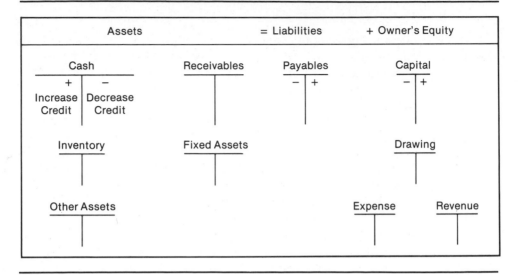

Since account balances may be affected in only two ways, the teacher points out that increases in an account are placed on the *balance* side, and that decreases are placed on the side opposite the balance side. Therefore, the student, by recalling these rules, can easily determine the balance side of any asset, liability, and capital account form of balance sheet. Since each asset item and its corresponding balance appears on the left-hand side of the balance sheet, the balance side for all asset accounts is the left-hand side. Likewise, since the liability and capital items and their corresponding amounts appear on the right-hand side of the balance sheet, the balance side for all liability and capital accounts is the right-hand side.

Liability, capital, income, and expense transactions are analyzed using similar procedures. The teacher points out that income is an increase in capital and that expense is a decrease in capital. Because such transactions are numerous, they are not placed in the capital account. Rather, income and expense are recorded in separate income and expense accounts (temporary capital accounts). This prevents the capital account from becoming cluttered with many amounts that would make difficult a quick determination of the total amount of each income and expense. In determining whether income and expense are to be debited or credited, the teacher points out that income is an increase in capital and that expense is a decrease in capital. Therefore, income transactions mean an increase in capital that is recorded in a separate income account. The income account (temporary capital) then is credited because all increases in any account go on the balance side. Likewise, when an expense transaction occurs, the decrease in capital is placed in a separate expense account. This expense account (temporary capital account) is debited because all decreases in any account are recorded on the side opposite the balance account.

Wunsch[15] suggests that students memorize the following three-step procedure for recording any business transaction: (1) increases in any account are recorded on the balance side, decreases in any account are recorded on the side opposite the balance side; (2) assets appear on the left-hand side of the balance sheet, liabilities and capital appear on the right-hand side of the balance sheet; (3) income is an increase in capital; and expense is a decrease in capital.

Using the foregoing suggestions in presenting the basic principles of debit and credit, an accounting teacher would proceed as follows in analyzing and planning a business transaction in T accounts:

a. Transaction: Paid cash, $200, for a new office desk.

b. Step 1: What is the name of each account affected?

c. Step 2: What is the classification of each account affected?

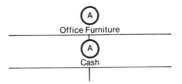

d. Step 3: How is the balance of each account affected?

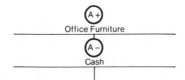

At this point, the teacher must use the plus sign and the minus sign to determine which account gets the debit and which one gets the credit. As Office Furniture is an asset that is being increased, it is debited for $200 because all increases in any account go on the balance side (the balance side of all asset accounts is the left-hand side because assets appear on the left-hand side of the balance sheet). Furthermore, as Cash is an asset that is being decreased, it is credited for $200 because all decreases in any account go on the side opposite the balance side (the side opposite the balance side of all asset accounts is the right-hand side, as the left-hand side is the balance side according to the placement of assets on the balance sheet).[16]

JOURNALS

There are four methods used to process business data in offices: manual, mechanical, punched card, and electronic data processing. Since most businesses generally use a combination of two or more of these methods, it is important that students become familiar with each. Current accounting textbooks include these methods in presenting content. The increased use of machines, including computers, makes it necessary for instruction to reflect current trends in accounting in business.

The impact of electronic data processing on accounting influences what to teach about journals. Students should be aware of the various names given the list of transactions that are not necessarily in the form of a manually prepared columnar form called a journal. "A listing of sales invoices may be called a sales journal by one business, an invoice register by another business, or a sales invoice listing by a third business. And in a journalless accounting system, the listing is called a binder."[17] Therefore, teachers should emphasize the *concept* of a journal, stressing the need for a listing of source documents. The journal offers an illustration of how accountants provide the data about daily business transactions.

Weaver suggests the following procedure in implementing the learning principle of simple to complex: "In covering the accounting cycle for the first time, introduce the concept of the journal. Then when introducing the special journals in the second cycle, point out the other terms used for a journal. After the second cycle has been completed, introduce the binder used in the 'journalless' system. And after the accounting principles have been taught and non-manual data processing methods are being introduced, point out how the concept of the journal is maintained in mechanical, punched card, and electronic data processing methods."[18]

Instructional approaches that focus on "why before how"—such as the equation approach—emphasize what is happening in a transaction before the process of journalizing the results of the transaction.

The journals should not be used during the first few weeks of the accounting course. The sequence of topics discussed should follow a pattern such as the following: "First, stress the fundamental elements and the accounting equation. Second, teach the analysis of balance sheet transactions and income statement transactions. Third, teach the use of accounts as a device to record changes brought about by the transaction. Fourth, introduce the recording of the transactions in a chronological sequence—in this case, in a journal. In this pattern of instruction, the student learns how to analyze transactions before he is confronted with the mechanics of journalizing."[19]

WORKSHEET: ADJUSTING AND CLOSING ENTRIES

The worksheet serves to bring accounts up to date, to classify them, and to adjust those accounts that are not up to date so that financial reports reflect a correct condition of the business. Usually you will find that an eight-column worksheet is sufficient in first-year accounting to introduce a few adjustments.

In teaching the worksheet, remind students to analyze the adjustments, using a T account before recording their adjusting entry on the worksheet. Explain the importance of keying their adjusting entries, using letters instead of numbers for this purpose. Remind students that the worksheet, as a working paper, is done in pencil. If possible, prepare an overhead transparency for a blank worksheet, then proceed through the recording of adjustments on the worksheet with students writing on worksheet paper provided to them.

In testing students, distribute duplicated worksheet forms to save time. Allow them to use round numbers to minimize arithmetic errors.

Boynton recommends the following steps for teaching the worksheet:[20]

1. Teach the trial balance.
2. Introduce the worksheet—its purpose and form.
3. Start to classify the amounts in the trial balance columns by extending them into the balance sheet columns.
4. Teach prepaid adjustments before dealing with the merchandise inventory account.
5. Extend amounts that are now adjusted (the up-to-date amounts for each account) to the balance sheet and the income statement columns.
6. Compute the net income or loss.
7. Prepare the income statement from the worksheet.
8. Prepare the balance sheet from the worksheet.
9. Record adjusting entries from the worksheet.
10. Record closing entries from the worksheet.

After the six-column worksheet is taught, closing entries are usually presented. Demonstrations of closing entries should be kept as simple as possible. Explain that the income statement columns of the worksheet provide all the information needed to close the income accounts, the cost accounts, and the expense accounts, and to close the net income into the capital account. Emphasize that the proprietor's capital account includes the balance of his or her drawing account.

All the necessary information for recording both the adjusting and closing entries is available on the worksheet. Use an overhead projector to show a completed worksheet on the screen while you use the chalkboard to demonstrate journalizing (1) the adjusting entries from the information in the adjustments column and (2) the closing entries from the information in the income statement columns.

After the adjusting and closing entries have been posted, the post-closing trial balance proves the equality of debits and credits before beginning the record of transactions for the next fiscal period. Point out to students that (1) nothing appears on the post-closing trial balance except permanent accounts and (2) the main purpose of the post-closing trial balance is to see if the ledger is correct after it has been closed.

FINANCIAL STATEMENTS

It is important to explain to students the need for separate income statement, capital statement, and balance sheet. Illustrate that all information needed to prepare the income statement and balance sheet is obtained from the appropriate columns of the worksheet. Explain that the statements are essential in order to analyze the current condition of the business. Emphasize that the financial reports are prepared in ink. Teach students to begin at the top of the income statement columns of the worksheet, checking off each amount in these columns as it is used on the income statement. Follow a similar procedure in demonstrating the preparation of the capital statement and the balance sheet. (Transparencies can be used effectively in this stage of the course to show the source of figures for the financial statements.)

Emphasize the order in which the three financial statements are prepared: (1) first, the income statement, to determine the net income or the net loss; (2) second, the capital statement, to determine the ending amount of the proprietor's capital, which is needed in the preparation of the third statement; (3) third, the balance sheet, which must come last because it uses the amount of the proprietor's capital as shown on the capital statement.

VOCABULARY AND CONCEPT DEVELOPMENT

The new vocabulary to be mastered in accounting is challenging. Research by Calhoun and others has shown the readability level of textbooks to be high, with some chapters in high school texts rated at a postsecondary level.

The following illustrate some of the methods that business teachers may apply to teach special and general accounting vocabulary effectively:

1. Introduce vocabulary words before students begin reading assignments. Include special and general terms with which students may have difficulty.
2. Present the words visually (chalkboard, posters, bulletin board displays, transparencies, and so on) as well as orally.
3. Illustrate each word by using displays, transparencies, and other visuals. This step is important, for as much as three-fourths of what an individual learns is through seeing.
4. Relate the word meanings, when possible, to student experiences, using commonplace terms such as "owns – owes = net worth."
5. Have students give examples demonstrating their understanding of the words. (Students prepare lists of assets, liabilities, and so forth.)
6. Prepare displays showing word meanings that are visible to students for as long as they are needed.
7. Use new words and have students use them in oral or written discussions and activities to help develop new words as part of their speaking vocabulary. Check student pronunciation to be sure that they are pronouncing words correctly.
8. After introducing and discussing new words, provide opportunities to assess student understanding. Include opportunities to demonstrate understanding of words, such as labeling, giving examples as needed.

9. Periodically review word meanings, pronunciation, and recall of words. For example, "You own 100 shares of stock in XYZ Company. If the company makes a profit, you receive a check; this payment is an example of ———."

The following exercise, developed by Caldwell,[21] provides an excellent example of learning material designed to teach accounting terminology.

ACCOUNTING VOCABULARY

Name ————————————

Date ————————————

Find the hidden accounting terms in the following statements:
1. Seeking to calm his nerves, the golf *pro fit*fully practiced his shots.
2. This pipe line extends over many an acre, ditch after ditch.
3. After six hours of work, she etched the beautiful pattern.
4. When Jack comes in, vent or yodel your greetings all at once.
5. Part of the Army's problem is to adjust men to the various climates.
6. The little tot almost fell from the swing.
7. John was thrown out, standing only two feet from home plate.
8. The meeting had to adjourn a little later.
9. The players led Gerry off the field.
10. "The jury will adjourn almost immediately," proclaimed the judge.
11. You must obey the law as set forth in the constitution and by the courts.
12. Just ahead loomed the Valpo station.
13. Harry chewed the tobacco until he saw his aunt approaching.
14. Santa Claus was accosted by hundreds of eager children.
15. After he was wounded, the knights led Geraint away from the jousts.
16. The general's aide bitterly denied the accusation.
17. "Now, my little chicken, try to untie those knots."
18. We will have a Christmas party on our new winter estate.
19. Robin Hood thought his partner's ale somewhat weak.
20. You cannot go in vest and shirt sleeves.
21. The advertising put out by the Linco men was original and clever.
22. The matter must come to an end or secession is sure to follow.
23. To cap it all off, we forgot the pickles and the olives.
24. "The duplex pen sells at only $5.95," intoned the salesman.
25. If even half is calmed, the other half of the audience will settle down.
26. The fracas has not promoted the friendships we so carefully tried to foster.
27. Lord Hotspur chased around the battlefield, seeking Prince Hal.
28. "Are cords and cardboard all that you will need?"
29. He will not budge till we tell him he may have his own way.

Whitaker suggests that the development of verbal skills is an important part of accounting instruction. Students need to be able to "(1) ask and answer questions about accounting terms and procedures when interacting with teachers or peers, (2) talk with potential employers about accounting, and (3) communicate with other employees or supervisors."[22]

To demonstrate the ability to communicate effectively about accounting, each student should be able to "(1) define the term or describe the procedure; (2) relate the term or procedure to other words on the list for which the student has already achieved competency; (3) give concrete examples of the term or how the procedure is followed; (4) explain how the term or procedure is related to the overall accounting system; and (5) respond to the evaluator's question until the evalutor determines that the student understands and can correctly use the term or procedure to talk about accounting.[23] Demonstrating these competencies requires a one-to-one setting which is not always feasible. The following procedure, a variation of the Keller Plan (a personalized system of instruction), provides one way to incorporate verbal training without significantly increasing the workload of the business teacher:

1. Adopt the following behavorial objective: Given a list of accounting terms and procedures, the student will demonstrate verbal competency for each word and procedure on the list.
2. Prepare a list of accounting words and procedures and group the list to parallel the written examination material. Two blank spaces should be included next to each term, as in the following example:

	Student Tutor	Teacher
Asset	_____	_____
Ledger	_____	_____
Account	_____	_____
Post	_____	_____

The five criteria for verbal competency should also appear on the word list.

3. Prepare a wall chart with student names along the vertical axis and accounting terms and procedures along the horizontal axis.
4. When the course begins, the teacher is presumed to be the only individual capable of evaluating the verbal competence of students. The teacher evaluates students when they feel they are ready on particular terms or procedures. If competency is demonstrated for a term or procedure, the teacher initials that word on the student's sheet. The student then puts an "X" on the wall chart for each term and procedure competently verbalized.
5. After a student has achieved verbal competence for a term or procedure, that student becomes a tutor for that word and will evaluate the verbal competence for other students. The student tutor will initial another student's list when that student has demonstrated compe-

tence for the term or procedure. Students are responsible for keeping their line on the wall chart correctly marked.
6. When a student is ready to be evaluated on a specific term or procedure, the wall chart is used to determine which students are competent and can evaluate performance for that word. The teacher should evaluate only when no students are as yet competent for the term or procedure, in the case of disputes over student tutor evaluations, or periodically to assess the evaluations of the student tutors.
7. Evaluations can occur at any time or place, whenever a student is prepared and a student tutor is available.[24]

MATHEMATICS SKILLS

The use of adding machines, calculators, computers, and so forth, sharply decreased the amount of mathematical computation done by bookkeepers and accounting clerks. Nevertheless, accounting students should be able to quickly and correctly complete basic processes involving adding, subtracting, multiplying, and dividing. Even with the use of machines, the students need to be able to choose the appropriate arithmetic process as well as estimate the results and determine whether an answer is approximately correct. Boynton[25] suggests that there are only a few arithmetic problem areas in bookkeeping/accounting. In the main, these center around (1) computing the terms of sales and purchases, (2) computing valuation accounts—depreciation and bad debts, and (3) computing interest and discount. Brief systematic exercises such as the following can help students to acquire and maintain competence in the basic skills. Practices and drills should also incorporate vertical as well as horizontal addition/subtraction problems.

ADDITION COMBINATIONS

The number combinations below form the basis of all addition. To add rapidly and accurately, practice adding them *mentally* until you can go through the entire group in less than twenty-five seconds. Do not place answers on this paper.

	a	b	c	d	e	f	g	h	i	j	k	l	m	n	o
	4	7	1	3	2	4	7	4	5	2	4	7	9	1	3
1.	9	7	8	8	5	5	9	3	6	9	6	2	5	7	5

	a	b	c	d	e	f	g	h	i	j	k	l	m	n	o
	1	7	1	2	3	6	5	6	4	4	2	8	7	2	6
2.	6	8	5	6	3	9	8	3	4	1	3	6	4	4	6

	a	b	c	d	e	f	g	h	i	j	k	l	m	n	o
	6	8	1	9	5	2	5	9	9	9	3	1	8	4	2
3.	7	2	1	9	7	1	5	3	1	8	7	3	8	8	2

SUBTRACTION COMBINATIONS

Practice *mentally* subtracting the combinations below until you can complete the group in less than fifty seconds. Do not place answers on this paper.

	a	b	c	d	e	f	g	h	i	j	k	l	m	n
4.	4	12	15	14	11	16	13	6	9	11	16	7	5	14
	2	5	7	6	2	8	6	4	5	8	9	4	3	7

	a	b	c	d	e	f	g	h	i	j	k	l	m	n
5.	9	8	10	9	2	8	13	15	4	17	9	10	10	12
	2	4	7	8	1	6	5	9	3	9	6	4	2	6

	a	b	c	d	e	f	g	h	i	j	k	l	m	n
6.	7	6	11	12	11	12	13	10	8	14	7	3	5	18
	1	3	4	8	5	3	9	1	3	5	2	1	1	9

	a	b	c	d	e	f	g	h	i	j	k	l	m	n
7.	7	13	3	11	5	7	14	16	14	11	7	11	12	15
	3	6	2	3	4	5	8	7	9	6	4	9	4	6

	a	b	c	d	e	f	g	h	i	j	k	l	m	n
8.	9	13	12	10	13	7	15	8	10	9	9	11	17	12
	7	4	9	9	8	6	8	5	8	3	4	7	8	7

Source: J. Edward Caldwell, "Initiative Makes the Difference: Techniques for Motivating Accounting Students" (Cincinnati: South-Western Publishing Company, 1978).

WRITING SKILLS

The application portion of the accounting course (practice sets, simulations, worksheets, and workbooks) necessitates student writing. The teacher should stress the importance of neatness, legible penmanship, and accuracy. (Some students may need to print rather than use cursive handwriting.) Instructional modules covering penmanship, basic math facts, and vocabulary offer a means through which the teacher can provide individual instruction, either developmental, remedial, or review.

Regardless of how the class is organized for instruction—whether it is conducted on an individualized, small-group, or large-group basis—the teacher should (1) provide ample explanations with illustrations as needed; (2) offer opportunities for students to demonstrate their understanding of concepts and to apply knowledge in a variety of settings; (3) have students explain the "why" of activities and processes; (4) provide instruction in a systematic manner so that students can master each step before moving on the the next; (5) periodically summarize concepts, rules, and principles; (6) relate individual steps in the accounting cycle to the overall cycle (a wall chart containing the steps is helpful); (7) provide remedial work, review, exercises in math, handwriting, and vocabulary through instructional modules and small-group instruction; (8) offer opportunities for students to progress at their own pace through instructional modules, simulation materials, and practice sets.

module 10.2
LEARNING ACTIVITIES

1. Review at least one accounting textbook and tell which instructional approach is used. Do you agree with this approach? Why or why not?
2. Prepare a mini-lesson covering the theory of debit and credit. Be ready to demonstrate the lesson in class.
3. Begin a collection of materials and techniques to use in teaching (a) the journals, (b) the worksheet, (c) adjusting entries, (d) closing entries, and (e) the financial statements.
4. Begin a collection of materials and techniques to use in (a) vocabulary/concept development and (b) math review, remediation, and development.
5. Prepare a mini-lesson for the first or second day in the accounting course.
6. Read an article on the influence of electronic data processing on accounting. Summarize the article and submit it to your instructor.
7. Review a set of business simulation materials. Report on (a) whether you would recommend using the material, (b) when it should be used in the course, (c) length of time needed to complete the material, and (d) type of students for whom you would recommend the material.

module 10.2
SELF-TEST

1. Identify and explain three different ways to provide for individual differences.
2. Briefly explain the following approaches to accounting instruction: journal, account, balance sheet, equation, and systems approaches.
3. List three instructional techniques you might employ in the initial stages of the accounting course.
4. Explain how you would go about teaching the worksheet, adjusting and closing entries, and the financial statements.
5. Identify five methods for teaching vocabulary development in accounting.
6. How can the accounting instructor improve basic math skills of students in the accounting course?

module 10.3
EVALUATING INSTRUCTION IN ACCOUNTING

An important and sometimes difficult responsibility of the business teacher is to assess the extent of learner achievement in accounting. Both formal and informal evaluation help the teacher and the student to determine the progress that has been made toward achieving mutually identified objectives. Evaluation is educational feedback for judging the effectiveness of learning. As a teacher of bookkeeping/accounting, you may want to use a combination of measures to assess student progress and to serve as a basis for awarding grades.

After completing this module, you should be able to (1) describe the kinds of measures appropriate for evaluating achievment in accounting, (2) construct short-answer test items, (3) identify behaviors to be observed through informal evaluation, and (4) list the criteria to be included in arriving at a course grade.

INFORMAL EVALUATION

Informal evaluation techniques, such as observation, checklists, and student self-evaluations, are appropriate tools for analyzing some forms of student behavior. You should use planned and systematic procedures if the results are to be worthwhile. You may want to plan a schedule so that a certain number of students are observed each day. Prior to beginning the observations, list the behaviors to be assessed. A checklist will help you to maintain consistency in student observations. Spend a few minutes explaining the importance of the behaviors to be observed. For example, in addition to identifying work habits as a behavior, explain what constitutes good work habits, such as beginning work promptly, having materials available, planning work effectively, and using equipment correctly. Other examples of behaviors that might be observed include the ability to follow directions, compatibility with others, neatness, cooperation, initiative, punctuality, and dependability. The teacher should indicate on the date(s) observed the extent to which a given student exhibited these behaviors. This could be done by using a scale with point values ranging from 1 to 5, or by using headings such as *excellent, good, fair, poor,* or *not observed.*

One of the ultimate goals of education is for students to become independent learners with the ability to evaluate their own performance. Therefore, an important phase of any evaluation plan should be self-evaluation. A checklist, completed periodically, could include questions such as the following:

Do I have my material and supplies ready when class begins?
Am I prompt in completing assignments?
Are my written assignments neat and legible?
Do I work without disturbing others?

The following personal balance sheet is an example of an appraisal procedure that can form the basis for intelligent student self-analysis and improvement.

There are frequent opportunities in accounting classrooms for students to work in groups or in committees and, in so doing, to evaluate the performance of other members of the group. Such opportunities arise in connection with practice sets, arrangement of field trips, preparation of bulletin boards, and use of simulation materials. Students respond well to evaluation by peers, although

MY BALANCE SHEET

What are you worth? Check your score.
Add assets and subtract liabilities to find your net worth.

	POSSIBLE SCORE	MY SCORE
Assets:		
Honesty	50	
Sense of Humor	50	
Enthusiasm	50	
Personal Apperance	50	
Dependability	50	
Cooperation	50	
Smiles	50	
Courtesy	50	
Total Assets	400	
Liabilities:		
Dishonesty	40	
Selfishness	40	
Discourtesy	40	
Laziness	40	
Lack of Self-reliance	40	
Pessimism	40	
Bad Judgment	40	
Total Liabilities	280	
Proprietorship:		
My Net Worth		

Source: Lloyd L. Garrison, "Evaluation in Bookkeeping, Accounting, and Business Arithmetic" in *Evaluation of Pupil Progress in Business Education,* Estelle L. Popham, ed. American Business Education Yearbook, Vol. 17 (Somerville, N. J.: Somerset Press, 1960), p. 246.

some students may be reluctant to evaluate others. The committee member being evaluated must be identified, but the student may exercise a choice about signing his or her own name to the evaluation. It is important that students assist in the formulation of criteria to be used in evaluation by peers. To provide for uniformity in answers, the questions may be structured with choices such as *yes, no,* or *to a limited degree.* Such questions as the following can be used in group evaluation:[26]

> Did this person attend all of the planning and work sessions?
> Did this committee member take an active part in formulating the final
>   report or results?
> Do you feel that this person assumed a full share of the work involved?
> How cooperative was this member in terms of the various duties and
>   responsibilities of the committee?
> In terms of the contribution of the other members of the committee, how
>   would you rate the performance of the committee member—first,
>   second, third, or fourth?

FORMAL EVALUATION

Testing in accounting should include two aspects: (1) knowledge of principles, theory, concepts, and terminology and (2) skill in the application of principles and theory. Short-answer tests are appropriate for measuring knowledge—the whys of accounting— while problem tests are better used to measure the application of principles and theory—the hows of accounting. To limit achievement tests to short-answer types, however, presents a distorted picture of a student's real accomplishment. Both published and teacher-made tests are essential to provide a comprehensive measure of student achievement.

Published tests

Several good published tests are available; these are usually short-answer type tests that accompany the textbook, and can be purchased at nominal cost from the publisher. Since these tests are limited to the content of the textbook, you should prepare additional test items covering course content not included in the text. Review the items on published tests in advance to be sure that the content matches that included in the course and that the vocabulary is appropriate for your students.

Teacher-made short-answer tests

Even if you choose to use published tests, there are times when you will want to construct your own test items. True-false, multiple-choice, matching, classification, and supply-type short answer are examples of appropriate times for measuring knowledge. Hardaway suggests that "the more advanced the course, the greater becomes the emphasis that is placed on theory and principles and the less the emphasis placed on practice."[27] Chapter 4 provides suggestions for constructing test items as well as procedures for planning and evaluating tests.

Problem tests

In addition to the short-answer tests designed to evaluate knowledge, the testing program should include problem-type tests to measure whether the student knows how to apply accounting principles in practice. Teachers have tended, in the past, to rely on short-answer tests because of their availability from publishers and their ease of scoring. However, a sound evaluation approach should reflect all course objectives.

Construction of problem-type tests is relatively easy since the problems should be similar to those the students have been working. However, there are several questions the business teacher must answer before constructing a problem test. How long should the problems be? Should I give a series of short problems or one long one? How will I score the problem? Will an error early in the problem that results in other errors be deducted more than once? Should the same number of points be deducted for each possible error? Should time be a factor in the test? If the slowest student can complete the problem(s) within the time allowed, are the accelerated students challenged? Should tests be varied according to student ability?

Many business educators feel that by using a series of short problems instead of one long problem, the teacher can eliminate some of the difficulties related to problem-type tests. Each short problem should be designed to measure one principle or concept or a part of a larger problem. The following is an example of such a problem.

Lamar's Appliance Center purchased a truckload of television sets for a promotional sale. The invoice, dated August 1, is for $15,000. The terms are 1/10, n/30. Since the store bought in volume, a 10 percent trade discount is allowed. If the bill is paid on August 8, what amount does Lamar's Appliance Center pay for the truckload of television sets?

Some authorities in bookkeeping and accounting recommend the use of mini-problems that incorporate several or all steps in the accounting cycle. Note that even though the following problem is simplified, students must have an understanding of principles and the ability to apply them.[28]

MINI-PROBLEM: THE COMPLETE ACCOUNTING CYCLE[28]

Bell Realty Agency's transactions for the month of July are listed below:

July 1. Bill Bell invested the following in his new real
estate business: Cash, $2,000; Office
Equipment, $500.

1. Paid cash, $175, for July rent.

31. Purchased new typewriter on account from
Allen Equipment Company, $550.

31. Paid Cash, $75, for utilities bill.

31. Received cash, $1,800, for commission earned
during July.

Instructions:

1. Record the transactions. Use a two-column general journal. Omit explanations.
2. Post the journal. Use skeleton T accounts. Omit dates and posting references.
3. Prepare a trial balance. Use six-column worksheet paper.
4. Complete the worksheet.
5. Prepare (a) an income statement and (b) a balance sheet.
6. (a) Record and post the closing entries; (b) balance and rule the accounts, and (c) prepare a post-closing trial balance.

SCORING THE TEST.   In order to score problem tests as objectively as possible, the teacher prepares a key or master sheet showing the possible point deductions for each type of error. The simplest type of scoring is to allow one point for each item, process, or ruling involved in solving the problem. A natural weighting of points, allowing one point for each item in the problem, is illustrated in the following journal entry:

On January 1, 1979, Terry Driscoll invested $10,000

in a plumbing business.

						Points
1979 January	1	Cash		10,000		(5)
		Terry Driscoll, Capital			10,000	(2)
		Invested cash in plumb-				
		ing business				(1)
					Total	(8)

In the above example, one point is allowed for the year, month, day, debit account title, debit amount, credit account title, credit amount, and explanation. If posting had been completed, two more points would have been added for posting the references.

Some teachers believe the weakness of one-point scoring is that certain errors deserve larger penalties and, thus, they assign varying penalties for different errors. So that a student is not penalized several times for one error (and its subsequent errors), you may wish to deduct only once for a given error regardless of the number of subsequent errors.

"Another evaluation process focuses on a sense of achievement, not just on details. A record is kept of the number of problems correctly completed over a given period of instruction. These problems may be completed in class, on tests, or for homework. All problems incorrectly completed must be corrected. At the end of the instructional period, students having the largest number of initially correct solutions are awarded the high ratings, and those with only a few receive low ratings. If the teacher desires to give more weight to certain problems, such as those on tests or particularly difficult homework assignments, he may increase their value to two or three instead of one. Thus if a student correctly completes four test problems valued twice as high as homework problems, he receives a score of eight for that test. A record of students' accomplishments kept over several semesters establishes minimum standards. This procedure emphasizes the completed problems as business emphasizes completed records, and what constitutes an acceptable solution is important too. Accuracy of results, correctness of method, and neatness of appearance are basic requirements."[29]

Business simulation sets

Short-answer tests are used to reveal student understanding of the information in simulation sets. In these "open book" type tests, students find answers to questions in the books and accompanying working papers that are included in the simulation. Test items should be constructed that require students to analyze the books, thus testing their ability to interpret as well as keep the books. Items could cover content such as the amount of cash sales for a given period of time, terms of invoices, date notes are due, amount of merchandise purchased on account, balances of accounts, and net profit.

GRADING

Business teachers vary in their philosophy and procedures for grading. Some view accounting as pyramiding and, consequently, put major emphasis on what students know at the end of the grading period. Others average all tests and work completed by students. Regardless of the grading plan the teacher chooses, it should be established prior to beginning the course and explained to students at the outset.

Factors that may be considered in arriving at a grade include tests and exams, simulation sets, written problems and assignments, practice sets, work habits, attitudes, and teacher judgment. One grading plan is as follows:[30]

Written problem assignments	1/4
Tests and quizzes	1/4
Practice sets	1/8
Final/midterm exams	1/4
Other elements	1/8

module 10.3
LEARNING ACTIVITIES

1. Construct one each of the following types of test items:
   a. multiple-choice
   b. short-answer
   c. true-false
2. Design an observation checklist that you might use in an accounting class, or design a self-evaluation checklist appropriate for student use.
3. Prepare a grading chart listing the factors that will make up the grade and weight of each for an accounting course.
4. Individually or with a partner, construct a test, including both short-answer and problem items, that would be appropriate for one module or topic in accounting.
5. Select a simulation set and construct a short-answer test that would assess student interpretation of data.

module 10.3
SELF-TEST

1. Briefly describe the plan you would use for evaluating student performance in accounting. Identify the educational level and give some attention to objectives, organization, content, and interpretation of the plan.

SUMMARY

Accounting is made up of both knowledge and skill. For students to acquire these, the teacher must provide a variety of instructional procedures and activities through which students can apply the knowledge gained.

When planning for individual differences, the teacher should specify the performance goals, present printed material in small segments with ample explanation and illustration, give explanations prior to making reading assignments, provide opportunities to apply knowledge gained, and build in teacher-student assessment.

The teacher will want to use a variety of printed and nonprinted materials in teaching accounting. These include textbooks, workbooks, simulation sets, filmstrips, transparencies, and charts. An overhead projector is an invaluable tool for presenting visual material in the accounting classroom.

Instructional approaches are generally classified as journal, accounting, balance sheet, equation, and systems approaches. The equation approach which emphasizes *why* and *how* is currently used in a number of texts; the systems approach is used in conjunction with other approaches.

A fundamental part of accounting instruction is the development of a firm foundation in the basic principles of debit and credit. Students need to learn the *why* as well as the *hows* relating to debit and credit. This means that the instructor provides explanations for processes rather than having students memorize rules.

Teaching the worksheet, adjusting and closing entries, and the financial statements involves a sequential and orderly procedure of building on previous student learnings.

What to teach about journals is influenced both by the instructional approach and the impact of electronic data processing. Teachers should stress the concept of a journal, including the various terms used for a journal, as well as "journalless" systems.

The new vocabulary and concept load in accounting is high. The teacher must incorporate a wide variety of techniques to make sure that students understand the many terms that are prerequisite to understanding concepts and principles.

Even with the increased use of nonmanual data processing, students should be able to complete basic mathematical computations. Instructional modules dealing with basic computations can be used to provide individualized instruction as needed.

A sound instructional program in accounting must incorporate both knowledge and skill. Opportunities must be provided for students to apply the knowledge gained. Students should understand why as well as how a transaction is completed.

An evaluation plan for an accounting course should include both formal and informal procedures. Short-answer tests, published and teacher-made, are appropriate for evaluating knowledge of theory, principles, concepts, and vocabulary. Problem-type tests are more appropriate for measuring application of knowledge. Several short problems are usually better than one long problem.

Student self-evaluation and teacher assessment of factors such as work habits, neatness, and the ability to follow directions can be accomplished through checklists and rating scales. The evaluation plan should be determined prior to beginning the course. Students should be familiar with the factors contributing to their grade and the weight of each.

References

[1] Henry Kaluza, "Teaching Accounting Concepts in Introductory Accounting Courses," *Business Education World* 52, no. 4 (March–April 1972): 14.

[2] David H. Weaver, "Implementing Career Education Concepts in the Accounting Program," *Business Education World* 54, no. 3 (January–February 1974): 13.

[3] *Mississippi School Bulletin: Business Education for Mississippi High Schools* (Jackson: State Department of Education, Division of Instruction, May 1976), pp. 16–17, 25–26.

[4] Weaver, "Implementing Career Education Concepts," p. 12.

[5] *Mississippi School Bulletin,* pp. 26–27.

[6] James M. Smiley, "Accounting Concepts and the First-Year High School Accounting Program," *Business Education World* 54, no. 1 (September–October 1973): 15.

[7] Lewis D. Boynton, *Methods of Teaching Bookkeeping-Accounting*, 2d ed. (Cincinnati: South-Western Publishing Company, 1970), pp. 119–20.

[8] J. Marshall Hanna, "Meeting Individual Needs in High School Accounting," *Business Education World* 55, no. 2 (November–December 1974): 29.

[9] David H. Weaver, J. Marshall Hanna, M. Herbert Freeman, Edward Brower, and James M. Smiley, *Accounting 10/12,* 3d ed. (New York: Gregg Division, McGraw-Hill Book Company, 1977), p. 110.

[10] Boynton, *Methods of Teaching,* p. 103.

[11] Ibid., p. 104.

[12] Weaver et al., *Accounting 10/12,* p. vi.

[13] Henry Kaluza, "Teaching the Modern Concept of the Accounting Process: The Systems Flowchart," *Business Education World* 53, no. 2 (November–December 1972): 19.

[14] Andrew J. Potts, "Teaching the Rules of Debit and Credit," *Business Education World* 54, no. 5 (May–June 1974): 27.

[15] Michael R. Wunsch, "Issues in Teaching Accounting" in *Business Education Yesterday, Today, and Tomorrow,* Ruth B. Woolschlager and E. Edward Harris, eds. National Business Education Yearbook, No. 14 (Reston, Va.: National Business Education Association, 1976), pp. 147–48.

[16] Ibid., p. 148.

[17] David H. Weaver, "A Potpourri of Comments About Journals," *Business Education World* 51, no. 1 (September–October 1970): 8.

[18] Ibid.

[19] Ibid.

[20] Boynton, *Methods of Teaching,* pp. 429–35.

[21] J. Edward Caldwell, "Initiative Makes the Difference: Techniques for Motivating Accounting Students" (Cincinnati: South-Western Publishing Company, 1978).

[22]Bruce L. Whitaker, "Accountants Need Verbal Skill Training," *Business Education Forum* 32, no. 7 (April 1978): 27.

[23]Ibid., p. 28.

[24]Ibid.

[25]Boynton, *Methods of Teaching,* p. 309.

[26]Lloyd L. Garrison, "Assessing Evaluation Techniques" in *Developing Vocational Competency in Bookkeeping and Accounting,* Eastern Business Teachers Association Yearbook, Vol. 40 (Somerville, N.J.: Eastern Business Teachers Association, 1967), p. 239.

[27]Mathilde Hardaway, *Testing and Evaluation in Business Education* (Cincinnati: South-Western Publishing Company, 1966), p. 250.

[28]Boynton, *Methods of Teaching,* p. 261.

[29]Ibid., pp. 269–70.

[30]Harm Harms and B. W. Stehr, *Methods in Vocational Business Education* (Cincinnati: South-Western Publishing Company, 1963), p. 372.

SUGGESTIONS FOR FURTHER STUDY

Brown, Kenneth W. "Competency-Based System for Accounting Instruction." *Business Education Forum* 31 (April 1977): 17–18.

Calhoun, Calfrey C., and Horner, Barbara. "Readability of First-Year Bookkeeping Texts Compared with Students' Reading Level." *Business Education Forum* 30 (October 1975): 20–21.

Fairchild, Charles. "Use of Practice Sets in Accounting Instruction." *Business Education Forum* 30 (February 1976): 19–20.

Francis, Robert M. "A Practical Approach to Financial Analysis." *Journal of Business Education* 52 (March 1977): 257–58.

Garrison, Lloyd L. "Individualizing Accounting Instruction." *Journal of Business Education* 52 (December 1976): 112–14.

————. "Using Simulation Sets in High School Accounting." *Balance Sheet* 59 (October 1977): 74–75, 86.

Geeding, Dona. "Accounting Simulations: Basic Systems." *Journal of Business Education* 52 (October 1976): 16–18.

Graham, John E. "Competency-Based Accounting Instruction." *Journal of Business Education* 52 (January 1977): 184–87.

Hubbard, John R., Jr. "College Preparatory Accounting." *Balance Sheet* 58 (February 1977): 240.

Klein, Donald. "An Alternative Model for Teaching Auditing." *Collegiate News and Views* 29 (Spring 1976): 3–4.

Mallue, Henry E. "The 'Time' Approach to Teaching Accounting." *Business Education Forum* 31 (January 1977): 24–27.

Meyer, Robert H. "Testing and Grading in High School Accounting." *Business Education Forum* 30 (April 1976): 17–18.

Musselman, Donald. "Notes and Interest—A Good Topic for Role Playing." *Balance Sheet* 59 (November 1977): 107–10, 137.

Musselman, Donald, and Musselman, Vernon A. *Lesson Plans in Accounting.* Danville, Ill.: The Interstate Printers & Publishers, 1978.

Nanassy, Louis C. "Current Research in Bookkeeping/Accounting and Basic Business Subjects." *Balance Sheet* 58 (March 1977): 280–81.

Thomas, Edward G. "Analyzing Financial Statements." *The Secretary* 37 (February 1977): 6–8, 14.

Wilson, David. "Break the Routine: Teach Taxes." *Business Education Forum* 31 (March 1977): 25, 28.

chapter 11

TEACHING BUSINESS MATHEMATICS

Business math is the practical use of mathematics as a tool. It contributes to the general education of all students by developing the basic mathematical skills and knowledge needed by individuals in their personal lives. It contributes to the vocational component of business education by developing competencies needed by individuals as workers, and may be considered a related skill for courses such as accounting, basic business, consumer economics, and office practice. Surveys indicate that approximately one-half of our adult population cannot determine the best buy on products such as boxes of detergent, and that fewer than one-quarter of all adults can balance a checkbook. Consequently, the development of such skills in the business education program becomes increasingly important.

module 11.1
OBJECTIVES AND CONTENT

Every day, in both our private and professional activities, we are required to use mathematical skills. In today's business environment, increasing numbers of young people find themselves in careers that require them to assemble, manipulate, and interpret all kinds of numerical data. These skills can be acquired or reinforced through the course in business mathematics.

After completing this module, you should be able to (1) identify the objectives for a course in business mathematics and (2) specify topics that should be incorporated in a business mathematics course.

OBJECTIVES

Business math is offered as a quarter, semester, or year-long course at the secondary and postsecondary levels. At the secondary level, it is open typically to students in any grade. In some programs, it is a prerequisite to accounting. The objectives of business math should reflect both personal and vocational applications, and should be reviewed and revised periodically to reflect current trends. For instance, students should learn to use metric system terminology; to solve and interpret mathematical problems in both English and metric systems; to interpret mathematical data such as interest, payroll deductions, graphs, charts, and so forth; and to use calculators to perform calculations.

Countless numbers of objectives could be written. You should write or select those objectives that provide students with the academic and vocational skills they will need. The following examples illustrate the kinds of terminal objectives that are appropriate in business math:[1]

1. Given a list of problems, the student should be able to add, subtract, multiply, and divide integers, decimals, and fractions, with a high degree of accuracy. The student should be able to apply these mathematical skills to practical applications; for example, preparation of bank reconciliation statements, maintaining a checkbook, determining means and other averages. He should be able to estimate answers by approximation and compare the answers with the actual, calculated solutions. He should be able to read a problem carefully, select the mathematical process or processes necessary for proper solution, and then solve the problem correctly.

2. The student should be able to change percents to fractions, write percents as decimals, represent fractions as percents, and apply this knowledge to business transactions.

3. The student should be able to solve practical problems which arise in an individual's daily economic life, such as determination of cash discounts, simple interest, compound interest, bank discounts, maturity date and maturity value of notes, installment plan carrying charges, and actual costs of owning a home or a car.

4. Given examples of graphic data, the student should answer a list of interpretative questions with 80 percent accuracy. The student should be able to differentiate between bar graph, line graph, and circle graph by writing a definition of each and showing an example. Given graph paper and specific business data to be shown in graphic form, the student should be able to prepare the type of graph requested.

5. Terminology used in merchandising will be correctly defined by the student. He will also correctly compute markups, markdowns, selling prices, gross profit, and trade discounts in accordance with standards set by the teacher.

6. The student should be able to compute interest on a savings account, determine premiums and cash value of a life insurance policy, determine cost of an investment in stocks, bonds, or real estate. The student should be able to compare methods of depreciation that might be used in determining income from real estate investments. From these computations and comparisons, the student will identify and compare investment possibilities.

7. The student should be able to describe the binary number system and its relationship to the computer, and write the binary equivalent of decimal numbers or vice versa.

8. The student should be able to list the conversions of measurements from English to the metric system of the units of length and weight, and correctly answer simple questions such as:
   a. How far is 100 m in the English system?
   b. It is 20 km between two villages in France. How far is this distance in miles?
   c. How many centimeters should there be in a 12-inch ruler?

9. Given time cards or narrative information, the student should be able to complete a payroll register, which includes computing regular and overtime pay for hourly and salaried employees, determining deductions an employer is required to make, listing deductions an employee may authorize, and identifying gross pay and net pay. Tax tables may be used.

10. Given narrative problems pertaining to daily living, the student should be able to compute the perimeter and area of a rectangle and triangle, the volume of a rectangular solid, and the circumference of a circle. The student should be able to solve problems involving use of common tables of weights and measures.

School systems are recognizing the importance of business mathematics concepts for all students as evidenced by their inclusion in basic skills needed by high school students. The following sample objectives for tenth grade students in Georgia are measured in statewide achievement tests.[2]

TENTH GRADE CRITERION-REFERENCED OBJECTIVES: MATHEMATICS

Number   *Objective*

1. Knows when to use addition, subtraction, multiplication, and division

2. Adds, subtracts, multiplies, or divides numbers written as decimals, mixed numbers, fractions, and percentages

. . . .

6. Computes simple and compound interest on savings accounts, loans, and service charges on installment buying

7. Can compute sales tax, profit, discount, cost, and selling price

8. Reads, interprets, and completes state and federal income tax forms and withholding exemption forms

9. Prepares computation for wages, reconciling a checkbook, and completing a bank deposit slip

CONTENT

The content of business math courses is sometimes organized around the mathematical application of business and personal situations, such as "Mathematics of Accounting" and "Records Management" or "Consumer

Math" which includes banking procedures, payroll, financial statements, depreciation expense, and consumer credit. Or content may be organized around topics such as income, measurement, discounts, investments, and income tax. All courses should have available, for those requiring it, a review of fundamental processes. The following topics are typical of those the business teacher may select in designing a course:

> banking, payroll, financial statements and analysis
> measurement, depreciation expense, consumer credit
> interest, installment loans and buying
> investments, taxes, insurance, stocks and bonds
> business ownership and bankruptcy, promissory notes
> statistics and display of business data, costing procedures
> pricing policy and return on investments, trade discounts, cash discounts
> preparing merchandise budgets, markup and markdown.
> transportation charges, commission sales, inventory, and turnover.

The content of business math is of importance to all business students since it focuses on topics not covered in general math or other business education courses.

module 11.1
LEARNING ACTIVITIES

1. Your school does not presently offer a course in business math although the faculty believes that such a course is needed. New courses have to be approved by the assistant superintendent in charge of curriculum and, ultimately, the local board of education. Prepare the following to be submitted:
   a. a brief justification for the course
   b. general course objectives
   c. content to be included.
2. Several states, including Pennsylvania, Oregon, and Florida, have identified objectives or basic skills that students should master prior to graduation from high school. Individually, or as a group activity, secure a copy of these objectives (or check with your state department of education to determine if your state has identified exit or other objectives for high school students). Report to the class on those objectives related specifically to business math.
3. Identify objectives or basic skills related to business math that you feel all persons leaving high school or postsecondary school should possess.

module 11.1
SELF-TEST

Note: The objectives in this module can be measured adequately by the activities.

module 11.2
INSTRUCTIONAL APPROACHES IN BUSINESS MATH

One of the major problems confronting teachers of business mathematics is to provide instructional materials and techniques appropriate for a diverse group of students. Age and achievement differences among students accentuate the need to make adaptations in both materials and processes of instruction. The use of calculators in the business math class, metrics and its implications for business education, and reading skills essential for success in math provide other examples of areas of concern for business teachers that are treated in this module.

After completing this module, you should be able to (1) identify and explain at least six different factors that should be considered in planning for individual differences, (2) describe the use of calculators in the business math class, (3) explain and illustrate three categories of basic instructional tasks in the math class, (4) specify the reading tasks related to business math and demonstrate their development, and (5) explain the role of metric instruction in business math.

INDIVIDUAL DIFFERENCES

The business teacher should expect students with a wide range of achievement backgrounds to enroll in a high school or postsecondary course in business math. Some students will be proficient in the fundamental processes of addition and subtraction, multiplication and division, while others will have knowledge of areas such as interest and measurement. To organize and conduct the class as one group is to invite boredom for those students who have previously mastered the skills, and frustration for those who have not.

The teacher may use instructional modules, programmed texts, worksheets, small-group instruction, commercially prepared kits, and teacher-directed lessons to provide for student differences. (See Chapter 5.) The activities in the course generally fall into three areas: computation, application of knowledge to problems, and interpretation of data either computed by the student or already available. All three kinds of activities will not necessarily be included in each module or assignment. Some modules will focus on fundamental operations such as vertical and horizontal addition; others, however, such as a module on income tax, will incorporate all three kinds of activities.

Several factors are important if the student is to achieve in an individualized program. The following are equally important in modules or teacher-directed instructional groups.

Pretest

As a diagnostic tool, the pretest is important in business math since some students will have already mastered the particular skill or knowledge under study. The pretest should incorporate activities similar to those the student is asked to perform in the module.

Terminology and symbols

Mathematics consists of many terms and symbols that will be new to the student as well as general terms, such as *foot* or *yard,* that have special meanings when applied to business math. Be sure to provide opportunities for the student to demonstrate understanding of the terms and symbols used in the module.

Explanations

One of the criticisms of some of the individualized math material is that it lacks adequate explanations for the student and is more appropriate for follow-up practice than for initial instruction. This weakness can be corrected by including ample explanations and examples, using both printed and audiovisual materials.

Practice

Each module or assignment must include several exercises in which the student practices the skill, under supervision if possible. Business-oriented or consumer-type problems should be used.

Immediate feedback

Build into your individualized program a plan for students to know as soon as possible whether their responses are correct or not. Include appropriate procedures for reviewing the processes and explanations for problems that have been answered incorrectly. The most effective instruction takes place immediately following the point when the student makes an error.

Reading level

Since an individualized program uses a variety of written (non-printed) materials, the teacher has to decide whether the reading level of the materials is appropriate for the students. For those deficient in reading skills, rewrite directions and explanations in a simpler manner and use nonprinted instructional materials, such as transparencies, slides, and tapes.

Word problems

Prior to beginning an individualized approach, students must know how to read word problems. Since this is a difficult area for many students, step-by-step procedures with accompanying practice should be planned.

In addition to individualized material for the content of the course, the teacher should assemble material or modules covering fundamental skills such as horizontal and vertical addition, subtraction, multiplication, division, fractions, decimals, percentage, and the process of solving word problems. For maintenance of skills already developed, the teacher may find it helpful to incorporate two or three drill exercises in each module.

For motivational purposes, the teacher may want students to begin with topics of current interest. "An effective individualized learning system should permit shuffling and sequencing of topics so that the teacher can capitalize on each student's current interest or needs. Few students will be excited if the course is started with a review of the fundamental processes. But some students may become interested in beginning with a topic for which they see immediate value—such as computing automobile insurance premiums or the arithmetic involved in an installment purchase of a motorcycle."[4]

Gunther suggests the use of mathematics laboratory cards to provide for individual differences as well as opportunities to apply principles, understandings, concepts, and skills to businesslike settings. He labels cards A–1, A–2, B–1, B–2, C–1, C–2, and so forth, with C cards the most difficult. The following are examples of laboratory cards that teachers can assemble or design with a zero budget:

> A–1 You are the star salesman at a large used-car lot. Find out what rate of commission such a salesman usually is paid. Your sales for the last sales period were as follows: two cars of the "luxury" class, nearly new; three family sedans, middle priced, two years old; four compact cars, three years old; three fun cars, two or three years old; two "clunkers." Use car ads from a newspaper to locate cars and prices fitting these descriptions. Find out how much your commission would be on these sales. Report any observations you may have about used-car prices.

> C–2 Obtain the annual report of a corporation in a field that interests you. Suppose that you are the president of that corporation and that its board of directors asked for your analysis of the probable course of the corporation over the next three years. Using the annual report for data, prepare your report to the board.[4]

These cards can be made to merge with textbook work so as to reinforce concepts included in the course.

CALCULATORS

Business math classes should reflect the increased use of calculators and computers in business. This does not mean that students do not know how to perform fundamental operations, but it does reflect a shift in emphasis. With the aid of calculators, the teacher can emphasize applications and interpretations since students do not spend excessive time in completing their calculations.

There are at least two weaknesses to consider in the use of calculators and computers in the instructional program: The machine cannot determine whether the numbers punched into it are correct, and the calculator cannot determine what mathematical process to use. To counteract the first weakness, the teacher should emphasize the skill of estimation. For instance, if the student were determining the actual cost of a $375 portable television set carrying a 10 percent discount, he or she should know immediately that $37.50 is the discount and that $40 subtracted from $375 would mean that the set costs approximately $330. However, if the student punched .01 rather than .10 into the machine, the discount would be $3.75, for a cost of $371.25. The student's estimated answer of $330 should result in rechecking of the computation for errors and, if no errors were found, rechecking of the estimation. A considerable difference in the estimation and the computed answer should serve as a signal to students of a possible error. The teacher should plan for mental and paper-and-pencil estimation problems to be included in the instructional program at frequent intervals. This skill must be taught and usually begins with principles of rounding. Many of the business math textbooks contain exercises on estimation that can serve as guides to the teacher.

Students with learning disabilities and mixed dominance (see Chapter 5) should be especially careful to check numbers for transpositions; in such cases, 375 may be read and recorded as 357.

Help in overcoming the second weakness—deciding what mathematical process to use—is provided for the student in the step-by-step process of solving word problems as well as periodic review of key terms. The teacher can include exercises in which students identify the mathematical processes they would use but do not actually complete the problem.

These two weaknesses should not discourage teachers from using calculators in business math classes. "It is no longer feasible or realistic to conduct business math classes without modern equipment. As a matter of fact, the lack of such equipment in itself gives a musty air to the subject, making it even more difficult for students to have an interest and respect for it. The price of calculators has decreased to the point where a battery of them can and should become standard equipment in the business math classroom."[5]

INSTRUCTIONAL TASKS

The business math course includes at least three categories of instructional tasks: helping students to develop understanding and mastery of new concepts, relationships, and skills; maintaining understandings and skills previously attained; and securing maximum transfer of learning for personal and professional use.

Developing new skills and knowledge

The key word in this category of tasks is "new" since, considering the range of individual differences, "new skills" vary among students. For the teacher to go through the motions of explaining content that students already know is a waste of time. Diagnostic testing is of prime importance to determine "new skills" for each student. (See Module 11.3.)

To develop new skills, the teacher plans lessons or modules that incorporate the following components:

PURPOSE.   Specify the purpose for learning the skill or knowledge, relating it as nearly as possible to personal or career objectives of the student.

TERMS AND SYMBOLS.   Introduce students to the terminology (general and specific) and symbols that are needed to master the skills in a given lesson or module.

NEW SKILLS.   Explain thoroughly and demonstrate the new skills. Two of the most common faults in teaching math involve "telling" students and assuming that they understand the content, and covering too much in too short a time period. The development of a new concept or skill is a slow process, requiring practice, drill, and review.

PRACTICE.   The presentation of the new skill should be immediately followed by opportunities for students to practice it under teacher supervision. Whether students are working on an individual basis or have been grouped for instruction, the teacher should observe them during practice, giving help as needed. Teacher observation should include the process used in completing a problem as well as the actual computation. The most effective time to provide remedial or corrective instruction is at the point when the student makes an error.

EVALUATION.   Incorporate a posttest to determine whether students have mastered the skills incorporated in the module assignment before going to another topic. Provide material for those students needing additional review and practice.

Maintaining skills and understanding

In addition to developing new skills, periodic reviews and drills are necessary to maintain mastery. Drills and reviews differ in their purposes. Drills are concerned with the *automatization* of relatively detailed processes; for instance, a student may practice (drill) on the multiplication tables until he or she knows them automatically. Review has two functions: one is the fixation and retention of facts, concepts, and processes, while the other is the organization of details into a coherent whole so that students see the relationship of the various parts to each other and to the whole. For example, the teacher could plan a review lesson on how to figure commissions, with each step related to the ultimate goal. The review could include the processes of changing percentages to decimals and multiplication as well as the problem-solving step of knowing how to arrive at the solution.

Drills are an important part of mathematics instruction and should be developed and implemented according to learning principles discussed in earlier chapters. Specifically, they should be (1) related to interests and needs of students; (2) short, probably no more than five to ten minutes in length since practice distributed in small amounts is more meaningful than an extended period; (3) special, concentrating on a particular skill. Initially, drills should be completed under close supervision so that mistakes can be detected and eliminated. Spend some time relating the purpose of the drill to the total operation. Too frequently the tendency to overemphasize proficiency in mechanical skills at the expense of developing understanding is a characteristic of drills.

In developing a maintenance program of drill and review as part of the total instructional program, the teacher should remember these guidelines:

1. Select materials that include significant skills, principles, concepts, relationships, and problem situations. Omit the trivia that may be interesting but not essential.
2. Distribute drill and review sessions throughout the course at increasing intervals and decreasing amounts.
3. Build or select drills that are diagnostic so that the student can detect his or her own weaknesses.
4. Assemble a variety of supplemental practice materials that can be used for remedial work.
5. Design each set of drills for uniform scoring and record keeping so that students can keep records of their own progress.

Securing transfer of learning

The final step in the instructional process requires the student to use skills and knowledges to solve problems. (See Chapter 2, "Transfer of Training.") Transfer of learning is not automatic; the teacher must provide activities that enable students to apply their mathematics skills and knowledges in businesslike situations, pulling together a variety of skills into realistic problem-solving situations.

READING SKILLS

The ability to compute correct answers is directly related to the student's ability to read and interpret problems. There are at least four major classes of reading tasks involved in math materials: (1) understanding symbols and specialized devices, (2) understanding general organization of the material, (3) developing the vocabulary, and (4) reading to solve the problem.

Understanding symbols

Math symbols are, in effect, a language that must be learned to the point of automation if the student is to be proficient in their use. The importance of symbols can be dramatized to students in an activity such as the following:

Directions: Solve the following problems quickly, using this symbol code: $+$ = divide; $-$ = multiply; $\times$ = subtract; $\div$ = add.

$6 \times 2 =$	$9 + 3 =$
$4 - 1 =$	$7 \times 5 =$
$8 + 4 =$	$9 - 3 =$
$6 \div 2 =$	$8 \div 4 =$

(Note how many students will fail to follow the directions!)

Activities such as the following can be used to teach symbols:

$I = P \cdot R \cdot T$ (Interest equals principle times rate times time.)
$I = P \times R \times T$ (Put in written form.)
Interest equals principle times rate times time. (Put in symbol form.)
$I =$ (I'll start and you complete the sentence. Interest equals. . . .)

Understanding organization

Spend a few minutes explaining to students how the material (module, textbook, assignment sheet, programmed material, and so forth) is arranged, including any special features.

Developing vocabulary

Vocabulary is the backbone of the instructional material and requires a systematic study of words. The business math teacher is concerned with developing both the technical vocabulary and the interchangeable or common vocabulary. When developing the technical vocabulary related to math, make few assumptions that students know the words, and be sure to include some form of vocabulary evaluation in your pretests. Pronounce the words carefully and correctly; if possible, write the words as you pronounce them. (See Chapters 9 and 10 for suggestions for teaching terminology.)

An effective way to introduce new topics in math is through vocabulary. An equally important task is the development of interchangeable vocabulary, that is, common words with multiple meanings. For instance, terms such as *yard, foot, table, product, root, proper, solution,* and so on, have meanings unique to math as well as meanings that are equally unique to other fields.

Solving problems

Many students have difficulty reading and solving word problems. Teachers can help by presenting skills that make reading to solve problems easier. Alert students to key words in the problems that give clues to procedures to be used, words such as *minimum, average, annual, share equally, combined,* and *per.* If pretests indicate that students are having difficulty with word problems, begin with verbal problems. Read a brief problem to the students, have them tell what they are to find out, the processes to be used, the mathematical sentence, and estimated answer. This approach helps students to learn the process of solving word problems before they have to read the problem. (You may present the problem on a transparency so that students can follow as you read.)

Until students become proficient in solving problems, have them answer questions such as the following as part of the problem-solving process:

1. Before solving the problem:
   a. What am I asked to find out? (Amount of discount or total payment)
   b. What information am I given? (This step helps students to pick out relevant information in the problem—total price, $120; discount rate, 5 percent)
   c. What mathematical processes will I use? (Multiply)
   d. What is the math sentence? ($120 \times .05 =$)
   e. What is my estimated answer? ($6.00)
2. Solve problem.
3. Compare estimated and computed answers.
4. Check computations and/or estimate if there is considerable variance between estimate and answer.

METRICS

The changeover to metrics is a gradual process with much being learned through daily use. Business math classes should include instruction in the use of the metric system. Students need to learn the meaning of terms such as *liter, meter,* and *gram,* as well as six prefixes: *milli* (one-thousandth), *centi* (one-hundredth), *deci* (one-tenth), *deka* (ten times), *hecto* (one hundred times), *kilo* (one thousand times). Since the system is based on tens, the math processes involve multiplying or dividing in multiples of ten. Teaching fractions becomes of decreasing importance in the metric system, while decimals become increasingly important.

Initially it will be necessary to teach students to convert from the English system to the metric system. Later, as students become more familiar with metric measurements, less emphasis will be placed on teaching conversions. To help students "get a feel for metrics," point out how the new units compare to the familiar measures of the English system: 1 liter = approximately 1 quart; 1 meter = slightly longer than a yard; 1 kilogram = about 2 pounds. A rule of thumb for converting Celsius (temperature) to Fahrenheit is to double the Celsius temperature and add 30; conversely, subtract 30 from Fahrenheit temperature and divide the remainder by 2 to get Celsius temperature. To help students "think metric," include a variety of exercises involving estimating and measuring to check results.

module 11.2
LEARNING ACTIVITIES

1. Begin a collection of drills and problems to use in providing for student differences in your classes.
2. Prepare a module or learning package for teaching a math fundamental. (The evaluation portion can be one of your activities in the next module.)
3. Outline a mini-lesson for teaching vocabulary words or symbols of your choice. Be prepared to demonstrate.
4. Design a visual for use in teaching metrics.
5. Select a math word problem and prepare a work sheet for developing skills in solving the problem.
6. Select one page, or portion, from a math book and rewrite it to simplify the reading level.
7. Outline a format you could use for a business math lesson.

module 11.2
SELF-TEST

1. Name and briefly explain at least five factors to be considered in planning for individual differences.
2. Summarize three categories of basic instructional tasks.
3. Defend or refute the use of calculators in business math.
4. Name and summarize four reading related tasks in math.

module 11.3
EVALUATION OF STUDENT PERFORMANCE

Evaluation of student performance in business mathematics is an ongoing process involving daily observation by the teacher, diagnostic testing to assess individual strengths and weaknesses, and mastery testing to determine the absorption of content in the module or unit just completed. The evaluation plan should allow for both student self-evaluation and teacher evaluation of student performance as a basis for the next step in the instructional program.

After completing this module, you should be able to (1) explain and illustrate diagnostic testing in business mathematics, (2) list and give examples of three general types of items that might be included on a math test, (3) construct sample objective items for a business math test, and (4) explain and demonstrate a scoring plan for business math tests.

Since business math is a performance or skill subject, the student's daily work serves as a means of evaluation. Through observation and teacher-student interactions, the teacher can become aware of difficulties and provide "on-the-spot" instruction and/or remediation. Immediate feedback on the solving of problems allows students to evaluate their own performances, noting areas of strength and weakness.

DIAGNOSTIC TESTING

Students enter business math classes with varying degrees of skill; thus, it is important for the teacher to assess individual performance so as to plan appropriate instruction based on student strengths and weaknesses. Teacher-made or commercially prepared diagnostic tests can help the teacher and students to identify specific strengths and weaknesses.

At least two types of diagnostic tests may be used effectively in business math:

1. Module or chapter pretest. These tests contain a representative sample of items found in a given instructional unit. (Be sure to include word problems, interpretation items, vocabulary, and application/decision-making items, as well as computation where appropriate.) Some textbooks include pretests as part of each chapter.

2. Fundamental operations. These tests measure student competency in fundamental operations, such as addition, subtraction, multiplication, division, decimals, and fractions. They may be given at the beginning of the school year or as part of a series of tests. However, since student performance in the business math course is partially dependent on the ability to perform fundamental operations, the teacher must identify at an early point those students needing extensive review and those needing only limited review.

When constructing the tests, you may want to group together those items measuring the same competency, or list the item number related to a given competency on a master sheet. Decide the number of items students must answer correctly to satisfactorily master the competency such as five of seven or four of five. When scoring, consider more than the answer; try to identify the competency that the student has not mastered, such as grouping or multiplication tables.

To help compile results into usable form after scoring the test, prepare a form on which you list student names on the left axis and the competencies across the right axis. Indicate by a plus or minus sign (+ or −) whether the student demonstrated mastery on each concept or competency. (Remember that you probably assigned three to five items to measure each competency and you specified the number of items to be answered correctly to demonstrate mastery.) A horizontal review of results gives a summary of individual performance on all concepts, competencies, and objectives, while a vertical review shows group and class performance on each. The teacher can then identify those students needing additional instruction. This same approach to analysis of data can be used with posttests or mastery tests following instruction. The form below is illustrative:

| | COMPETENCIES | | | | |
NAME	ADDITION VERTICAL 1-COLUMN	ADDITION VERTICAL 2-COLUMN	ADDITION HORIZONTAL 1-COLUMN	ADDITION HORIZONTAL 2-COLUMN	ETC.
Mary Allen	+	+	+	+	
Bob Brown	+	−	+	−	
Sue Davies	+	−	−	−	

MASTERY TESTS

The majority of items on a business math test are performance items. Occasionally, however, the teacher may want to include some multiple-choice or true-false items to conduct a quick check of comprehension.

1. When 17.35 is divided by 10, the answer is (a) 1735, (b) 1.735, (c) .1735, (d) 173.5.

    ———

2. A company received a bill with the following notation: 2/10, n/30. This means the company can deduct 2 percent of the bill if it is paid within ten days of the

    date of billing. (True or false)   ———

One of the mistakes sometimes found in math tests is that the items measure other than the content of the course. This is particularly true in word problems where the teacher is using businesslike applications or interpretation items. For example, "a couple filing a joint federal income tax return claims three children as exemptions. What is the amount of exemption for the children?" Students who have not had a unit of instruction on income taxes could not solve the problem although the process (multiplication) might be well within their capability range. Sometimes word problems are so long and include so many technical terms that the test becomes a reading test rather than a math test.

Test items in mathematics generally cover three types of skills: computation, application or problem-solving, and interpretation. Computation problems are generally associated with fundamental operations:

Add: 2,475
         1,293
         <u>3,541</u>

Subtract: 24.1
            <u>9.87</u>

Multiply: $3/4 \times 1/2 =$

Divide: $25.75 \div 0.5 =$

Estimate the sum: 392
                     210
                     <u>475</u>

Round off these numbers to the nearest tenth: 683, 77, 101, 44

Application items are generally word problems in which the students select the correct process and complete the computation:

Alan is temporarily employed at Circular Bonding Company. His take-home pay is $101.47 per week. The job will last for eight weeks. Alan plans to deposit 90 percent of his earnings in his savings account. How much will Alan have deposited in his account at the end of three weeks? Eight weeks?

With computation time reduced by the use of calculators, interpretation problems are also included in the instructional program and should be evaluated. The following is an example of an interpretative item:

Directions: The graph on page 430 depicts the units produced and the units scrapped during the month of August. What conclusion can you reach regarding the relationship of units produced and units scrapped?

SCORING THE TEST

The weight or number of points assigned to each problem on a math test should be in proportion to the steps required to complete the problem. Natural scoring, that is, 1 point for each operation selected correctly and 1 point for each operation computed correctly, is recommended.

Sample: A watch is priced at $59.50 plus excise tax of 10% and a local sales tax of 4%. For what amount should you write a check to pay for the purchase of the watch?
Step 1. $59.50 \times .10 = 5.95$
Step 2. $59.50 \times .04 = 2.38$
Step 3. $5.95 + 2.38 + 59.50 = \$67.83$

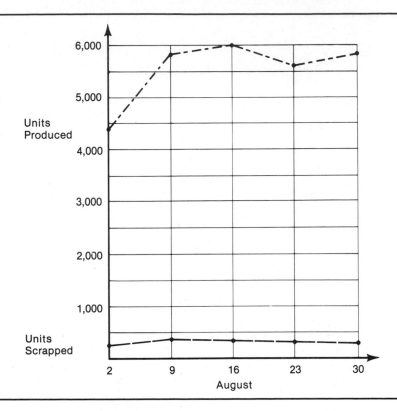

By allowing 1 point for each process selected correctly, and 1 point for each operation computed correctly, the student would earn 6 points. However, if in Step 2 the student had given the answer as .24 rather than 2.38, that answer and the final answer (5.95 + .24 + 59.50 = 65.69) would have been incorrect and the student would have earned 4 points.

When preparing the test, prepare a key showing the processes, the answers, and the points for each of the test items:

1. X 5.95
    X 2.38
    + 67.83

One point for each process and computation equals 6 possible points.

module 11.3
LEARNING ACTIVITIES

1. Outline a diagnostic test for use in business math. List the competencies to be included, the number of test items for each competency (use any material to help you identify the competencies), and the number of items to be answered correctly to indicate mastery. Prepare the form you will use to summarize the data.

2. Prepare one sample item for each of the following tasks: computation, problem-solving, and interpretation.
3. Construct at least two different objective-type items for use in business math.
4. Review a pretest or mastery test that accompanies a current business math text. What percentage of the items·involves computation? application? interpretation? How does this compare with the actual content of the chapter?
5. Construct a pre/post test to accompany the module you designed for Module 11.2.

module 11.3
SELF-TEST

1. Why are diagnostic tests important in business math?
2. Explain a scoring plan you would endorse for use in business math.
3. Why are daily teacher observations beneficial in business math?

SUMMARY

Business math contributes to both the general education and vocational preparation of students. Each day, individuals in their personal and business lives are confronted with situations that require the use of mathematical skills in computation, application, and interpretation. Objectives and content in business math should focus on the use of math as a tool so as to reflect the skills and knowledges needed by individuals as consumers and workers.

The achievement and ability levels of students enrolled in business math vary considerably, presenting a challenge to the teacher. When assembling or developing materials to provide for these individual differences, the teacher should consider several factors that can affect student success; these include pretest, terminology, explanations, practice, immediate feedback, readability/reading level, and word problems. Modules covering fundamental operations will be beneficial for students needing remediation or additional practice.

A current trend in math instruction involves the use of calculators. Their use cuts down on the amount of time students need to complete basic computations, allowing more time for application and interpretation. The instructional program is generally centered about three major categories: developing mastery of new skills, knowledge, and concepts; maintaining previously learned skills, concepts, and knowledge; and transferring skills and knowledge to personal and career use.

The ability to compute correct answers is directly related to the student's ability to read and interpret the problems. There are at least four major classes of reading tasks: comprehending symbols, understanding organization of material, developing vocabulary, and reading to solve problems.

Business math classes should include instruction in metrics with emphasis on terms such as *liter, meter, gram, Celsius,* and six metric prefixes, plus practice in estimation and problem solving using the metric system. Initially, students must learn some of the metric units that are similar to more familiar measures in the English system, such as meter (about 1 yard) and liter (approximately 1 quart).

Evaluation of student progress in business math is an ongoing process with the teacher observing student performance daily and offering immediate help as needed. Diagnostic tests provide the teacher and students with information to plan an appropriate instructional program. Module or chapter pretests and tests of fundamental operations are examples of diagnostic tests.

Most test items in business math are computation, application, or interpretation items requiring students to (1) complete an operation, (2) read a problem, select the correct process, and complete the computation, and/or (3) interpret data already available or computed by the student. Some problems call for the student to complete all three processes. Occasionally, the teacher may want to use a few multiple-choice or true-false items.

The weight or points allowed for each test item should be in relation to the number of steps required to complete the problem, with a point allowed for each process correctly selected and a point for each operation correctly computed. Thus, more involved problems receive more points, and a student earns points for parts of an item answered correctly.

References

[1] *Handbook for Business Education in Iowa* (Des Moines: Iowa Business Education Association and State Department of Public Instruction, 1972), p. 117.

[2] *Tenth Grade Criterion-Referenced Objectives, Mathematics* (Atlanta: Georgia State Department of Education, 1978).

[3] Robert A. Schultheis, "Individualizing Instruction in Business Arithmetic," *Journal of Business Education* 51, no. 3 (December 1975): 111.

[4] John L. Gunther, "Laboratory Techniques for the Business Mathematics Class," *Journal of Business Education* 47, no. 5 (February 1972): 191, 192.

[5] Esther D. Flashner, "Maintaining High Standards in Business Mathematics and Accounting," *Business Education World* 55, no. 3 (January–February 1975): 16.

SUGGESTIONS FOR FURTHER STUDY

Carr, Glenna D. "Using Tape Analysis to Teach Arithmetic and Office Machines." *Business Education World* 51 (January–February 1971): 14–15.

Fiber, Larry R. "Business Math in Transition." *American Vocational Journal* 50 (March 1975): 40–42.

Huffman, Harry. "How Business Teachers Should Plan for Metrication." *Business Education Forum* 28 (December 1973): 17–19.

Karnes, Delbert D. "Challenge for the Business Mathematics Teacher." *Journal of Business Education* 51 (October 1975): 25–26.

Odom, Jeffrey V. "The Current Status of Metric Conversion." *Business Education Forum* 28 (December 1973): 5–7.

Selden, William. "Metrication." *Journal of Business Education* 50 (February 1975): 198–202.

Stull, William A. "A Team-Competitive Approach to Teaching Merchandising Mathematics." *Balance Sheet* 58 (March 1977): 255–56.

Swindle, Robert E. "Individualized Progression in Business Mathematics. *Journal of Business Education* 49 (March 1974): 239–40.

Voelker, Pamela. "A Motivational Technique for Business Math." *Balance Sheet* 59 (September 1977): 11–12.

chapter 12

TEACHING BUSINESS MACHINES

The amount of paper work to be processed and the increasing number of machines used in business indicate the need for training students in the operation of office machines. Office machine instruction, while not an end in itself, is a means by which employees more effectively and efficiently handle the increasing amounts of paper work.

module 12.1
OBJECTIVES AND CONTENT

The business worker of the present and future must be skilled in a wide variety of machines, including calculating, reproduction, word processing, and data processing equipment. Consequently, business education programs at the secondary and postsecondary levels must include appropriate training for students on representative machines.

After completing this module, you should be able to (1) explain curriculum organizations used to develop machine skills, (2) identify objectives associated with the business machines instructional program, and (3) specify content to be included in a business machines course.

Schools differ in curriculum organization used to develop machine skills. In some schools, business machines is a separate course open to all students; in others, typewriting is a prerequisite. In still other schools, business machines is part of the content of other courses, such as office practice, business math, accounting, or advanced typewriting. Under the latter arrangement, enrollment is not open to all students. As a separate course, office/business machines is usually offered at the eleventh or twelfth grade level, close to application time for students planning to enter the labor market after high school graduation.

Business machines are also incorporated in skills labs at the secondary and postsecondary levels. In these individualized programs, students develop skills in typewriting, shorthand, and office machines while working simultaneously under the direction of a master teacher and one or more assistants.

The objectives of the business machines course vary, depending on length and whether it is a unit of instruction within other courses or a separate course. Examples of desirable student outcomes are as follows: (1) to develop marketable skills in the use of adding machines and calculators; (2) to demonstrate proficiency in machine transcription; (3) to exhibit behaviors characteristic of successful office employees, such as good work habits, dependability, accuracy, and neatness. Each school will expand or limit its particular objectives depending on available time for instruction, accessible equipment and materials, and the career objectives of students.

The content of the business machines course usually includes calculators—ten key, printing, rotary, electronic, electronic printing; adding machines—ten key, full key; copying-duplicating machines—copier, fluid duplicator, mimeograph duplicator, offset duplicator; and dictating-transcribing machines. Students develop skills in operating the machines, in using machines in businesslike applications, and in selecting appropriate machines or equipment for a specific job.

If a separate course in office machines is not offered, how can these skills be developed? Training in the use of calculators can be introduced, to a limited degree, in accounting and business math classes. In some advanced typing classes, a mini-unit on reprographics is incorporated. Some time may be spent in advanced shorthand-transcription on machine transcription. A unit on office machines is usually included in an office practice course.

module 12.1
LEARNING ACTIVITIES

1. Select an educational level of your choice, a school size and business education department size of your choice. Write a letter of justification to your school administrator for (a) new office machines as equipment for a separate course or (b) new office machines to be used in an existing course.
2. Specify the office machines objectives for your choice in Activity 1. List the machines to be included. (If you choose an integrated approach, list the machines to be included in each course.) Be specific, indicating each type of machine, such as ten-key adding, electronic printing, and so forth.
3. Review the literature or interview several business teachers or the state director of business education to determine how office machines skills are developed.

module 12.1
SELF-TEST

1. Briefly justify teaching office machines at the secondary and/or postsecondary levels.
2. List the types of machines to be included in an office machines course.
3. Specify at least three different kinds of skills to be treated in office machines instruction.

module 12.2
CONDUCTING THE COURSE

Effective instructional programs in office machines provide for skill development on the machines and equipment used in business and reflect the changes brought about by automation. Selecting and maintaining modern equipment and guiding students in appropriate instruction necessitate a close working relationship between the school and the business community.

After completing this module, you should be able to (1) identify criteria for selecting office machines, (2) specify three major areas of instruction in office machines and summarize the content of each area, (3) explain the role of individualized instruction in office machines, and (4) summarize key responsibilities of the office machines instructor.

SELECTING MACHINES

The first step in purchasing equipment or machines for a business education department or for a business itself is to determine need. Need is a logical outgrowth of program objectives. Surveys of machines used in the employment community, follow-up studies of graduates to determine machines and equipment used on the job, and a review of the literature help the business teacher to establish the need for specific machines.

After the needs have been identified, the business education staff specifies the kind and number of machines. Several factors should be considered during the selection process, including the purpose of instruction, available space, cost of the machines, projected enrollment, use of one brand or several brands, and the separate course versus the integrated approach. Kinzey [1] offers these suggestions to business teachers in selecting equipment:

1. The machines selected should be basic in nature. However, they should not be so specialized that employers prefer to train their own operators, nor so complicated they they are inappropriate for classroom use. They should never be so simple that training in their operation is a waste of time.
2. The machines should be appropriate for training beginning office workers. Placement opportunities for trained operators should be good, or operation skill should be valuable to those students entering beginning office jobs.
3. Any machine should be typical of its class in its technique and operation. . . .Choose the model having the features that are needed for instruction. . . .Unnecessary features often add to the cost.
4. The maintenance cost as well as the original price of the equipment should be considered. Economical and readily available maintenance service is of primary importance in the selection of any piece of equipment for classroom use.
5. There should be adequate room in the laboratory for the use of the machine. Convenient and safe electrical outlets should either be available or easy to install.

6. Whenever the budget is very limited, the possibility of renting equipment should be investigated. Sometimes renting is less expensive than buying. It may provide the use of a variety of machines for about the same cost as the purchase of one machine. Also, it may provide more up-to-date equipment and it affords a trial period on which to base future purchasing decisions.

Olson recommends that several types of cost be considered in purchasing machines.[2]

1. Cash outlay cost must be justified as a budget item for a particular year. (After writing the specifications, you will probably want to use formal bidding procedures.) If the cost is too much for one year's budget, consider a lease-purchase plan. Under a lease-purchase arrangement, the institution becomes the owner of the equipment after the lease-purchase period expires. By leasing, the factor of obsolescence becomes the responsibility of the vendor who will have to keep the equipment up to date.
2. Annual cost is determined by estimating the number of years the equipment is likely to last and the trade-in value at the end of its *useful* life in the program. Subtract the trade-in value from the cost and divide by the number of useable years. Add estimated annual maintenance cost to this figure.
3. Cost per student is determined by dividing the annual cost by the number of students who will use the machine.

Machine maintenance is available through several plans. You may (1) sign a maintenance agreement for a flat fee covering service on the machine as needed—usually such agreements reimburse both the cost of labor and parts; (2) call a service person for each repair as needed—a per-call arrangement tends to be more expensive on an individual basis; (3) employ a district or local service staff provided the school system is large enough to justify employment of one or more persons. You will have to check with your administrator about the school policy in effect on maintenance of machines and equipment.

MAJOR INSTRUCTIONAL AREAS

Instruction in office machines typically includes calculators and adding machines, copying and duplicating machines, and machine transcription. Word processing equipment, including the magnetic tape or magnetic card electric typewriter, text editing and composing equipment, and other automatic typewriter-actuated equipment, are coming into use in some schools.

Calculators and adding machines

The ten-key keyboard is commonly used in calculators and adding machines. Students need to learn the keyboard by touch and to develop speed and accuracy in its use. Paced drills should be used to develop speed and accuracy. Machines such as the tachistoscope or controlled reader can be used to project numbers at a continuous pace. First, you project the problems at a slow speed; then, after students have checked their answers, repeat the problems at a faster pace. For the final drill, drop back to a slow speed. Always have students check their papers for number of correct problems. Teacher-paced drills can be conducted with a stopwatch and a series of problems having a cumulative digit count and the correct answers. Students work for one to five minutes, starting over again if they complete the drill before the time is up. By tape recording the starting and stopping commands along with the elapsed time, students can participate in teacher-paced drills on an individual or small-group basis. To figure the gross speed, divide the total number of digits by the number of minutes.

Rhodes [3] has developed numeric timing copy for office machines students to attain ten-key stroking skill. He recommends weekly measurements of students' numbers-a-minute stroking skill. All students using the same numbers timing copy are administered five one-minute trials; the best of each student's five trials is scored. For a class of twenty-five students, usually only one or two will fail to achieve a correct total on one of the five timing trials. The majority of the instruction time devoted to number timings involves guided timings, each student striving for an individualized goal. Five one-minute guided timings are administered daily for the first four days of the week, followed by the weekly measurement on the fifth day. At the end of a twelve-week quarter, the normal distribution of student numbers-a-minute rates indicates that an A student should key at approximately fifty numbers-a-minute, with the D student keying at approximately twenty-five numbers-a-minute.

Instruction on calculators and adding machines should include characteristics of the different machines. For example:

The ten-key adding-listing machine—widely used for the adding and subtracting function, the ten-key touch operation has been adapted to bookkeeping machines, keypunch machines, and electronic calculators as well as to the telephone. It is a good choice for classroom instruction.

The full-key adding-listing machine is appropriate for addition and subtraction of long listed amounts. *Not* operated by touch, the zeros on the full-key machine need not be depressed.

The printing calculator is an economical, basic ten-key machine designed to perform fundamental operations of arithmetic with speed and accuracy.

The rotary calculator is a full-key, nonprinting machine that was widely used before electronic calculators. It has a speed disadvantage when compared to the electronic calculator On nonprint machines, it is necessary to check results by repeating the problem.

The electronic calculator is a ten-key machine characterized by speed, efficiency, and quietness. Models vary in degree of sophistication of function. Available in both battery and electrically operated models, the electronic calculator has programmable functions and internal memories. It is available with visible screen or printing features.

Instruction on the electronic calculator, as on all machines, involves motor and mental skills in operating the machine and using it as a tool in problem solving. In order to perform these tasks effectively, Bormann[4] recommends that students develop an understanding of fractions, percentages, decimal equivalents, rounding procedures, business problems (amount and percent proration; invoice extensions and totals; depreciation; simple and compound interest; payroll; amount and percent of change; inventory; income tax; standard deviation; selling price, cost, and markup; and so on). Students should also be able to apply proficiently the operating controls, the problem-solving process, and fundamental electronic operation. The following business problem illustrates how basic electronic operations are related to the solution:[5]

Problem 1. Borrowed $950 at 7.5% interest for 90 days. (Assume 365-day year.) Determine the maturity value of the loan.

Solution

maturity value $= P + I$

$$I = \frac{P \times r \times t}{365}$$

Electronic Operations

950 × .075 × 90 — Multifactor Multiplication: use transfer operation

6412.5 ÷ 365 — Combined Successive Calculations: use transfer operation
Division: use automatic operation

950 + 17.57 — Combined Successive Calculations: use transfer operation
Addition: use automatic operation

answer $= \$967.57$

Reprographics: Copying and duplicating machines

Curriculum offerings in the area or reprographics vary, depending on the level and objectives of instruction, available equipment, and amount of time for instruction. The content of reprographics focuses on three major areas: operation of machines, application of skills to businesslike settings, and decision making regarding the process most appropriate for the specific job. Four major types of machines should be included: copiers, fluid duplicators, stencil duplicators, and offset duplicators.

COPIERS. "Instruction should include the use of various types of copiers, their main features, their initial cost, cost of maintenance, per copy cost, and operator cost."[6] Schools, depending on size, probably have at least one copier for demonstration purposes or for students to operate. The simplicity of operation and the availability of copiers greatly reduce the time required for instruction. If several types of copiers are available in your community, have students make copies on different machines and bring them to class to compare for quality. (The original copy for student use should be typical of that used in business—letter, memo, table, form.)

STENCIL AND FLUID DUPLICATORS.   The amount of emphasis on stencil and fluid duplicating depends on their use in your geographic or employment area. Preparation of fluid masters and stencils is normally included in typewriting courses; however, modules covering preparation should be available for students who need to review the procedures.

Initial instruction focuses on the fluid duplicating process, parts of the machine, and operating the machine, including simple maintenance and care in running copies typical of those in business offices (cards, sheets of varying lengths, both sides of paper, and bulletins). In addition, students should know about various types of machines and their features, cost of machines and their maintenance and operation, advantages and disadvantages, and speed of operation. Problems should be presented in which the student decides between using the spirit or stencil duplicating process.

OFFSET DUPLICATOR.   The use of the offset duplicator in business has increased significantly in the past decade. One of its advantages is that the copy looks almost like an original. Because of the costs of the machine, supplies, and maintenance, many schools cannot afford an offset machine. In companies using offset machines, duplication for all departments is usually done in a centralized location by full-time operators. Even though the majority of office workers will not operate offset equipment, they should understand the basics of how the offset process produces a copy so that they will know why the original must be prepared in a certain manner, why corrections have to be made using specific techniques, and why placement on the page is important. "Students need to know types of projects for which it is frequently used; types of offset masters and features of each type; cost of equipment and maintenance cost; per copy cost; type and amount of training needed to be an offset operator; observation and explanation of how tabletop and large offset duplicators produce copies."[7]

Machine transcription

The increase in use of word processing systems should result in increased emphasis on instruction in machine transcription. Machine transcription is more difficult than shorthand transcription since the student has not heard the material before, names are not spelled out, punctuation is apparent, words may be blurred, and word endings such as "s" and "ed" and beginnings such as "b" for "d" may not be clear. For these reasons, machine transcription speed may not be as high, initially, as transcription of shorthand. On-the-job training will, of course, reduce these problems.

A planned instructional program for machine transcription should include these elements:

1. Familiarity with types of transcription equipment and the advantages and disadvantages of each.
2. Proficiency in operating the transcribers used for instruction. Meyer proposes that the following elements be stressed:
   a. "Typing from what is heard rather than what is seen."[8]
   Initially, students listen to the entire letter before beginning to transcribe. Later they scan the belt or tape to understand the content of the message. As the student gains experience and familiarity with the dictator's voice and style, previewing or scanning may not be necessary. Students should practice listening and typing in thought units, striving toward continuous typing. If a word is unclear, students can listen to the entire sentence or paragraph and choose an appropriate word; if there is doubt about a word or if it is a proper name or figure, they can leave a space and check with the dictator.
   b. "Use of correct grammar, sentence structure, punctuation, capitalization, and number form."[9]
   Through the context of the sentence and knowledge of fundamentals of good English, the transcriber can usually determine word endings, such as singular-plural, past-present tense, and so forth. (See Chapter 9.)
   c. "Correct spelling and vocabulary."[10] Remind students of the importance of correct spelling. Each student should have ready access to a dictionary and know how to use one. (See Chapter 9.)
   d. "Proofread."[11] Good proofreading habits are essential to good transcription. Students need to proofread for accuracy in typing, English fundamentals, and content.

Word processing equipment

Word processing refers to a managed system of people, procedures, and equipment for the rapid handling of written business communications. The development of the automatic typewriter had a significant effect on the evolution of word processing. The automatic typewriter is an electric typewriter that records words or symbols on a magnetic tape or card or displays them on a screen as in a video-text editing machine. The recorded material can be played back with little human assistance at a high rate of speed. Corrections are made by backspacing and striking over the error. The automatic typewriter can also be classified as a text editing typewriter. Many of the newer machines are compatible with photocomposition equipment, copying equipment, and the computer.

The cathode-ray tube (CRT) editing device differs from the automatic typewriter in that it allows a typist to "type" text onto a television screen where the image is displayed. The CRT keyboard controls allow insertion and deletion in the text. Printing is performed after the text has been created, edited, and verified on the screen.

One of the best examples of the use of electronic technology is the Computer-Stenograph Machine Shorthand System. A video unit connected to a computer allows super-fast processing of machine shorthand notes. English translations of machine shorthand can be seen on this telescreen instantly from the computer, or can be recalled to the screen at any time thereafter. Copy editing is done right on the screen, prior to the printout if desired, making it possible to do visual corrections on speeches, reports, or other compositions before they are transcribed—a business innovation that saves work, time, and money.

In view of the increasing use of word processing equipment by business and industry, business education programs should strive to obtain basic equipment such as the magnetic card selectric typewriter or the newer electronic typewriter by IBM for demonstration and familiarization training. In large programs, as time and budget allow, text editing equipment, composers, and computer terminals may be possible, thereby allowing for more extensive and specialized training.

Comtutor, a computerized typing program, combining a mini-computer with a cathode-ray tube screen monitor and a standard IBM keyboard terminal to instruct, exercise, guide, test, and evaluate student typists has been developed by the Comtutor Company of San Diego. Test statistics indicate that Comtutor-taught students develop typing skills more than 50 percent faster than by other methods.[12] The computer monitors each student's progress on an exercise-by-exercise basis. Students work independently, at their own speed. Comtutor registers student typing errors and typing rate per minute and displays the appropriate information on the screen for immediate feedback and reinforcement. A complete record of each student's progress is maintained in the computer's memory bank throughout the program. This record includes number of times each exercise is typed, completion time and number of errors per exercise, and typing rate in *wpm.* The record is available to the instructor at any time. The program allows the instructor more time for personal student attention since the computer also does all proofreading, calculations, and record keeping, and eliminates the need for makeup classes. During nonclass hours, the system can be used for administrative functions such as accounting, payroll, attendance reports, class schedules, placement reports, grade reports, and student rosters. The Comtutor educational system includes both the hardware and the software. The mini-computer has a 32,000 word memory bank and a storage capacity of 5,000,000 words and is capable of monitoring up to sixty-four students at the same time.

INDIVIDUALIZING INSTRUCTION

Office machines is an appropriate course for individualizing instruction. The number and variety of machines plus the variation in student achievement means that the teacher should have a means of providing for individual differences. Even with a rotation plan in which several students are working with the same type of machine simultaneously, multimedia instructional packages can facilitate learning in office machines labs. (See Chapter 8.)

An individualized office machines course should contribute to the educational needs of the brightest students as well as slower learners. Course content can readily be adjusted to meet student needs by altering the number of machines introduced, by providing problems of varying degrees of difficulty, and by changing the amount of decision making regarding which machines are appropriate for which jobs.

Sound-slide presentations, sound filmstrips, and film loops are effective means of presenting content on an individual or small-group basis. Students needing to review directions, explanations, or instructions may replay the audiovisual media as often as necessary. If the teacher is freed from routine explanations, he or she is available to help students on an individual basis, to observe operation of the machine, to administer tests, or to provide on-the-spot instruction.

Instruction on any machines should include the following minimum units: (1) an introduction, including the purpose of the machine, its use in business, and its cost; (2) the parts of the machine; (3) operation of the machine—during this phase, the student begins simple activities to develop skill in operation, including drills; and (4) culminating or application activities designed to pull together the skills in an activity that integrates prior learnings. (See Chapter 5 for information on the development of modules.) Culminating activities incorporate decision making in which students have to decide which machine to use, how to solve a given problem, and so forth. Illustration 12.1 provides an example of a learning activity in which the student is introduced to the operational parts of three machines. Illustration 12.2 is an example of an application activity.

RESPONSIBILITIES OF THE TEACHER

The office machines teacher is the key to the success of the course. There are several teacher responsibilities that underlie a successful program:[13]

1. Keep abreast of equipment trends in the office and tailor the machines room accordingly.
2. Equip the machines room with machines that will be used in offices of the immediate future as well as offices of the distant future.
3. Anticipate and plan opportunities for achieving related machine objectives in your course, such as time budgeting, basic arithmetic, arithmetic verification, applied business problems, and independence.
4. Be prepared to instruct on each machine in the room both by explanation and demonstration.
5. Individualize student programs and instruction.
6. Take a defensible position on the issue of multibrand machine teaching versus single-brand teaching.

illustration 12.1
INTRODUCTION TO MACHINE OPERATIONS

Sample Problem Number	VICTOR		MONROE		FRIDEN	
	Enter on Keyboard	Depress Function Key	Enter on Keyboard	Depress Function Key	Enter on Keyboard	Depress Function Key
(1)					Set Program Dial at 0.	
			Set Decimal Selector at 2.		Set Decimal Selector at 2.	
	Clear machine.	C ALL	Clear machine.	CD	Clear machine.	C
1.95	1 ● 95	+	1 ● 95	+‖	1 ● 95	+‖
1.95	Depress again.	+	Depress again.	+‖	Depress again.	+‖
1.95	Depress again.	+	Depress again.	+‖	Depress again.	+‖
7.50	7 ● 50	+	7 ● 50	+‖	7 ● 50	+‖
+ 7.50	Depress again.	+	Depress again.	+‖	Depress again.	+‖
	Copy subtotal (20.85) from visible display screen. *Do not clear machine.*		Copy subtotal (20.85) from visible display screen. *Do not clear machine.*		Copy subtotal (20.85) from visible display screen. *Do not clear machine.*	
12.75	12 ● 75	+	12 ● 75	+‖	12 ● 75	+‖
9.95	9 ● 95	+	9 ● 95	+‖	9 ● 95	+‖
	Read total (43.55) in visible display screen.		Read total (43.55) in visible display screen.		Read total (43.55) in visible display screen.	

Source: Paul Pactor, *Comprehensive Business Machines Course, Book II: Electronic Calculator* (Belmont, Calif.: Fearon-Pitman Publishers, Inc., 1976), p. 15. Reprinted with permission of the publisher.

illustration 12.2
APPLICATION ACTIVITY

Compute the following gasoline cost sheet; determine the number of gallons needed for each vehicle, the gasoline cost for each vehicle, and the total gasoline cost.

Vehicle Number	No. Miles Driven	÷	Avg. Miles per Gal.	=	Gallons Gas Needed	X	Cost per Gallon	=	Gasoline Cost
2-47	1224		12		102		.78		79.56
2-53	964		18						
2-54	2060		25						
2-55	372		10						
2-59	4716		11						
3-60	750		15						
3-61	3642		22						
							Total		

7. Establish a fair and sound grading procedure.
8. Explore novel ways of enriching the learnings of your students.

module 12.2
LEARNING ACTIVITIES

1. Using this module and other resources of your choice, prepare a list of criteria you will use in selecting office machines.
2. Write a script for a mini-lesson on a calculator, duplicator, transcribing machine, or automatic typewriter to demonstrate one or more operating parts or the use of the machine to solve a problem or prepare a business document. Describe the media you would use in the completed module.
3. Using this module, office machines textbooks, course guides, and other resources of your choice, outline the topics you would include in an office machines course lasting twelve weeks.
4. Begin a collection of materials that you can use to show students the variety of available office machines. Underline key descriptive features of the machines.
5. Describe and/or sketch an instructional display (bulletin board, for example) for use in reprographics.

module 12.2
SELF-TEST

1. Name three major areas of instruction in office machines.
2. Justify an individualized instruction program in office machines.
3. List at least five responsibilities of an office machines teacher.

module 12.3
EVALUATION OF STUDENT PERFORMANCE

The content of office machines can be divided into two major phases: information about the machines (such as parts, cost, and use) and proficiency in operating the machines. To measure these two types of content, you will want to use both objective items and performance items.

After completing this module, you should be able to (1) describe types of test items appropriate for evaluating student performance in office machines and (2) construct at least two objective and two performance-type test items.

OBJECTIVE TESTS

A limited number of objective items should be used to assess student knowledge about machines. The following multiple-choice items, are examples of objective items:

1. Spirit duplicating involves the same process as (a) fluid duplicating, (b) liquid duplicating, (c) direct process duplicating, (d) all of the above.
2. The carbon sheet behind the master contains a dye called (a) crimson dye, (b) copy dye, (c) aniline dye, (d) carbon dye.
3. The first step in running the spirit duplicator from layout to finished copy is (a) prepare a master, (b) prepare a layout, (c) get the spirit duplicator ready, (d) put the master on the duplicator and run copies, (e) remove the master and clean up.

Another type of objective item is labeling. The student labels the operating parts of a ten-key adding machine, for example. A modification of this type of test item requires the student to show the parts of the machine to the instructor. Illustration 12.3 is an example of a checklist the teacher might construct for testing knowledge of operating parts.

PERFORMANCE TESTS

The items included in performance tests should be typical of those completed by the student. Several short items are generally preferable to one long one. Both speed and accuracy are considered in the performance test. Speed is an indication of the student's skill at the machine, while accuracy is an indicator of mastery of the machine.

Reprographics

Evaluation items usually include preparation of a stencil and duplicating master sheets and running copies. Explain to students the criteria you

illustration 12.3
**TEACHER CHECKLIST FOR STUDENT EVALUATIONS:
TEN-KEY ADDING MACHINE**

Student Name_____ Date_____

Check each of the following items as the student completes each task.

		Satisfactory	Unsatisfactory
I.	Locate and explain the purpose of each of these machine parts:		
	1. Add Bar (plus bar)	_____	_____
	2. Backspace Key (if applicable)	_____	_____
	3. Clear Key (correction lever)	_____	_____
	4. Credit Balance Signal (if applicable)	_____	_____
	5. Digit or Column Indicator	_____	_____
	6. Minus Key	_____	_____
	7. Non-Add Key	_____	_____
	8. Paper Tape	_____	_____
	9. Platen or Twirler Knob	_____	_____
	10. Repeat Key (multiplication lever)		
	11. Subtotal Key	_____	_____
	12. Total Key (bar)	_____	_____
II.	Demonstrate proper posture Demonstrate proper hand position over the home-row keys	_____	_____
III.	Demonstrate ability to enter numbers on the keyboard using the touch method	_____	_____
IV.	Demonstrate ability to use the clear key or correction lever.	_____	_____

will use in evaluating copy, such as correct spelling, no typographical errors, directions followed, proper vertical and horizontal placement, sharp lines and letters, clear copy and copy not offset.

Illustration 12.4[14] is an example of a performance testing sheet for teacher use in determining student proficiency in operating the stencil duplicator.

Machine transcription

Evaluation of machine transcription centers around speed and accuracy since both are essential in developing a marketable skill. The following procedures may be used to assess speed and accuracy. Divide total words (five characters equals one word) by total transcription time to calculate gross words per minute. Accuracy is figured by dividing the number of words by the number of errors. Errors are defined as misspelled or wrong words, punctuation

illustration 12.4
PERFORMANCE TESTING SHEET:
HOW TO OPERATE THE STENCIL DUPLICATOR

To Be Filled Out by the Instructor

Did the operator do or check the following:

Circle One

1. Check the ink supply?   yes   no

2. Prepare the paper table and paper properly?   yes   no

                                           Circle One

    Paper loading lever down?   yes   no
    Left guide rail adjusted?   yes   no
    Paper on feed table?   yes   no
    Right guide rail adjusted?   yes   no
    Paper forward as far as possible?   yes   no
    Feed rolls adjusted (1/4 to 1/2
      inch inside guide rails)?   yes   no
    Side guides and back stop on the
      receiving tray adjusted?   yes   no
    Counter set at zero?   yes   no

3. Remove and store the protective cover
    properly?   yes   no

4. Attach the stencil properly?   yes   no

5. Start and stop the stencil duplicator
    properly?   yes   no

                                           Circle One

    Motor switch turned on?   yes   no
    Paper loading lever in up position?   yes   no
    Copies run?   yes   no
    Paper loading lever in down position? yes   no
    Motor switch turned off?   yes   no

6. Remove and store stencil properly?   yes   no

7. Replace the protective cover properly?   yes   no

8. Remove the blank paper and finished
    copies?   yes   no

9. Completed in twenty minutes or less?   yes   no

10. Placement correct:

                                           Circle One

    Vertical?   yes   no
    Horizontal?   yes   no
    Proportion between items?   yes   no
    Copy clear? (no offset)   yes   no
    Sharp lines?   yes   no

11. Number of typographical and spelling
    errors: 0   1   2   3 or _____

448

errors, poor erasures, carbon copy errors, and poor setup. By keeping a record of student test results each year, it is possible to arrive at a grading scale based on prior performance. A scale should be constructed for each test during machine transcription, and should be revised and kept up-to-date in line with current student performance.

The following is an example of standards recommended by Corgan for the first test (belt 5 from a series of 20 tapes from IBM in which there was a total of 4 tests):[15]

WORDS PER MINUTE		WORDS PER ERROR
27.5+	A+	250+
25.5–27.0	A	220–249
24.0–25.0	B+	190–219
22.0–23.5	B	160–189
20.5–21.5	C+	130–159
18.5–20.0	C	100–129
16.5–18.0	D+	70– 99
15.0–16.0	D	40– 69
14.5 and below	F	39 and below

These standards are for a college course in machine transcription. You will have to establish a scale appropriate for your students. Initially, until student test scores can be collected, you will have to set a temporary scale.

Adding-calculating machines

Tests of these machines also incorporate speed and accuracy. Those available from publishers usually recommend a time limit. Tests may be scored on the basis of number correct. The sample shown in Illustration 12.5 is extracted from an achievement test on the electronic calculator in the University of Georgia course in business machines.

module 12.3
LEARNING ACTIVITIES

1. Construct a minimum of two objective test items and two performance items for a business machine of your choice.
2. Read at least one article on evaluation of office machine instruction and report on the article to the class.
3. Interview a business teacher, at any level, and report on the evaluation plan used by that teacher.

module 12.3
SELF-TEST

1. Justify the inclusion of multiple-choice items, checklists, and performance items in evaluating student work in office machines.

illustration 12.5
ACHIEVEMENT TEST: ELECTRONIC CALCULATOR

You will be timed for 25 minutes to complete 50 problems. Do not write on the test copy. Record your answers on the score sheet as you work the problems.

ADDITION AND SUBTRACTION: (Record all necessary decimal points in the answers.)

$4.87	18.137	17.287	470 1/4
5.98	39.873	9.3415	67 1/2
4.78	- 27.145	.748	298.789
3.45	48.185	30.5815	67.71
2.17	- 59.258	29.6295	8.125
7.11	60.417	8.7407	388.167
4.60	73.528	9.9417	498.3/8
4.88	- 50.427	29.9514	34 3/4
5.71	94.748	37.2105	14.45
6.28	- 12.857	8.814	315.1558
(1)	(2)	(3)	(4)

MULTIPLICATION: (Record all decimal places in the products.)

23.776 x 10.96 = (5) _____

.78 x 2.76 x 16.5 = (6) _____

(45.8 x 27.7) + (18.6 x 25.9) = (7) _____

DIVISION: (Record four decimal places in the quotients.)

97,286 ÷ 458 = (8) _____

(196.75 ÷ 5.7) + (198.56 ÷ 6.8) = (9) _____

MIXED OPERATIONS: (Set the decimal control at 4.)

(189 + 254.7 - 79.38) x 47.87 = (10) _____

(869 + 188.6 - 54.25) ÷ 17.16 = (11) _____

(124.73 x 39.93) + 25.5 - 21.57 = (12) _____

(9,886 ÷ 17.5) + 289.78 - 76.35 = (13) _____

(29.78 x 241.55) - 25.45 = (14) _____

(8,495 ÷ 24.16) x 20.78 = (15) _____

PERCENTAGES: (Round results to two decimal places for dollars and cents.)

13 1/2% of $2,379.75 = (16) _____

$2,759 is __(17)__ % of $5,288

$2,768 is 18 1/2% of (18) _____

DISCOUNTS AND NET AMOUNTS: (Round results to two decimal places for dollars and cents.)

8 1/2% discount of $2,579 = (19) _____

$3,759 less discount of 34% = (20) _____

$4,875 less 15%, 12%, 9% = (21) _____

SUMMARY

Office machines instruction, at the secondary and postsecondary levels, is directed toward developing skills in adding-calculating machines, copying-duplicating machines, and dictating-transcription machines. Students should learn how to operate the machines, to use them in businesslike situations, and to select the appropriate machine for a specific task. Office machines are offered as individual courses, as units of instruction within other courses, or as part of a skills lab involving individualized instruction.

Office machines equipment and accompanying instruction should reflect the present and future business office. Before selecting the machines, you should identify criteria that incorporate course objectives, student objectives, space, enrollment, time, and budget.

Instruction in machines can be classified into four major areas: calculating-adding machines, copying-duplicating processes, dictating-transcribing equipment, and other word processing equipment. Within each of these areas, instruction should include an introduction (purpose of the machine, its uses in business, and cost); parts of the machine; operating the machine; and culminating activities.

The nature of the office practice course lends itself to individualized instruction. You will need self-instructional materials to accompany each machine so that you are available for analyzing student needs, prescribing appropriate instruction and individual assistance as needed.

Office machines instruction can be divided into two phases: information about the machines and proficiency in operating the machines. To assess student performance, you will want to include both objective and performance-type items. Performance items should be typical of those in the instructional unit and should measure both speed and accuracy.

References

[1]Vera G. Kinzey, "Office Machines Equipment Selection," *Journal of Business Education* 50, no. 4 (January 1975): 145–46.

[2]Milton C. Olson, "Basic Principles in Equipment Selection," *Business Education Forum* 26, no. 4 (January 1972): 15.

[3]George S. Rhodes, "Numbers-a-Minute Timing for Office Machines Students" (Unpublished manuscript, August 1978).

[4]Thomas M. Bormann, "Electronic Calculating: Processing of Thoughts," *Journal of Business Education* 48, no. 7 (April 1973): 303.

[5]Ibid.

[6]Nancy Groneman, "Current Duplicating Processes," *Journal of Business Education* 53, no. 7: 304.

[7]Ibid., pp. 303–4.

[8]Lois I. Meyer, "Learning to Transcribe from Machine Dictation," *Business Education Forum* 30, no. 5 (February 1976): 15–16.

[9]Ibid.

[10]Ibid.

[11]Ibid.

[12]*AICS Compass* (Detroit, Mich.: Association of Independent Colleges, May 1978), p. 5.

[13]David E. Gootnick, "Responsibilities of the Office Machines Teacher," *Business Education Forum* 27, no. 4 (January 1973): 36–37.

[14]Calfrey C. Calhoun and Norma N. Givens, *Office Occupational Program: Machines*—The Development of an Individualized Instructional System for Selected Multi-

occupational Programs in the Area Comprehensive High Schools of Georgia (Athens: Department of Business Education, University of Georgia, 1975), p. ST: PP4:4–5.

[15]Virginia E. Corgan, "Clerical Office Procedures," *Business Education Forum* 26, no. 3 (December 1971): 45.

SUGGESTIONS FOR FURTHER STUDY

Dohleman, Lee. "What I Look for in an Electronic Calculator." *Business Education Forum* 27 (March 1973): 32–33.

Giordano, Al. "Paired Instruction—A Graduated Complementary Method of Instruction in Business Machines Calculation Courses." *California Business Education Journal* 10 (May 1975): 19–21.

Kinzey, Vera G. "Individualize Office Machines Instruction with Performance Objectives." *Balance Sheet* 54 (December 1972–January 1973): 170–71.

McMurtry, David C. "Office Machines: Multi-Make vs. Uni-Make Instruction." *Journal of Business Education* 49 (October 1973): 23–24.

Quinn, Mildred Louise. "Combining Business Math and Clerical Office Machines." *Business Education Forum* 29 (April 1975): 21–23.

part four

TEACHING INFORMATION-PROCESSING BUSINESS SKILLS

chapter 13

TEACHING DATA PROCESSING

That computers have affected the lives of nearly all of us is indisputable. Their impact has been experienced in areas as widely separated as space research and preschool instruction. This impact is even more remarkable when the computer's brief history is recalled. In 1950, there were fewer than a dozen electronic digital computers in worldwide use. By the late 1960s, over 40,000 were in operation and the number is expected to exceed 100,000 during the 1970s.[1]

Computer applications have penetrated, directly or indirectly, almost every aspect of human affairs. They are used to design schools, to aid in their construction, and to help in operating them. Computers made possible the planning and building of spacecraft, their launching, control, and navigation to other planets. Computers also have been applied to less exotic but nonetheless significant roles in the functions of business, government, law enforcement, education, commerce, and science. Computerized Social Security and income tax deductions touch the lives of nearly all citizens. The seemingly unlimited usefulness of the computer itself has been augmented by the rapidly accelerating development of peripheral equipment, data communications, and word processing systems. This, in turn, has brought into use extensive networks in which a single computer, located in one city, services terminals in other cities across the nation. It has also brought about the development of the microprocessor or minicomputer, a stand-alone system with numerous applications whose cost is now within the reach of every school system.

Common use of the term *data processing,* like the use of *astronaut, radar, antibiotic,* and so on, is a phenomenon of the twentieth century, though the two words from which it is formed have been in our language for many centuries. *Data* is the plural form of the Latin *datum* which means a "fact or piece of information." *Processing* is a verb form applied to any manipulating or changing of raw material by hand or machine. Then, the term *data processing* means the "manipulating or changing of facts or bits of information by hand or machine."

The phenomenal development of computer technology has created an increasing demand for competent data processing personnel. Consequently, individuals who are knowledgeable about computer capabilities are enjoying increased career opportunity and flexibility. The concept of "careers related to consumers" is fast becoming an important educational consideration as schools recognize their responsibility in preparing students to work and live in a computerized society. The area of data processing appeals to both college and noncollege-bound students. The computer is a tool that can fit into existing curricula and help convert routine courses into exciting experiments. Business educators are now in the forefront of attempts to develop business-related applications of the computer. Their efforts are reflected in courses at the middle school/junior high, secondary school, postsecondary vocational technical school, and college and university levels.

module 13.1
PLANNING AND IMPLEMENTING DATA PROCESSING COURSES

This module is designed to help the teacher develop or expand a program to introduce all students to general computer capabilities, to provide certain students with a problem-solving tool, or to prepare business students for entry into the job market upon graduation. After completing this module, you should be able to (1) list and briefly describe three categories of data processing objectives, (2) describe potential student populations for which each category is designed, (3) identify general objectives for an introductory course in data processing, (4) specify courses appropriate for secondary and/or postsecondary data processing programs, and (5) name and explain the steps in establishing a data processing program.

OBJECTIVES

Data processing objectives can be classified into three general areas: (1) computer literacy, (2) problem solving, and (3) job entry. The first category, computer literacy, is general education, designed to acquaint students with computer uses and abilities. The second category focuses on developing problem-solving skills as related tools for careers in engineering, mathematics, science, accounting, as well as in data processing. Job entry, or vocational competency, concentrates on preparing students to enter the labor market in the data processing occupations. These three categories are found, in varying degrees, from middle school through college and university levels.

Computer literacy

The objectives of courses designed to promote computer literacy vary at different educational levels and on the same level. Factors such as number of courses offered, availability of equipment and supplies, teacher preparation, employment demands, and potential enrollment influence the selection of specific objectives. General areas of computer literacy appropriate for introductory courses include:

1. Introduction to systems thinking and the systems approach.
2. Basic levels at which data is processed—manual, mechanical, punch card, and electronic.
3. Knowledge and appreciation of the development of data processing techniques, specifically including the stored program digital computer.
4. Basic concepts of data processing.
5. Uses of data processing, both personal and business.
6. Social impact of technological advances in computer technology.
7. Terminology associated with the field of data processing.

Computer literacy can be developed through separate course(s) in data processing or by incorporating concepts into existing courses. Some educators believe that separate courses are the most effective approach since many teachers lack the technical knowledge about data processing to effectively integrate appropriate content into existing courses.

The relationship of particular programs to the field of data processing, however, may be effectively demonstrated by incorporating data processing topics or units into existing courses. For instance, the economic impact and the effect of data processing on employment should be explored in courses such as general business, business law, consumer education, and economics. Simple flowcharts can be introduced as one means of tracing the flow of products and raw materials used in production. Patent and copyright protection of computer programs can be examined in business law. A unit on data processing is usually incorporated in business math, accounting, and office practice. Business teachers must know the principles of data processing to effectively integrate them into existing courses.

Hardware, such as computer terminals, is not essential to developing computer literacy. However, the availability of a computer can enhance understanding. Field trips to computer installations as well as speakers who describe the uses of data processing in their businesses can be of great value.

Problem solving

Many students will enter non-data processing professions in which a background in data processing is helpful. These students develop problem-solving skills and, at the postsecondary levels, higher level skills in the use of data processing in their various occupations. The following are examples of the wide range of jobs in which data processing knowledge is utilized: aerospace engineer, athletic director, attorney, chemical engineer, insurance actuary, physicist, teacher, telephone installer, writer and editor, weather forecaster. Table 13.1[2] illustrates some of the data processing topics as well as the business areas in which these topics are specifically appropriate.

table 13.1
DATA PROCESSING IN BUSINESS

	ACCOUNTING	PRODUCTION	GENERAL BUSINESS	OFFICE	DISTRIBUTION
PROGRAMMING SKILLS					
Flowcharting	X	X	X	X	X
COBOL	X				X
FORTRAN		X			X
PL/1	X	X			X
RPG	X		X		X
BASIC	X	X	X		
Decision Tables		X			X
AUTOMATED APPLICATIONS					
Inventory	X	X	X		X
Production Scheduling	X	X			X
Accounts Receivable	X		X		X
Accounts Payable	X		X		X
Sales Analysis	X		X		X
OPERATING SKILLS					
Computer Room Operations				X	
Data File Handling		X	X	X	
Source Document Preparation	X	X	X	X	X

Job entry

The third major goal is to prepare students for data processing occupations. Some of the major job opportunities available to graduates of effective high school programs include

> tab operator—operates alphabetic and numeric keypunch machines, similar in operation to an electric typewriter, to transcribe data from source material to data cards; electronic data processing peripheral equipment operator—operates dictaphone, adding machine, calculator, and other office equipment in addition to the keypunch machine, performs general office duties requiring the use of bookkeeping, business writing, and arithmetic; coder/programmer—flow charts program specifications, prepared usually by a systems analyst, codes the flowcharted data into a program language, uses selected data to test and correct the completed computer program; terminal operator—operates terminal and off-line equipment to communicate between user and remotely located computer facility.[3]

Postsecondary programs are designed to prepare students for various jobs, such as business applications programmer, scientific applications programmer, systems software programmer, business systems analyst, or computer operator. In general, persons preparing for careers as scientific programmers, systems analysts and designers, and systems software programmers will enroll in four-year programs to acquire the necessary skills in data processing as well as the needed related courses.

CURRICULUM PATTERNS

A variety of curriculum patterns in business data processing can be found at the various educational levels.

Middle/junior high school

Career exploration courses at the middle/junior high school level provide opportunities for students to explore various computer careers and to form a basis for opinions and feelings about them. Illustration 13.1 provides a sample package introducing students to the work of the data coder.

Secondary level

Data processing curricula at the secondary level vary from one-semester introductory courses or the inclusion of data processing principles and concepts into existing business subjects to three-year vocational programs. One high school designed a course in data processing that combined both general education and vocational objectives. For some students, the course was vocational in that they were trained for clerical-type jobs such as keypunch or machine operators. Other students acquired knowledge and experience to help determine whether or not they wanted to pursue further training in the area. For those students whose career objectives included occupations in which data processing is used, the course provided a background for other computer programming courses. The first section of the course, six weeks, dealt with card machines; the second section, ten weeks, focused on wiring. Flowcharting and development of program logic were emphasized in the next ten weeks, during which time students learned to write their programs in Basic and to use the computer terminal. Behavioral objectives for this section of the course included the following:

1. Upon completion of the unit on computer programming in BASIC, the student will be able to block diagram and write a computer program to perform arithmetic, accounting, and looping functions.
2. The student will demonstrate his knowledge of programming by finding the errors, and correcting them, in a program containing errors.
3. The student will further demonstrate his knowledge of flowcharting and programming by translating a flowchart into a computer program.[4]

During the final ten weeks, students studied COBOL programming. Behavioral objectives for this section included:

1. The same objectives for COBOL as those listed for BASIC.
2. The student will be able to list and explain six methods of input and five methods of output for an electronic computer system.
3. Given a set of problems in addition, subtraction, multiplication, and division in the binary coded decimal system, the student will be able to complete them with 90 percent accuracy.
4. The student will demonstrate his understanding of bases by changing decimals into hexadecimals and by changing hexadecimals into decimals with a grade of 90 percent.
5. The student will demonstrate a sound grasp of the data processing terminology by a grade of 90 percent on a vocabulary test.[5]

A secondary curriculum that incorporates three major goals of data processing instruction might include courses in introduction to data processing, data entry, programming, cooperative work experience, advanced programming, and data processing applications.

Postsecondary level

Data processing at the postsecondary level is generally vocationally oriented with its major goals to train persons for careers in data processing or to provide students with related problem-solving skills and knowledges needed in their professions.

> Typically the vocational business data processing program will include courses in the following areas: introduction to data processing, assembler language programming, procedural language programming (such as COBOL), programming systems, systems design and development, programming applications, advanced programming techniques, field project or work experience. The number of courses and their content will vary with each program; therefore, this is not intended as an inclusive listing by specific course title, but to illustrate the breadth and types of training provided in these programs.[6]

Some colleges and universities recommend that business majors take at least one course in data processing before graduating. One decision that must be made is whether or not students will have access to the computer. In many schools, courses in data processing incorporate "hands-on" experience; when large numbers of students enroll in programming courses, this is not always feasible. "The usual procedure in such cases is for the students to turn the programs in to a central location on campus. The programs are run on the computer and later returned to the student programmers. In many of the courses where this procedure is followed, students may not see the computer during the quarter. In schools that offer a program designed to provide the student with skills necessary for employment, at least one course should be designed to give 'hands-on' experience in operation of the computer console.

Operation of the computer can usually be taught in two to six weeks depending on the complexity of the computer."[7]

PROGRAM PLANNING

Certain events should take place if an effective data processing program is to be implemented. Adequate time devoted to appropriate *planning* results in a sound instructional program. The following illustrate steps in program planning.

DETERMINE NEEDS.   To provide input for deciding whether or not to offer data processing programs, the school system or department should conduct a comprehensive needs assessment. Such a study would identify educational needs and interests of students; specify employment needs, both present and projected; indicate data processing equipment being used; clarify support (including financial) of board of education, dean, or administration.

IDENTIFY OBJECTIVES.   This step involves determining the general program goals and objectives as an outgrowth of data from the needs assessment. Specific student objectives would be developed as courses are selected.

FORM ADVISORY COMMITTEE.   The advisory committee can prove invaluable in determining a need for data processing programs, providing technical assistance in establishing a program, and serving as a link between the school and the community. (See Chapter 16.)

DETERMINE ORGANIZATIONAL STRUCTURE.   The school or college has to determine whether data processing will be incorporated into an existing department, such as business education, or whether it will become a separate program.

SELECT STAFF.   Personnel with appropriate training should be selected or employed early enough to be involved in program development.

DESIGN CURRICULUM.   Based on general program goals and needs assessment, the curriculum should be outlined, including plans for evaluation of the program.

DETERMINE FACILITIES, EQUIPMENT, AND MATERIALS NEEDED.   Using available data, the facilities, equipment, and materials essential to operation of a program should be selected. Equipment, including the computer, should be selected to complement program objectives. (Do not buy or lease a computer and then try to design an instructional program to fit it.)

MAKE EQUIPMENT AVAILABLE. This part of the procedure involves deciding which alternative to use with regard to acquisition of hardware: purchase, lease, terminals (time sharing), and so forth.

PUBLICIZE PROGRAM. Part of the planning process should include familiarizing faculty and students with the data processing program and its goals. A comprehensive program that incorporates computer literacy, problem solving, and job entry goals will have something to offer every student.

module 13.1
LEARNING ACTIVITIES

1. With a team member, design a brochure or information sheet for faculty and students describing a data processing program at the secondary or postsecondary level that incorporates the three major goals of data processing instruction.
2. The business education department staff believes that an introductory course in data processing would be of value to all students. Prepare the rationale and general objectives for an introductory course that you would submit to the administration for consideration.
3. Using this module and other references of your choice, prepare a list of data processing courses you would recommend for a secondary school program.
4. Interview a business educator, such as a professor at a teacher-training institution, a state or local supervisor of business education, or a department head at a secondary or postsecondary school, regarding the status of data processing instruction. Write a report of your interview.
   Or
   Invite a business educator to speak to the class about data processing instruction, giving special attention to trends and projections.
5. Invite one member of the class to contact the state supervisor of business education for a copy of the data processing guide for secondary and postsecondary levels. Report to the class on the suggested curriculum for each educational level. Compare these courses to those listed in your college catalog.

module 13.1
SELF-TEST

1. Briefly describe the various student populations for which data processing instruction is appropriate.
2. List the steps you would use in planning a data processing program. Explain the importance of each step.
3. For each of the following items, specify the category of data processing objectives that applies:
   a. Jack Hopkins plans to pursue a career as an accountant.

   Category: _____

illustration 13.1
DATA CODER

OBJECTIVES

The data coder records information to be processed by data processing machines. Information is recorded on sheets of paper or cards from which it is then keypunched into standard cards or from which it is read directly by special machines. This PLACE will give you the chance to explore this occupation by:

1. RECORDING INFORMATION TO BE KEYPUNCHED.
2. RECORDING INFORMATION ON A MARK SENSED CARD.
3. REACTING TO STATEMENTS THAT DEAL WITH THE OCCUPATION OF A DATA CODER.
4. IDENTIFYING THE ACTIVITIES AND REQUIREMENTS OF A DATA CODER.
5. EXPRESSING YOUR FEELINGS ABOUT THE OCCUPATION OF A DATA CODER.

You are to do all of the following.

ACTIVITIES

A. In this activity you will record information to be punched by a keypunch operator.

   1. Listen to the cassette tape marked "Data Recording."

   2. Assume you are employed as a data coder for a paint corporation. The corporation runs a daily sales analysis report with subtotals by user code, type code, container code and color code. All the information needed has been recorded on sales slips like the one shown in figure 2a. Condense the information for processing by recording the information from figure 2a in code form. Use the standard color codes given in figure 2b and the standard container, type and use codes given in figure 2c. Record your information on figure 2d.

illustration 13.1 (continued)

FEEDBACK

If you did not record all the information correctly, look up those codes which you missed again before going on to the next activity.

Color	Container	Type	Use	Quantity
09	2	2	2	030
15	5	2	2	010
32	3	1	2	018
04	2	2	2	045
27	5	2	2	028
21	5	2	1	135
23	5	1	1	010
03	3	2	2	012
36	2	1	1	118
33	2	1	2	014

B. In this activity you will record information on a mark-sensed card.

1. Read the following sections in FUNDAMENTALS OF DATA PROCESSING by Wanous, Wanous and Wagner.

    (A) "Numeric Code"--pages 64-65
    (B) "Alphabetic Code"--page 66
    (C) "Mark-Sensed Recording"--pages 100-101

2. Record the following information on the mark-sensed card in figure 1a of this package. A chart showing the punches which make up each alphabetic character also given in figure 1a.

    student number = 141 (columns 1-3)
    student name = Price Richard (columns 4-19)
    grade code = 1 (column 20)
    subject number = 203 (columns 21-23)
    department number = 13 (columns 24-25)
    semester hours = 2 (column 26)
    semester = 1 (column 27)

illustration 13.1 (continued)

FEEDBACK

Turn to figure 1b of this package and check your coding. If you had any coding errors you may want to read your resource material again.

C. Complete the following checklist by placing a check or an x in the box that shows your feelings.

	YES	NO
1. Coding data is boring.		
2. Coding data is time-consuming.		
3. Coding data requires specialized skills.		
4. Coding data involves a lot of logical thinking.		
5. Coding data is easy.		
6. Data coders could easily make mistakes if they are not alert.		
7. Coding data all the time would strain my eyes.		
8. Coding data involves too much repetition for me.		

D. Read the following resource: PLACE Card, "Data Coder."

illustration 13.1 (continued)

E. Complete the following self-check quiz.

	YES	NO
1. A person who has a good memory would be more efficient as a coder than a person who has a poor memory.		
2. It is necessary that a data coder know how to type.		
3. The data coder usually works in a pleasant environment.		
4. Specialized training is required for entry into the occupation of a data coder.		
5. Advancement opportunities for the data coder are good.		
6. The work of a data coder involves much physical labor.		
7. The data coder performs many different tasks.		
8. A data coder should have good vision.		
9. The job of a data coder requires someone with leadership abilities.		
10. The salary of a data coder is much higher than that of the average office worker.		

FEEDBACK

If you missed more than two, you may want to look at your resource material again.

1. Yes. A person with a good memory could code the data faster because memorized codes would not have to be looked up.

2. No. The majority of data to be processed is handwritten.

3. Yes. The work area is usually quiet and air-conditioned.

4. No. A data coder usually receives on-the-job training, no previous specialized training being required.

5. No. Advancement is usually very limited without further training.

6. No. The work requires little physical labor. The job is performed while seated.

7. No. The data coder has only one primary task--that of recording information.

8. Yes. The reading and recording of data can be very straining on the eyes, especially if vision is bad. Also, good vision is necessary if data is to be read and recorded accurately.

9. No. The data coder may lack leadership. The important qualification is the ability to follow directions.

10. No. The salary of a data coder is fairly low. It is comparable with that of a clerk-typist.

illustration 13.1 (continued)

F. Complete the following statements with the word or words which <u>you think</u> are the best examples of <u>your feelings</u>.

   1. The thing I liked best about the work of data coder is _____

       _____.

   2. The thing I liked least about the work of a data coder is _____

       _____.

   3. I (would/would not) like to become a data coder because _____

       _____.

FEEDBACK

Be prepared to share the answers you gave in activity F in a small group discussion.

Figure 1a
MARKED-SENSED RECORDING

CARD CODE FOR THE ALPHABET

A .. 12-1	J ... 11-1	S 0-2
B .. 12-2	K .. 11-2	T 0-3
C .. 12-3	L .. 11-3	U ... 0-4
D .. 12-4	M .. 11-4	V 0-5
E ... 12-5	N .. 11-5	W ... 0-6
F ... 12-6	O ... 11-6	X 0-7
G .. 12-7	P ... 11-7	Y 0-8
H .. 12-8	Q .. 11-8	Z 0-9
I ... 12-9	R .. 11-9	

illustration 13.1 (continued)

Figure 1b
MARKED-SENSED RECORDING

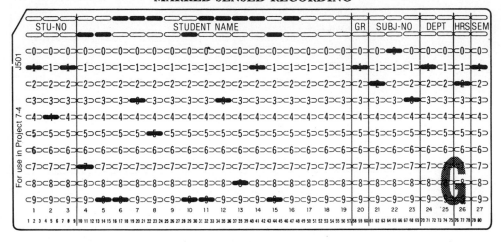

Figure 2a
INVOICE

CUSTOMER   ABC Hardware

State Street

Toccoa, Georgia   30577

QUANTITY	DESCRIPTION	UNIT PRICE
30 pints	Avocado interior paint	$ 1.50
10 gals	Sky blue interior paint	10.00
18 quarts	Pecan interior stain	2.50
45 pints	Harvest gold interior paint	1.50
28 gals	Ivory interior paint	10.00
135 gals	White exterior paint	10.00
10 gals	Brown exterior stain	8.50
12 quarts	Spanish red interior paint	3.50
118 pints	Redwood exterior stain	1.25
14 pints	Oak interior stain	1.25

Figure 2b
COLOR CODES

01 gray	10 pale pink	19 purple	28 coppertone
02 flame red	11 hot pink	20 lavender	29 turquoise
03 Spanish red	12 rose pink	21 white	30 silver
04 harvest gold	13 midnight blue	22 black	31 walnut
05 pale yellow	14 royal blue	23 brown	32 pecan
06 bright yellow	15 sky blue	24 off-white	33 oak
07 mint green	16 burnt orange	25 beige	34 cherry
08 apple green	17 orange	26 burgundy	35 maple
09 avocado	18 peach	27 ivory	36 redwood

illustration 13.1 (continued)

Figure 2c

CONTAINER CODES	TYPE CODES	USE CODES
1 half-pint	1 stain	1 exterior
2 pint	2 paint	2 exterior
3 quart		
4 half-gallon		
5 gallon		
6 3-gallons		
7 5-gallons		

Figure 2d
SALES ANALYSIS DATA

COLOR CODE		CONTAINER CODE	TYPE CODE	USE CODE	QUANTITY		
1	2	3	4	5	6	7	8

b. Mary Johnson wishes to become a computer operator after completing her training at the vocational technical school.

Category: _____

c. Helen Monroe is completing her master's degree in nursing.

Category: _____

d. Daniel Sims is uncertain of his career objective at this time.

Category: _____

e. Margaret Porter has retired and is enrolled in courses at the local college.

Category: _____

module 13.2
IMPLEMENTING DATA PROCESSING PROGRAMS

In addition to providing computer literacy courses for business students and offering education in computer programming skills to non-data processing majors, business teachers offer specialized educational programs for those intending to work as professional data processors. After completing this module, you should be able to (1) characterize the hardware, software, and manager relationships of manual systems, unit-record systems, first-, second-, and third-generation computers; (2) describe the educational implications of a typical minicomputer installation; (3) explain how a business teacher might decide about which type of hardware to lease or purchase; (4) describe the problem-oriented approach to teaching unit-record data processing; (5) explain the programming exercise approach to teaching programming; (6) describe the steps in the comprehensive problem approach to teaching programming; (7) spell out the systems orientation approach to teaching data processing; (8) give several examples of how data processing concepts can be integrated into other business education courses; (9) differentiate among data processing at high school, technical school/junior college, and college and university levels; (10) explain the concept of computer word processing and its implications for business education; (11) describe the AVT plan for individualizing instruction in data processing; and (12) explain several tools for evaluating the effectiveness of the data processing program.

HOW HARDWARE DEVELOPED

The matrix by Humphreys[9] shown in Table 13.2 provides an excellent interpretation of how data processing has developed over the past thirty

table 13.2

HISTORICAL DEVELOPMENT OF INFORMATION SYSTEMS

ERA	HARDWARE	SOFTWARE	MANAGER RELATIONSHIP
Manual system	Office Equipment Filing cabinets	Knowledge of system Intuitive judgment	Intimate, firsthand No technical training necessary
Unit record	Sorters Collator Reproduce-punch Accounting machine Summary punch Keypunch/verifier Batch processing	Technical assistance on board wiring Problems Card layout Forms design	Once-removed Acts through DP trained person who knew operation and wiring of unit record equipment Must be able to specify request
First-generation computer	650-fixed word No on-line processing Batch processing	Machine language SOAP Board wiring Forms design Programming	At least once-removed Works through pro- grammer for re- quests and results For first time, could get "all the facts"
Second-generation computer	1400-commercial 1620-scientific on-line capability for card read Punch magnetic tape Printing (600 lpm) Core storage Batch processing	RPG Program packages Systems support General programming	At least twice-removed Works thorugh sys- tems analyst who, in turn, works through programmer *Exception reporting* developed.
Third-generation computer	360 Teleprocessing Data cell On-line processing	Generalized operations Data base concept	Generally twice- removed Words through sys- tems analyst who, in turn, works through programmer Conceptual idea of *on-demand* reporting "Real time" systems
Future			Intimate, firsthand through remote terminal operation No training necessary Will be conversational mode

years. The rows of the matrix represent different eras. Four columns complete the vertical arrangement of the matrix: a column for hardware, the second column, defined as anything relating to actual data processing equipment; software, the third column, lists any programming and/or systems work used to support the hardware; and in the fourth column, the manager relationship is explained.

IMPLICATIONS OF THE MINICOMPUTER FOR THE BUSINESS TEACHER

The relatively low cost of a minicomputer system now makes it possible for small businesses and schools to install computers. Stand-alone mini-computers are expected to account for a major portion of the growth in the computer industry. Brooks and Behling feel that in the near future, most secretarial and clerical personnel will be employed in positions directly affected by data processing terminology, and thus the role that computers play in processing words and data should be an integral part of every business curriculum.[10]

The demand for programmers and other personnel to operate the minicomputer system will grow in direct proportion to the increase in the numbers of computers being installed. The most common languages that students who will be employed as minicomputer programmers should be taught are BASIC and COBOL, which are used by a majority of the minicomputer installations. Students also need a good background in bookkeeping/accounting and basic business principles and programming. "Hands-on" experience is highly desirable, with additional on-the-job training being provided after the student is employed.

A typical minicomputer installation consists of a keyboard (similar to a typewriter keyboard with control buttons) for inputing information, a screen (like a small television screen) for displaying the instructions, a printer for outputing information, a telephone for telecommunications, and one or more devices for memory. Several minicomputer terminals can communicate electronically through telephone lines to form a communication network. These terminals may be located as close together as the same room or as far apart as different states. Since the input (information) is entered primarily through use of the keyboard, good typewriting skills are necessary to ensure that data will be entered efficiently and accurately.

Business students who obtain positions in banks, insurance companies, department stores, and elsewhere using the cathode-ray tube (CRT) can readily transfer the knowledge gained while using the minicomputer to functions performed on the CRT. As a general educational benefit, students will be able to better understand electronic funds transfer and the "cashless" society which are rapidly becoming part of our daily lives. Many data processing "experts" predict that minicomputers will be as common in the home as television or telephone within the next decade. They will be used to pay bills and order merchandise electronically. If this prediction comes true, instruction concerning minicomputers may become part of the general school curriculum. Brooks believes that business teachers are best prepared for providing instruction on minicomputers whether the instruction is offered to complement the secretarial or clerical program, organized into a one- or two-year program to train operators and programmers, or offered in the future as part of the general education curriculum. The increased usage will lower the price of minicomputers even more—much like electronic calculator prices decreased as production increased.

Business teachers who are not familiar with minicomputers can attend university-sponsored summer workshops or seminars provided by computer manufacturers or study the programmed instructional materials available from computer manufacturers and publishing companies In some instances, instructional units for students are also available from the manufacturer. Business teachers must become aware of the computer's capabilities and limitations to better prepare students to enter a business world where minicomputers are likely to become a standard machine, as important and common as the typewriter or calculator.

HARDWARE AND CURRICULUM

Business and office educators are increasingly finding ways to include vitally needed data processing education in high schools and colleges across the country. Some have initiated one or two courses, while others have complete programs supported by data processing equipment (referred to as "hardware").

Berryman points out that hardware is important because business educators must provide the types of activities and learning situations that will most adequately prepare people for the data processing world of work.[11] Teachers should be concerned with obtaining equipment for use in teaching solid, fundamental concepts that are applicable to as many brands and models of hardware as possible. If the equipment has been selected with this in mind, there should be a fairly high degree of transfer-learning achievement present.

Probably the most important factor making hardware selection complex is that most people's knowledge is incomplete—maybe inaccurate. Even one quite familiar with the field may have a difficult time deciding which type of hardware to lease or purchase, given the normal limitations involving costs, program objectives, administrative demands, delivery schedules, and so forth. One approach is to obtain advice from business people who have already selected their equipment. (But keep in mind that their reasons for selection may be quite different from yours.) Another approach is to investigate what other schools have done; perhaps their needs are similar. Ideally, a combination of approaches usually generates sufficient information upon which to base a decision.

What should the hardware in an instructional program be capable of doing? What should the curriculum be designed to do? A review by Berryman of literature in the field, new job openings, discussions with data processors, and observations led to the following items as minimum considerations when planning an effective data processing program:[12]

1. Unit-record programs, using punched-card equipment exclusively as terminal programs, are outdated. There is only a demand for a limited number of operators in this area. The day of the fully equipped unit-record installation is all but over. Most data processing shops are computer-oriented. Proponents of this kind of program must realize that it is a limited approach toward up-to-date business data processing education.

2. Emphasis on these types of languages is needed: COBOL, Assembler, Basic, a Report Program Generator, and perhaps some FORTRAN. These languages will provide higher transferability to other languages the graduate may encounter while giving valuable skills necessary to obtain gainful employment. Some states are requiring the COBOL language to be taught in business data processing programs.

3. In addition to card systems, instruction in magnetic disk and/or magnetic tape systems is necessary. A computer system that is of any size will require basic knowledge in one or both of these areas.

4. Emphasis should also be placed on common data processing systems such as accounts receivable, inventory, billing, and so on. An overview and a fairly good understanding of systems design will help the data processor at the entry level to more clearly understand his or her role and will aid in further understanding as he or she proceeds up the ladder.

In short, then, hardware and curricula coincide; they must be directed toward the same goals. What the student learns in the classroom must be applied on the hardware, and these endeavors can be justified only if they are typical of the kinds of activities being performed in today's modern data processing installations. Once the educational objectives are determined and justified for a given program, great care must be taken to select the hardware that will assure the attainment of the objectives. Of course, all things being equal, the catalyst for any successful program is the instructor. Without a teacher thoroughly grounded in the field, hardware and curricula will be of little value.

TEACHING DATA PROCESSING

During the 1960s, a large number of business education data processing programs were begun, both on the secondary and postsecondary levels. Their purpose was to train technicians and to provide a source of supply to meet the need for data processing personnel. The early curriculum patterns that were developed served as models for numerous new programs. The teachers for these programs came from industry, colleges and universities, and the public schools. Business teachers gained their knowledge of data processing by attending manufacturers seminars, through government-sponsored institutes, and intensive home study programs.

Teaching punched-card concepts

As indicated previously, the current need for teaching punched-card concepts has been a subject of concern to business educators. Many feel that, with the introduction of low-cost minicomputers capable of performing most punched-card functions at greater speed, it is questionable whether the need for this highly specialized training will continue. Before extensive training is offered, community needs should be assessed by consultation with your advisory committee and perhaps a survey of the job opportunities available. Because some business educators feel that they can justify its place in the business curriculum, let us examine briefly the teaching of unit-record knowledge and skill.

The *problem-oriented approach,* described by Westley,[13] is most commonly used when one of the course objectives is to provide an introduction to unit-record data processing rather than a high degree of vocational competence (where an intensive machine approach may be used).

During the beginning of the unit-record course, the teacher discusses each of the machines in nontechnical terms. The purpose is to enable the student to learn the characteristics and the basic functions of each machine and its relationship to the other machines. Flowcharting is introduced to help provide a graphic presentation of these relationships, to describe the flow of data through the machines, and to illustrate the need for adequate documentation of solutions to data processing problems.

Each student is given the description of a simple data processing problem to be solved using unit-record equipment. He or she plans the solution, using flowcharts to describe the sequence of machines and processes that will be followed. Record layouts, printer design forms, and wiring diagrams are prepared and submitted to the teacher for approval. It may be desirable to have several problems that require the use of different combinations of machines for their solution. This ensures more efficient use of equipment and eliminates waiting time for the student.

After each step is completed, the student in cooperation with the teacher determines whether the desired outcomes at that point have been met. After all steps are completed, the entire solution is tested, using test data usually prepared by the teacher. If the results are incorrect, the student must determine the cause of the errors and make the necessary corrections. Once the solution is successfully tested, the complete "package" is submitted for evaluation. The contents of the "package" may vary considerably, depending on the teacher's requirements. Usually it would include a problem narrative, input and output formats and descriptions, wiring diagrams, a systems flowchart, operator instructions, a sample of the test data, and a copy of the final output(s).

Teaching programming techniques

If programming of business applications is taught in the business education department, it should be justified for its vocational objectives. Except as a possible tool for solving mathematical-type problems, it is unlikely that it can be justified for its personal-use value. The business programmer is concerned with developing solutions to business data processing applications. The programs he or she writes are likely to be used over and over again on a regular, scheduled basis—payroll and inventory, for example. The following outline by Westley[14] suggests some of the topics that might be covered in a programming logic, problem-solving unit or course. These topics should give the student an idea of some of the activities a programmer performs making it possible to decide whether or not he or she likes this kind of work before committing a great amount of time and effort.

1. Symbolic representation of programming logic
   a. Systems flowcharting
   b. Functional flowcharting
   c. Detail or logic flowcharting
   d. Flowcharting and program documentation
2. Problem-solving techniques using flowcharts
   a. Input and output logic and techniques
   b. Looping concepts
   c. Indexing
   d. Subroutines
   e. Table logic and techniques
   f. Decision table logic
3. File processing
   a. File organization
   b. File updating logic
   c. File access methods
   d. Detection and prevention of file process errors

The *programming exercise approach*[15] to teaching programming consists of using a series of short problems, each of which is designed to present a particular programming concept, technique, and/or instruction. Each subsequent exercise builds on the previous one, gradually working into more complex problem situations. The teacher introduces only those language elements necessary to solve successfully the exercise currently being developed. For example, in a symbolic assembler language course, a first problem might be to write a program to make a copy of a deck of cards that have been previously punched. Such an exercise teaches the use of input and output instructions, looping, and simple data description entries. The second problem expands on the first by requiring a count of the number of cards read, an accumulation of certain data on the cards, and a summary card punched containing the accumulated amounts. This introduces students to the use of arithmetic instructions and the additional data description entries necessary for defining work areas. A third problem introduces printed output and the instructions related to the printer. In each problem, the student is required to submit a flowchart prior to coding the solution, as well as a modified flowchart reflecting the changes made in the process of debugging or correcting programming errors. Advantages to this approach are that each student can work at his or her own pace, allowing the faster student to progress more quickly, and freeing the instructor to work with those students who need attention.

The *comprehensive problem approach,* also described by Westley,[16] begins with an overview of the features of the particular programming language. The student is presented with language elements, language structure, coding system, hardware considerations, and various syntax rules he or she will be using. (It should be noted that the success of this approach depends upon the student's possessing the ability to understand the logic necessary for solving typical business applications problems. If the student has not had this training, it is necessary to delay presentation of specific language considerations until sufficient skills in computer logic problem solving have been developed.)

Following overview of the language, the student is led through a carefully preplanned applications problem. The problem description is presented, discussed, and analyzed so that there is a clear understanding of problem objectives, inputs, outputs, and processing requirements. From this discussion, a logic flowchart for the problem solution is developed by the class under the guidance of the instructor. This flowchart serves as a guide for coding the solution. To give them the opportunity to learn the proper use of program coding forms, students fill out their own coding sheets for the problem solution. The first items coded are usually the input and output data descriptions. Then the coding of the individual instructions that will process the data are written. The instructor and the class work through the coding cooperatively, discussing each instruction and item of coding as it occurs. In this way, students learn the use of specific instruction in relation to a specific need. The coded program is keypunched into cards creating a deck commonly known as the source program deck. A precompile listing of the cards is then made to identify keypunch and other detected errors that may have occurred. It is particularly desirable to have a prelist if the student keypunches his or her own program. Corrections are made in the source deck and, with the necessary control cards added, the program is compiled. These control cards should be provided by the instructor in order to avoid long explanations that are not necessary for beginning programming students.

After the program is compiled, the student receives a copy of the printed output from the computer. There will usually be a listing of the source program (source deck entries), a list of errors and their location in the program, and a listing of the machine language or object program. Each error is examined to determine the changes necessary to correct it. This process is known as *debugging* the program. It is at this point that the student realizes the degree of care and the level of accuracy demanded of a programmer. It may be necessary to repeat the compile and debug steps several times until all errors detected by the computer have been corrected. Attaining a "clean compilation" does not mean, however, that the program will run. It merely indicates that all syntax and clerical errors have been eliminated. There may still be logic errors. These are detected by attempting to execute the program, using test data prepared in advance for the program. After all the logical and clerical errors have been corrected, the program is given the final test. The process of "walking" the students through the complete programming cycle may require more time with some groups than with others, and it may take away some of the "glamour" of computer programming. After this initial exposure, students are given additional problems to introduce them to additional language elements and instructions in a variety of programming situations.

The systems orientation approach[17] goes a step further in orienting the student to the field of data processing. Rather than introduce programming language, the instructor begins with a typical data processing systems problem. The objective is to show that a data processing system is a composite of a number of smaller problems, each of which requires a solution. The writing of a single program is not an end in itself, but rather only a small part of the overall solution. For example, the typical payroll system is composed of a number of subprograms. One produces the payroll register, another prepares the payroll checks, while yet another processes the year-to-date information and maintains the files. The basic idea is to develop the instructional program around one or more small systems. The specifications and interrelationships of each of the programs are developed cooperatively by the class under the guidance of the instructor.

The first program in the system and the related language consideration are presented in much the same manner as described in the comprehensive problem approach. The second and subsequent programs are then programmed by students. It is desirable to divide the class into small groups, with each writing the programs for only a part of the system. After all of the programs are tested and debugged, the entire system is tested. This technique brings out very clearly the need for accurate and complete documentation as well as the ability to work effectively with others. The systems orientation approach requires a great deal of planning if it is to be effective. A primary advantage is that the student learns programming in a realistic systems-oriented programming environment, realizing that the program is not an end in itself, but only part of a larger problem. He or she learns to work cooperatively with others, develops the ability to communicate ideas, and is given the opportunity to develop programming skills and creativity in solving business data processing problems with a computer.

A successful example of the teaching of electronic computer programming is cited by Phillip L. Gocker of Kimberly High School, Kimberly, Wisconsin.[18] Officials at the high school and area vocational/technical school worked out an arrangement in which high school students could run the programs they had written and keypunched, using the area school's IBM 360 computer. This cooperative venture gave high school students practical experience in writing programs, keypunching them, and debugging them when necessary. A flat rate charge for this service based on actual running time plus the number of programs was established. Through this experiment and joint venture, high school enrollment has grown from two one-semester offerings to four one-semester classes, each with expanded programming time.

The question of objectives in computer programming is addressed by Aukerman who feels that business educators should not be preparing specialized producers of data processing information except in designated technical curriculums.[19] Aukerman further states that we should educate our students in data processing principles classes at all education levels for the intelligent use of data processing information. In other words, we should be preparing wise consumers of computer output rather than programming specialists.

> . . . computer programming should give the student an appreciation of the complexities of computer programming, the ability to actually write simple programs, and an understanding of the type of information a programmer must have available in order to solve a business problem. The important point to remember when teaching an introductory computer programming course to nontechnical business students is that they should be able to understand computer programming; they should not be expected to perform as full-fledged, efficient computer programmers. Perhaps an acceptance of that statement and an adherence to its meaning will better allow business educators to prepare students to understand the inner workings of business data processing in an ever-changing atmosphere![20]

INTEGRATING DATA PROCESSING INTO OTHER COURSES

While instruction in the more technical aspects is best presented in a data processing course, there are numerous ways of integrating data processing concepts into other business education courses. In integrating these concepts into other courses, the emphasis should be on the *why* rather than the *how.*

TYPEWRITING.   Introduce students to career materials describing employment opportunities in data processing occupations requiring typewriting skills. Classroom demonstrations of various keyboard-operated equipment can be arranged to familiarize students with the keypunch, automatic typewriter, flexowriter, and teleprinter. You may wish to have students plan a card layout from which their names and addresses could be printed and, using a blank card and the layout they have designed, let them fill in the appropriate data by blanking out the correct combination of punch positions on the card. The cards can be run through an interpreter or accounting machine to have the data printed either on the card or on a sheet of paper.

Benno Sydòw, an instructor at Kellogg High School, Roseville, Minnesota, motivates typing students by having them type on a computer terminal.[21] The computer program is a timed drill that requires the user to type a previously entered sentence rapidly and correctly. When the sentence is typed correctly and within the allotted time, the program prints out the number of seconds and words per minute. The BASIC program can be changed to add the student's name, put in a variety of sentences for skill building, or store students' scores from one week to the next, thereby indicating progress. The program is as follows:[22]

```
LIS
TYPE

10   REM BENNO SYDOW, KELLOGG HIGH SCHOOL, ROSEVILLE, MN, APRIL 1975
20   DIM A$(72),B$(72)
30   A$="IT IS RIGHT THAT WE DO WELL."
40   PRINT "INSTRUCTIONS (YES OR NO)";
50   INPUT B$
60   IF B$(1,1)#"Y" THEN 120
70   PRINT "AFTER THE GO HAS BEEN PRINTED TYPE THE FOLLOWING"
80   PRINT "QUICKLY AND ACCURATELY: PRESS CARRIAGE RETURN AFTER"
90   PRINT "TYPING PERIOD"
100  PRINT
110  PRINT A$
120  PRINT "GO"
130  ENTER LEN(A$)/2,T,B$
140  PRINT
150  IF T=-256 THEN 220
160  IF B$=A$ THEN 190
170  PRINT "LETTERS INCORRECT"
180  GOTO 230
190  PRINT "TIME = ";T;"SECONDS"
200  PRINT "WPM = ";LEN(A$)*12/T
210  GOTO 230
220  PRINT "TOO SLOW, PRACTICE!!!"
230  PRINT "AGAIN (YES OR NO)";
240  INPUT B$
250  IF B$(1,1)="Y" THEN 120
260  END
GET-TYPE
RUN
TYPE


INSTRUCTIONS (YES OR NO)?Y
AFTER THE GO HAS BEEN PRINTED TYPE THE FOLLOWING
QUICKLY AND ACCURATELY:  PRESS CARRIAGE RETURN AFTER
TYPING PERIOD


IT IS RIGHT THAT WE DO WELL.
GO
IT IS RIGHT THAT WE DO WELL.
TIME  =  4        SECONDS
WPM  =  84
AGAIN (YES OR NO)?Y
GO
IT IS RIGHT THAT WE DO WELL.
TIME  =  3        SECONDS
WPM  =  112
AGAIN (YES OR NO)?N

DONE
```

SHORTHAND AND TRANSCRIPTION.   Develop shorthand outlines for common data processing terminology. Discuss the meanings of these terms and the context in which they may be found. Prepare dictation materials using these terms for a variety of correspondence situations. These activities should be included as a regular part of speedbuilding and transcription practice. Terms and their definitions are readily available from data processing equipment manufacturers, data processing books, and periodicals.

OFFICE PRACTICE.   Principles of data collection, preparation, and retrieval that are automated may be illustrated through films and filmstrips, magazines, books, and brochures from manufacturers. Students can use a teacher-prepared unit of filing and sorting, using punched and interpreted cards to illustrate that the filing theory is the same whether manual or automated methods are used. Students can also develop a panel discussion of the data processing functions of recording, classifying, sorting, computing, summarizing, communicating, and storing, comparing manual methods with the way these functions are performed by machines. Manufacturers can be invited to demonstrate text-editing equipment such as the stand-alone, software-oriented, programmable word processing system consisting of a keyboard, video display screen, printer, and dual station diskettes that are part of an integrated office system.

BUSINESS LAW.   Invite a representative from your local police department for a presentation of some of the data processing equipment being used by various law enforcement agencies. Topics such as "Invasion of Privacy by the Computer" can be used for a written and/or oral report by students.

BUSINESS MATHEMATICS.   Discuss and give examples of how automated data processing equipment has taken the drudgery out of payroll computations. Have students work various business problems and show how the computer will perform the same operations in a fraction of the time. Prepare flowcharts of the steps involved in solving mathematical problems. Develop exercises using various number bases such as binary and octal and the conversion from one base to another. Ask your local Radio Shack dealer to illustrate the completion of tasks such as inventory, general ledger posting, payroll, and accounts receivable with the TRS–80 microcomputer.

GENERAL BUSINESS.   The chapter on communications might be supplemented with a discussion of the automatic billing procedures that result from the completion of a direct dial, long distance phone call. The unit on transportation might include a discussion of the color coding system on railroad freight cars and the optical readers used by railroads in their locator and billing system for freight car accounting. A variety of business simulation programs and management games can be used to increase student interest and participation in class.

BOOKKEEPING AND ACCOUNTING. After completing the accounting cycle, introduce the ways in which the various activities can be accomplished by machines. Take a field trip to a business where the accounting process is largely automated. Examine and discuss checks and bank statements from a local bank. Explain the use of MICR (Magnetic Ink Character Recognition) coding along the bottom of the check. Several publishers are marketing materials that use the computer to supplement the teaching of accounting. Access to a computer is required, which could be a limiting factor.

CONSUMER-ECONOMIC EDUCATION. The economic impact and the effect of data processing on employment should be explored in these subjects. In teaching the stock market, a comparison of the growth of an industry would be relevant to the students' study. The use of computers for projections, predictions, and simulations as applied to management is directly related to economics. Use of computers in selecting investments is increasing and should be acknowledged as a business application of the computer.

Articulation of instruction

As data processing instruction progresses in educational institutions, programs in the high school will emphasize training for initial employment. In this category, there will be preparation for machine operators of various types. For example, operators of input machines can be trained in high schools, as well as the data typist, file clerk, sorting machine operator, and teletype operator. The high school can also prepare junior programmers or programmers' aides and operators. Included in this category are those students who wish to prepare for positions as programmers, systems analysts, and other higher level positions for which additional training is required.

Technical schools are developing programs for maintenance personnel, sales and managerial jobs. Programmers and systems analysts will also be trained at these institutions. Basically, these jobs provide the labor market with persons who can assume higher level jobs.

The four-year college graduate and the graduate student will be involved more in the area of software development. Since technological advances have gone beyond the capabilities of individuals to utilize equipment to the fullest, development of software will be receiving more attention in the future.

The development of computer-assisted instruction will require persons trained in many disciplines—behavioral scientists, mathematicians, instructional programmers, software experts, and engineering personnel. One of the frontiers of electronic data processing lies in the development of software to utilize the computer as a tool of learning. Business educators must become aware of the impact this development can have on business education. Business educators should be specialists in the development of programs and in the use of hardware involved.

COMPUTER WORD PROCESSING

Computer word processing is the merging of word processing with an electronic data processing computer system. The components of any word processing system are the same as those of a computer system: input, storage, processing, control, and output. Automatic typewriting systems are generally built around existing electric typewriters or communications terminals and may be classified as stand-alone units, shared-logic systems, and time sharing. They utilize a storage medium to contain text that generally will be typed, edited, or updated a number of times.

STAND-ALONE UNITS.   From the mechanical automatic typewriters of the early 1900s, which resembled the player piano, present technology has developed "stand-alone" equipment. This equipment consists of an electric typewriter with an electric hookup to a small-scale, special-purpose computer brain, with a magnetic tape cartridge or punched paper tape for storage. The stand-alone configuration is intended for desktop mounting or is available embedded in an integral desk.

Other technological developments incorporated into stand-alone word processing systems include cathode-ray tube viewing screens which allow scanning of an entire page of a document before sending it to a storage media (input) or printing hard copy (output). Magnetic cards, magnetic tape cassettes, magnetic disks or diskettes, and internal memories controlled by microprocessors provide immediate access to over 10,000 characters. For the most part, these systems are also produced as stand-alone units for use in computer systems.

SHARED-LOGIC SYSTEMS.   Stand-alone units have been incorporated into minicomputer-based systems for multiterminal/typestation in-house installations. Since they comprise a small-scale, time-sharing network, they are sometimes called shared-logic systems. The in-house, shared-logic system may support up to several dozen concurrent users, dependent upon system power and individual user workload. The shared-logic system may also include a photocomposition typesetting service which composes pages for typesetting. Input to the composition program may be output from a text-editing time-sharing system or may have been created in computer-readable form on some other system.

TIME SHARING.   Commercial time sharing is available for work processing applications, as well as the traditional electronic data processing applications. In both, multiple users have access simultaneously to a large central computer CPU (Central Processing Unit), yet each user appears to have sole access. Access is made by dialing the vendor's telephone number and using a password to establish communication between the CPU and the user's terminal (often a teletype unit).

TRAINING PERSONNEL. The typical automatic typewriting system can be operated by typists after training sessions ranging in length from several hours to several days. While almost any typist can learn how to operate an automatic typewriter, the most sophisticated text-editing systems should be managed by more "machine-oriented" personnel. It is the business educators of today who have a great responsibility to teach students about the concepts of electronic data processing, such as the application of computer word processing, to better prepare them for the future.

A major life insurance company has a screening procedure for word processors that provides clues for today's business educators as to content of this "machine-oriented" education. At this company, personnel for the word processing center were selected on the basis of a typewriting test requiring fifty words or better per minute, a standard spelling test, a proofreading test, and a standard word usage test. The basic skills of spelling, punctuation, grammar, and word choice are essential for positions at the machine operation level. For positions such as document originator or editor, additional skills in organization of writing and paragraphing are also important. As more companies use computer word processing for reprographics, the knowledge of graphic arts, in addition to basic skills, will be most beneficial.

The computer system is one configuration that can be used to accomplish word processing. Input can be implemented from paper and pencil, live shorthand dictation, dictation using recording equipment or electronic note taking (machine shorthand to magnetic tape). The output process may involve automatic typewriters, camera-ready copy for copiers, or reprographic equipment. Distribution may be accomplished through communications-oriented automatic typewriters, telephone interconnect equipment, facsimile (FAX), or physical delivery systems such as mail or messenger service. As editing and word processing become additional functions of the computer system, and as the interface between departments of the modern office is facilitated by technology, possibilities for integrated systems for automated business communication and information handling become realities.

METHODS OF INDIVIDUALIZING

One of the best-known plans for individualizing the teaching of data processing is the AVT (Audio-Visual-Tutorial) system developed and practiced at Lansing Community College, Lansing, Michigan. Weller and Edwards[23] describe AVT as a plan that completely individualizes instruction for every student participating. It utilizes audiovisual equipment and materials, the learning carrel, and tutorial assistance to guide each student at his or her own pace until the concepts and skills of a course or program are mastered. Easily adapted to the range of intellectual, emotional, environmental, and physical capabilities among individuals, the plan adjusts for differences in prior education, present extraschool activities, and future goals of each participant. It is an economically feasible system that can be tailored for all age groups from pre-school to graduate school and for any subject matter area.

There are no routine lectures or demonstrations because all instruction is provided in carefully prepared audiovisual units to be used by the student. Each of these units is mastered to an acceptable standard before the student progresses to the next one. There are no sets of papers or tests to be graded, as each paper is graded in an individual conference with the student involved. As a result of these conferences, on a one-to-one basis, the teacher becomes acquainted with the student as a person with abilities, desires, and hang-ups. The teacher can use his or her professional knowledge and skill to help each student achieve, instead of using group techniques that inspire some but invariably turn off others completely.

This system not only makes it possible for the professional teacher to avoid a lot of takehome work, but it also can free some important daytime hours for many types of professional development. Office hours are not always filled with student conferences because much of the advising and all course problems are handled in the AVT laboratory. There is more time for regular "housekeeping" chores, reading, writing, and the important obligation of finding out how data processing is being used in the community.

The experience of Weller and Edwards in teaching COBOL and FOR-TRAN under the AVT system resulted in their recommending that all courses be conducted on a laboratory basis with facilities available to students as many hours each day or each week as feasible. The time involved will be dependent upon each student's need, motivation, and external activities. Students do not necessarily have to be scheduled at the same time each day or the same days each week, except possibly for reporting purposes.

When the student arrives at the learning center, he or she is required to punch a time card giving the date, time, and unit. The student then receives the next audiovisual unit for the course and goes to an independent study carrel equipped with the necessary hardware to view and listen to the short, concise lesson. Whenever possible, students will actively perform some task along with the instructions.

Upon completion, the student takes the work to an instructor to learn whether or not it was done correctly, thus obtaining immediate feedback and a chance to correct any faulty practices or erroneous concepts before they become deeply entrenched. This tutorial aspect of each course may well be the most significant because every student gets the individual and undivided attention of the instructor as many times as there are units in the courses. If a satisfactory score is obtained on a quiz for the unit, the student can continue on to the next unit. Otherwise the unit must be repeated or reviewed. Having the exercises checked and giving a unit quiz prevents the student from waiting until the last minute and then cramming, with little understanding or retention.

When the AVT unit cycle is completed by the student, he or she signs out of the laboratory, indicating the time of departure. The student could, however, remain in the lab and proceed to the next unit of the course if he or she had the time and the desire to do so. To further teach and to test the student, programs are assigned to be coded, punched into source decks, and batched to be run on the computer. These programs draw together the contents of several units and provide a test of student understanding of those units.

Use of instructional television

At Oklahoma State University[24] television is used for presenting the basic material in the computer programming course. By allowing graduate assistants to develop the material in the TV lessons (at the same time applying the material according to the particular needs of students), the course is standardized, yet tailored as necessary for different groups of students. In addition, television can be used quite effectively for projecting close-ups of computer cards and output to large numbers of students and for showing computer equipment in operation.

Use of gaming and simulation

Use of the computer for gaming and simulation represents a valuable and exhilarating instructional experience for both student and teacher. Through computer simulation, the student can experiment and gain experience, test alternative solutions, and observe answers to "what if" type questions. Computer gaming and simulation serve to extend exposure to laboratory experimentation and decision making.

EVALUATION

Because of changing technology in the data processing field, there is a need for continued redesign of the data processing program to assure that it meets current needs of the community and students. Such redesign, of course, is based upon evaluation. The purpose of evaluating a data processing program is to assess achievements and make improvements. The process of evaluation should be continuous and include analysis of pertinent reference groups. Evaluation should, therefore, be both descriptive and judgmental. This section covers a few of the methods and techniques that are helpful in evaluating.

Surveys

There are many types of surveys. Data can be gathered from interviewing and from mailed questionnaires. A survey of employers who hire people for their computer centers often reveals useful information, for example, on entry requirements, employment standards, promotional opportunities, and earnings. Employers who have hired program enrollees (both graduates and nongraduates) should be able to make valid judgments of their preparation and formal training while in school. An equipment survey may facilitate course revisions, hardware replacement, and expectations for students.

Cooperative office education programs

The broad category of cooperative programs includes two basic types. First, the traditional part-time work experience programs in which the student spends a portion of the day in school and a portion of the day working in an approved training or work station. Second, the internship program, in which a student spends a quarter or a semester working full time for an employer in an approved, directly related occupation and alternate periods in full-time study. Either type of program facilitates evaluation, although part-time employment seems more popular, especially with high school students.

The business teacher assigned to coordinate the cooperative program has several opportunities to gather data for evaluation. Useful information might be obtained, for example, when locating, inspecting, and approving employment stations during the development of a training plan and while selecting and placing students. As the cooperative program becomes operational, additional information can be collected when supervisory visits are made. At each stage in the development and operation of this kind of activity, objectives should be reviewed and modified where necessary. At the close of the work experience period, teachers, students, and employers should be expected to evaluate their experiences and the program in general. These evaluations will provide information that will help to identify strengths and weaknesses and to point out needed revisions.

Follow-up

A follow-up study is another of the many evaluative tools that may be used. For example, it could be designed to gather data relative to those who were employed in directly related, related, or unrelated occupations; those who are attaining success or failure; as well as elicit opinions relative to needed program revisions, such as courses, course content, requirements and electives, texts, equipment, staff, and salary data. The follow-up study should include former program enrollees; more meaningful data can be gathered from this group than from program graduates only. Data from graduates fails to take into account students whose studies were terminated before completion.

Even more meaningful than a follow-up study would be a follow-up program that may be designed as a continuous procedure in which enrollees are followed up automatically six months after an academic year ends, and program garduates are followed up twice more on an annual basis.

Advisory committee

Members of your advisory committee can make valid judgments about quality and appropriateness of the data processing program. Since the purpose of the advisory committee is to give advice, it can render valuable assistance in such areas as curriculum, course content, staffing, teaching, and learning materials, guest lecturers, installation visits, and training or work stations for cooperative students. Members of the advisory committee could be asked to evaluate the program on a formal or informal basis.

Evaluation of students' work is necessary both on an interim and an end-of-course basis. Such evaluation is tied to performance goals for the course and to the grading system endorsed by the school. Evaluation is a continuous process of collecting information from all pertinent reference groups (students, employers, advisory committee members, teachers, and administrators) for the purpose of making judgments about the effectiveness of the data processing program. Program results should be compared to program objectives, to standards, and to other comparable programs. Once this has been accomplished, strengths and weaknesses will be identifiable and decision making for program improvement more easily accomplished.

module 13.2
LEARNING ACTIVITIES

1. Plan a field trip with your class. Identify in advance the applications you wish to observe. The tour should include an explanation, by company personnel, of the processing steps the class will see. The class should view actual input documents, keypunching operations and card production, steps involved in transferring card data to tape or disk, and the controls imposed for balancing and accuracy. The responsibilities of computer operators in running the job, examples of computer output for the application, controls on output, and the final disposition of reports or documents produced should all be thoroughly reviewed.

2. Write a paper on the evolution of computer systems beginning with Eckert's model at the University of Pennsylvania in 1947. Emphasize the hardware, software, and manager relationships involved.

3. Collect literature and visit a minicomputer installation (such as Radio Shack's TRS–80 or the IBM System 7 or the Honeywell 700). Make an oral report to your class about the educational applications of the minicomputer.

4. As a business teacher considering the purchase or lease of data processing hardware, draw up a questionnaire containing the items you would need answered in order to make the right decision.

5. Make an outline of the steps involved in one of the following:
   a. problem orientation approach to teaching unit-record data processing
   b. comprehensive problem approach to teaching programming
   c. programming exercise approach to teaching programming
   d. systems orientation approach to teaching data processing

6. Ask two business teachers (other than data processing teachers) how they incorporate concepts of automation and data processing into the courses they teach.

7. Interview a data processing teacher at the high school, community college, and college levels to determine the objectives and scope of the data processing program. Then prepare a written report comparing similarities and differences in the programs.
   Alternate Activity 7: Prepare the above report by drawing the information from a study of catalogs or other materials prepared by the schools.

8. Invite a sales representative to talk with your class about word processing systems. Ask the representative to explain the differences among stand-alone units, shared-logic systems, and time sharing.

9. Read and summarize an article from a professional business education journal describing a multimedia plan for individualizing instruction in data processing.
10. Outline the components of one or two plans for evaluating the effectiveness of the data processing program at a given level.

module 13.2
SELF-TEST

1. Define the following terms:
   a. hardware
   b. software
   c. unit-record systems
   d. first-generation computer
   e. second-generation computer
   f. third-generation computer
2. Describe some of the educational implications of the trend toward minicomputer installations.
3. Identify briefly two of the procedures a business teacher might use in deciding which data processing hardware to recommend for purchase or lease.
4. What factors would determine whether or not you might recommend the teaching of unit-record data processing in a given school?
5. Describe (a) the exercise approach and (b) the comprehensive problem approach to teaching programming.
6. Give several examples of how data processing concepts can be integrated into courses outside the data processing area.
7. Differentiate among the emphasis of data processing at high school, technical school, and college levels.
8. Explain the meaning of the term "computer word processing."
9. Describe the AVT plan for individualizing instruction in data processing.
10. Describe one of the methods commonly used to evaluate data processing programs.

SUMMARY

Computers have affected the lives of all of us either personally or professionally. Thus, data processing is emerging as an important part of the business education curriculum. Data processing instruction may involve three general goals: computer literacy or general education appropriate for all students; problem solving or related instruction for students whose career objectives include occupations using data processing; and job entry or preparation for careers in data processing. All of these goals are incorporated in varying degrees from the middle/junior high school through college and university levels. Programs range from one-semester introductory courses or units incorporated into existing courses to three- or four-year programs.

Certain steps should be taken if an effective instructional data processing program is to be planned and implemented: determine the need; identify the program and course objectives; form an advisory committee; determine the organizational structure for the program; select the staff; design the curriculum; determine the facilities, equipment, and materials needed; make the equipment available; and publicize the program.

In thirty years, data processing has evolved from manual systems of processing data to unit record-keeping systems to first-, second-, and third-generation computers. Today the computer industry is shifting toward the production of stand-alone minicomputers that offer the possibility, because of lower cost, for more hands-on training of individuals. Once the educational objectives for a data processing program are determined, care must be taken to select hardware that will realize attainment of the objectives.

Methodology in data processing centers around a comprehensive problem-oriented approach in which each exercise builds on the previous one, gradually working up to more complex problem situations. A high level of care and accuracy is essential in successfully developing and executing a program. Careful and complete documentation and the ability to work well with others are important in developing successful programmers.

Data processing can be integrated effectively into almost any business course either on a supplementary basis or as a vehicle for improving motivation and interest of students. Applications of computer word processing open up new opportunities for the machine-oriented individual and for administrative specialists. The content of data processing lends itself well to individualized, multimedia instructional approaches and to such techniques as gaming and simulation.

Through the use of surveys, cooperative office education programs, follow-up studies, and advisory committees, program results can be compared to program objectives, and decisions for improvement can be more readily made.

REFERENCES

[1] *Computers and Careers,* Central Texas College, Kileen, Texas (Washington, D.C.: U.S. Government Printing Office, 1973), p.1.

[2] Richard W. Brightman, *The Computer and the Junior College Curriculum* (Washington, D.C.: American Association of Community and Junior Colleges, 1970), p. 10.

[3] *Computers and Careers,* p. 5.

[4] Emma Jo Spiegelberg, "Data Processing for High School Students," *Business Education Forum* 28, no. 5 (February 1974): 46.

[5] Ibid.

[6] John W. Westley, "Data Processing," in *Changing Methods of Teaching Business Subjects* (Washington, D.C.: National Business Education Association, 1972), pp. 177–78.

[7] Lloyd D. Brooks, "Four Issues in Teaching Data Processing," *Business Education Forum* 26, no. 4 (January 1972): 40.

[8] Data Processing Mini-Course, "The Development of an Individualized Instructional System of Mini-Exploratory Courses in Career Education," (Athens: The University of Georgia, Department of Business Education, 1974), pp. 41–51.

[9] Neil J. Humphreys, "An Introductory Course in Systems Analysis," *Business Education Forum* 26, no. 1 (October 1971): 64–65.

[10] Lloyd Brooks and Robert Behling, "Minicomputers in the Business Teacher's Future," *Business Education Forum* 32, no. 4 (January 1978): 26–27.

[11]Terry E. Berryman, "Business Data Processing: Hardware and Curriculums," *Business Education Forum* 25, no. 2 (November 1970): 47–48.

[12]Ibid., p. 48.

[13]Westley, "Data Processing," pp. 169–70.

[14]Ibid., p. 170.

[15]Ibid., p. 171.

[16]Ibid., p. 172.

[17]Ibid., p. 173.

[18]Phillip L. Gocker, "Data Processing Can Be Taught in the High School," *Business Education Forum* 25, no. 3 (December 1970): 58–59.

[19]Richard Aukerman, "Business Students and Computer Programming," *Business Education Forum* 32, no. 2 (November 1977): 27.

[20] Ibid., p. 28.

[21]Benno Sydow, "Using the Computer Terminal to Motivate Typing Students," *Business Education Forum* 29, no. 7 (April 1975): 25–26.

[22]Ibid., p. 26.

[23]Stephen A. Weller and Ronald K. Edwards, "AVT System in Data Processing," *Business Education Forum* 27, no. 2 (November 1972): 58–60.

[24]Eugene Bailey, "Use of Instructional TV in Computer Programming," *Business Education Forum* 28, no. 1 (October 1972): 28–29.

SUGGESTIONS FOR FURTHER STUDY

Clark, James F. "Computer-Aided Instruction for Vocational Typewriting." *Business Education Forum* 32, no. 5 (February 1978): 28–29.

Felske, Herbert P. "Comprehensive Computer Program Requires Thorough Planning." *Business Education Forum* 32, no. 8 (May 1978): 36–37.

Gocker, Phillip L. "Programming Can Be Taught in the High School." *Business Education Forum,* 25, no. 3 (December 1970): 58–59.

Hallam, Stephen F. "The Advantages of Teaching More than One Programming Language." *Business Education Forum* 27, no. 3 (December 1972): 31–32.

Hamed, Charles J. "The Business Teacher's Role in Automated Data Processing." *Business Education Forum* 24, no. 8 (May 1970): 27.

Harvey, Alvina. "Data Processing for Ninth Grade Students." *Business Education Forum* 29, no. 2 (November 1974): 27–29.

Kaczmarski, Raymond. "Keypunch Takes on New Look." *Business Education Forum* 26, no. 2 (November 1971): 52–53.

Lambrecht, Judith J. "Curriculum Guidelines for High School Data Processing." *Business Education Forum* 32, no. 3 (December 1977): 29–31.

Leeson, Marjorie. "Walkthroughs Help Achieve Valid Computer Programming." *Business Education Forum* 33, no. 3 (November 1978): 24–28.

———. "Where Will the Minicomputer Lead Us?" *Business Education Forum* 29, no. 5 (February 1975): 21–23.

Ruge, Gerale D. "Use of a Mobile Classroom in the Teaching of Data Processing." *Business Education Forum* 24, no. 4 (January 1970): 32–33.

Schrag, Adele F. "Computer Terminals in the Classroom." *Business Education Forum* 26, no. 5 (February 1972): 48–49.

part five

TEACHING BASIC BUSINESS/ CAREER SKILLS

chapter 14

TEACHING BASIC BUSINESS COURSES

The general area of basic business is "coming of age" as a major component of business education. In many states, competencies in areas such as consumer education, economics, and the private enterprise system are mandated as requirements for high school seniors or as part of a core of competencies for all students.

Module 14.1 covers the rationale, objectives, and content of four basic business courses. Module 14.2 reviews elements of planning the instructional program in basic business. Module 14.3 includes a description of several instructional strategies appropriate for basic business subjects. Module 14.4 deals with evaluation procedures for basic business education.

module 14.1
OBJECTIVES AND CONTENT FOR BASIC BUSINESS

The area of basic business may be described as education *about* business that contributes to the general education of all students. Four courses that may be classified as basic business are included in this module: (1) consumer education, (2) economics-private enterprise system, (3) business law, and (4) general business.

After completing this module, you should be able to (1) identify the purpose and objectives of the basic business courses, (2) recommend grade placement and duration of each basic business course, and (3) select appropriate instructional topics and units for each course.

CONSUMER EDUCATION

Consumer education is the development in people of the capability for (1) achieving maximum use of and satisfaction from resources, (2) evaluating alternatives in the marketplace, (3) understanding rights and responsibilities as consumers in society, and (4) fulfilling their role as participants in a free enterprise system. Individuals and families are constantly making decisions about the use of their resources.\The choices they make as they purchase goods and services are largely determined by their values and goals. The market is growing increasingly more complex, and many persons both young and old are not prepared to decide among the alternatives available.

Consumer education is needed from kindergarten throughout the school program to help develop the attitudes, knowledges, and skills necessary to perform the buying, borrowing, investing, protecting, sharing, and saving functions for effective citizenship.

Objectives

The overall objectives for a consumer education course may be basically the same, regardless of grade level. Individual expectations, however, will vary, depending on students' ability level, maturity, prior knowledge and training in consumer education. Calhoun and Boyd[1] list the following general objectives which may serve as a guide for devloping your own objectives.

1. The student will recognize the importance of estimating income and expenses, clarifying values and goals, making decisions and financial plans.
    a. Students will list sources of income, keep records, and estimate income in real and hypothetical case studies.
    b. Students will be able to determine how money is spent, keep personal expense records, and estimate expenses in real and hypothetical cases.
    c. Students will clarify values and become aware of how personal goals influence financial decisions.
    d. Students will be able to apply the decision-making process to financial decisions in real and hypothetical cases.
    e. Students will be able to formulate and evaluate real or hypothetical spending plans.
2. Students will acquire skills that are necessary to make rational decisions when buying for themselves and for their families.
    a. Students will identify the skills and knowledges necessary to make rational decisions when buying for themselves and their families.
    b. Students will develop shopping skills which will make them more discriminating consumers.
    c. Students will investigate sources of information about products and services and will recognize the need for obtaining information before making a purchase.
    d. Students will recognize the need for consumer protection and will be able to identify the kinds of protection available to the consumer.
3. Students will be able to state valid reasons for using credit, to identify the types of credit and compute the cost of credit.
    a. Students will identify the concepts of borrowing and credit and will be able to list and evaluate reasons for borrowing or using credit.

    b. Students will be able to list and evaluate different sources and types of consumer credit.

    c. Students will be able to determine how much credit costs and how to shop for credit.

    d. The student will be able to identify criteria for establishing a good credit rating and will recognize the procedures for using credit wisely.

4. Students will recognize the need for protecting assets, the types of protection available, and the importance of choosing the type of protection most suited to one's means and needs.

    a. Students will be able to identify their assets and will be aware of the need for protecting those assets.

    b. Students will be able to explain the purposes of various types of insurance and will be able to list the criteria for selecting insurance.

    c. Students will be able to demonstrate a knowledge of types of insurance by selecting the type that is most suitable for various situations.

    d. Students will be able to name and describe the governmental and private consumer protection agencies and legislation aimed toward protecting the consumer.

    e. Students will understand the importance of wills and estate planning as a means of protecting one's estate and heirs.

5. Students should develop positive attitudes toward investing their resources as a means to achieve future goals.

    a. Students will be able to state several valid reasons for individual and family saving and investing and will realize that saving is a desirable habit.

    b. Students will develop an awareness that the amount to be saved is an individual matter which is determined by one's values, goals, and the amount of money available.

    c. Students will be knowledgeable about the various means available for saving or investing and will be able to make wise decisions based on factors such as safety, liquidity, convenience, and earnings.

6. Students will understand why every citizen must share in the cost of public services by paying taxes.

    a. Students will be able to list the various public services that are available to them and their parents.

    b. Students will be able to enumerate the various types of taxes needed to finance public services, and to explain the relationship of taxes to services rendered.

    c. Students will be able to describe tax collection procedures, explain how decisions are made for allocating such monies, and list ways individuals may help to reduce taxes.

    d. Students will improve their understanding of the American economic system with particular emphasis on the consumer sector, the role that consumers play in the allocation of resources in our market economy, and consumer responsibility toward the economy.

Content

        Textbooks in consumer education are plentiful. Typical of the broad topics recommended for consumer education classes are these from

Graf:[2] Consumer Information, Food, Consumer Credit, Transportation, Consumers in the Marketplace, Consumer Aid and Protection, Consumer Services, Housing and Shelter, Insurance, and Management and Family Income. Calhoun and Boyd[3] organized their Consumer Education Resource Guide around these six major topics: Financial Planning, Buying, Borrowing, Protecting, Investing and Saving, and Sharing. The following topics appropriate to consumer education are identified in *Consumer Education in an Age of Adaptation:*[4] the Consumer and the Economy; Values and Goals; Occupation and Income; Management of Resources; Economic Choices; Consumer Information; Advertising, Selling Aids and Motivators; Buying Goods and Services; Housing; Consumer Credit; Insurance Protection; Savings and Investments; Taxes; Consumer Grievances; Consumer Protection; Consumer Rights and Responsibilities; and the Consumer and the Environment. When planning and implementing a course, avoid an overemphasis on buying products such as groceries. If possible, maintain a balance among the topics. When dealing with topics such as buying and advertising, focus on the *principles* involved rather than on individual products.

Although there are numerous consumer education textbooks available, it is important to review the content carefully for accuracy. Current changes in laws, rules, interest rates, insurance regulations, and the like will result in the content becoming quickly outdated.

ECONOMICS

Economic understanding is a generally accepted goal in American education but one that is quite lacking in its realization. Bishop points out that

> the logic supporting the goal is founded upon the politico-economic system of the United States which gives each individual a unique role to play in the decision-making process both in the realms of personal and collective decisions. The implications of the logic are: (a) economic understanding is needed in personal decision making so that each individual, in his exercise of choice, can maximize his personal welfare and thereby tend to maximize the welfare of society as a whole, and (b) economic understanding is needed in the collective decision-making process so that each individual, in the exercise of his participatory right in a democratic society, will have a sound basis for evaluating the issues in terms of alternative courses of action.[5]

Economic concepts are incorporated in courses such as general business, business principles and management, and consumer education (consumer economics). At the high school level, a separate course in economics is probably most appropriate at the twelfth grade level. At the postsecondary levels, general economics courses are usually offered in the freshman-sophomore years.

Economics is basically concerned with how people use resources (which are limited) to fulfill their needs (which are unlimited). The study of economics is not designed to impose on students a "set of values," but rather to develop skills whereby students arrive at their own decisions.

Objectives

Objectives for an economics course will vary among schools, depending on the length and level of the course, as well as the maturity and ability of students. Daughtrey suggests the following objectives:[6]

A course in economics should help the student
1. develop an understanding of the basic economic problem, of the fact that all societies face the same problem, and of the fact that all societies do not solve the problem in the same manner.
2. increase his understanding of the American economy, its characteristics, goals, strengths, weaknesses, and problems.
3. develop a realization that solutions to economic problems as well as others must be couched in terms of goals and values.
4. acquire an elementary knowledge of economic principles relating to local, state, national, and international economic problems to enable him to base his voter decisions on analysis and better understanding of these problems.
5. improve his ability to use an analytical approach to solve problems in economics and in his personal life and to reason logically instead of emotionally.
6. broaden his vocabulary to understand the more common economic terms used in the press so that he can read and interpret the more thoughtful sections of newspapers and magazines.
7. increase his ability to read comprehendingly and interpret intelligently those statistical materials, tables, graphs, and other graphical economic presentations of economics which are directed to the general public.
8. broaden his appreciation of the fact that many social problems stem from economic issues and that an understanding of the issues may provide a better means of alleviating the problems.
9. appreciate the differences between economic systems and thereby increase his understanding of and loyalty to the democratic way of life as opposed to those systems where freedoms are eliminated or are severely abridged by the state.
10. appreciate the relationships inherent in economic activity.

Content

A review of economics textbooks reveals lack of consensus in the topics included and the amount of emphasis placed on each. Content, however, seems to focus on these areas: organizations, operation, and goals of the American economy; problems and issues of our society; the roles of the individual, the producer, and the consumer in the economy; measuring the performance of our society; the government and international economics; and comparison of the American economy with other economic systems.

One teacher organized a one-semester course in "free enterprise" from an entrepreneur's point of view around these topical areas: History of Free Enterprise, Organization of a Business, Beginning a Business, Internal Management Problems, External Factors Affecting a Business, Owning and Operating a Corporation, the National Economy, Unions, Problems of Business: Energy, Pollution, and Organized Crime. It is your responsibility to select the objectives and topics that make up the course. Your course will be more successful if you involve the students, in some way, in this original determination of objectives. For example, you can allow them to help you identify criteria to be used in the selection of units or topical content areas to be covered. Topics should be timely and information should be readily available from a variety of sources. A study of the topic should improve the basic skills of all class members, as well as provide opportunities for the student to work independently and with a group. The study should allow for creativity in developing and reporting learning outcomes. These and other criteria help to generate interest in the study of economics.

You will want to consider at least two factors in planning an economics course: (1) Much of the content is difficult and controversial. For example, deciding whether or not to build a major dam for hydroelectric or recreational purposes can become quite involved. Proponents and opponents present convincing arguments about its effects on the economy and the environment—and an important learning activity involves examining the effects of each decision. (2) Many students enroll in the course with limited experience and skill in decision making and problem solving. These are skills that are essential to basic business courses, and time and practice must be provided for students to develop them.

BUSINESS LAW

Business law deals primarily with the rules of conduct governing the business relationships of individuals and organizations. The course is usually taught at the eleventh or twelfth grade level and is open to all students.

Objectives

The objectives of a business law course tend to focus around these points: (1) to teach respect for the law, (2) to set forth in simple language the chief laws dealing with business transactions, (3) to assist students in acquiring better understanding of the legal principles governing their personal and business affairs, (4) to acquaint students with their legal rights and duties, (5) to furnish useful information to students who plan to enter the business world or who are already working full- or part-time in business firms, and (6) to provide exploratory material for those who contemplate entering law school.[7]

Content

The content of business law changes to reflect the complexity of business and current social change. There is heavy emphasis on law and the individual as evidenced through such topics as insurance, motor vehicles, home ownership, and credit. Contractual agreements comprise a large segment of textbooks as reflected in the study of personal property and risk, formation and operation of business contracts, sales of personal property, commercial paper, contracts of employment, bailments, torts, real estate, and business organization.

There are two related areas of concern in teaching business law. One is the amount of new specialized vocabulary. (See Chapter 9 for suggestions on the teaching of vocabulary.) Understanding the vocabulary is essential to understanding the content. A second area of concern is the technical nature of the content. You need to bring to the course certain fundamental knowledges. Be careful, however, not to make the course too technical, but rather select units and content that are appropriate for the students and their objectives.

GENERAL BUSINESS

Offered at the ninth or tenth grade level, general business may be the student's first encounter with business education. Primarily concerned with building a firm understanding of the business and economic environment in which all of us live, general business is open to all students and contributes to the general education objectives of each student.

Objectives

From the teacher's point of view, students should develop understandings and appreciations in general business related to (1) some of the characteristics of our economic system and how it is changing; (2) how businesses are organized and how they operate; (3) the need for well-trained workers and the necessity for considering careers in which each individual can make the greatest contribution to personal, civic, social, and economic well-being; (4) the marketing function of business and the development of consumer efficiency in obtaining and using economic goods and services; (5) how individuals and families can efficiently manage their money and problems caused by changes in the price level; (6) the function of banks and how to use their services; (7) the function of credit and how to use it intelligently in the management of personal and family business finances; (8) the nature and causes of economic risks and an understanding of how insurance protects the individual from the risks of loss of property or earning power; (9) the importance of having a savings plan and the special problems caused by changes in the price level; (10) the importance of communication and transportation and how available services may be used; (11) the rights and responsibilities of workers, investors, managers, and the government in our economy; and (12) the need for a thoughtful career choice and the means of finding and applying for a job. An analysis of these objectives reveals that, through general business, students develop an awareness of the business world and its implications for the individual.

Brown enumerates these objectives, stated in terms of student performance:[8]

1. Describe the characteristics of the private-enterprise system of the United States; its production, marketing, and consumption functions.
2. Identify changes in the economic system that have occurred and will occur, such as business cycles.
3. Describe major ways in which business firms may be organized and describe the characteristics of each of these forms of business organization.
4. Evaluate ways in which an individual can contribute to our economic system as a producer, a consumer, and a citizen.
5. Formulate a plan for efficient money management by individuals and families.
6. Describe the problems in individual, family, and business money management caused by changes in the nation's economy.
7. Explain the functions of banks in our economic system and assess ways in which individuals can use the services of banks intelligently.
8. Analyze the role of credit in the business world and explain how to plan wise use of credit in managing personal finances.
9. Define economic risk, list some of its causes, and describe how insurance protects the individual from loss of property and earning power.
10. Describe the role of savings and investments in the economic system and personal lives of consumers and ways in which savings and investments may be accumulated.
11. Describe the various types of insurance available to an individual and evaluate situations in which a person should have various types of insurance coverage.
12. Determine the rights and responsibilities of workers, investors, business firms, and the government in the American economy and describe the role of each in the operation of our private-enterprise economy.
13. Assess the need for careful career choice and analyze various careers available to an individual.
14. Investigate how to locate and apply for a job.

Content

The content of general business varies among schools and from year to year in the same school. Topics usually include the American business system, the roles of business and government, banking, money management, credit, insurance, saving and investing, travel, communication, transportation, and career information. Topics of contemporary interest, such as environment and energy, may also be included.

When planning and implementing a course in general business, you need to revise and update instructional materials frequently to avoid the use of inaccurate material. Check the content of all material for appropriateness for students. You will want to update your own professional preparation in the topical areas incorporated in the general business course. Attending workshops, seminars, and conferences; reviewing periodicals and other current materials; and enrolling in college courses are excellent means of keeping yourself current in general business content.

module 14.1
LEARNING ACTIVITIES

1. As a high school department chairperson, you are responsible for outlining a plan for selecting appropriate basic business courses to be offered at your high school.
   a. Briefly describe a high school of your choice as to location (rural, urban, suburban), size, employment community, description of student population, and extent of business program.
   b. List the business courses you would recommend for the high school you describe. Give the duration of each course and the recommended grade level(s). Describe the prerequisites, if any, for each course.
2. The business education department of your high school is preparing a brochure describing business courses and activities. You have been asked to write a brief description of five basic business courses including economics, consumer education, general business, business law, and business principles and management.
3. Using different resources, outline the general objectives and topics for a basic business subject of your choice.
4. Prepare a list of basic business-related competencies that should be demonstrated by *all* students.

module 14.1
SELF-TEST

1. Select two basic business courses and justify their inclusion in the general education requirements of all students.

module 14.2
THE INSTRUCTIONAL PROGRAM IN BASIC BUSINESS

Implementing the instructional program in basic business courses is a challenging task for business teachers. The contemporary content and the wide variety of instructional techniques and materials provide the basis for courses that are interesting and relevant for all students.

After completing this module, you should be able to (1) explain the importance of motivation, reading abilities, and current material in basic business courses; (2) illustrate a plan for individualization; (3) prepare or describe one activity for developing thinking skills at each of six levels; (4) explain or prepare an activity for developing concepts, generalizations, and facts; (5) outline a plan for developing positive attitudes in the framework of basic business courses; and (6) name and explain at least four principles underlying skill development in basic business courses.

PLANNING FOR INSTRUCTION

A crucial factor in the success of any business course is advance teacher planning. In addition to selecting objectives and topics, determining the time allocation and amount of emphasis for each topic, assembling materials, and identifying instructional strategies, your planning should also include efforts to motivate students toward the development of thinking skills, understandings, and attitudes.

Motivation

One of your first concerns as a basic business teacher is to establish a learning environment that will motivate students to want to learn. Keep in mind that motivational techniques appropriate for one group of students are not necessarily appropriate for other students. Some students in basic business courses may not recognize an immediate use or application of the information under study. Therefore, initial motivational activities should encourage every student to become involved in the learning process. Normally, students are more interested in activities in which they participate. An example of a motivational technique that might be used to introduce a unit on the monetary system is Barter Day. On this day, students are instructed to bargain with each other to exchange an item for one owned by someone else. Each person is to make at least one exchange. After the activity, lead a discussion centered around questions such as: Why did you trade something of greater monetary value for something of lesser monetary value? What techniques did you use to persuade someone to exchange objects with you? Did you have to settle for something you did not really want? If several persons wanted the same item, how was its trade finally resolved?

You may wish to begin a collection of motivational activities, identifying the topical areas for which each is appropriate. Guest speakers, films and filmstrips, current newspaper and magazine articles, field trips, and demonstrations provide excellent examples of ways to initiate a topic in basic business. After using an initiatory activity, make notes regarding its effectiveness and ideas for changing it if used later.

Reading

Students with a wide range of reading abilities should be expected to enroll in basic business courses. Consequently, many different print and nonprint materials are more appropriate than one set of books. Within the same topical area, students may use a variety of sources to gain similar information. A student handicapped by inadequate reading skills should not be denied the opportunity to learn about a given topic. Include vocabulary development as part of the group or individual instructional activities. As a basic business teacher, you will want to be continually alert to alternate instructional materials and techniques that fit the needs of your students.

While topics and objectives of basic business courses may remain primarily the same for several years, the actual content must be updated frequently. Changes in our economic system, in our value system, and in legislation, for example, can quickly render material out-of-date and incorrect. Be alert to the relevancy and timeliness of the content of basic business. One of the most frequent complaints of students in these courses is that the content is often out-of-date.

Individualization

Planning for individual differences is as important in basic business courses as in skills courses. The fact that portions of the content may be more appropriately developed through interactions of groups of students, and that demonstrations, speakers, and films may be presented to the entire class does not mean that basic business courses cannot be individualized. A key factor to remember in planning for student needs is that individualized instruction is not synonymous with individual instruction. Thus, at times, total groups, small temporary groups, or pairs may be the best organization available to you to provide for individual needs.

The nature of the content in basic business courses lends itself to the use of a wide variety of methods and techniques. Likewise, the heterogeneous groups normally enrolled in basic business courses present a challenge to the teacher to (1) evaluate student strengths and weaknesses both with regard to basic skills (communicational and computational) and prior knowledge of the subject matter under study and (2) plan appropriate instructional strategies. Individual learning packages, activity sheets, individual and small-group projects, discussion groups, contracts, and differentiated assignments are examples of strategies that provide for individual student needs.

Within the framework of one topic, you may plan an introductory motivational activity for the total class; have several appropriate learning activity packages in which some of the activities require teams of students working together; assign projects to temporary groups that are composed of a cross section of students, with reports to the total class; provide one-to-one or small-group instructional sessions for students who need additional assistance or reteaching; offer students the opportunity to plan one or more activities to meet objectives; and plan summary sessions to integrate and synthesize the separate knowledges, attitudes, skills, and appreciations gained. You may wish to refer to Chapters 3 and 5 for earlier discussions on planning and individualization that are appropriate for basic business subjects.

Developing thinking skills

Basic business instruction should be designed to help students use their thought processes in acquiring significant understandings, building constructive attitudes, and developing essential skills. Individuals who are able to use their higher thought processes rather than simply to memorize information and repeat it will be more successful as consumers, as producers, and as citizens. Levels of thinking parallel Bloom's taxonomic levels of the cognitive domain. (See Module 5.2.) You will need to plan activities and questions to develop these higher-order skills. Initially, it may be necessary to work with the student, using modules or teacher-directed activities, one or more high-level activities before making independent assignments. The following illustrate activities, assignments, or test items at various levels of the cognitive domain.

Knowledge, the lowest level of thinking, includes the recall or recognition of information previously encountered. *Example:* List four ways in which banks serve consumers.

Comprehension includes translating information from one form to another and interpreting the relationship between two or more facts, concepts, or generalizations. *Example:* Read the article describing the changes in postal rates for first-class mail over the past fifty years. Prepare a graph to picture these facts.

Application includes applying what one has learned in one setting to other situations. This means recognizing the similarities in the new problem to previously encountered problems and selecting an appropriate method of attack. *Example:* Mary and James Roberts wish to purchase a new stereo but they do not have sufficient cash. What options for financing are available to the Roberts? Which would be the most economical? Why?

Analysis, an important part of critical thinking and problem solving, involves determining how something is organized. *Example:* Andrew Camp bought a new clothes dryer with a ninety-day warranty on all parts and labor. Two months later, the dryer would not work. Mr. Camp called the local appliance dealer to repair the machine. *Select by underlining the statements that are unrelated to the problem:* The machine was under warranty. The machine was avocado-colored. The local dealer was obligated to repair the machine. Mr. Camp paid cash for the machine.

Synthesis is the process of putting together ideas or material to create a new pattern or structure. *Example:* Prepare an original commercial to advertise your favorite shampoo, breakfast cereal, or other product of your choice.

Evaluation, the highest level of the thought process, requires that a person use all other thought processes in making judgments. *Example:* Read the following contradictory statements about the energy crisis. Which statement is probably the most accurate based on the value of each statement. (Identify your criteria for determining the value of each writer's statement, such as the age of the statement, qualifications of the writer as an expert on the topic, and so on.)

One of the tasks of the school is to help students develop the skills necessary for locating, selecting, processing, and evaluating information. The following principles underlie the successful development of basic business skills:

1. Basic business skills require students to think. Students have difficulty in developing basic business skills unless they have perfected their thought processes.

2. Students should read basic business materials creatively and with comprehension. To read creatively, the student communicates with the author by adding ideas to those presented, and by agreeing or disagreeing with the ideas presented.

3. Students improve their ability to perform a skill over a period of time. They develop skill gradually as a result of a succession of appropriate learning experiences. Students may be introduced to problem-solving techniques in career exploration classes in the middle school and develop these skills to a higher level with guided practice in basic business courses at the secondary and postsecondary levels. Skills must be practiced correctly with a desire on the part of the student to improve the performance.

4. Skills should be taught in situations that require their use. Simulations, problem-solving experiences, role playing, and work experiences are examples of types of learning activities that provide students with opportunities to develop skills effectively.

5. A skills program should provide for individual differences. To achieve optimum student growth, classroom goals and teaching strategies must be planned to provide for the unique needs, interests, experiences, and abilities of the individual learner.

You may want to use the following model in guiding students in problem-solving, decision-making, value-oriented activities: (1) identify the problem and data pertinent to it; (2) state alternatives open to consideration in solving the problem; (3) indicate at least one consequence of pursuing each alternative, and describe how the people involved might feel as a result; (4) state what you would do if you were faced with these choices and had to make a decision, and explain why you would do so; (5) describe how you would feel if you did this; and (6) state what you believe may be a valid generalization about how people behave and/or feel in such situations.

Developing understandings and attitudes

The activities of basic business courses should be constructed so as to develop three types of learnings: understandings—concepts, generalizations, and facts; attitudes—values, appreciations, and ideas; and skills (treated in the previous section).

You are responsible for selecting (in conjunction with students whenever possible) the concepts, facts, and generalizations to be included in each course. Concepts are the ideas and meanings represented by words, terms, or other symbols for classes or groups of things. Concepts, best developed through involvement, vary in complexity. Low-level concepts are general ideas about concrete things. Students have no difficulty with the concept of transportation and can give concrete examples of modes of transportation. As they become more knowledgeable, they expand their concept of transportation to include transportation systems and worldwide modes of transportation. As you develop concepts in basic business, begin at a level that students understand before introducing more sophisticated, abstract concepts.

Middle-level concepts are general ideas that are somewhat abstract; they may combine a number of smaller ideas that are either abstract or concrete. *Corporation, labor union,* and *standard of living* are examples of middle-level concepts. Activities such as Barter Day give students firsthand experience with trading. High-level concepts are large, general ideas that are very abstract. They combine smaller abstract ideas. Examples include *democracy, value, interdependence.* The concept of *interdependence* can be illustrated by listing several personal possessions of a student. Then, in small groups, individually, or as a total group, name businesses, services, and individuals needed to get the item to the student.

Facts provide special information. Teachers use strategies such as lectures and discussions, reading assignments, films and filmstrips, slides, speakers, demonstrations, tape recordings, posters and other displays to present facts. While some statements of fact provide information very useful in itself, facts are important in that students can learn to make general rules or generalizations from them. Generalizations are conclusions that are drawn from groups of related facts. They express abstract, fairly permanent relationships among concepts. To comprehend a generalization, students must not only understand the facts and concepts it contains, but they must also be able to see the relationship of the various concepts-facts to each other and to the whole. An understanding of a generalization may be developed in two main ways: (1) Students can discover a generalization for themselves by examining groups of facts; this is called the *inductive approach.* (2) Students may cite specific facts that support a generalization given by the teacher or stated in an activity, or give examples that illustrate the generalization; this is the *deductive approach.* After appropriate instruction, students may be given a generalization such as the following and told to list facts or cite illustrations to support it: "In a free economic system, the demands of consumers determine what things will be produced."

Students may be given statements of fact, such as "When an item is no longer purchased, the manufacturers cease to produce it. Market surveys indicate that many consumers would be interested in buying —— if the price is reasonable." From these statements, students could formulate a generalization. Remember that their wording may be different from your wording. Check, however, to make sure that the generalization made by each student can be supported by the fact statements.

A second type of learning involves the formation of attitudes. There is considerable evidence that students need opportunities to develop values and attitudes. General Motors Corporation of Detroit, Michigan, has begun a series of workshop training sessions for high school vocational teachers and counselors to give them firsthand knowledge about job requirements, including work habits. The need for improvement in the instructional and guidance program is supported by the fact that of 6,900 hourly workers employed in 1977, 1,200 did not last through the ninety-day probation, not because of a skill deficiency, but because of chronic absenteeism and tardiness.

Simulations, role playing, case studies, youth organization memberships, and work experience programs provide excellent examples of experiences through which youth develop positive attitudes. Classroom rules dealing with promptness, neatness, working with others, and dependability are other ways to develop good habits and work attitudes. Whenever possible, develop such rules or guidelines jointly with students, discussing the need for each. It is important to remember that the teacher should not try to impose values and attitudes on students, but rather should provide ample opportunities, problem-solving skills, and information on which students build their own values and attitudes.

In general, you should be concerned with the growth of attitudes about learning, one's self-concept, other peoples and cultures, democracy, the physical world, work, the American economic system, the enrichment of life, and so forth. Bloom and Krathwohl identify levels of attitude achievement that can be used as a basis for instructional activities (see Chapter 5).

module 14.2
LEARNING ACTIVITIES

1. Select one topic from any basic business course and outline your plan for providing for student differences. Be as specific as possible. Use any resources you wish.
2. Begin a collection of activities and instructional strategies for developing thinking skills. Include at least one for each level of the cognitive domain. Specify the basic business course or topic for each activity.
3. Prepare an activity to use in developing a concept, generalization, or fact. Identify the content area and grade level for which the activity is appropriate. Be prepared to teach this activity to the class.
4. Select a basic business course and a topic and prepare an introductory lesson designed to stimulate student interest in the subject matter. Be prepared to teach this lesson.
5. Using the decision-making steps in this module (or a modification of your choice), work through the problem-solving process using a problem you have identified.

module 14.2
SELF-TEST

The objectives in this module are measured through the Learning Activities.

module 14.3
INSTRUCTIONAL STRATEGIES FOR BASIC BUSINESS

Basic business subjects lend themselves to the use of a wide range of instructional techniques, resource materials, consultants, and speakers. Chapter 5 includes a description of several instructional techniques that are appropriate for use with basic business subjects. This module focuses on the use of classroom questions, a sample learning activity package, and a selection of teaching-learning activities that illustrate various teaching techniques for basic business education.

After completing this module, you should be able to (1) identify an effective procedure for developing questions for group discussions; (2) describe a learning activity package as an appropriate tool for teaching topics in the basic business area; and (3) illustrate other activities and techniques appropriate for use in basic business courses.

CLASSROOM QUESTIONING

The success of group discussions, informal student evaluations, or the introduction of a new topic depends to some extent on your ability to construct meaningful classroom questions. In the preceding module, you reviewed the levels involved in the thinking process. In composing or selecting questions for instruction or evaluation, you will want to keep these levels in mind to ensure the development of appropriate outcomes. There are simple questions as well as difficult questions in each level of the cognitive domain. Some teachers erroneously think that slow students should restrict their efforts to memory questions. Not so! Students need variety in their educational diet.

To assess your abilities in composing questions, look back over some of the materials you developed for use in class or incorporated into learning packages. Now categorize them, using Bloom's taxonomy. If you find yourself giving a disproportionate emphasis to a question relating to a specific level of the domain, make an effort to emphasize other types of questions. Good questions are difficult to compose. Sometimes a carefully formulated series of questions does not bring the expected responses from students. If this happens, study the questions to determine whether they are too difficult, improperly constructed, or if additional instruction should have been offered. Discard questions that cannot be repaired and save good ones. This means that each year you will start with a larger file of questions. (Do you notice the similarities in this procedure to constructing test items?) Some teachers use the same questions from one year to the next, failing to evaluate, discard, or revise questions as needed.

In addition to knowledge about the thinking levels, you should read extensively in the field to develop mastery of the subject matter. Such mastery is critical to basic business courses where content changes frequently and where printed material may become outdated or incorrect within the time span of the course.

During the process of studying available material (this should include more than a student textbook) and identifying course objectives, be especially alert for generalizations, values, skills, and other major ideas. From these can come the higher-level questions. As a basis for good questioning, present subject matter from as many sources as possible. The majority of classes use a textbook as a major source of information for most students, whether in an individualized or traditional setting. Material in the textbook can be expanded in a number of ways:[9]

1. A contradiction to information offered in the text
2. A different interpretation or evaluation than offered in the text
3. Additional evidence to support a point made in the text
4. A different line of reasoning to arrive at a conclusion made in the text
5. A new example of the use of a generalization, value, definition, or skill developed in the text
6. More recent or accurate information on a topic presented in the text.

Occasionally teachers fall into the habit of directing questions to only a few students in each class. Periodically, you may want to chart classroom participation for a day or two to determine whether there are students you are not involving in group discussions or who do not voluntarily participate. One study of slow learners at the high school level revealed that some students went through the entire school day without any teacher calling them by name.

LEARNING ACTIVITY PACKAGES

Learning activity packages offer a framework to provide for differences in student interests, abilities, and achievements. The sample LAP, Illustration 14.1, could be used in a general business or consumer education course. As you read through the LAP, note the information for the teacher, the multimedia material, and the activities that include both individual and group assignments. Developed by Alexa Bryans under the author's direction at the Center for Family Financial Education, University of Georgia, this LAP, one in a series of fifty, is particularly appropriate for grades seven through nine.

illustration 14.1
PART I: TEACHER'S EDITION FRAUDS AND SCHEMES

Rationale: Students should equate protection with more than private or government-sponsored programs for the individual. It is hoped that students will also relate protection to the many consumer agencies and that they will see the advantages of having and using these agencies to help protect them and to help prevent their becoming victims of some fast-talking salesman. This package is designed to help students become familiar with consumer agencies and how they can help protect people and their money from frauds and schemes.

Objectives: By the time the student finishes this package he/she will be able:
1. To list "do's" and "don't's" that will help protect people and money.
2. To identify five consumer protection agencies and determine the classification of each agency and name the type of protection provided.
3. To define terms related to consumers and their rights.
4. To realize the importance of having and using consumer protection agencies.

Prerequisites: Students should master these packages before they work through the package on Frauds and Schemes: (1) Assets that Need Protection, (2) Why People Buy Insurance, (3) Insurance for the Property Owner, (4) Insurance for the Automobile Owner, (5) Health and Accident Insurance, (6) Life Insurance, (7) Insurance for Income Security, and (8) Developing an Insurance Program.

References

Films
"The Big Con," California Department of Justice, Ken Nelson Productions, 3718 Sunset Boulevard, Los Angeles, Calif. 90026
"Consumer Protection," Coronet Films, 65 E. South Water St., Chicago, Ill. 60601
"Dr. Quack's Clinic" Slides, Photo Lab, Inc., 3825 George Avenue, N.W., Washington, D.C. 20011
"A Reason for Confidence," Associated Films, 600 Grand Avenue, Ridgefield, N.J. 07657

Booklets
"Advertising," Franklin Watts, Inc., 575 Lexington Avenue, New York, N.Y. 10022
"Consumer Information Responsibilities of the Federal Government," Committee on Government Operations, House of Representatives, Washington, D.C. 20402
"Consumer Protection," Consumers Union, Inc., 265 Washington Street, Mt. Vernon, N.Y.
"Guide to Federal Consumer Services," President's Committee on Consumer Interests, Superintendent of Documents, U.S. Government Printing Office, Washington, D.C. 20402
"Your Money and Your Life," U.S. Dept. of Health, Education and Welfare, Social & Rehabilitation Service, 400 Maryland Ave., Washington, D.C. 20201

Books
DeBrum, S.; Haines, P.; Malsbary, D.; and Daughtrey, A. *General Business for Economic Understanding.* 11th ed. Cincinnati: South-Western Publishing Company, 1976; pages 159–68.
Price, Ray G.; Musselman, Vernon A.; and Hall, J. Curtis. *General Business for Everyday Living.* 4th ed. New York: McGraw-Hill Book Company, Gregg Division, 1972; pages 212–40.

illustration 14.1 (continued)

Special Instructions: To give the student an understanding of the basic principles involved in frauds and schemes, this package will include:

1. An activity for pupils to demonstrate their concepts of terms concerning consumers.
2. A group activity concerning consumer agencies and their functions.
3. A group activity for pupils to express their concepts of the four consumer rights.
4. A crossword puzzle utilizing many terms consumers may encounter.
5. An activity for listing do's and don't's that may help consumers protect themselves.
6. Questions for thought and discussion.

The preassessment should be administered before any vocabulary is presented. If students do not achieve 100 percent accuracy, they should be instructed to work through the package.

Secondly, the vocabulary words given below should be presented to the students on more than one occasion before the students work through the package.

The vocabulary that the students need to master in order to complete this package is as follows:

1.	Faulty	(failing to do what is expected; imperfect)
2.	Estimates	(calculations of what the costs of work done by another will probably be)
3.	Approved	(regarded as good or satisfactory)
4.	Off-brands	(a brand name not generally known about; not knowing of the company that makes the product or performs the service)
5.	Unreliable	(not trustworthy; proven not to be dependable)
6.	Unauthorized	(not given authority; not justified; not given official permission)
7.	Mislead	(to lead astray; to lead into error)
8.	Incurable	(not curable; cannot be corrected)
9.	Fraud	(trickery; dishonesty; cheating)
10.	Extortion	(getting money by force or threat)
11.	Profiteering	(making large profits by charging too much money for goods or services)
12.	Quackery	(the act of pretending to have medical skills that one really does not have)
13.	Unsafe Health Practice	(any act in which a person does not try to protect his health or the health of others)
14.	Schemes	(underhanded plots or plans to deceive or take advantage of another)
15.	Informed	(having much information, knowledge, or education)
16.	Deceitful	(dishonest; deceptive; misleading)

Instructions for Evaluation: All activities in this package, with the exception of the preassessment, the crossword puzzle, and the list of do's and don't's, are group- or class-centered activities. The students should not be graded on any group or class activities. The teacher should guide all group activities, but the students should do the actual work themselves.

illustration 14.1 (continued)

The postassessment is provided to help ensure that the student has achieved the basic objectives set forth in this package. The student should *NOT* be allowed to look back in the package while taking the postassessment. If the students do not achieve 100 percent accuracy in this section, they should be instructed to work through the package again until they feel that they are able to answer all questions correctly.

The keys to the preassessment, the crossword puzzle, and the postassessment are given at the end of the teacher's section of this package.

The student should NOT see the key to the preassessment as the answers are incorporated in the postassessment, and the package is designed to help the student arrive at the correct answers.

The student should not be graded on questions about attitudes and values. These questions are designed to help the student examine his or her attitudes and values for personal use.

Consumer Agencies

Given below is a list of consumer agencies that you may wish to have students investigate for the services each may offer. It is a more comprehensive list than the one in the student's section.

Federal Agencies: Federal Trade Commission, Food and Drug Administration, Interstate Commerce Commission, Public Health Services, Post Office Departments, Social Security Administration.

State Agencies: Attorney General's Office, Small Claims Court, State Consumer Services Agency.

Local: Health Department, Police Department, Fire Department, Highway Department, Building Inspector (Building Codes).

Consumer-Directed Agencies: Consumer's Research, Inc., Better Business Bureau, Consumers Union, Council on Consumer Information, Chamber of Commerce, Retail Merchants Association, Underwriter's Laboratory.

KEY TO PREASSESSMENT

1. Consult the list of do's and don't's given in the text section of the *Learning Activities* of the Student's Package.
2. Consult the list of agencies in *Learning Activities* of the Student's Package. Answers to this question may vary depending upon the student's choice.
3. a. Fraud is trickery, dishonesty, or cheating of another person.
   b. Schemes are underhanded plots or plans to deceive or take advantage of another person.
   c. Profiteering is making large profits by charging too much money for goods or services.
   d. Quackery is pretending to have medical skills or other skills that one really does not have.
   e. Extortion is getting money by force or threat.
   f. Unsafe health practices are acts in which a person does not try to protect his health or the health of others.
4. It is better to be protected (by being informed) BEFORE an incident takes place. The answer to this question is left to the discretion of the individual student.

illustration 14.1 (continued)

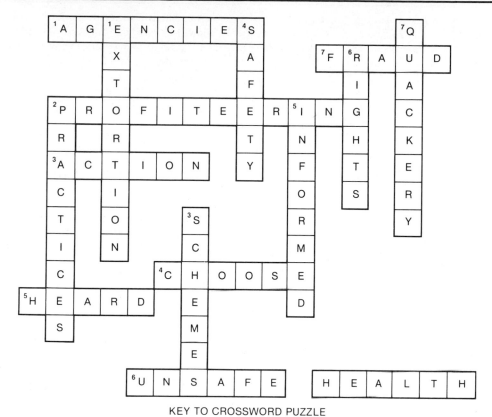

KEY TO CROSSWORD PUZZLE

KEY TO POSTASSESSMENT

DO'S

1.
2. ⎰ Consult the list of do's and don't's given in the text section
3. ⎱ of the *Learning Activities* in the Student's Package.
4.

DON'TS

5.
6. ⎰ Consult the list of do's and don't's given in the text section
7. ⎱ of the *Learning Activities* in the Student's Package.
8.
9. ⎧ a. Consult the list of agencies in the *Learning Activities*
   ⎨ b. in the Student's Package. The answer to this question
   ⎩ c. will depend upon the student's choice.

illustration 14.1 (continued)

10. (See "Key to Preassessment")
11.   "
12.   "
13.   "
14.   "
15.   "
16.   "

PREASSESSMENT

Read the following questions. Answer as many of the questions as you can. Check your answers with your teacher.

1. List four "do's" and four "don't's" to follow that will help protect you and your money.
2. There are many private and government-sponsored agencies that help protect consumers. But in order for these agencies to be helpful to a person, the person must be informed—he or she must know about the agency and what the agency can do to help protect him or her. Answer these questions:
   a. Name five consumer protection agencies.
   b. Tell whether the agency is private, local, or government-sponsored.
   c. Name some of the types of protection each agency provides.
3. Define the following terms:
   a. Fraud
   b. Schemes
   c. Profiteering
   d. Quackery
   e. Extortion
   f. Unsafe health practices
4. Do you think it is important for consumers to have agencies to help protect them *before* and *after* they buy goods and services? Give reasons why or why not.

POSTASSESSMENT

Read the following paragraphs. Answer all questions and fill in all blanks. Check your answers with your teacher.

Claire ordered an AM-FM clock radio at a "special—once in a lifetime price." She saw the ad in a magazine. The ad required that Claire send the money for the radio when she sent the order. She knew nothing about the company. Two months later, she received a used, broken radio. She wrote the company about this radio, but her letter was returned. It seems that the company had moved, and no one knew where. Claire had to take the $30 loss.

Claire could have avoided all this trouble if she had taken the time to be an "informed consumer." List four do's and four don't's that might have helped protect Claire and her money.

DO'S	DON'T'S
1. _____	5. _____
2. _____	6. _____
3. _____	7. _____
4. _____	8. _____

illustration 14.1 (continued)

There are many private and government-sponsored agencies that could have helped Claire. If she had been an informed consumer, she might have checked with these agencies for help.
9. a. Name five consumer protection agencies.
    b. Tell whether the agency is private, local, or government-sponsored.
    c. Name some of the types of protection each agency provides.

Define the following terms:
10. Fraud
11. Schemes
12. Profiteering
13. Quackery
14. Extortion
15. Unsafe health practices
16. Do you think it is important for consumers to have and use agencies such as the Better Business Bureau, the State Consumer Service Agency, the Food and Drug Administration, and the Federal Trade Commission to help protect them and their money? Why or why not?

illustration 14.1
PART II: STUDENT'S EDITION FRAUDS AND SCHEMES

Overview: Most sellers follow honest sales practices. But as a consumer, you must be aware that there are dishonest people who will try to take your money by selling you faulty goods and services. The best way to protect yourself and your money is to be aware of your rights as a buyer and to know what you are entitled to expect when you purchase goods and/or services.

Objectives: By the time I finish this package, I will be able:
1. To list "do's" and "don't's" that will help protect a person and his money.
2. To identify five consumer protection agencies and determine the classification of each agency and name the type of protection provided.
3. To define terms related to a consumer and his rights.
4. To realize the importance of having and using consumer protection agencies.

References: To help you reach your objectives on frauds and schemes, use as many of the following resources as needed to do the suggested activities.
Films: "The Big Con," "Consumer Protection," "Dr. Quack's Clinic," "A Reason for Confidence."
Booklets: "Your Money and Your Life"; "The Protectors, The Story of the Food and Drug Administration"; "Advertising"; "Consumer Protection"; "Guide to Federal Consumer Services"; "Consumer Information Responsibilities of the Federal Government."
Books: General Business for Everyday Living, 1972, pp. 212–40. *General Business for Economic Understanding,* 1976, pp. 159–68.

Learning Activities: Read the following paragraphs, then do as many of the activities as you can.
You have learned about personal and group insurance in the last several packages, but insurance is not the only type of protection offered to consumers. There are many private and government agencies that work to help protect consumers. In order for these agencies to work best, they must have the needed facts presented to them by citizens who know when to report and what to report.

illustration 14.1 (continued)

In 1962, President Kennedy pointed out that consumers have rights and also responsibilities. Unless a person practices these rights, he cannot expect to be helped by other agencies. Here are the RIGHTS and RESPONSIBILITIES:

1. The right to *safety.* (Products and services *should not* be dangerous when used as directions instruct.)

2. The right to *be informed.* (The consumer should be able to find out about all products and services he may use, and he *should try* to find out.)

3. The right to *choose.* (The consumer should be able to choose the product or service that he wants to buy, and he *should shop around* and compare before he buys.)

4. The right to *be heard.* (If a product or service does not do what it is supposed to do, the consumer *should report* to the proper agency for action against the selling company.)

In one of the activities following this section, you will learn about some of the agencies to which you can report a business or person who is not being truthful in business dealings.

Here are some "do's" and "don't's" to help you protect yourself and your money:

DO

... Say "No" to door-to-door salesmen.
... Be aware (through advertising) of quality and prices of products and services.
... Get estimates on appliances, TV, auto, and home repairs.
... Shop around before buying goods or services.
... Go to approved medical persons for dental work, eyeglasses, hearing aids, reducing aids.
... Consider the total cost when ordering records or anything by mail.
... Be careful of "all sales final," "as is," "going out of business," "get rich quick," "home employment."

DON'T

... Buy off-brands unless they are guaranteed.
... Join record or book clubs if you can buy them cheaper locally.
... Send money in chain letters.
... Deal with unreliable and unauthorized dealers.
... Be mislead by mail that says you have won a prize or have been specially selected.
... Pay for unordered merchandise.
... Buy cures for any incurable diseases such as cancer.
... Sign contracts in which you pay out money unless you understand all the terms and your responsibilities.
... Pay for merchandise left for neighbors or friends unless the person specifically tells you that he is expecting a delivery.

Here are some examples of terms that you, as a consumer, should be familiar with:

Fraud: Mr. Brown sold Alice a painting for $50. He assured her the painting was an original painted by the artist De Roe. Two weeks later Alice saw four other paintings just like hers in Mr. Brown's store. Mr. Brown had tricked Alice into buying the painting.

illustration 14.1 (continued)

Extortion: Mr. Wallace received a telephone call telling him that unless he paid the caller $100,000 the caller would burn his home down. The caller is trying to get money from Mr. Wallace by threatening him.

Profiteering: Mrs. Mack has the only gas station in the small town in which she lives. Therefore, she charges all her customers 10¢ more for each gallon of gas then the gas stations in the nearby towns. Mrs. Mack is making large profits by taking advantage of others.

Quackery: Mr. Watts moved to another state and decided that since no one knew who he was he would pretend to be a doctor. So he put up a sign with Dr. Watts on it and opened a small office. He had had some training as a male nurse, so no one knew the difference for a while. Mr. Watts is pretending to have skills that he really does not have, and this could be very dangerous for his patients.

Unsafe Health Practices: Marie had stomach pains for a week, and she went to the doctor. The doctor gave her a prescription and told her to follow the directions carefully. When Betsy, a friend of Marie's, had trouble with her stomach, Marie told Betsy to take the pills the doctor had given her. Betsy should never take any medicine that has been prescribed for someone else. Betsy was being very foolish when she took the pills because they could have made her very sick.

Schemes: Paul and Don and several other boys were going to summer camp. Paul and Don had been before and knew that you were not allowed to buy candy at camp. Paul and Don planned to take 50 candy bars with them to sell to the other boys for 30¢ each. They decided to hide the candy in one of the other boy's truck so that they would not be blamed if the candy were found. Paul and Don were planning to take advantage of the other boys by being unfair or underhanded.

Define each of the following terms: (1) Fraud, (2) Extortion, (3) Profiteering, (d) Quackery, (5) Unsafe health practices, (6) Schemes.

Now write a short paragraph giving an example of *each* of the terms you have just defined. Or find articles in the newspaper of examples of each of the terms. Bring these articles to class.

Choose one of your paragraphs or articles to share with your classmates. Then discuss with the class ways in which the situation could have been stopped had the person been an "informed consumer."

Prepare and present group reports on protection provided for the consumer by the agencies listed below:

Federal Agencies: Post Office Department, Social Security Administration.

State Agencies: Small Claims Court, State Consumer Services Agency.

Local Agencies: Health Department, Police Department, Fire Department.

Consumer-Directed Agencies: Better Business Bureau, Chamber of Commerce, Retail Merchants Association.

Your report should include: (1) Whether the agency is private or government-sponsored; (2) what the agency does to protect consumers; (3) how one should go about reporting an incident to the agency.

Earlier in this package we mentioned the RIGHTS and RESPONSIBILITIES of consumers as outlined by President Kennedy. They included the right to *safety,* to *be informed,* to *choose,*

illustration 14.1 (continued)

and to *be heard.* Now, divide into four groups and prepare a panel discussion or a talk on one of the rights listed above—how it can help protect you and your money. Present your "Right" to the rest of the class for discussion. Be sure to include these points in your presentation: (1) Why every consumer should use these rights; (2) why it is the responsibility of every consumer to use this right; (3) how every consumer may go about taking advantage of this right, and (4) why it would help if business and industry also practiced the same right concerning consumers.

Postcheck:
1. On a separate sheet of paper, list at least four "do's" and four "don't's" that will help protect you and your money.
2. Complete the following statements that summarize what you have learned about consumer rights and responsibilities.
3. Now, enter your answers to the statements in #2 in the crossword puzzle that follows.

Across:
1. There are many private and government _____ set up to help protect consumers.

2. _____ is making profits by taking advantage of someone.

3. Consumer protection agencies may take legal _____ against businesses that try to deceive the public.

4. One of the rights of consumers is the right to _____ .

5. Another consumer right is the right to be _____ .

6. An example of an _____ practice is taking medicine without reading the label.

7. _____ is defined as trickery, dishonesty, or cheating another person.

Down:
1. _____ is the act of getting money by force, threat, or the like, or to charge too much money for something.

2. Unsafe health _____ can be very dangerous to a person.

3. _____ are underhanded plots or plans.

4. Another consumer right is the right to _____ .

5. Another consumer right is the right to be _____ .

6. President Kennedy outlined four consumer responsibilities and _____ .

7. A person who pretends to have medical skill or any other skill that he really does not have is practicing _____ .

illustration 14.1 (continued)

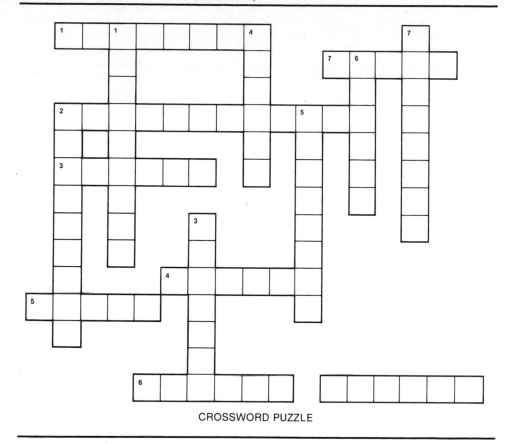

CROSSWORD PUZZLE

Questions for Thought and Discussion

You were taught in other packages that advertising may be helpful or harmful. You must be an informed person to be able to take advantage of helpful advertising and to avoid getting "taken in" by harmful advertising.

Find two advertisements in a newspaper, on TV, and/or on the radio. One advertisement should be helpful, the other one should be harmful or deceitful. Discuss the advertisements in class. Be sure you can answer the following questions:

What makes the advertisement helpful? or

What makes the advertisement harmful?

Does the advertisement represent an act of fraud, profiteering, schemes, unsafe health practices, or quackery? If so, which one?

We have been talking about "informed consumers."

1. In your opinion, what must a person know in order to be considered an "informed consumer"? Why?

2. In your opinion, is it more important for a person to be informed *before* or *after* another person has been untruthful in a business dealing? Why?

INSTRUCTIONAL ACTIVITIES

The activities described in this section are examples of the wide range of instructional techniques you will find appropriate for basic business courses:

1. *Debate* the following: The federal government should regulate the percentage of annual increase allowed for hospital care.
2. Invite a lawyer to *speak* on recent legislation affecting consumers.
3. Prepare a *report* covering the features of national health insurance plans.
4. Prepare a *chart* depicting the change in the value of gold on the European market during the last decade.
5. *Apply* for a Social Security card.
6. Prepare a *collage* or *exhibit* depicting the problem of pollution.
7. *Organize* and operate a company.
8. *Survey* members of the community to find out the impact of such buying incentives as trading stamps, premiums, coupons, prizes, and contests. *Construct* your own instrument.
9. Use a *brainstorming* session to determine how average citizens can cut the cost of public services.
10. *Interview* the school superintendent for cost figures on lost and damaged textbooks, equipment, material, and damaged school property. List the things the school could have bought with that money.
11. Select a country and *investigate* its system of *taxation*. *Compare* its income, sales tax, and property taxes with that of the United States. Follow up with a comparison of services offered by the governments of each country.
12. Draw a *pie chart* showing how federal, state, and local dollars are spent.
13. If a tax referendum is to be voted on, *discuss* which *services* could be eliminated or reduced. Discuss the implications of cutting services such as education, law enforcement, health, welfare, recreation, or transportation.
14. Write an *essay* on "Life in the United States Without Taxes."
15. Make a *list* of *necessities* that are provided by tax dollars; contrast these with a list of necessities that are not provided by taxes.
16. Prepare a *list* of *vocabulary* words on income taxation that have been selected from federal and state tax forms.
17. *Compare* the advantages and disadvantages of *investing* $5,000 in the following: (a) local savings and loan association, (b) savings account in commercial bank, (c) municipal bonds, (d) annuity, (e) life insurance, (f) credit union, (g) common or preferred stock.
18. Select a *stock* or several stocks in which you might "invest" $1,000. Follow the stock for two weeks in the newspaper. It may be "sold" and other stocks "bought" during this period. Keep a written record of the amount of money you have "earned" or "lost."
19. Invite an attorney to *talk* with the class about *estate planning* and taxes on estates.
20. In small groups, *research* and *report* on the following types of *life insurance*: term, straight life, limited payment, endowment, and group life.
21. *Plan* and *budget* for yourself for one month. Compare your actual expenses with the budgeted amounts.

module 14.3
LEARNING ACTIVITIES

1. Select one topic from a basic business area of your choice and prepare five questions you might use in group discussion.
2. Select a topic in the basic business area and begin the construction of a module (learning activity package). Ask another student to review your package.
3. Add to your collection of activities for teaching basic business courses. Classify each according to the content area in which it may be used.

module 14.3
SELF-TEST

The objectives in this module are measured through the Learning Activities.

module 14.4
EVALUATION OF BASIC BUSINESS COURSES

Evaluation in basic business courses includes evaluation of and by students, as well as evaluation of courses and materials both by students and the teacher. The measurement of learning outcomes in these courses is more difficult than in the skill areas of business education because attitudes and concepts are not immediately apparent. A variety of evaluation techniques is available, however, and each must be selected to fit the particular objectives and needs of a learning situation.

After completing this module, you should be able to (1) cite at least six to eight ways to assess student progress, (2) outline a sample evaluation plan, (3) construct three types of test items, (4) design or select a sample student self-evaluation instrument, (5) outline a form for student evaluation of topic or instructional packet, and (6) develop criteria and evaluate supplementary basic business material.

EVALUATING STUDENT ACHIEVEMENT

Evaluation of student achievement in basic business courses takes as many forms as there are teaching techniques. In addition to formal testing, the teacher incorporates a combination of activities such as reports, projects, contracts, learning packages, case studies, simulations, worksheets, and class participation in the evaluation process. Since written tests measure only a portion of a student's overall performance during a grading period, the teacher has to develop and acquaint students with an evaluation plan for the grading period that specifies what factors or tasks will be assessed and the relative weight of each. Illustration 14.2 shows an evaluation plan and a basis for grades developed by Brown.[10]

This plan illustrates the variety of activities included in student evaluation in a given grading period. The teacher selects the activities appropriate for each grading period for his or her students and the content area. By incorporating a variety of activities, the teacher gains a better view of overall student performance.

Formal test items contribute to the evaluation of student performance. Teachers use a variety of objective-type items, including multiple-choice, classification, matching, true-false-neither, short answer, and completion as well as cases, problem situations, and some essay or discussion questions. (Chapter 4 discusses techniques for constructing test items.)

When writing essay or discussion items, keep these points in mind: Do not use discussion questions to evaluate knowledge that can be tested with objective items. Generally speaking, recall or memory questions should not be in

illustration 14.2
SAMPLE EVALUATION PLAN

TASK	EVALUATIVE CRITERIA	PORTION OF TOTAL GRADE
Five written tests	For each test, standards for letter grades are established according to school criteria or class performance in total	10% for each test
Completion of a contract	Criteria for each letter grade set up in the contract for satisfactory completion of a specified set of activities	15%
Completion of a Learning Activity Package	Criteria for posttest scores established for the package	15%
Small-group work	Group evaluation of total group and individual members completed at the end of the group work	10%
Homework assignments (During the 9 weeks, a variety of assignments may have been given on 18–20 occasions)	Points awarded on each homework assignment according to number of items on assignment and difficulty of total assignment; a grading scale for total points was set up during the grading period	10%
	Total	100%

essay or discussion form. Before correcting papers, decide on elements that should appear in the answers plus as many approaches and responses as you consider correct. When scoring tests, write comments and corrections on essay responses; although this is time-consuming, it is perhaps more meaningful to the student than a grade.

The following sample test incorporates both a case and objective items. Note that the questions are presented in a more natural setting than the traditional objective item.

Published tests, almost always in objective format, are generally available for each textbook. When using these tests, check to see that the items correspond to objectives you selected for your course and are appropriate for the reading level of your students, deleting and adding items as needed.

Another element in evaluation is student self-evaluation. Attitude inventories, opinionnaires, pretests, and checklists in which students rate their own efforts on a topic give them an opportunity to become part of the evaluation process.

EVALUATING THE COURSE

Course objectives, content, instructional techniques, and materials should be reviewed annually to ensure that they are current, accurate, and reflect the needs and interests of students. Student evaluation should be incorporated into each instructional packet or series of packets on a given topic. This

illustration 14.3
SAMPLE TEST ITEM

The Johnson family decided to move to another state. They sold their home and hired the Ace Moving Company to transport their goods to their new location. Mr. Johnson drove to the new state while Mrs. Johnson took an airplane. When the Johnsons arrived in their new location, they read the newspaper ads for new homes. They purchased a new home with a mortgage guaranteed by the federal government. Federal agencies regulate many of the situations the Johnsons were involved in. Indicate the one agency which regulates each situation.

  A. Interstate Commerce Commission
  B. Federal Trade Commission
  C. Federal Housing Assistance
  D. Housing and Urban Development
  E. Environmental Protection Agency

  ____1. Transportation of their goods by the Ace Moving Company
  ____2. Having safety equipment on their car
  ____3. Nondeceptive newspaper advertisements for housing
  ____4. A federally guaranteed mortgage
  ____5. Information about the nature and cost of closing and settlement of their housing purchase
  ____6. Water quality standards in their new community

Source: David Graf, *Teaching Consumer Education,* Delta Pi Epsilon Rapid Reader No. 2 (St. Peter, Minn.: Delta Pi Epsilon, Gustavus Adolphus College, 1977), p. 47.

feedback, often in the form of a checklist, gives students a chance to rate the topic as very interesting, quite interesting, of average interest, not very interesting, or dull (or use descriptions of your choice). They also rate the material and instructional techniques and objectives as very helpful, quite helpful, and so on, and make suggestions for improving the topic or packet, for revising the material and techniques, and for adding or deleting objectives. By comparing the average rating of each topic quarterly, by semester, or annually, the teacher can measure the effectiveness of revisions.

Teacher evaluation as well as student evaluation of a course are very important. The effective teacher attempts to improve a course each time he or she teaches it. On a master set of materials or in the lesson plans, you can make specific notes regarding changes—additions and deletions of objectives, topics, materials, and instructional techniques. Be alert as to how well your objectives and materials meet the needs of slower students or those who are more advanced. Note whether more time should be devoted to a topic. Write suggestions for improving instructional packets. List additional objectives that should be added and those that should replace others currently used. Follow up on student evaluations with your own appraisal. Begin a list of materials needed to improve instruction. Evaluation systems are of most value when complete data is used in their appraisal.

Part of your evaluation responsibilities fall within the area of supplementary materials and resources—including printed material, audiovisual, human, and environmental. Some teachers find it helpful to establish criteria for determining the probable value of materials and resources. Your criteria might include the following: (1) Is the material appropriate for the topic? (2) Is the material current? (3) Is the material accurate? (4) Does the material aid in realizing course objectives? (5) Is the material appropriate for the performance level of the students? (6) Is the material attractive? (7) Can the material be used within the time limits of the course? (8) Is the material financially feasible for the school?

module 14.4
LEARNING ACTIVITIES

1. Select a basic business subject, identify a topic, and outline an evaluation plan for assessing student progress. Use any resources of your choice.
2. Write three sample test items, each of a different type and for a different basic business course. Use Chapter 4 as well as other content material.
3. Construct a brief checklist that could be included in an instructional packet for students to use in assessing their perceived level of performance on the packet.
4. Begin a collection of self-evaluation instruments for use with students, such as attitude scales, opinionnaires, tests measuring knowledge of economics and consumer education.
5. From the literature, select a test of economic understanding or consumer education and administer it to a group of students. Report to the class on student performance.

6. Design a brief evaluation form for students to use in assessing an instructional packet. Incorporate objectives, materials, and instructional techniques.
7. Select one resource or material that might be used in a basic business course. Specify the criteria for evaluating its effectiveness. Evaluate the resource or material and report your findings to the class.

module 14.4
SELF-TEST

The objectives in this module are measured through the Learning Activities.

SUMMARY

Basic business courses are assuming importance as educators recognize the contribution of these courses to the general education of all students. Examples of courses that are classified as basic business include consumer economics, economics, business law, and general business. These courses are offered at different grade levels in the high school and for different periods of time. In selecting objectives and content for these courses, you should consider their grade placement and duration; the ability, achievement, and career goals of students; and other basic business courses they are taking.

When planning the instructional program in basic business courses, the teacher selects objectives and topics, determines the relative importance of each topic and establishes the time allocation, assembles a wide variety of print and nonprint materials, outlines possible instructional techniques, and formulates an evaluation plan. Other factors that should be given specific attention include motivation, reading level of learners, use of current material, and individualized activities for the course.

An important outcome of the instructional program is the development of thinking skills. Activities should be planned to lead students to develop higher-level thinking skills. Basic business courses are also concerned with the development of understandings (facts, concepts, generalizations), attitudes (values, appreciations, ideas), and skills in locating and using information.

Instructional strategies in basic business courses draw on a variety of techniques, materials, and resources. The twenty-one instructional activities included in this chapter suggest numerous ways for students to realize course objectives. Effective use of classroom questioning by the teacher can do much to stimulate student interest, and efforts should be made, over a period of time, to help students develop higher-level generalizations, values, and skills. Learning activity packages, such as the sample in this chapter, provide another means of adjusting content to individual interests, achievements, and needs.

An integral part of the instruction in basic business subjects is the evaluation of student performance. Since formal tests indicate only a portion of student performance, the teacher should develop an evaluation plan that incorporates a variety of assessment devices. Student self-evaluation, as well as teacher evaluation, can be included. Part of the overall evaluation is examination of the course itself—the objectives, materials, and instructional techniques. These should be assessed in light of student needs and interests both by the teacher and by students. Recommended changes can be reviewed and incorporated into courses when appropriate.

References

[1]Calfrey C. Calhoun and Fannie L. Boyd, *Consumer Education Resource Guide* (Athens: University of Georgia, College of Education, 1972).

[2]David Graf, *Teaching Consumer Education,* Delta Pi Epsilon Rapid Reader No. 2 (St. Peter, Minn.: Delta Pi Epsilon, Gustavus Adolphus College, 1977), p. 3.

[3]Calhoun and Boyd, *Consumer Education,* p. iii.

[4]Sally R. Campbell, *Consumer Education in an Age of Adaptation* (Chicago: Sears, Roebuck and Company, 1971), pp. 11–19.

[5]Walter L. Bishop, "Factors Affecting the Level and Development of Economic Understanding of Community College Students" (Ph.D. diss., University of Georgia, 1974).

[6]Anne S. Daughtrey, *Methods of Basic Business and Economic Education* (Cincinnati: South-Western Publishing Company, 1965), pp. 387–88.

[7]Kenneth E. Goodman, Francis J. Radice, William G. Williams, *Today's Business Law,* Teacher's Manual and Key, 4th ed. (New York: Pitman Publishing Corporation, 1975), p. 1.

[8]Betty Jean Brown, *Teaching General Business,* Delta Pi Epsilon Rapid Reader No. 1 (St. Peter, Minn.: Delta Pi Epsilon, Gustavus Adolphus College, 1977), pp. 1–2.

[9]Norris M. Sanders, *Classroom Questions* (New York: Harper & Row, 1966), p. 159.

[10]Brown, *Teaching General Business,* p. 29.

SUGGESTIONS FOR FURTHER STUDY*

Bonnice, Joseph. "Examining the Implications of Recent Research in Consumer Education." *Business Education World* 57 (January-February 1977): 30.

———. "Teaching-Learning System for Consumer Education." *Business Education World* 57 (March-April 1977): 24.

Boulden, Alfred, "The Business Teacher's Role in Teaching Law." *Journal of Business Education* 52 (May 1977): 344–45.

Butler, Tommie; Henry, Mavis; and Musick, Joseph A. "A Secondary School Adventure in the Free Enterprise System." *Business Education Forum* 32 (November 1977): 22–23.

Campbell, Sally R. *Educator's Guide to Teaching Auto and Home Insurance* (New York: The Educational Relations Division, Insurance Information Institute, 1977).

Chizmar, John R.; Hiebert, L. Dean; and McCarney, Bernard J. "Assessing the Impact of an Instructional Innovation on Achievement Differentials: The Case for Computer-Assisted Instruction." *Journal of Economic Education* 9 (Fall 1977): 42–46.

*These references, published in 1977, are examples of a variety of materials abailable for teacher use in the basic business areas. In addition to these resources, check listings in the *Business Education Index.* Also, contact major companies such as Sears, J. C. Penny, General Mills, Ford, General Motors, as well as banks, federal savings and loan associations, and insurance companies for free and inexpensive materials.

Clow, John. "Teaching Student Rights and Responsibilities in the Business Law Course." *Business Education World* 57 (November-December 1977): 23–25.

Cox, Jerry R. "Vary Classroom Activities for Basic Business Students." *Business Education Forum* 32 (March 1977): 13–14.

Daughtrey, Anne S., and DeBrum, S. Joseph. *General Business in the Curriculum.* Cincinnati: South-Western Publishing Company, 1977.

DeLozier, M. Wayne. *Cases in Consumer Behavior.* Columbus: Merrill Publishing Company, 1977.

Garman, Thomas, and Gummerson, Ronald. "Value of Topics in Consumer Education." *Journal of Business Education* 52 (April 1977): 328–31.

Hendricks, Arthur. "Creating a Slide Presentation or Photo Book in Consumer Education." *Business Education World* 57 (May-June 1977): 30.

Hermann, Robert. "Relating Economic Ideology to Consumer Protection: A Suggested Unit in Consumer Education." *Business Education World* 57 (September-October 1977): 13–15.

Hopkins, Charles, and Price, Ray, eds. *Developing Economic Understanding Through General Business and Advanced Basic Business.* (New York: Joint Council of Economic Education, 1977).

McClintock, Richard. "Six Business Commandments." *Tomorrow's Business Leader* 8 (Winter 1977): 6.

Master Curriculum Guide in Economics for the Nation's Schools. Joint Council on Economic Education, 1977.

Mattson, Drew. "Economics in Post Secondary Business Schools." *Balance Sheet* 59 (November 1977): 115–17, 119.

Messerman, Robert. "Business Law: The Awakening Effect of an Introductory Course." *Journal of Business Education* 52 (October 1977): 16–17.

Mintz, Herman, *Dramatizations for Business Classes.* (Portland, Me.: Walch Publishing Company, 1977).

Nelson, Robert, and Bober, Gerald. "Small Business Ownership: A Neglected Career Option." *Business Education World* 57 (March-April 1977): 22–23, 30.

O'Grady, James P., and O'Reilly, J. Michael. "Mock Negotiations: A Labor-Management Experience." *Journal of Business Education* 52 (January 1977): 180–81.

Powell, William. "Teaching Thinking Skills in the Business Classroom." *Business Education Forum* 52 (December 1977).

Schaefer, Julie C., and Paradis, Edward. "Help the Student with Low Reading Ability." *Journal of Business Education* 52 (January 1977): 160–62.

Swenson, Dan H. "Structure: A Key to Getting Started in Basic Business." *Journal of Business Education* 52 (December 1977): 132–33.

Tonne, Herbert A. "Consumer Education in the School." *Journal of Business Education* 52 (January-February 1977): 30.

Watson, Gwen S. "Learning Activity Centers in the Basic Business Classroom." *Journal of Business Education* 52 (April 1977).

Whitney, Eugene P. "Our Other Responsibility: Basic Business Survival Skills." *California Business Education Journal* 12 (February 1977): 11–12.

Wyllie, Eugene. "The Indiana Consumer Education Project." *Ball State Journal* 48 (Spring 1977): 12–17.

chapter 15

TEACHING BUSINESS/CAREER EXPLORATION IN THE MIDDLE GRADES

Career education at the middle/junior high school is one of the newer areas of responsibility for business education. The importance of career education is noted in Section 3 or Public Law 95–207, the Career Education Incentive Act of December 1977:[1]

> In recognition of the prime importance of work in our society and in recognition of the role that the schools play in the lives of all Americans, it is the purpose of this Act to assist states and local educational agencies and institutions of postsecondary education ... in making education as preparation for work, and as a means of relating work values to other life roles and choices (such as family life), a major goal of all who teach and all who learn by increasing the emphasis they place on career awareness, exploration, decision making, and planning and to do so in a manner which will promote equal opportunity in making career choices. . . .

module 15.1
GOALS AND OBJECTIVES OF CAREER EXPLORATION

Exploration is a crucial phase in career education. The skills and knowledge acquired during this phase become the foundation for decision making at later levels. The major thrust at the middle school level is toward having the student explore various occupational clusters to become familiar with the preparation requirements and available educational opportunities. After completing this module, you should be able to (1) explain the relationship of career education at the middle school to career education at the elementary, secondary, and postsecondary levels, and (2) identify objectives, concepts, and goals of career education at the middle school/junior high level.

CAREER EDUCATION MODEL

Career education, which is better described as a concept rather than an additional course, should be an ongoing component of the educational program of all students regardless of their ultimate career objectives. Illustration 15.1 shows the broad goals of career education at the various educational levels. It is important to note that the middle school/junior high emphasis is on orientation and exploration. The overall objectives of this model focus on helping students to develop (1) a comprehensive awareness of career options; (2) a concept of self that is in keeping with a work-oriented society, including positive attitudes about work, school, and society, and a sense of satisfaction resulting from successful experience with these areas; (3) personal characteristics, such as self-respect, initiative, and resourcefulness; (4) a realistic understanding of the relationships between the worlds of work and education to assist individuals in becoming contributing members of society; and (5) the ability to enter employment in a selected occupational area and/or to go on for further education.[2] Objectives 1–4 are introduced at the middle school/junior high level.

Table 15.1 provides a breakdown of the USOE Career Education Program Model by objectives, depth and scope, courses or curricula, and location of instructional facilities for each educational level. It summarizes career education at the various educational levels.

CAREER EDUCATION GOALS

The U.S. Office of Education Policy Paper, "An Introduction to Career Education," expresses the outcomes of career education from kindergarten through the postsecondary level as follows.[3]

Career education seeks to produce individuals who, when they leave school at any age or at any level, are:

Goal 1: Competent in the basic academic skills required for adaptability in our rapidly changing society

Goal 2: Equipped with good work habits

Goal 3: Equipped with a personally meaningful set of work values that foster in them a desire to work

Goal 4: Equipped with career decision-making skills, job-hunting skills, and job-getting skills

Goal 5: Equipped with specific occupational skills and interpersonal skills at a level that will allow them to gain entry into and attain a degree of success in the occupational society

Goal 6: Equipped with a degree of self-understanding and understanding of educational vocational opportunities sufficient for making sound career decisions

Goal 7: Aware of means available to them for continuing and recurrent education

illustration 15.1
**USOE COMPREHENSIVE CAREER EDUCATION SYSTEM:
SCHOOL-BASED MODEL**

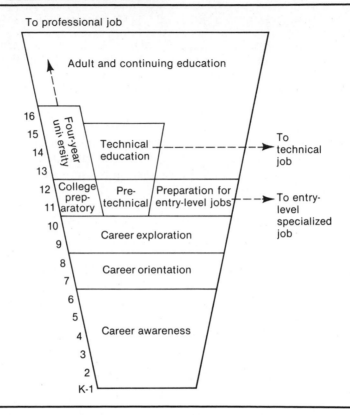

Source: ERIC Clearinghouse on Vocational and Technical Education. *Career Education Practice,* Information Service No. 65, VT 017 221. (Columbus: The Center for Vocational and Technical Education, The Ohio State University, December, 1972), p. 19.

Goal 8: Either placed or actively seeking placement in a paid occupation, in further education, or in a vocation consistent with their current career decision

Goal 9: Actively seeking to find meaning and meaningfulness in work through productive use of leisure time

Goal 10: Aware of means available to themselves for changing career options—or societal and personal constraints impinging on career alternatives.

CAREER EDUCATION CONCEPTS

Such statements of objectives as that listed above help to provide a rationale for career education at all levels. Middle school business teachers should be familiar with these goals in order to understand why the middle school is an important component of the total career education program. The Wisconsin Career Development Scope and Sequence Model identifies the following concepts as vital for the middle/junior high level:[4]

table 15.1

CAREER EDUCATION PROGRAM MODEL
(USOE CONCEPTUALIZATION)

GRADE	OBJECTIVE	DEPTH AND SCOPE	COURSES OR CURRICULA	LOCATION OF INSTRUCTIONAL FACILITIES
Elementary (grades K-6)	To develop an awareness of the occupational world	General understanding with unrestricted exposure to all fields of work; guidance and counseling for career development	Integrated as part of total program	Every elementary school
Early secondary (grades 7-10)	To stimulate occupational interest and provide exploratory and prevocational experiences	Acquaintance with many specific occupations; opportunities for practical experiences; guidance and counseling for career development continued	Continue integrated program and provide separate courses that include experiences related to all fields of work	Every middle and high school
Late secondary (grades 11-12)	To provide specific training for a grouping of closely related occupations and further exploratory experiences for those needing it	Training for job-entry skills; guidance and counseling for career development continued; placement services provided	Separate courses with skill development objectives; program offerings will be dependent on student interest and labor demands	High schools, area centers, private occupational schools, and business and industry
Postsecondary	To provide advanced specific occupational education and training	In-depth training; many advanced technical offerings; guidance, counseling, and placement services provided	Separate courses; offerings dependent on student interest and labor demands	Community colleges, state colleges and universities, private occupational schools, business and industry
Adult	To provide occupational training, upgrading and/or retraining	Training for specific employment needs of individual; job counseling for adults; placement services provided	Offerings dependent on demand; many short-term programs and universities,	Local schools, area centers, community colleges, colleges private occupational schools, business and industry

Emphasize that (1) an understanding and acceptance of self is important throughout life; (2) persons need to be recognized as having dignity and worth; (3) occupations exist for a purpose; (4) there is a wide diversity of careers which may be classified in several ways; (5) work means different things to different people; (6) education and work are interrelated; (7) individuals differ in their interests, abilities, attitudes, and values.

Develop the concept that (8) occupational supply and demand have an impact on career planning; (9) job specialization creates interdependency; (10) environment and individual potential interact to influence career development; (11) occupations and life styles are interrelated; (12) individuals can learn to perform adequately in a variety of occupations; (13) career development requires a continuous and sequential series of choices; (14) various groups and institutions influence the nature and structure of work.

Introduce the idea that (15) individuals are responsible for their career planning; and (16) job characteristics and individuals must be flexible in a changing society.

Exploration is a crucial phase of career education. The skills and knowledge acquired during this phase become the foundation for decision making at succeeding levels. The major thrust at the middle school/junior high level is toward having the student explore various occupational clusters (families) and become familiar with the preparation requirements and educational opportunities available for obtaining the necessary training.

The U.S. Office of Education has identified the following occupational clusters as those into which career education will ultimately be integrated at all levels of the educational program:

Business and Office Occupations
Marketing and Distribution Occupations
Communications and Media Occupations
Construction Occupations
Manufacturing Occupations
Transportation Occupations
Agri-Business and Natural Resources Occupations
Marine Science Occupations
Environmental Control Occupations
Public Service Occupations
Health Occupations
Hospitality and Recreation Occupations
Personal Service Occupations
Fine Arts and Humanities Occupations
Consumer and Homemaking Occupations

Within each cluster, specific occupations may be perceived as existing on a particular rung of a career ladder; thus, occupations may be viewed both individually and in relation to each other within the cluster. During the exploratory phase, the student should examine not only the opportunities available within a cluster of occupations but also the life style and work style implications of each occupation.

Illustration 15.2 shows how career education concepts are treated in the career development continuum. The chart is valuable in that it provides a "rule of thumb" in planning career education experiences.

Drawing on the overall goals, objectives, and concepts of career education, the teacher then selects or prepares objectives and goals appropriate for the local school. The following are some examples of goals selected by a school system:[5]

illustration 15.2
**CAREER DEVELOPMENT PROGRAM PLANNING
SCOPE AND SEQUENCE**

FACTORS	AWARENESS K-3	ORIENTATION 4-6	EXPLORATION 7-9	PREPARATION 10-12-Adulthood
Self-understanding				
Decision-making				
Work World				
Societal Understanding		INTRODUCE	DEVELOP	EMPHASIZE
Economic Understanding				
Career Planning				
Leisure and Avocational Planning				
Occupational Preparation				
Employability and Employment				

Source: Harry N. Drier, Jr. "Career Development Construct for Educational Change," in *Career Education,* Third Yearbook of the American Vocational Association, ed. Joel H. Magisos (Washington, D.C.: American Vocational Association, 1973), p. 80.

The pupil will be able to recognize the relationship between his or her personal characteristics and broad occupational clusters. (Self-Awareness)
The pupil will be able to describe occupational clusters in terms of tasks performed and skills required. (Career Awareness)
The pupil will be able to recognize the effect of selected psychological, sociological, and economic aspects of society on individuals and their careers. (Career Awareness)
The pupil will be able to relate levels of educational preparation and courses of study to specific occupational pursuits. (Career Preparation)

CAREER EDUCATION OBJECTIVES

The Georgia State Department of Education identified these objectives for career development at the eighth-grade level.[6] They are measured by a criterion-referenced test near the end of the eighth grade.

1. Given a particular situation, the student can identify characteristics which may ensure success or failure.
2. The student recognizes how the ability to get along with people affects getting into, keeping, and advancing in a job (interpersonal relations).
3. The student recognizes how personal characteristics may impede and/or facilitate work on the job.
4. The student recognizes how self-confidence influences personal aspirations.
5. The student recognizes that certain things about oneself can be or will be changed and that such changes can affect one's chances for participating in and successfully completing various educational and vocational activities.
6. The student will recognize that work is an integral part of a life style and that through career planning one can improve and/or change his or her life style.
7. The student will demonstrate a knowledge of behaviors which are indicative of a sense of responsibility for one's own actions and decisions.
8. The student recognizes that career goals in many occupations are achieved only through experiences and/or additional training.
9. The student recognizes that different occupations require different educational preparation, and that there may be alternative routes to the same occupation.
10. The student recognizes the wider variety of educational and occupational opportunities available to those who complete high school and to those with advanced and/or specialized training as compared to persons who do not complete high school or who lack skill training.
11. The student will demonstrate knowledge or skills which are important in obtaining a job.

12. The student recognizes that s/he is influenced in some manner by every school subject area s/he encounters, and s/he has some knowledge of the application of subject matter to everyday life, including one's work.

13. The student will be familiar with several major sources of vocational and educational information and be able to judge generally how accurate, reliable, and helpful certain sources and pieces of information are.

14. The student will recognize some of the ways in which the availability and/or desirability of specific educational and vocational opportunities are being influenced by social, economic, and technological trends.

15. The student will recognize that within an occupational area or group there are a wide variety of career choices.

16. Given several occupational fields (job families), the student will be able to identify some of the factors about the job fields which could influence career choice.

17. The student will recognize how various experiences such as leisure-time activities, volunteer work, and part-time jobs can be useful in choosing educational and vocational goals.

18. The student recognizes the interdependency of immediate decisions and long-range goals.

19. The student can recognize the influence of a group of friends on his or her personal decisions.

20. The student can identify important decisions and choice points that face people who pursue various educational and vocational choices.

module 15.1
LEARNING ACTIVITIES

Note: The following is an ongoing activity for the entire chapter.

1. As business education supervisor, your immediate task is to revise the career education program's business education component for three middle schools in your system. During the past two years, the program has lost sight of its intended objectives and has become a one-semester typewriting course.

    Part I. Write a brief purpose and justification of career education at the middle school level. Then list the objectives you consider appropriate for your school system.

module 15.1
SELF-TEST

1. Briefly explain the relationship of career education at the middle school, elementary school, high school, and postsecondary school levels.

module 15.2
IMPLEMENTING AND EVALUATING CAREER EXPLORATION

Career exploration, a unique and important part of the total career education program, is relatively new to the curriculum and its content and methodology are not clearly established. The business teacher must plan and implement a course that will help students to acquire skills needed in exploring a variety of careers, examining self, and making decisions.

After completing this module, you should be able to (1) summarize the characteristics of middle school/junior high students; (2) identify topics and organizational plans for career exploration; (3) identify six content areas to be included in exploring a career field; (4) explain, demonstrate, and assemble at least two different instructional activities for each of the areas identified in number 3; and (5) outline a plan for evaluating career exploration experiences.

STUDENT CHARACTERISTICS

Student characteristics during the middle school years differ from those of the elementary and high school years. Between childhood and adolescence, boys and girls face pressures from biological, social, and psychological fronts. They become aware of themselves and the physical changes taking place in their bodies. There is some evidence that sexual changes occur about a year earlier than they did a century ago. Today's children grow taller than their parents. These factors make youth *seem* bigger, older, and more able to handle adult responsibilities. Teachers and parents often look at the "physical" youth and treat them as though they were older than they really are.

Middle school students feel a need for recognition and acceptance by peers. "These youngsters are searching for status and recognition in society. The social classes of the students and the cultural background of the family group play a very significant part in the child's life. The child from a lower socioeconomic status may realize that children from the families of a higher income bracket seem to have a definite advantage. Research shows that middle- and upper-class families seek to instill in their children a greater motivation to achieve, which is an important factor in their growth. Often children from a lower socioeconomic group are sensitive because of their dress, speech, or habits which may differ from some of their peers."[7]

Socially, youth are acquiring adult roles through trial and error. The career education classroom can provide excellent opportunities for students to explore and assume, temporarily or through simulated activities, their adult roles. Psychologically, this is the period during which youth acquire an identity. They narrow and focus their personal, occupational, sexual, and ideological commitments to the point where they are perceived by others to be adults. Intellectually, they come to school knowing more than previous generations and possessing greater intellectual sophistication. The mind is developing to its adult capacity at this time.

Middle school students exhibit a wide range of interests. They are often moody and loud, displaying markedly different reactions and behavior patterns to the same stimuli. At this age they are fascinated by realism and facts, and they begin to question the right of adults to dominate. They seek prestige. Most enjoy group enterprises but find some satisfaction in working alone.

Perhaps the biggest problem affecting early adolescent youth is pressure —pressure that comes from parents, who are overanxious about their child's future; from teachers, who either do not know or do not implement child growth and development principles; from dominating peers, who demand conformity and set their own standards; from grades and homework, with the emphasis on college more than a muted background; and from the family, which requires a new role of the early adolescent.[8]

Teachers should use these and other characteristics of students within the eleven-to-fifteen-year-old range as a basis for developing meaningful career education programs.

IMPLEMENTATION

The objectives of career education at the middle school are achieved through separate exploration courses as well as existing academic courses. In a well-planned program, each teacher should assume responsibility for developing career education concepts, especially as related to that teacher's particular content area.

After developing career exploration objectives, the teacher then selects topics relating to business and office careers. An organization pattern is selected based on his or her preference. Possible organization includes Data Processing, Management and Finance, Clerical and Secretarial; Secretarial, Clerical, Data Processing, and Accounting; or Clerical, Secretarial/Stenographic, Accounting-Data Processing, and Business Ownership.

Regardless of the content organization, there are several areas of emphasis that should be incorporated into each career field. These include:

1. an examination of the career field, the context in which it is performed, and its contribution to the world of work;
2. skills, knowledges needed in the career field, including courses and educational levels in which they may be attained;
3. occupational outlook, career ladders, including the local, regional, and national job opportunities;
4. job tryout experiences involving simulations, role playing, observations, and limited hands-on experiences;
5. assessment of student interests, abilities, attitudes, aptitudes, values, and achievements in relation to the career cluster under study; and
6. decision-making processes which should be closely related to self-assessment.

Each teacher should select the organization, career fields, amount of emphasis, and instructional activities appropriate for the students involved.

Introducing the course

Most of the courses that students enroll in relate to specific skills and knowledge to be learned, such as mathematics, English, or business law. Career exploration classes, on the other hand, are concerned with learning about careers, self-assessment, and the process of decision making. In a new program of career exploration, one of your responsibilities is to convince students, parents, and sometimes other teachers of the value of career education for each student.

What are some techniques that you might use to interest students in exploring careers? The following are suggestive of those used by experienced career exploration teachers.

1. Have students list as many different jobs as they can in five minutes.
2. Have students pretend they are parents and write down careers they think would be appropriate for their son or daughter.
3. Show a film or filmstrip about careers in business.
4. Prepare a slide presentation of local office employees on the job.
5. Have a panel of local persons employed in business tell about their jobs.
6. Invite a panel of parents employed in business and office occupations to tell about their jobs.
7. Plan a field trip to a business, showing office employees at work.
8. Arrange a day on the job where students can experience firsthand the details of a business career.
9. Arrange afterschool or summer work experience where students can earn as they learn about business and office careers.
10. Secure several copies of publications such as the *Occupational Outlook Handbook* and have students skim them to get a feel for the wide range of job opportunities available to them.
11. Have a small-group or total-group discussion on "How I Plan to Decide on a Career."
12. Watch a career development television program such as "Bread and Butterflies" which includes short-term, long-term, and subject-area activities.

Instructional techniques

Based on student characteristics, opportunities in your employment community, and the abilities, achievements, aptitudes, and interests of your students, you will want to plan activities that meet individual needs. Illustration 15.3 is an example of an individualized instructional module developed at the University of Georgia through which students may explore a job in the clerical job cluster. In an earlier module, students would have viewed a filmstrip about office workers, read about careers in a modern office, visited a local business (completing a field trip form to guide their observations), dis-

illustration 15.3
THE RECEPTIONIST TEACHER'S GUIDE

I. Materials and Equipment
Equipment: None.

II. Learning Resources
Activity A: script (included in this teacher's guide)
Activity C: Book: *A Career in the Modern Office.* Available from: McGraw-Hill Book Co., Gregg Division, New York, N.Y. 10020

Book: *Concise Handbook of Occupations.* Available from: J. G. Ferguson Publishing Co., 6 North Michigan Avenue, Chicago, Il. 60602

PLACE CARD

Job: Receptionist

Duties: The main duty of a receptionist is to receive visitors, direct or escort visitors to the proper office, and maintain records of visitors. The receptionist may perform other functions. These may include operating a switchboard, typing, filing, and other general clerical work.

Work Environment: Almost all large and medium-sized offices, businesses, industrial plants, and public buildings have jobs for receptionists.

Educational Requirements: High school education is preferred and may be required by some companies. A background in business courses, especially typing and clerical procedures, would be helpful.

Personal Requirements: Pleasant disposition, outgoing personality, poise
Neat appearance
tactful, courteous, cheerful

Salary: $90 to $110 per week

Sources of Additional Information: Local receptionists

Vocabulary: Tact—Public Relations—Poise

SCRIPT FOR RECEPTIONIST

You are a receptionist in the Hughes Company. Your main duty is to greet callers when they come in and show them to the office of the person they wish to see. You also provide information and may do other tasks such as answering the telephone and typing.

A visitor enters the office. The receptionist is busy typing labels for file folders. The receptionist immediately stops typing and turns to greet the caller.
Receptionist: (with a smile and a pleasant voice) Good morning, may I help you?
Caller: Yes, I'm Mr. Hall. I have an appointment to see Mr. Kelly.
Receptionist: (checks appointment schedule and confirms appointment on schedule.) One moment, sir, and I will ring Mr. Kelly's office. (Receptionist rings Mr. Kelly's office on the intercom telephone line.) Mr. Hall is here for his nine o'clock appointment. (Pause.) Yes, I will show him in. This way, sir, the first door to the right. (Receptionist gets up and shows Mr. Hall to Mr. Kelly's office and returns to desk to continue typing the labels.)
Another visitor comes in.
Receptionist: Good morning, may I help you?
Caller: Yes, I would like to see Mr. Nash. I'm Jack Timmons.

illustration 15.3 (continued)

Receptionist: (Checks appointment schedule and finds no appointment for Mr. Timmons.) Do you have an appointment, sir?

Mr. Timmons: No, I don't, bit I would like very much to see Mr. Nash.

Receptionist: One moment, sir. I'll see if he is busy. May I tell him the nature of your business.

Mr. Timmons: Yes, my company, Smith Industries, is handling the new manufacturing device for him.

Receptionist: (Calls Mr. Nash's office.) Mr. Timmons of Smith Industries is here and wishes to see Mr. Nash about the new manufacturing device his company is handling. (Pause.) Mr. Timmons, Mr. Nash is busy at this moment and will see you in a few minutes. Would you be seated and I will show you in when he is ready. (A few minutes pass and the intercom buzzes.) Yes, I will show him in. (Turns to Mr. Timmons.) Mr. Nash will see you now, sir. This way. His office is the second door to the left. (Gets up and shows Mr. Timmons in. Returns and resumes typing.)

Another caller comes in.

Caller: I'm James Morris of Walter, Incorporated. I would like to see Mr. Kelly.

Receptionist: (Checks appointment schedule.) Do you have an appointment, sir?

Mr. Morris: No, I don't.

Receptionist: One moment, sir. I will check to see if Mr. Kelly can see you today. (Pause. Calls Mr. Kelly's office.) Mr. Kelly is busy at the moment, Mr. Morris, but he will be glad to see you this afternoon at two o'clock if you care to come back then.

Mr. Morris: I have a plane to catch at 11:30.

Receptionist: Perhaps you would like to make an appointment for another time.

Mr. Morris: All right. Anytime next week would be fine.

Receptionist: I'll check with Mr. Kelly's secretary to see if Tuesday at 10:00 would be suitable. (Pause.) Yes, that will be fine. I'm sorry you were not able to see Mr. Kelly today and I will see you next week.

The receptionist's job is mainly one of public relations. Her main function is to greet and help people who come to the office. She may perform other duties which may include answering the telephone, filing, and typing. In this package of activities you will explore the occupation by:

OBJECTIVES

1. ACTING OUT THE ROLE OF THE RECEPTIONIST.

2. REACTING TO STATEMENTS THAT DEAL WITH THE RECEPTIONIST'S OCCUPATION.

3. IDENTIFYING THE ACTIVITIES AND REQUIREMENTS OF A RECEPTIONIST.

4. EXPRESSING YOUR FEELINGS ABOUT THE OCCUPATION OF A RECEPTIONIST.

illustration 15.3 (continued)

ACTIVITIES

A. After finding a classmate who is also interested in this occupation, act out the role of a receptionist by using the script provided at the end of this package.

When you complete the exercise, go on to the next activity.

B. Read the following statements about the work you did in Activity A and circle the answer you believe to be correct.

YES NO 1. The main duty of a receptionist is to type letters.

YES NO 2. A receptionist should greet callers in a pleasant and friendly manner.

YES NO 3. All visitors who come to the office have appointments.

YES NO 4. A receptionist usually sits there with nothing to do until the next caller arrives.

YES NO 5. The receptionist is usually the first person a caller sees when entering an office.

Check your answers with the answers below.

illustration 15.3 (continued)

FEEDBACK

1. Yes. The receptionist's main duty is greeting callers.

2. Yes. The receptionist may be required to perform other duties when not greeting callers.

3. No. Since the receptionist greets all callers coming into the office, she should have an outgoing personality.

4. No. The receptionist is usually sitting down most of the time.

5. Yes. Smaller offices usually do not require the services of a receptionist.

E. When you have completed answering the following phrases, place your name on this sheet and turn it in to your teacher at the end of class. She may arrange a group discussion for you to share your feelings.

1. The thing I like best about the job of the receptionist was

_____.

2. The thing I liked the least about the job of the receptionist was

_____.

3. I think being a receptionist in a business is important because

_____.

4. I (would, would not) like to be a receptionist.

illustration 15.3 (continued)

FEEDBACK

1. No. The main duty of a receptionist is to greet callers.

2. Yes. The receptionist represents the company and should always be friendly and pleasant.

3. No. Not all visitors who come to the office have an appointment and many times the receptionist will have to tell the visitor that he cannot see the person he wishes to see. This requires tact and poise.

4. No. While a receptionist's main duty is to greet callers, she may be assigned other tasks which she may do while not greeting callers.

5. Yes. The receptionist is usually the first person a caller sees when entering the office. It is for this reason that she should present a neat appearance and pleasant disposition.

C. Read the following:

1. PLACE CARD--Receptionist

   and/or one of the following

2. "The Receptionist", A Career in the Modern Office, pp. 125-128.

3. "Receptionist", Concise Handbook of Occupations, p. 245.

D. Read the following statements about the activities and requirements of a receptionist and circle the answers you believe to be correct.

YES NO 1. A receptionist is usually responsible for greeting callers.

YES NO 2. The receptionist may have other duties such as opening and sorting mail, answering the telephone, or typing.

YES NO 3. A receptionist should be a shy, quiet person who does not like to meet people.

YES NO 4. The receptionist's job requires much physical activity.

YES NO 5. Receptionists mainly work in large and medium-sized offices.

Check your answers with the answers on the next page. If you miss more than two, you should re-read the resources provided.

cussed clerical and secretarial careers, and selected four occupations from the cluster they would like to explore further. Illustration 15.3, The Receptionist, is one of twelve occupations they might choose for additional exploration.[9]

The following activities are appropriate examples for implementing the areas of emphasis discussed earlier in this module. The secretarial cluster is used as an example.

1. The Career Field
   a. View filmstrips, slides, and films on secretarial careers such as legal secretary, medical secretary, court reporter, educational secretary, executive secretary, stenographer, and secretary in a small office.
   b. Brainstorm or hold a small-group buzz session during which students list reasons why secretaries are important in business.
   c. Present a skit about a day in business when the secretaries were all out on strike.
   d. Interview a secretary and an employer regarding the role of the secretary in business; prepare a report for the class.
   e. Prepare a display showing different secretarial jobs. (You may want to begin a collection of magazines and brochures as a source of pictures for the students to use.) Some students may want to take photographs of secretaries on the job.
   f. Read one or more articles on a career as a secretary.
   g. Individually or in small groups select one television program to watch and list each secretarial career depicted in the program. Describe the duties performed by each individual.
   h. Begin a careers notebook to be continued throughout the course containing information about the career cluster, skills and knowledges needed, personal interests, values, and aptitudes.
   i. Write a brief report or tell the class about one or two secretarial jobs you would like best and one or two you would like least; give reasons for your choices.
   j. Prepare a list of advantages and disadvantages of a job as a secretary.
2. Skills and Knowledges
   a. Read articles describing what secretaries do and prepare a list of tasks they perform.
   b. Look at a filmstrip, film, or slides about a secretary and list the tasks performed.
   c. Visit an office and observe the tasks performed by the secretary; report on your trip to the class.
   d. Invite a secretary to visit the class and tell about the different skills, knowledges, and personal traits used on the job.
   e. Prepare charts listing skills and knowledges used by secretaries in specialized situations, such as legal offices, medical offices, and government offices.
   f. Invite a high school senior or vocational-technical school/junior college business student to tell about the business courses and other courses they have taken, or will take, and the skills and knowledges they have acquired.
   g. Interview a worker in the secretarial field using questions such as the following: What special interests or skills do you need for your job?
      What other occupations can you enter with your knowledge and training?
      What channels can I use to get this job—training, college, or experience?
      What type of person do you have to be in order to like and be successful at your job?

What are the jobs you have held and which ones have led to the one you hold now?

What types of interests do you have and how did they help you decide what job you wanted?

What school subjects do you use in your work and how?

How has your particular job changed over the past ten or twenty years? What do you think it will be like in another ten years?

How does this job support your way of living in terms of income, knowledge, working hours, and leisure time?

Are your hobbies like or different from your job?

Why is this job important to you? What satisfactions do you get from it?

What are the most important duties of a secretary as you view the job?

3. Job Opportunities and Career Ladders

Much of this content will be integrated with discussions and activities related to Phases 1 and 2.

   a. Read articles, job descriptions, and publications such as the *Occupational Outlook Quarterly* and prepare a chart showing various jobs in the secretarial field, including those requiring little training, moderate amounts of training, and high levels of skill and knowledge.

   b. Read the classified ads for several days and prepare a display or make a report on job opportunities in the secretarial field.

   c. Invite a speaker from the State Employment Service or a local employment agency to discuss job opportunities in the secretarial field.

   d. Read the Department of Labor publication in your state and prepare a report or chart on job outlook, salaries, demand and supply in the secretarial field.

4. Activities and Simulations

You will want to assemble, construct, or purchase as many activities of varying difficulty levels as possible through which students can become familiar with careers in the secretarial field.

   a. Write the script and, if possible, videotape a play about careers in the secretarial field.

   b. Try out office machines used by the secretary, including the typewriter, calculator, duplicating machine, and copier.

   c. Role play situations involving interpersonal relations such as getting along with the supervisor and with co-workers.

   d. Spend some time in an office, performing simple tasks or observing the secretary at work.

   e. Rotate the job of class receptionist. (You may need to arrange visits by other teachers to the class to give the receptionist some experience.)

   f. Complete activities; such as outlined in item g, which illustrate the tasks performed by a secretary.

   g. Preparing an agenda.

   Your employer, Mr. Baker, the high school principal, has asked you to prepare the agenda for the August faculty meeting. Using the information below, prepare an agenda. Make necessary corrections and set up the agenda in good form.

   Agenda, meeting of faculty, August 20, 19—

   I will make some introductory remarks and welcome the faculty and make introductions.

Old Business we will need to consider should include:
- Report on mainstreaming and the i.e.p. (individualized educational program)
- Report on work-experience programs in business and distributive education
Advantages
Possible problem areas
Support of business people
- Report of the physical education department
New programs
Athletic schedule for fall quarter
- Scheduling
Suggested changes in scheduling
Scheduling assignments

New Business to be taken up:
- Parent-teachers association
Appointment of committee to work with PTA officers
Suggestions
- System-wide grading
Problems with present system
Proposed changes
- Other new business to be introduced from the floor
Meeting will be held at 9:00 A.M. in Mell Auditorium.

h.   One business teacher reports the following approach to career exploration:

Since the eighth grade year is the first year students in Fulton County attend high school, this course took the approach of introducing the student to his new school. I began to guide my students through exploratory experiences as they learned about their work environment (their school) and several career opportunities which related to each curriculum department within the school (English, mathematics, business, and so on). The first day of class I informed the students that they were a part of the entire school operation since they were workers who were currently engaged in the occupation of STUDENT. I introduced myself as PERSONNEL MANAGER, not teacher. The principal was the MANAGER and the assistant principal was the ASSISTANT MANAGER. An interesting activity occurred when our school principal met with the students on the third day of class and compared his duties as principal with those of a manager.

During the first two weeks of the course, the students became familiar with their work environment. This feat was accomplished through such activities as completing a work environment layout as the students toured the school; preparing job descriptions for the occupations of student, personnel manager, manager, and so on; meeting with various workers in the school such as manager (principal), assistant manager (assistant principal), counselor, department chairmen, custodians, and bus drivers; and preparing an organization chart for the school.

Not only did the students become familiar with their work environment within the local school, but they also explored careers related to the entire county school operation such as Board of Education, superintendent, assistant superintendents, and curriculum directors. They also discussed such topics as school financing, food services, and health and safety services.

Each student completed an application form in which s/he applied for the position of STUDENT. Applications for Social Security numbers were completed. Each STUDENT signed a contract in which s/he made an agreement with the PERSONNEL MANAGER and MANAGER to perform certain requirements in the course. The PERSONNEL MANAGER agreed to remunerate with a grade comparable to the work performed.

After being introduced to their work environment, the students began to explore various careers. The careers were presented to the students by first introducing them to a curriculum department within the school. Each career was also presented to the students as belonging to one of the fifteen occupational clusters as defined by the U.S. Office of Education. The students then explored various careers which depended upon training from the curriculum department being considered through such activities as making posters, interviewing, listening to and conversing with guest speakers, writing skits, participating in skits, preparing slides, and videotaping.

Careers relating to every department within the school were explored. A job description for each career explored was given to the students. These job descriptions, along with all other handouts and work completed for the course, were compiled in a notebook called MY WORK WORLD.

This career education course was unique in its approach. Rather than concentrating on careers related to business education only, this course introduced students to careers in many fields. However, the importance of business education in each career was mentioned so that each student could gain an appreciation for the importance of business skills and knowledges in all careers.[10]

5. Self-Assessment and Decision Making
    These two phases are treated together since both processes are closely related. Developing decision-making skills is one of the most important objectives of career exploration, and continued emphasis should be placed on maintaining and extending this skill throughout the secondary and postsecondary levels.
    a. You may want your students to complete the "feedback" sheets in Illustration 15.4 for one or more occupations as a means of summarizing job requirements and opportunities as well as their attitude toward a given job.
    b. In the process of self-assessment and decision making, students should examine both life style and work style. Attention should be given to the impact of career choice on personal values and the kind of life style to which one aspires. The student should be encouraged to examine such questions as the following in collecting information:[11]
        What are the demands of this job on my "discretionary time"?
        How much traveling will I be expected to do?
        What are the demands on my privacy?
        How much time will I have with my family?
        How much time will I have for community involvement?
        Can I keep physically fit?
        Will I be able to develop and maintain close friendships?
        Will I be expected to move frequently from one geographic area to another?

illustration 15.4
SCALE FOR MEASURING KNOWLEDGE AND ATTITUDE
·TOWARD JOBS

Job Title _____ Name _____

FEEDBACK

I. The Job and Preparation

1. Does this job require a college education? Yes   No

    a. If yes, how many years of college? _____
    b. Do you have to keep going to school to keep up to date in this job? Yes   No
    c. What kinds of courses must be studied? _____

    _____

2. Does this job require a special training or apprenticeship program? Yes   No   How many years are required? _____

3. Does this job require a high school education? Yes   No   Is it best to have one for this job? Yes   No
    a. What kinds of courses should be studied in high school? _____

    _____

4. Does this job require that one have experience before entry? Yes   No If yes, what kinds of experience? _____

    _____

    a. How does one obtain this experience? _____

    b. Must one be licensed or have special certification to perform in this job? Yes   No
        1. If yes, what kinds of licenses and certificates? _____

        _____

        2. How does one get them? _____

5. What other things might one do to prepare himself for this job?

    _____

    _____

6. How does one enter this job? _____

    _____

7. How much money might be needed to prepare for this job? _____

========== HOW DO YOU FEEL ABOUT THE JOB?==========

A. Do you like going to school? Yes   No

B. Do you like to study? Yes   No

C. What kinds of things do you like to study? _____

    _____

illustration 15.4 (continued)

FEEDBACK

D. Will these studies help you in this job? Yes   No

E. Would you want to continue going to school for the length of time required to prepare yourself for this job? Yes   No

F. Do you think that the job is worth the money it would take to prepare for it? Yes   No

G. Where might you raise the money to prepare yourself for this job?

_____

H. To what schools would you go to prepare yourself for this job?

_____

I. Where can you get more information about preparing for this job?

_____

J. What can you do now to prepare for this job? _____

_____

K. Is your achievement in the related subjects good enough to prepare you for this job? Yes   No   Maybe

------------------------------NEXT CATEGORY------------------------------

II. <u>The Job and Working Conditions</u>

1. Where do you find this kind of job? (government, large city, small city, private industry, single ownership) _____

_____

2. How many hours a day would you have to work? _____

3. How many hours a week would you have to work? _____

4. How long would your vacations be? _____

5. Does this job involve working with many people? Yes   No

6. What kinds of clothes would you wear to work? _____

_____

7. With what kinds of people would you work? _____

_____

8. How many years of education would these people have? _____

9. Would you shave or put on make-up before going to work? Yes   No

illustration 15.4 (continued)

FEEDBACK

10. What would your working area look like? (inside-outside, hot-cold, clean-dirty, quiet-noisy, crowded-spacious) _____
_____

11. What kinds of tools, equipment, or machines would you use in this job? _____
_____

12. What kinds of tasks would you be doing on this job? _____
_____
_____
_____

13. What kinds of skills and knowledge would you need to do this job?
_____
_____
_____

14. Does the worker specialize in some particular part of this job?
Yes   No   If yes, what part? _____

15. How many bosses might you have? _____ How many people would you boss? _____

16. Are there more men than women in this job? Yes   No

17. Would you be working with more men than women, women than men or equal? _____

18. How physically hard would this job be? _____

19. Would your hours be regular hours such as 8:00 to 5:00? Yes   No

20. Would you be working alone or with several people? _____

21. Would you earn a regular, guaranteed salary or would you earn a commission based on how much you work or sell? _____

22. Is there a lot of pressure to meet deadlines or to get things done?
Yes   No

23. Would you meet lots of people on this job? Yes   No

24. What is the salary range for this job? _____

25. What things might affect the salary? _____

illustration 15.4 (continued)

FEEDBACK

26. What are some fringe benefits that you would earn? _____
_____

================ HOW DO YOU FEEL ABOUT THE JOB ================

A. Would you like regular 8:00 to 5:00 working hours and very little or no overtime? Yes   No   If it paid extra money, would you like it? Yes   No

B. Would you like irregular hours? Yes   No

C. Would you like all your week ends free for recreation? Yes   No

D. Do you like to clean up and dress up for work? Yes   No

E. Do you like to work with other people who are well dressed? Yes   No

F. Do you like to work by yourself? Yes   No

G. Do you like to meet new people? Yes   No

H. Is this a man's job or a woman's job? _____

I. Do you like to work indoors with little moving about? Yes   No
   Lots of moving about? Yes   No

J. Do you like to work outdoors with little moving about? Yes   No
   Lots of moving about? Yes   No

K. Do you like to work under pressure to meet deadlines? Yes   No

L. Would you like to be the leader of people on the job? Yes   No

-----------------------------NEXT CATEGORY-----------------------------

VIII. The Job and the Community

1. Do you know someone who has this job? Yes   No

2. Do you like people who have this job? Yes   No

3. What kinds of cars do people with this job drive? (new-old, big-small) _____

4. Do people with this job live in big houses? Yes   No

5. Do people with these jobs tell other people in your church, school or neighborhood what to do? Yes   No

illustration 15.4 (continued)

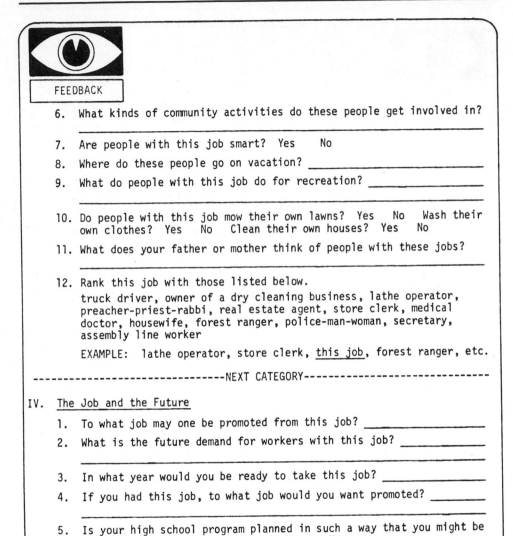

FEEDBACK

6. What kinds of community activities do these people get involved in?
   _____

7. Are people with this job smart? Yes   No

8. Where do these people go on vacation? _____

9. What do people with this job do for recreation? _____
   _____

10. Do people with this job mow their own lawns? Yes   No   Wash their
    own clothes? Yes   No   Clean their own houses? Yes   No

11. What does your father or mother think of people with these jobs?
    _____

12. Rank this job with those listed below.
    truck driver, owner of a dry cleaning business, lathe operator,
    preacher-priest-rabbi, real estate agent, store clerk, medical
    doctor, housewife, forest ranger, police-man-woman, secretary,
    assembly line worker

    EXAMPLE: lathe operator, store clerk, <u>this job</u>, forest ranger, etc.

-------------------------------NEXT CATEGORY-------------------------------

IV. <u>The Job and the Future</u>

1. To what job may one be promoted from this job? _____

2. What is the future demand for workers with this job? _____
   _____

3. In what year would you be ready to take this job? _____

4. If you had this job, to what job would you want promoted? _____
   _____

5. Is your high school program planned in such a way that you might be
   preparing yourself for this job? Yes   No

6. Can you wait until you have prepared yourself for this job before
   earning the money necessary to buy a new car? Yes   No

-------------------------------LAST CATEGORY-------------------------------

V. <u>The Job and Me</u>

1. Does this job pay enough money for me to buy the things I want?
   Yes   No

illustration 15.4 (continued)

FEEDBACK

2. What would you like <u>least</u> about this job?_____
    _____

3. What would you like <u>most</u> about this job? _____
    _____

4. Would dad and mom want me to take this job? Yes   No

5. Would they be proud of me in this job? Yes   No

6. Would my friends think highly of me in this job? Yes   No

7. Would I be proud of myself in this job? Yes   No

8. Is this job a challenge to me? Yes   No

9. Would this job keep me away from my family? Yes   No   My church?
    Yes   No   My recreation? Yes   No   Community clubs? Yes   No

10. Would I have to travel a lot in this job? Yes   No   Would I like
    this? Yes   No

11. Do I see myself in this job in the future? Yes   No

12. What are some advantages of this job? _____
    _____
    _____

13. What are some disadvantages of this job? _____
    _____
    _____

14. What personal characteristics should a person with this job have?
    _____
    _____

15. Do I have these characteristics? Yes   No

16. I might like this job. Yes   No

17. Complete the following scales:
    A. "Job Rating Scales"

illustration 15.5
JOB RATING SCALE

Job Prestige

| very low | low | middle | high | very high |

Salary

| very low | low | middle | high | very high |

Working Conditions

| very low | low | middle | high | very high |

Preparation Required

| very low | low | middle | high | very high |

Future Outlook

| very low | low | middle | high | very high |

•Likewise, in selecting a work style that has the most meaning, the student should answer questions such as:

How important is autonomy at my job?

Should my job be an integral part of my nonworking life?

Do I want routine work or do I want work that requires constant decision-making skills?

Do I want opportunities for a good deal of creativity in my job?

•At the middle school level, the emphasis is on developing the *process* of examining one's interests, values, goals, and attitudes in relation to various occupations, not on making the decisions themselves. One activity appropriate for using decision-making skills is for the teacher and students to prepare a list of questions to be used as a guide in selecting courses, extracurricular activities, and clubs for the upcoming school year.

•A checklist as shown in Illustration 15.6 can be used to help students to determine their own work values:

illustration 15.6
WHAT ARE YOUR WORK VALUES?

Ideas about the characteristics of a desirable work place vary greatly. What are your work values? The following inventory consists of twenty items, each item describing the two extremes of a major work characteristic. To work with people vs. work alone. For each item, check the space which best describes your own work values.

	Very Important	Moderately Important	Not Important		Not Important	Moderately Important	Very Important	
Work for organization	___	___	___		___	___	___	Self-employment
Work alone	___	___	___		___	___	___	Work with other people
Structured environment; well-defined duties and responsibilities	___	___	___		___	___	___	Unstructured work: room for creativity and initiative
Close supervision	___	___	___		___	___	___	No supervision
Low level of responsibility; no critical decisions	___	___	___		___	___	___	High level of responsibility; makes key decisions
Short hours: maximum eight hours per day	___	___	___		___	___	___	Long hours and weekend work usual
Guaranteed regular hours	___	___	___		___	___	___	Possible overtime
Variety of duties every day	___	___	___		___	___	___	Similar duties every day
Challenges and risks in work	___	___	___		___	___	___	Work offers security
Fast pace; high pressure	___	___	___		___	___	___	Slow pace; low pressure
Visible end products: specific achievable goals	___	___	___		___	___	___	Can't see results of work, long-range goals
Work indoors in pleasant environment	___	___	___		___	___	___	Work outdoors in all weather and conditions
Willing to relocate anywhere	___	___	___		___	___	___	Work in specific geographical area
Work for large business	___	___	___		___	___	___	Work for small business
High prestige and status	___	___	___		___	___	___	Low prestige and status
Many opportunities for advancement and professional development	___	___	___		___	___	___	Few opportunities for advancement and professional development
Live close to work	___	___	___		___	___	___	Live half hour or more from work
Close work with machines	___	___	___		___	___	___	Little work with machines
Early retirement	___	___	___		___	___	___	Work opportunities after 65
Frequent travel	___	___	___		___	___	___	Little or no travel

1. What special interests or skills do you need for your job?

2. What other jobs can you do with your knowledge and training?

3. What ways can I get this job—training, college, or experience?

4. What type of person do you have to be in order to like and be successful at your job?

5. What are all the different jobs you have had and which have led to the one you have now?

6. Do you think that your mistakes have helped you to make better decisions?

7. What types of things (interests) do you like to do and how did they help you decide what job you wanted?

8. What school subjects do you use in your work and how?

9. How has your particular job changed over the past ten or twenty years? What do you think it will be like in another ten years?

Source: Career World, Teacher's Edition, vol. 5, no. 5 (January 1977).

---

c. Have students prepare a summary of the career field cluster. On one chart, list the major skills and knowledge needed to perform various jobs. On another chart, list the courses and levels of formal training normally needed to acquire the necessary skills and knowledge. On a third chart, summarize the significant work tasks and characteristics. Have each student examine his or her interests, academic abilities, grades in school, aptitudes, and values, and prepare a paper giving his or her reaction to a specific job cluster (or to specific jobs within the job cluster) as a possible professional career, (reasons must be based on self-assessment versus career requirements). Encourage students to be as specific as possible (that is, "A receptionist works with other people; I prefer to work alone").

d. Conduct group sharing sessions in which students are encouraged to discuss their observations of job performances and job conditions; how they felt about themselves while performing or observing the work under study; what personal needs they feel would be met or hindered by such work; what aptitude they feel they might have for such work; and how they think one goes about preparing for such work.

e. Ask students to list the decision-making situations they encountered yesterday and to discuss how they arrived at a decision.

f. Outline the steps involved in decision making. Use this process to solve an immediate problem that affects the group.

EVALUATION

The teacher must incorporate several types of evaluation as an ongoing component of the career exploration program. The changing nature of business careers, both emerging occupations and existing jobs, necessitates frequent examination of the content of the exploration program to assure its accurate representation of the job market in the business-office cluster. Advisory committees composed of representatives from business and industry as well as parents and business educators can help the teacher in program assessment. The business teacher is responsible for keeping up-to-date on employment opportunities and the nature of business-office jobs. Publications from national, state, and local labor departments are helpful in assessing the current job market.

Evaluation of materials

Program goals and objectives and student abilities, achievements, and interests are key factors in establishing criteria for selecting new materials and for periodic assessment of materials on hand. Checklists may be designed to ensure systematic and uniform assessment of all materials. You will want to have material of varying difficulty levels, since within the same class you will have students with a wide range of abilities. Increasing amounts of print and nonprint career education material are appearing on the market, and most of it is attractive and interesting. The key factor is to assess the *appropriateness* of all materials in terms of your objectives and your students.

Student evaluation

Student evaluation focuses on content, activities, interests-values-attitudes, and processes. For many middle school/junior high students, assessments of interests and processes are new experiences.

Content tests emphasize knowledge of an occupation. The following illustrates a true-false item of a content nature:

——T ——F   The receptionist is usually responsible for greeting callers.

——T ——F   The receptionist's job requires much physical activity.

Activities, including role playing, simulation, hands-on experiences, and worksheets, are important tools through which students learn about the world of work. Observation of student activities can also offer one means of assessing student performance. Be careful, however, *not* to put too much emphasis on grading these activities. The intent is for students to *explore*, not to master specific skills and knowledges. Simulated interviews may be used to measure skills in applying for a job, for example. Prepare 3 x 5 cards describing the job openings. Allow students to apply for the job of their choice. Other staff members from your school or a nearby high school, local businessmen, or school administrators could serve as interviewers. Students might or might not be offered a job on the basis of the interview and accompanying résumé. By videotaping the interviews, students are able to evaluate one another's performances as well as their own, using a checklist.

Interests, values, and attitudes checklists and rating scales may be used both as pre- and posttests to reflect student change. These should not be used for a grade, but as a means of having students examine change in their personal behaviors.

Decision-making skills are best measured through application problems in which students are expected to arrive at decisions using the techniques learned in class. For example, students may be given a problem and directed to work through all the steps in the decision-making process to arrive at a choice. For example, Ed Dills, seventeen years old, will be a senior in the upcoming school year. He has a summer job at a local plant paying 1½ times the minimum wage. The plant manager has offered Ed a permanent job if he does not return to high school. Evaluation of this or other decisions is based on students' abilities to follow a logical decision-making process and to arrive at a reasonable conclusion. The *process* is more important than a *correct* answer.

Work habits, attitudes, and interpersonal relations are vital to overall job performance. You may want to establish businesslike criteria for classroom performance, such as promptness, neatness, following directions, working without disturbing others, and so on, as a means for evaluating student behavior in the course. Checklists should be completed both by the students and the teacher.

module 15.2
LEARNING ACTIVITIES

Part II (Continued from Module 15.1)
- A. Outline the topics, in an organizational plan of your choice, for the career exploration course.
- B. List the areas of emphasis for the topics in "A" above.
- C. Prepare or describe at least one activity for each area of emphasis. (Minimum of five total activities. The activities should be related to all topic areas.)
- D. Outline an evaluation plan for the career exploration course.

module 15.2
SELF-TEST

1. Summarize the characteristics of the middle school/junior high student with respect to social, physical, psychological, and intellectual factors.

SUMMARY

One of the goals of education at all levels is preparation for work regardless of the individual's career objective. At the middle school/junior high level, the career education emphasis is on *exploration* which involves examining career clusters (job families) in relation to one's interests, abilities, aptitudes, attitudes, and values. Using available goals and objectives as guides, the teacher develops specific objectives for the local school, making adaptations as needed on the basis of the school's unique characteristics and needs.

The physical, social, psychological, and intellectual characteristics of middle school students differ from those at the secondary school level. Business teachers need to be aware of these characteristics and to use them as a guide in developing a career exploration program involving the business and office occupations. The organization of topics should reflect opportunities in the state, regional, and national employment communities. Areas of emphasis include an examination of the career field, skills and knowledges needed, the occupational outlook and career ladders, real and simulated job tryouts, self-assessment and decision making. A variety of group and individual activities are appropriate for meeting individual needs.

References

[1]Career Education Incentive Act, Section 3, Public Law 95–207, December 13, 1977, (Washington, D.C.: U.S. Government Printing Office).

[2]Calfrey C. Calhoun and Alton V. Finch, *Vocational and Career Education: Concepts and Operations* (Belmont, Calif.: Wadsworth Publishing Company, 1976), p. 126.

[3]Kenneth B. Hoyt, *Monographs on Career Education: Perspectives on the Problem of Evaluation in Career Education* (Washington, D.C.: U.S. Government Printing Office, 1976), pp. 30–37.

[4]Harry N. Drier, Jr., "Career Development Activities Permeate Wisconsin Curriculum," *American Vocational Journal* 47, no. 3 (March 1972): 40.

[5]*Evaluation Report of Career Education for Rural Georgians: Crisp and Liberty Counties*, Missouri Evaluation Projects (Columbia: University of Missouri, 1976).

[6]Career Development Objectives, Eighth Grade (Atlanta: Georgia State Department of Education, 1978).

[7]Douglas R. Jones, "Pressures and Adolescents," in *Education for the Middle School Years: Readings*, eds. James E. Hertling and Howard G. Getz (Glenview, Ill.: Scott, Foresman and Company, 1971), p. 32.

[8]James E. Hertling and Howard G. Getz, "Middle School Years: The Early Adolescent, Instruction," in *Education for the Middle School Years: Readings* (Glenview, Ill.: Scott, Foresman and Company, 1971), p. 26.

[9]The Development of an Individualized Instructional System for Mini-Exploratory Courses in Career Education at the Middle/Junior High School Level: Clerical and Secretarial Mini-Course (Athens: Department of Business Education, University of Georgia, 1974).

[10]Carolyn Vickery, "Eighth Graders Explore Their Work World," *Georgia Business Education Association Armchair Bulletin* 10, no. 1. (January 1978): 3–4.

[11]Lucille T. Stoddard, "Career Education and the Lifestyle Concept," *Business Education Forum* 32, no. 7 (April 1978): 12.

SUGGESTIONS FOR FURTHER STUDY

Anderson, Marcia; Stitt, Thomas; and Nystrom, Dennis. "Occupational Orientation and Exploration Programs." *Journal of Business Education* 51 (February 1976): 228–30.

Baggett, Harry. "Studying Life-Styles of Office Workers in Career Education." *Balance Sheet* 57 (February 1976): 200–2.

Green, Edna M. "Experiences with Exploring and Discovering the World of Business." *Balance Sheet* 57 (April 1976): 304–5.

Keller, Arnold. "Career Education: Success for the Potential Dropout." *Clearing House* 51 (October 1977): 70–72.

Noble, Carol G. "Helping Students Recognize Personal Qualities for Job Success." *Journal of Business Education* 52 (January 1977): 164–67.

Patterson, Clarissa M. H., and Phillips, Priscilla M. "Motivational Techniques for Career Awareness and Job Exploration." *Business Education World* 56 (May–June 1976): 25.

Price, Margaret, and Maurello, Marty. "Consider a Career in Government." *Today's Secretary* 79 (February 1977): 23–25, 30.

Rauch, Verda. "Expanding Your Offerings with Mini-Courses." *Journal of Business Education* 52 (February 1977): 211–12.

Stallard, John J., and Hilton, Margaret J. "Career Education: Decision-Making Strategies." *Journal of Business Education* 52 (May 1977): 366–67.

Steagall, Paul, Jr.; Agee, Janice; Janney, Debra; and Murray, Sue. "Teaching Business Exploration." *Virginia Business Education Association Newsletter* (February 1977): 16–17.

part six

GUIDING RELATED BUSINESS INSTRUCTION

chapter 16

WORK STUDY PROGRAMS IN BUSINESS EDUCATION

Many secondary and postsecondary schools have work programs for their students. These programs are of two general types: cooperative work programs (cooperative education) and noncooperative work programs. Cooperative work programs are instructional programs in which the school and employers jointly provide learning experiences to prepare students for initial office employment. Such programs are referred to in this chapter as cooperative office education. Both the in-school and on-the-job activities focus on the student's career objectives. Chapter 16 will examine characteristics of cooperative work programs, review cooperative program goals, and explore the procedures for establishing and maintaining effective cooperative programs.

module 16.1
CHARACTERISTICS AND GOALS

Module 16.1 introduces the distinguishing characteristics of cooperative work-study programs, the types of programs in use, and their goals. After completing this module, you should be able to (1) contrast cooperative and non-cooperative work-study programs, (2) list six characteristics of cooperative work-study programs, (3) describe three types of cooperative work-study programs, and (4) formulate goals for an office education work experience program.

Cooperative work programs have six distinguishing characteristics, all of which must be met for a program to be "cooperative." "Students in the cooperative program (1) participate in learning experiences based on a specified career objective, (2) work part-time in a training station selected on the basis of that same career objective, (3) receive pay and school credit for on-the-job training, (4) have constant school supervision, (5) participate in this program for at least one year, and (6) take in-school courses which relate directly to their on-the-job training."[1]

There are several types of noncooperative work programs, some of which may be offered in the same school with cooperative programs: *Exploratory programs,* which are designed to acquaint students with employment opportunities and requirements. Students (who may or may not be paid) observe or try out various jobs for a few days, weeks, or a semester. *Sheltered workshops,* which are designed for individuals who cannot function in a normal work environment. These persons perform certain jobs under supervision in a sheltered setting. *Work-study programs,* which are designed to help students remain in school or college by means of part-time jobs which may or may not be related to the students' career objectives.

Business teachers work directly with cooperative programs, providing in-school related instruction and supervising on-the-job training. Secondary programs usually combine work and instruction daily, with school in the morning and on-the-job training in the afternoon. At the college level, the on-the-job training may follow the secondary pattern or may be an all-day job for a few weeks with weekly seminars on the campus. This chapter will focus on the cooperative programs, known as cooperative office education (COE), cooperative vocational education (CVE), vocational office training (VOT), or other similar names. Some of the procedures and techniques described may also be appropriate in other work programs.

TYPES OF COOPERATIVE PROGRAMS

Cooperative programs may be offered for separate vocational areas, such as business education, distributive education; for combined areas, that is, one program such as diversified cooperative training (DCT) serving several vocational areas; or for special needs students, in which the focus of the program is on acquiring a job, holding a job, and developing entry level skills. "To point out the differences between the regular cooperative program and the cooperative program for the disadvantaged, we might examine the traditional motto used in cooperative education. In the cooperative vocational program, the motto is learn while you earn—with the emphasis on *learning.* However, in the cooperative program for the disadvantaged, the motto should be revised to earn while you learn—with the emphasis on *earn.* Hopefully, when the disadvantaged student is earning money and has made progress in developing appropriate work attitudes, s/he will be motivated to acquire occupational skills and may transfer to the cooperative vocational program."[2]

After surveying the employment community, the faculty, and the students, the administration makes a decision to offer: (1) no cooperative work program, (2) separate work programs for various vocational areas, (3) joint cooperative programs, and/or (4) special needs work programs.

GOALS

If a cooperative business program is to be implemented, one of the first tasks of the business teacher is to specify program goals which form the basis for specific student objectives. The following are examples of goals for cooperative programs for business students:[3]

1. To present, develop, and refine the office skills necessary for job competency.
2. To promote the feelings of self-respect and achievement in students.
3. To provide a laboratory in which students practice the skills, knowledges, and attitudes learned to make the classroom instruction more meaningful and relevant.
4. To provide an opportunity, through the use of local businesses, for the students to acquire additional skills and knowledges not possible or practical in the classroom.
5. To provide an opportrnity for students to make social adjustments and to develop the ability to work cooperatively with coworkers and superiors.
6. To develop sound concepts of personal money management through experiences gained from wages received from training stations and related instruction.
7. To encourage good attendance in school and on the job.
8. To make learning meaningful and practical to students who may be inclined toward quitting school and to provide for financial assistance.
9. To provide a situation in which community needs for office employees may be more satisfactorily met.
10. To encourage graduates of the high school to become employed and remain in the community.
11. To guide the students in selecting the particular job most suitable to them in terms of their interests, aptitudes, and abilities.
12. To stress the importance of being neat, prompt, and dependable.
13. To emphasize the importance of being able to follow directions and accept supervision.
14. To develop good work habits and attitudes; to aid in the development of such personality traits as punctuality, dependability, accuracy, tact, adaptability, poise, and a sense of responsibility that makes for efficient work with a minimum of supervision.
15. To prepare the students for full-time employment following graduation and to give them a background of training which will contribute to rapid advancement on the job.

module 16.1
LEARNING ACTIVITIES

1. Follow-up studies of graduates of Russell High School reveal that a majority of the students enter the labor market after graduation. Assume that you are the business education supervisor for the school system. After meeting with the business education faculty at Russell High, you have been asked to investigate the possibility of establishing a cooperative office education program. Prepare the following material to submit to the school superintendent, building administrator, and board of education.
   a. Statement requesting permission to establish a cooperative program to include:
      (1) definition of cooperative office education

        (2) rationale for cooperative education

    b.   Goals for the cooperative office education program

2. Arrange with your instructor to invite your state supervisor in charge of cooperative office occupations programs to visit the class to discuss the organization and guidelines for cooperative office education in your state. Ask him or her to explain the provisions for cooperative office education programs in the state plan for vocational education.

module 16.1
SELF-TEST

1. Differentiate between a cooperative office education program and other types of work experience for students.

module 16.2
ESTABLISHING A COOPERATIVE EDUCATION PROGRAM

The success of a cooperative office education program depends, to a significant extent, on how thoroughly the business teacher plans for the initial establishment of the program. In this module, you will become familiar with the basic procedures involved in establishing such a program: (1) acquire administrative approval; (2) determine the need for and interest in the program among students and the employment community; (3) select a qualified teacher-coordinator; (4) submit a cooperative program application to your state business education office for approval; (5) begin publicity efforts to acquaint students, parents, faculty, and employers with the cooperative office education program; (6) select the advisory committee; (7) arrange for necessary facilities, equipment, and program; (8) establish criteria and select training stations; (9) establish criteria and select student-learners; (10) develop individual training plans; and (11) place students on the job.

    After completing this module, you should be able to (1) identify the procedures for establishing a cooperative office education program and (2) summarize the tasks involved in each of the procedures.

ACQUIRE ADMINISTRATIVE APPROVAL

    The first step in setting up a cooperative office education program is to secure the support of the school administration. Before meeting with the administrator(s), you should prepare a written proposal including the rationale for the program; its goals and objectives; the benefits to students, school, and community; the proposed curriculum; equipment, facilities, and materials needed; personnel needs; and the number of students to be served. Administrative support from both the school and the system is essential to the success of the program.

DETERMINE NEED FOR THE PROGRAM

Since cooperative education involves the combined efforts of the school, students, teachers, and the employment community, it is necessary to know the interest of these groups in such a program. Can the employment community support a cooperative program; that is, are there sufficient potential training stations? Will firms accept the philosophy of cooperatively supervised on-the-job training correlated with classroom instruction? Are there enough students to support a program? Community and student feasibility surveys should be administered to determine needs. From the city directory or similar publication, secure a list of local businesses. Send each firm a survey instrument along with an explanatory letter. (Your state business education supervisor can assist you in constructing or adapting an instrument.) Illustrations 16.1[4] and 16.2[5] provide examples of business and student surveys. To personalize the survey, ask for an interview when the survey form is completed in order to answer questions or clarify information. In large communities, business teachers from several schools may want to cooperate in conducting the survey.

The first step in constructing the instrument is to decide the purpose of the survey and the type of data needed. Topics usually included are willingness of business persons to participate, types of businesses, size and location of businesses, types of equipment and machines used, and entry requirements for office employees.

In addition to the business community questionnaires, survey tenth- and eleventh-grade students to determine their interest in such a program. This instrument should include questions about career objectives, past/present work experience, business courses taken, extracurricular activities, and interest in participating in the cooperative office education program.

SELECT QUALIFIED TEACHER-COORDINATOR

During the early planning stages, a teacher-coordinator should be identified. This business teacher will have to meet specified criteria which usually include a proper certificate and one or more years of teaching experience and one year or its equivalent of actual work experience. The teacher-coordinator should clearly understand his/her responsibilities which include tasks such as

illustration 16.1
SAMPLE BUSINESS SURVEY
VOCATIONAL OFFICE TRAINING PROGRAM

SURVEY OF JOB OPPORTUNITIES IN BUSINESS AND OFFICE OCCUPATIONS

Name of Firm_____ Phone_____

Address_____

Type of Business_____ Business Hours_____

Name of Person
Completing Questionnaire_____ Position_____

How many full-time office employees are employed by your firm?

_____Male   _____Female

How many high school students do you now employ part-time?

_____Male   _____Female   _____None

What education is required of your beginning full-time office workers?

_____Grade School   _____High School   _____College

Do you give job entrance tests?   _____Yes   _____No

If yes, what types of tests are administered?_____

_____

Skill standards required_____

_____

Do you have a training program in your business?   _____Yes   _____No

Are there any particular types of office occupations in which you have
difficulty securing workers?   _____Yes   _____No

Types of office occupations_____

Approximately how many employees have you in the following classifications?

_____Filing Clerk   _____Typist
_____Receptionist   _____Clerk/Typist
_____Mailing Clerk   _____Stenographer
_____Keypunch Operator   _____Secretary
_____Bookkeeper   _____Transcribing Machine Operator
_____Other   _____Calculating Machine Operator
_____   _____Duplicating Machine Operator

illustration 16.1 (continued)

If a program were initiated in the high school where students worked part-time and attended school part-time, would you be interested in employing one or more students in your business part-time?

_____Yes   _____Number   _____No

If no, comments: _____

_____

Check the kinds of learning experiences that your business could provide for the student-learner:

_____Telephone Usage   _____Ten-Key Adding Machine
_____Filing   _____Full Keyboard Adding-Listing Machine
_____Automatic Typewriter   _____Electronic Calculator
_____Electric Typewriter   _____Printing Calculator
_____Dictation   _____Offset Duplicator
_____Machine Transcription   _____Spirit Duplicator
_____Typing - Cutting Stencils _____Stencil Duplicator
_____Bookkeeping   _____Payroll Records

Others_____

_____

_____

_____   _____
Signature of Coordinator   Date

_____   _____
School Address   School Phone

_____   _____
Home Address   Home Phone

helping students identify their career objectives, and determining whether or not these objectives could be met by the cooperative program;

contacting local employers, evaluating their training potential, and convincing them to employ and train students;

placing students in jobs on the basis of the students' career objectives;

working with students and employers to plan the students' total vocational instructional program;

visiting the students on the job to supervise their progress, and to assist the employers in their training endeavors;

providing the in-school related instruction;

usually, serving as a sponsor to a student vocational organization; and evaluating their programs on a continuous basis.[6]

illustration 16.2
STUDENT INTEREST SURVEY FORM

Name_____ School_____

Address_____ Date_____

Date of Birth_____ Telephone_____

Parent or Guardian_____

Occupation of Parent(s) or Guardian_____

_____

Have you worked before?_____ Where?_____

What were your duties?_____

Are you employed now?_____ Where?_____

What are your duties?_____

What business subjects have you completed?_____

_____

_____

Business subjects to be taken in senior year_____

_____

Extracurricular activities_____

_____

What are your plans after graduation?_____

_____

Are you interested in preparing for an office occupation while attending
high school?   _____Yes   _____No

Would you be interested in a cooperative office education program which
involves going to school part-time and working part-time?   _____Yes _____No

Are you interested in additional information about the vocational office
training program?   _____Yes   _____No

SUBMIT COOPERATIVE PROGRAM APPLICATION TO STATE

The teacher-coordinator works closely with the state supervisor in completing applications and other forms necessary for program approval and operation. Teacher-coordinators of cooperative office education programs generally have extended contracts that provide for an additional month of employment. This month, sometimes split into two weeks before the opening of school and two weeks after closing, is used for placing students on the job, developing specific job instruction for each student, and compiling files and reports. Teacher-coordinators may also be reimbursed for travel to professional meetings where improvements in cooperative programs are discussed.

BEGIN PUBLICITY EFFORTS

At the outset, it is necessary to have two-way communication so that students have an opportunity to determine whether the program, as described by the teacher-coordinator, will meet their needs. The teacher-coordinator must also disseminate information to parents of prospective students, preferably through face-to-face conversations. Likewise, personal visits to business persons are necessary to establish a link between the school and potential training stations. It is important, in these initial visits to employers, to establish the idea that the program is primarily one of training. Direct contacts with other faculty members in the school are essential to the successful initiation of a cooperative program. The guidance staff can be of assistance in interpreting the program to prospective student trainees and in providing data about the occupational interests and abilities of students. Newspaper articles are effective in the organizational stages as a means of getting information to students, parents, and business persons. The most effective publicity, however, will come from a carefully planned program of systematic contacts with business education classes, individual students, parents, the school administration, and the business community.

SELECT ADVISORY COMMITTEE

Lay advisory committees are important to vocational education as emphasized by the 1968 Amendments of the Vocational Education Act of 1963 which established funds for federal and state advisory committees and defined their functions. The advisory committee for a cooperative office education program should be composed of five to twelve members, representing various areas within the school and community such as education, civic organizations, business, and office occupations employees. You will want to meet with the building administrator regarding the makeup of the committee, talk with the potential committee persons, and have the building or system administrator write each person asking him or her to serve. The length of the term should be staggered initially, some for one year, some for two years, so that a nucleus of competent individuals can be maintained. "The duty of the committee is strictly advisory; educational policy remains under the control of the superintendent of schools. The advisory committee should remain a sounding board for advice on operating procedures. The committee may be asked for advice on public information programs and may assist in these activities. It may suggest sources of training stations and sources and types of instructional materials, assist with youth club affairs, provide resource personnel for related classroom instruction, recommend minimum standards for students, assist with the employer appreciation banquet, and identify adult education needs."[7]

ARRANGE FOR EQUIPMENT, FACILITIES, AND INSTRUCTIONAL PROGRAM

The business education program, which includes cooperative education, should be designed to provide students with general and specific skills needed in the labor market. As a teacher-coordinator you will want to show evidence to the administration, the advisory committee, students, and the employment community that your business curriculum is appropriate for preparing students for employment. Your state business education department probably has recommended curriculum, equipment, and facilities for business education programs. If the curriculum, facilities, and/or equipment are inadequate, you will need support from the administration in securing what is needed.

SELECT TRAINING STATIONS

The first step in choosing training stations is to determine the selection criteria. While specific criteria will vary, these general areas should be included: adherence to laws and regulations, relevance to career objectives of students, desirable firm (business) characteristics, appropriate working conditions, adequate on-the-job supervision, acceptable location and wages, adequate length of participation (preferably school year), appropriate equipment and facilities. Check with the local and/or state supervisor of business education to make sure your criteria are consistent with federal guidelines and state and local plans.

After preparing the criteria, begin personal visits to possible stations identified in the community survey. Talk with the employer (manager or his or her representative), visit the work area, and, during one of your visits, speak with the person who will be the on-the-job supervisor. This is the time to answer questions about the cooperative program, and to explain the employer's responsibilities.

Evaluate each potential training station, using a checklist or evaluation form on which you list the firm's name and address, type of business, contact person, phone number, criteria and the degree to which each is met, and comments. This data will help you in matching student-learners to possible training stations.

SELECT STUDENT-LEARNERS

Of prime importance to the success of a cooperative office education program is the selection of qualified students. The necessary criteria should be identified, and parents and students should understand them fully. (The administration should understand that cooperative business education is a culminating course, based on satisfactory accomplishment of prerequisites. If adequate numbers of students desire a work program, but lack prerequisite skills, then the school system should consider a work program for the disadvantaged. See Module 16.1.)

Criteria for selection should reflect legal restrictions, time requirements for on-the-job training, interpersonal skills, academic skills, career goals, and character traits. To avoid any parental and/or student misunderstandings, you may want to send home a letter describing the criteria for the student and parent(s) to sign and return to you. You will also want to design or adapt a student application form for potential enrollees. This form should include data such as:

Personal Data, including name, address, birth date, parents' name; availability of transportation.

Educational Background, including courses taken, both general and business education.

Competencies, such as typing speed, dictation speed.

Career Objective, including long-range and short-range goals as well as future training plans and reason for wishing to participate in a cooperative business education program.

DEVELOP TRAINING PLAN

The training plan is an individualized statement of work which serves as a guide for both in-school and on-the-job instruction. While the plan should be prepared cooperatively by the teacher-coordinator, employer, and student-learner, the teacher-coordinator is responsible for developing the plan. Sources such as the *Occupational Outlook Handbook* and the *Dictionary of Occupational Titles* are good references for developing a training plan which usually includes these parts: title of job, job description, career objectives of student, areas of experience and training, details of specific areas of training and experience indicating where the instruction is to take place, project (if assigned), and activities for career development. Training plans should be examined frequently and amended as needed. An abbreviated training plan is shown in Illustration 16.3.[8]

PLACE STUDENTS ON THE JOB

A major responsibility of the teacher-coordinator is to place students in training stations that most effectively prepare them for their career objectives. By reviewing the students' applications and the types of learning experiences that can be provided at the training stations, the teacher-coordina-

illustration 16.3
TRAINING PLAN

I.   Title of Job: Stenographer-Clerk

II. Job Description: Stenographer for office manager. Duties
     include taking dictation, transcription, and other typewriting,
     operating adding machine, and performing a variety of related
     clerical duties.

III. Career Objective: Executive Secretary

IV. Areas of Experience and Training:

     A. Shorthand and Transcription
     B. Typewriting
     .   .   .   .
     G. Assembling Materials

V.   Details of Specific Areas of Training and Experience:

		Instruction	
		In Class	On Job
A. Shorthand and Transcription			
1. Learn to take dictation efficiently		x	x
3. Study files for examples of previous correspondence			x
G. Assembling Materials			
1. Learn to organize materials rapidly		x	x
4. Learn to use collator			x

VI. Project: Prepare a portfolio of sample office-type production
     work and personal data

VII. Career Development:

     A. Read each issue of <u>Today's Secretary</u>
     .   .   .   .
     D. Participate actively in FBLA Club

---

tor can make tentative placements. When possible, arrange for each student to talk with at least three potential employers.

Prior to setting up student interviews with prospective employers, plan orientation sessions for students. Some of the activities and content to be included in these sessions are job qualifications in relation to student competencies, application forms and résumés, letters of application, and appearance and procedures in the interview. Role playing, simulation, and other learning situations in which students can practice these skills should be provided. It may also be helpful to invite a personnel manager to speak to the class about the interview procedure. (Your students should have Social Security numbers and may need to secure work permits.)

While the in-school instruction on job orientation is proceeding, the teacher-coordinator schedules the interviews and prepares job interview cards that introduce the student to the employer. Illustration 16.4 depicts an interview card.

The training station sponsor or employer should be provided with pertinent information about each student to be interviewed. The employer should not make any commitments to a student at the interview session. After all students have been interviewed, the employer may want to speak with additional students or may be prepared to select the student-learner. In any event, selection is usually done in close cooperation with the teacher-coordinator. When the student is placed at a training station, the employer, parent, and teacher-coordinator may sign a training agreement. (See Illustration 16.5).[9]

module 16.2
LEARNING ACTIVITIES

1. With two or three other class members, construct or revise a questionnaire to use in (a) surveying businesses or (b) surveying students to determine the need for an interest in a cooperative program.
2. One of your responsibilities as teacher-coordinator is to meet with prospective employers to explain cooperative business education programs. Outline what you would say to a prospective employer.
   OR

illustration 16.4
JOB INTERVIEW CARD

School Name

Address

This card introduces _____(Student name)_____

who wishes to be interviewed for a part-time job as part

of the cooperative business education program.

Appointment Time_____   Appointment Date_____

Firm_____

Address_____

_____

illustration 16.5
SAMPLE TRAINING AGREEMENT

Student's Name_____Birth Date_____ Age_____

Student's Address_____ Telephone_____

School_____ Telephone_____

Training Station_____ Telephone_____

Address of Training Station_____

Training Supervisor_____ Position_____

Dates of Training Period: From_____ To_____

Average Number of Hours of Employment: Per Day_____ Per Week_____

Student-Learner's Rate of Beginning Pay_____

Career Objective_____

Basic skills, attitudes, and knowledge needed in this occupation:

Major areas of experience and training to be provided at training station:

Major areas of related instruction to be provided in class:

RESPONSIBILITIES

The STUDENT-LEARNER considers this job experience as contributing to his/her career objectives and agrees:

1. To be regular in attendance, both in school and on the job.
2. To perform training station responsibilities and classroom responsibilities in an efficient manner.
3. To show honesty, punctuality, courtesy, a cooperative attitude, proper health and grooming habits, appropriate dress, and a willingness to learn.
4. To conform to the rules and regulations of the training station.
5. To furnish the teacher-coordinator with necessary information about the training program and to complete promptly all necessary reports.
6. To consult the teacher-coordinator about any difficulties arising at the training station or related to the training program.
7. To participate in those extracurricular school activities that are required in connection with the VOT program.

You have been invited by the business teachers at a nearby school to talk with them about beginning a cooperative business education program. Outline the presentation you would make, explaining the procedures for establishing a program.

3. Specify the objective(s) and prepare one visual aid you can use as you orient students for their interviews with prospective employers.

The PARENTS of the student-learner, realizing the importance of the training program in attaining the student-learner's career objectives, agree:
1. To encourage the student-learner to carry out effectively his/her duties and responsibilities.
2. To share the responsibility for the conduct of the student-learner while training in the program.
3. To accept responsibility for the safety and conduct of the student-learner during travel to and from the school, the training station, and the home.

The TRAINING-STATION, recognizing that a training plan is being followed and that close supervision of the student-learner will be needed, agrees:
1. To provide a variety of work experiences for the student-learner that will contribute to the attainment of career objectives.
2. To endeavor to employ the student-learner for at least the minimum, listed number of hours each day and each week for the entire training period.
3. To adhere to all federal and state regulations regarding employment, child labor laws, minimum wages, and other applicable regulations.
4. To assist in the evaluation of the student-learner.
5. To provide time for consultation with the teacher-coordinator concerning the student-learner and to discuss with the teacher-coordinator any difficulties the student-learner may be having.
6. To provide available instructional material and occupational guidance for the student-learner.

The TEACHER-COORDINATOR, representing the school, will coordinate the training program toward a satisfactory preparation of the student-learner for his/her occupational career objective and agree:
1. To see that the necessary related classroom instruction is provided.
2. To make periodic visits to the training station to observe the student-learner, to consult with the employer and training sponsor, and to render any needed assistance with training problems of the student-learner.
3. To assist in the evaluation of the student-learner.

Additional Comments:

By_____   _____
        Employer   Parent

_____   _____
    Job Supervisor   Student-Learner

                                           DATE_____
_____
    Teacher-Coordinator

4. Develop the rough draft for a brochure summarizing the key information that students, parents, and employers need to know about a cooperative program in office education.
5. From your nearest U.S. Employment Office, pick up a federal bulletin covering specific child labor standards. Report to your class on the standards governing age

requirements, work permits, permits to employ, minimum wage laws, hours of work, compulsory school attendance, and Social Security.

6. Develop a training agreement form which could be used for a cooperative office education program. You may adapt a form already in use in your local school system or you may develop your own form.

7. Make a list of the qualifications a student should possess in order to be accepted for the cooperative program. Develop the list into an evaluation form to screen students for a cooperative office education program.

8. Develop a list of the criteria you would recommend for prospective training stations. Using these criteria, develop a checklist to screen potential employers.

9. Role play a situation in which you assume the part of a teacher-coordinator. Ask a classmate to play the role of an employer who is not familiar with a cooperative program. You want to convince him or her to provide a training station for your cooperative office education program. Ask the class to critique the conversation.

module 16.2
SELF-TEST

1. The objectives in this module are measured through the Learning Activities section.

module 16.3
MAINTAINING A COOPERATIVE EDUCATION PROGRAM

After the cooperative program is established, the teacher-coordinator is responsible for its smooth and effective operation. The three aspects described in this module need to be carried out continuously in order to improve the quality of the program. Providing related instruction, supervising on-the-job training, and evaluating students and the overall program constitute vital phases of the cooperative office education program.

After completing this module, you should be able to (1) identify the activities essential to maintaining a cooperative office education program and (2) demonstrate and/or explain how each activity can be accomplished.

PROVIDE RELATED INSTRUCTION

The training provided in school for cooperative students can be classified as general related instruction and specific related instruction. The training plans that specify what is to be taught (content), when it is to be taught (sequence), and where it is to be taught (school or job) help the teacher-coordinator to plan the related instruction. Initially, the emphasis is on general topics; later, the major emphasis shifts to specific instruction. By reviewing the training plans, you will be able to identify both the general and specific topics that should be included.

General related instruction is based on topics of interest and concern to all students in office occupations. Instructional units may incorporate interpersonal skill development, appropriate dress and grooming for the office, receiving and handling visitors, handling incoming/outgoing mail, communication services, operation and maintenance of office equipment and supplies, arranging itineraries and transportation services, general office financial records, and work habits and attitudes.

Specific related instruction topics vary among students, depending on achievement levels, career objectives, and training station requirements. Specific instruction usually includes topics such as advanced typing and shorthand skills, filing, communication and computational skills, office machines operation (specific machines or higher level of performance), office procedures, and transcription. Both individual and small-group instruction will probably be necessary. The very nature of the in-school instruction lends itself to effective implementation of individualized instructional programs. Over a period of a few years, you will be able to purchase and/or develop a wide range of materials appropriate for both specific and general related instruction.

SUPERVISE ON-THE-JOB TRAINING

A major responsibility of the teacher-coordinator is supervising on-the-job training which is accomplished through regularly scheduled visits. Each visit should be planned for a specific purpose. Obviously, one purpose is to become more familiar with employment conditions and student assignments and responsibilities through observation of the student's work. Other specific purposes include:

> gathering information which will help you to evaluate student progress;
> determining how you can provide the student with additional related help in the classroom;
> determining what additional training activities are needed by the student;
> determining what, if any, changes need to be made in the student's training plan;
> determining what, if any, problems exist that need to be addressed;
> determining the adequacy of the training program;
> determining whether safety, health, and legal requirements are being met.[10]

The frequency with which you visit student-learners will vary depending on the amount and quality of supervision/instruction provided by the on-the-job supervisor, the number and kinds of duties performed by the student-learner, the number and location of the training stations, the competencies exhibited by the student-learner, and the preference of the employer. Visits should be scheduled, however, at least once a month. Remember to confirm dates and time of visits with the employer.

Plan for each visit. Identify the main purpose; specify what you need to accomplish with the on-the-job supervisor; assemble current individual training plans; review previous observation reports and student reports. During the visits, abide by some general guidelines previously agreed upon by you, the employer, and the student-learner. Your guidelines could include the following:

Make appointments for visiting the training station.
Keep information about the business/firm confidential.
Observe only in the areas of the business approved by the employer.
Make suggestions/recommendations to the student-learner in private.
Avoid interfering with the student-learner at work.
Have on-the-job supervisors periodically evaluate student-learner performance.
Conduct conferences with on-the-job supervisors in a professional manner, avoiding controversial issues.

EVALUATE STUDENT LEARNING

Evaluating student performance is an important responsibility of the teacher-coordinator. Chapter 4 and the content-area chapters include suggestions that are appropriate for evaluating in-school instruction.

The employer (or on-the-job supervisor), the student-learner, and the teacher-coordinator should participate in evaluating student on-the-job performance. Student performance in the areas of skill development, attitudes and work habits, and personal traits and characteristics are usually assessed. The individual training plans indicate many of the specific objectives or competencies.

The employer or supervisor completes written progress reports, often in the form of a checklist with comments. These should be filed on a regular basis, monthly, each six weeks, or whatever time period is chosen. The employer's report may be a checklist specifying skills and knowledges, such as typewriting, shorthand, filing, proofreading; work habits and attitudes, such as accuracy, the ability to follow directions, cooperativeness; and personal traits, such as appearance, speech, manners, patience, and dependability. Student performance in each area may be rated on a scale: *Unsatisfactory, Poor, Average, Above Average, Superior,* or *Needs Help, Weak, Average, Good.* Variations include listing assigned tasks performed by the student as specified by the training plan; the section of the checklist dealing with skills would vary for each student. Another format is to list phrases that describe possible behaviors. The employer/supervisor checks those that most accurately describe the student-learner. An example of this format is as follows:

Cooperation
_____Always cooperates eagerly and cheerfully
_____Usually cooperates eagerly and cheerfully

————Cooperates willingly when asked
————Cooperates reluctantly

Other general information included on the employer form is student name, period of time covered, days present or absent, days tardy, name of company, comments and signature of supervisor. Remember to acquaint students with the criteria for evaluation being used by the employer.

Students should complete two forms—a weekly report form and periodic self-assessment forms. The weekly form includes the student's name, date, firm/business, hours worked daily, tasks performed, and may include comments on special achievements or problems. The student should know when to submit the weekly reports. Check for neatness, accuracy, and promptness in completing and turning in reports. These are work habits that are important on the job. Periodically, students should complete self-assessment forms. A checklist such as the one used by employers may be appropriate. In addition, you may want to have students identify specific improvements needed.

The teacher-coordinator should complete a form each time he or she visits a student. The visit form may be general in nature, listing the date and time of visit, purpose of visit, and comments. Illustration 16.6 is an example of a detailed report on which are listed the tasks from the training plan that the student is undertaking.[11] You may need to use both types of forms during the year; at least monthly, complete the detailed form.

GRADING. During the planning stages for cooperative education, the teacher-coordinator should specify how student grades will be determined. This includes identifying the factors that will compose the grade and deciding the relative weight of each. Elements of the program that lend themselves to a grade include the in-class instruction, the employer rating, and the teacher-coordinator rating. Each element should be weighted as to its relative importance; for instance, related instruction, 40 percent; employer rating, 20 percent; teacher rating, 40 percent. A point system is easy to manage when compiling scores: A = 5 points, B = 4 points, C = 3 points, D = 2 points, and so on.

The average of student performance on related instruction is converted to points as follows:

Test 1	3 points
Test 2	4 points
Project	4 points
Activities	3 points
	$14 \div 4 = 3.50$

Employer and teacher-coordinator ratings can be converted to numbers by equating each criteria to a number, such as Superior = 5, Above Average = 4, Average = 3, and so forth. Then, average the ratings.

To find a student's course average, multiply each number rating by the weight of that factor and divide by 100 as follows:

illustration 16.6
COORDINATOR'S OBSERVATION/EVALUATION REPORT

Training Station_____

Supervisor_____ Student_____

Date_____ Time of Visit_____

Points to Observe and Evaluate   Comments

1. Attitude of the supervisor and other
    workers toward the student-learner:

2. Specific tasks and skills in which
    the student-learner is engaged:

    Tasks:

3. Personal appearance, characteristics,
    and traits:

4. Interest in work and ability to work
    with others:

5. Strengths and weaknesses and problems
    encountered:

Other comments: (1) Need for related subject matter, (2) Intensified
and/or additional on-the-job experiences, (3) Training plan adjustments,
(4) Need for conferences, (5) Student-learner comments, (6) Supervisor
comments, and (7) Other.

Related Instruction   40% x 3.50 = 140.00
Employer Rating   30% x 4.53 = 135.90
Teacher Rating   40% x 4.12 = 164.80
                          ──────────────────────
                          440.70 ÷ 100% = 4.41 (B)

EVALUATE THE PROGRAM

Commitment to quality business education implies that the teacher-coordinator systematically evaluates the program. The success of cooperative office education is best viewed in terms of student success. Are students employed in positions related to their career goals? To what extent have students progressed toward their career objectives? How are graduates who completed cooperative office education competing in the labor market with students who did not participate in a cooperative program?

Abbreviated follow-ups of graduates should be completed each year with in-depth follow-ups every three to five years. The annual follow-ups ask for employment status, additional education or training, and relationship of current employment to career objectives. In-depth follow-ups include employment and promotions, education and/or training, salary, graduate's opinion of the value of specific courses and training, primary tasks performed, and recommendations for changing the cooperative program.

In addition to follow-up studies of students, the teacher-coordinator should examine staff qualifications, curriculum, student organizations, and cooperative program operation. Illustration 16.7 provides a sample instrument that is appropriate for the evaluation of a cooperative program.

module 16.3
LEARNING ACTIVITIES

1. Using this module and other sources, construct or modify one of the following forms:
   a. employer evaluation of student-learner
   b. student-learner self-evaluation
2. Invite a training station sponsor to speak to the class. Prepare a list of questions you would ask the employer. Submit the list to your instructor.
3. Develop your own coordinator's observation/evaluation report form. You may adapt one already in use in your local school system or you may adapt the one shown in this module.
4. Arrange to observe the related instruction class in your local high school. Report on the method of instruction, the materials used, and the subject matter covered during the class.

module 16.3
SELF-TEST

1. Why is evaluation of students' on-the-job performance such an important part of the teacher-coordinator's responsibilities?
2. What tools should be used for determining the quality of the cooperative office education program?
3. Why is it important to involve the employer in the planning of a cooperative program?
4. How does the continuous updating of the training plan affect the content of the related instruction class?
5. Compute a course grade for a student, using the following data:
   a. Point System
      5 points = A
      4 points = B
      3 points = C
      2 points = D
      1 point = F
   b. Determine the relative weight of each of the three components of job performance.
   c. Related Instruction Grades: 95, 73, 83, 88, 72, 94, 98.
   d. Employer Ratings (Superior, Above Average, Average, Poor, Unsatisfactory)

illustration 16.7[12]
SAMPLE EVALUATION CHECKLIST

The suggested checklist is scored by rating the criteria with the appropriate numerals listed below:

4 - Condition or provision is present to a very satisfactory degree.

3 - Condition or provision is present to a satisfactory degree.

2 - Condition or provision is present to a fair degree.

1 - Condition or provision is present to an unsatisfactory degree.

0 - Condition or provision is not present.

Notations should be made of compensating features or particular shortcomings.

The following suggested rating can be used for classification according to total points:

200-220 Excellent: The entire program seems to be functioning in the best possible manner.

165-199 Good: The overall program seems to be functioning in a satisfactory manner.

110-164 Fair: The program appears to meet the minimum requirements with some areas that need improvement.

55-109 Poor: The program seems to be functioning below normal with a number of areas needing attention.

EVALUATION CHECKLIST

1. General Objectives

   a. Has a good written statement of objectives been developed?   ( )

   b. Are the objectives adjusted to meet changing conditions in the community?   ( )

2. Coordinating Teacher

   a. Does the coordinator meet the state's requirements?   ( )

   b. Does the coordinator have suitable personal qualifications?   ( )

   c. How effectively does the coordinator promote the VOT program?   ( )

   d. Has a friendly and mutual relationship been established between students and coordinator?   ( )

   e. Is the coordinator an active participant in school and community affairs?   ( )

illustration 16.7 (continued)

3. Organization of the Program

    a. Is VOT an integral part of the curriculum?   ( )

    b. Are students given an opportunity to take preparatory
       courses?   ( )

    c. Is freedom given to the coordinator in the development of
       the program?   ( )

    d. Is provision made for protecting the best interests of
       students?   ( )

    e. Is class enrollment limited so as to provide time for
       adequate individual instruction?   ( )

    f. Does the student receive school credit for training
       received in a training station?   ( )

    g. Is scheduling of work experience done to the advantage
       of students and businesspersons?

4. Advisory Committee

    a. Is the Advisory Committee composed of individuals who
       represent such groups as employees, employers, educators,
       parents, or other interested groups?   ( )

    b. Are the duties of the Advisory Committee confined to
       counseling and advising the school?   ( )

    c. Are the school administrator and the coordinator ex-officio
       members of the Advisory Committee?   ( )

5. Selection and Placement

    a. Does the coordinator have access to and use of school
       records?   ( )

    b. Does the coordinator secure information about students from
       guidance counselors and from other teachers?   ( )

    c. Does the coordinator investigate previous work records?   ( )

    d. Do prospective students have an opportunity to counsel with
       the coordinator?   ( )

    e. Are students counseled to enter the program on a basis of
       their abilities and interests?   ( )

    f. Does the training station provide well-organized learning
       situations?   ( )

    g. Is there provision for an adequate number of diversified
       placement opportunities?   ( )

    h. Does the training station serve in an advisory capacity to
       the school?   ( )

illustration 16.7 (continued)

i. Does the training station pay the student-learner a salary commensurate with ability and with other employees with similar training and ability? ( )

6. Instructional Program

    a. Is instruction aimed at the present needs of the students? ( )

    b. Is there good rapport between coordinator and students? ( )

    c. Are adequate records of student progress available? ( )

    d. If one text is used, are other reference books available? ( )

    e. Are a variety of instructional methods used; for example, conferences, discussions, projects, and so on? ( )

    f. Are current materials used in the classroom? ( )

    g. Is there a variety of office machines available? ( )

    h. Are there sufficient machines for instruction? ( )

    i. Is there sufficient room for classroom instruction and a room available for guidance activities? ( )

    j. Is there a club which provides for the development of leadership and participation in group activities? ( )

7. Coordination of the Program

    a. Does the coordinator have sufficient time for coordination? ( )

    b. Is the coordinator permitted to use coordinating time only for coordinating duties? ( )

    c. Does the coordinator visit each training station periodically? ( )

    d. Is the student's immediate supervisor contacted by the coordinator to determine the student's progress? ( )

    e. Does the coordinator use information obtained to adjust problems that arise relative to the program? ( )

8. Public Relations

    a. Has the program been presented to various employer and employee groups in the community? ( )

    b. Have the services of leaders in business and education been used to present the program to community groups? ( )

    c. Have parents of students been acquainted with the program? ( )

    d. Do the teachers understand and appreciate the program? ( )

illustration 16.7 (continued)

e. Is consideration given to the work-study program in
scheduling?   ( )

f. Are the guidance counselors informed about the place
of the program in the total school program?   ( )

g. Do students have an opportunity to learn about the program?   ( )

h. Does the local school administration support the program?   ( )

9. Follow-up

a. Does the administrator counsel with the coordinator and
require periodic reports?   ( )

b. Do the school administration and the coordinator use the
services of the state department in evaluating and
improving the program?   ( )

c. Is a follow-up survey conducted each year?   ( )

d. Are adequate records kept of former students?   ( )

e. Is the program adjusted in the light of the evaluation
and follow-up findings?   ( )

f. Are recommendations made for curriculum development as
a result of follow-up findings and the evaluation of
the program?   ( )

Total Points _____

Rating 1	*Rating 2*	*Rating 3*
Average	Above Average	Above Average
Above Average	Superior	Superior
Average	Average	Above Average
Poor	Poor	Average
Above Average	Superior	Superior

e. Teacher Ratings (scale same as for employer ratings)

Rating 1	*Rating 2*	*Rating 3*
Average	Average	Above Average
Above Average	Superior	Superior
Poor	Average	Above Average
Unsatisfactory	Poor	Average
Above Average	Superior	Superior

SUMMARY

Cooperative and noncooperative work programs are found in many secondary and postsecondary schools. Cooperative education involves the joint efforts of the school and employers in providing learning experiences designed to prepare students for employment. In noncooperative programs, school instruction and job experiences may not be related. Business education teachers normally work closely with cooperative office education programs, such as Cooperative Office Education, Vocational Office Training, and Cooperative Vocational Education.

Effective cooperative office education programs depend, to a large extent, on thorough planning. Systematic procedures such as the following should be used when establishing a program: (1) acquire administrative approval, (2) determine need for the program, (3) select qualified teacher-coordinator, (4) submit application for approval of program to state department of education, (5) begin publicity for the program, (6) select an advisory committee, (7) arrange for appropriate facilities, equipment, and instructional program, (8) select training stations, (9) select student-learners, (10) develop individual training plans, and (11) place students on the job.

Maintaining a successful cooperative office education program requires that the teacher-coordinator provide appropriate related instruction, supervise on-the-job training, and continuously evaluate both students and the program. If the program is to be effective, then the teacher-coordinator must ensure that instruction and training stations are appropriate for student career goals.

References

[1]The Center for Vocational Education, The Ohio State University, *Establish Guidelines for Your Cooperative Vocational Program,* Module J–1, Professional Teacher Education Module Series (Athens, Ga.: American Association for Vocational Instructional Materials, 1978), p. 11.

[2]Ibid., p. 12.

[3]Adapted from Coordinator's Manual, *Vocational Office Training* (Atlanta: Georgia Department of Education, Business and Office Education Service, 1970), p. II–B–2.

[4]Ibid., pp. V–E–4, 5.

[5]Ibid., p. V–E–6.

[6]The Center for Vocational Education, *Establish Guidelines,* p. 8.

[7]Ralph E. Mason and Peter G. Haines, *Cooperative Occupational Education and Work Experience in the Curriculum,* 2d ed. (Danville, Ill.: Interstate Printers and Publishers, 1972), p. 150.

[8]Adapted from Coordinator's Manual, *Vocational Office Training,* pp. V–Q–2, 3.

[9]Adapted from Coordinator's Manual, *Vocational Office Training,* pp. V–P–2, 3.

[10]The Center for Vocational Education, The Ohio State University, *Coordinate On-the-Job Instruction,* Module J–7, Professional Teacher Education Module Series (Athens, Ga.: American Association for Vocational Instructional Materials, 1978), p. 6.

[11]The Center for Vocational Education, The Ohio State University, *Evaluate Cooperative Students' On-the-Job Performance,* Module J–8, Professional Teacher Education Module Series (Athens, Ga.: American Association for Vocational Instructional Materials, 1978), p. 9.

[12]Adapted from Coordinator's Manual, *Vocational Office Training,* pp. VII–B–3, 4, 5.

SUGGESTIONS FOR FURTHER STUDY

Allen, Thomas R., Jr. "The Role of the Coop Coordinator in Post-Secondary Education." *Balance Sheet* 59 (September 1977): 9, 39.

Campbell, Donald, and Peele, Mark. "Individualized Training Plans for Coop Students." *American Vocational Journal* 50, (May 1975): 29–31.

The Center for Vocational Education, The Ohio State University. Performance-Based Teacher Education Modules: Category J: Coordination of Cooperative Education; Category A: Program Planning, Development, and Evaluation; Category G: School-Community Relations. (Athens, Ga.: American Association for Vocational Instructional Materials, 1978.)

Herr, Edwin L. "Decision-making and Employability Skills and the Role of Cooperative Work Experience." *Business Education World* 57 (March-April 1977): 11–13.

Herwick, Mary Jo. "Streamlining Cooperative Office Education Student Selection." *Journal of Business Education* 53, (October 1977): 22–26.

Meyer, Warren G.; Crawford, Lucy C.; and Klaurens, Mary K. *Coordination in Cooperative Vocational Education.* Columbus, Ohio: Charles E. Merrill Publishing Company, 1975.

Ricci, Fred A. "Enlist Industry Participation in Cooperative Programs." *Business Education Forum* 30 (April 1976): 9–10.

———. "Job Descriptions for Cooperative and Distributive Education." *Journal of Business Education* 52 (April 1977): 322–25.

chapter 17

WORKING WITH STUDENT ORGANIZATIONS

Student organizations are important components of business education programs. They may be viewed as extensions of formal class activities since they provide opportunities for students to develop new affective, cognitive, and psychomotor skills needed for personal and occupational growth, and to practice and extend existing ones. They provide an excellent opportunity for students to develop leadership ability and to expand their knowledge of business through local, state, and national contests, service projects, and business-related activities of various kinds. Largest of these groups, and open to all business students, is the Future Business Leaders of America, sponsored by the National Business Education Association. FBLA's college counterpart is Phi Beta Lambda. The Office Education Association, sponsored by the U.S. Office of Education and the American Vocational Association, serves students who are preparing for business office careers in reimbursable programs at high school and postsecondary levels. The Future Secretaries Association, sponsored by the National Secretaries Association, maintains high school and postsecondary chapters for business students planning careers as secretaries. Pi Omega Pi is a national business teacher undergraduate honor society. Delta Pi Epsilon is a national honorary graduate business education fraternity with research, leadership, scholarship, and service goals.

After completing this chapter, you should be able to (1) prepare a rationale for a student organization, (2) outline a plan for organizing a new chapter of a student organization, (3) explain or prepare a draft of procedures for developing leadership skills among officers and members, (4) design forms for use in scheduling and planning activities and meetings, (5) suggest guidelines for fund-raising projects, and (6) explain the role of evaluation in student organizations.

Many high schools and colleges throughout the country have active chapters of business education-related student organizations. One of your responsibilities as a business teacher may be to advise one of these student organizations. Whether you are serving as an adviser for an existing organization or establishing a new chapter, one of your first steps is to obtain a copy of the official handbook to familiarize yourself with the purposes, goals, and objectives of the club. Contact the state supervisor of business education for a copy of the handbook. A next step is to specify, preferably in writing, your rationale for the organization. Your attitude toward the organization, its purpose and role in the total business education program, forms the basis for your leadership as an adviser. This is an excerpt from a rationale statement:

> I believe that a student vocational organization is an integral part of the total educational program because it provides real-work experiences through which students can learn certain essentials of living that might otherwise be omitted from their instructional program. I believe that the organizational goal of self-motivation is worthwhile because I have known many, many students who have improved their scholarship through their involvement in a student vocational organization. I believe that the adviser is a key person in the organization. The adviser is responsible for planning activities that help students develop into healthy, mature adults and leaders in their community. As an adviser I will do everything possible to promote the organization.[1]

When preparing your statement, remember that a rationale is a statement of your belief followed by reasons for the belief.

ORGANIZING A STUDENT GROUP

If you have the responsibility for establishing a student organization, there are several groups with which you must work. First, the school administration has to approve and support the organization. For instance, if you want to establish a Future Business Leaders of America chapter, the school administrator must have such information as the need for the club; target population for which it would be appropriate; organizing process; facilities required for meetings; recommended meeting times; teacher and student time required; type of activities involved—local, state, national; and finances necessary for operating the organization.

After securing the permission of the administration, contact your business education state supervisor who is responsible for working with youth organizations. This individual will provide you with the necessary information and material to organize a chapter. An adviser and/or officers from a nearby chapter will also assist you in developing plans for your group.

No organization can be a success without the enthusiastic support of students. An important step, then, is to enlist interested students and provide them with opportunities to participate in FBLA activities. Spend some time in class describing the goals and objectives of FBLA; invite students from other FBLA chapters to visit your school to talk about their experiences with the organization. Since this is an ongoing activity not limited to the initial organization of a chapter, develop systematic plans for enlisting new members in your chapter. Students should be fully aware that participation in FBLA provides opportunities to complement the instructional program. You, as an adviser, will be helping members to get involved in meaningful activities and projects as soon as possible. Students should be actively involved in planning the new chapter. Select a committee of students, or ask for volunteers to work with you in nominating temporary officers, recruiting members, preparing the bylaws and constitution, and planning the initial meeting.

Since FBLA is a high school organization, you may want to send a letter to parents of potential members telling them briefly about the organization and how it will benefit students.

The organizational meeting is important because of the impact it has on prospective members as to the worth of the club. The temporary officers (selected by the planning committee) will work with you in planning and implementing this meeting. This first meeting may incorporate such business items as establishing the chapter, adopting the constitution and bylaws (if they are developed at this point), selecting a nominating committee for officers or electing officers if the planning committee presents a slate to the group, setting meeting time and dates, determining amount of dues, and planning the next meeting. The organization handbook will have suggestions for items of business to be included at the organizational meeting.

Active chapter officers are essential to the success of the organization. Some time should be spent, perhaps at the end of class or during a meeting, in discussing the duties associated with an office and the responsibilities of each individual who accepts an office or committee membership.

DEVELOPING LEADERSHIP SKILLS

One of the purposes of business education student organizations is to develop leadership qualities among its members. FBLA, OEA, FSA, and PBL can provide numerous leadership development opportunities for individual members that cannot be accomplished in the regular instructional program. The adviser has an important role in achieving these purposes. "Your responsibilities in preparing students for leadership roles in the student vocational organization will include assisting in the election and installation of officers, conducting leadership training sessions for officers, assisting students in advancing within the available degrees in the student vocational organization, and sending student representatives to district, state, regional, and national student vocational organization activities."[2]

Through participation in the various service, social, fund-raising, and educational activities, each member—not just the officers—can have opportunities to develop leadership skills. Planned leadership training sessions for chapter officers and members are important. In addition to covering the specific duties of each officer, the sessions can emphasize the skills that officers need to carry out their responsibilities. Training sessions should focus on working in/with a group, learning parliamentary procedure, and developing communication skills, both oral and written. Role-playing and simulation activities in these areas can be incorporated into the training sessions.

Many student organizations provide for student advancement based on achievement of identified goals. FBLA members, for example, can earn three levels of membership based on successively higher achievement: assistant, supervisor, and leader. Each member should be aware of the requirements for advancement and encouraged to become involved in working toward achieving the various membership levels. As students complete requirements, the adviser should promptly file the proper forms and provide school and community recognition of these student achievements.

Leadership qualities can be promoted through student participation in activities at district, state, and national meetings. Acquaint your students with the opportunities for participation and competition (both group and individual) and help them develop the necessary skills and knowledges needed. Contests cover areas such as typewriting, shorthand, data processing, accounting, parliamentary procedure, public speaking, job interview, and so forth, as well as chapter projects, posters, scrapbooks, and exhibits. Participation in district, state, regional, and national meetings and contests either as an officer or a contestant is a positive motivational device for members at local levels.

PLANNING ACTIVITIES

Well-planned program activities appropriate to the interest and ability levels of members are essential if the student organization is to be successful. The following guidelines can be helpful to you and your officers in planning and selecting chapter activities:[3]

> Encourage a well-balanced program of activities. A chapter which emphasizes sports activities, for example, at the expense of civic or educational or leadership activities, will do little for student personal growth and understanding.

> Keep the activities on the level of members. An interesting and student-centered program, developed by students under your supervision, will encourage member participation and club growth.

> Encourage selection of activities that will challenge every member. Activities should have sufficient scope and depth to bring out the best in each member. They should not be beyond students' abilities, but sufficiently difficult and significant to merit recognition by members and others outside the club when successfully completed.

> Ensure that most of the activities relate in some way to the educational objectives of the vocational program. Activities which encourage personal growth, occupational understanding, and recognition for achievement will assist the student in becoming a better employee, a better student, and a better citizen.

> If either the chapter or adviser is new, do not undertake too many activities. Work toward accomplishing some student vocational organization objectives through the program of activities, but do not expect to accomplish everything until both the adviser and the chapter have gained experience and a more extensive program can be undertaken.

Avoid planning activities beyond the financial capability of your program. Many activities require financing. Good planning involves providing methods of securing or raising funds to pay these costs, and/or planning activities which require little or no expenditure of funds (particularly if school policy prohibits fund-raising activities).

All activities should be clearly stated and understood by the members. Anyone reading the written plan should be able to see how the activities assist in achieving chapter goals. In addition, the plan should reflect careful consideration of the following questions:

What efforts and commitments on the part of members are necessary?

What special student training is needed?

How many members will be involved and profit from this experience?

What committees are needed to plan and carry out this activity?

Guide your officers in setting up a monthly calendar listing each activity or meeting and its date. The officers may decide that detailed activity sheets are helpful in the efficient operation of the chapter's program. Such a planning sheet might include the activity; the chapter goal to which it relates (this helps the officers to select activities appropriate to chapter goals); specific items to be considered or tasks to be completed (such as time and place of activity, practice sessions needed, persons to be invited, special materials or equipment needed); and committee members or individuals responsible for each activity.

An important point in activating projects is to determine the funds needed for their implementation and to develop plans for securing them. Check with the administrator regarding school policies on fund raising. Some school systems limit the number of fund-raising projects a club may engage in each year. Once you and the officers decide on the fund-raising projects, have them approved by the administration. Projects should be considered in light of their potential profit, duration, and skills needed by students. Projects often used for fund raising include car washes, bake sales, candy sales, flea markets, calendar sales, dances, Christmas tree sales, Santa helpers at local department stores, paper/aluminum drives, faculty-student ball games, and raffles.

Activities associated with fund raising provide students with excellent opportunities for using their skills and knowledge in a business environment. For instance, students will be involved in decision-making activities (Which project will net the most profit considering the time and effort required?), selling, preparing budgets, keeping records of funds collected and spent, organizing financial statements, and compiling reports for the chapter and the school.

EVALUATING THE CHAPTER

Evaluating the chapter's activities, goals, meetings, training programs, and projects should be an ongoing process since evaluation is the key to improvement. Evaluation should focus both on procedures (How efficiently were meetings conducted? How well were projects organized? How effective were membership campaign techniques?) and outcomes (How much money was raised? How many contestants "placed" at district and state events? How many members were enrolled?) and should involve the adviser, the officers, and the members in one or more types of appraisal. As the adviser, you must evaluate the ongoing activities and operation of the chapter. You and the officers will probably want to develop an evaluation plan that includes both the techniques to be used and the means for utilizing data gathered to improve the chapter. Reports submitted to state or national headquarters are one means of evaluation. Monthly evaluations of chapter meetings and activities provide clues to the health and vitality of the organization. Periodically, all members should be involved in assessing the chapter's effectiveness in meeting its goals and serving its members.

Advising a student organization requires time and effort by the business teacher. An active chapter, however, can add significantly to the educational experiences of your students.

Illustrations 17.1,[4] 17.2,[5] and 17.3 are examples of evaluation forms that have been used successfully to evaluate business education student organizations.

LEARNING ACTIVITIES

1. Oakland High School is a new comprehensive high school. The business education department believes that an FBLA or OEA chapter would strengthen the program. You have agreed to serve as faculty adviser.
   a. Write a rationale for the organization.
   b. Outline the content of a speech you can make to business students explaining the value of the organization to each of them.
      OR
      Prepare a draft of a letter to be sent to parents of prospective members, telling them about the organization and how participation could benefit students.
   c. List at least five different fund-raising projects that the club might use.
   d. Outline a plan for a leadership training program for new officers and other interested members.
   e. Design or modify forms you might use in scheduling and planning activities.
   f. Outline an evaluation plan involving adviser, officers, and members.
2. In cooperation with other members of the class, contact a state business education supervisor for information on the goals and objectives of various student organizations, such as FBLA, OEA, FSA, PBL. Each committee should prepare a report on one of the organizations.
3. Interview a student member of a business education organization as to its contribution to his or her education experiences.
   OR
   Interview a business teacher who is an adviser to a student organization regarding the role of business education clubs in the overall curriculum.

SELF-TEST

1. Develop a brief statement of rationale for a business education student organization of your choice.

illustration 17.1
MONTHLY PROJECT EVALUATION

Project_____ Business Club_____

Committee_____ School_____

Chairperson_____ City_____

Number on Committee_____ Chapter Adviser_____

Date Project Initiated_____ Scheduled Completion Date_____

Chapter Goal Project Designed for_____

How many meetings have been held?_____

How many subcommittee meetings have been held?_____

Current status of project?_____
_____
_____
_____

What has helped the project?_____
_____
_____
_____

What (if anything) is impeding the project?_____
_____
_____
_____

Recommendations_____
_____
_____
_____
_____

Copies to: Chairperson, Adviser, Committee File

2. Identify the steps you would take in organizing a new chapter of a student organization in your school.
3. How does the business teacher assist student members of a club in developing leadership skills?
4. Identify three guidelines you would use with chapter officers in
   a. planning and selecting chapter activities
   b. choosing fund-raising activities
5. What is involved in effective evaluation of the business education student organization?

illustration 17.2
MONTHLY EVALUATION

Month/Year_____

Adviser_____

School_____

Club_____

Number of students enrolled_____

Number of student organization members_____

Meeting dates_____

How many members were present_____

This meeting was _____ Chapter _____ All School

List the Agenda for the Meetings

1. _____   5. _____
2. _____   6. _____
3. _____   7. _____
4. _____   8. _____

What committees were appointed or reported to the group?

1. _____   5. _____
2. _____   6. _____
3. _____   7. _____
4. _____   8. _____

What activities were planned or carried out?

1. _____   5. _____
2. _____   6. _____
3. _____   7. _____
4. _____   8. _____

STATE BRIEFLY HOW THIS MEETING OR ACTIVITY CARRIED OUT THE YEARLY PROGRAM
OF WORK OR CHAPTER GOALS.

SUMMARY

Student organizations are important components of the business education program at the secondary and postsecondary levels. Through organizations such as FBLA, OEA, FSA, and PBL, students have opportunities to develop new skills and apply existing ones. The attitude of the adviser toward the organization is a major factor in its success. Successful chapters of school

illustration 17.3[6]
OVERALL EVALUATION

STOP AND EVALUATE YOUR CLUB

	Points		
ACTIVE COOPERATION	3	2	1
Are our members interested, active, cooperative, and informed?			
Are our advisers referred to for advice?	___	___	___
Does each member appear or assist with an activity during the year?	___	___	___
Is a real effort made to find the abilities of each member?	___	___	___

PROGRAM OF WORK

	3	2	1
Are our activities based on club purposes?	___	___	___
Has a program of work been planned by our club?	___	___	___
Is our program of work organized so that it is easily understood by all members?	___	___	___
Is our program of work planned early in the year and are later activities carried out according to this plan?	___	___	___
Is the club part of the business education program?			

GOOD ADVERTISING AND PUBLICITY

	3	2	1
How have we interpreted our club program to the community and school?	___	___	___
Have we completed activities which help to strengthen the school in our community?	___	___	___

CLUB ACTIVITIES

	3	2	1
Are we promoting training of students for the business world?	___	___	___
Have our activities helped our members grow in social graces?	___	___	___
Are our money-making projects educational and related to the club goals?	___	___	___

organizations provide students with varied opportunities for involvement in activities that promote the development of leadership skills. Chapter activities should be selected that are appropriate for members, and periodic evaluations should be incorporated as a basis for improvement.

References

[1]The Center for Vocational Education, The Ohio State University, *Develop a Personal Philosophy Concerning Student Vocational Organizations,* Module H–1, Profes-

illustration 17.3 (continued)

Points

DEMOCRATIC COOPERATION AND UNDERSTANDING

Have we promoted democracy and the development of
  creative leadership in school and community life? ___ ___ ___
Are opportunities provided for all members to learn
  to participate in group work?
Are our meetings orderly, well-planned activities? ___ ___ ___
Do the members clearly understand club goals,
  objectives, and values? ___ ___ ___
Do our members recognize the opportunity for personal
  growth through the club? ___ ___ ___

OPPORTUNITY TO LEARN

Is effective use made of the Handbook and other
  releases from the State Office? ___ ___ ___
Do experiences provide opportunities for all
  members to develop leadership abilities? ___ ___ ___

COMPLETION OF WORK - A SUCCESSFUL CLUB

Are accurate reports kept on file? ___ ___ ___
Are necessary reports and dues sent promptly to
  the State Adviser? ___ ___ ___
Do we participate and assume our responsibilities
  in the State Organization? ___ ___ ___
Do our projects help us achieve the goals we set? ___ ___ ___
Do we use what we learn from our evaluation for
  future plans? ___ ___ ___

Excellent	65-79 points
Average	41-64 points
Below Average	Below 40 points

sional Teacher Education Module Series (Athens, Ga.: American Association for Vocational Instructional Materials, 1977), p. 17.

[2] The Center for Vocational Education, The Ohio State University, *Prepare Student Vocational Organization Members for Leadership Roles,* Module H–3, Professional Teacher Education Module Series (Athens, Ga.: American Association for Vocational Instructional Materials, 1977), p. 3.

[3] The Center for Vocational Education, The Ohio State University, *Assist Student Vocational Organization Members in Developing and Financing a Yearly Program of Activities,* Module H–4, Professional Teacher Education Module Series (Athens, Ga.: American Association for Vocational Instructional Materials, 1977), p. 8.

[4] The Center for Vocational Education, The Ohio State University, *Supervise Activities of the Student Vocational Organization,* Module H–5, Professional Teacher Education Module Series (Athens, Ga.: American Association for Vocational Instructional Materials, 1977), p. 13.

[5] Ibid., p. 14.

[6]Ohio Office Education Association, *Club Handbook* (Columbus : Ohio Office Education Association, n.d.), pp. 25–26.

SUGGESTIONS FOR FURTHER STUDY

Daggett, Willard. "Student Organizations—FBLA, A Competent Part of a Complete Business Education Program." *Sincerely Yours* 30 (November 1975): 20.

Fullenkamp, Sharon. "Youth Clubs—Future Business Leaders of America." *Ohio Business Teacher* 34 (March 1974): 21–25.

Groneman, Nancy, and Reicherter, R. F. "Toward One Business Student Organization." *Business Education Journal* 25 (Fall 1977): 11–14.

Jones, Rufus. "FBLA and PBL in Mississippi." *Mississippi Business Education Journal* 4 (March 1976): 66–67.

Schlotzhauer, Virginia. "Parliamentary Procedure Tips." *Tomorrow's Business Leader* 8 (Winter 1977): 4.

INDEX

603

Checklists, 74–75
  for bookkeeping and accounting teaching, 404
  for evaluation of cooperative work-study program, 586–89
  for preliminary lesson plan, 145
  for student evaluation of ten-key adding machines, 447
Classroom(s). *See also* Facilities; Individualized labs
  atmosphere, 25, 57–58
  physical conditions, 32
Clerical aides, 604
Clerical workers, expected increase in number of, 14–15
Closing entries in bookkeeping, 397
COBOL. *See* Curriculum for data processing teaching
Cognition stage of skill learning, 39
Cognitive domain, learning activities in, 103, 104–6
Cognitive objectives
  defined, 100
  relationship to affective objectives, 101
Colleges and universities. *See also* Postsecondary vocational-technical centers
  business education in, 6–8
  typewriting teaching in, 179–80
Committees, in office business class, 334. *See also* Advisory committees
Communication skills teaching. *See* Business communication skills teaching; Shorthand and transcription teaching; Typewriting teaching
Communication tasks, 346–47
Communications cluster, in model office, 325
Community colleges. *See* Colleges and universities
Competencies
  for beginning teacher, 97–98
  involving concepts, 22
Competency-based learning systems, 45–47
Competition, as motivator, 35–36
Comprehension
  in development of thinking skills, 506
  reading, 369
Comprehensive problem approach to programming, 477–78
Computation-related business skills teaching. *See* Bookkeeping and accounting teaching; Business machines teaching; Business mathematics teaching
Computer-Stenograph Machine Shorthand System, 442
Computers. *See also* Calculators and adding machines teaching; Data processing teaching
  availability for data processing teaching, 457
  secretarial jobs and, 13

Comtutor, 442
Concepts learning
  in basic business course planning, 508–9
  in bookkeeping and accounting teaching, 398–401
  in discovery-cognitive learning, 22–24
  and educable mentally retarded, 164–65
Concomitant learnings, job instruction sheets and, 331
Concrete learning, 36
Confidential information, 611
Connotative meaning, voice tone and, 350
Consumer education, 495–98
  content, 497–98
  data processing and, 482
  objectives, 496–97
Consumer education learning activity package on frauds and schemes, 511–25
  student's edition, 517–21
  teacher's edition, 512–17
Content
  of business machines course, 434–35
  of business mathematics course, 416–17
  of speech, 350–51
Contracts, in office practice teaching, 333–34
Controlling function of teacher, 96
Cooperation, in classrooms, 25
Cooperative student experiences, 130
Cooperative work-study program
  administrative approval for, 568–69
  arranging for equipment, facilities, and instructional program, 574
  characteristics of, 565–66
  determination of need for, 569, 570–71
  evaluation of, 584–85, 586–89
  and evaluation of data processing learning, 487
  evaluation of student learning, 582–84
  goals of, 567
  instructional approach to, 580–81
  publicity for, 573
  selection of advisory committee for, 573–74
  selection of students for, 575
  selection of teacher-coordinator for, 569, 571
  selection of training stations for, 574
  state supervisor and, 573
  student job placement in, 575–77
  supervision of on-the-job training, 581–82
  training plans for, 575, 576
  types of, 566
Copiers, use of, 439–40
Correct Words a Minute (cwam), 210, 227
Course planning, 119–26
  for business machine teaching, 436–45
  for data processing, 461–62
  and identification of instructional units, 120–25
  and selection and/or writing of course objectives, 120

To the owner of this book:

We hope you have enjoyed MANAGING THE LEARNING PROCESS IN BUSI-
NESS EDUCATION. We would like to get your reactions to the book in order
to improve future editions; won't you take a moment to fill out this questionnaire for us? Thank you.

Your school:_____

Your instructor:_____

Department of: _____

Course title:_____

What did you like most about MANAGING THE LEARNING PROCESS IN BUSINESS
EDUCATION?

_____

_____

_____

What did you like least about it?

_____

_____

_____

Was the entire book assigned for you to read?

_____

_____

_____

If not, what parts or chapters were NOT assigned?

_____

_____

_____

Was there anything that you found particularly difficult to understand?

_____

_____

_____

If you have any other comments, we would be delighted to hear them.

_____

_____

_____